Starting an Online Business All-in-One For Dummies®, 2nd Edition

4-09

P9-BBU-022

Timeline for Your Online Business

Action	Completion Date
Finalize or validate business idea.	
Write a formal business plan.	
Select a business name.	
Register business name.	
Choose domain name.	
Register domain name.	
Identify business location.	
Check zoning laws (if home based).	
Set up office.	
Decide organization status of company.	
Legalize business structure.	
Obtain business license.	
Set up business bank account.	
Meet with accountant to review tax requirements.	
Obtain employer identification number (EIN).	
Secure business and health (or other types of) insurance.	

Action	Completion Date
Secure funding (if using outside sources).	
Apply for sales tax certificate (if applicable).	
Select hosting service.	
Select Web developer.	
Select distributor or drop shipper.	
Create content for Web site.	
Select products and finalize services.	
Develop Web site.	
Add shopping cart or other e-commerce applications.	
Obtain merchant account.	
File trademarks and copyrights.	
Submit site to major search engines.	
Initiate marketing plan.	
Test (and correct) all site functions.	
Launch site to public!	

Important Web Sites You Need to Know About

Web Site	URL	What You Can Do
Electronic Copyright Office	www.copyright.gov/register	Register your site's content.
Internal Revenue Service (IRS)	www.irs.gov/formspubs/index.html?portlet=3	Access and print publications and forms.
Internet Crime Complaint Center	www.ic3.gov/complaint	Report online fraud and e-mail abuse.
Patent and Trademark Office	www.uspto.gov/main/trademarks.htm	Search the trademark database.
U.S. Postal Service	https://sss-web.usps.com/cns/landing.do	Print postage and ship from your computer.
Small Business Administration (SBA)	www.sba.gov/financing	Find financing information and loan applications.

Starting an Online Business All-in-One For Dummies, 2nd Edition

Cheat Sheet

Site Launch Checklist

Are you ready to take your Web site live? Before you push that last button to make your site a reality, be sure to check off each box (as it applies to you) on this list:

- ❑ My site map (or the layout and structure of all my Web pages) is complete.
- ❑ The site map matches my Web pages — exactly.
- ❑ Each Web site page is displayed and is fully accessible.
- ❑ Every link throughout the site works properly and opens the appropriate page.
- ❑ All graphics and photos are loaded quickly and completely, and the images are crisp and clean.
- ❑ My content is free of misspellings and grammatical errors.
- ❑ Pricing information and product or service descriptions are correct.
- ❑ Pages with online forms or registration information function when I press the Submit button, and the information is sent (in the specified format) to the designated point of contact.
- ❑ Text boxes or drop-down boxes on forms and other pages work correctly.

- ❑ Buttons for top-level menus work. (Ensure that these buttons, like the one that returns users to your home page, function properly on every single page.)
- ❑ Special commands that are spelled out with coding language (HTML or PHP, for example) show up properly when the site loads.
- ❑ My credit card processor or other payment service option is in place and working.
- ❑ All e-commerce-related functions, such as my shopping cart, operate correctly.
- ❑ Include any membership icons or logos (such as Better Business Bureau or Chamber of Commerce member emblems).
- ❑ I tested my site for browser compatibility and screen resolution.
- ❑ My site was tested using a dialup connection and a broadband connection.
- ❑ Contact information using my e-mail address or phone number is clearly displayed and easy to find.
- ❑ The copyright symbol and current year are prominently placed at the bottom of every page.

Tips for Building Loyal Online Customers

- ✔ Offer multiple ways for customers to communicate with you (including e-mail, phone, real-time online support, and online forums).
- ✔ Respond to customer e-mail within 24 hours.
- ✔ Engage customers by providing ways to interact with your site (such as participating in online communities, writing product reviews, and commenting on blogs).
- ✔ Make customers feel special by sending coupons and other exclusive offers to your registered users or frequent buyers.

- ✔ Give customers several different payment options to make buying easy.
- ✔ Offer free shipping — no strings attached.
- ✔ Collect personal customer information (with permission) and use it to send special offers or gifts on birthdays and anniversaries and other special occasions.
- ✔ Find creative ways to thank customers for visiting your site, and for making a purchase.

For Dummies: Bestselling Book Series for Beginners

Starting an Online Business
ALL-IN-ONE
FOR DUMMIES®
2ND EDITION

by Shannon Belew and Joel Elad

WILEY

Wiley Publishing, Inc.

Starting an Online Business All-in-One For Dummies®, 2nd Edition

Published by
Wiley Publishing, Inc.
111 River Street
Hoboken, NJ 07030-5774

www.wiley.com

For general information on our other products and services, please contact our Customer Care Department within the U.S. at 877-762-2974, outside the U.S. at 317-572-3993, or fax 317-572-4002.

For technical support, please visit www.wiley.com/techsupport.

Wiley also publishes its books in a variety of electronic formats. Some content that appears in print may not be available in electronic books.

Library of Congress Control Number: 2009922581

ISBN: 978-0-470-43196-2

Manufactured in the United States of America

10 9 8 7 6 5 4 3 2 1

WILEY

About the Authors

Shannon Belew is the co-owner of several online businesses: allbizopps.com, allsmallbiz.com, avespamedia.com, bizoffice.com, todayshomeoffice.com, top10workathome.com, and workathome1.com. Bizoffice.com is a nationally recognized, award-winning global provider of resources for small and home businesses. Shannon writes the *Huntsville Times* column "Today's Home Office"; has written magazine and newspaper articles; and founded the public relations firm aVespa Media, Inc. Her clients have appeared in such venues as *Inc.* magazine. She has also consulted for an Internet provider, advising companies on developing and reengineering their online presence.

Joel Elad was a fan of the Internet before most people had ever heard of the World Wide Web. He sells online as a PowerSeller on eBay with an impeccable customer satisfaction rating. He also runs his own e-commerce businesses: JoelElad.com focuses on selling educational products such as books and DVDs about selling online, and NewComix.Com, which he co-founded in 1998, focuses on selling new comic books, Japanese manga, DVDs, and action figures. He was the lead instructor for the Learning Annex in New York and California for classes about eBay and advanced Internet sales, and he's an educational specialist trained by eBay. He also contributes to *Entrepreneur magazine,* TrendGrinder.com, and SmartBiz.com.

After earning his MBA from the University of California–Irvine with an emphasis on entrepreneurship and information technology, Joel co-authored five bestselling books focusing on online activities, including *Web Stores Do-It-Yourself For Dummies* and *LinkedIn For Dummies* (both from Wiley Publishing). He's now a consultant to e-commerce companies, a trainer to thousands of eager students at seminars and workshops, and a guide for helping people attain the freedom of growing their sales and establishing their own online presence.

Dedications

Shannon: This book is dedicated to my family: my son, Holden; my daughter, Wiley; and my husband, Tom. Thanks for your relentless encouragement, love, and patience — and for always reminding me what is most important in life.

Joel: This book is dedicated to the hardest-working man I will ever have the privilege of knowing — my dad. Thanks for showing me the value of planning and discipline, as well as love. You will always be my inspiration.

Authors' Acknowledgments

Shannon: Since becoming a published author, I have realized that two groups of people deserve the most thanks once a book like this one is published: the team of people that helped produce it and the great people who are kind enough to buy the finished product!

That said, my sincere thanks to the entire team at Wiley Publishing that made this book a reality, not once, but twice. This includes Rebecca Whitney, Jim Kelly, Rebecca Senninger, Kyle Looper, and my co-author, Joel Elad. I am convinced that this is one of, if not the, most talented and caring group of people I could ever have the privilege of working with, or knowing. A special thanks to Rebecca Senninger and Kyle Looper for their continued guidance.

Thanks also to all of those who choose to read this book and who are inspired to become entrepreneurs. It is your ingenuity, creativity, and passion to follow a dream that not only makes this world go 'round but also inspires the rest of us to follow in your footsteps.

Of course, I can't leave out another important group of people. Thanks to my in-laws, Jim and Freida Belew, for their support and love. Most importantly, thanks to my parents, Ron and Janice Sanders, for inspiring me. You have always encouraged me to stay on track with my dreams, even through the many ups and downs of this crazy life. Every entrepreneur should be so lucky to have parents like you in her corner.

Joel: I'd like to give a big thank you to Anthony and Yvonne Choi, James Marchetti, Anita Cohen-Williams, and Hans Park for the contacts, information, and support I needed along the way to fill in the gaps.

A special acknowledgement goes to my usual co-conspirator, Michael Bellomo, who put me on the path of being an author and keeps me going with a bizarre sense of humor mixed with a powerful dose of inspiration.

Most of all, I have to thank the Wiley team, which has been truly inspirational: Kyle Looper and especially Rebecca Senninger, whose patience and guidance helped make this book possible.

Publisher's Acknowledgments

We're proud of this book; please send us your comments through our online registration form located at http://dummies.custhelp.com. For other comments, please contact our Customer Care Department within the U.S. at 877-762-2974, outside the U.S. at 317-572-3993, or fax 317-572-4002.

Some of the people who helped bring this book to market include the following:

Acquisitions and Editorial

Project Editor: Rebecca Senninger

Acquisitions Editor: Kyle Looper

Copy Editor: Rebecca Whitney

Technical Editor: Jim Kelly

Editorial Manager: Leah Cameron

Editorial Assistant: Amanda Foxworth

Sr. Editorial Assistant: Cherie Case

Cartoons: Rich Tennant
(www.the5thwave.com)

Composition Services

Project Coordinator: Patrick Redmond

Layout and Graphics: Samantha K. Allen, Reuben W. Davis, Andrea Hornberger, Melissa K. Jester, Sarah Phillipart, Christin Swinford, Christine Williams

Proofreaders: Caitie Copple, Christopher M. Jones

Indexer: Sharon Shock

Publishing and Editorial for Technology Dummies

    Richard Swadley, Vice President and Executive Group Publisher

    Andy Cummings, Vice President and Publisher

    Mary Bednarek, Executive Acquisitions Director

    Mary C. Corder, Editorial Director

Publishing for Consumer Dummies

    Diane Graves Steele, Vice President and Publisher

Composition Services

    Gerry Fahey, Vice President of Production Services

    Debbie Stailey, Director of Composition Services

Contents at a Glance

Table of Contents

Introduction

For two decades, the Internet has continued to prove itself a viable tool for building, managing, and growing a business. Little doubt remains that you can make money online and find success in doing so. In fact, since beginning our own online endeavors, we have had the privilege of meeting and working with a variety of entrepreneurs — people who, much like you, share a dream of finding economic independence by running their own businesses. As you might have guessed, many of them found success on the Internet.

The Internet provides not only a legitimate resource for starting your own business that offers a steady source of income for your family but also a nearly endless source of ideas and opportunities to market and grow your company. It can even give you the flexibility to work from home, the freedom to work part-time, or the ability to earn an additional source of income to help make your life more enjoyable.

Now we want to share with you the knowledge and tools we picked up along the way and provide you with a few shortcuts to help further your own online endeavors.

About This Book

We first wrote this book in 2006 to cover the many different ways you can start or expand a business by using the Internet. For this second edition, we took great care to update all the key information that has remained valid in the past couple of years. We also searched out many of the new opportunities that have evolved since then, such as mobile commerce, social networking, and blogging as a legitimate revenue maker. For that reason, among others, we encourage you to use this book as a resource and return to it whenever you need it most.

In addition to providing you with details regarding specific online business strategies and moneymaking opportunities, the book covers basic offline information. It's the stuff that every small-business owner needs to understand, such as how to apply standard accounting principles and keep up with the legal side of running a business.

Of course, using this book doesn't guarantee that you will make a lot of money — or any money, for that matter. The book provides you with just enough knowledge and inspiration to keep your online business dreams on track. Running a business is hard work. It takes persistence, dedication, and perhaps an equal mix of patience and luck.

What You Need Not Read

You should at least browse through *every* section of this book. Even if your e-commerce skills are more advanced, it never hurts to have a refresher course on some of the business basics. Considering that the Internet touches many different aspects of people's lives, you never know what unexpected tidbits of information you might discover.

Nonetheless, some parts of this book certainly aren't required reading — you know, the extra stuff. Typically, these sidebars and paragraphs are marked with Technical Stuff icons. They provide a little more detail because sometimes you need just the meat of an issue.

If you don't think that this "extra stuff" is necessary information, you have our permission to skip it. We know — you don't need our permission. This is your book now. Use it in the manner that's most helpful to you and your online business.

Foolish Assumptions

While we wrote this book, we assumed a few things about you:

✦ You're a smart, inquisitive person who is seeking information about running a business on the Internet.

✦ You have an entrepreneurial spirit and are a bit of a risk taker — at least in the area of starting a business.

✦ You may be looking for ways to use the Internet to build an existing brick-and-mortar business or to increase online donations for a nonprofit organization.

✦ You're comfortable using computers and browsing the Internet.

✦ You use e-mail regularly.

✦ You're willing to find out about new technologies.

✦ You want to use Web sites and online technologies to build a brand.

✦ You want to use the Internet to make money.

✦ You have bought items online and maybe even sold a few things.

How This Book Is Organized

To ensure that you can access the right information, when you need it most, this book has 11 *minibooks*. Each one addresses a general business topic (such as marketing) or a specific area of online business (such as selling on eBay).

Because this book is a *reference tool,* it works best if you can quickly flip to the sections that most apply to you — regardless of whether you're starting, growing, or expanding a business online. This section provides a glimpse of the material you find inside.

Book 1: Online Business Basics

From the best way to finance your venture to fine-tuning your business plan, Book I touches on everything. You might already know some things but need a review of other issues. Or, you might simply want reassurance that your idea is viable. Book I explains how to validate your online business concept, and even provides inspiration to nudge you forward in the right direction.

Book II: Legal and Accounting

Book II is all about protecting your assets. Find out whether you should operate as a sole proprietor or incorporate, and then set up a good record-keeping system to keep your online business on track. Don't forget to review what the IRS expects of you, now that you're a business owner. You find this information, and more, to ensure that your *i*'s are dotted and your *t*'s are crossed.

Book III: Web Site Design

Your Web site is a key factor in creating a viable online business, and design and functionality rules are continually evolving for the Web. Book III shows you how to enhance functionality and incorporate good Web design principles to build a truly inviting and user-friendly site. An important part of attracting your audience and knowing how to keep them is the wording you use throughout your site. It's time to write online content with *zing,* and this book shows you how to do it.

Book IV: Online and Operating

Maybe you're not sure which shopping cart software is best for your online store or you want to know whether affiliate programs can earn you more money than selling e-books on your own. In Book IV, you explore the best profit structure for your site and choose products that sell. Merchant payment solutions, back-end inventory management systems, and other e-commerce necessities are covered in this book.

Book V: Internet Security

You know about spam and you've been warned about identity theft, but there's much more to understand about online security. If your Web site isn't locked up tight, a few unwanted visitors will sneak in and take over. Book V shows you how to implement basic security measures, such as firewalls, spam filters, and adware blockers. Then it talks about denial-of-service

(DoS) attacks, spoofing, and credit card fraud. We also help you develop a security plan to protect yourself — and your customers — from the most recent security threats.

Book VI: Boosting Sales

Are you ready to rev up your e-commerce engine? Book VI shows you how to implement online public relations to increase exposure to your site and gives marketing tips that help convert visitors to buyers. You find detailed information about using search engine optimization (SEO) and paid search advertising to increase sales and about using traffic analysis software effectively to reveal important patterns about your customers' shopping habits.

Book VII: Retail to E-Tail

You're an experienced brick-and-mortar retailer ready to expand your business to the Internet. Before rolling out the welcome mat to your online customers, you need to check off a few items on your to-do list. Book VII explains why you should develop separate online store policies, how to convince your regular customers to shop with you online, and how to maximize online sales without cannibalizing your in-store profit. You also find out how to incorporate some of the most recent online trends, such as mobile commerce, to help market your business and build sales.

Book VIII: Storefront Selling

Can you say "eBay?" It stands to reason that a book about online businesses isn't complete without a section on eBay. It also makes sense that many viable eBay alternatives are also included so that you understand how to maximize your online auction opportunities. In Book VIII, you find all the basic information you need in order to start selling on eBay and other online auction sites and storefronts (such as Amazon). All of them are worth checking out. This minibook also highlights sites such as CafePress and Spreadshirt.com that help you sell custom products from online stores that are easy to set up.

Book IX: Fundraising Sites

E-philanthropy is a popular buzzword among nonprofits of all sizes. The idea of attracting an online donor base to increase funding is also practical and cost efficient. Getting your organization started in fundraising by way of the Internet is the goal of Book IX. Find out how simple additions to an existing Web site can increase donations or determine whether a full-fledged online campaign is warranted.

Book X: Niche E-Commerce

One of the best ways to grow a business online is to stumble across a trendy idea that's just beginning to take off. It's the type of idea that makes others say, "I wish I had thought of that!" This type of specialized product or service is often popular because it's targeted to a specific customer base, or *niche market*. The Internet enables online businesses to market to niche audiences inexpensively. Although Book X doesn't provide a list of guaranteed bestsellers, it gives you a glimpse of some lucrative niche markets. Tweens, blogging, and social networking (like Second Life) are just a few of the areas covered in this book to help you discover how to capitalize on hot new niche markets.

Book XI: E-Commerce Advanced

Book XI is for online business owners who have been around for a while and are facing the decision of where to take their business next. Your site might have celebrated a ten-year anniversary or passed a significant revenue milestone, or maybe potential buyers want to it. For you, Book XI discusses everything from taking your business to the next stage of growth to handling an occasional dip in sales. It also shows you the best approach for a site redesign, reveals marketing strategies to increase your customer base, and reviews strategies for taking on a financial partner to expand the site.

Icons Used in This Book

These icons call attention to important details:

Check out this helpful hint. We picked up this information somewhere along the way.

This friendly reminder serves up important information. Whenever you see this icon, know that this information is something worthwhile to keep in mind as you move forward.

Pay special attention when this icon appears. It could save you from making a fatal error — at least in your online business!

You can usually understand an idea without having to know its behind-the-scenes details. Even when we point them out with this icon, feel free to skip them and move on.

Book I
Online Business Basics

The 5th Wave   By Rich Tennant

"Oh, we're doing just great. Philip and I are selling decorative jelly jars on the Web. I run the Web site and Philip sort of controls the inventory."

Contents at a Glance

Chapter 1: Starting from Scratch

In This Chapter

✔ **Recognizing when the time is right**

✔ **Understanding the different types of online businesses**

✔ **Gathering your thoughts and getting started**

*O*nce upon a time, start-up businesses that operated over the Internet were considered risky ventures with uncertain futures. No longer is that the case! Consider how many different ways you interact with businesses over the Internet every day: You probably buy gifts for friends and family members, look up health-related information, make vacation travel arrangements, and even buy music or pay bills online using a Web-enabled mobile phone. Each of these interactions also represents a business opportunity by which people earn a living on the Internet.

In fact, U.S. online retail sales are expected to reach $335 billion by 2012 for e-commerce goods sold, according to studies done by Forrester Research. With more than 238 million people now using the Internet in the United States alone (according to Internet World Stats at www.internetworldstats.com), many potential customers are willing to be Internet consumers. Why shouldn't you be the next person to take advantage of this rapidly growing market and start an online business? In this chapter, we answer that question, describe the kinds of businesses that exist online, and motivate you to get started.

What Are You Waiting For? Start Your Business Now!

You might have dreamed for years about starting an online business. Or, perhaps you woke up just yesterday with a brilliant idea. What are you waiting for? The truth is that the most difficult part of beginning a new endeavor is making the decision to do it. You can easily get bogged down with excuses for why your business won't happen. To keep you motivated and on track, here's a list of the Top 10 reasons to start an online business *now:*

✦ **You can gain financial freedom.** One major incentive for owning any business is the potential for a better income. The Internet offers the opportunity to create your own wealth.

✦ **You have unlimited customer reach.** No geographical boundaries exist when you run a business over the Internet. You can choose to sell your products or services within your community, within your own country, or to the entire world.

✦ **It's affordable.** You can now create a Web site inexpensively and some-times for free. The cost to maintain your site, secure products, and cover related expenses is often relatively low. This low start-up cost is especially evident when you compare the start-up costs of an online business and a traditional bricks-and-mortar business.

✦ **Your schedule is flexible.** Part time, full time, year round, or seasonal: Your schedule is up to you when you operate your virtual business. You can work in the wee hours of the night or in the middle of the day. An online business affords you the luxury of creating a work schedule that works for you.

✦ **Novices are welcome.** As the Internet has grown, *e-commerce* (a type of business activity conducted over the Internet, such as sales or adver-tising) applications have become increasingly simple to use. Although you benefit by having experience with your products or services, the process of offering those items for sale online is easy to understand. You can set up shop with little or no experience under your belt!

✦ **You can start quickly.** From online auctions like eBay to storefronts powered by Amazon.com, the tools that can help get you started are readily available, essentially overnight. Many of these sites (such as Amazon) handle all the details for you — they set up the Web site infra-structure, manage the payment and shopping cart system, and even pro-vide easy access to merchandise.

✦ **You can expand an existing business.** If you already own a business, the Internet provides you with the most economical and most efficient way to expose your business to a huge new group of customers and increase sales.

✦ **No age barriers exist.** You might be retired and itching for extra income, or perhaps you're a teenager who's only beginning to consider career opportunities. Online businesses provide economic opportunities for entrepreneurs of all ages.

✦ **A variety of ideas qualify.** As proven time and again, the Internet sup-ports a broad range of business concepts. Although some ideas are better suited to long-term success, almost all your ideas have potential.

✦ **Everyone else is doing it.** Okay, maybe your parents wouldn't approve of using this logic. It's certainly true, though: People around the world are finding success and more financial freedom by starting businesses online. It's one leap you should be proud to take!

If you're still hesitant, consider this bonus reason: The information you need in order to take your business online is *right at your fingertips* — literally. This book gives you most of what you need to get started. Whatever else you require, such as information about conducting business in your specific state or regulations for your specific industry, is out there on the Internet (put there by some other enterprising entrepreneur, no doubt). You have no more excuses!

Choosing Just the Right Business

After you decide to start your own online business, you have to take a look at the different categories of online businesses from which you can choose, which we conveniently provide in this section.

Not all online businesses will explode like Amazon or eBay. But even if your business never grows into a megastore, you need to plan for the long haul. You want your business to succeed and survive. Also, selecting the right type of online business is just as important. Losing interest or lacking an understanding of your chosen business area can hinder the growth of your new online business. Putting some thought into the type of online business you want to pursue pays off.

Creating online businesses for today and tomorrow

The secret to e-commerce success is to create a business that will stand the test of time. Sure, some people take advantage of relatively short-lived trends and make a mint (the Pet Rock and Beanie Babies, for example). The odds are small, however, that you can create the same magnitude of buying hysteria with a product or service. Still, hundreds of thousands of entrepreneurs are quietly and steadily making a respectable living by using the Internet, and their ideas will find a market for many years. They're not making millions of dollars a month, but they're paying their bills and making a profit.

The widely used term *online business* can be used in different ways. It sometimes refers to a company that operates only over the Internet and has no other physical location from which to sell goods or services. It can refer to a traditional brick-and-mortar business that also sells over the Internet. In this book, an online business is any entity (or person) using the Internet, in whole or part, as a source of income for itself, its business, or its organization (such as a club or a nonprofit agency).

Finding a business that's your type

You can pursue a variety of businesses to earn money online. Almost all types of income-generating opportunities fall into one of two categories:

✦ **Business to consumer (B2C):** Customers are typically the individual consumers who make up the general public. They buy products or services designed for personal use.

✦ **Business to business (B2B):** Customers are most likely other businesses. They might buy steel by the ton, employee uniforms, or anything that would be used primarily by a company.

Crossover between the two categories can occur. Sometimes, either type of customer can use the products or services you offer, as is the case with office supplies. And, with more businesses now shopping online, this crossover occurs frequently.

Knowing whether your primary customers are individuals or businesses helps you to create more effective marketing campaigns. Typically, these two groups buy from you for very different reasons. By marketing to each individual group, you can better target your advertising messages for increased sales. You may find that your primary customers require (or respond better to) one type of marketing, different from your secondary customers.

You find within each of the two primary categories the different types of businesses you can operate. Here are a few examples of the ways in which you can generate revenue online:

✦ **E-tail:** When you have a *brick-and-mortar* store (a physical building from which to sell retail merchandise) and you offer those retail products for sale online also, you have an e-tail site. You're responsible for hiring the resources and purchasing the tools needed to sell your wares over the Internet. One successful example of an e-tail site is the Barnes & Noble bookstore — you can buy your books online or visit the brick-and-mortar store.

✦ **Storefront:** This term is commonly used to refer to any Web site where you sell merchandise but lack a physical location for customers to visit in person (brick-and-mortar). (Offline, the retail industry uses this term to describe the outside of a building, which includes its signage, front door, and overall image.) In this book, a *storefront* is a one-stop shop for setting up an online presence to sell products. Yahoo! and CafePress. com are examples of storefronts. CafePress.com, for example, provides you with a custom page that displays all your wares. This page has a structure, though, that matches the overall CafePress.com site. Think of it as a flea market or one of those small kiosks you see in the mall — you get your very own little shopping area that you can customize, and visitors to your page see your merchandise and can learn a little about you if you choose to include personal information about yourself or your business. Good storefront providers offer the following:

  • *Templates for your Web site:* You don't need to build a site from scratch. Many storefront providers provide you with wizards or HTML files that you can customize for your storefront.

  • *Hosting options:* Many storefront providers have a variety of options for you, some free and some for a fee. These can include elements such as shopping cart systems, phone support for your storefront, discounts on fees if you pay rent by the year rather than monthly, and more.

- *A shopping cart solution:* The method that customers use to purchase products from you.

- *Payment options (possibly) and even products, in some cases:* The ability to accept online payment (credit card or debit card) is an absolute must. But other options allow payment to be deferred or even allow financing of purchases.

- *An auction:* The way your customers buy products is somewhat different when you auction items to them. Your customers can bid on the final purchase price, as opposed to buying at a price you set. (eBay, the daddy of all online auction sites, has become so popular, however, that it has blurred the lines among auction, storefront, and e-tail. We discuss eBay in Book VIII, Chapter 4.)

✦ **Service business:** You don't have to sell products to have an online business. From doing taxes to writing brochures, most professional services can be sold online, just like physical products.

✦ **Content site:** In the earliest years of the Internet, people assumed that it would always be a resource for free information. More and more, that point of view is changing. Charging a fee for all types of content and information products has become an accepted business model. And you find that as your site becomes more popular with visitors, options such as paid advertisements on your site can generate income.

✦ **E-commerce application:** If anything lends itself for sale over the Internet, it's technology. E-commerce (or electronic commerce) applications continue to provide lucrative growth for innovators. Think of e-commerce as any type of technology product that makes doing business online (and offline) easier. Inventory programs, shopping cart solutions, and payroll-management software are all examples of innovations that would fit nicely in this category.

In Book IV, we explain how to create a revenue model for your business; you can apply this model to any of these types of businesses.

As you can see, you have no shortage of opportunities to satisfy your urge to start a business. After you officially decide to take the plunge, you can narrow the field and get started.

Getting Started

Even after reading this entire chapter, you might still consider having an online business to be a dream — a vision for your future. At this point, you might want to test the water to see whether it's right for you, just as you dip your toe into a pool before diving in. At some point, though, you have to decide to go for it. To that end, this checklist describes what you need to do to begin wading into your own online business:

+ **Make the decision to commit.** Although you don't have to quit your day job yet, you need to acknowledge that you're ready to pursue your goal. Say aloud, "I want to start an online business!"

+ **Set clear goals.** Write down *why* you want this business and what you expect to gain from it. These goals can be related to financial objectives, lifestyle goals, or both. If you know what you're looking for, you can also more easily choose the right business to meet your needs.

+ **Talk with your family.** After you commit to your idea and establish your goals, share your plan. If you're married or living with a partner, you must talk about your vision for the future. After all, your dream for an online business affects that person's life too. Discussing your plans with family is also a helpful step in making your business a reality.

+ **Create an action timeline.** Unlike the broad goals you set in the first item in this list, writing down specific action steps can help you realize tangible results. From researching business ideas to obtaining a business license, assign a targeted date of completion to further ensure that you make each step happen. (Figure 1-1 shows an example of an action timeline for use with your business.)

+ **Identify a business.** As we show you in the preceding section, you can choose from different types of businesses to operate online. Before going any further, however, you have to decide which business to pursue. Narrow your choices by thinking about what you enjoy doing or which specific qualifications you might already possess. Consider your professional experience and your personal desires. You might even have a hobby that can be developed into a moneymaking business.

+ **Develop your business idea.** Define your idea and determine how you will turn it into a profitable online business. (Read Book I, Chapter 2 when you're ready to evaluate whether your idea is feasible.)

After you make it through this checklist, you're ready to go to work and transform your dream into a legitimate business.

(Sample) Start-Up Action Timeline for Your Online Business

Start date: January 15
Estimated start-up date: June 30

Action	Completion Date	Status/Comments
Finalize/validate business idea	1/30	
Write a formal business plan	2/15	
Select a business name	1/30	
Register business name	2/15	
Choose a domain name	1/30	
(if different from corporate name)		
Register domain name	1/31	
Identify business location	2/01	
Check zoning laws (if home-based)	2/05	
Set up office (computer, telephone, and so on)	2/15	
Decide organization status of company	1/30	
(sole proprietor, incorporation)		
Legalize business structure	2/28	
(file incorporation papers)		
Obtain business license	2/05	
(and other necessary permits)		
Set up a business bank account	2/05	
Meet with accountant to review tax requirements	2/10	
Obtain Employer Identification Number (EIN)	2/15	
Secure business insurance/health insurance/other	2/28	
Secure funding (if using outside sources)	3/31	
Apply for sales tax certificate (if applicable)	3/01	
Select:		
Hosting service	3/02	
Web developer	3/02	
Distributor/drop shipper (if applicable)	3/30	
Create content for Web site	4/29	
Select products and/or finalize services	5/20	
Develop Web site	6/10	
Add shopping cart/other e-commerce applications	6/15	
Obtain merchant account	6/15	
File trademarks and/or copyrights	6/16	
Submit site to major search engines	6/17	
Initiate marketing plan	6/20	
Test (and correct) all site functions	6/28	
Launch site to public!	6/30	

Figure 1-1:
A timeline
for starting
your online
business.

Chapter 2: Turning Internet Dreams into Reality

In This Chapter

✔ **Training yourself to think like a netrepreneur**

✔ **Evaluating your business idea's chances for success**

✔ **Scrutinizing your future customers**

✔ **Picking apart your competitors**

Congratulations! After you make the emotional commitment to get started, you have to shift gears and concentrate on the next set of actions that will make your Internet business a reality. From evaluating the potential success of your idea to identifying who will buy your products, you gain in this chapter the tools to help get your idea off the ground. In the process, you find out what it means to think in terms of operating a business online. In this chapter, we get you to think like a netrepreneur and start your business on the right track.

Thinking Like a Netrepreneur

Using the Internet to conduct business is similar in many ways to operating a traditional company. *Profitability* (or how much money you make after subtracting your expenses), taxes, and customer feedback are examples of factors that affect your business whether it's online or off. Some exceptions, however, set apart an online business. Even the most experienced entrepreneur can get caught in the trap of forgetting those differences. Particularly important are your attitude and how you approach the business as a netrepreneur.

As you read this chapter, you see the term *netrepreneur* frequently. You often hear it used in the business community, too. The term developed in response to the growing number of people moving their businesses online. The term combines *Net,* the slang term for Internet, with the word *entrepreneur,* which is someone who assumes the risk and rewards of a new enterprise. *Netrepreneur* (or the variation *netpreneur*) simply refers to an innovative business owner, like you, who conducts business online.

Adjusting your attitude slightly and viewing business from behind the lens of a netrepreneur isn't difficult. Doing so is simply a matter of recognizing that the Internet changes the way you can and should operate your online business.

When you think like a netrepreneur, you

✦ **See the invisible storefront.** Although the doors, walls, and even the salesclerk for your online business might be invisible, they definitely exist. In fact, every part of your Web business leaves a distinct impression. Yet rarely do you hear or see the response to your storefront directly from customers. Consequently, and contrary to popular belief, a Web site demands your continual care and attention — new products to add, bugs to fix, replying to e-mail, and more.

✦ **Understand who your customers are.** Even if you don't personally greet your online visitors, don't be fooled: The Internet offers the unique opportunity to learn and understand almost everything about your customers. You can learn where else they shop, how much time they spend on your site, what products they're interested in, where they live and work, how much they earn annually, whether they are parents, and which magazines they read. Netrepreneurs collect and use this information regularly in an effort to increase sales and better serve their customers. (When you're ready to meet your customer, turn to Book VI, where we explain how to get and use this wealth of customer information.)

✦ **Respond to fast and furious changes.** The way people use the Internet to buy, sell, or search for products and services changes rapidly. Also, the rules for operating an online business as imposed by both the government and the business world in general are modified almost daily. Sustaining success online means that you must take the initiative to keep up with new trends, laws and regulations, safety and security concerns, technology, and even marketing tools.

✦ **Speak the language.** Communicating to your customers through a Web site can be challenging. Your buyers want and expect quick and easy access to information. Because attention spans are limited, content should always be relevant, easy to find, and to the point.

As an entrepreneur, you must choose your words carefully. Your site's content, including the words you use on your Web pages, serves two purposes:

• It helps sell your products or services to visitors.

• It plays a big role in *search engine optimization,* or the way you can increase visits to your site by placing higher on the list of rankings by Internet search engines.

✦ **Know when (or whether) to innovate.** You might be able to develop a new or different method for doing business online, although it's probably not necessary. Innovative tools already exist, and you can often find them on the Internet quickly and cheaply. You don't need to re-create the wheel — you just have to know how to find and apply the tools that are already out there.

✦ **Reap repeated rewards.** Establishing multiple streams of revenue or maximizing a single source of revenue is a common practice online. For instance, you might have an outstanding information product for sale on your site. The same product can just as easily be sold on other Web sites in exchange for a small percentage of earnings. Or, you can choose to add another netrepreneur's product to your site and pay that person a percentage of earnings. (To begin increasing your earnings, read about affiliate programs in Book IV.)

Putting Your Business Idea under the Microscope

Every successful business begins with that first idea. From fast-food restaurants to selling cosmetics from home, Ray Kroc first dreamed of hamburgers, and Mary Kay visualized selling makeup door to door. Your dream for an innovative new business is no exception. Maybe you have several unique concepts to choose from or are already firmly set on a single one. Either way, how do you decide whether you should quit your day job and focus on your brilliant idea? You have to pick apart the idea, observe closely, and determine whether it merits a full-time (or even a part-time) business. This section describes the three methods you can use to decide whether your idea has real potential.

Using informal research to verify your idea

The best place to begin gathering information is from sources closest to you. Be prepared to receive varying opinions — both positive and negative. Use this input as a general gauge of whether to continue reaching out to the next source of information. You and your idea are in the center, surrounded by three rings from which to collect input. If the ring closest to you provides mostly positive input, proceed to the next ring. (See Figure 2-1.)

Ring 1 consists of your friends, family, and co-workers. Ask them these questions:

✦ Have you ever heard of this type of product or service?

✦ Would you buy this product or service?

✦ Do you think that it's a good idea?

✦ What challenges do you think I will encounter?

✦ What are the benefits?

✦ Can you envision me selling this product or service? Why or why not?

Three Rings of Decision

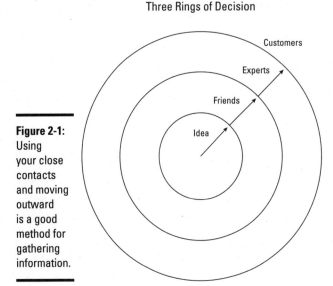

Figure 2-1:
Using
your close
contacts
and moving
outward
is a good
method for
gathering
information.

In Ring 2, seek input from industry professionals, investors, other entrepreneurs, and organizations that offer support to small businesses. Ask questions similar to those listed for Ring 1. Because of the experience the people in Ring 2 have, you should give more weight to their responses. Small-business support resources include

✦ **Small Business Administration (SBA) at www.sba.gov:** The SBA, a government-sponsored organization, helps small business owners with loans, navigating paperwork, free seminars, and other services.

✦ **Small Business Development Center (SBDC) at www.sba.gov/sbdc:** The SBA provides its services through local branches.

✦ **Chamber of Commerce at www.uschamber.com:** From small towns to large cities, all local chambers help owners develop their small businesses.

✦ **SCORE at www.score.org:** This network of retired executives counseling small businesses matches small-business owners with business-exec retirees who volunteer their time to help small businesses develop and prosper.

✦ **Women's Business Center www.onlinewbc.gov:** The SBA has a special group dedicated to women who want to create small businesses.

In Ring 3 are your potential customers. Ask them these questions:

✦ Would you use this product or service?

✦ Have you used something similar?

✦ How much would you be willing to pay?

✦ How often would you use it?

✦ Where would you normally go to buy this product or service?

✦ Would you order it over the Internet?

If you find that you're receiving a majority of positive feedback from sources in all three rings, you can consider your idea worthwhile. Or, at least you have enough validation to continue to the next phase of your evaluation process.

Applying a SWOT analysis to your idea

Another popular method for determining the pros and cons of an idea is referred to as *SWOT analysis.* (SWOT is short for strengths, weaknesses, opportunities, and threats.) Companies use it for several reasons, including as a decision-making tool for product development. The simple process also lends itself to a more thorough investigation of your business idea. This section covers how you can put your idea to the SWOT test!

Create your own SWOT chart by following these steps:

1. **On paper, draw a cross (or a box divided in half both horizontally and vertically) to create four separate quadrants, as shown in Figure 2-2.**

2. **Label the upper-left quadrant as** Strengths.

3. **Label the upper-right quadrant as** Weaknesses.

4. **Label the lower-left quadrant as** Opportunities.

5. **Label the lower-right quadrant as** Threats.

   After you draw and label the chart, you can begin to fill in the details.

6. **In each quadrant, write down the factors that influence or contribute to each of your four SWOT categories.**

Strengths and weaknesses are considered *internal* factors that control or specifically contribute (good or bad) to the business concept. Opportunities and threats are *external* factors that are influenced to some extent by the environment or are otherwise outside of your control.

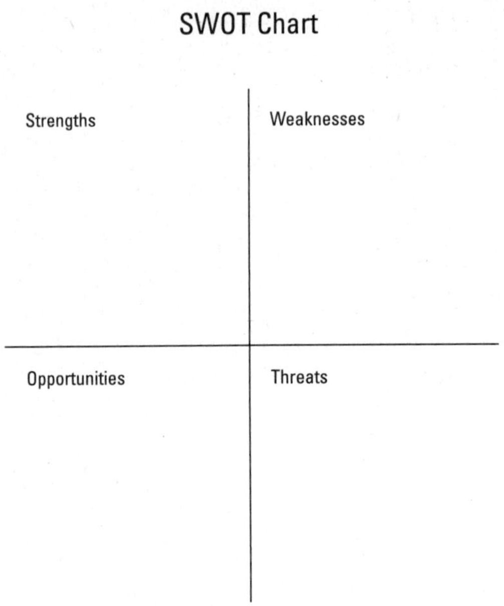

SWOT Chart

Strengths   Weaknesses

Figure 2-2:
Start your   Opportunities   Threats
SWOT chart
to help
investigate
your
business
idea.

7. **Analyze the information you filled in. Ask yourself the following questions to start developing your SWOT analysis:**

   Strengths

   - What advantages does the product or service offer?
   - Do I have expertise in this business or industry?
   - Can I get a patent to protect the idea?

   Weaknesses

   - How much does developing the product cost?
   - Is getting suppliers difficult?
   - Am I learning a new industry from the ground up?

   Opportunities

   - Does my idea take advantage of a new technology?
   - Is my product or service in demand?
   - Have changes in policies or regulations made my idea necessary?

   Threats

   - Does my product or service have established competitors?
   - Do my competitors sell the product or service for less than I can?
   - Will changes in technology make my product obsolete?

Use the feedback you receive from your informal research (during the Three Rings exercise) as factors in your SWOT quadrants. Combining other people's opinions with your own provides a more comprehensive — and useful — SWOT analysis.

8. **After you fill in the categories of your first SWOT analysis, take a look at which quadrants have identified the most, or most significant, factors.**

    The strengths and opportunities that are listed indicate the advantage you might have in the marketplace. If you're lucky, they outweigh your weaknesses and challenges. Perhaps you can now see what you must do to offset those disadvantages if you really want your idea to work.

Whatever the outcome of your analysis, you should have a better feel for the value of your business idea after viewing the completed SWOT analysis.

Choosing the best idea for YOU

Perhaps you have no trouble dreaming up new ideas for a business. Instead, your challenge is deciding which *one* to pursue. Unlike the SWOT analysis or feasibility study, no established test determines which of your many pursuits is best suited for you. This decision is much more subjective and personal. However, you can ask yourself a few questions to get guidance. For each of the following questions, choose the answer that best reflects how you feel. Total the points to show your numerical score. Take this quiz for every business idea you have on your plate. Don't forget to compare your final scores.

Neutral or none	Not much	Somewhat	Very much
(0 points)	(1 point)	(2 points)	(3 points)

- Does this idea interest you?
- Does this product or service *excite* you?
- Do you have experience with this product or service?
- Does it require a large investment?
- Do you have money readily available to fund the concept?
- Will starting this business require you to alter your lifestyle?
- Are you willing to change your lifestyle for this idea?
- Does this business reflect your personal goals?
- Does this idea reflect your professional goals?
- Can you imagine owning this same business in ten years?
- Did your idea pass your feasibility test?

Creating a feasibility study to validate an idea

After your idea gains a nod of approval from friends and family and the SWOT analysis indicates that your product has merit, your idea must jump through one more hoop for complete validation. A *feasibility study* is a somewhat formal, written process that helps you determine whether your idea is realistic. The goal of the study is to provide you with final proof, so to speak, that your business concept is viable.

A feasibility study answers these basic questions:

✦ Will the product or service work?

✦ How much will it cost to start?

✦ Can your idea make you money?

✦ Is the business concept *really* worth your time and energy?

A feasibility study kicks your analysis up a notch. It relies on in-depth research to provide more detailed answers to questions in five primary areas:

✦ **Your product and service**

- What is the product or service?

- How will my customers use it?

- Where or how will my customers buy it?

- How is it designed, and how is it delivered to my customers?

- Am I testing to ensure that my product works correctly? (Describe these tests in detail.)

✦ **Your experience (including your management team's experience)**

- Who is my management team?

- What experience do I and my employees have?

- What are my specific skills and credentials?

- Which skills am I missing, or in which areas am I weak?

- How much time can I devote to my business?

✦ **The market in which you're competing**

- What is the demand for my product?

- Who are my customers? (What is the target market?)

- How big is the size of the market I'm selling to?

- What is the status of the market? Is it growing or stagnant?

- Where and how can I reach those customers?

+ **Your competition**

  • Who are my primary and secondary competitors? (Describe each of your competitors in detail.)

  • How do my competitors market their products or services?

  • What makes me different or better than my competitors?

  • Is my product easy to copy? How can I prevent it?

+ **Your costs**

  • How much does it cost to make my product or produce my service?

  • What other business costs do I have?

  • What amount of money do I need to start?

  • Do I have access to funding?

  • When will I make a profit?

Now you know how much information you have to gather in your feasibility study. As you answer all these questions, make sure that you back up those answers with detailed research. Then write your results in a one-page summary that discusses what you discovered. Your summary should answer the five basic questions in each category and provide proof of whether you have a viable idea. After the validation process is complete, you can turn your attention to the next piece of the business success puzzle: potential customers.

Identifying Your Market and Target Customer

The terms *target market* and *target customer* are ultimately defined as the entities that buy your product or service. Although these phrases are sometimes used interchangeably, *market* is often used to describe a collection of individual target customers.

The target represents the people who are most likely to buy or use your product or service.

Classifying your customer

Knowing your target customer is an important advantage when you begin marketing. As we explain in earlier sections in this chapter, recognizing your primary customers lends credibility to your business concept. The more you know about your target customers, the more easily and cost-efficiently you can build your business and market to these folks.

How do you decide who this person is or who the groups of people are? You can describe or segment your customers. The two most common classifications are

+ **Demographics:** Age, income, gender, and occupation are examples of common factors used to describe your customers.

+ **Psychographics**: Music choices, hobbies, and other preferences make up this category. Usually, psychographics reflect lifestyle choices.

You can also describe your customers in other terms, such as these categories:

+ **Benefits:** Describe why customers use your product or service. For example, customers might need it for medical purposes, or they might receive a luxury benefit, where they don't *need* the product or service but choose to invest in it for perceived benefits.

+ **Geographic preferences:** Point out where people live. The location can include a specific neighborhood, city, state, region, or even country. Customers can also be segmented according to home (or residential) locations versus business locations.

+ **Use-based preferences:** Specify how frequently customers want or need your product.

Typically, your target market includes customers described by a mixture of the terms and categories in this list. For instance, if you sell cotton-candy-flavored lip gloss, your target market might be described this way:

Girls

Ten to 14 years old

Live at home, in households having a combined annual income of $50,000 or more

Listen to pop music and participate in at least one extracurricular activity per week

Buy makeup products at least monthly to enhance appearance

Depending on what type of product you sell, your target market most likely includes a wider mix of customer types — not just one.

Going to the source

In the preceding section, we talk about what a market description might consist of. Where do you get the information to build this type of description, though? You can use any or all of the following methods to gather information for your customer profile:

+ **Survey potential (or existing) customers.** Conduct a focus group in which you interview a small group of likely customers. Or, distribute a survey or registration form online to gather the data.

✦ **Observe competitors' customers.** Stake out your competitors by visiting them online. You can often discover exactly what competitors think about their own customers just by reading through their sites. (This information is often readily available on competitors' Web sites, in sections labeled About Us or Company Information.) For competitors with retail locations, visit their stores and observe the customers and their habits in person.

✦ **Use published market research.** To identify the types of customers most likely to buy your products, read about trends in reputable market reports. You can find much of the research for free online. Larger research firms charge a fee (which can range from several hundred dollars to several thousand dollars per report) for detailed reports. If this is something you're interested in, start with companies such as Gartner Group (www.gartner.com) or IDC (www.idc.com).

Use this information to pinpoint exactly who your customer is.

Competing to Win: Analyzing Your Competition

If you're serious about developing a successful online business, you need every advantage possible. That means getting to know not only who your customers are but also who else is after their business. Start by writing down a list of your top three to five competitors.

Keep this list on hand, and document basic information, such as

✦ Web site address

✦ Physical address (if they have one) and number of locations

✦ Annual sales

✦ Number of employees

✦ Types of products or services offered (with full description)

✦ Strengths and weaknesses

✦ Copies of ads, flyers, and brochures

✦ Special promotions (especially online offers)

✦ Pricing information for products or services similar to yours

As a quick and easy way to keep up with your competition, visit their Web sites and sign up for their newsletters and other promotional offers by e-mail.

Be sure to maintain a list of your secondary competitors, too. These companies don't sell your exact products or services but come close enough to compete for your customers' dollars.

Hooray! You completed your due diligence and have a fat file of information about all your stiffest competition. What now? This kind of data does you no good when it just takes up space in a filing cabinet. Use it to your advantage.

Sift through your collected information again to refresh your memory (because you probably have lots of information), and follow these steps:

✦ **Compare apples to oranges.** Using the information you collect, compare both your strengths and weaknesses to that of the competition. (You can even do a complete SWOT analysis on each one of your competitors!) This comparison identifies where you fit in the marketplace relative to other players in your area of interest.

✦ **Plan your marketing strategy.** You have access to your competitor's marketing material, so use it to define your own marketing strategy. Play up your company's strengths in ads; advertise in markets that your competitors missed; and plan to educate your customers on the benefits that separate you from your competition.

✦ **Create a competitive pricing model.** Maybe you discovered that you can beat a competitor's price. Or, perhaps your research shows that you *must* price lower to survive. Use pricing data of a competitor to map out the best pricing model for your product or service.

✦ **Determine growth models and financial requirements.** Suppose that a major competitor is ready to partner with a big distributor. Although you might not be able to compete immediately, this information helps you plan for growth. Use this knowledge to better understand your competitors' growth and financial strategies, and then adjust yours accordingly.

The old cliché is still accurate: Knowledge is power. Don't let good information go to waste. Use what you learn to differentiate yourself and win points with your customers.

Chapter 3: Getting Real: Creating a Usable Business Plan

*O*ne big complaint from entrepreneurs, especially those running small companies is "Why do I have to write a business plan?" Quite honestly, you don't. Several entrepreneurs even chose not to create written guides for their businesses. Some are doing just fine, and others are struggling.

In this chapter, we tell you why having a business plan is a good idea and show you all the benefits you can reap from not only having one but also reviewing and updating it regularly.

We can't possibly cover everything about writing and using a business plan in this chapter. After all, entire books are devoted to business plans. In fact, a good one to look into is *Business Plans For Dummies,* 2nd Edition, by Paul Tiffany and Steven D. Peterson (Wiley Publishing).

Understanding the Value of a Plan

Starting and managing a business without a business plan is, like it or not, the same as searching for a buried treasure without a map: Although you know that the gold is in the ground somewhere, you're wasting an awful lot of time by randomly digging holes in the hope of eventually hitting the jackpot. Without a plan, the odds of success aren't in your favor.

Why, then, do people resist using this tool? They resist it for two reasons:

✦ **Having a plan involves a great deal of work.** Don't despair: You can minimize the amount of work involved, which we get to momentarily.

✦ **They don't understand the importance of having a plan.**

To help you overcome your business plan angst, we provide these reasons for having a plan — you can decide whether to take another step without one:

✦ **You can more easily secure money:** This goal is probably the most common reason for the creation of a business plan. If you decide to ask strangers to lend you money, whether those strangers are bankers or private investors, they want to see a plan. Lenders have a better chance of protecting (and recouping) their investments when a formal strategy documents your projected income and profits. Even if you're counting on family members for a loan or are using your own funds, having a business plan confirms that you have thought about how to use the money wisely.

✦ **A plan creates a vision that gives you a well-defined goal:** Coming up with a great idea and transitioning it into a viable business opportunity can be challenging. Having a written plan forces you to fully develop the long-term vision for your product or service. With those clearly defined goals in place, you stand a much better chance of accomplishing your vision.

✦ **A plan can provide timeless guidance:** Done correctly, this document provides a concrete plan of operation for your business — not only during your start-up phase but also for three to five years down the road. Keep in mind that the plan might need occasional tweaking (as discussed at the end of this chapter). However, investing the time now to create a strong foundation ensures that you have a barometer to help you make decisions for managing your company.

Chances are that at least two of the three reasons on this list are valuable to you. Even if you don't plan to attract investors, you're already forming a picture about what your company looks like, and you're setting goals to make sure that you get there. The only remaining step is to make your thoughts more permanent by writing them down in a business plan.

Recognizing That the Parts of the Plan Make a Whole

A traditional business plan is sectioned into seven or eight major parts. At first, that number of parts might seem a bit overwhelming. Consider, however, that most experts recommend keeping a finished business plan to fewer than 20 pages. (You can usually get by with many fewer pages.) When you break down that recommendation, each section becomes only 2 or 3 pages long, which translates to 5 or 6 paragraphs per page. It's not so much after all!

Each part plays a critical role in your overall plan. Although each section can almost stand alone, the sections work together to present a complete picture, or vision, of your business. Don't even think about omitting one of them!

Depending on your main purpose for having a business plan, you can develop sections with more diligence. For example, if you're seeking outside funding, make sure that the Financials section is as thorough and accurate as possible.

Before you start writing, get a sense of the scope of your plan by reading these brief descriptions of the basic parts you need to cover:

✦ **Executive summary:** Although this part comes first in your plan, you typically write it last. This brief page does just what it says: It highlights the major points from each of the other parts of the plan. This page is usually the first one that investors and other advisors read, and how well it's written can determine whether they turn the page or show you the door.

✦ **Business or product description:** This section provides a detailed description of your overall business and your product or service. You should include a *vision statement* (or *mission statement*), which summarizes your goals for the business. When you describe your product or service, don't forget to pinpoint what makes it a unique and viable contender in the marketplace.

✦ **Market analysis:** Provide a thorough description of your target market. In this case, discuss both the overall industry in which you're competing and the specific customers to whom you're marketing. Don't forget to include a description of any market research you conducted.

✦ **Competitive analysis:** In much the same way as you describe your target market in the market analysis, in this one you provide an in-depth view of your competitors in that market. The more detail you can provide, the better, to show exactly how well you understand (and are prepared for dealing with) your competition. Address your competitors' weaknesses and also state how you can counter their strengths.

Don't double up on your work. Use information you gather during your SWOT analysis and feasibility study (see Book I, Chapter 2). Adapt the research and results of both to include in the market-analysis and competitive-analysis sections of your business plan.

✦ **Management team:** Whether you're flying solo on this operation or working with a team, highlight the expertise that you and your executives bring to the table. Include summaries of your key professional experience, educational and military background, additional certifications or completed training programs, and all other relevant accomplishments. Remember to include a copy of your full résumé.

✦ **Operations:** Here's where the "rubber meets the road." Use this section to describe your marketing and operations strategies. Then detail *how* you plan to implement these strategies in your business. Think of the Operations section as your chance to prove that you know how to convert innovative ideas into a successful business.

✦ **Financials:** Start talking money. In this section, you include projections (or estimates) of how much money the business will earn and your expenses, or costs of doing business. This combination is typically referred to as a *profit-and-loss statement.* For the first year, break down this information for each month. (This listing demonstrates how far you must proceed into your first year before you start making money and indicates where seasonal slow points might occur, with smaller amounts of income coming in.) After the first year, show your projections annually. (See Book II for complete descriptions of legal and accounting requirements.)

When you're pursuing outside funding, try to be optimistic about your financial projections. Don't be unrealistic, and don't be too conservative, either. If you're using the plan only internally, you can play it safe and estimate your future profits toward the lower end.

✦ **Appendix:** Consider this area a catchall for important documents that support portions of your business plan. Place copies of your loan terms, patent or copyright documentation, employee agreements, and any other contracts or legal documents pertaining to your business.

You might wonder, of course, whether you can specifically use a separate business plan format with an online business. No, not really. As you can see from the descriptions in the preceding list, each part or section of the plan is generic. You can use almost any business plan template, tailor it slightly to your specific type of business, and achieve the same results.

Having a "sample" plan written for an organization similar to your online business is helpful. Check out one of the business-planning resource centers on the Web, such as Bplans (www.bplans.com), to locate a sample plan specifically for online businesses to use as a guide. (See Figure 3-1.)

Figure 3-1:
Find sample
business
plans at
sites such as
Bplans.com.

Getting Help to Write the Plan

Even though you will probably feel better about writing a business plan after you read the rest of this chapter, more options can help make writing one easier. When creating a plan feels like more than you can handle alone, the solution is to hire a professional to write it for you or purchase business plan software that walks you through the process.

Don't think that a business plan template or other software package is cheating. Your goal is to get your business off the ground — don't close any doors or turn away any help. The money you spend on your business plan is an investment that has the potential to pay back many times; the time you spend on your business plan can likewise shorten the time you must spend later in preparing your business for success.

Determining when to hire a professional

Not everyone needs outside help to construct a solid business plan. If you're starting the business part-time or you plan to be a one-person company for a while, the plan doesn't necessarily have to be lengthy and complicated.

As a *sole proprietor* (one-person company), part-time operator, or home-based business owner, you might write a condensed version of the business plan, with the same sections but less detail. Rather than use a 20-page document, you might be able to achieve the same objective in only 8 pages.

Alternatively, if you need to secure a large amount of money for your online business start-up, it just might pay (literally) to get help — especially if you plan to *pitch* (sell) your business idea to savvy investors, such as venture capitalists. Bringing in a seasoned business plan writer helps you

+ Add polish to your plan

+ Remember to include pertinent information

+ Phrase the wording of your business plan in the best possible way so that you speak the language of investors

If you're pressed for time, getting assistance might also speed the process for you. Additionally, if you commit to using the business plan to its full potential (as a long-term operational guide), hiring an experienced consultant almost guarantees that your plan is a top-notch piece of work.

Knowing what to expect from a business plan consultant

After you decide to seek assistance with your plan, you might be surprised to find that you're still expected to contribute information. Business plan writers are often referred to as consultants, and for good reason: You consult these folks to get advice and guidance on how to make the most of your plan.

A consultant translates your thoughts into the final written document. Consultants aren't mind readers, though: You're still responsible for providing all the initial information, often in written form.

You might be wondering how much this service costs. After you realize that you're still doing a good bit of the work, your expectations on price might change. Regardless of the amount of work you must contribute, however, writing the plan still takes a great deal of time, and you're paying for the consultant's expertise. Expect to pay the minimum national average of $1,500 to $5,000 for a business plan written by a professional.

Keep in mind that wide variations might still exist, on both ends of the price scale, for this service. Much of the final price depends on

+ Your requirements for the plan

+ What you can contribute (to save the consultant time)

✦ The consultant's experience level

✦ The complexity of the business concept

✦ The amount of research required to substantiate the plan

Although a more knowledgeable consultant might charge a higher hourly fee, she could complete the project much sooner because of her experience. A consultant who "lowballs" the price of the project might not fully understand the amount of time involved and might try to increase the quoted price later.

When you're working with a professional, the length of time to complete your plan depends on several factors. Here are some examples:

✦ How much information you can provide

✦ How quickly you can provide the information

✦ How extensive the plan is that you need

✦ How available and easily accessible the facts about your business are

If you decide to hire a professional, check first with experienced advisors who offer free assistance. Your local Chamber of Commerce or SCORE (Counselor's to America's Small Businesses) might provide enough to support writing the plan yourself. The Small Business Administration (SBA) offers an online tutorial for writing a business plan at www.sba.gov. (See Figure 3-2.)

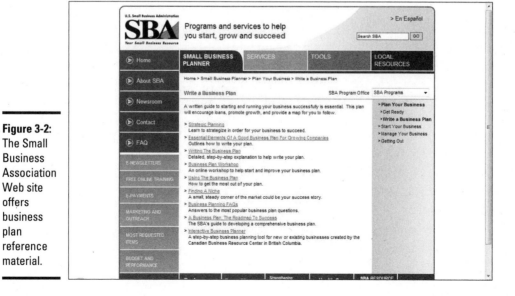

Figure 3-2:
The Small
Business
Association
Web site
offers
business
plan
reference
material.

When you're ready to hire a professional, keep these points in mind:

✦ Look for someone with experience in your product or service industry.

✦ Find a consultant who's comfortable with, and knowledgeable of, online businesses.

✦ Review samples of other business plans the consultant has written.

✦ Ask for written testimonials and references you can contact.

✦ Get a firm price quote.

✦ Agree on a reasonable timeline for completing the plan.

✦ Put your final terms into a written contract, including specifics of what you're responsible for providing.

Using a Business Plan Today, Tomorrow, and Always

Ignoring your business plan or forgetting to maintain it is the same as failing to plan. To ensure that your business plan passes the test of time, consider these suggestions for ways to use it:

✦ **As reference material:** Refer to your plan often. Rereading your original plan is a good way to make sure that you're staying on track.

✦ **As a decision-making tool:** When major operational issues occur or expansion opportunities arise, turn to your business plan. Decide whether the issue at hand fits your original goals and timeline before taking action.

✦ **As a troubleshooter:** When problems surface, minimize your frustrations. Use your own words of wisdom to resolve your problems. Take a look at your plan to see where the hiccup is. More than likely, you addressed potential problems in the Operations section of your business plan.

✦ **As a vision guide:** After your business is running, you can easily lose sight of the big picture. Concentrating on daily tasks and problems can derail your overall progress. Check your plan frequently and refocus your vision.

Every January, schedule at least two business plan preview sessions for the coming year. If necessary, pencil in a date and time on your calendar. (Block out three or four hours.) Do this task semiannually or quarterly, depending on whether you made, or will make, significant changes to your business.

Chapter 4: Finding Money to Fund Your Online Start-Up

In This Chapter

↙ Getting started with little or no money

↙ Selling others on your idea

↙ Searching for alternative money sources

↙ Avoiding start-up costs with an upfront investment in an existing business

One of the most important choices you make when you're creating a company is how to fund your brave new endeavor. The amount of money you have available and where it comes from truly helps you begin defining the rules by which you must operate the business.

If you borrow $25,000 from a bank, for example, right away you know what's at stake. Each month you *have* to come up with at least enough money to cover that loan payment or else you risk jeopardizing your personal credit record (if you're a sole proprietorship and aren't incorporated). On the other hand, if you borrow $5,000 from your in-laws, you're potentially inviting additional decision-makers into your business because there's no such thing as "silent" in-laws.

Whether you need $500 or $500,000 to get your business going, this chapter shows you various financing options and describes what each one means to the future of your business.

Bootstrapping the Low-Cost, No-Cost Site

We don't lie to you: Just like starting a political campaign, having plenty of money available makes things easier when you're starting a business. Fortunately, having a lot of money isn't a requirement to start an Internet business. If you don't have access to megabucks, you can always *bootstrap* your new business. (The term comes from the idea of pulling yourself up by your own bootstraps, or making your own way.) In the case of financing your entrepreneurial dream, bootstrapping is a matter of making a little money go a long way.

Making the leap to the bootstrapping lifestyle

One of the first rules of bootstrapping is to hang on to other sources of income for as long as possible. In other words, keep your day job! You might have to design your Web site during lunch breaks or work past midnight to prepare customer orders for shipping. Although keeping a regular job while starting a business can mean a grueling schedule, it provides you with much-needed financial security in the early stages of building your company.

Try something between maintaining a full-time job and starting a business. Many entrepreneurs worked part-time jobs at night so that they could dedicate themselves to their new businesses during the day.

If you're the all-or-nothing type, perhaps you want to throw yourself completely into the business or you're confident enough in your idea that you just *know* success (cash!) will materialize. You should still plan for alternative sources of income. Look for freelance work, short-term consulting jobs, or whatever else it takes to keep money coming in while building your business.

Saving money to make money

Making sure that cash is coming into your business is only your first step. Learning to conserve your cash is the second rule of bootstrapping. Controlling the *outflow* of money, or how that money is used, is quite important.

Here are some ways that any good bootstrapper can conserve cash:

✦ **Become frugal.** Spend only when absolutely necessary, and then buy "on the cheap." Rather than buy brand-new office furniture, for example, find what you need by shopping garage sales, thrift stores, and eBay!

✦ **Budget wisely.** Create a financial plan that helps you track income, expenses, and projected sales. By monitoring the money you have coming in and going out every day, you're less likely to get into trouble. Book II shows you exactly how to establish this type of budget and set up your accounting procedures.

✦ **Use other people's money.** Rather than borrow money from banks or investors, "borrow" money from your suppliers and customers. You can negotiate terms with vendors that allow you to pay for supplies 30, 60, or 90 days out (in other words, after you receive them). Then ask customers to pay for your product or services up front or in "Net 15" days. This strategy lets you use your customer's money, rather than cash out of your pocket, to pay off your expenses.

✦ **Sacrifice for the business.** The cash coming into your business should be just that — money for your business. If you're using revenues to support your personal lifestyle, the business doesn't stand a chance. Bootstrappers commonly forfeit luxuries and even downgrade their living circumstances while growing a company. Could you live in a smaller house for a while or drive a less expensive car?

✦ **Inspire, don't hire.** The early stages of building your company can be overwhelming, with lots of hats for you to wear. Rather than hire full-time employees, inspire others to work with you *gratis* (for free). Not everyone wants or needs immediate compensation, so sell people on your skills as a leader and get them excited about where your company is headed. The promise of a job (after you're on more stable financial ground) may be enough to get someone working five or six hours a week right now. Some individuals are willing to work for free, in return for a recommendation from your company. A lot of people design comple-mentary Web sites, in exchange for using those businesses as client referrals. By seeking out this type of synergistic swap, you can avoid hiring employees in the beginning.

✦ **Find a mentor.** Hiring a consultant can break the bank before you even open your doors for business. Mentoring is an alternative way to get advice from established professionals that costs you absolutely nothing. These experts probably won't do the work for you. They can advise you on critical decisions, introduce you to other professionals and suppli-ers, and sometimes even help you find your first customers. People are generous with their time, especially when you ask them to share their personal expertise with you.

Getting resourceful

In addition to locating experts or finding cash, you need to identify other means of getting what you need. Check out these resourceful alternatives to help you jump-start your online business:

✦ **Barter and trade:** One way to keep a lid on your spending and still acquire supplies and services is to trade with other companies. Rather than pay a professional to write copy for your Web pages, for example, barter with a writer for her service. *Barter,* or trade, is a method of paying for products or services, without using cash. When you *barter,* you exchange your services or products for those of another person (or company). This method of conducting business has become so popular that you can now join formal barter-exchange organizations, such as Southern Barter (see Figure 4-1). Membership is usually free. You can find barter organizations online that serve your specific state or region or find one that has a national reach.

The Internal Revenue Service (IRS) doesn't mind bartering, as long as you record on your taxes whatever you receive as income. Any transac-tion involving the exchange of a product or service that doesn't involve cash changing hands is considered "barter" by the IRS. The IRS advises that both you and the other person agree ahead of time on a fair market value (the price you would normally pay for the service or product). That amount should appear as income for both of you when you com-plete Form 1099 (as shown in Figure 4-2). You can read the complete guidelines for how to report bartering as income on the IRS Web site (www.irs.gov).

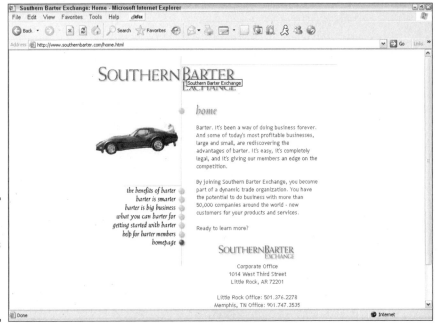

Figure 4-1: Online communities let you barter goods and services.

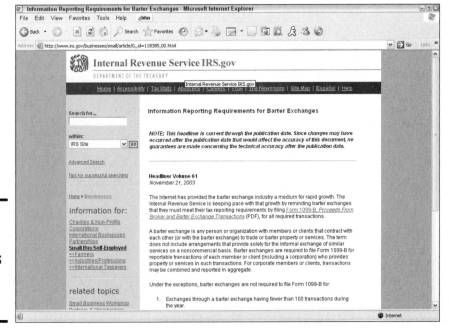

Figure 4-2: When bartering, use the IRS 1099 Form to show income.

✦ **Try out trial versions before you buy.** When you stock up on necessary software for your online business, don't rush to buy expensive off-the-shelf products, which can cost several hundred dollars. Instead, use free demonstration (demo) versions that are good for a specified period. Eventually these free trials run out of time, so budget accordingly if you anticipate needing to make a more permanent software purchase.

Visit the Web sites of the companies that produce or distribute your favorite software to see whether you can find demo or trial versions.

✦ **Use freeware.** This type of software is distributed for free over the Internet. Independent software developers and small companies typically offer software applications, graphics, games, and developer tools at no cost to you, and with no strings attached. Even if you don't find a recognizable brand-name product, you might find one that has similar features. Be aware that freeware almost never has technical support, so if you use it, you're on your own!

Here are several Web sites that keep a list of available freeware:

- Tucows.com: www.tucows.com (see Figure 4-3)

- MajorGeeks.com: www.majorgeeks.com

- Free-Downloadable-Software.com: www.free-downloadable-software.com

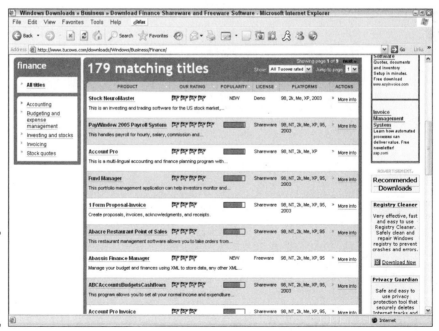

Figure 4-3:
Search for free software at Tucows.com.

A bootstrapping success

Started with $100, TicketsNow.com became a major industry competitor, and its founder became a multimillionaire. How did this accomplishment come about?

After three years of college, Mike Domek ran out of money and enthusiasm for his formal education. Deciding instead to gamble as an entrepreneur, he wrote a personal check for $100 and incorporated his new business. He managed to buy a few office supplies and a two-line phone system and then converted his one-bedroom apartment to an office. Mike's company specialized in locating premium seating and sold-out tickets for major events, such as rock concerts and sporting competitions.

The business was customer-service-intensive, and before long, Mike realized the inefficiency of the business. So, in 1999, he moved the business to the Internet. This strategy gave his customers the option of searching for event tickets themselves and then purchasing them online. Mike was pinching pennies to self-fund growth for the company.

The risk paid off. Online-event ticket sales grew to be a billion-dollar industry. Mike's company became the world's largest online marketing place for premium ticket sales and in January 2008 he sold the company to Ticketmaster for $265 million. That's not a bad return on a $100 investment!

Looking at the pros and cons of bootstrapping

Bootstrapping may sound like you're flying by the seat of your pants (or your boots), but it's quite the opposite. It requires adopting a rigorous thought process that includes detailed and innovative planning.

Although bootstrapping may seem painful, consider the alternative of bringing in other investors or borrowing money. Is it worth the sacrifice? Take a look at how this approach can affect your business now and down the road, and then decide for yourself:

✦ **You retain ownership.** Keeping full ownership or controlling interest of the business is one of the most important benefits of bootstrapping. You get to make all the decisions, without having to run them by investors or shareholders or even lenders first. You also choose how and when the company grows. And, if you need to bring in capital (money) down the road by selling shares of your company, you don't jeopardize your control. You can sell off a minority interest and maintain controlling interest.

✦ **You can make quick decisions.** Typically, you don't have layers of departments or managers within a bootstrapper organization. You can make decisions without getting bogged down by bureaucratic red tape. That's an important advantage over competitors, especially when you're heavily into the research-and -development (R&D) process. Your organization can offer new products or make other changes much faster than many of your competitors can.

✦ **You assume minimal risk.** Without putting much money on the line, your risk (or what you can afford to lose) is greatly reduced. You also have the most to gain, though, because your investment and risk factor are small. This motivating factor can spur you to success.

✦ **You maintain a cash-is-king mindset:** Being frugal pays off now and later. Initially, your conservative decisions assist you in building a positive cash flow for your business. As a bootstrapper, you tend to hold on to those same decision-making philosophies in an effort to maintain your cash reserves as the company expands. This mindset may help to keep your online business debt free.

Finding the Perfect Investor

Not everyone has what it takes to grow a successful company from nothing or while operating on a shoestring. Or, maybe your business concept requires a significant injection of capital right from the start. If so, you have other alternatives to bootstrapping. The most popular approach is to find an investor.

Investors, either individuals or a group of individuals, buy into your idea and provide the money you need in exchange for stock (or a percentage of ownership) in your business. You can choose from several types of investors; each type comes with its own pros and cons, of course. The trick is to find the best type of investor for your needs.

Turning to your friends and family network

You're probably familiar with the idea of turning to friends and family, or the *F&F network,* for start-up funds. A major advantage of this strategy is that you have a lot of flexibility in how you structure the terms of the agreement.

The simplest method is to simply ask for a loan. You need a certain amount of cash, and your mom or best friend is happy to oblige. As a bonus, the interest amount on the loan is usually minimal or non-existent, and the time for repaying the money is open ended — not a bad deal.

An alternative is to take on your friends and family as investors. In other words, you give up a percentage of shares or stock in the business for the amount of money they agree to provide. On the upside, you don't repay that money. However, if you no longer want those people to own a piece of your business, you have to buy back their stock to get rid of them.

Here are some advantages of acquiring investors from your F&F network:

✦ **You can easily obtain the money.** You have an established circle of friends and family members who already know and trust you. Sometimes, you don't even have to sell them on your business idea — let alone show them your business plan. They just want to help you.

✦ **You can get cash quickly.** Unlike going to a bank or venture capitalist, you don't have to jump through any "lending" hoops or participate in a series of drawn-out meetings. Friends and family may be able to get their hands on cash quickly and hand it over to you sooner.

✦ **You have a potentially large pool of investors.** You can easily find small amounts of money from lots of different sources. If you need $50,000, you can get 10 friends to contribute $10,000 each rather than try to find one person who can contribute the entire amount.

This method has a few disadvantages too, of course:

✦ **You can have problems with unstructured terms:** Because you know each other, you tend to keep things informal. That opens the door to uncertainty and inconsistency and big misunderstandings. Be wary of taking on friends and family members as investors without structured, written agreements that clearly define the terms of their investments in your company or the payback terms of your loan.

✦ **You may give up too much stock:** You want to gratefully reward those who take a chance on you, especially when you're close to them. For that same reason, however, you can end up giving away too much interest in your company. Or, if you turn to a large group of friends to invest, you may have to ante up a large block of stock for a small amount of cash. This uneven exchange can put you in a precarious position as the company grows.

✦ **The business can interfere with relationships:** Taking on your most trusted circle of friends or family as investors can lead to heated disagreements, hurt feelings, and your fair share of misunderstandings. Damage to these friendships or relationships with family members isn't easy to repair.

Finding angels

If the uncertainty and lack of structure of the friends-and-family (F&F) network bothers you, turning to an angel may be more appealing. An *angel* investor can be an individual investor or a group of investors who are willing to put money into start-up or young companies.

Several important differences separate angels from other types of investors. Angels usually bridge the funding gap. Raising more than $100,000 or $200,000 from friends and family is tough, yet a venture capitalist usually isn't interested in investing less than a million dollars, especially in a company without a track record. An angel meets what you might call midlevel funding needs.

Another important difference is that an angel investor typically doesn't take an active role in a company. An angel wants to provide capital, not run the business, although that person sometimes becomes a member of an advisory board or board of directors. (We discuss the board of directors as part of your formal business structure in Book II.) In addition to taking this hands-off approach toward your business, an angel is less likely to demand an immediate return on an investment. Whereas your father-in-law may expect to recoup his money in a couple of years, an angel's target return may be five years.

Over the past decade, this network of investors has become more careful, performing due diligence and examining every aspect of the proposed business — many lessons from the 1990s dot-com bust were learned, and investors aren't simply throwing money at every Internet business opportunity that appears. Although angels are usually more willing to take risks on new, unproven businesses, the overall requirements for investing are increasingly the same as those used by venture capitalists (as outlined in the next section).

A hands-off approach to long-term lending sounds great, right? It's not all roses, though. Among the negative factors in seeking money from an angel is that he often requires a larger stake in a business. Having a higher percentage of ownership in a company offsets his risk. When the return on investment comes, it equates to a significant amount of money for your angel. Also, acquiring money from angel networks is getting tougher. Increasingly, angels are using the same or similar funding guidelines as those of venture capitalists. An angel expects you to have a polished business plan, an experienced management team, and an *exit strategy* (a way for the angel to recoup his initial investment and then some).

If the negative side of working with an angel doesn't bother you, how do you locate one? Examine your own network of colleagues, friends, and family — ask if they have any contacts that might be interested. If that strategy doesn't provide any leads, search for angels at the regional or national level. Here are some places to begin your search:

✦ Chamber of Commerce or other local business-support organizations

✦ Professional associations (local and statewide) focused on technology

✦ Your accountant, banker, or attorney (who often works with or knows angels)

✦ Investment clubs

Online resources for angel networks and entrepreneurs include

✦ AngelInvestorNews.com: www.angel-investor-news.com

✦ Funding Universe: www.fundinguniverse.com

✦ Go Big Network: www.gobignetwork.com

✦ NBAI.net (Network of Business Angels and Investors): www.nbai.net

✦ vFinance.com: www.vfinance.com

Venturing into the world of venture capital

Venture capital (VC) funding isn't the easiest route for securing money for your business. Maybe you remember the stories of the dot-com era when millions of dollars were thrown haphazardly into Internet start-ups. Well, in spite of that bursting bubble, venture capitalists are still out in force; getting their money, however, is much more difficult now.

To be honest, we don't recommend even considering venture capital as a resource for a brand-new company. This type of funding is designed for businesses that need an aggressive (or very large) amount of money to support the next level of business growth. Venture capitalists are institutional investors (professionally managed funds) that invest anywhere from $500,000 to $10 million or more in a company. Most often, this investment is made in preparation for an initial public offering (IPO) on the stock market, a sale, or a merger with another company.

Suppose that you're thinking big and are intrigued by venture capital as a funding source. How do you know whether your company is ready to pursue VC money? Although the funding criteria vary among venture capitalists, most of them generally expect the following from your company (and you):

✦ **It has already used seed money.** Your company is long past the point of obtaining money from friends and family as part of its start-up stage. Seeking money from a venture capitalist means that you have already gotten additional rounds of financing from angel investors and are now ready for a more substantial investment boost.

✦ **It has a proven track record.** Establishing a history of success is a necessity for venture funding. Investors expect your company to have experience under its belt and proof of the underlying business concept. Having an offline (brick-and-mortar) business that has financial records that can be verified greatly increases your success of finding funding.

✦ **An experienced management team is in place.** Being the sole employee of a company isn't a good thing when you're seeking venture capital. Instead, you *must* have a seasoned team of executives with the experience to take your company to the next level.

✦ **It's in a "hot" industry.** Venture capitalists invest in more than a company — they invest in an industry. And, some industries or markets are hotter than others at any given time. Just as Internet companies were the favorites of the late 1990s, biotechnology (biotech) companies were the darlings of the past few years. Your business doesn't have to fall within the top three industries of interest, although it certainly improves your chances for funding.

✦ **It's in a high-growth stage.** Securing venture capital means that your company is no longer in an early growth stage. It's now positioned for significant earnings. Although the amount can vary, a good rule is that your company can achieve annual revenues of $25 million within a 5-year time frame.

✦ **You're willing to relinquish control.** If you don't have in place a top-notch team of heavy hitters (including yourself), relinquishing executive control may become a condition of funding. If you previously held the title of CEO and president, you can expect to be replaced by an outsider of the venture capitalist's choosing.

If you're serious about pursuing venture capital, you should do a few things first:

1. **Start making connections early.**

   Go to seminars on venture capital funding (usually sponsored by professional organizations in your community) and meet the venture capitalists involved in giving the presentations.

2. **Contact other companies that have recently secured funding.**

   Seek out other small businesses and ask for referrals to VC firms. This is also a good time to ask questions and get a general understanding of what the process may be like for a company similar to yours.

3. **As you're building these networks, start your own form of record-keeping.**

   Securing venture capital is a tedious, time-intensive process. The sooner you begin to understand the process, the more likely you are to be successful when the time comes.

4. **Begin making a list of potential venture capital firms.**

   Keep track of the companies in which they invest, how much they invest, and in which industries they most actively invest.

When you're ready, two established resources can assist you in locating and learning about venture capital firms that might be a good match for your business:

✦ *The Directory of Venture Capital & Private Equity Firms, 2008 Edition:* This extensive guide at `www.greyhouse.com/venture.htm` offers direct access to more than 2,300 venture capital and private equity firms worldwide. In addition to presenting basic overview information about each firm, the guide also lists extensive contact information, including phone numbers and e-mail addresses. Grey House Publishing, the publisher, offers a hardbound copy and an online database by paid subscription.

✦ *The Money Tree Report:* This quarterly report lists detailed information about venture capital funding in the United States. It's a collaborative effort between PricewaterhouseCoopers and the National Venture Capital Association with data from Thomson Financial. For information, and to review the quarterly reports, visit the Web site at www.pwc moneytree.com.

Check your local library for a copy of either resource on this list. Although you may get stuck with an older edition of the book, you can save the out-of-pocket cost of several hundred dollars that you would spend for a more current edition, and many of these resources stick around for a while.

During economic downturns, or when the economy is generally weakened, both venture capitalists and angel investors become increasingly selective about where and how they invest. It becomes even more important for you to have a solid business plan with a strong roadmap to a return on investment.

Checking Out Alternative Financing

When all else fails, a diligent netrepreneur still has a few other financing options. Alternative financing gives you one more option, although it's not necessarily your best or first choice. These options can help you open your doors for business, so to speak. Many times, you end up combining a variety of these sources to fund your great idea:

✦ **Credit card:** For better or worse, a credit card is a popular choice for funding a business. More than 80 percent of small businesses have used personal and business credit cards as a source of money, according to the Small Business Administration (SBA). As lending tightens from banks and other traditional resources, credit cards can sometimes provide the only source of fast cash for a new or growing business. Although credit cards may be a quick and easy alternative, they can also be expensive. Some credit card companies charge interest at 20 percent or more. In addition, they can slap you with hefty fees for late payments or for exceeding your credit limit. Financial advisors also caution that fully paying down the balance of your credit cards can take decades when you're making only the minimum monthly payments.

To make the best use of credit cards, look for cards that offer rewards based on your spending or total balance. Credit card companies often give reward points for every dollar spent, which can be used to cash in on gift cards to office supply stores or buy merchandise that can be used in your business (such as digital cameras and even computers).

Consider moving balances with high interest terms to another card. Credit card companies often offer limited introductory low- or no-interest rates for transferring your balances from other cards. If these offers don't come in the mail, don't be afraid to call credit card companies (including your existing one) to negotiate for a better rate.

✦ **Retirement cash:** A personal savings plan, such as a 401(k), has long been a source of money for someone opening a start-up business. Before draining your account, consider the penalties for early withdrawal and seek advice from your accountant on the pros and cons of this source of funding.

✦ **Home equity loan:** Following a period of rock-bottom interest rates and what was a seemingly endless housing boom, banks and other lenders have now pulled back from their creative borrowing options. As a home-owner, you can still "cash out" the equity in your house, use it for other purposes, and pay it back at a fixed interest rate over 5, 10, 15 years or more. Similarly, you can refinance your home and use the additional funds for other purposes, such as starting a business! Another option is to open a home equity line of credit. It gives you a fixed amount of money that you're approved to borrow. You take out the money only as you need it, though, rather than in one lump sum. However, all these options have become increasingly difficult to obtain after the banking and housing meltdown of 2008. Now you must have fantastic credit scores, among other things, to qualify for a loan. You can still use a home equity loan as a funding source — just be prepared to jump through a few extra hoops to get the money!

Book I
Chapter 4

Finding Money to
Fund Your Online
Start-Up

Borrowing money against your house is always risky! Many business experts hesitate to recommend this method as an option because of the potential loss and the emotional toll of losing your home. Consult with your accountant, or other financial advisors, before making this decision.

✦ **High-interest loan:** Some specialized lenders finance loans (even high-risk ones if you have poor credit) at high interest rates. These rates are usually similar to, or higher than, credit card rates. When all other options fail, this method may be a possibility; be cautious, though, about taking this route.

✦ **Microloan:** If you're looking for a smaller amount of capital, several sources exist. For example, the SBA has a Community Express (or Small Loan) Program for small businesses. The low-interest loans are typically for amounts less than $100,000 and are usually closer to $5,000 or $10,000. You don't need collateral, or even a complete business plan. However, you have to participate in a consultation with an SBA-approved technical advisor, and you must have good credit. The loans can sometimes be obtained the same day you apply. To find out who offers loans in your area, contact your state or regional SBA office or visit www.sba.gov. Other microlenders include private organizations, such as Count Me In (www.countmein.org) a nonprofit lender that provides lending and other resources and Accion USA (www.accionusa.org), a nonprofit lender that loans as much as $25,000 to small businesses.

✦ **Grant or award:** If your business concept is innovative, you may want to search out grant opportunities or contests offering financial rewards. *Grants* are monetary awards that you don't have to repay. For instance, in the Idea Happens contest that Visa USA sponsored, the company gave

$25,000 in seed money to 12 young entrepreneurs who submitted the best ideas for new businesses. Other organizations — such as business magazines, office supply chains, and other large retailers — often sponsor business-plan-writing contests with financial payoffs, or they award cash and prizes as part of their general business contests. No all-in-one resource tracks this sort of thing, so you have to do your homework by diligently searching the Internet and thumbing through business publications for opportunities. However, the shot at free money may be well worth your time!

Be wary of Web sites that charge for a list of "free money" resources from government grants. Although legitimate grants are available, you don't have to pay for them: You can obtain a list for free from the Catalog of Federal Government Assistance, at the U.S. government's grant site: www.grants.gov (see Figure 4-4).

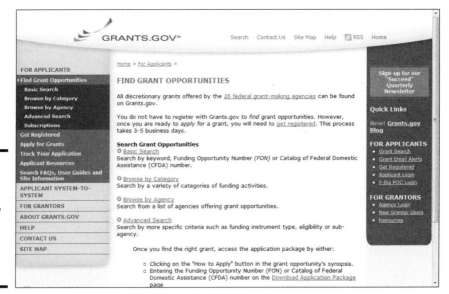

Figure 4-4:
Check out Grants. gov for any potential grants for which you can apply.

✦ **Incubator:** This type of entity or organization, established to support entrepreneurial development, usually provides shared resources for businesses. Sometimes, *shared resources* refers to a physical location (such as an office building) or simply refers to access to volunteer or hired professionals that are shared by the organization's entrepreneurs. Although incubators don't traditionally provide start-up money (in fact, they take only a small percentage of stock in exchange for their services), they're still considered an alternative funding source because an incubator provides your business with a range of tools, resources, and services for free, or for a reduced fee. Because this is money you would otherwise spend during your start-up phase, the amount of savings and the invaluable assistance (which can accelerate the growth of your business) translates into free investment dollars.

Locate technology and small-business incubators in your area by contacting the National Business Incubation Association at www.nbia.org to locate technology and small-business incubators in your area.

Taking a Shortcut: Purchasing an Existing Site

Securing financing for an online business takes time and persistence — there's no doubt about it. If you're interested in a completely different path, you can take a shortcut. Have you considered purchasing an existing Web site? Don't get excited — you don't have to march up the virtual steps of Amazon.com or eBay and put an offer on the table. (To be realistic, you would be laughed right out the door.) Somewhere between the people dreaming of starting a business and the giants dominating the Internet, hundreds of thousands of other mom-and-pop businesses have already established a small presence online. Many of them are doing quite well, others are struggling, and some just don't have any sense of direction. Those latter categories provide you with the largest opportunity to jump-start your online dreams.

Stop dreaming, and take a look at the benefits of scooping up an existing site to launch your business. You can

+ **Override start-up costs:** Finding an existing online business means that you don't have to worry about all the initial costs and hassles of getting the site started. Maintaining or building an existing site is usually cheaper than starting from scratch.

+ **Eliminate time to market:** Although you may have a business up and running in just a few weeks, establishing yourself in the market and gaining a presence in the search engines takes much longer than that. Buying a ready-made site (even a fledgling one) removes at least some of this concern.

+ **Gain established customer base:** The theory "Build it and they will come" has repeatedly been disproved when it applies to Web sites. Purchasing an online business that has existing customers is a definite perk.

To make sure that the site you're considering buying has real value when it comes to customers, ask to see proof of a current e-mail list or database of customers or members (not just a log of daily visitors).

What makes an existing site a smart purchase?

Buying an existing online business is basically the same as purchasing any other type of business: You have to do your homework and determine whether it's truly a wise buy. Find answers to these questions about a business before you sign on the dotted line:

- Is the online business a viable business model?

- Does the purchase include any existing inventory or customer contracts?

- Even though the site is established, does its concept pass your feasibility test?

- Is the site generating revenue? How much? (Ask for financial statements verified by a certified public accountant.)

- What expenses does it incur?

- Can you reduce the amount of overhead by making different management decisions?

- Can you increase the percentage of profit by making different management decisions? If so, how long would it take to implement these changes?

- How long has the site been established?

- What is the annual percentage of revenue growth? (How much more money does it make over the previous year?)

- How many people visit the site each day? (Ask for verification.)

- Does the owner maintain any logs or records verifying the number of visitors and other stats?

- What are the site's popularity rankings in all the major search engines?

- What, if anything, has the owner previously done to increase rankings?

- Has the site been featured in any magazines or other Web sites?

- How many other Web sites link to this site, and vice versa?

- If a product is being sold, does it have a dedicated supplier? Does it have other supplier sources?

- If it's an information product or a service business, do you have the skills and staff to duplicate it?

- Does the site have a poor reputation? Or, has it had lots of unhappy customers?

- Is the site in good standing with the Better Business Bureau and other organizations?

- Does it have a current business license?

- Are its taxes current?

- Has its URL expired, or is it about to?

- Does it have a valid Secure Sockets Layer (SSL) certificate to allow protected, properly encrypted transactions over the Internet?

- Which hardware and software, if any, are included with the sale?

- Do you gain any proprietary software in purchasing the site?

- Why is the current owner willing to sell?

- Can you create your own site and generate similar results in a short length of time, for less than the selling price?

✦ **Get a site for a steal:** Do your homework and you can purchase a site for very little money. Look for businesses in which the owners have these characteristics:

- They have grown tired of the site or are bored by it.

- They have no time to maintain it.

- They ran out of money after putting the basics in place.

- They're in a cash crunch.

These factors don't necessarily mean that the business is bad — it just means that it was under poor management!

✦ **Negotiate payment terms, with no out-of-pocket costs:** Even if you end up with a large (but reasonable) price tag, you still have a money-saving alternative. For instance, offer to make a small down payment on the site. Then let the owner know that you will make monthly payments until the balance of the sale price is paid in full. (If the site is producing revenue, you can use a portion of that income to cover the payments, so only the deposit comes out of your pocket.)

✦ **Lease to own:** In this strategy, the seller retains ownership of the site and you manage it. You pay the owner a set monthly fee, plus a percentage of the profits, until the sale price is paid.

Chapter 5: Creating Policies to Protect Your Web Site

In This Chapter

✔ Establishing a customer service pledge

✔ Developing policies for operating your business

✔ Delivering the goods as promised

Customers are the reason you're in business. All too often, though, their role in your success is an afterthought. Even though you spend a great deal of time thinking about what they can do for you, sometimes you forget about what they expect of you, until a problem surfaces.

In this chapter, we show you how to invest the proper time into the "care and feeding" of your most important business asset — your customer.

Taking Care of Customers

Consider the process of starting your business. You think about your future customers, right? You anticipate who will buy your product. You research their needs and painstakingly detail how to meet those needs in your business plan. You develop a marketing plan that explains how to reach your customers, and you calculate, dollar for dollar, how their spending translates into profit for you. Something is missing, though: Where in all that research and planning is your pledge to your customers — your vow of how you will treat them? Most business plans don't include this type of pledge, unless one of your company's competitive advantages is defined as an unprecedented level of customer service.

I pledge to you

What is a customer pledge, and how do you develop one? A *pledge* to your customers is a *written* guideline of what they can expect when doing business with you. The pledge should be the basis of your overall customer service philosophy.

Start your customer service pledge internally, and make it something used only by you. From there, you can create an external (public) customer service pledge.

Put it in writing

How do you create a customer pledge? Here are a few simple steps you can follow to get going:

1. Answer a few general questions about how you really feel about customers (be honest!):

   - How do you view your customers? Do you know them personally or speak with them on the phone, or are they completely anonymous?

   - How important are customers to you and your business?

   - How important is repeat business?

   - What are you willing to do for customers every single day?

   - What are you *not* willing to do for your customers?

2. Define realistic parameters of how you plan to communicate with your customers every day, as shown in these two examples:

   How can customers contact you? Can they

   - Send e-mail 24 hours a day?

   - Call a toll-free phone number and leave a message 24 hours a day?

   - Call a long-distance number within set business hours?

   - Write a letter and send it by snail mail (through the U.S. Postal Service)?

   When and how will you respond to customers?

   - Immediately when you respond only by e-mail?

   - Within 24 hours when you respond by phone or e-mail?

3. Identify what, if anything, is special about the way you treat customers. For example, do you call customers personally to make sure that they received their orders? Or, do you invite them to regular online sessions to discuss how your products or services could improve?

4. Draft a written document detailing your customer service pledge for your internal use. The document can consist of a short list of bullets or several paragraphs based on your previous answers. This guideline is your personal reminder of how you incorporate customers into your business every day.

5. Write a pledge to your customer. The pledge, which can be as general or specific as you choose, should reflect your internal customer service philosophy but be a written document that can be read and judged by the customer about how your business responds. (Figure 5-1 shows the PuzzleHouse customer pledge as an example.)

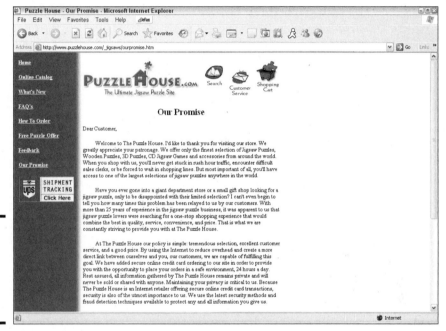

Figure 5-1:
This online
retailer
pledges to
care for its
customers.

Putting Policies in Place

As you might expect, creating your customer service pledge is only the beginning of the customer care policy. To manage your online business successfully and legitimately, you have to put several policies in place. The government mandates some policies, and others are the result of common sense to minimize confusion for yourself, your employees, and the people you do business with. For example, when working with franchise organizations, one of the most critical components of doing business is the *policy manual,* a small booklet filled with written policies establishing an unwavering set of guidelines and procedures for operating. The policy manual serves as an easy reference tool when you have questions about how to operate.

Policies are equally important to customers, employees, and vendors. Although you don't have to create a formal manual filled with your policies, you must write them down somewhere. In many cases, you should also publish them on your Web site, to protect yourself from misunderstandings and reassure your customers about how you do business.

Privacy policy

A *privacy policy* details how you collect, treat, and use the information you receive from customers and from other people who visit your Web site. This policy not only covers information that customers knowingly provide but also applies to the use of *cookies,* or the information files that Web servers create to track data about people and the online sites they visit. Your privacy policy, like the sample policy from the Better Business Bureau (see Figure 5-2) should clearly state your commitment to customer privacy and data security. To find the sample policy, go to `www.bbbonline.org/Privacy/sample_privacy.asp`.

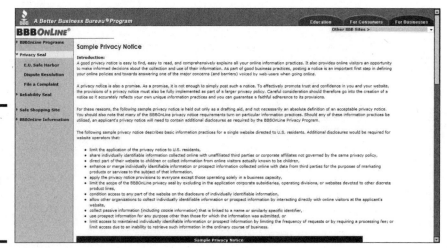

Figure 5-2: Use this sample privacy policy from the Better Business Bureau.

A privacy policy is a requirement for your online business if you're based in the United States. The U.S. government's Federal Trade Commission (FTC) mandates this policy. The policy must be properly labeled on your Web site and easily accessible within your site.

Your privacy policy should include these elements also:

✦ A description of *how* you collect information from your site visitors and customers

✦ Details of *what* information you collect

✦ An explanation of what you do with the information and how and where you store it

✦ Disclosure of whom you might share customer information with

✦ Instructions for how visitors or customers can change their information or remove it from your records

Your policy on how you handle a customer's credit card data should be in line with the requirements of the Payment Card Industry Data Security Standard (PCI DSS). As an online retailer, you're required to comply with certain regulations for handling and storing sensitive customer data under the PCI DSS, or else you could face a steep financial penalty. To find out more, visit www.pcicomplianceguide.org.

User agreement or terms and conditions

Increasingly, sites are implementing user agreements. Just like a written contract, this agreement specifies terms or conditions by which you allow visitors or customers to use your site. You might choose to post on your site a static (unchanging) page that simply lists these points. However, a more legally binding version of this agreement requires visitors to acknowledge that they have read the terms and agree to abide by them. Usually, before visitors are allowed to go to certain areas of your site or make a purchase, they're forced to click a button verifying that they agree to the terms.

When you're creating your site's terms and conditions, you should include this information:

✦ **How visitors or customers can or cannot use your site:** Rules that apply to not only your customers but also your employees, such as posting personal information (phone numbers or physical addresses, for example) on a discussion forum

✦ **Who is allowed to view your site:** Whether visitors meet age or U.S. citizenship requirements, for example

✦ **Which other policies are in place:** Shipping, returns, or complaint procedures, for example

✦ **Legal and liability issues:** For example, details of responsibility by you and third parties for providing information and taking actions, and for specifying geographic location where legal disputes will be settled

Shipping policy

Your shipping policy should clearly explain the details of how and when customer orders are handled and shipped. Although you can determine some conditions of this policy, you must also comply with the FTC's mail or telephone-order merchandise rule.

According to the FTC, your online site must

✦ Ship an order within the timeframe you promised at the time of ordering or as stated in your advertising or on your Web site.

✦ Ship a product within 30 days after it's received, unless you specify an earlier timeframe.

✦ Give notice to a consumer as fast as possible whenever you cannot ship that person's product when promised.

✦ Include a revised shipping date in the delay notice you send to a customer.

✦ Allow a customer to agree to a delay or to cancel an order and provide a description of the time required for a refund.

Return policy

Include in your return policy the conditions under which you allow customers to return a product or decline a service. Will the customer receive a full or partial refund from you? A good policy should protect both you and your customers. Be specific about your return policy so that customers clearly understand (and aren't surprised by) your rules. Your policy should include these elements:

✦ **Time limit:** Set the maximum number of days within which a return will be accepted.

✦ **Conditions of use:** Maintain the right to reject a return if an item shows obvious signs of use, for example.

✦ **Restock fee:** Explain any fees incurred by restocking a returned item.

✦ **Exceptions:** Specify any items that cannot be returned.

✦ **Shipping responsibility:** Determine who pays for the cost of shipping when a product is returned.

✦ **Refunds issued as cash or credit:** Decide whether to issue store credit rather than give cash back.

✦ **Third-party rules:** Direct customers to consult the return policies of third-party vendors if you sell their items.

As e-commerce grows, so does the problem of customers taking advantage of online retailers. Let your return policy protect you by limiting the number of days you agree to accept returns. Customers must have enough time to evaluate products (three to five days is a reasonable length of time) but not use it indefinitely before demanding their money back.

When you're selling products through a third-party vendor, such as a storefront or an auction site (like Yahoo! or eBay), be sure to check whether the company has a mandated return policy. The vendor site's policy can override your internal return policy.

Safety for young users

Whether or not you plan to sell to children, establish a policy about minors. If your site is targeted to children under 13 years old or has a separate section for kids, your Web site must comply with the FTC's Children's Online Privacy Protection Act, or COPPA (see Figure 5-3). This rule requires you to

✦ Post a privacy policy on the home page (the first page) of your site and link to the privacy policy everywhere that you collect personal information.

✦ Notify parents about how you collect information.

✦ Get parental consent before collecting information.

✦ Allow parents to see the information you collect about their children and let the parents change or delete details.

✦ Maintain the confidentiality, security, and integrity of the information you collect.

Other online policies

Other polices you may want to include on your Web site are the following:

✦ **Message board or chat room policies:** In these areas of your site, visitors and customers can share their opinions, ideas, and concerns. If your site offers these communication options, set up some basic guidelines for how you operate each one. Your policy should specify such items as who can participate and whether someone must register (or sign on as a member) first. Also, indicate who is monitoring these activities and in what manner. The policy should clearly specify which type of material is inappropriate for posting, and how and when you might remove it.

✦ **Exporting:** If your site sells to customers outside the United States, you might be subject to special government regulations by the Commerce Department and Defense Department and possibly other departments. What you sell (or export) and where you sell it (which countries) might be tightly regulated. If you believe that this is the case with your business, you should seek advice from your attorney about developing an exporting policy.

✦ **Spam:** Depending on your type of business, you can include a spam policy within your privacy policy. This policy states whether your site does or doesn't distribute marketing e-mail and how you respond to it.

✦ **Endorsement and linking to other sites' policies:** Whether you sell products or services from other sites, provide links to sites not owned by you, or allow other sites to link to yours, you're smart to notify customers about it. Your linking policy should simply state how external links are used and whether you endorse the information found on these linked sites. Provide customers with a way to notify you of problems with external sites or violations to your policy.

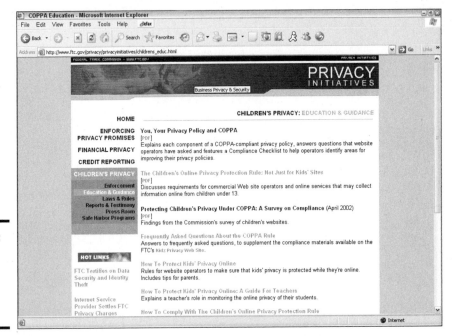

Figure 5-3:
Provide a policy for how you deal with minors.

Delivering On Your Promises

After you establish your basic principles of operation, you have to deliver on them. *Executing,* or following through, on the policies you create isn't easy, but it's essential for several reasons.

These policies represent promises to your customers and determine what customers come to expect from you. Failing to meet these expectations compromises your reputation and, ultimately, eats away at your sales.

Equally important are the consequences when you fail to deliver and then incur a legal liability. The government mandates and monitors several policies. Even a small oversight can land you in hot water with both your customers and federal laws!

Nobody's perfect, and you might fail to deliver on a promise now and then. If you fail, be sure to follow these steps:

1. **Notify your customer immediately.**

2. **Apologize for your mistake.**

3. **Correct the problem.**

4. **Offer a partial or full refund, a free gift, or a discount on future purchases.**

Chapter 6: Setting Up Shop: Everything You Need for Online Efficiency

In This Chapter

✔ Organizing your work space

✔ Stocking your office with necessary equipment

✔ Maximizing the power of your computer

✔ Selecting applications to enhance desktop performance

✔ Choosing software to increase productivity

✔ Identifying the best method for accessing Internet service

*Y*ou're going to be spending a lot of time with your online business, so you might as well be comfortable while you do so. From the chair you sit in to your filing system, you need to spend a little time setting up your office with the correct equipment and software, as well as Internet access. (That last one is obvious, eh?) Spending time up front on creating an efficient workspace can save you plenty of time later.

A Floor Plan for Success

You might work from a cramped bedroom in your modest home or in a spacious high-rise office complex. Either way, maximizing your work space can be an important step toward obtaining true efficiency in your business.

Follow these steps to create a floor plan for your office space:

1. **Make a list of how you will use your space.**

   Ask yourself these questions:

   - Do I need a desk? How much desk space do I need?
   - Will I store paperwork and files in a central filing system or use some other method?
   - Will customers visit my office?
   - Do I need working space for employees?

2. **Make a list of all your office furniture, equipment, and accessories (including office supplies and other items that should be stored but remain accessible).**

If you're sharing the space with others, make sure that you account for their belongings too. Or, if your office performs double duty as a bedroom or dining room, include on your list the non-work-related furniture that will remain in the room while you work.

3. **On a sheet of paper, sketch out the dimensions of the room with lines that represent your walls, and then draw all your furniture and large office equipment in position within those walls.**

Rather than literally draw your furniture, you can draw different shapes and label them (see Figure 6-1).

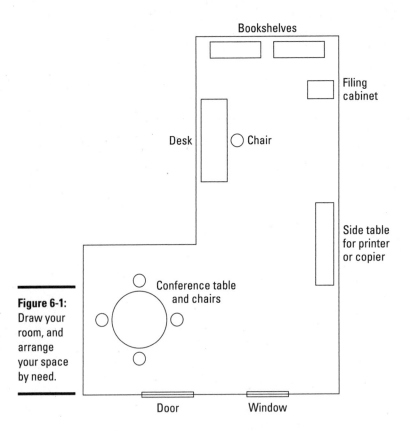

Figure 6-1:
Draw your
room, and
arrange
your space
by need.

4. **Arrange the furniture and office equipment in a way that best meets your needs, based on the list you created in Step 1.**

This arrangement should be based on function.

After your room has been put on paper, based on how you want it to function, you can put the measurements to the test (see Figure 6-2).

When you arrange your furniture, address storage needs for your office supplies. If you don't have designated architectural space (like a closet or built-in bookshelves), you have to bring in storage (such as file cabinets, baskets, and removable shelving).

5. **Measure all pieces of furniture and major equipment.**

Using the room dimensions on your paper, compare measurements to see whether everything fits. If you run out of room, keep trying different arrangements until you find a floor plan that fits both your needs and your measurements.

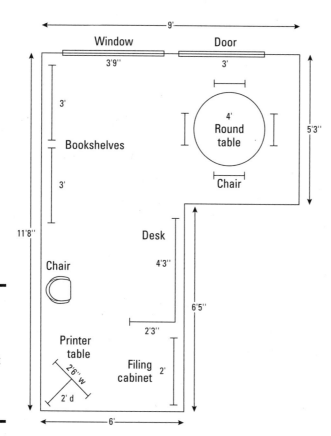

Figure 6-2: Precise measurements ensure that everything fits in your space.

If your real furniture doesn't fit the room's function-based paper layout, consider getting rid of some items. You want the room to function based on your needs, as opposed to forcing everything you own to fit in the office space. Get rid of unnecessary pieces of furniture, or trade them for small pieces if space is at a premium. Sharing home furniture with your office (double-duty) makes sense if space is limited — and makes good financial sense, too.

Must-Have Equipment

You no longer have to invest several thousand dollars in big, clunky pieces of equipment because both the size and the prices of these items have dropped tremendously. The prices of all-in-one items such as fax, copier, printer, and scanner are dropping and, obviously, take less space.

Make form follow function

Rather than think about your office equipment in terms of a collection of cartridges and cords, think of each piece in terms of the function it provides. You need access to some key functions (equipment) to run a business.

This list describes the functions most businesses need access to most often:

✦ **Printer:** Although most of your correspondence can be conducted online, you still need to print invoices, offline marketing materials, and hard copies (printouts) of items for your files. You can choose from a laser printer (which uses a laser to draw the images) or an inkjet printer (which sprays ink on the page). A laser printer is designed for more demanding, high-volume print jobs. An inkjet is usually more affordable and has superb quality for a small office. You can purchase a decent inkjet printer now for less than $50. More money buys you a faster printer: Slow printers can handle 1 page per minute (ppm) and higher-end printers can handle more than 10 ppm.

Rather than compare only printer functions, be sure to also compare ink cartridge requirements before you buy a printer. An ink cartridge is often almost as expensive as the printer itself; a $50 printer can require a $30 ink cartridge, for example. Be sure to find out

- Whether the printer requires a particular brand of cartridge

- How much the cartridges for that printer cost

✦ **Fax software:** Sending a facsimile is a necessity, even with the explosive use of e-mail. Rather than purchase a separate fax machine, consider buying fax software (so that your computer acts as the fax) or sign up for a Web-based fax service and receive faxes as attachments to your e-mail.

TIP

You can easily find and compare fax software and services on the Internet. Check out Shopper.com (www.shopper.cnet.com) to compare software bargains. Or, sign up for Web-based services at eFax (www.efax.com), where you can use the service for free as long as you use a nonlocal number and send or receive a limited number of pages each month.

✦ **Copier:** Having access to a small copier can be a good investment for your office. When you shop for a copier, decide which features you need:

- Do you want color printing, or is black-and-white print suitable?

- Will you use a *duplexing* feature, which prints both the front and back of the page?

- Is *collating* (automatically stacking and binding papers as they print) a big deal?

Also look for copiers that

- Add large amounts of paper to trays at one time so that you're not continually refilling them

- Have a quick warm-up time (the time it takes the equipment to prepare to print) so that you can start copying quickly

- Are suitable for small to mid-size print job volumes.

✦ **Scanner:** This piece of equipment, which is particularly useful when you frequently work with photos and other images, allows you to scan images or documents into your computer for manipulation or storage or to send as files or faxes to others. Most scanners come with custom software you must install, or try the Windows Scanner and Camera Wizard (found in the Windows Control Panel). You can choose from several types of scanners:

- *Flatbed:* This model, the most common and the most versatile, can scan books or three-dimensional objects in addition to paper and photos.

- *See-through vertical scanner:* This scanner style is often recommended for use with digital photography because of its quick scan time and ability to fully display images as you scan them.

- *Sheet-fed scanner:* You might prefer this type if you need to quickly scan multiple documents (and don't need to scan books or other bound material).

✦ **All-in-one device:** If you occasionally need access to a range of office equipment, you might want to invest in an all-in-one, or multifunction, machine. This type of machine, which is growing in popularity, is especially appealing for small-office or home-office use. The machine serves as a printer, scanner, copier, and fax machine, all from a single unit. It's a great space-saver in your office, too.

✦ **Digital camera:** You might not be used to including a camera in the category of business tools. Yet, in building and maintaining an online business, having a digital camera might be a requirement, especially if you have an eBay store or any other e-tail type of store. The camera then becomes a necessity to take product pictures that you can upload to your site. (Some printers and all-in-one devices come with memory card slots built in. You can take your memory card out of your camera and insert it directly into the device for printing!)

Revving up with a powerful PC

One important piece of equipment for your new online business is a computer. It's the heart and soul of your office because all your valuable data resides on it and you use it to communicate with folks in all kinds of ways. How do you know whether your existing computer makes the grade now that you're a netrepreneur? Should you upgrade or buy new? If you buy a new one, how can you be sure that you're investing your dollars wisely? Although those questions are tricky, luckily, they have simple answers.

Jumping into the upgrade-versus-purchase debate

Overall, the cost of purchasing a computer is outrageously low. You probably receive promotions advertising new desktop computers for as little as $299! By the time you calculate your time or pay somebody else's labor fee and buy parts, can you truly upgrade an existing computer for that price?

Desktop or laptop: Deciding on a computer

Even if you're sold on the sleek, compact size of a laptop, consider these factors before you make a final purchase:

Budget: Although desktop computers can be bulky, they're packed with options at rock-bottom prices. Comparatively, you pay for the convenience and size that a laptop offers. It's usually double the price of a desktop with similar capabilities.

Capability: You can run the same applications on both a desktop and a laptop. If you work with a lot of graphics, though, the laptop screen might not do them justice. When you're working in one location, you can connect your laptop to a larger monitor, of course — just remember that it costs extra!

Convenience: Putting a price tag on convenience is difficult. Whether you need to tote your computer from room to room or from city to city, a laptop is your best portable solution.

Comfort: Adjusting to a smaller screen size, button-size mouse, and more compact keyboard space isn't always easy. You might be more comfortable with the larger components offered on a desktop. You can attach a USB mouse or keyboard to a laptop to overcome this problem.

Some laptops are just as powerful and full-featured as desktops. They're slightly larger and heavier, with wider screens and full-size keyboards. Although they can be considered portable, the size and weight put them closer to desktops than laptops.

Not so fast. You have to compare apples to apples by looking at more than just the price tag. Compare capabilities. That off-the-shelf computer for $299 is probably a bare-bones, stripped-down model — probably no more powerful than that old machine you used for the past couple of years! Sure, the new one might work a bit faster; to get comparable features, though, you most likely have to add memory, hardware, and other applications to truly address your needs. By the time you upgrade your new computer, you've sufficiently passed its original $300 price threshold to make you reconsider buying new.

If you have the skills and the comfort level to take apart your computer, add components, and then put Humpty Dumpty together again, upgrading can be a cheap and relatively easy solution.

If you're serious about building or upgrading your own computer, check out *Building a PC For Dummies,* 5th Edition, by Mark L. Chambers (Wiley Publishing). It tells you how to create your own, custom computer.

Taking the plunge: Buying new

You might be more comfortable buying a computer with all its parts already assembled. You can still design a custom computer, by choosing the options you want and letting a computer retailer customize it for you. Or, you can purchase an off-the-shelf machine that's already loaded and ready to go.

How do you decide which computer is right for you? The simplest way to approach this decision is by backing into it. Follow these general guidelines:

1. **Decide how you will use the computer.**

   You're running a business with it, of course. Be specific about which type of activities you're using it for, such as accounting, word processing, keeping a database of customer records, or storing digital photos of your products.

2. **Identify the specific software applications you're using for each of those activities, such as Peachtree, Microsoft Word, Microsoft Access, or Photoshop.**

   Each of these applications recommends system requirements, including available memory and processor speed, that are necessary to run them.

3. **Match and compare the requirements in Step 2 to the computer you're considering purchasing.**

   Look closely at not only the computer's processor but also the hardware and features that come with the computer, including these items:

   - Hard drive space
   - Operating System (Windows, Mac, Linux/Unix)
   - Memory capacity (RAM)

- CD-ROM or DVD (read-only)

- CD-ROM RW or DVD-RW (allows you to save data to a disc)

- Modem

- Networking card (preferably wireless-ready)

- Monitor (with the option for a flat screen)

- Keyboard and mouse (wireless, to avoid clutter on your desktop)

- External speakers

- Installed software

4. **Compare the support service and warranties.**

   Does the manufacturer or retailer offer you customer support? Be sure to find out whether this service is included in the cost of your purchase, and whether it limits the amount of support you can receive before a service fee kicks in. Find out exactly what is covered under the warranty and for how long. You might have to purchase an extended warranty to cover some computer parts. Keep in mind that some manufacturers require you to ship back your hardware versus sending a repairperson to your location. Before making a purchase, determine whether on-site support is important to you.

Do you happen to have a computer with a small amount of memory? USB *memory sticks* are portable (and cheap) storage components that use external USB flash drives that plug in directly to your computer. You can then use them to transfer or store files. It's like having an extra hard drive, except that this one can literally fit into your pocket. About the size of a small pen or keychain, this type of memory stick can be attached to your keychain for easy portability. If you need to transfer data between computers, this tool is invaluable for your office. You can get an 8GB stick for less than $50.

Don't hesitate to eliminate your learning curve before making your first computer purchase. The unlimited number of choices, and the never-ending list of computer-speak acronyms, can leave you frustrated. To make sure that your final selection is the best one, delve into the book *Buying a Computer For Dummies,* 2006 Edition, by Dan Gookin (Wiley Publishing).

Let somebody else do the hard stuff

Another option is to not even keep equipment on hand if somebody else can handle a service for you. Many places offer fax, printing, binding, and other services to small businesses at competitive prices.

If you can't afford to purchase the equipment right away, locate a small-business service center close to your office. You can find them in copy stores, such as FedEx Office (formerly Kinko's), or in retail office-supply stores, such as Staples.

Tools for Your Desktop

Your computer is unpacked. You're ready to explore a world of business opportunity. Before you dive in, make sure that you have these basic — but necessary — applications on your desktop, ready to run.

Inventory the built-in (supplied) programs to determine which ones work for you and which ones don't. Using the built-in software can save you money, but don't sacrifice your need for functionality by using an inferior product. Buy what you need to get your jobs done.

Searching for a Web browser

Your *Web browser* is the software that lets you travel from site to site across the Internet. You enter a site's address, or *URL (Uniform Resource Locator),* and the browser displays the site or page on your computer screen. For an online business, this is an absolute requirement.

Microsoft Internet Explorer remains the dominant browser, with an estimated 90 percent of computer users relying on it. Netscape Navigator, at one time the most popular browser, is no longer considered a viable alternative, unless you have an earlier version. That's because Netscape, managed by AOL, is no longer being supported by AOL. However, Mozilla's Firefox Web browser is rapidly gaining in popularity. Its increased security features are appealing and its variety of features user-friendly. Google also has its Chrome, which is possibly the fastest loading of the bunch and is free to download at `chrome.google.com`.

Keep in mind that a browser is typically already included when you purchase a computer, although which browser varies based on your operating system. You can always download a different browser to your computer or update an older version of your existing browser. Get started downloading the browser of your choice by going to these Web sites:

✦ **Microsoft Internet Explorer** is at `www.microsoft.com` (see Figure 6-3).

✦ **Mozilla Firefox** can be downloaded at `www.mozilla.org` (see Figure 6-4).

✦ **Chrome** is available for download at `www.google.com/chrome`.

Figure 6-3:
Internet Explorer, the most used browser.

Figure 6-4: Mozilla is another browser option.

Put access to all the major browsers on your desktop, especially as you begin creating and maintaining your business Web site. Then you can check for consistency among page views displayed with different browsers. For example, Internet Explorer might display your Web page in a slightly different way than Mozilla. The difference might be subtle, or it might cause the loss of pertinent product information or graphics. (We talk about these and other Web design details in Book III.)

Sending and receiving messages with e-mail

E-mail is a painless way to communicate with customers, vendors, and employees. Unfortunately, the popularity of this communication tool has led to a bigger problem: How do you keep up with, sort, store, and reply to all these messages? And, what's the best way to combat spam, viruses, and other harmful or annoying applications to your inbox?

You can resolve these issues by finding a good e-mail program. In addition to acting as an organizer and a system for filtering junk mail, your e-mail system should be simple to use and pack a few added features.

One of these e-mail programs might meet your communication objectives:

✦ **Thunderbird:** The e-mail program designed by Mozilla automatically detects and sorts junk mail. Packed with features, it also offers an enhanced three-column view of your e-mail. Figure 6-5 shows you the Thunderbird multicolumn view. Download Thunderbird for free at Mozilla.org (`www.mozilla.org/products/thunderbird`).

✦ **Gmail:** Google Gmail is a popular, and free, e-mail option. Not only does Gmail boast one of the highest storage capacities (which means you don't have to delete old mail in order to make room for new mail); it also offers some other cool features. In addition to one of the best spam-blocking capabilities, it also automatically sorts messages based on conversations, utilizes Google search technology to make it easy to find e-mails, and includes built-in chat. You can access your Gmail from your mobile phone by redirecting your phone's Web browser to a Google app. Did we mention that Gmail is free? Take a look for yourself at `www.mail.google.com`.

✦ **Outlook or Outlook Express:** Microsoft created two versions of its
e-mail messaging system:

- *Outlook Express:* The simpler version often comes free with your
computer. The program's limited functions are suitable for your use
at home or in your small business.

- *Outlook:* If you need more capabilities accessible by more users, this
version might be a better choice. Outlook comes with Microsoft Office.

The Outlook family of products has had security flaws that left people's
computers vulnerable to viruses and other risks. You can obtain security patches (or a fix to the problem) if you have an older version of the
e-mail program. To compare features and download the most recent version, go to the Microsoft site (www.microsoft.com).

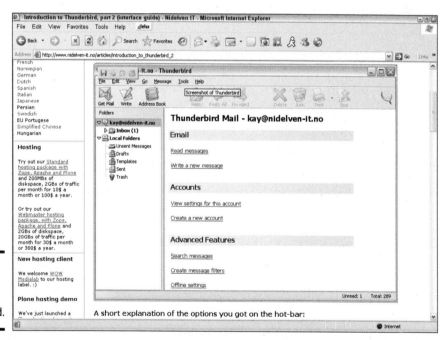

Figure 6-5:
View your
e-mail with
Thunderbird.

Using document-viewing software and other useful applications

As you begin using the Internet and your computer to communicate, you might
find that several programs come in handy. Frequently, you receive a document
as an attachment to e-mail or on disc. Depending on the program the sender
used to create the document, it can be in any of a number of formats: a Word
file, a PDF (portable document format) file, or an image saved in one of a slew

of formats, such as a TIF, GIF, BPM, or JPEG. Even if you don't have exactly the same program as the sender of the file, you can still open and view these files if you have the right software.

We suggest installing the following programs on your desktop so that you're prepared to receive and view information in a variety of formats:

+ **Adobe Acrobat (Reader):** *PDF files* are electronic documents that you might receive in e-mail or download from a Web site. To view, print, or search PDF files, you must have the free reader software loaded on your computer. To get the software, go to the Adobe Acrobat Web site (www. adobe.com) and download it.

+ **WinZip:** When you need to send or receive large files, even lots of them, this utility feature works to compress files so that you can more efficiently send them in e-mail. WinZip allows you to zip (compress) and unzip files and complete folders. It's available for $29, or you can download a trial version. Use it free for 21 days. When you're ready to purchase WinZip, go to www.winzip.com. (*Note:* Windows XP and Vista come with a compatible compression program built-in; you might not need to purchase a compression program if that one suits your needs.)

+ **Movie and audio player:** If you ever visit news sites, such as CNN, you probably come across video or audio clips in news stories that you can view or listen to online. More Web sites are offering audio and video clips, whether as part of an online small-business training course or a preview of a newly released Hollywood movie. To hear and see these clips, you must have a viewer or player installed on your computer. Microsoft includes Windows Media Player as a built-in player for the Windows operating system.

Apple makes the easy-to-install player QuickTime Player, which works on either a PC or a Mac (Macintosh computer). To install the player, follow the download instructions at the Apple Web site (www.apple. com/quicktime/player). Or, try RealPlayer, which also works on multiple platforms. It's available at www.real.com/freeplayer.

Your Essential Software Toolkit

Most businesses require some robust software programs to handle their core business activities, such as generating printed letters and invoices, juggling finances, designing marketing pieces, and making sales presentations. As you might expect, your choice of business software is almost endless. Some essential programs, however, are important to add to your computer now.

When you buy a new computer, be aware that some basic software packages, such as Microsoft Works, are often included with the system. If the included software isn't your first choice, negotiate with the salesperson to trade out for different software. Or, when you order online, look for deals that let you add software programs at the time of purchase, for less than the full retail price. This list describes some core software packages you should consider:

✦ **Word processing software:** Working with documents, either creating or reading them, is standard procedure in business. Depending on how frequently you're using documents, a few word processing software solutions are available. For instance, your computer might come with WordPad, a simple, easy-to-use program. For extended features, however, try a more advanced program, such as Microsoft Word (`www.office.microsoft.com`) or WordPerfect (`www.corel.com/word perfect`). If you're looking to save money, there are a couple of free options. Take a look at Google's word processor called Document (`www.docs.google.com`), or try the leading open-source word processing option, OpenOffice (`www.openoffice.org`).

✦ **Graphics or imaging software:** Any time you work with images, graphics software becomes a necessity. You can use this software for everything from creating logos to editing digital photo images. Your computer might come with a basic paint program that allows you to draw images and do basic photo editing, and it's fine for occasional use. Depending on your needs, though, you can also explore more advanced graphics software, such as Paint Shop Pro (`www.paintshoppro.com`) or Adobe Illustrator (`www.adobe.com/illustrator`).

✦ **Presentation software:** This type of software allows you to create a professional presentation using text and graphics and applying special effects to the content. PowerPoint (`www.office.microsoft.com/powerpoint`), part of Microsoft Office, is one of the most recognized presentation software products. Its ease of use makes it a good match for use in your businesses. You can create information on individual slides that can be viewed one by one or run in sequence in a slide show. Google Presentation (part of the Google Docs family) is also a nice option for presentation software.

✦ **Financial software:** Keeping track of business financial information requires specialized software. Financial software handles items such as payroll, invoicing, and profit-and-loss statements. Popular products include Quicken (`www.quicken.com`) and Microsoft Money at `www.microsoft.com/money`.

Connectivity: Today's Internet Options and More

Considering the variety of Internet service choices you have and the number of providers that are in business, now is certainly a great time to start an online business. You can select a plan that truly meets your needs and that doesn't break the bank. One area that you should *not* skimp on for your online business is your Internet service. After all, it (along with hosting for your site) is the backbone of your business.

Here are some of your connection options:

✦ **Dialup:** Using a dedicated phone line and modem, dialup was once the most common method of accessing the Internet. It's now considered quite limiting with its poor modem-transaction quality and slow 56 Kbps connection speed. The advantage that remains is price. It provides a cheap alternative for you to access the Internet; a dialup provider often charges less than $10 a month for service. However, unless you still live in a rural area where other connection options are limited (or non-existent), you may want to pull the plug on dialup!

✦ **Broadband:** A very high-speed Internet broadband connection can be as much as 70 times faster than dialup. Broadband works by carrying many different channels of data over a single wire, or source. As a matter of fact, the continued growth in e-commerce is credited to the ever-expanding number of consumers who have access to a broadband connection in their homes. That access to significantly increased speed makes shopping online faster and easier.

When you or your customers consider using broadband, you're likely to use one of two types:

- *DSL:* Digital Subscriber Service gives you a high-speed connection by using a normal phone line and digital modem capabilities. Don't worry about your phone line being constantly busy, though: After special equipment is installed on your end, your phone line can be used simultaneously for accessing the Internet and for regular voice communication. Because phone companies providing the service were slow to establish access to all areas, you might live in a neighborhood that simply cannot support the DSL option.

- *Cable modem:* Much like DSL, cable provides a very high-speed connection. Typically considered faster than DSL, it's chosen by many users for its outlandish speed. However, cable modems use *shared* bandwidth, whereas DSL uses *dedicated* bandwidth. This shared network is also associated with the higher security risk of cable. The reasoning is that you're more vulnerable to people breaking into and accessing your information over a shared network. (When you want to read more, we discuss these and other security issues in Book V.)

Although pricing plans for cable modems and DSL fluctuate, plan to spend at least $20 per month. Cable companies aggressively compete for business, with some offers as low as $19 per month for the first six months. Shop around for the best deal before you settle on a service provider.

Book II
Legal and Accounting

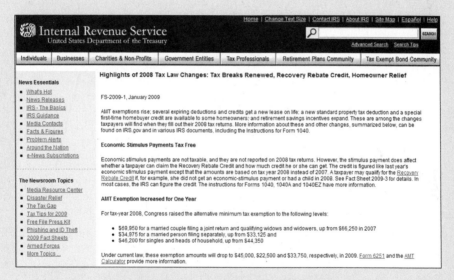

Internal Revenue Service
United States Department of the Treasury

Advanced Search   Search Tips

SEARCH

| Individuals | Businesses | Charities & Non-Profits | Government Entities | Tax Professionals | Retirement Plans Community | Tax Exempt Bond Community |

News Essentials

- What's Hot
- News Releases
- IRS - The Basics
- IRS Guidance
- Media Contacts
- Facts & Figures
- Problem Alerts
- Around the Nation
- e-News Subscriptions

The Newsroom Topics

- Media Resource Center
- Disaster Relief
- The Tax Gap
- Tax Tips for 2009
- Free File Press Kit
- Phishing and ID Theft
- 2009 Fact Sheets
- Armed Forces
- More Topics ...

Highlights of 2008 Tax Law Changes: Tax Breaks Renewed, Recovery Rebate Credit, Homeowner Relief

FS-2009-1, January 2009

AMT exemptions rise; several expiring deductions and credits get a new lease on life; a new standard property tax deduction and a special first-time homebuyer credit are available to some homeowners; and retirement savings incentives expand. These are among the changes taxpayers will find when they fill out their 2008 tax returns. More information about these and other changes, summarized below, can be found on IRS.gov and in various IRS documents, including the Instructions for Form 1040.

Economic Stimulus Payments Tax Free

Economic stimulus payments are not taxable, and they are not reported on 2008 tax returns. However, the stimulus payment does affect whether a taxpayer can claim the Recovery Rebate Credit and how much credit he or she can get. The credit is figured like last year's economic stimulus payment except that the amounts are based on tax year 2008 instead of 2007. A taxpayer may qualify for the Recovery Rebate Credit if, for example, she did not get an economic-stimulus payment or had a child in 2008. See Fact Sheet 2009-3 for details. In most cases, the IRS can figure the credit. The instructions for Forms 1040, 1040A and 1040EZ have more information.

AMT Exemption Increased for One Year

For tax-year 2008, Congress raised the alternative minimum tax exemption to the following levels:

- $69,950 for a married couple filing a joint return and qualifying widows and widowers, up from $66,250 in 2007
- $34,975 for a married person filing separately, up from $33,125 and
- $46,200 for singles and heads of household, up from $44,350

Under current law, these exemption amounts will drop to $45,000, $22,500 and $33,750, respectively, in 2009. Form 6251 and the AMT Calculator provide more information.

Keep up to date with the ever-changing
tax laws on the IRS Web site.

Contents at a Glance

Chapter 1: Minding the Law

In This Chapter

✓ Keeping your business within the law

✓ Determining whether you can legally work from home

✓ Obtaining the necessary licenses to operate your business

For good reason, the world has more lawyers than the U.S. national debt has dollars: Lots of laws are out there, and many of them pertain to how you should run your business.

One of the first things you discover in owning a business is that you cannot avoid certain specific legal requirements. An Internet business is subject to not only traditional laws imposed on any company but also further regulation. As with the rest of the Net, these rules change quickly, and the burden to keep up is on you.

In this chapter, we review the basic laws so that you can start setting up shop.

We're not lawyers, and laws differ from state to state. So, if you're the least bit concerned, consult a local attorney to answer any of your questions.

Keeping Your Business Legal

Whether you have an online business or an offline business, you must do certain things to set yourself up and operate legally. If you already have a business that you're taking online, this advice is probably old news to you. But if you're starting your online business from scratch, read on.

Admittedly, quite a few business-related laws exist. At first pass, they can be a bit overwhelming. Like everything else in business, though, you take one step at a time and, before you know it, you arrive. The same is true with the legalities of operating an online business. Start out on the right foot by getting up to speed with these basic requirements.

Depending on the type of business you're conducting over the Internet, additional laws or regulations might apply to you. Several good sources to help you research this information include

+ A trade association within your industry

+ Your local Chamber of Commerce

+ The Small Business Administration (SBA)

Federal tax identification number

If you have employees or your business is a corporation or partnership, you need a federal tax ID. Officially known as an employer identification number (EIN), this 9-digit number is used to identify a company whenever its owner files certain forms and tax returns.

You can apply for a federal tax ID by calling 1-800-829-4933. An authorized agent walks you through the process and then issues an EIN to you. The easiest method, however, is to apply online at the IRS Web site: `https://sa.www4.irs.gov/sa_vign/newFormSS4.do`. Or, if you prefer, you can download the required Form SS-4 and submit the application by regular U.S. mail.

The EIN is requested on many different types of business documents, from bank accounts to loan applications. If you don't have a federal tax ID number, you can use your Social Security number instead.

Resale certificate

If you sell any type of product, your state might require that you collect and pay a sales tax on every sale. If so, you need to apply for a resale certificate (often associated with buying wholesale). Be aware that the amount of sales tax to collect, the dates the tax is due, and the rules of collection vary by state. For that reason, you should check the regulations for the state in which your business is physically located. Because exceptions to the rules often exist or other details can be difficult to understand, also consider talking with a certified public accountant.

Business bank account

When you first begin to operate a business, you might be tempted to run all your money through an existing personal account. Trust us: This technique happens quite often and is rarely a good idea. Why do people do it? If you're just testing out your business idea, opening a separate account might seem unnecessary. Or, perhaps you view it as a way to save some money on bank fees. Unless you plan to maintain your idea strictly as a hobby, however, you need to open a business bank account immediately. Otherwise, it becomes too easy to commingle personal and business expenses. How can you possibly separate them if they share a bank account?

Health department permit

If you manufacture, package, or distribute food-related products as part of your online business, you need a permit from the health department. The permits (along with any necessary on-site inspections) are handled by your city or county health department. However, you might also be subject to certain regulations of the Food and Drug Administration (FDA). For instance, if you're making and selling homemade jelly over the Internet, you might be required to meet certain labeling standards that detail ingredients and nutritional information. You can obtain a complete food-labeling guide, along with other details of starting and operating an online food business, at the FDA Web site: `www.cfsan.fda.gov/~comm/foodbiz.html`.

You can get a small-business food-labeling exemption if you don't exceed certain annual sales levels or if you don't make nutritional claims in your advertising.

When you open a business account, the bank needs specific information, such as a copy of your business license, your federal tax ID number or Social Security number, and, possibly, proof of incorporation if you want your legally incorporated business name on the account.

Consider opening two bank accounts: one for all your daily transactions and the other for dealing with sales tax, employee withholding, and other regular tax payments. Keeping these items separate and using simple money transfers from one account to another can help you keep your payroll/employee finances separate and easier to manage. Meet with your bank's manager to find out what perks may be available when opening one or more business accounts. Banks are very competitive and often agree to waive certain fees or offer free checking for a period of time.

Employee forms

When you hire others to work for your company (even if you are your only employee), the IRS wants to be in the know, and that involves forms, of course. You should be familiar with several forms required by the IRS:

✦ **Form W-9:** When you hire independent contractors (non-employees), consultants, or self-employed individuals to perform work, have them complete IRS Form W-9. This form provides you with the information you need to report earnings to the IRS and generate a Form 1099 (see the next bullet point) that reports their earnings at the end of the year.

When you're hiring independent contractors, be sure to check the IRS definition of what constitutes a contractor (versus an employee). For instance, if you have workspace available at your office for the contractor or require the person to work a set schedule, you could cause an independent contractor to be considered an employee. If that's the case, you're responsible for withholding taxes. You can even be fined (with interest) if you don't withhold wages and the mistake is discovered later.

✦ **Form 1099:** If you hire someone (other than an employee) to do work for your company, you need to send that person a Form 1099 at the end of the year. You're required to complete this form only if you paid the individual $600 or more. If you're not incorporated and provide a service for another company, you receive, of course, a Form 1099.

If you barter or trade services or products with another company, the IRS expects you to report, on Form 1099, the value of that trade as income.

✦ **Form W-4:** If you have employees, they must fill out Form W-4s so that you can withhold, report, and deposit their correct amount of employment-related taxes. You're responsible for *withholding,* or taking out, money for income tax, Social Security and Medicare, and federal unemployment taxes (FUTA).

✦ **Form W-2:** By the last day of January following the end of each calendar year, you're responsible for sending this form to your employees. A W-2 reports the total income an employee earned from you during the preceding calendar year, along with the amount of money you withheld for various taxes during the year.

Zoning for Business (at Home)

Your home is the ideal place to start an online business. Your home is quick and easy to set up, and it equates to low overhead. Before you convert that spare bedroom into an office, however, you need to determine whether you're allowed to operate a business from your home.

The answer typically comes down to a single word: *zoning.* Most cities and towns have zoning ordinances that define how a particular piece of land or group of properties can be used. They further specify which types of activities can occur there. For example, some neighborhoods are zoned for residential, which means that only single-family homes can be built in that area. Other areas might allow multifamily (apartments) residential. In the area of commercial or business use, the zoning becomes more complicated because businesses are often separated by types of industry. An area might also be labeled *mixed use,* which allows both residential and some types of limited commercial activity.

How do you decide whether your residential neighborhood is zoned for business? Check with your city's licensing or planning department. When you provide your address, the city clerk can tell you whether your neighborhood has any restrictions that would prevent you from opening your business.

Payment Card Industry (PCI) Data Security Standard

Effective June 30, 2005, a regulatory procedure went into effect for all online retailers. The Payment Card Industry Data Security Standard is a set of guidelines for all e-commerce merchants with internal payment-processing systems. It helps ensure that merchants keep customer data secure when they're collecting, processing, and storing personal and financial information.

The release of this standard is in response to the ongoing increase in identity theft and stolen credit card numbers obtained from Internet sites. Credit card companies, under pressure to tighten security measures, collaborated to issue this worldwide security standard. (Previously, each major card company had its own standard.) This solution is more encompassing and reaches all levels of e-commerce merchants, regardless of the number of monthly transactions they handle. (If you make fewer than 20,000 merchant transactions per year, *validating* your compliance is optional.)

Failure to comply with the standard can result in some outrageous penalties, including fines of up to $500,000 per incident or possible cancellation of your merchant account. Overall, the measure to increase the protection of your customers' data is a good one. Unfortunately, it's one more regulation that even very small companies must comply with to avoid penalties. The requirements of the standard stipulate that companies must

- Install and maintain a firewall configuration to protect data
- Not use vendor-supplied defaults for system passwords and other security passwords
- Protect stored data
- Encrypt the transmission of cardholder data and sensitive information across public networks
- Use and regularly update antivirus software
- Develop and maintain secure systems and applications
- Restrict business access to data based on job description and needs
- Assign a unique ID to each person who accesses the computer used for financial data
- Track and monitor all access to network resources and cardholder data
- Regularly test security systems and processes
- Maintain a policy that addresses information security

As part of the validation process, you might have to complete a self-assessment questionnaire. You can find more information online at the MasterCard merchant site: `http://sdp.mastercardintl.com`.

Book II
Chapter 1

Minding the Law

Some cities and counties make zoning maps, along with a detailed list of city ordinances, available online. If your city has a Web site, start there first!

Assuming that all goes well and you find no restrictive ordinances, you'll be in business quickly. But sometimes this isn't the case and your home-based business isn't allowed. Then you have to ask for a *variance,* or an exception to the zoning ordinance. Fortunately, because millions of people are working from home now, many cities have already established criteria for such exceptions. Even if your neighborhood isn't specifically zoned for business, therefore, your city might allow small home-based businesses if they meet certain conditions.

To grant a variance, cities and counties want assurance that your business doesn't have

✦ High-volume street traffic

✦ Increased activity (by customers) in and out of the home

✦ Large trucks on-site (delivery trucks or company vehicles)

✦ Required additional parking

✦ Exterior signage

✦ The use or storage of harmful chemicals

✦ Warehousing of a large number of products

✦ The on-site sale of products to the public (such as what takes place at retail locations)

✦ Employees (usually more than 3 or 4) working on-site

These conditions are in place primarily to ensure that your business activities don't adversely affect your neighbors or have an effect on residential property values. Luckily, most Internet-based endeavors don't create such nuisances. Be sure to reiterate this point with city planners when you're pursuing a variance request for your business.

If your business involves storing and shipping large numbers of products, you might want to lease an off-site storage facility or arrange to have your products shipped from a distribution facility. It not only eases concerns from city officials initially but is also a good preventive measure to keep your neighbors happy.

Increasingly, zoning isn't the only concern when you're starting a home-based business. Many cities are now requiring home occupational permits. If you want to operate from your home, you're required to have this permit — no matter what your business. The good news is that certain occupations or business types are often automatically granted permits (and computer or Internet-related businesses are almost always included). However, you might have to qualify for a permit based on a long list of conditions that are similar to the criteria used in seeking a zoning variance (noise, traffic, on-site sales, and employees, for example). When you apply for a home occupational permit, you might also be asked to provide a list of all your neighbors and their addresses. The city then sends notice of your intent to operate a business from your home and gives your neighbors an opportunity to object. Even with this caveat, obtaining a home occupational permit can be much easier (and faster) than having to get a zoning variance granted. When you apply for the permit, expect to pay a small fee, ranging from $1 to $75.

A home occupational permit doesn't take the place of a business license. To operate legally, you must have both. See the next section to find out how to obtain the all-important business license.

Is that all you have to do? Not quite. Even if your home clears municipal zoning ordinances and home occupational permits, other obstacles can stop you from operating a home-based business:

+ **Your homeowners' association:** Residents of subdivisions, condominiums, and some neighborhood communities often have homeowners' associations. If you're in this group, some restrictive covenants (or rules) probably govern your home and what you do to it, with it, and in it. The rules might also cover operating a business from your house. Read your covenants or bylaws carefully because even if your city doesn't restrict your business use of your home, these covenants might. If a problem exists, you can always go to the board of directors that manages your homeowners' association and try to obtain an exception.

+ **Landlords:** If you lease an apartment or house, the rental agreement might prohibit you from conducting any business activity on the property. Review your lease thoroughly for clauses that specify how you can use the property.

If you choose to ignore legal restrictions concerning how your property can be used, you're taking a considerable risk. If your business activity is discovered, city officials could shut down your business, your homeowner's association could impose steep fines (and even put a lien on your home), or your landlord could evict you.

Obtaining Business Licenses

Regardless of where your business is located, you need a license to operate it. A *business license* is a piece of paper granting you the right to do business within a city, county, or state. Licenses are typically valid for a one- or two-year period and are nontransferable. (If you sell the business, the license is void.) You have to pay a fee when you apply for your license. The amount is often based on the type of business you operate and can range from $25 to several thousand dollars.

You (and not a city clerk) should specify which business category you fall under when you apply for your license, because a category specifically for an Internet-based, or *e-commerce,* business might not exist. Instead, you have to select a broad category based on the specific activity conducted through your site. Some categories can require steep licensing fees and might not, in fact, apply to you. Scour the entire list and the accompanying fees. Then choose the one most related to your business and with the lowest fee.

In addition to obtaining a city-issued license, you might be required to have a license for the county in which you're operating your business. This license is similar to a city license but is often less restrictive and less expensive. Be aware that some occupations (building contractors, realtors, and other professional service providers, for example) might further require that you obtain a state license. Although you probably don't need a state license to operate your online business, you can double-check by visiting your state's Web site.

To help you find out where to go for your city and county licenses, the SBA offers an online list for all 51 states. You can find the Where to Obtain Business Licenses list at the SBA.gov site: `www.sba.gov/hotlist/license.html`. Each state is divided into counties, and the list gives you the locations and phone numbers of where to go to apply for a license.

Chapter 2: Choosing the Right Foundation: From Partnerships to Corporations

In This Chapter

✔ Deciding which business form is best suited to you

✔ Establishing yourself as a sole proprietorship

✔ Evaluating alternative legal structures when other owners are involved

✔ Operating by the rules of incorporation

✔ Modifying your ownership structure

At the top of every start-up checklist is a line item that reads "Establish the formal structure of your business." This line means that you start by deciding how you want your company legally organized. You can be the sole owner or have 2 partners or 50 shareholders. Each form of business has definite advantages and disadvantages, depending on your goals for the business.

Read the information we provide in this chapter about all these options before making your final decision.

Strategizing for the Best Organization

Choosing how to set up your business is easier than you might think. Considering that you have only four primary choices, the odds of narrowing the selection quickly are in your favor. Yet one of the most frequently asked questions when someone is starting a business is "Which structure is best for me?" To get started, you need to resolve four key issues:

✦ **Ownership:** Deciding who ultimately owns or controls your company is a primary influence on your choice of legal structure. A second factor is the number of people who control the business. Some forms of business are limited by both the number of owners and the type of owner (individual or corporation) it can have.

✦ **Liability:** You must choose where you want the legal responsibility for the business to reside. Deciding whether you're comfortable accepting full liability for the actions of the company or whether you need the protection (or veil) of a corporation is an important choice.

✦ **Taxes:** Each of the business structures is subject to various forms of taxation. For instance, you might pay a self-employment tax based on your earnings. Or, you could be taxed on the dividends paid out to all owners from the business. In the case of one type of incorporation, you might even experience *double taxation* — paying tax as the business and again as an individual stockholder.

Because the tax issues are so complex, first talk with a tax attorney or certified public accountant to determine which option best fits your specific circumstances.

✦ **Funding:** The way in which you finance the growth of your company can play a significant role in determining its structure. If you're *bootstrapping* (self-financing) the company, any of the structures might work for you. However, if you seek outside financing from angel investors or venture capitalists, you need the option of having stock available for distribution. If another business entity plans to own stock in your company, your choice of business structure is severely limited. See Book I, Chapter 4 for more info on how to fund your business.

Now that you understand these four primary areas of concern, you should have a better idea of where your specific requirements fit in. To make your final decision, read the detailed descriptions in the following sections for each business entity.

Operating Alone as a Sole Proprietor

If you're interested in simplicity, look no further. A sole proprietorship is recognized as the quickest, easiest, and least expensive method of forming a business. The main caveat is that only one person can operate as a sole proprietor. You and the business are literally the same entity. The upside of that arrangement is the ease of getting up and running. With the mere act of conducting business (and obtaining a license), you're considered a sole proprietor.

The downside of being a sole proprietor is that potential legal ramifications exist. Because you and the company are one, you're fully accountable for the losses of the business along with any legal matters. Whether the business is involved with lawsuits or problems with creditors, you're personally liable. No corporate protection is available — your personal assets (such as your home) can be sold and your personal bank accounts used to pay off creditors.

As a sole proprietor, you're also responsible for all taxes. The profits and losses of the business are listed on Schedule C on your personal tax return. And, you pay self-employment taxes (Schedule SE), which is a combined Social Security and Medicare tax. It's calculated as a percentage of your earnings, and as of the 2009 tax year, the percentage is 15.3 percent (12.4 percent for Social Security and 2.9 percent for Medicare).

A maximum amount of earnings is subject to Social Security tax. You're taxed 12.4 percent on only the first $102,000 of your combined wages, tips, and net earnings.

In addition to obtaining a business license and paying taxes, you have to address two other topics of interest if you're considering operating as a sole proprietor — how to

+ Register your company name

+ Form a sole proprietorship with your spouse

We discuss these topics in the next two sections.

Fictitious name registration

Unless you choose to operate your company under your exact legal name (or use your last name), you need to register a *fictitious* name with the state. The name of your company is different from that of its legal owner (you). Suppose that your name is John Smith and you decide to name your company Online Information Services. By registering that fictitious name, you become John Smith *dba* (*doing business as*) Online Information Services. Your business name should then appear on your checking account, business license, and any other legal documents.

Check with your city and state governments to determine how you should register your fictitious name. Some states require only that you submit an application and pay a small filing fee. Others mandate that you publish in a newspaper your intent to use the fictitious name before you begin to use it.

Husband/wife sole proprietorship

Togetherness is a wonderful thing, as you and your spouse might have found out when you got married. You and your spouse might even want to operate a business together. Does this mean that you no longer qualify for the simplified structure of a sole proprietorship? That depends.

The IRS legally recognizes a sole proprietor as having only one owner. If a spouse is working for the company, the IRS expects you to treat that person as an employee (which means that you have to pay payroll taxes). Alternatively, if your spouse has an active ownership role in the company, the IRS treats the business as a partnership (which means that both of you are taxed separately on the income). However, some tax advisors suggest that you can still file as a sole proprietor even if your spouse participates in the company. When you file a Schedule C on your joint tax return, all business income is viewed as one sum for both of you, although the IRS still views your business as belonging to a single owner.

To avoid paying payroll taxes, you can classify your spouse as a *volunteer.* Your spouse is then only occasionally active in the business and doesn't get credit toward Social Security.

If the IRS determines that your spouse works regular, consistent hours, it could mean instant classification as an employee. At that point, you might be responsible for paying a hefty sum of back taxes and penalties. Always consult a professional tax advisor to ensure that you're operating within the allowable classifications designated by the IRS.

Sharing the Load with a Partnership

In some ways, a general partnership is similar to a sole proprietorship: It's relatively simple and inexpensive to form. Issues of liability and taxes reside fully with its owners. The primary difference with a partnership is that it allows you to have multiple owners.

Although the terms of this type of partnership can be based on a verbal agreement, you should spell out the conditions in writing, for two reasons:

✦ **Dispute resolution:** Having the specific details of your original agreement in writing is handy if a dispute arises between you and your partner (or partners).

✦ **Proof of partnership:** If something happens and a written document cannot be produced, you and your partners are assumed to share equally in all aspects of the business. Proving otherwise in a court of law, or to the IRS, could prove difficult.

When you define your partnership, the basic agreement should address these areas:

✦ **Structure:** Shows what percentage of the company is owned by each partner

✦ **Control:** Defines which partner is responsible for which part of the daily management of the company

✦ **Profits:** Detail the division of profits and losses and the timeframe for distributing profits to the partners

A partnership arrangement brings up certain questions that you must consider at the beginning of a partnership:

✦ How much money and time will each partner contribute, and how will decisions for the company be made?

✦ What happens if one partner stops contributing, can no longer be actively involved, or wants out of the partnership?

✦ Can you buy out the interest of another partner, or will the partnership be dissolved automatically when a dispute cannot be settled?

✦ How will ownership be transferred if one partner dies or is involved in a divorce (especially if the partners are married to each other)?

✦ How will an owner's share in the company be redistributed?

These questions are tough to answer. You probably don't want to believe that anything will go wrong between you and your partners. Unfortunately, for one reason or another, partnerships go sour all the time.

The most successful partnerships are those in which issues such as these were openly discussed and agreed on up front. Likewise, individual owners who have survived a failed partnership have done so because a written agreement was in place. Considering that you and your partners are personally liable for the actions of your company, a formal partnership agreement is your best chance for avoiding problems.

Limited Liability Company (LLC)

If you prefer entering into a business using an entity that offers a bit more legal protection to you and your partners than a partnership, a limited liability company (LLC) might interest you. (Although some states also recognize a limited liability partnership, or LLP, the LLC is more common.)

The LLC combines the flexibility of a partnership with the formal structure and legal protection provided by a corporation. As in a general partnership, income is passed through to the individual partners, and profits can be distributed according to your agreement. (Note that profit doesn't have to be split equally among partners.) An LLC allows you to have an unlimited number of partners, and permits you to raise money for the business by taking on investors (including other corporations) as members. Additionally, members or partners of the LLC aren't personally liable for the actions of the corporation.

If you choose to form an LLC, you have to file with the state, although the requirements typically aren't as stringent as they are in a corporation. (You're not required to maintain bylaws or keep minutes of annual board meetings, for example.) However, the requirements for forming an LLC vary by state, so you have to research those requirements for the state in which you file.

Making It Official with Incorporation

One option to consider when you're establishing a business is whether to incorporate. A *corporation* is a legal entity that's separate from the individuals who create or work for it. Stock in a corporation is issued to individuals or to other business entities that form the ownership of the company.

Different flavors of corporations

Depending on your situation, you can choose one of two types of corporation:

+ **C corporation (or "C corp"):** This traditional form of a corporation typically offers the most flexibility when you're seeking investors. A C corp is allowed to have unlimited shareholders, usually with no restrictions on who they are. The downside is the way in which this status of corporation is taxed. In a concept commonly referred to as *double taxation*, the business is taxed first on its income and then its individual shareholders must also pay tax.

+ **S corporation (or "S corp"):** Electing to have Subchapter S status is an option for your company if you have a limited number of shareholders (as few as just you and usually no more than 35). The shareholders must all be individuals (they cannot be corporations or other business entities), and they must be legal U.S. residents. You also have to agree to operate the business on a calendar year for tax purposes. The advantage of becoming an S corp is that you avoid double taxation. (Profits and losses are passed through to shareholders.)

The choice to incorporate

The biggest advantage to incorporating is that it offers legal protection to its owners. As an individual shareholder, you're not personally liable, as you are with a sole proprietorship or general partnership. You might find that a corporation offers significant tax advantages, too. If you're seeking investment capital or plan to take the company public with an initial public offering (IPO), a corporation gives you the most flexibility to do so.

Incorporating has a few disadvantages, too. For starters, you must file or register your corporation with your state. This process involves a large amount of paperwork, which takes some time. To file, you have to submit articles of incorporation that state (among other information)

+ The purpose of your business

+ The name of the company

+ The name of the owner

+ The company's location

You also have to submit bylaws, which describe how the company is run, and a list of officers, or the people who direct the company in its daily decisions, such as a president, secretary, and treasurer.

After your corporation is approved by the state, your responsibilities don't end there. To maintain the corporation's status, you're required to issue stock, hold annual board meetings (with its officers), and record minutes of these meetings. These formal requirements of a corporation can be cumbersome for you, especially when you're starting a new business. In addition, a corporation has to file separate tax forms, which are typically more complicated than an individual return. You could be doubling your efforts — and your expense — while trying to comply with taxes.

If the corporate veil is pierced, you can be held personally responsible for the debts and legal concerns of your corporation. This situation happens when you don't properly uphold the requirements of your corporation. Any protection offered by the corporation is therefore forfeited.

Forming a corporation isn't the cheapest method of starting a business, either. If you hire an attorney to file the necessary paperwork with the state, expect to spend close to $1,000 or more in legal expenses and filing fees. Even if you elect to incorporate yourself or do it through an online service, it can still cost several hundred dollars. You pay, at the least, an initial filing fee with the state and then an annual fee to maintain your status.

Changing Your Organization as It Grows

Just because you select one form of structure when you're starting your business doesn't mean that you're stuck with it forever. As with other decisions you make along the way, you might find that your growing company warrants a different legal structure at some point. Of course, the ideal situation is to select a structure that gives you the most flexibility at the time you start up. Sometimes, though, that's not reasonable. The next-best plan of action is to understand when and how you should change your organization.

Perhaps the best indicators are those related to money and ownership. As a small-business owner, if you use your money better through different tax strategies, waste no time making the transition. Many businesses start out as sole proprietorships because that option is simple. When the owner hits a certain level of income, however, it makes sense to incorporate based on the amount of self-employment taxes being paid. The advantage of saving several thousand dollars outweighs the compliance burden of incorporation. As they say, it's a no-brainer!

Then there's the matter of owner status. As a sole proprietor, if you take on an additional owner, you have to convert to a partnership or some form of corporation. Similarly, if you're operating a general partnership and then decide to seek out other owners for investment purposes, forming a corporation and offering stock might make sense.

You can much more easily switch from a sole proprietorship or partnership to a corporation than vice versa. After you incorporate a business, you're expected to meet payroll and wage-related tax requirements as defined by the IRS, and you're expected to hold shareholder meetings. If you decide that you cannot maintain a formal corporation or that it's no longer the best structure for your company, you cannot simply stop meeting these requirements. Instead, you must follow certain procedures to legally dissolve the business before you can change its official ownership status. The Small Business Administration (SBA) offers detailed instructions for this process at www.sba.gov/smallbusinessplanner/exit.

Before changing the status of your business, *always* consult with your certified public accountant, attorney, or other trusted business advisor. Consider your options carefully!

Chapter 3: The Trademark-and-Copyright Two-Step

In This Chapter
✔ **Understanding trademarks and the law**

✔ **Establishing copyrights and your right to be covered**

✔ **Registering your work**

✔ **Hiring lawyers to do it for you**

*Y*our business is important to you, and protecting your hard work and assets is probably high on your list of concerns. From your company logo to your business documentation to your Web site, making certain that your intellectual property (IP) is protected from improper use, plagiarism, and defamation is a never-ending process.

In this chapter, we show you how to protect your investment by registering for trademarks and filing your copyright.

Understanding Why Trademarks and Copyrights Matter

Creating a distinctive name, symbol, or phrase for use in your business can involve a lot of work. After all, branding companies are paid tens (or hundreds) of thousands of dollars to come up with the right names for new products or services. The same hard work and amount of time invested applies to a written work of art, a clever body of text used on your Web site, or an original piece of artwork: If you go to the trouble of developing unique content, it's probably worth protecting it as your own.

To understand how to protect yourself, you have to enter the Land of Legalization. Start by wrapping your brain cells around some extremely important words, as defined by the U.S. government:

✦ **Copyright:** A form of intellectual property law that protects original works of authorship, including literary, dramatic, musical, and artistic works, such as poetry, novels, movies, songs, computer software, and architecture. The Library of Congress registers copyrights, which last for the life of the author plus 70 years.

✦ **Patent:** A property right granted by the government of the United States to an inventor that excludes others from making, using, offering for sale, or selling the invention throughout the United States or importing the invention into the United States, in exchange for public disclosure of the invention when the patent is granted.

✦ **Trademark:** Protects words, names, symbols, sounds, or colors that distinguish goods and services from those manufactured or sold by others and that indicate the source of the goods. Trademarks can be renewed forever, or as long as they're being used in commerce.

Obtaining one of these legal stamps to claim something as your own is a fairly painless process. Taking this precaution can eventually translate into dollars gained. Not having a product or logo protected makes it easier for someone to copy or steal your idea. That's money out of your pocket! Although having a trademark or copyright might not prevent others from infringing on your work, it certainly makes it easier to go after them in court if they do.

Although the rules for these protective marks are the same whether you're conducting business online or off, the Internet has increased the stakes in some instances. Having your information readily accessible by millions of people around the globe makes it much easier for others to "borrow" from your hard work. That's all the more reason to make the effort to officially protect your information.

Making Your (Trade)Mark

Do you have to register your work to be protected? No. You might be surprised by this answer, but a federal trademark isn't a necessity. Suppose that you design a symbol to be used as the logo for your online business. By placing that logo on your site, and using it there and on any other business materials, you have established rights to it. So, why bother to officially register it? Obtaining federal registration acts as a notice to the public that you own the mark. It can also assist you if you decide to take action in a federal court to stop someone else from using your work. Also, if you want to register your logo outside the United States, the official registration provides the basis for you to do so.

Even if you choose not to formally register your work, you can use the trademark symbol anyway. After you establish that brilliant tagline or artistic logo, go ahead and place the trademark symbol (^{TM}) near your work. However, you cannot use the symbol showing that the work is officially registered until you apply for registration and receive final notification that your mark is registered. At that time, you can use the registered symbol (®). Figure 3-1 shows examples of how to use these symbols properly.

Having a registered trademark doesn't prevent others from infringing on its use. After your work is registered, it's up to you to enforce it.

Figure 3-1:
Trademark
and
registration
symbols
show
ownership.

Protecting Your Investment with Copyrights

As with trademarks, you don't have to file for copyright protection to claim your written work as your own. Copyright protection is in place at the time you create your work. However, if you choose to file a lawsuit against someone for using your information, the U.S. Copyright Office advises that you need the formal certificate of registration as proof of ownership.

The good news is that copyrighting your information isn't expensive. Filing fees, at this time, are $35 per work if filed online and $45 per work if filed by other means; a group of material typically costs a minimum of $45 (or $15 per individual work within the group).

If you choose to register, certain rules pertain specifically to Web sites and other material (such as documents you offer for download) distributed online. For instance, you can copyright any original information you include on your site.

Here are some other variables:

✦ You can protect computer programs you have written.

✦ You can protect entire databases.

✦ You *cannot* copyright your domain name for your site (such as `www.mysiteisgreat.com`).

✦ If you decide to send out an electronic newsletter to your customers each week, it's protected under copyright laws, as long as the information is original.

The rules become more complicated when you discuss the period over which a work is protected or the amount of work that can be copyrighted. For instance, the original words on your Web site pages are protected.

However, if you make updates to any of your pages and change that information, it isn't protected. In other words, you aren't given an unlimited copyright to your site's content. If you change the information (which you should do to keep your site fresh and current), you must file another application and pay another filing fee.

Here's an exception to this rule: An online computer program may be treated separately. Online work that's continuously updated can be classified as an automated database, which can have a single registration that covers updates over a three-month period (in the same calendar year). Or, if you have material, such as an e-newsletter, that's updated daily or weekly, you might qualify for a group registration (or a single registration that covers multiple issues). Unfortunately, blogs or online journals don't fall under the group-registration option at this time.

For complete details about copyrighting your online work, check out the official site for the U.S. Copyright Office and its section about electronic content, "Copyright Information for Online Works": www.copyright.gov/circs/circ66.pdf. As with all advice in this book, when it comes to legalities, we highly advise you to consult an attorney if you have any questions or concerns about any actions you need to take.

The Digital Millennium Copyright Act

The Digital Millennium Copyright Act (DMCA) became law in 1998. This legislation is part of the World Intellectual Property Organization (WIPO) Copyright Treaty, which countries around the world had previously agreed to adopt. Its intent is to provide enhanced copyright protection, specifically within electronic media (the Internet). Generally, the DMCA makes illegal the use of technology to copy or pirate digital material, such as software, music, and video. The DMCA further prohibits you from selling or distributing technology that could permit this type of activity.

How does the DMCA affect you? The answer depends on your type of business. If your Web site distributes music in any way, this law requires that you, as a Webcaster, pay appropriate licensing fees for that right. If you're a nonprofit organization, a library, or an Internet service provider (ISP), you gain some added protection if someone uses your system to distribute copyrighted material. If you're the owner of copyrighted material and discover an infringement, you can report it to the ISP that's transmitting the information and request that the material be removed. Other than in these situations, the DMCA might not be a concern for you. You should be aware of it, though, because this piece of legislation has been controversial. As court cases evolve, you might discover that you're more affected than you thought.

Establishing Registration Yourself

As we point out in the preceding section, establishing your work as your own is as simple as creating it and using it. When you're ready to take the extra step to obtain proof of ownership, you can easily file for a trademark or copyright yourself.

Getting your trademark

You can apply for a federal trademark all on your own. Follow these steps to work through the registration process:

1. **Go to the Web site of the United States Patent and Trademark Office:** `www.uspto.gov`.

   The main page of the site lists current news and information about trademarks and patents. Along the left side of the page is a list of topics from which you can choose more information.

2. **Under the Trademarks category, click the File Online Forms (TEAS) link.**

   This step takes you to the Trademarks Electronic Application System (TEAS) page. The left side of the page contains links to detailed information about enhancements to the system and important notices. The right side of the page contains links to the application forms.

   At the top of the File Online Forms page, the Where Do I Start link provides complete filing information for first-time filers. You can also access a link that shows you each page in the registration process so that you know exactly which information you need to file. You should visit these links before you start the registration process.

3. **In the upper-right corner of the page, under the word *Form,* click the TEAS Tutorial link.**

   A step-by-step guide to the online filing procedure opens, as shown in Figure 3-2.

4. **Complete all steps.**

   After you complete the application tutorial, your mark is officially submitted for approval.

   Have your credit card ready when you file online. A $325 filing fee, per item, must accompany your online application.

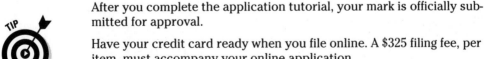

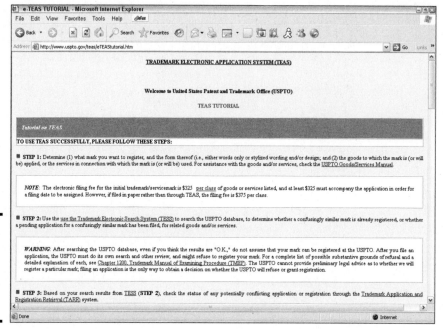

Figure 3-2:
Use the
tutorial
to file
trademarks
online.

5. **Check the status of your application by calling 703-305-8747 or going to the Trademark Application and Registration Retrieval (TARR) system at** `http://tarr.uspto.gov`.

Wait at least 25 days before checking the status of your application. It takes that long for the trademark databases to be updated.

Filing for copyright

To file an application for obtaining a federal copyright of your work, follow these steps:

1. **Go to the Web site of the U.S. Copyright Office, at** `www.copyright.gov`.

   The home page shows you a list of choices to get information, as shown in Figure 3-3.

2. **Click the How to Register a Work link.**

3. **Click the Electronic Copyright Office (eCO) icon and then click the Continue to eCO button.**

Figure 3-3:
Self-file your copyright at the U.S. government's copyright site.

4. **Register with the Electronic Copyright Office.**

5. **Select the Register a New Claim link under the Copyright Services menu tab on the right side of the page.**

The resulting page provides a list of specific steps of how to register a copyright.

6. **Follow the three steps as outlined on the site.**

These steps include completing an online application, paying the filing fees, and uploading your work using an accepted file format. Tutorials for each stage help you complete the filing process successfully.

If you have trouble filing electronically, you can also send the completed application and copies of your work, along with the designated filing fee, to this address:

Library of Congress Copyright Office
101 Independence Avenue, S.E.
Washington, D.C. 20559-6000

After your registration is approved, you receive a certificate of registration (usually in four or five months).

Retaining Professional Assistance

Hiring an attorney who specializes in trademarks, patents, or copyrights can be a good idea if your situation is complex or you're not comfortable handling the applications on your own. If you're pursuing registration in foreign countries, hiring an attorney who's familiar with international laws is invaluable. Because U.S. copyright and trademark laws are recognized in some, but not all, countries, using an attorney can ensure that you're fully protected.

You can expect to pay big bucks for the expertise of a professional. An experienced attorney might charge anywhere from $175 to $250 (or more) per hour for her service. This money is in addition to any filing or application fees you might have to pay. For this fee, you can expect a trademark attorney to conduct a thorough search of existing and pending marks that might conflict with yours. The attorney should also complete all forms on your behalf and act as the primary point of contact with the United States Patent and Trademark Office or the U.S. Copyright Office.

To protect your investment, follow these tips when you're hiring a professional:

✦ Look for an attorney who specializes in intellectual property, or trademarks, copyrights, and patents.

✦ Get referrals from others you know who have used attorneys to register their businesses.

✦ Clarify which portion of the work is conducted by the attorney and which part is handled by legal aides (or junior partners).

✦ Discuss the attorney's rate and whether you're billed up front.

✦ Ask for a written statement or estimate of how much you can expect the process to cost.

✦ Confirm that the attorney is licensed.

You can search for an attorney in your area by using the referral guides on these Web sites:

✦ **American Bar Association (ABA):** Visit www.abanet.org to locate attorneys in your area that can help you with your specific legal needs.

✦ **FindLaw:** FindLaw, at www.findlaw.com, can also help you locate local attorneys that specialize in various legal subjects, including trademark policies.

Chapter 4: Accounting for Taxes (And Then Some)

In This Chapter

✔ Keeping up with IRS expectations

✔ Tracking your profits and losses

✔ Finding software to make accounting a snap (or as close as it gets)

✔ Choosing a professional to ease your mind and protect your pocketbook

✔ Paperwork: Deciding what stays and what goes — and when

*U*nless you have a penchant for numbers, along with a love of crunching them, accounting is probably the least fun part of owning a business. Even so, we also recognize that it's one of the most necessary business functions. Why? It boils down to these two issues:

✦ **Taxes:** The Internal Revenue Service (IRS) demands that you keep accurate records of the monetary side of your business. That way, you're sure to contribute your fair share of taxes to Uncle Sam.

✦ **Profitability:** IRS aside, *you* need to understand how well (or not so well) your business is doing financially. Then you can make good strategic decisions for its future — and yours!

Dread it as you may, you have to embrace accounting. Okay, perhaps not embrace it, but you can at least learn to appreciate its value and commit to keeping up with it. To help prepare you for that financial road ahead, we start by introducing you to some basics of accounting. Before long, you may even look forward to balancing your checkbook. (Hey, anything is possible.) If you find that you just can't hack the accounting life, we also advise you on how and when to choose a professional to help you out.

The Tax Man Cometh — Again and Again

You've probably heard the saying that nothing in life is certain except death and taxes. Suffice it to say that the latter is at least predictable. As a business owner, you can count on the tax man regularly showing up on your doorstep. Rain or shine, without fail, taxes come due at certain times of the year whether you like it or not.

In Book II, Chapter 1, we give you a glimpse of what to expect of the tax man when we discuss the pros and cons of various ownership structures for your business and how each form is taxed. Regardless of which type of business structure you choose, you face many tax-related requirements when you run an online business.

For starters, several types of federal and state taxes are likely to apply to you, as we describe in the next few sections.

Income tax

You pay income tax on the money your business earns. Almost every type of company has to file an annual income tax return. (The exception is the partnership, which files only an information return.)

The important thing to know is that federal income tax is a pay-as-you-go system — the IRS doesn't want to wait until the end of the year to receive its cut of your money. Instead, you must pay the amount of taxes that are due every quarter. Because you don't always know the exact amount to pay in time to file by the IRS deadline (maybe an overdue invoice comes in at the last minute or a refund has to be issued), you can *estimate* the tax amount for each quarter and then submit that dollar amount. Table 4-1 lists the appropriate IRS form to submit when you're estimating taxes, along with many other forms that the IRS says you need, according to the type of organization you create.

Table 4-1	IRS Tax Forms Based on Business Type	
Organization Type	*Potentially Liable For This Type of Tax*	*Form or Forms Required*
Sole proprietor	Income tax	1040 and Schedule C1 or C–EZ (Schedule F1 for farm business)
	Self-employment tax	1040 and Schedule SE
	Estimated tax	1040–ES
	Employment taxes: Social Security and Medicare taxes and income tax withholding	941 (943 for farm employees)
	Federal unemployment (FUTA) tax	940 or 940–EZ
	Depositing employment taxes	8109

Organization Type	Potentially Liable For This Type of Tax	Form or Forms Required
Partnership	Annual return of income	1065
	Employment taxes	Same as sole proprietor
Partner in a partnership (individual)	Income tax	1040 and Schedule E
	Self-employment tax	1040 and Schedule SE
	Estimated tax	1040–ES
Corporation or S corporation	Income tax	1120 or 1120–A (corporation) 1120S (S corporation)
	Estimated tax	1120–W (corporation only) and 8109
	Employment taxes	Same as sole proprietor
S corp-oration shareholder	Income tax	1040 and Schedule E
	Estimated tax	1040–ES

Employment tax

Your tax responsibilities don't end, of course, with reporting your income. Employees play a role, too. Whether you have one person (even if that's you!) or a hundred people working for your company, if you hire employees to work in your online business, you're responsible for paying certain taxes on behalf of those employees. Even if they work only part-time, you still have to keep up with the paperwork and pay up.

These obligations are commonly referred to as payroll taxes. You must file *withholding forms* (along with the accompanying payment) to both the IRS and your state treasury department. The types of taxes you pay on behalf of your employees include

✦ Medicare and Social Security taxes (as part of the Federal Insurance Contributions Act, or FICA)

✦ Federal income tax withholding

✦ Federal unemployment tax (FUTA)

Calculating the withholding amount can be complicated: You start with the information submitted by your employee on a Form W-9 and then use the tables in IRS Publication 15, *Employer's Tax Guide* (Section 16). It's available at www.irs.gov/pub/irs-pdf/p15.pdf. If you're still not sure how to calculate this amount, your financial advisor (bookkeeper or accountant) can easily do it for you.

With calculated withholding amounts in hand, you need to fork over payroll taxes every quarter. You must file Form 941, *Employer's Quarterly Tax Return,* by the last day of the month that follows the end of the quarter. Table 4-2 shows the payroll due dates for both paper filing and electronic filing.

Table 4-2	Due Dates for Payroll Taxes	
Quarter Ends	*Normal Due Date*	*Extended Due Date*
March 31	April 30	May 10
June 30	July 31	August 10
September 30	October 31	November 10
December 31	January 31	February 10

In addition to providing payroll dates, the IRS Web site for small businesses offers easy access to almost every other type of tax form you need to submit. The site even contains an online learning center so that you can further educate yourself about all tax and business start-up issues, as you can see in Figure 4-1.

The rule of filing quarterly has some exceptions. Always check with your accountant or CPA to confirm that you're filing properly. Otherwise, the IRS can slap you with hefty penalties and interest (never a good thing!).

If you believe that your employment taxes are $1,000 or less (equal to annual earnings of $4,000 or less), you may be eligible to submit payroll taxes annually. For more information, visit the IRS Web site at www.irs.gov/businesses/small/article/0,,id=152104,00.html.

You might want to file electronically. (Come on — if you're running an online business, you ought to be set up for filing online, right?) Although the process is fairly easy, some paperwork is involved. In other words, don't assume that you can wait until the day before your taxes are due to sign up!

To start making online payments, go to the IRS Web site for small businesses at `www.irs.gov/businesses/index.html`. Follow the e-file link. (It should be on the left side, under the heading IRS Resources.) The documents you're looking for is Form 4419, Application for Filing Information Returns Electronically (FIRE). Before you can file your taxes, you must submit a request to do so. An IRS-approved online vendor can submit your request for filing online, or you can submit your own manual request.

Even in you submit a manual request, you still must use an online vendor to submit your payroll taxes, so we recommend saving yourself from the hassle of duplicating steps and let an online vendor handle the application request for you.

Before you can complete the manual or online vendor application, you must have an employer identification number (EIN).

Make sure that you account for the slight turnaround time for processing your application. The IRS should receive your application by the 15th of the month that precedes the next quarterly payroll filing deadline. For example, if you want to start filing electronically for the second quarter, the IRS must receive your application by March 15.

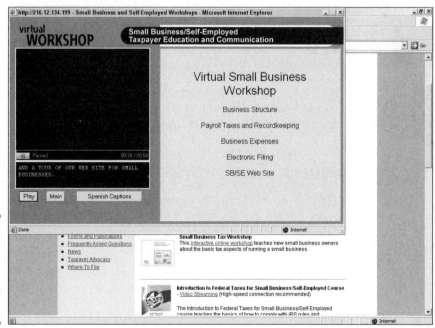

Figure 4-1:
You can take quick online tax classes from the IRS.

Sales tax

Another tax responsibility is that of tracking and collecting sales tax from your customers and then submitting it to the appropriate state and local agencies. If you sell (or manufacture) products, you probably have to deal with this issue.

You may be wondering whether you can, of course, avoid sales tax because you're selling products online and not within a particular state. Although federal legislators are debating this issue, for now it comes down to this guideline:

> If you sell to people in any state where you have a physical presence (and sometimes that can be the tiniest remote office), you must collect tax from customers originating from that same state.

The flip side of this issue is that individual states are becoming more aggressive about collecting sales tax from Internet-based companies. Yet a lot of uncertainty remains about how this obligation will play out in each state. Rest assured that this issue will get passed around legislatures like a hot potato! Our advice is to stay on top of the most current information at both the state and federal levels and to have your accountant continually keep you updated.

You're also liable for filing and paying other state-related taxes (not just sales tax). Because the amount varies greatly across states, check with your accountant to find out which taxes apply to your online business. Or, you can contact your state's revenue department to learn more.

The Federation of Tax Administrators (FTA) Web site has a direct link to the appropriate agency Web sites for each state. Find the link at www.tax admin.org/fta/link/default.html.

By the Numbers: Accounting Basics

Although we freely admit that accounting isn't our favorite activity, some elements of it are enjoyable. For example, at the end of every month, you have the opportunity to look at the profit-and-loss (P&L) statement to see how well your business is doing — on paper. It's like getting a checkup (for better or worse) and viewing a summary of every activity you performed during the month, as it relates to the bottom line of your business. If all is well, yippee! If you encounter problems, a profit-and-loss statement is bound to expose your points of weakness.

If you're still not sure what a P&L is, let alone what it means to your business, don't worry. You'll soak it up in no time, along with several other important pieces of financial information in the following sections.

Determining periods and methods

Before you can walk, you have to crawl. When you're starting a business, one of the first things you have to do is select your *tax year,* or the defined period that you use to provide an annual snapshot of the financial state of your business.

You can choose from several types of tax year:

✦ **Calendar year:** This method is defined by the wall calendar you buy at the beginning of every year. The 12 months that are encompassed start January 1 and end December 31. Your calendar-year accounting system follows the same pattern: Move from month to month and then start all over again on the next January 1.

✦ **Fiscal year:** Although this type of tax year also has a fixed 12-month period, it never ends on the last day of December — any other month, but not that one. For example, you could choose to run from October 1 to September 30 of the following year. Why bother? If you have a seasonal business, this method provides an opportunity to adapt your operational schedule to an accounting and tax schedule. If your peak season is at the end of the year, having to worry about reporting or paying taxes also can be cumbersome.

✦ **52-53-week:** In this variation of the fiscal year, you operate on a 52- or 53-week period rather than on a 12-month schedule. The catch is that your tax year must always land on the same day of the week (close to the end of a calendar month), thus requiring that an extra week be added to the period in order to end on the same calendar date each time.

A calendar year is probably the easiest reporting method for you to adopt. Depending on which type of business you form (an LLC or S corporation, for example), you may have difficulty getting the IRS to approve anything other than a calendar year. The IRS refers to it as a *required tax year.*

If you have good reason to think that the calendar year is a problem for your business, you must file a request (Form 1128) with the IRS to change your tax year. Unless an IRS code provides for automatic approval, be prepared to pay a filing fee for the change request.

Your next decision is to choose an *accounting method* for your business. You use this method to arrive at your income and expenses. Just as you choose your tax year, you select your preferred accounting method when you start your business. You're then expected to stick with it, unless the IRS approves a change.

Here are the two most common accounting methods for a business:

✦ **Cash basis:** Simply put, you report earnings when they're received and report expenses when they're incurred. The IRS says that you *cannot* use the cash method if any of these conditions applies:

  • You're a corporation (other than an S corporation) with average annual gross receipts of more than $5 million.

  • You're a partnership that has a corporation (other than an S corporation) as a partner, and the partnership has average annual gross receipts of more than $5 million.

  • You're a tax shelter.

  • You have inventory.

Special circumstances and exceptions to the rules always exist. Be sure to check with your CPA regarding which basis is best for your business.

✦ **Accrual basis:** In this method, your revenues can be reported when you earn them rather than when you receive the money (cash). Likewise, your expenses can be reported on the date they're owed, as opposed to the date on which you pay them. If you produce items or have inventory, accrual is considered the best way to provide an accurate picture of your financial status from year to year. Of course, that rule has some exceptions! You can use another method, even if you deal with inventory, if you are

  • A qualifying taxpayer who passes the gross receipt test (with less than $1 million in gross sales for each year of the test period)

  • A qualifying small-business taxpayer who passes the gross receipt test (with less than $10 million in average annual gross receipts for each year of the test period)

  • An eligible business as determined by the IRS

Also, you must *not* be

  • A tax shelter

  • Prohibited from using the cash method

And now, your balance sheet

No matter which accounting method you choose, you need to know how to make sense of your company's financial statements. A *balance sheet,* which is one of those statements, is a detailed summary of your business's financial status.

To understand your balance sheet, here are some terms you need to know:

✦ **Assets:** Everything of value that your business owns. Assets typically include

  • *Cash:* Available money in your bank accounts

  • *Accounts receivable (A/R):* The money that your customers owe you

  • *Inventory:* The monetary worth of whatever merchandise you have on hand

  • *Fixed assets:* Land, buildings, furniture, and equipment

  • *Miscellaneous:* A catchall term for anything that doesn't fit into any other category

✦ **Liabilities:** All the debts of the business. Liabilities can include

  • *Accounts payable (A/P):* The money that you owe suppliers, vendors, or credit card companies

  • *Accrued expenses:* Wages, payroll taxes, and sales tax, for example, that have been collected but not yet paid

  • *Noncurrent:* Notes payable to shareholders and the portion of long-term debt that isn't yet due, for example

✦ **Net worth or capital:** The amount of your ownership or equity or the amount you invested in your company

✦ **Revenue or sales:** All the income your business has earned, usually recorded over a specific period

✦ **Expenses:** Everything spent by your business, typically recorded (or totaled) for a specified period

Now you know all the essential terms that relate to a balance sheet. The next important point is that when a balance sheet is put together correctly, the bottom line must "balance" by using the following equation:

Assets = liabilities + net worth

That's it. See? It's not that confusing! To help you grasp how a balance sheet should look, check out the sample shown in Figure 4-2.

Balance Sheet
Ending December 31, 2005

	2005
ASSETS	
Current Assets	
Cash	$2,500
Accounts receivable	2,800
Inventory	5,500
Total Current Assets	**$10,800**
Fixed Assets	
Buildings	$ 0
Land	0
Furnitures and fixtures	1,200
Equipment	7,000
Accum. depreciation	(200)
Miscellaneous	0
Total Fixed Assets	**$8,000**
TOTAL ASSETS	**$18,800**
LIABILITIES AND SHAREHOLDERS' EQUITY	
Liabilities	
Accounts payable	$3,300
Taxes payable	500
TOTAL LIABILITIES	**$3,800**
Net Worth	15,000
TOTAL LIABILITIES & NET WORTH	**$18,800**

Figure 4-2:
A sample balance sheet.

A quick glimpse: The P&L

Unlike a balance sheet, an *income statement* (commonly referred to as a profit-and-loss statement, or P&L) provides a quick snapshot of your revenues and expenses. It's made up of *line items,* a sequence of items providing a monetary total for every category of revenues or expenses. When you compile the statement, you can see how much money your business earned (or lost) for that specific period.

You can create P&Ls on a quarterly basis. Looking at P&Ls monthly is more useful, however, because you can more easily spot any unusual fluctuations in your sales or expenses.

Suppose that you earn $750 in a month, which is deposited in your checking account. Then you withdraw (or spend) $800 that month. The bank also charges you $40 in overdraft fees for two bounced checks that were paid from your account. You have lost $90 for the month (you were short $50, plus $40 in overdraft fees).

Your P&L shows you the same type of information as your bank statement. If you pull up a record of your bank account online, you can see a list showing where your money went that month. By looking at your initial balance, and the checks you wrote against your deposits, you see whether you ended up with a positive balance (a profit) or a negative balance (a loss) over that period.

Check out Figure 4-3 to see what a P&L statement looks like.

In the example shown in Figure 4-3, notice two important characteristics of a P&L:

+ **The dollar value for each line item is shown as a percentage of your gross revenues (total earnings before anything is deducted).** Using percentages gives you a clearer picture of how much (or little) you're spending from your total earnings. For example, if you find that you're spending 32 percent for banner advertising and only 5 percent on keywords, consider whether that's how you intended to spend your advertising budget.

   Regularly review your P&L statement to track whether you're staying within your budget for the year.

+ **The total dollar amount and percentages from the preceding month and for the year to-date are included.** It's all on the same page. If the line item showing your Internet service fee jumps 50 percent in one month, you might want to investigate. See whether you accidentally made a double payment to your supplier or were mistakenly charged for a product and didn't notice it on the original bill. Don't laugh: You might be surprised at how easily events like these can slip past you!

Think of a P&L as a tool for keeping track of your business. Like the balance sheet, it provides an important glimpse of your business, over a specific period. If you review your financial statements regularly, you can catch mistakes and identify positive trends and then use that information to make critical decisions about the financial well-being of your online endeavor.

Income Statement (P&L)
For month ended July 31, 2006

		07/31/06
Income:		
Gross Sales:		$9,115.00
Less Returns		(0.00)
Less Other Discounts		(0.00)
		$9,115.00
NET Sales		
Cost of Goods Sold:		
Beginning Inventory	$500.00	
Add: Purchases	250.00	
Freight	50.00	
		800.00
Cost of Goods Available		
Less: Ending Inventory	(400.00)	
		-400.00
Cost of Goods Sold		
Gross Profit (Less)		$8,715.00
Expenses:		
Advertising	150.00	
Amortization		
Bad Debts		
Bank Charges	50.00	
Commissions		
Credit Card Fees	55.00	
Depreciation		
Dues, Subscriptions (Books)	15.00	
Insurance	145.00	
Interest		
Loans		
Maintenance		
Miscellaneous	40.00	
Office Expenses – General	137.28	
Operating Supplies	124.56	
Payroll (Wages & Taxes)	2,800.00	
Permits and Licenses		
Postage	95.00	
Professional Fees	275.00	
Property Taxes		
Rent	650.00	
Telephone		
Landline	289.00	
Cell	150.00	
Training/Workshops	20.00	
Travel		
Utilities	280.00	
Vehicle Expense		
Gas/Mileage	42.14	
Maintenance		
Web Site Fees	355.00	
Total Expenses		5,672.98
Net Operating Income:		3,042.02
Other Income:	0	
*NET INCOME (LOSS):		$3,042.02

*This is pre-tax income.

Figure 4-3:
A sample income (P&L) statement.

Choosing Software to Make Your Tasks Easy

Accounting software allows you to enter your daily financial activities, press a few keys at the end of the month, and — *voila!* — print your balance sheet and P&Ls. It's just a matter of picking the right software.

QuickBooks, the accounting software from Intuit (www.intuit.com), is a favorite among a majority of small-business owners because it simplifies the recordkeeping process for your business and is *extremely* easy to learn and use. Many people are already familiar with it, simply because they use it for personal accounting, too. But when you enter your local office-supply store to purchase a copy of the software, you may be in for a shock: Not only does QuickBooks have several versions for business applications, but lots of other types of accounting software selections are also available.

We don't want to sell you on a particular brand of software, such as QuickBooks. Instead, we want to help you understand which benefits and features to look for so that you can choose the best accounting software for your online business.

Going online?

The first consideration for choosing software is whether you want to use a Web-based service provider. As with the vendors who handle payroll taxes for you, those and many others also provide online accounting services.

One big advantage of a Web-based product is that the data is stored off-site and is easily accessible from any computer. Why does this matter? Well, if something happens to your office (such as a fire or a flood), you can still access your data from another location. Or, if you travel, you can manage your accounting details while you're on the road.

Another perceived advantage is pricing. Rather than pay several hundred dollars out of your pocket in one whack, you pay it out every month (sometimes as little as $20 a month). After a full year, of course, you've paid almost the full price of a box of software. That monthly fee can also include support and other benefits that over-the-counter accounting software might not offer.

What size are you?

When you're shopping for accounting software, one size doesn't fit all. In fact, the amount of revenue your business pulls in, along with the number of employees you hire, has a lot to do with which accounting program you should choose. As a small business, you want to find entry-level software that you can find at Staples or Office Depot, such as QuickBooks or Peachtree.

How much do you want to pay?

Ah, it's everybody's favorite question: How much do you want (or are you willing) to invest in your accounting program? You probably prefer leaning toward the lower side of the price scale. Luckily, most over-the-counter software packages suited to truly small businesses range from $40 to $400 for single users. The price fluctuation largely depends on these factors:

✦ **Brand:** As with most business products, you usually pay more when you're using a more widely recognized brand of software. Our experience is that Intuit's QuickBooks and Peachtree by Sage are a little pricier than the Bookkeeper brand of software (by Avanquest Software), for example.

✦ **Features:** Price is affected by not only the number of features offered with various accounting software programs but also the complexity of those features. Keep these questions in mind:

• Do you want software that easily integrates with your online banking system, even if it costs more?

• Must the software communicate with your offline point-of-sale system and your online inventory system? Or, do you just want to track your invoices and expenses and spit out occasional reports to pass along to your CPA?

The more you expect from your accounting software, the more you can expect to pay for it!

✦ **Industry:** Similar to the issue of the type of features that are offered, some accounting software is designed for your particular type of *industry*. Consultants, manufacturers, and retailers are all examples of some of the most common industries that use specific software. If you want accounting software designed for your kind of business, you can probably expect to pay closer to $400 (or higher).

Do you need support?

Another important part of your purchasing decision is the issue of support. One advantage of choosing software that has been around for a while is that the company is usually capable of providing decent support, both online and by phone.

Before purchasing your software, find out the terms for receiving ongoing support and compare the product across brands. Some software comes with unlimited online support, and others offer only 30-day support and then charge a fee after that.

In addition to being able to turn to your software vendor for support, you should know that your accountant or other financial advisors are better prepared to help you when you use software that they know how to use. For that reason, don't hesitate to ask for their advice before making your final purchase.

Hiring a Professional

Regardless of the type of accounting software you install or your own ability to number-crunch, at some point you might need or want to hire outside help. An array of tax and accounting professionals are available. In the following sections, we tell you how to determine which one is right for you.

**Book II
Chapter 4**

**Accounting for
Taxes (And Then
Some)**

Recognizing that it takes all types

Start by reviewing the types of professionals who can help you. They include

+ **CPA:** These initials after a person's name, which stand for certified public accountant, indicate that the person has passed a state-regulated exam and is recognized by the IRS as a paid preparer for submitting your tax returns. Typically, a CPA fully understands accounting methods and is well versed in tax regulations. Because tax laws are cumbersome and continually changing, a CPA might even specialize in a particular area. Examples of industry-based specialization are government, retail, and small business; or, specialization can be classified according to function, such as a CPA who specializes in mergers and acquisitions. Additionally, a CPA can legally conduct audits, whereas other accounting professionals cannot.

+ **Accountant:** For all intents and purposes, an accountant has the same basic skills as a CPA. The difference, of course, is the lack of a state-issued license or certificate. Even so, an accountant can assist in preparing your taxes and file them, too. And, like a CPA, a reputable accountant can advise you about financial decisions, and should be up to date on changing tax laws.

+ **Bookkeeper:** Someone in this category can manage the basic record-keeping activities for your small business, including these tasks:

  • Make deposits.

  • Log in accounts receivables.

  • Handle account payables.

  • Manage payroll.

  • Send out appropriate forms, such as W2s and 1099s, to employees and contractors.

In addition to being able to keep the books, this person should be comfortable with creating an income statement and a balance sheet each month. Of course, bookkeepers come with all levels of experience and education. (Some are professionally certified with a college degree, and others aren't.) A basic bookkeeper is usually the most affordable outside help.

✦ **Tax consultant:** This catchall term includes both independent advisors (who can range from accountant to CPA) and tax preparers, such as the folks at your neighborhood H&R Block office at tax time. Similar to a bookkeeper, this person's range of experience, knowledge, education, and certification varies.

✦ **Enrolled agent:** This type of federally licensed professional understands both state and federal tax laws. In addition to completing an exam issued by the U.S. Department of Treasury, she has also passed a federal background check. An enrolled agent can also gain licensure after having worked for the IRS for at least five years. She is certified in the eyes of the IRS to

  • Prepare your taxes

  • Assist you in long-term financial planning

  • Represent you in dealing with the IRS

✦ **Tax attorney:** Most tax attorneys don't handle general accounting functions. Instead, you hire an attorney specifically to deal with issues pertaining to the tax law — for example, to handle an audit requested by the IRS or to file corporate bankruptcy (which we hope that you never do!). Larger corporations might also keep a tax attorney on retainer or hire one in-house, if the company continually deals with complex tax issues. Your small business is less likely to need the services of a tax attorney regularly.

Attorneys, enrolled agents, and CPAs are the only professionals authorized to represent you with the IRS.

As a general rule, you need a full or part-time bookkeeper. If you're up to the task (and many small-business owners like it this way), you can wear that hat, too. If you aren't adept at follow-through or if numbers just plain scare you, consider hiring someone.

Depending on the experience (or inexperience) of the professional and the market rate in your community, you can hire a basic bookkeeper (often referred to as a *bookkeeper clerk*), for a fairly low hourly rate. (The rate can start in the range of $8–$12 an hour, depending on experience.) A more experienced person, such as a professional full-time bookkeeper or a professionally certified bookkeeper, charges a much higher hourly rate — or a mid-to-upper-end management-level salary if you hire the person full time.

When you interview bookkeeper candidates, use the free Bookkeeper's Hiring Test, available from the American Institute of Professional Bookkeepers, to qualify them. You can find and print the test at `www.aipb.org/testrequest.php`.

Knowing what to expect from your tax professional

In addition to having someone handle your daily financial recordkeeping, you should establish a relationship with a CPA, an accountant, or an enrolled agent. This type of professional should be available to assist you with these tasks:

+ Prepare and file your taxes.

+ Set up your accounting system.

+ Advise you on the legal organization of your company (and other start-up issues).

+ Compile (or review) financial statements.

+ Assist you in long-term financial planning for your business.

+ Address specific tax-law questions and concerns as they arise.

+ Ensure that the proper amounts and types of taxes are being filed.

+ Guide you in the completion of (or submit on your behalf) all quarterly tax documentation and other forms that might be required annually.

+ Answer questions and advise you about other general tax- and finance-related concerns.

These professionals typically charge a high hourly rate. (A CPA's rate can start at $125 an hour.) Make sure that you clarify how you're charged for time. (Some professionals don't charge for questions asked by way of e-mail, and others do, for example.)

Before you consult with your outside professional advisor, make a list of the specific questions or issues you want addressed. This list keeps you on track and ensures that you maximize the time spent with your advisor while avoiding running up steep bills.

Finding likely candidates

After you decide which type of professional you want to hire, your next step is finding one. Fortunately, you have lots of places to turn to for a head start on this task:

✦ **Referrals:** Ask business peers and family members whom they use or recommend. Ask for specific information, such as

- What do you like about the way this person does business?

- What expertise does the professional have?

- How long have you known him or used his services?

- How much does he typically charge?

✦ **Local organizations:** Area Chamber of Commerce chapters and other local business associations often make their membership databases available to the public. Although the organizations typically don't endorse one member over another, they can suggest which professionals might be best suited for your specific requirements and tell you whether any complaints have been registered against them.

✦ **Professional associations:** Industry or professional groups are a terrific place to start your search for a CPA or other accounting professional. You can check out this list of organizations to get started:

- American Institute of Certified Public Accountants: www.aicpa.org

- National Association for Enrolled Agents: www.naea.org

- American Association of Attorney-Certified Public Accountants: www.attorney-cpa.com

- CPA Associates International: www.cpaai.com

- American Institute of Professional Bookkeepers: www.aipb.org

- AGN North America (Association of Separate and Independent Accounting and Consulting Firms): www.agn-na.org

✦ **Classifieds:** When you're hiring a bookkeeper or an accountant, feel free to place a classified advertisement to find the best candidate.

When you place a help-wanted ad, you hear from better-qualified candidates if you're specific about the required job functions. We also recommend requesting that job candidates forward their salary requirements or salary history, along with their résumés.

✦ **Phone book:** If all else fails, the Yellow Pages usually has a substantial listing of potential financial advisors.

Narrow the field of reputable contenders by skimming advertisements for professionals who list specific certifications, licensures, and memberships in professional associations.

Choosing the best person for you

After you create a short list of possible candidates, how do you decide which one is best suited for your business? In addition to checking for proper accreditations and confirming hourly rates, you have to consider a few other issues when you're choosing a CPA, an accountant, an enrolled agent, or even a tax attorney:

✦ **Experience:** You want to know whether the person specializes in particular areas of accounting or tax law. You should also find out, however, what type of work now takes up the majority of the professional's time and also the type of work performed in the past. Two critical questions to ask are

• What areas do you most enjoy handling?

• In which areas do you have the most up-to-date knowledge?

Because definitive rules of taxation and the Internet are still somewhat up in the air, you're not as likely to find a professional who specializes in this area. Instead, look for someone who's eager and willing to stay informed on new issues and changes to the tax law. Preferably, choose someone who's committed to tracking down the answers to difficult or lesser-known tax questions.

Ask your CPA about changes in the tax law to determine whether you're affected. The IRS provides a quick summary of those yearly changes on its Web site at `www.irs.gov` (see Figure 4-4).

**Book II
Chapter 4**

Accounting for Taxes (And Then Some)

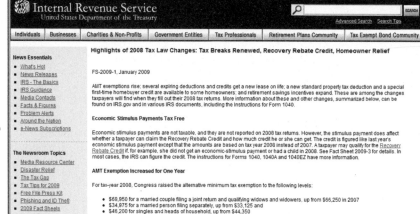

Figure 4-4: Track changes to the tax laws at the IRS site.

✦ **Availability:** A highly qualified independent professional often has a waiting list of clients. Although that's a helpful situation for the accountant, it doesn't help you. You need a professional who can work with you now. No matter what, it doesn't hurt to ask what the person's client schedule is like. For example, some professionals work part-time or have a four-day workweek. Others are eagerly growing their businesses and are available to answer your questions seven days a week. Nothing is wrong with either schedule; just find the one that you can live with as a client.

✦ **Firm size:** Size does matter, and sometimes a smaller firm is the better option. Even though some folks think that a large, recognizable accounting firm is the way to go, that's not always the case. If you have a small company, you might find yourself at the bottom of the totem pole when the firm prioritizes its clients. Your company's needs might get passed off to a junior accountant or other staff person. Unless your business is large enough to support individual departments (HR and marketing, for example), working with a large firm may mean less attention and higher rates. A smaller firm or an independent professional may give you more dedicated attention and be available immediately to answer your questions.

✦ **Philosophy:** Your financial advisors are ultimately your partners in business. Their professional views *must* complement yours. We're referring to not only ethics but also strategic philosophies. For example, if you're an aggressive risk-taker in business, you may think that a conservative accountant will hold you back. Alternatively, you may prefer a conservative outlook as a means to provide a system of checks and balances to your liberal financial outlook.

✦ **Work style:** This term refers to how a professional interacts with you and services your needs. For example, does the CPA insist that his firm file all required paperwork with the IRS, at a steep hourly rate? Or, does he prefer to help you get started and then encourage you to take care of everything yourself in order to keep your expenses in check? What are his preferred methods of communication? If your tax professional isn't a fan of e-mail, he might respond to your questions only by phone. Or, an assistant might serve as a middleman and rarely be available to talk with you without scheduling a formal appointment. Again, none of these issues has a right or wrong answer. It's a matter of which style best meshes with your personal preferences.

Spending the time to determine these concerns means a lot to the future of your online business. After all, this professional plays an integral part in your business as a trusted financial advisor. That's why we suggest taking your time to select the best match for you and your new business.

Following the Rules of Recordkeeping

After you find a CPA or other financial professional, that person no doubt instructs you on the rules of good recordkeeping. In the meantime, take our crash course to help you get started doing things right!

Dealing with all the paper

When we refer to *records* in the remainder of this chapter, we don't mean your account logs. Instead, we're talking about the physical records (the dreaded *paper trail*) that the IRS expects you to maintain. The thought of accidentally throwing out the wrong receipt or losing a copy of a question-able invoice can send chills up the spine of any well-meaning entrepreneur if the IRS comes calling. At the same time, your office space probably doesn't come with unlimited storage space.

How do you balance the need to hang on to important receipts with the need not to be overrun by the growing mounds of paper? The good news is that the IRS now recognizes electronic versions of financial records. You can therefore scan copies of receipts, invoices, logbooks, and other proof of financial transactions and save them as files on your computer or, better, back up these files to a CD-ROM or DVD. Then you get to throw out the hard copies! That's the easiest way to avoid the clutter that builds up with months and years of business transactions.

If you lose the electronic file and are audited, the IRS isn't sympathetic. The loss could cost you thousands of dollars — and possible jail time (in the worst-case scenario). We highly encourage you to make multiple copies and store one or more sets at another location or in a fireproof safe.

You can avoid the time it takes to scan and save critical documentation by hiring a company to do it for you. In addition to making electronic copies of your paper trail, these digital documentation specialists store the electronic files for you. You can also purchase digital documentation software that makes it easy to do yourself!

Storing records: How long is long enough?

Whether or not you "go digital" with your recordkeeping, one critical question remains: How long should you keep records? We should have a straight-forward answer for you, but we haven't found one yet. That's because the IRS states (in Publication 583):

You must keep your records as long as they may be needed for the administration of any provision of the Internal Revenue Code. Generally, this means you must keep records that support an item of income or deduction on a return until the period of limitations for that return runs out. The period of limitations is the period of time in which you can amend your return to claim a credit or refund, or the IRS can assess additional tax.

Huh? Well, the IRS says that you should keep records for as long as there's a possibility that it might audit you. We always heard that seven years is a safe bet. However, the true issue isn't the type of *documentation;* rather, it's the type of *situation* you encounter with the IRS.

For example, if you have employees, the IRS says that those tax records must be kept for at least 4 years from the period the tax becomes due or is paid, whichever is later. On the other hand, records about assets, such as property, should be kept until the period of limitations expires for the year in which you dispose of the property. Even tangible guidelines such as those, however, could be null and void if you're audited for a fraudulent tax return. In that case, all bets are off and you had better have ready access to *all* your records, from the beginning of time!

All these situations make up what the IRS refers to as a *period of limitations.* Table 4-3 gives you an overview of the rules for these time restrictions, as defined by the IRS.

Table 4-3	IRS Periods of Limitations
If You Do This	*The Period Is This Long*
Owe additional tax and the other situations in this table don't apply	Three years
Fail to report legitimate income and it's more than 25 percent of the gross amount on your return	Six years
File a fraudulent return	Unlimited
Fail to file a tax return	Unlimited
File a claim for credit or a refund after filing your return	Two to three years after tax is paid
File a claim for a loss from bad debt or worthless securities	Seven years

Keep these employee records safely filed away

The IRS advises that you retain any information related to employee taxes. Even if a record relates to someone who no longer works for you, keep the following documents for at least four years:

- Amounts and dates of all wage payments (including annuity and pension)

- Amounts of tips reported by your employees and records of allocated tips

- Fair market value of in-kind wages paid to your employees

- Employee information, including name, address, Social Security number, job title, and dates of employment

- Copies of Forms W-2 and W-2c that were returned to you (undeliverable, if mailed)

- Records of sick pay or other pay due to injury or absence (including the amount and weekly rate of payments that you or a third-party payer made)

- Copies of employees' income tax withholding allowance certificates (Forms W-4, W-4P, W-4(SP), W-4S, and W-4V)

- Dates and amounts of tax deposits you made, along with confirmation numbers for deposits made by Electronic Funds Transfer Protocol (EFTP)

- Copies of filed returns, including 941 TeleFile Tax Records and confirmation numbers

- Records of any fringe benefits provided to employees, including expense reimbursements paid

**Book II
Chapter 4**

Accounting for Taxes (And Then Some)

To play it safe, embrace the philosophy "When in doubt, hang on to it!" This technique is especially manageable if you have the limitless storage capacity for electronic documentation.

We hope that you never have to worry about an audit from Uncle Sam (the U.S. government). The thought that it's always a possibility, though, is certainly incentive enough to keep all your records in order!

Book III
Web Site Design

The 5th Wave   By Rich Tennant

"Just how accurately should my Web site reflect my place of business?"

Contents at a Glance

Chapter 1: What's in a (Domain) Name?

*I*n the offline world, the mantra of success for business is "Location, location, location!" It's not much different for your online business: Rather than use a numerical address on a building, though, you now use a virtual address or domain name. Usually, your online address includes your company's name or initials or some other derivation. A traditional business address is listed in the Yellow Pages, and your online address is listed with search engines.

As you might guess, securing the best possible domain name is an important piece of your overall online strategy because the name you select can influence how easily customers can find you. How do you get the perfect name to drive customers to your online place of business?

Not to worry: After using the information in this chapter, you'll find that choosing and registering your address is only a few clicks away.

Picking Your Online Identity

A *URL,* or *Uniform Resource Locator,* represents the unique address for each page on a Web site or document posted online. Your Web site might be made up of several Web pages, each with its own, unique URL.

Before you start creating Web pages, your first order of business is to determine your domain name, or the part of the URL that specifically identifies the name of your Web site (see Figure 1-1).

This list deciphers the elements in a URL:

✦ **Directories:** Shows up as you go deeper into the site

✦ **Documents:** At the end of the URL; identifies any documents you have on the page

✦ **HyperText Transfer Protocol:** Helps direct visitors to a named server

- ✦ **Registered domain name:** Always appears as part of the URL

- ✦ **Top-level domains:** Can include `.com`, `.net`, `.org`, and `.biz`. See the section "Varying the extension," near the end of the chapter, for more options

- ✦ **World Wide Web:** Indicates that you're on the Internet

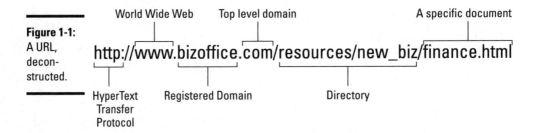

Figure 1-1:
A URL, decon-structed.

World Wide Web   Top level domain   A specific document

http://www.bizoffice.com/resources/new_biz/finance.html

HyperText Transfer Protocol   Registered Domain   Directory

REMEMBER

Although your Web site normally has only one domain name, it has more than one URL. The URL for the *home* page, or *entrance* page, of your site often looks the same as your domain name. Every page of your site, however, has a unique URL, such as

- ✦ `www.myveryfirstwebsite.com`: The home page

- ✦ `www.myveryfirstwebsite.com/index.html`: The home page (the same as omitting the `index.html` portion of the URL)

- ✦ `www.myveryfirstwebsite.com/services.html`: The Web page that contains information about the services you offer

Approaching your domain name carefully

You can take one of two opposing approaches when you select your domain name:

- ✦ **You have an existing business or have already named your start-up.** If that's the case, you usually should match (as closely as possible) your company's name to the domain name. Using your existing business name is simple, straightforward, and often quite effective.

- ✦ **The success of your online company hinges on the domain name itself.** Maybe you're starting an Internet company that sells *e-books* (electronic, downloadable information) telling readers how to start a business. In that case, your legal company name might be irrelevant. A more important consideration is to find a domain that clearly indicates your type of business or the customers you're targeting. In this scenario, your company name might be John Smith dba JS Enterprises. A more effective domain name for your business, however, might be `www.biz startup411.com` because it says what you do.

Understanding what a domain name should be

No matter what approach you take to choosing your online business name, consider the following list of common denominators in determining the best possible domain for you. A good domain name should have these characteristics:

✦ **It's easy to spell.** As anyone who depends on a computer's spell checker can testify, the average person doesn't do well in a spelling bee. That's why we're firm believers in avoiding hard-to-spell words in your domain name. Although `www.BriansBodaciousRibs.com` seems harmless enough, it's fairly easy to flub. Why not try `www.briansribs.com` or `www.goodeating.com`? The easier your domain name is to spell, the more likely customers are to find you without a hassle (and, when they do find you, the more likely they'll be in the mood to buy some of your bodacious eats!).

✦ **It's simple to remember.** Your domain name doesn't have to be catchy or trendy to work. Simplicity goes a long way in our crowded, overhyped world.

✦ **It's relatively short.** A shorter name is easier for customers to remember than a longer one. Consider the (fictitious) law firm Brewer, Mackey, Youngstein, Yale, and Associates. Its URL might be

    www.BrewerMackeyYoungsteinYaleandAssociates.com

Wow! That name takes a while to type, not to mention that you have to spell everybody's name correctly. Instead, consider the name `www.BrewerandAssociates.com`. See the difference?

✦ **It contains important keywords.** This characteristic is important for two reasons:

   • Using descriptive words in the domain clearly says what you do.

   • Using relevant words that frequently show up in search engines is potentially beneficial to your site's rankings. (We explain search engine optimization further in Book VI, Chapter 6.)

The law firm used in the preceding example can easily use *keywords,* or words that might be easily associated with the type of business, to create one of these domain combinations:

   • `www.legalfirmforhire.com`

   • `www.breweryounglawyers.com`

   • `www.attorneysbmyy.com`

✦ **It's alphabetically strategic.** Does your domain name begin with a number or start with a letter that's near the front of the alphabet? If so, your site is more likely to secure a spot at the top of directories and other reference lists. When you're promoting your site, this strategy gives you a slight advantage in getting noticed sooner. Don't get us wrong: A random string of numbers doesn't do much for your business.

Relevancy still counts. You can manage to use this strategy and remain true to your business. One author of this book used the same approach in naming a couple of sites. For instance, the search engine directory specifically for small businesses uses the domain www.allsmallbiz. com, and a site filled with categories of beach-themed products, information, and travel destinations is named www.365beach.com.

✦ **It's intuitive to customers.** You want a domain name to provide, ideally, a sense of who you are and an indication of the type of products or services you're selling. You don't need a *literal* translation, such as www. isellbooks.com — depending on your business, that approach could be detrimental to sales. What if you're selling to a highly targeted or specialized market (such as teenagers or radical sports fans)? A straightforward domain name is labeled as boring and undermines the image of your company, whereas an edgy or more creative name can win customers. For example, a bookseller specializing in romance novels might use a domain name such as www.romancingthepages.com or www. steamyreads.com. The point is that your customer base, whoever it consists of, should be responsive to your domain name.

Registering the Perfect Name

Congratulations: You chose your domain name, and you're ready to make it official. The next step is to register the name with a domain registrar. You can sign up using any company that specializes in domain registration. The registrar takes care of all the paperwork that's required in order to activate your new domain name, including these tasks:

✦ Submitting contact information

✦ Determining the duration of the registration period

✦ Listing your domain in the official Internet list of domains maintained by the Internet Corporation for Assigned Names and Numbers (ICANN) at www.icann.org

Who you gonna call?

Who registers domains? Your ISP (Internet service provider) might do it because many now provide this service along with hosting options. Or, you can use any other company or Web site that acts as a third-party affiliate for registrars. In other words, now you can register a domain name with almost anyone! Although finding a place to sign up is a piece of cake, Table 1-1 provides a brief price comparison of some of the top online registrars for standard .com extensions. Now you have a wide range of extension choices, from .com and .net to .biz and .tv, and they usually vary in price. For example, the new .mobi extension, for mobile use, costs significantly more, than a .com or .net extension, for example. *Remember:* All three registrars also offer services such as hosting, e-mail, Web sites, and more.

Table 1-1	Domain Registrar Price Comparison			
Company	*Registration Cost*			*Services Included*
	One Year	*Two Years*	*Private Fee**	
Network Solutions	$34.99	$29.99	$9.00	100 subdomains and free support
Register.com	$35.00	$35.00	$10.00	
Go Daddy	$10.69	$10.69	$8.99	Starter Web site e-mail, and blogcast

* Private registration prevents your personal and company information from appearing when someone looks up your domain info.

You may also be wondering, "Why would I want to pay Network Solutions $34.99 per year when Go Daddy charges me $10.69?" Sometimes, the answer lies in the services offered and the type of provider. Always compare services and fees to ensure that you're getting a good deal based on the services you want and need.

Let's make it official

After you make a decision about where to register, it's time to get down to business. To show you how painlessly you can reserve your domain name, we walk you through the process by using the GoDaddy.com service. (It's similar to almost any other registration service you might choose to use.)

Follow these steps to quickly register your domain name:

1. **Go to the Go Daddy Web site at www.godaddy.com.**

2. **Enter the name you want to register in the Start a Domain Name Search Here search box.**

Type only the name you want, and don't preface it with www. That part is already assumed by the registrar. (Some registrars' domain search boxes place the www. in front of the search box to remind you that typing that part isn't necessary.)

3. **To the right of the search box, click the arrow on the smaller search box to choose from a drop-down menu the extension (such as .com or .net) that you want for your name.**

The default selection for the box is .com.

4. **Click the Go button.**

Your search results page appears (see Figure 1-2). If your selected domain name is available, a small check box appears next to it. The cost of reserving the domain for a year appears next to the name. Below the available name is a list of similar names, along with other available extensions you can choose to register. You're notified if the name is already registered. Variations are offered if the domain name is already registered. (If the name isn't available, see the next section.)

5. **From the list of suggested additional domains, select any other name you want to register at this time by selecting the check box next to a domain name. When you finish, scroll to the bottom of the page and click the Continue button.**

You can have multiple working domains even when you have only a single Web site. Simply *forward,* or point all other extensions to, the designated domain of your choice. Use *masking*, a technique that hides (or masks) the other domains. Then, only your preferred domain is displayed when someone navigates to your Web site. Your ISP or registrar can handle this process for you.

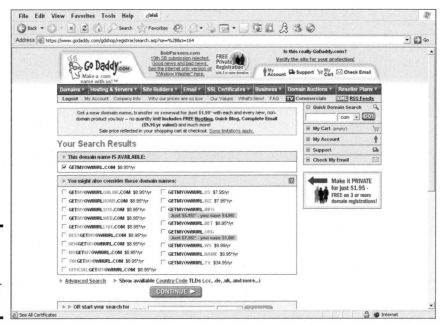

Figure 1-2:
Your
domain is
available for
registration.

When you're registering a `.com` extension, register the matching `.net` version if it's available. These extensions are still the two most common. If your site is successful, a savvy competitor is more likely to snatch up the `.net` version over any other. This statement is especially true if you have a descriptive domain name with a wide appeal (such as `partygoods.com`) or if it falls within a popular search category (such as `starwars fans.com`). If the `.com` version of your domain isn't available and you're registering another extension, one domain is plenty for starters. After your site grows, you can determine the value of registering other names.

6. **Before you can continue, you must log in to an existing account on the next page, labeled Domain Registration Information, or create a new Go Daddy user account.**

You provide basic information (your name, address, and e-mail address) to set up your account.

7. **When you finish logging in to your account, click the Continue button at the bottom of the page.**

Information provided in your registration is the same as that used to define your technical, administrative, and billing contact, unless you specify otherwise. Use these default settings for now. You can always change this information later, by using the Manage Your Account feature.

The next page summarizes the registrant information you entered when you created your account.

8. **If all elements look like they should, scroll down to the bottom of the page and click Continue.**

A few other questions are listed before nearing the bottom of this page. Skip any questions that aren't a required part of the registration process.

The page that appears gives you a few more registration and checkout options. For example, on this page you decide for how long you want to register the domain name: one year, two years, or more. You can choose whether you want the domain automatically renewed by the registrar before its expiration date.

You can pay a few dollars more to get a *private* registration, where your name, address, and other pertinent personal or business information aren't disclosed to anyone trying to find out who owns your domain. Unless you want the public to have access to the information included in the domain-registration directory (WHOIS), invest a few dollars to protect your identity.

9. **After completing the additional required fields, to avoid looking at other special offers and products for sale, select the Quick Checkout option at the bottom of the page and click the Continue button.**

The secure checkout page appears.

10. **After you read the domain registration agreement and terms of service, select the check boxes indicating that you have read both documents and agree to abide by each agreement.**

11. **Review your order as it's listed at the top of the page, and enter the requested billing information.**

Typically, requested information includes your credit card number and shipping information. A copy of your receipt is e-mailed to you along with additional information for how to access your new domain.

When you complete this step and print a copy of your receipt, you're finished. Congratulations — you now have a domain name that's all yours!

Book III
Chapter 1

What's in a
(Domain) Name?

Finding Out What to Do When Somebody Gets There First

We hope that the domain you want is the one you get when you register. Sometimes, though, your first choice for a domain isn't available. Nothing bursts a bubble faster than having this sort of event happen. Don't let it frustrate you, though. You still have several options.

Exploring your domain name options

When you initially search for your domain (as described in the preceding section), the registrar might tell you that it isn't available. Underneath that notification is typically a box containing a list of suggested alternative domains that the registrar has available. Don't be surprised if the automated system returns a few decent alternatives! At this point, you can choose one of the suggested runners-up generated by the registrar.

If you don't find a perfect match on the suggested list, the next-less-appealing choice takes you right back to the drawing board. Yep, you can start a brand-new search for an entirely different name.

Getting what you want — at a price

Starting from scratch again usually isn't your preference. After all, you might have fallen head over heels for a domain name and no substitute will work. In that case, you should know that you can pursue that domain name, even though it's already taken.

Here are the ways you can go in hot pursuit of your dream domain name:

✦ **Put the name on back order.** Think of this strategy as the official waiting list of domain names. A registrar keeps your name on file and notifies you when the domain you want expires and becomes available. Each registrar handles the process differently. For instance, some charge a small, upfront fee, and others charge a larger commission when you receive the domain name. Being first on the list doesn't always mean that you're assured of receiving the name, either. A few registrars now use an auction to sell the domain to the highest bidder when more than one person has indicated interest. (You're not required to participate in the auction and in some cases can specify a maximum bid.) Don't forget to check your registrar's back-order policies and procedures to make sure that you understand how a back-ordered domain is awarded.

✦ **Make an offer.** You might be too impatient to wait and see whether a domain expires in six months. The owner can decide to renew it, and then it's gone for at least another year. That's why several registrars have a *certified offer* option. You set a price to buy the domain name, and the registrar presents the offer to the existing domain owner on your behalf. Using this technique makes sense for a couple of reasons:

  • *You can find out quickly whether an owner is willing to give up a domain name.* The seller must respond within a specific length of time.

  • *Your name and personal information are kept private.* If the offer is accepted, you pay the registrar by credit card and the money is transferred to the seller. The registrar handles the entire process, including the transfer of the domain name. This type of certified-offer service often gives the seller the chance to respond with a minimum asking price. Then, if your first offer is declined, there's no beating around the bush. You find out how much the seller wants before she would consider selling.

  In most instances, a minimum asking price of about $100 is required, which is the downside of an offer scenario. The registrar also charges you a fee for using the service, regardless of whether your offer is accepted. The fee is typically a minimum of $50 plus a commission if your offer is accepted.

✦ **Contact the owner.** If you prefer to negotiate directly, contacting the domain owner in person is another option. Even though you lose your anonymity, you avoid paying service fees. Better yet, direct contact provides the opportunity to plead your case and use personal charm to try to get a good price for the name. (Okay, that's not always enough to sway a seller, but it might help.) Many companies have negotiated directly with sellers with much success. One domain owner, who no longer had an active site for the URL, gave away the domain. The moral of this story: It never hurts to ask.

If a domain owner has chosen a private registration, which keeps his contact information confidential, you might have difficulty locating him to make an offer. If the Web site for the domain is *active* (you can view it), search the pages for contact information. Although an e-mail address works, a phone number is preferable. You can keep calling until you reach a live person (who can then connect you with the owner).

Finding the owner of a domain name is easy to do when you use the WHOIS feature offered by registrars. The option to use WHOIS is typically provided to you automatically if your domain search shows that the name is already taken. Or, you can find a direct link for the WHOIS feature at the top or bottom of the registrar's home page. (Figure 1-3 shows you the information you can find about a domain order when you're using WHOIS.)

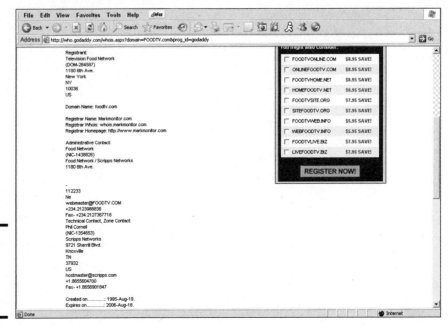

Figure 1-3:
WHOIS
reveals
domain
owners.

All the Good Ones Are (Not!) Taken

Approximately 55 million domain names are actively registered, according to WHOIS Source statistics (see `http://whois.domaintools.com`). At last count, more than 300,000 new domains are registered every day. Wow! No wonder people are tempted to claim that "all the good ones" are indeed taken (or are being held hostage for a huge ransom). Not true! Plenty of fantastic domain names are available. In fact, the continued popularity of the Internet has prompted lots of acceptable and creative alternatives for domain registration.

Varying the extension

Among the easiest ways to find a good domain name is to use an alternative extension. We can't deny that the old favorites `.com`, `.net`, and `.org` remain the most recognizable. More than a dozen extensions are now in use, and using these alternatives is no longer considered a stigma. (Table 1-2 lists, in order of the most common U.S. extensions, all the extensions you can consider for use.) Don't shy away from them. Looking through the list is a simple way to find the domain name of your choice!

Table 1-2	Extensions Used in Domain Registration	
Extension	*Use or Country Represented*	*Generally Used For*
.com	Commercial	General business
.net	Network	Internet business
.org	Organization	Nonprofit and trade association
.info	Information	Resource
.biz	Business	Small-business
.tv	Television	Entertainment, media
.name	Personal use	
.jobs	Business	Employment-related sites
.travel	Business	Travel-industry use
.ws	Former country code	Web
.bz	Former country code	Business
.cc	Former country code	Miscellaneous
.us	United States	
.vg	British Virgin Islands	
.co.uk	United Kingdom	Commercial
.org.uk	United Kingdom	Organization
.me.uk	United Kingdom	Personal
.de	Germany	
.jp	Japan	
.be	Belgium	
.at	Austria	
.com.mx	Mexico	Commercial
.co.nz	New Zealand	Commercial
.net.nz	New Zealand	Network; usually Internet providers
.org.nz	New Zealand	Organization
.gs	South Georgia, South Sandwich Islands	
.tc	Turks, Caicos Islands	
.ms	Montserrat	

**Book III
Chapter 1**

What's in a (Domain) Name?

View the complete country code list at www.iana.org/cctld/cctld-whois.htm.

Getting creative

Acquiring a domain-worthy domain name may involve a little creativity on your part. As you have probably seen for yourself, most general names (applying to very wide or popular categories) got scooped up during the first Internet craze of the 1990s. All the gems — Business.com, Politics.com, SportsFan.net — are long gone.

Don't let this information stop you! Keep in mind that the Internet is still in its infancy and there's plenty of room for domain names that are equally effective as those first category-busters. Here are four creative ways to find an outstanding domain name:

- **Make the domain name *very* specific.** One recent trend is that of niche (or specific) sites. You can find out more about growing a niche on the Net in Book X. For now, we want you to know that the same trend applies to domain names. Creating a more specific and telling name, rather than one that's very broad, serves you well in the search engine rankings and with your customer base. For example, `www.redsoxfans.com` is quite specific about its subject and audience.

- **Make the domain name creatively telling.** Ever hear that saying about thinking outside the box? Even though it's a cliché, it holds true with domain names: Sometimes, you're trapped into seeing only one way to describe something, and that usually means being literal. If you sell food and toys for cats, you're tempted to find a domain that says exactly that: `cattoys.com`. Rather than continuously circle around the same type of name, think about other ways that your products, services, or target audience are viewed. Make a list of terms and phrases that people use when they talk about these items. You can still be specific, but with a more creative tone. That cat site may do extremely well using a domain name like `mouseloversonly.com` or `thescratchingpost.com`.

- **Make the domain name perfectly meaningless.** Have you ever stumbled across a Web site with an outrageously different but perfectly applicable name (such as Google or Yahoo!)? Web sites with extremely odd, fun, or funky domain names can grow a following just like any other site. If you're in a business that lends itself to the less conservative approach, go with it.

- **Use add-ins.** If your domain name uses common words, finding an exact match available isn't all that easy. Not to worry: Just mix it up a bit. You can try abbreviating your words or using a couple of initials rather than spell out the whole thing. Or, you can break it up with a hyphen or two (Pearl-Earrings-For-You.com, for example). You can also add *inc* or *corp* to the end of your company name (only if you're incorporated, of course) or add another word that indicates the industry you're in — for example, SmithJewelersInc.com or SmithPearlsandDiamonds.com. Another trick is to include words such as *official, favorite, original,* or *popular* to the domain name (FavoritePearlEarrings.com, for example).

Chapter 2: Designing Customer-Friendly Sites

In This Chapter

✔ **Preparing for profitability**

✔ **Considering timeless design options**

✔ **Doing away with fluff**

✔ **Winning raves with function**

*Y*ou might have put most of your efforts into dreaming about and planning for your business. As you begin designing your Web site, though, you see your ideas come to life for the first time. Creating that first site is exhilarating! You have to stay focused, though. Otherwise, you risk becoming distracted by bells and whistles that can waste your time and money.

Experience has taught us that you can easily avoid certain common mistakes. The key is to develop a plan, keep it simple, and stick to it. If you follow these ground rules, you're rewarded with a Web site that's functional, timeless, and customer friendly.

Maximizing Performance for Profitability

You're in business to make a profit, so how does your Web site fit into that goal? Although the answer to this question might seem obvious, you can easily forget that your Web site is both a marketing tool and a vehicle for obtaining profits. The common denominator between those two points is a site that's functional for customers. When you maximize your customer's ease of use and experience with your site, everyone wins!

To get the most from your site, we recommend creating a *profitability plan*. The plan is all about efficiency. You start by strategically identifying the features, technologies, and products for sale that enhance profitability — and getting rid of those that don't.

Ideally, you want to develop this plan before your first site goes up. Then you can address profitability within every page of the site as it's built. Not to worry, though: You can apply the same methodology to an existing site. The process just might take a little more time if you need to restructure the site to meet your goals. Either way, maximizing your profit is worth the effort.

When you're ready to create a plan that maximizes your potential for profitability, follow these steps:

1. **Define the purpose of your site.**

   You should be able to voice that purpose in only one or two sentences. The purpose should reflect your site's role within your overall business. If you have trouble getting started, try answering these questions:

   - My Web site exists because _____.
   - I am creating (or planning) a Web site because _____.
   - When my site is complete, I want it to _____.

2. **Evaluate your revenue streams by listing all the ways in which you earn, or plan to earn, revenue from your site.**

   Be specific when you list the ways in which your site contributes to your revenues; for example, divide the list into two categories: direct revenue and indirect revenue.

3. **After you list your profit sources, assign a numeric value to them.**

   The numeric value is based on both sales volume and profitability. Of course, if your site isn't developed, you don't have a sales history. Instead, you rank items according to expected profitability. (You can go back later and cross-reference them by both profitability and best sellers.)

4. **Determine which applications or functions on your site contribute to your revenue sources, and then delete the ones that don't contribute.**

   This step helps you avoid wasting your time trying to maintain elements that don't contribute to profitability. Expect some items to affect sales directly, and others to influence them indirectly. For instance, a shopping cart or payment-processing method directly affects sales because customers use it to purchase products. On the other hand, a registration box that customers use to sign up for newsletters is an indirect contributor. (Although the newsletter doesn't lead to immediate purchases, by creating continued awareness, it helps future sales.)

5. **Compare your remaining list of products, services, and features with your site's purpose (as defined in Step 1) and omit the ones that don't directly contribute to it.**

   Items that don't directly reflect your site's original intent can cannibalize it down the road and eat away at your profits. By streamlining your revenue sources this way, you keep the site tightly focused on its target customer.

   You should understand now what adds value to your site (and to what degree).

6. **Strategically place features and revenue sources on your site map, which becomes your profitability plan.**

   Usually, a site map is representative of all the pages that make up your Web site. The *layout* indicates the placement of the pages. In this step, you're simply creating a site map that's based on profitability. In other words, specify where you want those "opportunities to purchase" to be placed on pages within the site. Is your largest revenue generator at the top of your home page, or do customers have to click through five pages to see it? If you receive indirect revenue when customers agree to submit a form page for more information, can they access the form from your home page? Is the form's location obvious, or do visitors have to search for it? Now you have a plan!

With your profitability plan in hand, you have a guide during the technical stage of building your site. (We address the technical aspect of developing your site in Book III, Chapter 3.) First, you have to tackle the style issue. No matter how much you plan for profitability, if your site isn't attractive, customers don't hang around long enough to make a purchase.

Looking Your Best

First impressions are lasting ones, or so the old saying implies. When visitors first see the design of your Web site, they decide what they think about it within the first few seconds of viewing your site. Often, a favorable impression is based entirely on the design elements you use. From classic to vintage or from plain Jane to modern, establishing that look sets the tone for your entire site.

Following basic design principles

When you're thinking about site design, consider these five major elements that contribute to a timeless look:

✦ **Structure:** The foundation of your site's design is its structure, or *layout*. Determining the layout of your site requires that you make decisions about these elements:

   • *Number of pages:* Consider the depth of the site (the number of pages that are necessary).

   • *Placement of the navigational toolbar:* Referred to as a toolbar, navigation bar, or menu bar (it's the series of buttons or links that visitors use to visit different areas of your site), it's commonly placed along the left side of the site or along the top — or in both places. You can also use right-side menu navigation. Figure 2-1 shows the different ways to use a navigational bar on a page.

- *Buttons, tabs, and links:* Buttons you can use on the navigation bar come in unlimited designs, shapes, and colors (depending on the software you use). Additionally, you can use text, rather than a button, as a link. You might also want to repeat a navigational bar in the form of tabs at the top of the page or even use links at the bottom of the page.

✦ **Color:** An influential design element is in the color scheme you choose to use. Do you go bold and bright or soft and understated, or do you stick to plain white or neutral colors? Another consideration is how to incorporate those colors (or lack thereof) into the site. You can use a color as a background for your entire site, to highlight sections of text, or to separate segments within your site by using borders or blocks of color.

The psychology of color choice is thought to influence everything from your customers' moods to their buying behavior. For more information on how color can affect customers, check out the research on the Pantone (a leading color company) Web site: `www.pantone.com/products/products.asp?idArea=16`.

Figure 2-1: This Web site has navigation bars on the left and bottom of the page.

✦ **Font:** The font type and size you use throughout your site makes a statement. With thousands of font styles to select from, you can send a variety of messages to your customers, and in the blink of an eye. Additionally, the text size you use contributes to not only the look of the site but also its readability. For example, text that's too small might not be easy to read. *Sans serif* fonts, which have hooks and loops on the letters, are also difficult to view when used online. Another concern is when choosing special fonts (usually you buy these): They might not be viewable by most Web users. Stick to the list of core fonts for the Web, which are available to most users.

Table 2-1 lists some core Web fonts you can choose from and explains what the styles say to your customers.

Table 2-1	Common Fonts for Your Site
Font	*Message It Sends*
Arial	I'm common and nondescript.
Comic Sans	I'm choosing whimsy over seriousness.
Courier New	I'm old-fashioned, from the era of newsroom typewriters.
Georgia	I'm classic and professional and layered with style.
Times New Roman	I'm quite traditional.
Trebuchet	I'm professional yet relaxed (similar to casual Friday in the workplace).
Verdana	I emit a friendly, modern vibe.

Book III
Chapter 2

Designing
Customer-Friendly
Sites

✦ **Images:** The use of photos and graphics (animated or otherwise) can complement your site, if they're used correctly. Images help draw readers' eyes to specific areas of your site and can help illustrate information and ideas. If you're selling products, high-quality images are a necessity, of course. When you're designing the site, think about how many images you'll use, what size they need to be, and where you might place them within the site for the best effect.

✦ **Media:** As the Internet continues to mature, more Web sites are incorporating video and sound clips. For some sites, this capability becomes an intricate design element. For others, whether to use some form of media becomes a functional issue: Can your customers even view video and sound clips? If that's the case, you must decide whether customers will view this type of media as adding to or detracting from your site's usability.

Making design choices

You must make a number of decisions when you develop the look and feel of your site. How do you choose which options make the most sense for you? Generally, one or more of these characteristics dictate a site's look:

✦ **Your industry or line of business:** If you're in a conservative industry, such as accounting or financial services, consider that subdued colors with a simple layout might appear to be more professional. Alternatively, if a potential customer is searching for a graphic designer, the customer might expect to see a bright, funky design with lots of colorful images. Figure 2-2 shows two different types of businesses and the designs they chose to reflect their particular image.

✦ **The types of products or services you offer:** Selling products or services that have a serious message (such as medical equipment) begs for a low-key design approach. And, the information your site contains might require many layers of pages to provide research or product information. On the other hand, products that are fun or made for recreational purposes might sell better if the site is light and whimsical and filled with product images rather than with product data.

✦ **An existing brand:** Particularly if you have an established business, your site's style or look might be predetermined by your company's store or product base. You want your site's image to be consistent with your established brand. In that case, you should pull design elements for your Web site from a logo, from marketing materials, or from the design of the existing brick-and-mortar location. You should, at the least, complement what you have in place.

✦ **Your customers' demographics and psychographics:** Age, gender, education, geographic location — the more you know, the more likely you are to create the appropriate feel for your site. It's certainly not unusual to design your site to fit the image of your target customer, especially with niche (or highly specialized) markets.

✦ **Your personal preferences:** Sometimes, which design elements you choose to incorporate depends on which ones most appeal to your personal taste. (You get a say in this process, after all). Okay, you shouldn't *always* design a site based entirely on personal preference. There's still nothing wrong, however, with throwing in a few elements that make your own heart sing.

The final consideration in designing your Web site is to create a timeless look, and we don't mean that you design a site once and never touch it again. A common pet peeve is a site on the Internet that's outdated and looks like an early-generation "brochure" site. That makes us instantly feel as though the company doesn't care about its business or its customers. The company probably has a Web site only because somebody told company employees that they needed one, so they turned one of their sales brochures into a basic three-page site, launched it on the World Wide Web, and never thought about it again.

Figure 2-2: These two companies chose Web site designs to reflect their different types of businesses.

If you want to create a Web site that's considered timeless, keep these three suggestions in mind:

✦ **Keep it simple.** Whether a site was developed in 1995 or 2005, trends change. Trust us when we say that trying to keep up with every new Web design feature that's rolled out becomes expensive and time con-suming. By keeping your design elements simple, and by using only one or two trendy features, however, you increase the design lifespan of your site. The best example we can offer is Google, shown in Figure 2-3. Its overall site design is clean and basic, which lends itself to its original purpose as a search engine. Finding the search box isn't a chore when you pull up the Google home page, considering that it's one of the first (and only) elements you see. To make the site seem less sterile, some small, animated graphics appear around the company's logo on holidays and special occasions. This level of basic design doesn't work for every type of Web site, of course, although it gives you an idea of what you can accomplish with an understated design.

✦ **Keep the information updated and relevant.** This advice includes everything from text and photos to hypertext links and copyright dates. Keeping the substance of your site current offers value. Also, you can easily overlook a graphical design that might be lagging a few months (or years) in the past.

✦ **Avoid images or graphics that visually date the site**. For instance, if you use photos of current events, or that are seasonal in nature, your site can quickly become dated. Similarly, photos of people can be telltale signs of an outdated site because of clothing and hair. The exception is if you intentionally use graphics or photos that evoke a retro feel or pro-vide relevant historical information.

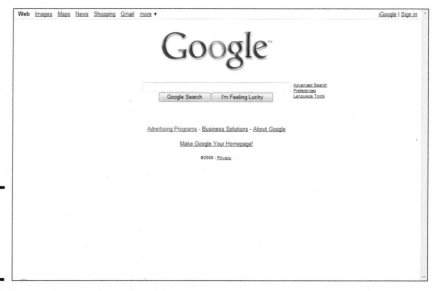

Figure 2-3:
The Google
site is
simple and
timeless.

Does your site design work?

Before finalizing your site's design, ask yourself these questions to determine whether your site makes a winning first impression:

✔ Does the design reflect your defined purpose for the site?

✔ Will the look of the site appeal to your customers and encourage them to buy from you?

✔ Does the site's design (especially colors and fonts) allow information and products to be easily seen? Or, do your eyes strain to look at text and images?

✔ Does the choice of layout, specifically the navigational bars, make it easy to locate information and move between pages?

✔ Is the site consistent with all other marketing and promotional tools you use?

✔ When a customer first views the site, will it promote the image you want customers to have of your company?

Before designing your site, do your homework. Search the Internet for competitors' sites and evaluate which design elements work and which don't. You can even gather a small group of prospective customers and ask which sites they respond to most.

Choosing Substance Over Style

In case your head is filled with hot design ideas, we should mention that a good site doesn't function by design alone. In fact, sometimes you can make your site even better by sacrificing trendy design elements. The good news is that if you agree to forego a few of those high-end elements, your budget gets to breathe easier. The bad news is that some folks are just flashy, and breaking old habits isn't easy.

Okay, if you haven't guessed yet, we're talking about the use of Macromedia Flash. It's the intense graphics-animation program that some people swear is a Web site must-have. You've probably seen the images of fast cars that pulse across auto dealers' Web sites. Or, maybe you noticed dancing fruit and animated paint splatters that mesmerize you while they move and twist seamlessly throughout a site — that's Flash animation. To be honest, its value is a point of contention among professional designers. Half of them agree that it's a beautiful, and perhaps even useful, tool. The other half thinks that the World Wide Web is better off without it.

Flash that's done well can be entertaining — and in some cases warranted. If you're looking for information quickly, though, or want to buy a product, having to continually trudge through Flash programs becomes annoying.

Our professional opinion is that the majority of business Web sites can do without Flash. Why? This list has some answers:

✦ **It's costly.** The added expense for developing Flash animation wreaks havoc on most design budgets. Also, if you need to update content frequently, the bills add up fast!

✦ **It lacks purpose.** In most cases, high-tech Flash animations are unnecessary and don't serve a legitimate function.

✦ **It's a time burden.** The time it takes to load, or the need for special software to play an animation, is often frustrating to non-broadband customers.

✦ **It's ego driven.** A desire to develop Flash often revolves around a Web designer who wants to flaunt his skill set, or a site owner who wants a jazzed-up site, as opposed to using a tool that suits the needs of the site.

✦ **It causes time delays.** Because the use of Flash can easily add to the development time of creating your site, using Flash adds not only cost but also time.

With so many reasons not to use Flash, you might be wondering whether you have any reasons *to* use it. Proponents of the development tool are quick to defend it. Here are some positive aspects:

✦ **What you see is what everyone sees:** Flash ensures that your page appears the same way no matter which browser displays it.

✦ **Flash shows off your products:** In some cases, Flash can quickly and efficiently transfer information and dynamic images from a database and take up less bandwidth. Product demonstrations can also be enhanced by using Flash. For some sites, particularly online retail sites, or e-tailers, Flash may even be a necessary tool to better showcase products. The tool can be entertaining and encourage interactivity.

✦ **Flash shows up in searches:** Because Flash images are searchable by Google and Yahoo!, your pages that use Flash can be indexed by the leading search engines.

✦ **Flash looks good when it's done well:** Flash, done well, can lend a professional, high-tech look to your site.

What we're saying is you don't have to completely shy away from using Flash, but be thoughtful in whether it will enhance your site design and usability.

Whether you're pro or con about the use of Flash, the decision to incorporate it on your site ought to hinge on two questions:

✦ Does Flash enhance your customer's experience when they're visiting your site?

✦ Will your sales increase as a result of incorporating Flash into your site design?

Counting on Function to Win Customers

Really, the two questions we discuss in the preceding sections should be used as a barometer whenever you consider function and your Web site. Whether you're talking about a shopping cart application or a registration box that lets customers sign up for your newsletters, function is what drives a customer's experience. If a particular function adds value for the customer, it's likely to increase your revenues, either directly or indirectly.

Understanding the customer experience

Think back to one of your recent visits to a Web site. Maybe it's one of your favorites, or one you visited for the first time. How would you rate your experience? Did you find what you wanted quickly and easily? Did you glean the information you needed? Did your browsing lead to a purchase? Or, were you frustrated by the whole thing and you chose instead to move on to another site? Well, guess what? Your customers think about the same issues every time they visit your site.

Ultimately, customer experience leads them to make two important decisions:

✦ Whether to make a purchase from you

✦ Whether to return to your site

For example, the Small Business Administration site (www.sba.gov) uses different functions to make locating facts, figures, and helpful business tools easier (see Figure 2-4). Throughout the rest of this chapter, we point out several examples of these functions (such as quick-loading pages, site search function, and live customer service).

Building function into your site

When you consider what's at stake with your business when you design your own site, you have to figure out how to use function to influence customer decisions. We suggest attacking function at three levels.

At the first level are *basic functions*. Customers expect this lowest, or base, level of functionality. Basic functions include these features:

✦ **Quick-loading pages:** Customers don't have the patience to wait for pages to load. Even if they're still using slower dialup connections, you're the one who's expected to ease that problem for them. If you don't anticipate customers having varying speeds of Internet access and account for that difference in your Web design, you just missed a potential sale.

Figure 2-4:
The SBA
site uses
customer-
friendly
functions.

✦ **Ease of navigation:** When customers go from page to page within your site, the navigation tools you provide should allow customers to

- Readily find and identify navigational buttons and links

- Immediately return to the home page, regardless of what page they're on

- Return to the preceding or last-visited page by clicking a link

- See pages and sections they have visited on the site by using a link history, usually at the top of the page

✦ **Working links:** All internal and external links to pages on your site should be valid and working. In other words, customers don't want to click a link and expect to find more information on a product, only to find a `Page Not Found` message. Broken links that go nowhere also diminish the credibility of your site and indicate that you don't update or maintain it.

✦ **Viewable images:** When you include photos and graphics on your site, be sure that the images — especially product images — load correctly and quickly. Additionally, avoid using grainy pictures or tiny images that are difficult for customers to see. (We provide more detail about working with images at the end of this chapter.)

✦ **Shopping carts:** Yes, this is a category unto itself (and we discuss it in detail in Book IV, Chapter 5). We list it as an interactive function because all too often small Web sites make the mistake of not even using shopping carts on their sites. Instead, customers are asked to call the company to place orders; or to print, fill out, and fax order forms to the Web site owner. That's a fatal mistake! You *must* provide a method for shopping and paying for items over the Internet.

✦ **E-mail contact:** Providing customers with a method other than a phone number to contact you is another basic function of your site. Offering an e-mail link is one of the easiest, although you can do it in several ways.

At the second level of site functionality are *interactive functions,* which actively engage customers with your site. Although this type of function isn't necessary to place an order, it can increase value and sales for your site. Samples of interactive functions include

✦ **Site search:** Give customers a tool that allows them to quickly search for information within your site. This function might not be as useful if your site is small. However, if you have a site filled with products or layers of data, customers appreciate having search capability.

Although customizable search functions are expensive, free versions are available. Try FreeFind.com at `www.freefind.com`. It offers a flexible and unlimited page-search function in exchange for displaying ads. An ad-free, subscription-based service is available starting at $19 per month. Google also has a comparable paid-search feature starting at $100 annually.

✦ **Downloadable documents:** If it's appropriate, consider offering your visitors the option to download information. You can offer PDF documents of articles, research papers, and detailed product reviews and manuals.

✦ **Forums:** Message boards, bulletin boards, forums (or discussion boards), and chat rooms are options that let visitors interact with you and with one another. Many people consider forums a free form of technical support; if your boards stay active and updated, this added function might keep customers coming back to your site.

✦ **Blogs:** These online journals provide another opportunity for customers to interact with you and others. In Book X, Chapter 3, we show you how blogs not only provide enhanced functionality for your site but also serve as proven marketing tools.

✦ **Member registration:** You can make registration free or make it a condition of accessing certain sections of your site. In return for signing up as members, visitors can receive newsletters, site updates, or e-mail messages announcing new products. Registration provides members with benefits and provides you with customer contact information — a win-win situation for both parties.

✦ **Newsfeeds and RSS:** Included in this category are scrolling links to your company's most recent news or press releases. Or, you can offer links (from external feeds) to top news stories that are relevant to your target customer. By using RSS feeds on your site, you allow customers to receive recently updated content, product information, and news.

The third level is reserved for tools and features that offer customers an *enhanced* experience on your site. Items of enhanced functionality often include

✦ **Online demonstrations and tutorials:** Depending on the complexity of the products or services you sell, online demos and Web-based tutorials can be useful. Customers receive the value of trying out the product or discovering how it's used, which often increases the likelihood of a purchase.

✦ **Live or 24/7 customer support:** The Internet never sleeps, and neither do some of your customers. Regardless of when they might be shopping on your site, your customer service is greatly enhanced if you can offer unlimited support. Although it isn't necessarily *technical* support, your customer might need to ask a question before making the decision to buy your service or product.

You don't have to set up a full customer call center to offer live or 24/7 support. Several companies have developed the service for even the smallest online retailers. Try LivePerson Pro software or Live Person Contact Center to instantly add live customer support to your Web site. A free trial is available at `www.solutions.liveperson.com/sb`. This tool offers pay-as-you-go pricing.

✦ **Geographic locators:** Okay, if you have physical locations in addition to your Web presence, geography-related tools are a plus. Your customers appreciate access to maps and driving directions, store locators using interactive maps of the United States (or other countries), and even product-locator searches based on zip codes.

Customizing a map for your site is easy using Google Maps (`www.google.com/lbc`) from its Local Business Center service. This free tool lets you create maps and driving routes that you can add to your site immediately.

✦ **Second-language viewing options:** Not all your customers speak fluent English. Savvy Web site owners offer customers the option to view sites in other languages. (Spanish, or Espanol, is one of the most popular alternatives in the United States.)

✦ **New media:** Video and sound clips serve a purpose, and these options have increasingly become standard. Giving access to information by using newer forms of media is still considered an unexpected bonus. Try adding podcasts (self-published broadcasts over the Internet) or Web conferences (conference calls over the Internet that allow for participant interaction). They're quite helpful for new product introductions.

Understanding the value of functionality is a major part of developing a customer-friendly site. It's also an opportunity to set yourself apart from your competition, by simply taking the time to plan.

Chapter 3: Building a Site without Spending a Fortune

In This Chapter

✔ Planning a well-structured business Web site

✔ Finding out how to build your own Web site

✔ Using HTML commands effectively

✔ Building Web pages with specific software tools

✔ Hiring the right professional to help you design your site

✔ Working with your professional designer

✔ Providing the right information at the right time

*I*n the early days of the Internet, simply having a Web site was a way to differentiate your business from the competition. As interest in the Web developed and grew, companies of all shapes and sizes focused their efforts on capturing people's attention with Web sites. Because of this growth in online competition, planning a site and building a distinctive design and proposition became increasingly important. After all, an outstanding site encourages current customers to stay with your business and promotes your site's presence to the new shoppers who come online every day.

The same basic principles of Web site design apply as much now as they did when the Web took off in the mid-1990s. Technologies used on the Web might come and go, but you don't have to include the latest and greatest technology on your site. Customers are drawn to sites that are simple, focused, easy to use, well organized, and *useful*. Everything else is just sound and fury.

In this chapter, we present the steps for creating a Web site that serves your business and your customers. We direct you to spend some time defining exactly what you want on your site, and then we show you ways to implement your ideas, either by yourself or with the help of a professional. In either case, we specify the issues you need to consider and the traps you need to avoid so that you can focus on designing your Web site and move on to the next phase of your business.

Mapping Your Route to a Successful Site

When people opt to build a new house or commercial building, they don't just hire a contractor, bring over the concrete and tools, and say "Go for it." Before construction even begins, they craft a carefully detailed plan that they review, edit, and approve. Your Web site should be treated the same way. The best sites aren't dreamed up by eccentric designers and thrown together quickly. Good sites require a clear road map from the people who run the business to ensure that the focus of the business is never lost.

Thinking about your Web site before you start its design is important. Start by making a list of all the functions you want to provide on your site. If you're tempted to believe that your site has just one function — to *sell stuff* — we encourage you to break down that function into subfunctions, by answering these questions:

✦ **What kinds of products do you want to sell?** The number and organization of pages you have on your site depends on the makeup and complexity of your products or services. For example, you should have at least one page for each category of product.

✦ **How many distinct categories of products will you sell?** You might need a separate page for each product category. Think about splitting up categories such as consumer electronics and computer products, for example.

✦ **Will customers be able to create an account on your site?** If so, you need to provide a page where customers can log in, update their personal information, view their orders, and enter payment information.

✦ **Will you provide customers with additional content, original or not?** Some Web sites make money by offering a subscription for their customers to read premium content such as special articles, interviews, and video, audio, and photo excerpts.

✦ **How will customers pay for their orders?** You need to be able to take credit card orders, and provide a mailing address if you accept personal checks or money orders.

✦ **Will you tell people about you and your business mission?** Some companies think that having a Web page about their mission statement isn't important, whereas others use this page as a way to connect with customers.

✦ **Will you provide instructions for using your Web site?** It has been a common practice for Web sites to create a page for Frequently Asked Questions (FAQ) to help their customers use the site properly and find everything that's available.

After you come up with your list of site functions, the next step is to draw a map showing the Web pages you need in order to accomplish those functions and showing how the pages relate to one another. At this point, don't even think about how the Web site or the individual pages will look; just identify the different pages that need to exist on your site. Assign each page to a box on your map, and check off the function that the page will handle. When you're done, you should have a map of your site that looks like a flowchart.

At the top of your map is the *home page,* which is your launch pad to the rest of the Web site (see Figure 3-1). This page answers all the basic questions that customers have about your business, just like the friendly receptionist in the lobby of a 50-story building. Whether this visit is the first — or the fiftieth — for your customers, the home page has to answer their questions in a clear, concise, organized way or be able to point them in the right direction quickly.

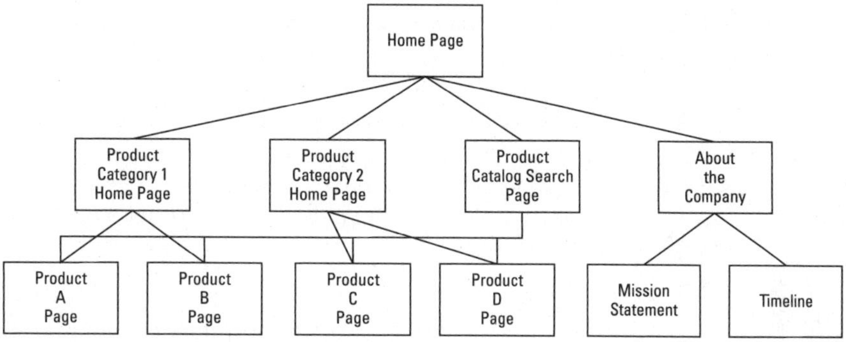

Figure 3-1:
The home page on your Web site leads into all your categories.

Home Page

Product Category 1 Home Page

Product Category 2 Home Page

Product Catalog Search Page

About the Company

Product A Page

Product B Page

Product C Page

Product D Page

Mission Statement

Timeline

You can build a Web page that holds a text version of the map you created and make it available to your customers. Just like a road atlas helps drivers follow their route, this *site map* helps your online customers find anything available on your site without taking a wrong turn — or, in this case, a wrong click.

Below the home page are your main category pages. Although your first draft might look like the one shown in Figure 3-1, the beauty of such a simple map is that your site plan can expand and grow from that basic model. As you design more complex and function-intensive Web sites, you can add more levels to your Web site map. When you build your site map this way, you can visualize how your entire site operates, because you capture how your pages support each other.

Site-builder checklist

Most e-commerce Web sites have a basic list of pages that they provide to their customers. As you're designing your own site, take a look at the functions that most sites provide and decide which types of pages are right for your business:

- ✔ Home
- ✔ Catalog
- ✔ Customer account
- ✔ Order information

- ✔ Frequently Asked Questions
- ✔ Content
- ✔ Map and direction (if you have a retail site)
- ✔ Checkout
- ✔ Payment processing (possibly on someone else's site)
- ✔ About Us or Company History (describes mission, purpose, or employees, for example)

Setting reasonable expectations

When your Web site is in the paper-and-pen phase of design, you might find that you're adding a bunch of boxes (pages) and dreaming up the ultimate Web site. After all, you haven't designed or written the pages yet, so creating a gigantic, robust, fully functional site for any customer is easy — *on paper*.

Although we don't want to take the wind out of your sails (or is that *sales?*), we definitely advise you to keep these expectations and guidelines in mind as you begin to turn your road map into your virtual store:

✦ **Don't put too much stuff on one page.** Avoid tying together several product lines. If your pages become bloated — too filled with information and graphics, for example — the page becomes too long for customers to read and takes too long to load and display on their screens.

✦ **Position key information at the top.** Keep your pages short, and put key information at or near the top of the page. Newspapers place key articles *above the fold* (the top half of the newspaper page) because not all readers take the time to flip over the paper to read the bottom half. On the Internet, if you're asking your customers to scroll down the page to see something important, you're taking the risk that they won't do it and might leave your site without seeing your business's main functions.

✦ **Keep the number of steps to a minimum.** One reason that customers come back to a site like Amazon is that they can find an item, click once, and have the item shipped to them. Customers turn to online shopping for convenience, so offer them a quick or smooth process to navigate the critical areas of your site. Even though some customers stay to look around, take advantage of your content, or use other functions, your site needs to appeal to the customers who want to get in, get what they want, and get out.

One way to check the complexity of your Web site is to look at your road map. If you have too many levels between the home page and a finishing point for placing an order, consider revamping your plan to provide a smoother path.

✦ **Remember that good design takes time.** If the world took six days to create, don't expect to have your site up in a day. Although the broad strokes of creating a Web site (such as creating the navigation bar and home page layout) can happen quickly, the refinement and fine-tuning of the site (such as defining button colors or the number of columns) can take much longer. Then again, fine-tuning can separate you from the competition in your customers' eyes. Give your designer enough time to do good work, but not free reign to create a masterpiece.

Avoiding common holdups in developing a site

The last part of any Web site design process involves looking at the site map and page count and then estimating how much time you need to create the site. Expert designers typically estimate a number (of hours, days, or weeks, for example), and then pad that number by adding extra time to complete the project. You might ask, "Why pad the estimate?" After all, if someone is just implementing your well-structured plan, what can go wrong?

You find a variety of reasons that developing your site can take longer than you expected. As you move from Web site design to implementation, beware of these traps:

✦ **Trying to design and build the site at the same time:** People like to dive in with only a few pages on their maps (*before* the design is complete) and then add pages as they build out their sites. The constant starting, stopping, and thinking about which extra pages are needed can slow you down when you're trying to build the site.

✦ **Not having the right capabilities for your site:** Some people envision having a graphics-rich, interactive, advanced Web site and then find out in the design process that their Internet service provider (ISP) can't support certain programs or supply bandwidth to display video properly. Careful planning helps you create specifications, which you can verify with your site provider to make sure that your site capabilities are what you want — before you buy.

✦ **Not updating the entire site when you make a change:** Even the most carefully laid Web site plans can require some modification when you implement them. Remember that good sites link back and forth between different sections. The last thing you want is to update one section without updating the links in the rest of your site. If this happens, your customers can get lost while surfing around — and might leave for good.

Book III
Chapter 3

Building a Site without Spending a Fortune

✦ **Forgetting about the message:** As your Web site grows and expands, you can easily lose focus on what the site should accomplish. At any time, you must be able to go back to your home page — or any other page — and determine the site focus by viewing the page for a few seconds. If you spend longer than 10 or 15 seconds interpreting the message, you're off track.

No matter how many changes you make, never let the message of your site get lost or obscured.

✦ **Not having the content ready:** You can have the plan built and promise to deliver your data or content to your Web site developer by a certain date. If you miss this date for some reason, you throw the developer's plans — not to mention the project's workflow — into chaos.

✦ **Not having a reliable developer:** The best-laid plans are just *plans* until someone turns them into a Web site. If you're depending on someone with specialized skills, make sure that she has the time available to deliver your site when you need it.

You Can Do It! Make a Build-It-Yourself Site

The thought of turning site maps, content lists, and other plans into a full-blown Web site can intimidate almost anyone — especially someone who has never created a Web page. To create Web pages in the early days of the Internet, you had to know the specialized computer code *HyperText Markup Language (HTML)* and be able to write that code by using a program such as Notepad. Now, however, you can find many tools to help you design your own site without having an extensive knowledge of HTML.

That said, knowing how to use some HTML is still a good idea because this knowledge gives you more control over the site-building process. Although Web site tools can create a lot of HTML code and help you build functions quickly, you might have to edit the work those tools do to make your site faster, smoother, and easier for customers to use. You have to direct these efforts to make sure that your site is an effective communications tool for your customers to do business with you. These Web site tools can help you get something done, but *you* have to provide the "why" of the Web page: Why is it being built, and why should customers use it?

A good first step is checking with your Web hosting company to find out which site development tools it provides. Most hosting companies have site design tools and templates that work with their servers, and can get you up and running with basic Web page designs. You can update those basic designs with your own content, labels, and products.

If your Web host doesn't provide any site-building tools or you're not happy with its offerings, don't worry — you have more options, as outlined in this list:

✦ **Free tools online:** You can find a number of free or inexpensive site-builder tools on the Internet. Table 3-1 lists some of these tools.

You might also find free Web tools from your Internet service provider (ISP). Companies such as AOL and EarthLink offer free Web hosting space and some basic tools for building your personal Web site. You can use these same tools to help create your e-commerce site.

✦ **Your word processor:** You can even use your word processor to build a Web site! Microsoft Word can save any document you create as an HTML file so that you can type your site map and create Web pages without much stress.

✦ **Advanced site-builder software:** Later in this chapter, the section "Going modern with Adobe Dreamweaver, and more" introduces some advanced, superfunctional programs that can help you build a rich, complex site for your business.

Table 3-1	Companies with Site-Building Tools
Company Name	*URL*
Creating Online	www.creatingonline.com
CoffeeCup	www.coffeecup.com
Trellian	www.trellian.com/webpage/
Web Express	www.mvd.com/webexpress
Web Monkey	www.webmonkey.com
Web Studio	www.webstudio.com

Using HTML: The old-fashioned way to build a page

Regardless of the Web design tool you use to build your Web site, you need a basic understanding of how HTML works. This understanding helps you edit your pages and figure out what your tools are creating.

Unlike software code that has to be translated, compiled, and otherwise prepared before a consumer can use it, *HTML (HyperText Markup Language)* code is written, saved as a file, and then interpreted by the program that reads the file. Usually, the software program that reads the HTML file is a Web browser, such as Microsoft Internet Explorer. The Web browser opens the HTML file and finds these two elements:

✦ **Text** represents the titles, headings, paragraphs, links, and other elements that you want customers to see when they visit your Web site.

✦ **Commands, or *HTML markup tags,*** tell the Web browser how to *mark up,* or format, the text that's in the file and, therefore, control how the text looks to customers.

The browser reads all the instructions that you place in these markup tags and draws the Web page on the computer screen the way you specify it. Because this language is uniform and structured, most Web browsers interpret the commands in the same way. Your customers see the same design regardless of the computer or operating system they're using.

Commands are marked in the HTML file by command-start and -stop symbols: the < and > signs. They look like this:

<command>

Typically, HTML commands are implemented by indicating, in this order,

✦ The start of the command

✦ The text that will be affected by the command

✦ The end of the command

For example, if you want a word to appear bolded on your Web page, you write

<B>*word*</B>

The <B> command indicates that you're turning on (starting) the Bold command. Adding a slash (/) to the ending command tag indicates that you're turning off the command. Your Web browser looks at this code and creates an effect as though you're holding down the Bold key, typing a word, and then releasing that key and moving on to the next section.

If you don't provide the command tag to end a particular command, the Web browser continues to format the rest of the file by using that command. If you put a <B> (the Bold command) in your file and then forget to end the command, the rest of the text in your Web page appears as bold text.

Every HTML file has certain essential commands that should always be present. The following listing shows a skeleton HTML file:

```
<HTML>
  <HEAD>
  <TITLE>Basic webpage title</title
  </HEAD>
  <BODY>
  The content of your Web page would go here.
  </BODY>
</HTML>
```

Always put the <HTML> tag on the first line of your HTML file. This tag tells the Web browser that it can find HTML code inside your file. Next, your Web page contains two sections: the *header* (marked by <HEAD>) and the *body* (marked by <BODY>).

Your header section should contain all the information that defines your Web page, which includes — but isn't limited to — these elements:

✦ **Title:** Your Web site title appears on the browser's title bar and should instantly tell customers the purpose of the Web page.

✦ **Function definitions:** For example, if you're creating a Web page for customers to search your catalog, make sure to define the function as a search page.

✦ **Author information:** Fill in the author's information, whether it's you, your business name, or your Web designer. That way, customers know whom to thank for a well-planned Web site, interesting content, and a creative design.

✦ **<META> tags:** This type of tag tells your Web browser the definition and keywords of your Web page. See Book VI, Chapter 6 for more information on these tags.

The body section contains everything else related to the Web page, especially anything visible to your customers, such as

✦ **Your content:** For example, a description and photographs of your products or services, and any information you're displaying for your customers.

✦ **Navigation information:** Usually, every Web page has a consistent set of links that can take your customers to every main section of your Web site with one click.

✦ **Links to other parts of your Web site:** If your Web page needs to reference another part of your Web site, make sure that the link is present in the page.

✦ **Links to other Web sites:** Many times, a Web site offers links to other Web sites that are complementary to theirs, or partners with them for co-promotion efforts.

✦ **Forms asking customers to fill in information:** For example, you need the name and shipping address of any customers who decide to order something or join your mailing list.

Sometimes, designers put all the information in the body and very little in the header section. Although your Web page still loads and presents itself to your customers, the lack of a divider between header and body information makes it harder to update your Web pages properly (for example, when you need to change some functions on your Web site) and maximize your outreach to the Internet community. Similarly, putting main content inside the header section can distort the display of your Web page because some Web browsers try to condense the header to the top of the screen. Figure 3-2 shows a Web page with the information properly distributed.

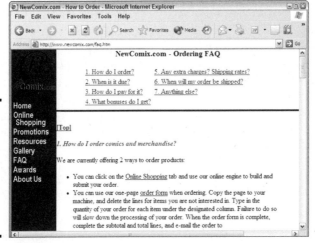

Figure 3-2:
The header and body information on this Web page is properly distributed.

Qualifying your HTML commands

Some HTML tags require markup instructions other than the caret signs (< and >) and the command name. These needy tags require specific information, known as *attributes,* that your Web browser uses to implement the command. Like the commands, these attributes are written inside the caret signs to separate the markup instruction from the regular text of the file.

Suppose that you want to provide a Web link so that when customers click the words *Order Here* from your home page, their Web browsers open your catalog page. Although the command for building a Web link is <A>, you have to assign the attribute of the destination page, which is known as *Hypertext REFerence,* or HREF. You would write the following HTML code:

```
<A HREF="catalog.html">Order here!</A>
```

You turn on the Web link command with <A, assign the destination cata log.html as your Web link (HREF), add the words Order here! as the text your customers see, and end the command with </A>. Notice that you do *not* have to close out the attribute separately; just define it within the carets surrounding the opening tag.

Table 3-2 shows some common HTML commands that have important attributes to define.

Table 3-2	HTML Commands That Require You to Assign Attributes	
Command	*Attribute*	*Element That It Assigns*
<BODY>	BGCOLOR	Background color
	TEXT	Color of text in the body
	LINK	Color of Web links
	VLINK	Color of visited Web links
<FONT>	COLOR	Color of the font
	SIZE	Size of the text that's using this font
<IMG>	SRC	Source of the image file

If you don't assign attributes such as background color or size, your Web browser uses the default attributes that the customer set up on her computer or that was supplied with the Web browser software. Typically, the link color is set to blue, visited links are set to purple, and the background color is set to white.

Using tables to organize your page

After you get the basics on how to set up a Web page, you want to find ways to organize all the text, graphics, and data that you present on your Web page. Specifically, if you want to show an array of products on your Web site, you organize the product photo, description, Buy Now button, and other specifics in a smooth, centered format. One popular way that Web site designers ensure a smooth presentation is to use HTML tables.

Originally designed to show numbers and data in a spreadsheet-style format, tables are now becoming the building blocks for aligning every element in a Web page. Many navigation toolbars, whether they run across the top or left side of a Web page, are in fact HTML tables that space the navigation commands evenly, no matter which Web browser or computer screen is being used.

The easiest way to build a table is to use an automated Web site builder, (such as the ones we discuss in the next section). However, understanding how tables are created in HTML helps you make any necessary edits, in case the builder tools don't properly create all aspects of the table.

Follow these steps to define a table in HTML:

1. **Type the** <TABLE> **command wherever you want to start building a table in your HTML file.**

2. **For every horizontal row you want to build in your table, type the** <TR> **command to start the row and the** </TR> **command to end the row.**

   You can assign as many rows to a particular HTML table as you want. Although there's no minimum number, you should try to put at least one row into each table you create.

3. **For each column cell you want within a row, type the** <TD> **command to start the cell and the** </TD> **command to end the cell.**

   Although you define the number of rows in the table, your Web browser interprets the number of columns in your table by counting the number of cells created with <TD> and </TD>.

   If you create different numbers of cells within your rows of a table, your Web browser tries to compensate by evenly spacing out the cells. This compensation can result in an uneven display, however. When necessary, create cells with no content by simply putting <TD></TD> in the necessary rows.

4. **Type the** </TABLE> **command when you're done building the table.**

Be careful if you build tables to place inside other tables. Every table on your page uses a <TABLE> command, and if you start building tables within tables, you might mix up the matching commands. If you don't provide the correct number of </TABLE> commands to end your tables, your Web browser tries to format the rest of your Web page into the tables you created, which can cause a disjointed appearance on your page.

To give you an idea of what a complete table definition looks like in HTML, we show you a basic 3-row, 3-column table that contains four different prices for a product:

```
<TABLE BORDER=1>
<TR>
<TD>JOEL'S SNOWBOARDS</TD>
<TD><B>UNPAINTED</B></TD>
<TD><B>PAINTED</B></TD>
</TR>
<TR>
<TD><B>MODEL 1000</B></TD>
<TD>$79.99</TD>
<TD>$129.99</TD>
</TR>
<TR>
<TD><B>MODEL 2000</B></TD>
<TD>$99.99</TD>
<TD>$179.99</TD>
</TR>
</TABLE>
```

Using this code sample results in something like the table shown in Figure 3-3.

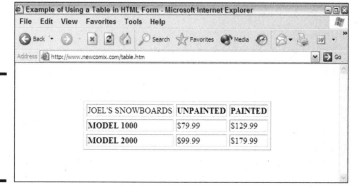

Figure 3-3:
This Web page has a 3-row, 3-column table.

Notice how the <TABLE> command has an attribute named BORDER. If you set the BORDER to 0, no lines are drawn between rows or columns. This way, your Web site visitors see only the contents of your table, not any defining lines.

By default, your table takes the entire width of your Web page. You can assign the WIDTH attribute to your <TABLE>, <TR>, or <TD> commands to manually space a particular cell, row, or table to appear on the Web page. Using the preceding example, suppose that you want the cell containing the painted price to occupy just 20 percent of your table width. To accomplish this task, you can use this line of code:

```
<TD WIDTH="20%">$129.99</TD>
```

You need to assign the WIDTH attribute for all cells in the table for that same column. Otherwise, you risk throwing off the spacing for the entire table.

Your tables can contain much more than just text. You can assign pictures, buttons, text fields, or whatever elements you want to your table cells. Just make sure that you're assigning an equal amount of content to each cell and keeping track of how much is in each one. You don't want to throw off the alignment of your table by putting three pictures in one cell and only one picture in the next cell.

Going modern with Adobe Dreamweaver and more

Web pages have many elements you can specify, and keeping track of them all is hard when you design pages using only HTML. The growing number of commands available in HTML fueled the need for software programs to help organize all these elements. These programs create the HTML commands automatically so that you can focus on the layout, design, and content of your Web page rather than worry about whether you defined all your table cells properly.

One of the most popular Web page design software programs is Adobe Dreamweaver. This program provides many buttons and menus to help you place HTML commands as though you're writing a paper in Microsoft Word. The software prompts you for specific information and then displays a sample of what your Web page will look like, as you're building the page. This way, you can try a command to see how it will look and then change it right there, if necessary, before continuing with your development.

The pros and cons of using automated site builders

You can use a Web site builder tool, such as Dreamweaver, to create sophisticated Web pages without having much specific knowledge, which is why millions of people buy these tools every year. However, keep in mind that using automated site builders isn't without a downside, and you can fall into certain traps if you rely solely on these tools.

Here are some reasons to use a site-builder tool:

✦ **Ease of use:** A builder tool is designed to make the process of creating Web pages as easy as possible. It looks like any other software program you're familiar with using and offers buttons, menus, and wizards to help you construct the building blocks of your Web page.

✦ **Wide array of options:** A builder tool is programmed with every HTML command that's available to use, and with functions that combine these commands. This combination gives you many options for creating your Web pages, and the tool's ease of use ensures that you don't have to search through documentation to figure out a specific name and definition for a function.

✦ **Total control:** You can rely on the code that a builder tool generates or insert your own code whenever it's needed. This type of program helps you easily validate your work by color-coding the commands in your file for easy visibility, for example.

Despite the attraction of all these features, you should also see the drawbacks of relying on a builder tool:

✦ **Unneeded code:** These programs have a particular way of inserting code into your HTML files, and sometimes they insert too much code or unnecessary code that Web browsers can interpret incorrectly. You must optimize your code after a builder tool creates it so that your pages load faster and cleanly.

✦ **Exclusive functions:** Some builder tools, especially Dreamweaver, offer powerful functions that you can insert into your Web pages. These functions are sometimes written with special commands that can be interpreted by only specific Web server programs. Web servers advertise this capability as including *extensions*, and whoever is hosting your Web site has to have the right extensions file for your Web pages to work properly.

✦ **Cost:** Full versions of Adobe Dreamweaver software can cost hundreds of dollars for one copy of the program. Although these versions offer a huge array of options, sometimes the cost isn't justified for the Web site you truly need for your business.

Creating Your Site with the Pros

One way that entrepreneurs get ahead is to understand their strengths and weaknesses: They focus on their strengths and have other people handle their weaknesses. Many people who want to operate their own online businesses aren't necessarily skilled Web site designers, and nothing is wrong with that. In the earlier section "You Can Do It! Make a Build-It-Yourself Site," we outline tools and technologies that can help you create your own site. You can choose another approach, however: Make the investment to have a professional Web site designer create your business Web site. The right interactions and communications with a professional designer can fuel an excellent site, and can even improve your overall business model so that increased orders and higher visibility help you recover the time and money you spend.

Some people consult with professional designers to create their sites and then give the business owners the tools to maintain their sites without any additional help. Other business owners contract with professionals to create and maintain their sites so that the designers can introduce new styles and functions as their businesses progress. Either approach can be beneficial for your business, and you should decide how much help you want, as either a one-time investment or an ongoing expense.

Seeking experience: Choosing the right Web site designer

Half the battle of finding a Web site designer is deciding that you need to hire one in the first place. The other half of the battle involves knowing where to look and talking to potential candidates until you find the right fit. Finding the right designer is similar to finding other specialists you need in order to solve specific problems. Whether you're looking for an auto mechanic, a plumber, a dentist, or in this case, a Web designer, consider these methods for finding a qualified professional:

✦ **Listen to word-of-mouth advice.** Talk to your friends, business associates, partners, or anybody you do business with online or in person. Find out which Web site designers they have used and solicit their opinions of these professionals.

✦ **See the work designers have done.** Look at Web sites that you like or enjoy. Most of the time, a small link or reference at the bottom of the home page or About Us page mentions whether a professional designer created the site. Follow the link back to the designer's site for more information.

✦ **Evaluate designers' portfolios.** Use search engines, read relevant magazines in your area, or look around to find a few companies. Then evaluate the samples or references they provide, to see whether their work for other people is good enough or fits the style you want for your own business.

Hooking up with a Web design firm

From the early days of the Internet, some Web design companies have focused on providing quality work for their clients. Going to a design firm gives you specific benefits for completing your project:

✦ **Reliability:** If a particular designer is having a bad day, week, month, or even year, a design firm can shift the workload away from that person and find backup or additional resources to cover the job. Design firms typically have contacts with freelance designers who come into the firm when needed to help tackle a big problem.

✦ **Coordination:** If several designers are working on your project, a design firm can coordinate the work and give you a single point of contact who communicates your ideas and tasks to the design team.

✦ **Experience:** Design firms have a portfolio of past projects and experience that lends itself to your project. They can bring their know-how and expertise to your project without having to navigate a large learning curve.

Going with a freelancer

When you ask around to find the right Web site design professional, you might be pointed toward talented individuals who work on a freelance basis and take on specific clients and projects that fit into their schedules. Some freelance professionals take assignments outside their full-time jobs, as a way to make some extra money. Others have enough clients to make their freelance jobs become their full-time careers.

Choosing a freelance designer over a design firm comes with its own set of benefits. A freelancer

✦ **Costs less to hire:** When you hire a design firm, part of the cost goes toward maintaining the overhead costs of the company. Although that overhead is beneficial to ensure the reliability of your project, if you're more flexible, a freelance designer typically charges less per hour or per project than the average design firm.

✦ **Works more nimbly:** You might find that a design firm you choose requires decisions and work to be done in various committees, with approval required at all stages by the firm's managers. This system can slow the progress of a Web site's development, and if speed is a top concern, a freelance designer who can focus on your project can produce a quicker result because the only approval that's needed is yours.

✦ **Provides a unique style:** Although designing a Web site is definitely a mixture of art and science, the creativity you want might not come from a firm that has developed procedures and processes for cranking out their various clients' Web sites. An individual freelance designer can bring her own quirky, creative, unique style to your project, which is what might draw you to this designer in the first place.

 You can use a Web site such as eLance.com to find the right freelance designer for your project. Simply go to `www.elance.com` and choose from qualified professionals (see Figure 3-4). Or, you can click the Post Your Job link to post your time and cost requirements and then receive bids from freelancers.

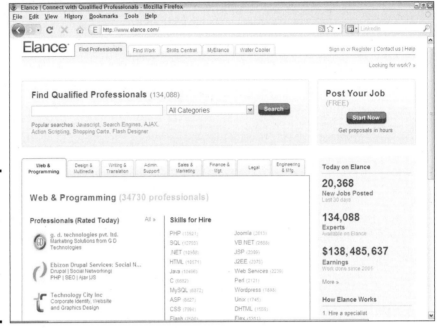

Figure 3-4:
Post your require-
ments on
eLance
so that
freelancers
come to
you!

Comparing apples to apples

While you're deciding whom to hire as your Web site designer, comparing quoted prices is a perfectly natural consideration for making up your mind. If you don't consider certain factors, however, they can skew the math and thereby make your comparison invalid.

For example, a price for designing a Web site is normally determined in one of two ways:

+ **Flat fee:** One price covers the complete site development.
+ **Per-hour pricing:** You're billed a rate per hour of development time.

Knowing a few key items from your designer or firm can help you compare prices more evenly. In this section, follow the advice that applies to your situation to find out the specific details.

If a designer or firm charges a flat fee for the entire project:

+ **Ask for a specific list of what's provided for that fee.** You might assume that the price you're quoted is the only fee you have to pay. Then you might find out at the end of the project that the flat fee excludes extras that you assumed were included, and be forced to pay more than you expected.

✦ **Ask what happens if someone has to spend overtime hours to complete the project.** One benefit of having a flat fee is knowing that you don't have to worry about the number of hours your designer is spending to build your Web site. This way, someone can't dawdle on a function to run up the bill, for example. Some design professionals offer a flat fee on the assumption that the project will take a maximum number of hours to complete. In this case, the contract stipulates that if the project exceeds that maximum number, the client pays more.

If a designer or firm charges by the hour:

✦ **Ask for time estimates on the various pieces of the project, function by function.** Web site design professionals might give you different numbers for the total number of hours needed. Rather than compare total numbers, you can compare detailed quotes to know whether one firm is spending more time on specific functions or one person is forgetting to factor in pieces that other designers know are essential.

✦ **Ask for limits to be put into place.** A Web site designer can easily quote a specific number of hours and then exceed that number and keep the bill running while you pay for his excesses. That's why you must establish limits for various pages, especially less-complicated pages. The designer should be forced, at the least, to call you if he needs to spend more time than quoted so that you can hear an explanation and make the decision.

Regardless of how you're charged, find out who pays if you find a bug or error in the work after the fact!

Sometimes, a Web designer can offer a lower quote because he refuses to cover the cost of fixing the work when the project is complete. Although the initial price is low, you could pay more if a lot of reworking or correction is needed, and then you don't save anything. Request assurances that the designer will spend the time necessary at the end, and specify that no one will be fully paid until the project is completed to your satisfaction.

Your best bet is to ask your designer to provide a full checklist of every action that's necessary to build your Web site and then to review that checklist as your site is being designed. To ensure that the review takes place, many people tie their designer's payments to the completion of the checklist. For example, when the designer can show that 50 percent of the items were completed, she receives 50 percent of the payment. This strategy helps prevent someone from receiving a full payment upfront and then quitting before completing all the agreed-on tasks.

Speeding up the process

Regardless of whom you choose to be your Web site designer, take the time to get the following "ducks in a row" to ensure that your designer is working as efficiently as possible — and costing you less in the end:

✦ **Prepare site specifications upfront.** First and foremost, you should have a clear idea of what your site should contain before your first meeting with the designer. Prepare a written road map of your site (as discussed in the section "Mapping Your Route to a Successful Site," earlier in this chapter) and notes on the various Web pages that you feel are essential to the your site. You can brainstorm with your Web designer about your Web site, but starting with your road map and making small changes is quicker and easier than if you're starting with a clean sheet of paper and spending hours writing down the basics.

✦ **Have your content already ready.** Make sure that the content you want for your site is already typed and available in electronic format. You're paying the designer by the hour, most likely, and you don't want to pay those rates for a skilled professional to type reams of data for you.

If necessary, hire a typist separately from your Web designer, and give that typist the sole responsibility of creating electronic text or Word document files with your information.

✦ **Establish firm milestones.** When you meet with your Web designer, work to establish rough dates for checking on the progress or establishing various milestones, which can be the end dates for specific portions of your site. Although some Web designers don't like specific hard-and-fast dates, you can reasonably expect to see portions of the project completed by certain dates. This way, you can see the progress of your site, make changes (if necessary) before everything is done, and ensure that the project is progressing.

✦ **Be readily available to assist the designer.** Make sure that you're available to answer questions and feed information to your Web site designer. Sometimes, the designer gets stuck while waiting days (or weeks!) to receive specific and necessary information from you. Even if you're incredibly detail oriented and spell out everything in advance, your designer sometimes needs to ask you a question, get approval for a change, or find out more information about your business before proceeding.

Keeping an eye on your business interests

When you hire a Web site design professional, the expectation is that you don't need to know how to use HTML or have any design skills. That is, after all, why you're hiring the professional. However, your design professional will have expectations about how you participate in the project, how your business operations are reflected in the site, and who owns the rights to the resulting site and its content. You must know your role in this process so that you can contribute to a successful site that contributes in turn to your business success.

Keep in mind the concept of scope when you're hiring someone to develop your site. *Scope,* in this case, refers to the amount of information and areas of concern that affect your Web site developer. She should operate within her role as specified in the contract or agreement between you and her.

Don't involve your developer in other aspects of your business or create expectations that she will contribute to your business plan. Keep the developer's activities focused on the job at hand so that she can deliver your site as specified.

Drawing up your contract or agreement with a Web site developer provides a learning exercise for both parties. Spell out exactly what you need, and specify whether other people, yourself included, are providing pieces of the puzzle (such as product databases) that interact with their work. This way, you both know the extent of the site developer's responsibilities.

Staying true to your business and customers

As the business owner, you determine how your site fulfills your business goals. Although an eager Web site developer might want to build something to highlight his specialties, they can conflict with your business purpose. If you're focusing on a pure e-commerce site with little extra content, you need to communicate that fact so that your designer doesn't hand back a content-rich, bloated site.

Know your customers and the audience you want your site to attract. Talented designers can build your site in different ways to appeal to different audiences, and you must point them in the right direction to "hook" the right people. Without any specific targets, your designer might produce something that speaks to every group but says nothing of value to any of them.

Supplying the designer with the right stuff

You can't just drive your car into a service station, toss the guy the keys and say "Fix it," and then walk away and expect to get your fully repaired car back hours later. The same situation applies to designing your Web site: You must provide the right information to your designer, and at the right time during the process, so that your site is built correctly from the start. Here are some tips:

✦ **Outline your business practices.** Your Web site designer isn't necessarily a businessperson and can't be expected to understand the intricacies of your business. You need to explain how your site should operate and why. If you have certain rules or exclusions for how you sell your goods and services, spell them out before development begins. For example, if you need to enforce a minimum order or disallow certain product combinations in the same order, those business rules must be a part of the proposal. Don't expect your designer to implicitly know how your business operates or understand its specific requirements.

✦ **Supply all relevant content.** At some point, you need to provide the content that will fill your Web site. This content consists of not only the names and descriptions of products but also any product databases, pictures, pricing information, or other data that has to interact with your site. Unless your designer is creating your company logo, you have to provide your logo, mission statement, contact information, and anything else that needs to appear on your site. Some of this information is spelled out in your agreement; other pieces, such as a customer database, can be handed in down the road, or even at the end of the process.

✦ **Make your systems available when needed.** Your developer also counts on having you and your computer systems available while building your site. This statement is especially true for more complex sites that operate on a Web server and communicate with programs such as a database, a supplier's inventory system, and a third-party payment solution. The quicker you can provide access, and the more documentation and notes you can provide about these interlocking programs, the quicker the designer can turn around and build you the correct Web site.

Clarifying who owns what

When you're hiring someone to design and build your Web site for you, establish the ownership of this work after it's complete. You might assume — because you're paying a professional to do the work — that this constitutes a work-for-hire agreement where you automatically own full rights to the resulting site and its content.

Never assume that you have a work-for-hire situation, and — as part of your contract — spell out the ownership rights of everything the Web developer provides to you. In addition, make sure that items such as photos, graphical images, and functions don't carry any unexpected royalties or licenses that you have to pay to use.

After the job is done, ask the Web designer for a copy of your Web site, either available online as a backup copy or on a CD-ROM. This way, if something happens to your Web server or you have a falling-out with your designer, you still have a full copy that you can use to keep your site running. Make sure that all the images, icons, logos, buttons, and other types of graphics — not just the HTML files — are included in your copy. If your Web designer also designed your company logo, ask for the logo in different file formats and sizes.

Chapter 4: Finding the Host with the Most

*O*ne of the many decisions you make when you're starting a Web site is where to host it. You might be wondering what a host does and why you even need one. A *host* site provides a place (a *server*) for your Web site and all the files that make up your site to reside. That host provides an address so that others can access it by using the Internet.

In this chapter, you discover the differences between a host and an Internet service provider, the different types of hosts and what they have to offer, legal agreements, and the decisions you make about becoming your own host.

Differentiating between an ISP and a Host

Try not to confuse a host with an Internet service provider. You need both! Allow us to explain the difference by using a car analogy.

Think of your Web site as a car. The color, interior materials, CD player, and sunroof are all parts of a car that are visible — and those visible elements are comparable to your Web site. Although the car's engine might be hidden away under the hood, it gives the car its power. You can rev it up with lots of horsepower to provide that extra oomph, even though the only folks likely to see this part of the car are you and your mechanic! Those under-the-hood works are the same as your hosting service. You can choose more disk space and other extras that give your site more power. If the engine isn't running, your car doesn't work; similarly, if your host's server is down, so is your Web site.

Where does your access to the Internet enter this picture? That's your driving lane, of course! You can stay in the right lane (the equivalent of dialup access) or hit the left lane for speed (broadband service). A tollbooth is the equivalent of the service provider that sells you access to the Net. As an added benefit, most ISPs provide both Internet access and Web hosting.

Determining What Makes the Difference for High-Performance Hosting

When you're gearing up for a high-performance Web site, you must decide how much horsepower — 'er, *hosting* power — you really need for the site. Horsepower translates into fast loading speeds, video and sounds playing without interruption, and images loading quickly. Consider these hosting options:

✦ **Disk space:** The size of your Web site files dictates how much disk space, or storage, you need from a host. If you use Flash, or plan to have a lot of pictures or graphics, count on needing more storage space. Typically, disk space is measured in megabytes (MB), and 500MB is enough for a basic commerce site. It's also no longer uncommon, though, for even a low-end hosting package to start out offering a minimum of 1 gigabyte (GB) of space.

✦ **Bandwidth:** This capability controls how much data, or information, a server can send and receive at any given moment. The higher the amount of bandwidth your host's server has, the more traffic (visitors) your site can support at one time. To give you an idea of how important bandwidth can be, consider this real-life example. When Victoria's Secret held its first lingerie fashion show over the Internet, a huge number of people simultaneously logged in to view the show. When the site's available bandwidth was exceeded, the site crashed, and many disappointed customers missed the provocative runway viewing! Most Web hosting companies offer a minimum of 5 to 10 gigabytes of space, but it's cost effective to add at least 150 GB.

✦ **Data transfers:** Every time someone views information from your site (including text, images, and video), that's considered to be a transfer of data. Think of it as traffic (or data) leaving your site. You can generally count on 1GB of data transfer being the same as 40,000 to 50,000 page views. Hosting plans generally allow for a specified number of transfers per month and then charge additional fees if you consistently exceed the limit.

✦ **Allowable languages:** Depending on which scripting language you use to create your site, you might have to find a host that supports that specific type. For instance, support of Hypertext Markup Language (HTML) is standard for all hosting services these days. Not long ago, people had a hard time finding a host that allowed Hypertext Preprocessor (PHP) scripting language, but it's now commonly supported.

If you hire an outside developer to create your Web site, be sure to ask which scripting language is being used to design the site. Or, ask whether you can specify which language is used. Then find hosting that supports it. Although this problem is rare, we have seen it happen. Better safe than sorry.

✦ **Database access:** If you plan to incorporate a database on your site (for inventory management, for example), the server must allow for it. Typically, you should ensure that MySQL or SQL (Standard Query Language) is available, which means that the server is set up to use this language to access and transfer information from your database. Don't be surprised if you're asked to pay extra for this feature.

✦ **E-commerce enabled:** Save yourself a headache later and confirm that your hosting plan supports e-commerce software, such as a shopping cart program, and that it supports the one you want to use. Many companies bundle hosting with a specific e-commerce solution (because they get a cut of the fees from those merchant programs). Either way, you're likely to pay more in hosting fees when you add an e-commerce feature to your site.

In addition to obtaining e-commerce software, you need a Secure Socket Layer (SSL) certificate. It ensures that you can safely transmit data over your Web site when customers make purchases. Check to see whether your hosting plan offers a *shared* SSL certificate, which covers all Web sites located on its server. Otherwise, expect to shell out more bucks to purchase an individual SSL for your site. If the hosting company doesn't offer the option, you can check www.verisign.com for more information on purchasing your own SSL.

✦ **Operating system:** Similar to your desktop computer, a server has an operating system, too. Deciding which one is right for you depends on what operating system you're using for your Web site. Two server options are available:

• *Windows:* When you're using Microsoft Access, Active Server Page (ASP), or any Microsoft-specific scripts, a Windows-based server is more suitable.

• *Linux:* This server software supports almost any type of scripting language. It's definitely a better match for your Web site if you use MySQL, PHP, or Perl.

The type of operating system you have on your own computer doesn't influence which server is best suited to host your Web site.

✦ **Redundancy and backups:** Let us get straight to the point — if your server crashes, you're up a creek without a paddle! You must back up your Web site, which means that your data is copied and saved to another location so that if one server goes down, your data is still available from the second source. Your hosting plan should include frequent, and preferably daily, backups to derail any impending crisis. To prevent backups from becoming necessary in the first place, you need a reliable server — not to mention a responsible host. When you're purchasing a hosting plan, determine which type of precautions a provider has in place to prevent its server from going down. Don't forget that the problem isn't always a matter of equipment failure. Power outages, maintenance checks, and other manmade or environmental conditions can cause a server, along with your Web site, to go out of commission. Redundancy is the best contingency plan because it means that your host has dual systems in place that allow information to remain accessible from a secondary source, even if the primary source goes out.

✦ **Web analysis:** To understand who your customers are and how they're using your site, chances are good that you need to know how many people visit your site each day, which parts of the site they frequent, and maybe even which other sites these visitors came from (based on IP addresses). To find out, you need some type of Web analysis software. If this feature isn't included with your hosting plan, ask whether any restrictions exist on the type of software you can use with the site, and whether you pay an additional charge for using it.

You can embed a small bit of HTML code into your home page (and other pages) and use Google Analytics for free.

✦ **Support:** No matter who you are, there comes a time when you need a little help. Although it's not easy to determine the quality of a host's support until you experience it, you can compare some basic features. Is support offered 24/7 (24 hours a day and seven days a week)? If not, what are the hours of the host's customer service center? Are both online support and phone support available? If online support is offered, make sure that it offers access to answers in real time, as opposed to waiting as long as 24 to 48 hours for a response to e-mail! Always confirm whether you're charged for live tech support and whether the charge is based on use by the minute, hour, or month. Those bills can rack up fast, even for a seemingly simple question!

✦ **Other:** A host can choose to make *beaucoup* (*lots* of) extra features available with your plan. If all other factors are equal, don't hesitate to compare this assortment of small prizes to find the host with the most! Mailboxes (for your e-mail) are a common feature that's always included, although the number of mailboxes offered varies greatly. Mailboxes might not even be a big deal to you. On the other end of the scale, though, competitive hosting plans now offer free tools that allow you to set up blogging, chat rooms, or discussion boards; easy content-management programs; polling or voting features that allow you to take surveys of your customers; calendars; and more — lots more!

Sorting Out Your Web Site Host Options

Although choosing a hosting plan can be overwhelming, after you begin researching all the options, you find that most hosts make comparing apples to apples easy. To ensure competitiveness, hosts often break down their plans into several categories. With a quick glance, you can determine whether a plan has all the elements you want.

Basic, or *starter,* hosting packages offer bare-bones necessities — enough to get, and keep, a simple site with minimal images up and running. When this level is all you need, you end up making your decision strictly on price. (We see it happen all the time.) What we consider to be the other *forced* option is when you require e-commerce capabilities. No matter what, you have to choose the plan that provides for this need. (Typically, no more than one e-commerce hosting plan is available from one source — so you need to shop around to get the best deal.) Again, when you're selecting among providers, your decision comes down to price and which e-commerce program is partnered with (or offered by) each host.

Mid-level plans usually leave the most room for uncertainty. These hosting options vary the most by both price and available features. To overcome indecision, make a list that prioritizes which items you need and which you're most likely to set up and use in the first three months of your site going live. Then again, budgetary decisions might rule in the end!

One more determining factor is the geographic location of the host. Although your site can be hosted by a company located anywhere in the world, its proximity offers a few advantages and disadvantages, according to its scope:

+ **Local:** Signing up with a company right in your backyard should truly be a consideration. Among the benefits of this arrangement are that you can schedule an on-site appointment with the provider and check out its facilities for yourself. Because you also typically are assigned to a specific salesperson, you have a primary point of contact who ends up knowing a lot about your business and its needs. This arrangement can be helpful, especially in the beginning, when you're making decisions about which features you do and don't need. The biggest disadvantage of this arrangement is price. Local hosting companies are often smaller than their larger, national online counterparts and cannot be as competitive. Additionally, if you live in a rural area or a small city, you might not have many — or any — locals to choose from!

+ **National:** Whether you host with a company in Topeka or Timbuktu, it usually doesn't matter whether it's half a world away from you. Although you might not get personal attention or an up-close look at its facilities, you can find some real deals. Not only are you likely to find palatable prices, but researching your options is also a breeze. Visit a host's Web site, click the link to show pricing, and — bam! — you have the 411 (that's *information*) to make a quick decision.

Here's one word of advice for when you're shopping nationally: If the company isn't a large, recognized provider, take extra precautions. When you're using any online service you're not familiar with, do your homework first. Check with the Better Business Bureau for complaints, and call to talk with a sales representative to get a better feel for how the company operates. Do the same with local providers; an unstable company can easily leave you without a connection!

Putting the Long-Term Contract in the Past

An important factor in choosing a host is the nature of your contractual obligations. Long-term contracts are a distant memory when it comes to hosting a Web site. If a host that you're considering requires this type of contract, consider other options first. You're likely to find an equally good deal with another host that requires nothing more than a monthly commitment.

Don't get excited yet: You're not free and clear of all rules and obligations. You still must abide by certain terms of agreement. You might have to pay a small setup fee, along with the first few months of service in advance, none of which is refundable. Or, you might be required to provide 30 days' notice before terminating service. More often than not, you pay monthly fees in advance of using the service, so plan ahead.

Because you always sign a paper agreement or click to accept an electronic document, a *contract* is still in place. Although it might not bind you to a block of payments over a specified period, it specifies the terms of your relationship with the host.

Always read the fine print of any contract, terms of agreement, or other legally binding document. You may find that some contracts limit what you can and cannot do on a Web site.

Serving Yourself: Don't Overlook Other Server Options

One decision you eventually have to make when you're selecting a host is whether you want to skip a hosting plan and rent your own dedicated server. In that case, your partnership with a particular hosting plan might require you to sign a contract — or two. To help you better understand what you might be getting into, we explain the different types of server options:

✦ **Shared server:** The hosting plans we explain earlier in this chapter are examples of how you use a shared server. In essence, you're using the same computer (or server) along with many other Web sites. Although that arrangement translates into lower costs, you have less flexibility in the types of applications you can run, because the server is configured with the same settings and applications to all who use it.

✦ **Dedicated server:** Gaining complete control over the type of server you use and the programs you install on it requires that you have a dedicated server. As its name implies, the bandwidth, memory, and storage space on this computer are dedicated entirely to *you*. You also typically gain root access, which means that you can configure the server to your specifications. This more expensive option is often used when you need to run special programs or when you have multiple sites or extremely high-traffic sites. The downside of using a dedicated server (in addition to the expense) is that you're responsible for installing software, handling regular maintenance, and fixing any unexpected problems or system failures that occur. We recommend tackling this server arrangement only if you're an experienced Web master or computer technician.

✦ **Co-location:** You might like the idea of owning a server but aren't in a position to manage or repair any problems that arise. If that's the case, co-location might be the answer. You provide the hardware (or the computer) and lease space *(rack space)* for it with a host company. The host company then installs the server and ensures that you have consistent access to the Internet, which is a big advantage of co-location. Depending on your physical office space, this situation is ideal for another reason: A server requires certain environmental conditions, such as being kept in a dry, cool (or temperature controlled) room, and co-location providers maintain data centers that meet or exceed these conditions. Because you own the equipment and are responsible for all other aspects of maintaining it, this option also requires that you have advanced skills.

✦ **Managed server:** Sometimes referred to as a virtual server, this option is a compromise to a dedicated server. Unlike with co-location, you lease the equipment, and the hosting company takes care of most server functions, including installing software and updates; handling security and maintenance; and acting as a troubleshooter for problems. If you have specific needs for your site and aren't proficient in maintaining a server, managed servers work well.

✦ **Virtual dedicated server:** Another take on limited maintenance but increased flexibility is what some hosts refer to as *virtually dedicated*. As with shared hosting, others use the server with you, but access is limited to a small number of customers. You gain dedicated space and control because the host uses walls or partitions on the computer to separate it into several virtual dedicated servers. Although your site is on a shared server, it has been configured to appear as a standalone, dedicated server with no other users.

As with hosting, the price and the exact services offered with each server package vary. And, because you're usually required to sign a long-term lease agreement, make sure that you understand what the price covers and what the responsibilities are for both you and the host company. Also, make sure that cancellation terms are clearly spelled out so that you can get out of the agreement if you're unhappy with the provider.

Chapter 5: Writing Content that Search Engines Want to See

One of us has written Web copy (that is, written content) for companies that sell everything from socks to ski boats. As varied as these companies and their products are, they all have one thing in common: Just like you, they use the Internet to sell products or services.

To achieve that goal, they depend on someone else to find the right words for their Web sites. Don't worry: When you're creating content for your own site, you don't have to hire a professional writer. You have to understand, though, what turns ordinary words into good Web copy. This chapter is devoted to helping you turn plain words into ones that sell.

Words Are Words — Right? Wrong!

How do you know what works when it comes to describing your products, welcoming your customers, and engaging in any other communication that requires the written word? Effective Web copy helps you accomplish these four objectives:

✦ Help search engines notice your site.

✦ Convince customers to visit your site.

✦ Elicit in your customers a desire to act (to buy stuff!).

✦ Entice customers to come back and do it all over again (buy more stuff!).

Now that you know what earns the official stamp of approval on your Web copy, it's time to start writing. You should know that not all words are created equal. Some words pack a wallop when they're delivered. Others hang in the air unnoticed.

With millions of words in the English language, picking the *right* ones for your Web site might seem daunting. Not so. Writing for the Web is easy if you use words, phrases, and sentences that are

✦ **Attention-getters:** *Bam!* Chef Emeril Lagasse knows how to get a viewer's attention. You have to do the same online. Visitors to your Web site are unforgiving. If you don't catch their attention quickly, they desert you in a heartbeat. Choose words, especially in headlines, that command attention and pique interest — all in a blink of the eye.

You have fewer than eight seconds to attract and keep the attention of your customer. That's how long the average person looks at a Web page before deciding to move on. The decision your customer makes to stay or leave depends on the information you provide. Make that information

- *Meaningful:* Don't waste words. Be brief and choose words that matter.

- *Easy to read:* Use short sentences. Don't bog down readers with too much detail.

Give customers a choice in seeking more in-depth information. If someone wants *all* the details, you can provide either a hypertext link to another page or a pop-up window. There, visitors can find complete product descriptions, case studies, or other background research. For those who want it, you make it easy to obtain.

✦ **Self explanatory:** Abbreviations, catchy product names, and industry lingo are fine. Don't assume, though, that customers will understand on the first read-through. When you use these types of words, define them in parentheses or link to a pop-up window that contains the complete information. Be *clear.*

✦ **Simple:** Say what you mean. Don't make your customers read between the lines or try to guess what you intended.

Getting Ready to Write for the Web

There's little doubt that words can affect the people who read them. Words are catalysts that move people to action. With that in mind, what do you want your customers to do when they visit your Web site? If you said "Buy stuff," think again. That's a given. You need to be more specific. Specifically, which *action* do you want customers to take when they're visiting your site? If you can answer that question, you can write words that sell.

Understanding who and why

To start writing for the Web, you have to determine these factors:

✦ **Your audience:** Before you write a single word of copy, take a moment to understand whom you're writing for. Who are your potential customers? Why are they visiting your site? What are they searching for — information or products? Specifically, what problem are they trying to solve, and how can you help them solve it?

✦ **Your customers' motivation:** In addition to knowing about your customers, you need to understand what motivates them to take action. Do they want to be entertained? Educated? Are their purchases based on emotional decisions? Or, do they simply want enough facts to validate their buying decisions? To some degree, their motivation might be dictated by what type of product you're offering, the age of your target customer, or the standard offering within your industry. Even so, understanding motivation helps dictate your writing style and the words you use. It also guides the tone of your writing. Your tone can be serious, whimsical, or no-nonsense. Your tone itself can motivate people to action.

✦ **Your customers' solution:** When you understand your customer's desires, needs, and motivations, you can provide a solution. Simply naming your product or showing a picture of it doesn't do the trick. You need to explain *how* your specific product solves your customer's problem and tell why your product provides the best solution. If it's the most efficient, cost-effective, or reliable one on the market, let the customer know. They're all part of the solution you offer. And, these benefits influence a customer's final decision to buy.

Okay, so you're convinced that your product answers the needs of your customer, and you're pretty sure that you know which features move customers to action. What else is there? Well, the next part of the equation is packaging the information in a way that customers can easily accept.

Understanding that packaging is everything

The first part of what we refer to as content packaging is *specifying the outcome* you want. Consider that every single page of your Web site serves a specific purpose. For example, a home page might convince a visitor to stay long enough to click a specific product link. Or, a source of information might encourage your customer to register as a member of your site. After you define the expected outcome for a page, it becomes easier to determine whether your content serves that purpose.

Another key to packaging your Web site information is making the content skimmable. Designing *skimmable* text simply means that you allow a customer to look over chunks of data rather than have to read every single word to get your message. People have short attention spans when they're surfing the Web. Reading content off a computer screen can strain their eyesight, too. That's why scanning content becomes the preferred method for online reading. By using a few simple tricks, you can still draw a customer's eye to details, even if they're speed reading.

Follow these suggestions to make your text scannable:

✦ Use short paragraphs.

✦ Highlight, or **boldface,** important words and phrases.

✦ Use bullets (like the ones in this list) to call out details.

✦ Include hypertext links to draw attention to a source of more information.

✦ Increase the font size of text to put emphasis on certain words.

✦ Incorporate graphics or images that complement the text and call attention to it.

 Eyetracking research is a popular method of studying how people read content on Web pages. Some researchers have noticed particular patterns and believe that users skim important content in an "F" shaped pattern. Go to Eyetrack III at www.poynterextra.org/eyetrack2004/index.htm to find details about this pattern and how to apply it to your own Web pages to make your Web copy more effective.

Getting organized

After you create killer copy that's skimmable, you're ready to transfer your final thoughts onto your Web page. Wait! You must complete one more step: Organize the information on the page in a way that makes sense. Your message should be simple, concise, and easy to understand. The most important factor is the order in which the information appears on a page. The text should lead visitors to take action (the specific outcome you identified earlier).

Figure 5-1 illustrates how you can incorporate these content strategies on the home page of your site. Because the desired outcome on this page is to have customers click a particular link to obtain more information about services, the content is organized in a way that leads customers to that final action — clicking to move to the next page.

Making a list and checking it twice

A single Web page can have an unlimited amount of information and choices, of course — filled with lots of links, buttons, and page sections. Your visitors can then choose from several possible actions on that one page. What do you do then?

You have to make a choice: Decide which actions take priority. You can do so by following these simple steps:

1. **Make a list of all possible decisions visitors can make when they're viewing your Web page.**

2. **Prioritize the different choices or actions, from most to least desired.**

   For example, it might be more important for visitors to click a page filled with products than to click a link to sign up for a newsletter.

3. **Place the content on the page in such a way that customers view the information in your preferred order (according to your prioritized ranking).**

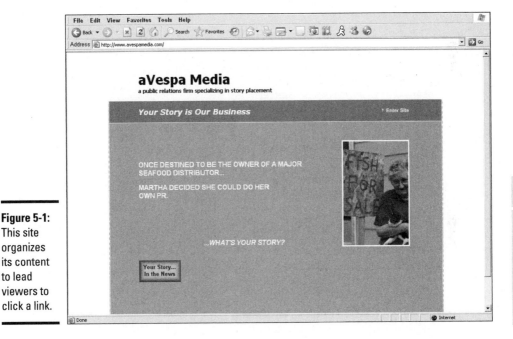

Figure 5-1:
This site organizes its content to lead viewers to click a link.

Figure 5-2 shows examples of two different ways to organize the content when you want multiple outcomes for a single page. In the first example, the goal is to encourage visitors to use the on-site search engine for opportunities of interest to them and to also lead visitors to click specific links on the site. The second example uses a strategy that puts more emphasis on having visitors view advertising first and then provides the search capability as an option. The site achieves this goal in the positioning of the various components (the ads and search function, for example) along with text placement on the page.

Figure 5-2:
Prioritize how you want content organized on a page.

Visitors to a Web site read information by starting at the top of the page and moving downward. As they do with printed offline text, they also read from left to right. Therefore, content you place at the top and to the left of your pages usually is noticed first.

Moved to Purchase: Turning Words into Action

After you identify the actions you want customers to take, it's time to choose the words that elicit those responses. Choose words and phrases that accomplish these tasks:

✦ **Evoke a feeling.** Decisions to make a purchase are often influenced by emotions. Words that help conjure those emotions and feelings are more likely to get a response. Keep in mind, however, that someone shopping for plain paper napkins isn't emotionally connected to the purchase. In this case, a straightforward explanation of the product probably works best.

✦ **Grab attention.** Some words naturally cause people to momentarily pause when they read them. *STOP! Don't go further until you read the next sentence,* for example, is an effective way to get your customer's attention long enough to introduce the next level of information. And don't forget *FREE!* — one of the most popular attention grabbers.

✦ **Identify a problem.** Customers are looking for products and services that answer a need. They're drawn to words that describe the problems they're trying to solve.

✦ **Contain buzzwords.** Every industry and consumer market has key words or phrases that are part of that market's lingo, such as *plug-and-play.* When you talk the language, your customer is more likely to hear what you're saying and respond.

✦ **Offer assurance.** Customers want to feel good about their decisions to buy your products or use your services. When you use words that offer comfort or reinforce the buying decision, customers are often encouraged to make a purchase.

✦ **Request a purchase.** If you don't ask a customer to make a purchase, your chances of having the customer make one are greatly diminished. This type of wording is often referred to as a *call to action.* The words or phrases ask the customer to make a decision at that point. A call to action is particularly effective when it immediately follows words that offer assurance.

Use the following list of words and phrases to grab a customer's attention, provide assurance, or ask a customer to take action.

Grab Attention	*Provide Assurance*	*Take Action*
Stop	Guaranteed	Buy now
Listen	Trial version	Order here
Urgent	Risk free	Click to order
Sale	No risk	Get more information
Half off	Free sample	Request information
Clearance	No obligation	Contact us
Reduced	Money-back guarantee	E-mail us
While supplies last	Success stories	Join today
Almost sold out	Testimonials	Subscribe
Secret	Loyal customers	Buy now, pay later
Confidential	Quality	Act now
Hot	Validated or tested	
Limited time only	Approved	
Proven	Referrals	

Making unsubstantiated or false earnings claims or false promises about products or services can subject you to fines and prosecution. For more information and legal guidelines, visit the Federal Trade Commission at www.ftc.gov.

Choosing Words that Search Engines Notice

Just as we suggest that you use industry buzzwords to talk to your customers, you can use these same types of words to "talk" to search engines.

Think about how search engines work to help promote your site. A search engine starts by classifying your site, or putting it into a group of similar sites. Then it ranks your site depending on how relevant it is for that particular category of sites. That level of relevancy makes the search engine useful when potential customers search for particular terms.

When you're ready to gain a thorough understanding of how to master search engines, check out Book VI, Chapter 6. For now, we simply want to make you aware of the importance of thinking about search engine rankings while you're writing the initial content for your site.

When you're writing content that's search-engine-friendly, remember these two brief rules:

+ **Think like a customer.** Scatter buzzwords, industry-specific phrases, and words that specifically relate to your type of business throughout your site's content. Incorporate the words that customers would use in conducting a search on Google or Yahoo!.

+ **Avoid saturation.** Keywords should be a natural part of your content, and not overly obvious. For instance, if you were to write just three relevant phrases repeatedly, the search engines would flag that as a problem and probably lower your ranking or throw you out of the listings.

Before writing your content, do your own search using a popular search term for your product or service. Then visit the top five sites that are listed in the returned rankings. Notice which words or phrases your competitors use, and consider finding a logical place for them in your content.

Chapter 6: Lights, Camera, Action! Taking Your Site Live

*A*fter taking the trouble to design a site, fill it with quality content, and find the perfect place to host it, you would think that that's the end of the story. We don't want to disappoint you, but you have to deal with another major phase before you launch.

In this chapter, we break this final stage into smaller segments to make it easy to follow. For one moment, let us summarize what all those segments mean in layman's terms: Test, test, and test again! Then, and only then, blast off!

Some Things to Know Before You Start Uploading

Both *launching* and *uploading* your site are terms used to represent the point when you finally make a site viewable by the public over the Internet. Before you upload your site to the Net, though, it should be fully functional. Your site design and content should be complete, your navigational tools should work properly, and all parts of it, even the smallest parts and pieces, must be in place and working.

Okay, you can throw caution to the wind and launch an incomplete site. We don't advise it, though. Why not? For one thing, it isn't professional. Not to mention that your customers become easily frustrated when form falls short of function.

An incomplete site diminishes your business's credibility.

The point is that a haphazardly constructed and prematurely launched Web site can cause you to lose customers. If a section or feature of your site isn't fully developed or functional, frustrated customers may never bother coming back again.

If you take away anything from this chapter, remember these two points:

✦ Fully complete your site before launching it.

✦ Make darn sure that every element works.

You should know about a few other helpful concepts before launching:

✦ **Little details count.** Bring out the magnifying glass when you're reviewing your site for mistakes before launching. Check for misspellings, broken links, malfunctioning applications and widgets, and other problem points.

✦ **Some functions are limited until after the launch.** A few features might fully function only after your site is live. For instance, forms frequently can be activated only after the site is up for good. Remember to check all forms after the site goes live and correct problems immediately.

✦ **Third-party data takes time.** If you use a newsfeed or syndicated content or another type of data from third parties, it might not be instantly available when the site launches. Sometimes a delay of several hours, or even a full day, occurs before you're entered into a customer database, the switch is flipped, and you go live. If the information isn't accessible after two business days, contact the service provider to report the problem.

✦ **Rankings aren't immediate (or guaranteed).** After your site goes live, you can submit it to be reviewed and possibly included in various search engines. (We go into the art of optimization in detail in Book VI, Chapter 6.) Right now, all we ask is that you remember that it takes a while for a search engine to scan and rank your site after it's up, so don't expect it to show up in the search engines right away. Even after your site is *spidered,* or reviewed, by the search engines, it may not appear anywhere near the top 100 listings. Initially, it may be that only people who type your URL in the Address field or your company name in a search engine will find your site.

✦ **Automated Web builders are different from designers.** If you launch (or your Web designer launches) your site, it's immediate. In other words, all the files are uploaded to the server at one time. Within minutes, you're finished and the site is on the Net. With automated Web builders or template programs, you might be required to publish your site page by page to the Internet rather than upload a complete file. (You can remove a page later if you see a mistake.) Be careful, though: Correcting problems to buttons or to the site's menu bar is sometimes difficult after the site is published.

Here's one last thing you should know: Sites look different to different people. We're not talking about personal style preferences. Instead, realize that the code or language used to design your site appears differently when it's viewed with various browsers. Your job is to test your content with every browser you can get your hands on and minimize the differences so that the site looks its best in any browser. In the next section, we suggest ways you can test for optimal conditions before launching your site.

Taking the Compatibility Test: Testing Screen Resolutions, Browsers, and Platforms

Compatibility testing is the fun part of launching a site. Any slight variation between code, and the way each browser interprets the code, makes a noticeable difference on the screen.

To illustrate this point, Figure 6-1 shows how command code displays differently when displayed in various browsers. Sometimes the differences can be subtle, and a matter of how much information displays on a typical screen. In this example, we captured shots of a site's home page in some of the most popular browsers, including Internet Explorer 7.0, Mozilla, and Google Chrome. When comparing screen shots, you want to not only ensure that all your code displays properly, but that the most important information is readily visible within the screen area, without visitors having to scroll down the page to view the information.

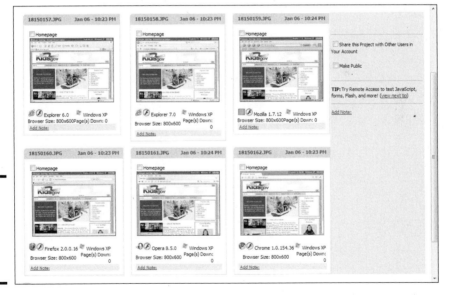

**Book III
Chapter 6**

Lights, Camera, Action! Taking Your Site Live

Figure 6-1:
Compare your site in more than one browser.

Many professional developers suggest staying away from FrontPage when designing your site. For instance, although Internet Explorer reads FrontPage with no problem (because both products are from Microsoft), FrontPage doesn't have a good reputation for displaying well in other browsers. Lots of extra code is often already built in, and sorting through it to remove what you don't need (especially if that extra code is the source of browser compatibility problems) is difficult.

Checking it out

How do you check for browser discrepancies? The obvious answer is to install every possible browser (or at least the mainstream ones) on your computer and run a trial version of your site in each one. Because you can download browsers for free, the only cost to you is your time.

Be sure to look for glaring inconsistencies that make your information difficult to read, prevent images from loading, or omit information completely.

Another issue to test for is screen resolution, or how your site looks in different resolution settings. (Don't confuse this term with the physical measurement of your monitor's screen.) By *resolution,* we mean the number of pixels (or miniscule dots) that make up an image on the computer screen. Standard resolution settings are 640 x 480, 600 x 400, and 1024 x 768. Within each resolution is a designated amount of viewable space, which can affect how your Web site looks on a computer. Computer users can choose which resolution to use on their computers.

Figure 6-2 displays a chart from AnyBrowser.com that shows examples of different resolutions and the viewable space in each one. Now is the time to check your work! We recommend adjusting your screen to each standard resolution to see how your site appears to visitors using that same resolution.

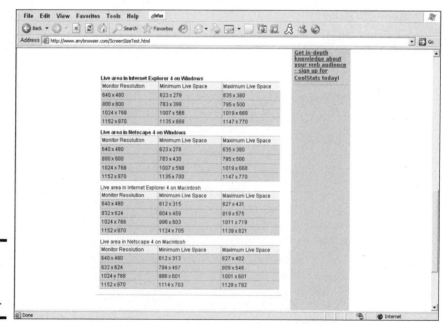

Figure 6-2:
View sites
in different
resolutions.

Testing on Mac, Windows, or whatever

If checking for browser compatibility and screen resolution isn't enough already, another major element is involved in testing your site. You have to test your site on different operating systems. For example, you might wonder what your site looks like using Macintosh OS X 10.4 (Tiger) when you designed it on a PC using Windows XP. And, we haven't even mentioned Linux!

Not everyone has access to multiple computers and operating systems to test for this feature. Instead, use a site that offers this service remotely (over the Internet) for free or for a minimal fee. BrowserCam.com (`www.browser cam.com`) uses screen captures to let you see your site on any operating system and in any browser.

Keeping people in mind

Even if you know the basic information to test for when you're launching your site, you always have to consider a growing list of issues. For instance, your site should be accessible for disabled viewers, according to the World Wide Web Consortium (W3C) Web Content Accessibility Guidelines (WCAG) and other government regulations. Complying with these guidelines involves using slightly different coding, color contrasts, and text options for images, for instance.

Web-based services, such as CynthiaSays (`www.cynthiasays.com`) or WAVE (`http://wave.webaim.org`), can quickly scan your site to confirm accessibility. Both services check the code behind your design as well as the viewable areas to check for proper functionality, according to WCAG standards.

Although you might not want to hear this advice right now, you should routinely test your site for these and other issues, long after you pass the initial launch stage. Keeping your site current and easy to use for the largest possible number of people is standard in the world of online business.

Taking a Trial Run

When a major company releases a software program, game, or Web site, it often has a limited distribution in a beta version. *Beta* means that the work is in test mode and is subject to change. A beta test, or a product in *beta mode,* is typically released to a large segment of the general public. As for *your* site, we suggest showing a beta version to a limited group of users in a trial run.

**Book III
Chapter 6**

**Lights, Camera,
Action! Taking
Your Site Live**

These users include (ideally) friends, family members, and a few prospective customers who are willing to provide you with honest feedback. Upload the site and run a live trial version of it for a day or two. Everyone then has a chance to visit the site several times before you take it down again for final changes.

Your beta users should be on the lookout for common errors you might have missed, features or links that don't work correctly, graphics that load improperly — or not at all — and the general appearance and overall ease of use of the site. (For instance, the site should be intuitive to visitors, and the names of the page links and buttons must make sense to other people, not just to you.)

Your site launch checklist

Before you push that last button to make your Web site live, be sure to check off each box (as it applies to you) on this list:

❑ My site map (or the layout and structure of all my Web pages) is complete.

❑ The site map matches my Web pages — exactly.

❑ Each Web site page is displayed and is fully accessible.

❑ Every link throughout the site works properly and takes me to the appropriate page.

❑ All graphics and photos are loaded quickly and completely, and the images are crisp and clean.

❑ My content is free of misspellings and grammatical errors.

❑ Pricing information and product or service descriptions are correct.

❑ Pages with online forms or registration information function when I press the Submit button, and the information is sent (in the specified format) to the designated point of contact.

❑ Text boxes or drop-down boxes on forms and other pages work correctly.

❑ Buttons for top-level menus work. (Be sure to ensure that these buttons, like the one that returns users to your home page, function properly on every single page.)

❑ Special commands that are spelled out with coding language (HTML or PHP, for example) show up properly when the site loads.

❑ My credit card processor or other payment service option is in place and working.

❑ All e-commerce-related functions, such as my shopping cart, operate correctly.

❑ I've included any appropriate membership icons, logos, or emblems (such as the ones used by members of the Better Business Bureau or Chamber of Commerce).

❑ I tested the site for browser compatibility and screen resolution.

❑ I tested the site using a dialup connection and a broadband connection.

❑ My contact information (e-mail address or phone number) is clearly displayed, and I made them easy to find.

❑ The copyright symbol and current year are prominently displayed at the bottom of every page.

Three, Two, One — Take Off!

NASA launches its space shuttle missions at certain times of the day, and under the most forgiving weather conditions. Although we guarantee that the weather outside isn't a concern for your launch, certain times are better than others for sending your site out on the Net.

Particularly when you're using a freelance Web site designer, you should have input about when your site launches. Because that person usually sends the files to the server on your behalf, request that your site be launched early in the week. That way, if a problem surfaces, you have plenty of time (during the workweek) to fix it. Frustration is quick to set in when you launch a site on Friday afternoon and discover a problem shortly thereafter that you have to live with for the whole weekend.

When you use an outside developer, you're asked to sign a waiver when the project is finished. The waiver says that your site is accurate and that all requested changes were made. You get a sense of finality when your site comes off a project-management list. Sign the waiver only when you're completely satisfied! The Web developer is then released from additional work after the site is launched. If your provider charges for maintenance (or changes) to the site, the signed waiver signals that the provider can switch you from the development stage to the stage of paying for Web maintenance, which can cost you.

Avoid launching the day before a long holiday weekend begins, regardless of whether you or someone else designs your site. Of course, larger Web sites might find that launching a site over a holiday is advantageous. The slower period gives the company an extended shot at a trial run — and one more opportunity to correct errors. If a site has been well marketed, the opposite effect can occur: It can be a hit by a large amount of traffic because more people are home and spending time on the Net. However, unless you spend a lot of money and effort investing in prelaunch publicity and advertising, high traffic flow shouldn't be an issue for you at the beginning — holiday or not.

Nothing has to be forever on the Web. If you discover a mistake after your Web site goes up, don't panic. You can easily and instantaneously make a correction. The Web is certainly not static, so updates are usually a snap.

Plenty of excitement should accompany your site's sendoff to the World Wide Web. This major accomplishment is the start of something potentially lucrative. Celebrate!

Book IV
Online and Operating

Pick a time for the mail carrier to
pick up your outgoing packages.

Contents at a Glance

Chapter 1: Determining Your Revenue Model

In This Chapter

✔ Acquiring and reselling tangible products

✔ Finding revenue sharing opportunities with affiliate sites

✔ Selling your professional services

✔ Distributing information for profit

✔ Creating a revenue stream by placing online advertisements

✔ Incorporating multiple sources of revenue for a healthy bottom line

Face it: Whenever you start an online business, you must answer one question before you answer any others — how will you make money?

You can have the most brilliant, original, or quirky idea ever conceived, but if you don't have a viable plan to bring in dollars, the concept doesn't hold water. The good news is that, with the Web entering its second decade, a number of viable ways to make money have emerged. In this chapter, we break down the various revenue models on which you can base your online business.

Selling Tangible Products

A natural choice for making money online is to sell some sort of product. You might already have a fantastic product, or you might need to search for a mix of products that you can buy and resell to others over the Web. Either way, selling a tangible product over the Internet has proven to be a successful online earnings model ever since e-commerce began taking off in the early 1990s.

Projecting how you'll make a profit

When you deal in tangible goods and services, the question of how to make a profit boils down to a simple four-word phrase: "Buy low, sell high." As entrepreneurs have known for thousands of years, you have to sell something for more than you originally paid for it in order to make money. Even if you're able to catch fish from the sea and sell them to big food suppliers, or if you're able to create works of art with the fruit of your talent, you still incur business expenses. A fisherman has to pay for a boat, fuel, and equipment. An artist has to buy paint, brushes, and canvas. No matter what you sell, you have to project how much you're going to spend in acquiring or producing the product, and how much you can reasonably get for it in the marketplace. The difference is your profit.

Before you even spend your first penny buying or producing tangible products to sell, take a moment and ask yourself some basic questions that will help you project your potential revenue:

✦ How much does producing or purchasing my product cost?

✦ How much is my overhead: the cost for utilities, rent, salaries, and transportation, for example?

✦ Can I price the product in such a way that it covers my overhead and purchasing costs and still remains competitive with similar products?

✦ Will added shipping costs skew (or diminish) that competitive price point?

✦ What volume of products do I need to sell each month in order to reach my desired profit margins?

✦ How much traffic (how many visitors) must I drive to my site *and* convert to customers in order to reach those sales goals?

✦ How much do I need to spend on marketing to attract that level of traffic?

Write all the projected expenses and income on a piece of paper. Do some in-depth thinking about whether you can make your business plan (that's what this is, after all) work successfully. If your profit isn't enough to make a living or at least make enough for your immediate needs, make adjustments now. That might mean finding more products, raising prices, or reducing expenses (or all of these). Run the numbers past any experienced businesspeople among your family or friends who can serve as mentors.

Knowing whether a product-based revenue model will meet your financial needs is difficult to know for certain — a lot depends on the product itself. In Book IV, Chapter 6, we show you how to research and further test your product ideas — whether you created the item or are buying products for resale.

Manufacturing and selling your own goods

In terms of sheer profit margin, you can rarely do better than creating your own products for little or no money and selling them online. If you're creative and enterprising, you can sell your own work by using e-commerce sites, auction sites such as eBay, and Web sites that have been set up to market a particular type of item (such as ArtQuest, at `www.artquest.com`, where artists can list their own works for sale).

There's virtually no limit on the kinds of items you can sell online. They range from delicately smocked dresses for children to funky, hand-strung beaded jewelry. Or, maybe you want to develop an original board game or peddle custom-designed iPod skins. Rest assured that all these products have a place on the innovative Internet.

As you might expect, a few characteristics give your personal handiwork a leg up on the competition, including

✦ **It's a quality product.** Without exception, consumers expect a product that's worthy of its price tag. When you're creating your own products, you have total control over quality. Make sure your designs are finished and your workmanship is of a high level before you put items up for sale.

✦ **It's original.** If your handmade product is a unique twist on a mass-marketed type of product, you can have rewards. Internet shoppers are always looking for products that are somewhat unique or slightly different from the items available in most retail stores.

✦ **It fits a niche.** Maybe your handmade product isn't completely unique but is part of a specialized, hard-to-find group of products (such as personalized cellphone or iPod cases or cases for fountain pens). Narrowing your product's appeal by audience is a good way to increase revenue potential. We discuss niche markets more in depth in Book X.

✦ **It has a built-in customer base.** Perhaps your product is designed to appeal to a specific group of people, such as a religious group that makes woven altar cloths for churches. Having a clearly identifiable existing customer base that you can market to makes selling your product that much easier.

When you're making a product from scratch, the way in which you earn money can vary. If your product meets one or more of these descriptors, chances are good that you will do well. At least you're off to a good start!

Buying tangible goods and selling them online

Even if you don't have the creative ability to craft your own products, you still have plenty of options for making money online. In fact, the overwhelming majority of online entrepreneurs are people who buy tangible goods at low prices and sell them online for a profit. You can either sell directly from your own Web site or allow another Web site to market your products.

Selling directly online means that customers come directly to you (by way of your Web site) to buy an item. There's no middleman. The marketing, publicity, and fulfillment are all up to you — in other words, it's a lot of work, but the rewards can be great. If you don't have any experience selling, it makes sense to allow other Web sites, such as eBay, to market your products. The

Web site brings you customers and provides you with systems for creating sales descriptions and receiving payments. Your host Web site charges fees for its services, but you don't have to do all the work.

Whether you sell directly or sign up with another Web site to sell your goods, you have to find a source for your products. Three of the most popular options — finding your own merchandise; finding a wholesale supplier; and finding a drop shipper — are described in the sections that follow.

Finding your own merchandise

Many people who sell online begin at home, or close to home. They begin by cleaning out their closets, their garages, and their attics. They sell off the extra merchandise in their own homes. Then they move on to the homes of their relatives.

Others scour flea markets, estate sales, garage sales, secondhand stores, dollar stores, and many other marketplaces, looking for treasures they can sell online at a profit. Sellers who are lucky enough to find a reliable source of desirable merchandise can make part or perhaps even all of their income. The problem is that the time spent searching, hauling, and bringing home the items to sell is considerable. Not only that, but there's the question of where to store all the products and the boxes used to ship them: You either have to delegate a room in your house for this purpose or rent warehouse space. It's hard to build up a sufficient inventory to make a living at selling online.

Buying wholesale

Owners of traditional retail stores are accustomed to buying their inventories wholesale or becoming distributors for particular products or brands. The same option is available for your online store. When you buy wholesale, you purchase products at a discounted price and then resell them to your customer base at a marked-up price. You're responsible for ensuring that these tasks are completed:

+ **Purchase inventory in bulk.** You can't buy just one clock radio. You have to commit to a whole case (or several cases) to get a discount.

+ **Warehouse the inventory.** The wholesaler doesn't let you keep all those cases of products at his place. You're expected to store the inventory you purchase for your site, even if you have to keep it around for several months. You have to find space for it in your home or rent a warehouse, and because online merchants tend to buy higher quantities of merchandise at wholesale than they do scouring flea markets, this proposition can turn into an expensive one.

+ **Ship the products to your customers.** Because you keep the merchandise at your place of business, you have to handle packaging and shipping each item (unless you hire employees to help you). See Book IV, Chapter 7, to find out more about packaging and shipping your products.

✦ **Handle returns and exchanges from customers.** If a customer is unhappy with a product or the item is damaged, it has to be shipped back to you to be dealt with accordingly.

The drawbacks for a small online business are probably obvious. Among the biggest is that your out of-pocket cash commitment is hefty. If you're just starting out, you take a financial hit right off the bat.

Of course, you have to have a place to store all these products, too. A garage or spare bedroom might suffice for a while, but eventually you need to rent other storage space. That overhead expense certainly eats into your profitability! Many online merchants find that that the third option that's listed for sourcing merchandise to sell — drop shippers — enables them to market their products without having to deal with having to store and handle inventory.

When you purchase merchandise from a wholesaler, you typically must provide some form of proof that you're a legitimate business (and that you're not buying for personal use). Wholesalers might ask you for a state-issued reseller's certificate or a federal tax ID number. And, if the wholesaler doesn't require these items, you might not be paying truly wholesale prices!

Going inventory free: Drop shipping

For many online entrepreneurs, the ideal setup is working with a *drop shipper,* a company that sells you merchandise at wholesale prices but only when you sell to a member of the public at a retail price you specify. You don't need to spend lots of money building inventory with a drop shipper; you're billed only when you make a sale. And, the drop shipper stores the inventory for you and ships your products as you sell them. Drop shippers are ready to provide you with a steady stream of merchandise, and you don't even have to worry about warehouse space. When you use drop shipping, you can select products from other manufacturers, set a price for each item, and then turn around and offer the products for resale on your site. You're able to focus on presenting and marketing the products while the drop shipper handles fulfillment.

The factor that makes this model especially attractive is that you don't buy or hold any inventory. Instead, you wait until a customer places an order from your site. After the payment has cleared, you forward an order to your drop shipper and pay for the product. (You're charged a wholesale or discounted price, whereas your customer pays you full retail price.) The drop shipper then sends the product directly to your customer. You make money on the difference between your cost for buying the product from the drop shipper and the price you charge your customer. As far as your customer knows, the merchandise is coming directly from you. Other perceived benefits include being able to offer excellent customer service and concentrate on marketing, rather than on manufacturing, the product. You don't have to deal with the headaches of managing inventory and shipping products. You can focus on the front end — the sales process.

What's the down side? Lots of companies claim to be reputable drop shippers, but many aren't trustworthy. You have to closely scrutinize certain issues to create a realistic picture of your income potential:

+ **Lack of control:** When you work with a drop shipper, you don't control how the merchandise is packed or shipped or how quickly it arrives. Discuss with the drop shipper which shipping method should be used.

+ **Possible inventory problems:** You depend on your drop shipper to have the inventory in stock when someone purchases it. If it's not there, you have to explain delays to your customers.

+ **Return policies:** Make sure your drop shipper accepts returns. If it doesn't, you'll be stuck with the bill when the customer expresses dissatisfaction and wants to send something back.

+ **Dealing with a lack of volume discounts:** Because you're not purchasing products in bulk, the discounted retail price is typically higher than when you buy wholesale. This price difference can translate to lower profit margins for you. If you sell consistently, you may be able to negotiate a lower price eventually, but at first your profit margin is less than if you purchase at wholesale and sell directly to the public.

+ **Handling less-competitive pricing:** To offset lower profit margins, you might be tempted to mark up the product's price significantly. The risk is that your product might not be price competitive in the marketplace. That's not a bad thing — as long as you can balance it with another value proposition (such as excellent customer service or a huge product selection).

+ **Balancing demand and value:** With profit margins a little tighter, you might search for drop-shipped products sold at the deepest discounts. Although your profit margin can rise because of this factor, if the product doesn't have mass appeal, it doesn't sell.

+ **Driving traffic:** When you pay more for a product (in exchange for the convenience of on-demand ordering), your profit becomes a true numbers game. You have to attract a much larger number of visitors to your site to realize the same, or similar, profit margins as a site that's buying wholesale (see the previous section) or selling custom products.

+ **Locating legitimate drop shippers:** One of the toughest obstacles to overcome is simply finding a reliable resource from which to buy your products. Some drop shippers or lists of drop shippers are outdated or otherwise incorrect or feature companies with steep (and unnecessary) setup charges and other fees.

A reputable resource for locating drop shippers and wholesalers is Worldwide Brands. You can access this well-researched list of drop shippers by purchasing a Product Sourcing membership from www.worldwide brands.com/wwb/main_Products.asp. Membership fees start at $299.

Selling Your Professional Services

Sometimes, of course, the issue isn't always which types of products you have to offer. Sometimes, you have to ask, "What can I *do* for you?" Another source for making money online is selling your services. Most online services fall into one of four key areas:

✦ **Creative:** These products are delivered as a service. For example, you might be a graphic artist who develops logos, a writer who is paid to create ad copy, or an artist who paints portraits from photographs that customers upload to your Web site.

✦ **Organizational:** If your site is an organization based on paid memberships, we consider it a service Web site. Typically, your members pay for access to a group of services in exchange for a renewable fee.

✦ **Professional:** These folks are accountants, attorneys, public relation agents — you get the idea. Whatever the service, not only do you market it online, but your customers also can purchase the service over the Internet.

✦ **Software-based:** A variety of Web sites provide software online that their visitors can use with their Web browsers. Sometimes called an application service provider (ASP), it's almost a hybrid of a service and a product. A company uses a Web site to sell software or a process that's delivered or managed as a Web-based service. Some examples are an online payroll-processing firm, a Web site hosting service, and a shopping cart program.

Whatever service you want to promote online, you need to have a clear picture of the benefits and downsides so that you can maximize your chances of success.

Understanding the pros and cons

You gain a distinct benefit, geographically speaking, from offering any type of service-driven revenue stream online. For example, if you're a graphic artist living in a small rural town, the number of people who regularly need your service is limited. By selling your services from a Web site, you can quickly broaden your prospective customer base.

Selling your professional services online has a downside, too. As you know, revenues from most service-based business are limited by the products you can produce — there are only so many hours in a day! Your final output (and income potential) is based on your, or your staff's, available billable hours. Of course, you can take action to minimize this type of effect on your revenues:

✦ Increase your hourly rate.

✦ Hire additional staff.

✦ Replicate your service as a Web-based deliverable product.

✦ Add complementary sources of revenue (other services or products) to your site.

For many professionals, the added visibility that comes with a Web site outweighs the disadvantages. And these days, professionals need to be on the Web just to keep up with the competition.

Building credibility

One of the most important issues for anyone who sells his services online is *credibility*. What experience or credentials do you have that help you stand out from the crowd? Although you can reach a larger number of prospective clients on the Web, you're also up against more competitors. And, when people purchase services over the Internet, they look for indications that you're legitimate and skilled.

Unlike meeting with a potential customer in your offline business, you don't always have the opportunity to establish a direct relationship with a prospective client. Your Web site serves as that introduction and relationship builder. If information about your service isn't available (or obvious), your potential customer will click through to a competitor's site.

Establishing your credibility isn't difficult. Your Web site can feature any or all of these items, to help solidify your reputation and put potential customers at ease:

✦ **Degrees or certifications:** Adding this information to your bio on the About Us page gives prospective customers a sense of security. If you have certifications in niche areas, this information is especially effective for building credibility.

✦ **Company history:** The issue of the number of years you've been in business is especially important if your Web site services are new but you've been in business offline for quite some time.

✦ **Clients:** Even if you don't have any heavy-hitter clients on board, a short list of named clients illustrates your legitimacy (and the fact that people hire you).

✦ **Case studies:** Describing how your service was used to help solve a customer's problem is an effective way to communicate a success story. A case study demonstrates the different ways your services can benefit someone.

✦ **Testimonials:** Whenever you finish a project that has gone well, ask your client to provide a testimonial. One or two sentences are plenty to let others know that you did a good job.

✦ **Recognition:** Any awards or kudos you receive definitely build confidence in your capabilities.

✦ **Press clippings:** Don't be shy. If you appear in a newspaper or magazine article, shout it from the rooftop or from your home page. Links to this type of publicity serve as validation from a third party.

✦ **Referrals:** Similarly, if other experts, service providers, or organizations tout your skills, let site visitors see that you're considered a leader in your field.

Add a link to your membership organizations at the bottom of your Web site's home page. Making these elements highly visible on your front page can encourage a new visitor to your site to hang around a little longer.

Adding the items in the preceding list to your site also helps you deal with another issue: When you run an online service company, you have to *market yourself,* just like you would market any product. Being hesitant about promoting your talent affects your earnings.

If you're not comfortable blowing your own horn or you just don't have time, hire a professional. Count it as part of your marketing expenses, as you would when you buy banner ads or Google AdWords.

Selling Information

The Internet holds so much information that simply finding the data you need the most is a time-consuming process. Some of the most successful businesses on the Web got their start by simply organizing the mountain of online content and making key information easier to find. The two most notable examples are Yahoo!, which developed one of the first indexes of Web sites, and Google, which created one of the most effective search engines ever.

When it comes to content, though, *almost anything* can be converted and packaged into some sellable format. Some online newspapers, such as the *Chicago Tribune,* charge a fee for accessing and reprinting articles from their extensive archives. But it's not just words: It's also music, games, videos (film), research data — you name it.

The subject of providing saleable content online holds so much promise that we dedicate an entire chapter to it. If this area interests you, Book IV, Chapter 3 shows you how to transition your expertise into e-books, Webinars, and other marketable online content-based products. Whether you create a Web site that organizes information or you sell articles or other information online, developing marketable content requires only four initial steps:

1. Originate.

   In this step, you create the product. It's a fairly simple and straightforward process to convert and save your words, music, or images to a media format.

2. Replicate.

   After you have an information product, your next step is to duplicate it for resale. It's basically a matter of converting content into a type of downloadable file that's distributed over an Internet connection. The file might be a PDF document, an image file, or even a link to a password-protected Web site that contains the information.

   The ease of duplication makes online content quite affordable. For one reason, the labor you used to create the original piece doesn't have to be repeated. Instead, it might take as little as one-tenth the amount of time to make and distribute a copy after you make a sale.

3. Disseminate.

   After the content is stored in the preferred format, you're ready to put it up for sale. You have lots of ways to make the content available for download: You can use standard shopping carts that integrate with content products, or you can use Web-based services that distribute content on your behalf.

4. Update.

   Making minor revisions or updating content is a matter of returning to the original document or file. After the corrections are made, you save the changes and then replace the old media with the most recent version.

Ease of production aside, you're probably curious about how much you truly can earn. Although that number is hard to pinpoint, we can share some trends with you. Revenues from paid content spending are expected to reach $3.1 billion in 2009, in the United States, according to Jupiter Research. The rate of growth is still considered slow, but is expected to remain viable, especially considering companies such as YouTube, Hulu, and iTunes, and even traditional media sites for major networks, have expanded the meaning of "content." It's no longer about only the written word; videos and music have skyrocketed into the arena of sought-after content. The new demand has also caused a tug-of-war to surface between the strategies of offering paid content versus offering free content that's subsidized by advertising. We think that paid content will continue to grow, and prominent media organizations are continuing to lead the way. For example, *The Wall Street Journal* (www.wsj.com) requires a full subscription to view its online articles. It charges $1.99 per week for full access.

Perhaps responding to growing preferences, content distributors big and small are also offering content in single quantities. One of the best known examples is the Apple iTunes store, which struck a chord with fans when it started selling downloadable songs for 99 cents apiece. Others, such as Napster (`www.napster.com`), promote multiple purchasing options. Like iTunes, it offers single songs for 99 cents or entire albums for $6.95. Napster also offers a monthly membership with unlimited downloads for $9.95 per month. Notice that your price point and potential revenue for this model largely depend on three factors:

✦ The type of content you're offering (and how it is traditionally packaged)

✦ The popularity of your content

✦ The way your content is being sold by your competitors

Placing Ads for Profit

Although paid programming is undoubtedly growing on the Web, it's not the only game in town. In fact, content is being used to sustain another tried-and-true Web business model: advertising. When you attract enough visitors to your Web site by providing marketable content, you can place advertisements and earn money from advertisers.

Looking at sites that sell

We know that you recognize the online billboard model. The content is good, and it's free. It's used to draw visitors to a Web site. The more eyeballs the content attracts, the more money that can be earned by selling ad space. Just like that, free content is turned into money in the bank! Several popular types of sites support earning revenues from ad dollars:

✦ **Portal:** This model was one of the original Web business models. This type of site provides a host of information on a specific area of interest. BizOffice (`www.bizoffice.com`) is an example of an information portal. It's targeted to small-business owners and home-based business owners and to anyone just starting a business.

✦ **Search engine:** Google and Yahoo! might have the market cornered, but niche search engines are making headway. For example, AllSmallBiz (`www.allsmallbiz.com`) narrows the search process to only small-business-related search topics.

✦ **Classifieds:** Personal ads are among the fastest-growing categories in this market. Sites that promote listings for jobs, household goods, or businesses for sale also attract visitors.

✦ **Information exchange:** This area includes blogs, user groups, and communities such as social networking sites, like MySpace (`www.myspace.com`) and Facebook (`www.facebook.com`).

Like the portal site, the ad-based business model has been around practically since the birth of the Internet. As the industry has matured, it has become standardized to a large degree (although it continues to evolve). It therefore has generally accepted rules or guidelines for

✦ Which forms of online advertising are acceptable

✦ How results of an ad campaign are measured

✦ Why and how a site should be audited by a third party to validate its traffic

✦ How much advertisers are typically prepared to pay for ad campaigns

To discover more information about current advertising guidelines and standards for the Web, we recommend visiting the Interactive Advertising Bureau (IAB) at www.iab.net.

Analyzing traffic patterns

After you examine Web sites that attract ad revenue, you need to improve your own Web site and analyze it so that you can determine whether it's attracting enough attention to make ad revenue a viable proposition. That depends. For the most part, your income is connected to the level of *traffic,* or number of unique visitors, your site receives. The level of traffic you receives depends on two factors:

✦ **Value:** The quality and appeal of your content have a direct effect on the number of visitors it receives. Sites that have engaging content, or deal with highly popular subject matter, are more likely to attract and retain visitors.

✦ **Promotion:** Because even good sites can go unnoticed, your number-one job (following content creation) is to market your site. This task runs the gamut from search engine optimization to public relations. You have to attract eyeballs in order to make money. (When you're ready to get serious about boosting sales by promoting your site, check out Book VI.)

Naturally, if your site has been up and running for a while (preferably, several months), you can use your traffic analysis data to gauge future traffic patterns. This strategy works even with a limited amount of historical data. Specifically, look at the percentage of growth in the number of visitors from week to week or from month to month. By multiplying this figure over several months, or even a year, you create a baseline calculation of the growth you can expect — assuming that no negative trend in visitor traffic takes place. This calculation doesn't account for spikes in visitor traffic following a higher search engine ranking or from marketing activities to promote your site.

How do you know when you reach a number of hits that's sufficient to start generating revenue from ad sales? Consider that most online *ad networks* (organizations that sell ad inventory on behalf of Web publishers) require that you meet a minimum traffic count before they will work with your site. For most Web sites, this cutoff is between 3,000 and 5,000 unique visitors per month. That's an average of approximately 100 to 166 visitors per day to your site.

With a start-up business, you obviously don't have the hard, cold data to estimate when you might hit those magic numbers. So, you need to *project* your site traffic. How? Take a look at the traffic patterns of sites that are similar to the one you're building. You can find some of this information from a third party, such as Alexa (`www.alexa.com`). This site, owned by Amazon, provides free information about Web sites, including traffic rankings. To access the information on Alexa, follow these steps:

1. **Go to the Alexa home page at `www.alexa.com`.**

   On this page, you see different features spotlighted (such as a Web site comparison graph and a "what's hot on the Web right now" list of sites).

2. **Enter the URL you want to know more about in the Get Info box and click the Go button.**

   For this example, we used the Small Business Administration site at `www.sba.gov`.

   You then see a new page that provides general information about the site, including

   • A summary of recent traffic ranking details

   • Snapshots of the site

   • A list of the sites' pages that people visited

3. **Go to the Traffic History Graph to compare your data to other sites.**

   On the page that appears, you see a graph detailing recent traffic patterns for the site, as shown in Figure 1-1. Below the graph, you find boxes to enter up to four site URLs that you want to compare to yours. Once you enter all the Web sites, click the Compare Sites button.

   Alexa estimates the traffic rank by using a combined measure of the number of users (the *reach*) and number of page views over a three-month period.

4. **Change the type of results displayed on the graph by clicking either the Rank or Page Views tab at the top of the graph.**

5. **Vary the results by period by clicking a time-range tab at the top of the graph.**

   You can view results for seven days, one month, three months, six months, or the max amount of data they have a available.

6. **To repeat the process for other sites, simply enter new URLs into the boxes at the bottom of the graph.**

**Book IV
Chapter 1**

**Determining Your
Revenue Model**

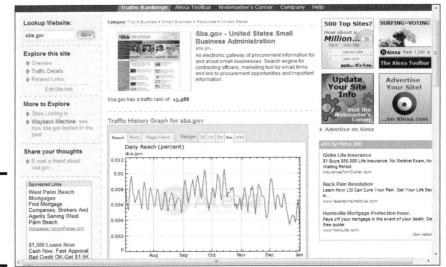

Figure 1-1:
Check
traffic
pattern
results.

Use the comparison tool, directly underneath the graphs, to compare results between two sites. Simply enter the URL of a competing site in the box under the graph, and then click the Compare Sites button. The new graph uses red and blue lines to show the difference between the two sites. Figure 1-2 shows you the result of a comparison between SBA.gov and IRS.gov.

Having access to this free information provides a good overview of traffic patterns for sites similar to yours. These results are in no way a guarantee of *your* level of visitor traffic. Many other factors influence the results, such as

✦ Age of the site

✦ Natural search rankings (in Google and Yahoo!)

✦ Amount of marketing designed to drive traffic

Additionally, keep in mind that these figures from Alexa are only estimates.

For more detailed information about ranking results, Alexa allows qualified Web site owners and developers to purchase data reports and get additional information. Find details by clicking the Webmaster's Corner tab at the top menu bar.

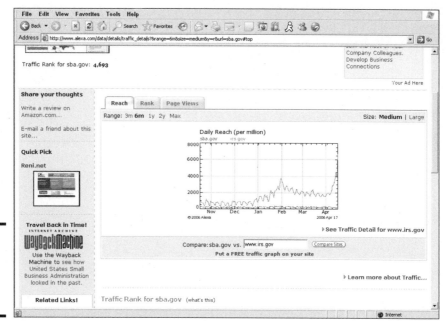

Figure 1-2:
Compare
the traffic
history of
sites.

Choosing ad formats

The types of advertising formats you choose to offer influence your ad revenue. Although a banner ad continues to be an old standby, savvy advertisers (and experienced media buyers) expect a variety of ad format options so that they can mix and match to find the best value for their investment:

✦ **Banner:** This standard, boxed ad usually appears at the top of your home page. Some sizes remain more popular than others. You can see samples of the most common banner-ad sizes in Figure 1-3.

✦ **Rich media:** Displayed like a banner ad, rich media uses Flash or other dynamic programming (including video) in the ad.

✦ **Pop-up:** This type of ad appears on the Web site page that your visitor is viewing.

✦ **Pop-under:** This type of ad opens behind, or underneath, your primary Web site. Visitors usually don't notice that a new window is open until they close or minimize the browser window.

✦ **Sponsorship:** Rather than offer a standard banner ad, your content-rich site can allow advertisers to "sponsor" certain sections. For example, on a site about raising children, a diaper company might want to sponsor the section targeted to infants or toddlers. You agree to place the sponsor's name and logo alongside the content or in another prominent location close to that content area.

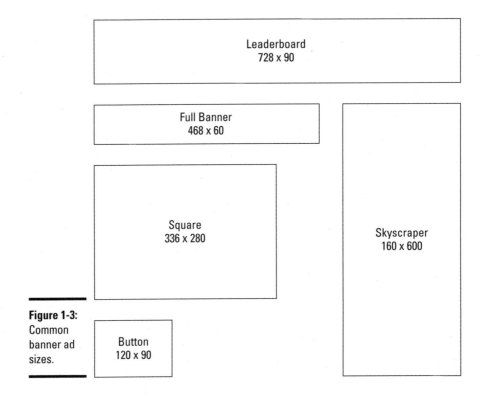

Figure 1-3:
Common
banner ad
sizes.

✦ **Text link:** You can embed a paid text link anywhere in your site. A visitor who clicks the link goes directly to the site being advertised.

✦ **Contextual:** This type of ad uses text links targeted to match the content of your site. The most well-known use of contextual ads is Google AdSense.

✦ **Referral:** Also called a lead generator, this format is usually set up as a form page that a visitor from your site completes and submits to the advertiser. The form information indicates further interest in the product and provides a sales lead.

✦ **24-hour buyout**: A newer trend, a buyout includes all types of ads that your site displays. The advertiser buys your *complete* ad inventory across your site for a 24-hour period (or, in some cases, more often than a single day). In other words, one company is your sole advertiser for the day.

Naturally, you might ask, "How much do I charge for ads?" Answering that question is tricky: Rates vary tremendously for the different online ad formats and how much advertising clout your particular site has. We can tell you that all formats are typically sold in one of three ways:

✦ **CPM:** Cost per thousand impressions. An *impression* is a single appearance of an ad in someone's Web browser window.

✦ **CPC:** Cost per click, or click-through. A *click-through* occurs whenever someone clicks an ad and goes to the advertiser's Web site.

✦ **Flat rate:** A fixed dollar amount that's paid regardless of results or number of click-throughs.

Although it's nearly impossible to say how much your specific site can charge, we can give you some idea of a typical range. For example, an average rate paid on a cost-per-click basis can run from several cents per click to a few dollars per click-through. A text link might bring in a flat fee ranging from $25 per month to several hundred dollars per month, regardless of the number of impressions. On the other hand, sponsorships or 24-hour buyouts might net several thousand dollars.

A quarterly ad price index report from PubMatic (www.pubmatic.com) shows costs for display ads across ad networks and small Web sites and predicts falling ad rates in late 2008. Here are some of the details:

✦ Entertainment sites cost an average of 33 cents per every 1,000 visitors (or eyeballs, as they're commonly referred to).

✦ Sports sites made 25 cents per thousand.

✦ Social networking sites earned the least for their ads at 22 cents per thousand.

✦ Business, finance, and technology sites brought in more money for their ads, which usually ranged from 60 cents to a dollar per thousand.

The magic variables seem to be both *traffic and site topic*. The more visitors you have and the more popular your site's topic, the more people pay for advertising on your site.

There's one exception, according to PubMatic. Smaller sites, those with fewer than one million page views per month, can earn as much as three times that of large, high-traffic sites with more than 100 million page views per month! This is because the smaller sites are typically niche sites with highly targeted content that reach a targeted audience who are more likely to click through on ads. You can find out about what it takes to start a niche site in Book X.

Estimating your revenue potential

To find the ballpark amount of what you can eventually earn, we recommend researching your closest competitors. Although this method is far from scientific, it's a start.

Begin by checking out your competitors' ad rates. You can usually find a link from the site's home page labeled Advertise with Us or similar wording. The link helps you find information that advertisers need to know, such as

✦ Number of unique visitors

✦ Visitor demographics

✦ Size and cost of available ad formats

Also note the type and number of ads running throughout the site. A quick calculation (multiply the number of ads by the ad rate) provides a *general* estimate of possible ad revenues for that type of site.

Getting it from Google

Another way to estimate one source of ad revenue is by using the Google Traffic Estimator tool, from Google AdWords (`www.google.com/ads`). By using this marketing tool, companies can bid on search terms that help direct traffic to their sites. Remember that these ads are contextual, based on content-specific keywords.

For a brand-new site, getting paid to display those search ads is a quick way to begin earning revenue. (Google AdSense is the name of the revenue-earning side of Google AdWords.) When you place the Google ads on your site, you're paid based on the number of click-throughs on the text links. This system is appealing not only because of the large Google audience but also because you don't have to sell the advertising space or set up and monitor banner ads. Google handles almost everything.

If you know how much an advertiser is potentially willing to spend on a keyword (that relates to the content on your site), you can form an idea of how much you can charge.

To get started on your quest for keyword data, sign up for the Google AdWords program. After you're approved, follow these steps to access the Google Traffic Estimator tool:

1. **Go to the Google home page at `www.google.com`.**

At the bottom of this page, under the famous Google search box, are several links.

2. **Click the Advertising Programs link.**

A split page appears, showcasing Google AdWords on the left and Google AdSense on the right.

3. **Click the Google AdWords link in the upper-left corner of the page.**

The Google AdWords home page appears, with a login box in the upper-left corner.

4. **Log in to your account by entering your e-mail address and the account password you chose when you signed up.**

If you have bought AdWords in the past, a report is displayed, showing your campaign history. At the top of the page are several tabs, including Campaign Management, the page you're on. Under these tabs are three other links.

5. **Click the Tools link.**

The next page lists some Google tools that help you optimize your ad performance.

6. **Click the Traffic Estimator link.**

On the new form page that appears, you can enter information to conduct a search (see Figure 1-4).

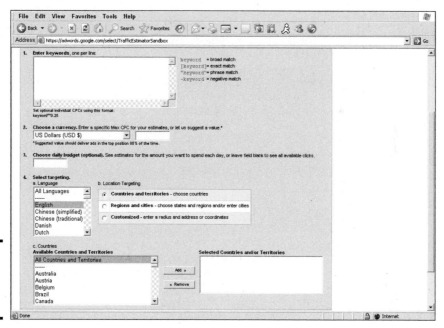

Figure 1-4:
The Google
Traffic
Estimator.

7. **In the large text box at the top of the page, type the search terms that relate to the site you want to research.**

You can enter many different terms at a time. Put each keyword term on a separate line. As an example, we used the search term *celebrities.*

8. **Choose which currency you want to use from the Choose Your Currency drop-down box.**

9. **Enter the total amount of money you want to spend on the CPC (cost-per-click) in the text box for each keyword.**

   Because you're not purchasing keywords, leave the maximum CPC amount blank. This way, you see the highest amounts being paid for search terms.

10. **Use the next set of drop-down boxes to select which languages and countries of origin you want to include in your search.**

    You can further narrow the search by choosing a customized type of search or searching by regions, states, and cities.

11. **After selecting one or more countries, click the Add button.**

    Clicking Add puts the designated country in a separate box. If you neglect to click Add, you see an error message as you proceed.

12. **After you enter all the data, press the Continue button to display your results.**

A chart appears that includes the estimated number of click-throughs per day, based on current advertisers using that term. The chart also estimates the cost per day for that keyword, and the maximum dollar amount you can expect for that term (for the top position). Figure 1-5 shows the results for the term *celebrities*.

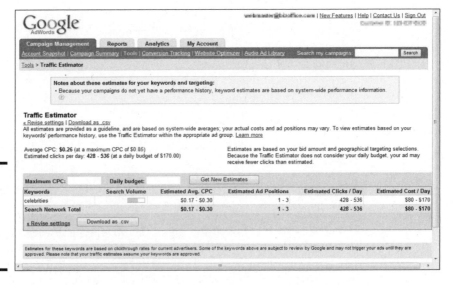

Figure 1-5: This tool gives you rates for keyword terms.

Okay, now that you have the information, you have to find out what it means for your business. If you're an advertiser, the amount is obviously what you can expect to pay for the keywords. Suppose that you're the owner of a content-based Web site about celebrity gossip, however, and you implement Google AdSense on your site. Based on the results you see in our example for the keyword term *celebrities,* advertisers are paying anywhere from 17 to 30 cents per click. Of course, you don't earn the full amount. To estimate the amount you might bring in for directing traffic to that same keyword, anticipate receiving no more than 50 percent of the total. (To be superconservative, count on only one-fourth the amounts shown.)

As we said, this tool isn't foolproof for determining future revenues. For starters, the data is still based on an estimate provided by Google. It further assumes that you have the traffic to support click-throughs for the Google ads placed on your site.

Either way, you're likely to find that Google AdSense can earn you a little bit of change — although not enough to fully support your financial needs.

Managing ad space inventory

You can choose to sell your site's entire advertising inventory. There's certainly nothing wrong with managing that kind of campaign yourself.

However, companies (especially agencies) purchasing ad space from you expect the process to be smooth. They want verifiable data that the ad ran and the impressions were served by your site to those who visited it. You therefore have to

✦ Place the ads efficiently.

✦ Monitor the campaign.

✦ Report your progress to your advertiser.

To make this process easier to manage, you need to implement a good ad-server program for your site.

An ad server program can be software that you install or a Web-based product supported by a third party. To make your task as simple as possible, we recommend the latter!

One ad server program that has been around for a while and is well respected is the DoubleClick DART for Publishers. By using this hosted, Web-based ad server program, you can manage and serve ads on your site. It has an extensive list of features and supports rich media, too. Do you want to know about pricing? It fluctuates based on impressions, so you have to call to get a quote. You can find more information at www.doubleclick.com.

Another alternative is using a service we like from ValueAd (www.valuead. com). Its product, AdXpress, is also a Web-based solution priced according to the number of impressions you serve. However, its Junior plan is absolutely free when you're serving as many as 50,000 monthly impressions. This solution is terrific for a smaller, start-up site.

Selling the space

Of course, part of handling your site's advertising involves selling it. You're completely responsible for these tasks:

✦ Seek advertisers.

✦ Respond to ad inquiries.

✦ Manage the back-end functions of each campaign that's run on your site.

You might also have other responsibilities, such as

✦ Negotiating ad rates

✦ Invoicing advertisers

✦ Seeking renewals for ad campaigns

If your time is scarce or handling these functions isn't your preference, you can contract with an *ad network,* a company that handles the advertising for your site from start to finish. Most networks work with you only if you provide a minimum number of page views per month, usually starting around 3,000 to 5,000. If you're interested, check out these established ad networks:

✦ **AdvertisingZ.com:** www.advertisingz.com

✦ **BurstMedia:** www.burstmedia.com

✦ **FastClick:** www.fastclick.com

✦ **ValueClick:** www.valueclick.com

As long as you can attract the eyeballs, using an ad network can be an effective way to increase your revenue potential. That's certainly the name of the game for using an ad-based earnings model!

Establishing an Affiliate Advertising Program

One of the most effective ways to take advantage of online advertising to enhance your income online is to set up an affiliate program. An *affiliate* agreement enables other sites to refer traffic to your Web site, usually in exchange for a small commission on each sale that originates from its referral traffic. You can set up an affiliate program that's based on one of these methods:

✦ **Pay-per-click:** You pay each time a link to your site or product is clicked.

✦ **Pay by lead:** You pay whenever a referred customer completes an online form, for example.

✦ **Pay by flat rate:** You pay a set fee as opposed to a percentage of each sale.

You might be interested in becoming an affiliate for others as a way to earn revenue, too. In Book IV, Chapter 2, we show you how to start adding existing affiliate programs to your Web site.

A big benefit of establishing your own affiliate arrangement is that you maintain control over how your product is distributed to your customers. You're still the one handling and shipping the product, even though both you and your affiliate are likely to have contact with the customer. Another inherent benefit is that affiliate programs serve as a cost-effective marketing tool for building awareness about your product or Web site.

Setting up an affiliate program isn't complicated, although you're responsible for keeping up with some critical functions:

✦ **Create and review affiliate guidelines.** You establish your terms and conditions as part of a legally binding affiliate agreement. You also must review affiliate sites to make sure that they comply with your guidelines for affiliates.

✦ **Track affiliate sales.** Providing working links for routing and tracking affiliate traffic is an essential part of your offering. You also need to keep up with ongoing totals of affiliate sales.

✦ **Report affiliate income.** In addition to providing regular earnings reports to your affiliates, you have to report their income for tax purposes. That process requires sending 1099 forms to affiliates each tax year and reporting their income to the IRS.

✦ **Offer marketing materials.** An affiliate program is more effective when you provide your resellers with enthusiastic support, including everything from banner ads to electronic newsletters advertising special promotions.

✦ **Keep in touch.** Affiliates are like any other type of customer: If you want them to keep doing business with you, you have to service them. Your job is to communicate with your affiliates to keep them interested in, and (you hope) successful in, your particular program.

Setting up and maintaining any one of the preceding items for your affiliates can appear daunting at first. Dozens of legitimate companies are available, however, to manage affiliate programs for you. These pay-for-performance marketing firms not only run your program but also actively solicit and qualify new affiliates on your behalf. Of course, they also take a cut of your sales in exchange for this service.

If you prefer to manage an affiliate program in-house, plenty of software programs can make your job quite easy. The affiliate-management software available from AffiliateWiz at `www.affiliatewiz.com` has lots of features, and installation support is included when you purchase the software license. Its software starts at $699.

If $699 is a little steep for you, consider an alternative, such as iDevAffiliate, available from `www.iDevDirect.com`. This company offers its basic affiliate-tracking software starting at $99 with no monthly fees or setup charges.

You can set up an affiliate program for any type of product or service your Web site offers. As long as you can afford to offer a percentage of sales anytime a "buying" visitor is referred to your site, affiliate programs can be effective for you.

Putting It All Together: Multiple Revenue Streams

Online ad revenues have certainly been on the upswing lately, proving again to be an exciting business model for your site. Who says that you have to choose only *one* source for earning the big bucks, though? Merging different online business models is smart business. The catch is deciding when and how to add different revenue streams to the mix. In our experience, you have to start by striking the right balance between your core customer base and your primary earnings strategy. At the same time, remember not to bite off more than you can chew, and focus on the sales strategies that you can handle comfortably so that you don't become overwhelmed before you even start out. Begin by identifying your *earnings anchor*. This primary money-maker provides you with a steady source of income. It's the type of business most closely linked to the identity of your site — and your target audience.

After you establish an anchor, you can look for *complementary* products or services. These items extend the value of your site and increase your earnings potential.

For example, the core customer base of CelebritySwagReport (`www.celebrityswagreport.com`) is people who want to find and buy the same trendy products that are given to celebrities as gifts (during award shows and for wedding gifts, for example) or purchased by celebrities for themselves or others. The earnings anchor is the revenue earned from selling the products featured on the site. The site is designed to highlight and sell the products first. Even within the earnings anchor, though, the site has three sources of revenue within the category of products:

+ Swag products that are sold directly, either by drop shipping or from inventory the owner maintains

+ Affiliate programs, which allow profit from a product that the owner might not otherwise be able to obtain

+ A line of promotional products that brand the site (such as T-shirts, mugs, and totebags)

As the site grows and attracts more visitors, the complementary earnings streams start to kick in. The first, advertising, includes everything from displaying Google AdSense to selling banner ads and sponsorships.

Another popular opportunity is using microcommerce (products under $5). Because the site offers content, it can sell subscriptions to customers who want to view exclusive reports, articles, and interviews. Likewise, this site's target audience makes the site a good fit for selling downloadable ringtones and other mobile products through an affiliate program. After the site has reached a certain level, it can feasibly add income by establishing an affiliate program for the site.

When you're determining what revenue streams to add to a site, and when, we recommend these two philosophies:

+ **Any added sources of income should complement, rather than take away from, your core business model.** Always remember who your target audience is, and make sure that you're appealing to their preferences or needs.

+ **Although a single earnings source might be necessary initially, it pays to diversify.** For example, try not to depend on one revenue stream (or product or service) for more than 60 percent of your total sales. If one of your sources suddenly takes a nosedive in its earnings potential, the rest of your revenue mix can compensate — at least temporarily.

Chapter 2: Making Money with Affiliate Programs

Affiliate programs, or revenue-sharing plans, have been around for quite some time, both online and off. Online versions became more than a passing fad when companies such as Walmart and Best Buy started offering them. A big-box retailer doesn't set up this type of program unless it has something to gain — usually, money. Affiliate programs, in a nutshell, pay you to send them customers. If a purchase is made by one of your referrals, you receive a small percentage of the profit.

Brand-name retailers aside, some affiliate programs are good, some are (admittedly) a little cheesy, and others are an outright bust. In this chapter, we help you sort out the winners from the losers so that you can earn affiliate income from your own Web site.

Looking at How Affiliate Programs Work

Revenue-sharing programs are simple to set up and easy to run as a sideline to your existing Web site. No kidding: Earning money through an affiliate program boils down to five steps:

1. Find a program that offers a product or service you like.

2. Sign up online by completing the affiliate agreement.

3. Place links to the program on your existing Web site.

4. Actively promote the affiliate program through banners, newsletters, and other suggested online marketing tactics.

5. Collect revenue.

On the surface, these steps are exactly what's required of you. Revving up the revenue stream takes a little more of your time and energy, of course. The amount of effort is minimal, though, compared to other online money-making strategies you might try.

Here are the secrets to building a lucrative affiliate marketing program:

✦ **Find a good match.** Think about your site's audience and the type of information they're looking for. Finding affiliate programs that offer products and services that appeal to your built-in customer base gives you a head-start toward success. Similarly, if you plan to create a Web site around affiliate programs, match your marketing efforts to that prospective customer. If your site is marketed to business owners, an affiliate program for a toy store doesn't go over well with your customers. However, a site created to appeal to the demands of working mothers, or home-based working moms, is a much better fit with a toy store.

✦ **Drive traffic.** One reason that the creator of the affiliate program is offering the opportunity is so that it can increase the number of potential customers who see its offering. How? By driving Web site traffic from one site (your site) to another (its site). For you, making money as an affiliate marketer depends on your ability to create large, continual streams of qualified visitors to the affiliate link by using a variety of marketing activities.

Notice that we didn't mention one word about finding a *quality* product or service. Sadly, that's because a lot of people have made good money with lowbrow programs. We're not saying that the programs were illegal, or even deceptive in nature. Rather, a few e-books weren't well written or were filled with old, outdated information. For a couple of software products, you could have found shareware equivalents and downloaded them for free. Still, all these items appeared to sell like hot cakes.

For whatever reason, quality isn't always a critical factor in the world of affiliate marketing. Or, at least it's something that can be overlooked. For the record, we believe that finding an affiliate program with a product or service that you would personally buy is important. Selling something that you believe in is so much easier than selling something you don't like!

Understanding some affiliate terms

When you're shopping for affiliate programs, you run into words or phrases associated with the affiliate process. Some you may recognize, and others are probably new to you. Become familiar with these concepts so that you can understand what's involved in participating in a successful affiliate program:

✦ **Affiliate:** An individual, a company, or a site that's paid money to promote another company's products or services

✦ **Pay-for-performance:** The process of rewarding a company or Web site (usually with money) for driving traffic to another site

✦ **Affiliate network:** A single company that oversees affiliate programs for multiple vendors and then recruits and approves affiliates on behalf of the companies they represent

✦ **Publisher:** The company or site that wants to be an affiliate

✦ **Advertiser:** A company or site that wants other sites (affiliates) to sell its merchandise

✦ **Merchant:** Another term for advertiser

✦ **Unique visitors:** A specific number of individuals who visit a site within a certain period, usually counted in a daily or monthly timeframe

✦ **Cost-per-click (CPC):** An amount of money an advertiser pays a site each time a visitor responds to an ad (specifically, by clicking a link or an ad)

✦ **Creatives:** Advertising material (usually, such items as banner ads, links, e-mail content, and pop-up ads) that you, the affiliate, use to promote items to visitors

✦ **Tracking tag (or tag):** A device, usually a link, given to an affiliate to keep up with the success of a campaign; allows visits to be tracked

✦ **Qualifying link:** An approved link given to an affiliate to place on a Web site to earn commissions

✦ **Required URL:** The specific Web site address where affiliate links must point to earn commissions for referred traffic, or visitors

✦ **Subaffiliate:** Another site that's managed under a single affiliate account; anything other than your primary Web site that's added to your account

✦ **AutoRenew:** A feature that automatically renews an affiliate's account upon expiration of the original term or length of time

Finding an affiliate program

Affiliate marketing programs are broken into three common sources, or places where they originate:

✦ **Retail sites:** Plenty of traditional retailers offer bona fide affiliate programs. Among some of the bigger names are Target, Macy's, Nordstrom's and Lands' End. Of course, each one is using an affiliate program to drive sales of its *online* business, not its brick-and-mortar version. One way to locate stores with affiliate programs is simply to make a list of your favorites and do the research. It takes time, but it's worth it.

A store with an affiliate program typically identifies the opportunity clearly on its Web site. Look for the Affiliates tab on a site's home page, or sometimes on the About Us page. Figure 2-1 shows the Target affiliate program.

✦ **Established online vendors:** Many branded names that are best known for delivering products via their Internet presence cater to affiliates. Topping the list are e-commerce giants such as Apple iTunes, McAfee (virus protection), and Dell (computers).

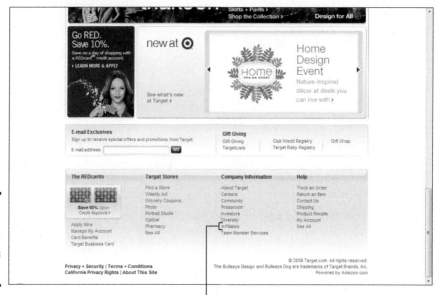

Figure 2-1:
Affiliate
links are on
the retailer's
home page.

Link to Affiliates page

✦ **Pay-for-performance networks:** In addition to searching independent sites, all-in-one sites can save you time. Pay-for-performance networks have assembled hundreds of (if not more) affiliate marketing programs under one roof.

An advantage of using a network is that you can apply for multiple programs at one time, and you can manage an unlimited number of your affiliate accounts in one place. Because major retailers often use networks to handle their affiliate programs, you're privy to exclusive promotions reserved only for the networks' affiliates. Networks are also a good way to locate category-specific programs, such as security software or gardening supplies, or to find lesser known products and services, such as e-books targeted to small businesses or coupon offers for pregnant women.

The networks on this list offer affiliate programs for just about everything under the sun:

- *AffiliateFuel.com:* www.affiliatefuel.com

- *Clickbank.com:* www.clickbank.com

- *CommissionJunction.com:* www.commissionjunction.com

- *LinkShare.com:* www.linkshare.com

- *TheBizOppNetwork.com:* www.thebizoppnetwork.com

Promoting affiliate programs is easy if you use the tools that are already created. When you're signing up as an affiliate, visit the community message boards that are often set up for affiliates. Find out what marketing tools (banner ads or newsletters, for example) other affiliates found successful. You can save time with your own efforts! If you're assigned to an affiliate marketing manager, don't hesitate to drop an e-mail and ask for suggestions based on your site's core audience. That person's job is to help make you successful.

Signing Up for an Affiliate Network

After you locate a specific program or an affiliate network that appeals to you, you can sign up. The process typically takes fewer than ten minutes.

Follow these steps to sign up for the LinkShare program, for example:

1. **Go to the site's home page at www.linkshare.com.**

2. **Click the Publishers link.**

   A page that describes CPA advertising appears.

3. **Click the Join Now button at the bottom of the page.**

   A new page opens, as shown in Figure 2-2, with a form for you to fill in basic information. The page has three boxes along the top, labeled with numbers. The boxes represent the steps you take to register.

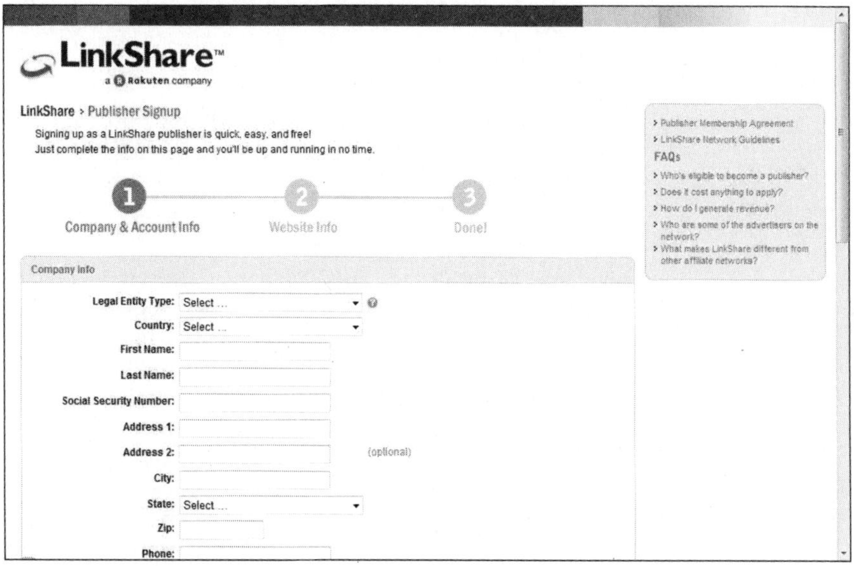

Figure 2-2:
Sign up
to earn
money as
an affiliate.

> **LinkShare**™
> a ⓡ Rakuten company
>
> LinkShare › Publisher Signup
>
> Signing up as a LinkShare publisher is quick, easy, and free!
> Just complete the info on this page and you'll be up and running in no time.
>
> **1** Company & Account Info   **2** Website Info   **3** Done!
>
> **Company Info**
>
> Legal Entity Type: Select ...
> Country: Select ...
> First Name:
> Last Name:
> Social Security Number:
> Address 1:
> Address 2:   (optional)
> City:
> State: Select ...
> Zip:
> Phone:
>
> › Publisher Membership Agreement
> › LinkShare Network Guidelines
> **FAQs**
> › Who's eligible to become a publisher?
> › Does it cost anything to apply?
> › How do I generate revenue?
> › Who are some of the advertisers on the network?
> › What makes LinkShare different from other affiliate networks?

4. **Fill in your company and account information, and click the Go to Step 2 button.**

    The form contains standard questions, such as company name, address, and employer identification number (EIN) or Social Security number. On this page, you're also asked to read the affiliate agreement and ensure that you agree with the terms.

5. **Enter the short security key that appears at the bottom of the page and click Continue.**

    A new page appears that asks for information about your Web site. On this page, you're also asked to complete information concerning how you want to receive payments.

6. **Fill in the payment information and click the Finish button.**

    Watch for an e-mail message from the company for further instructions and information about your new affiliate account.

You have the option of signing up for direct deposit, but only after you're paid at least one commission check. If you're interested in this option, look for direct-deposit instructions when you receive your first check.

Your approval for participating in an affiliate program may not come quickly. That's because every legitimate program has criteria for eligibility, although some are more lenient than others. For example, many affiliate programs don't process your application unless you have an active, or live, site. Others, such as AffiliateFuel.com, further require a minimum number of unique visitors.

Some affiliates review your site in detail before approving your application. AffiliateFuel also takes as long as ten days. Other programs provide immediate electronic approval as long as you meet basic requirements, such as

✦ An active Web site

✦ A valid Social Security number or employer identification number (EIN)

✦ Verification that your site doesn't violate any of the network's terms and conditions

After your approval with an affiliate network is confirmed, it's easy to apply for as many individual programs as you like. At LinkShare.com, for example, the merchants are separated by categories. After you open a category page, you see all merchant affiliate programs along with details for the program. After you check the boxes of the programs you're interested in, your application is automatically submitted. You then receive notification of acceptance (or not) in your e-mail.

As you grow your affiliate programs, use the account management tools that the network provides. Figure 2-3 shows an example of the account-reporting functions LinkShare provides.

Figure 2-3:
Online
reports
track your
affiliate
activity.

You can join multiple affiliate programs, and programs run by different affiliate networks.

Scouring for details

When you're perusing an affiliate marketing program that interests you, notice several things before signing up to participate.

Commission structure

Review the payout system for the program. It's usually a percentage of sales or a flat dollar rate. However, the amounts may be based on minimum sales levels, which isn't a best-case scenario. Alternatively, programs that reward you with larger commissions as your volume increases are beneficial. Or, if a product requires a recurring fee (such as a monthly subscription), you may receive a one-time payment rather than residuals. Knowing the payout rates comes in handy for comparing programs.

Method for payment

You may get to choose how and when to receive payment. Look for details, including the currency used for payment; a set dollar amount accumulated before being paid (often, a $25 minimum); monthly or quarterly distributions; and the option for direct deposit into your account.

Refunds

Find the program's policy for handling customer returns or refunds. Understand how and when that money is taken out of your account.

Recordkeeping

Established affiliate programs typically offer a simple but sophisticated accounting system.

(continued)

**Book IV
Chapter 2**

**Making Money with
Affiliate Programs**

(continued)

You can view your complete commission history in addition to what's in your account. Always confirm that the program provides this type of account review, and find out how frequently it's updated (in real time, daily, or only at month's end).

Tracking

One frustration occurs when an affiliate program doesn't provide an effective way to track statistics for your affiliate link. The best programs make it easy to understand how many click-throughs you get in addition to final purchases.

Cookies

For well-known sites that receive plenty of traffic on their own, having a cookie tracker in place for affiliates is important. You know that someone will inevitably go to a site after clicking your affiliate link and then leave without buying anything. The following week, that person might be ready to go back and make a purchase! With affiliate link cookies in place, the site can monitor the visits and offer credit for your original referral. Most cookies are good for 10 to 14 days.

Limits or exclusions

Larger programs may have restrictions on what products or services are included in an affiliate program. Or, you may have to follow strict guidelines for promoting certain products or using product images. Always read the fine print so that you're not caught off guard.

Penalties

Even an unintentional violation can lead to a slap on the wrist (such as a small monetary fine or a scathing letter) or to having your account turned off. Read the Terms and Conditions document carefully to understand how and when you may be penalized.

Restrictive marketing strategies

Affiliate marketers commonly specify how affiliates can and cannot market their programs. Most restrictions refer to e-mailing strategies that can lead to trouble for the affiliates as violations of anti-spam laws. Companies are cracking down on this issue because they're the ones being held responsible (legally) for your (the affiliate's) actions. To avoid having your account closed over a simple mistake, take a close look at which marketing strategies are prohibited or considered offensive.

Logos, banners, and content

Affiliate programs want you to do well, so they typically provide you with marketing tools. Before signing up for a program, peruse the marketing collateral that's at your disposal. Is it enough? Is there a variety? Are they quality pieces? Would you, or could you, really use them? This issue is important because you may be restricted from creating your own marketing materials and have to use theirs!

Avoiding Scams and Questionable Content

As you now know, even something as extremely popular as online poker can come with serious legal strings attached. After you join an affiliate program for something like that, you're at risk of paying the price if things aren't on the up-and-up. Last time we checked, claiming ignorance doesn't get you a Get Out of Jail Free card.

Illegal affiliations

Participation in any illegal affiliate programs is limited by the governing laws of your home state or country. You must know the law and then abide by it. To avoid becoming an outlaw, follow these safety tips:

✦ **Always read the terms and conditions of the affiliate agreement.** Affiliate programs might disclose legal caveats to you in easy-to-find warnings on their sites, but more than likely you can find them in the fine print. Read agreements carefully to determine your potential liabilities for participating.

✦ **Look for clues to the country of origin.** Affiliate programs that are run from foreign countries, or without a U.S. base of operations, may be a sign that the activity isn't permitted stateside. Or, when you sign up for an affiliate program, you may be asked to enter your country of origin. After doing so, watch for a message or special instruction that serves as a disclaimer about doing business in particular countries.

✦ **Conduct a search.** Although this tip isn't foolproof, you can start verifying the legitimacy of a program by doing a simple search. Enter in a search engine the name of the company you want to do business with or the type of program it is (online games, for example). Especially if it's a hot topic, you quickly find any red flags.

✦ **Investigate the company.** Although some specific products or subjects may be off limits, sometimes you run into companies that are blacklisted. Participating in an affiliate program with one of these companies can label you as "aiding and abetting." If something seems questionable, don't hesitate to check out the company further. Start with the Better Business Bureau Online at `www.bbbonline.org`.

✦ **Check with authorities.** The U.S. Department of Justice has information on a handful of questionable Internet activities, including online gambling and selling prescription medication online. Visit the site at `www.usdoj.gov/criminal/cybercrime/ecommerce.html`. The Federal Trade Commission is another source for validating illegal affiliate operations. You can access it at `www.FTC.gov`.

If you have any reason to suspect that a company is participating in an illegal activity or you have joined an affiliate program and believe it to be fraudulent, report it! Contact the Internet Crime Complaint Center at `www.ic3.gov` to file a concern online.

Questionable affiliations

Affiliate programs that are technically legal but considered somewhat shady or distasteful are a sore spot. The "shady or distasteful" part of that description may sound like a line from the *Leave It to Beaver* generation, but it holds true.

These affiliate marketing programs aren't completely on the up-and-up because of the validity of their offerings or their operational practices. For example, if a program has a long list of complaints registered by unhappy customers and affiliates, this company is skirting disaster. Or, maybe the program is connected to obscene or pornographic products and there's a question about how the material is being distributed.

For lots of reasons, think twice before affiliating with these types of organizations. Ultimately, it's your decision. Just be aware that your site's name and reputation become linked with any program you promote. With that advice in mind, here's a list of red flags to watch for when you review affiliate programs:

✦ **No money-back guarantee is offered.** Be wary of programs that don't provide product guarantees or some form of money-back guarantee to customers. As a prospective affiliate, this one definitely presents a red flag. You can get stuck holding the bag and taking the blame when your referred customers get burned.

✦ **Returning a product is especially complicated.** Nobody likes to deal with returns, but reputable companies offer return policies. Usually, you don't need an act of Congress to make the exchange!

✦ **Corporate information isn't readily available or verifiable.** Legitimate companies place contact information prominently on their Web sites. You can also cross-reference and verify company information by using domain-registration services and other affiliations.

✦ **Affiliates or customers are unhappy.** Monitor the parent site's message boards, or other community message boards, for tales of broken promises and disastrous customer service.

✦ **No support is offered.** The purpose of an affiliate program is to use other sites to drive more traffic and customers to your product. A company with that goal in mind provides resources and support to help affiliates be successful. Newsletters, contact information for technical support, links, banner ads, and other marketing materials are the norm in legitimate affiliate programs. If these items aren't mentioned, trouble might lie ahead.

✦ **A sign-up fee is required.** Signing up for most affiliate programs is free. If you have to pay to join or have your application "screened," run!

✦ **Scam associations are obvious.** You may find a company with no complaints that promotes the type of material that is often labeled as a scam or shows up on consumer watchdog lists. Work-at-home programs and business opportunities are often among the list of top offenders (although plenty of legitimate ones exist, too).

✦ **Legal proceedings have been initiated.** Although you might not have any concrete information, check for lawsuits that have been filed against a company, or any pending legal proceedings that might point to fraud in the making. You can check with the Better Business Bureau online or call your state's attorney general's office. This information might also show up in an Internet search.

Another source of telling information is a company's affiliate agreement, along with its policy for accepting affiliate marketers.

Look for affiliate programs that adhere to strict guidelines. A legitimate program typically turns down approval of a site or cancels an affiliate agreement that has any of these characteristics:

✦ **Inactive URL:** Because your site cannot be verified, the domain may not match what you entered or your site may be under construction.

✦ **Trademark infringement:** You have references to registered names or logos on your site.

✦ **Mismatched information:** The information you provide doesn't match your tax information, business license registration, or domain registration from other, legitimate resources.

✦ **Questionable content:** Your site contains pornography or obscene information; contains hate-oriented information; distributes or links to illegal substances; promotes gambling activities; or is otherwise deemed questionable.

✦ **Questionable recruiting:** Affiliates that plan to market a program by using aggressive e-mail campaigns can violate anti-spamming laws.

Chapter 3: Turning Information into Profit, from e-Books to Webinars

In This Chapter

✔ **Creating an information product**

✔ **Finding hot topics to write about**

✔ **Writing, formatting, and distributing an e-book**

✔ **Developing and promoting a Webinar**

Many people think that online sales involve physical products, where you put something in a box and ship it off to Jane Smith in Iowa, who ordered your product online. These eager sellers sometimes overlook the most valuable "product" they can offer the buying community: their knowledge. The old adage goes "Knowledge is power." Well, if power leads to wealth, knowledge also leads to wealth. Thanks to many of the technological advances of computers and the Internet, it's now much easier to build a system and earn money by sharing your information, knowledge, and techniques with people who desperately want to learn.

Information products are becoming one of the hottest categories of products you can find on the Internet. Unlike a physical product that has material costs (such as the cost of the paper for a book or the cost of microchips and a metal case for a computer), an information product can have zero physical costs. Unlike a television or car that has to roll off an assembly line and requires a certain amount of labor to produce one unit, you can make infinite copies of an information product — instantaneously — and meet whatever demand you have for your product. In the past, information products required postage, printing, transportation, and other fees to distribute information. Now you can zap an electronic version of your information product anywhere in the world with an e-mail message.

In this chapter, we talk about the world of information products and how you can create, benefit, and profit from them. We show you how to create your information product, research and refine your topic, and lay out the information in a clear and concise format. Then we show you how to make your information available to costumers by putting it into an *electronic book* (or *e-book*) or a World Wide Web seminar *(Webinar)*.

Creating Your Own Information Product

The best example of an information product is something you probably have in your car: a map. A map is simply a physical representation of highways, streets, intersections, and landmarks that tells you about a detailed but specific topic: how the roads in a certain area are laid out and intersect with each other. You then read and interpret the map to solve a specific problem — namely, how to move from point A to point B. Your information products should work in a similar manner. You simply organize a specific, complete set of information about a given topic, present it in a clear fashion, and collect money for distributing the information.

Finding hot topics

Which information should you sell? The answer varies, depending on your knowledge, experience, and goals. The topic of your information product is essential, so ask yourself a few questions to get started:

✦ **What am I good at?** Suppose that you're at a party or get-together and a friend or an acquaintance hears about your job and life story and asks, "Hey, how did you do such-and-such?" or "What did you need to know to get that opportunity?" That's a source for your information product.

If your life experience has trained you to excel at a difficult topic, such as assembling a complicated piece of equipment or laying out an interior design for a new home, you can capture and record that experience to help others and profit from the experience. People pay for experience all the time — if they didn't, every consultant in the world would be out of a job!

✦ **What are people having problems with?** If you notice that a number of people are having the same problem in one area, an information product to help solve that problem can be quite profitable.

Sometimes, the information is out there but it's hard to find, it's packaged poorly, or it isn't explained well. For example, someone who had attended driving school for a traffic violation found out how to legally challenge traffic tickets in court, exploit the most common loopholes that cause tickets to be dismissed, and even attend driving school more often than the law intended. He wasn't a born expert, but he learned what he needed to know and made money by presenting that information in an organized and clear fashion.

✦ **What areas of service does my business provide?** Sometimes, the best way to explain what your business does is to transfer some key functions or knowledge areas of your business into an information product, and use it to introduce clients to your business or get noticed in your community.

Real estate agents commonly package small information packets describing the top ten things that new homeowners should look for in new homes. By distributing this packet, an agent can provide instant value to a potential client, show experience in an area, and, hopefully, gain some business beyond what the packet explains.

Put together a focus group consisting of your family members and friends. Ask them which books they bought recently, which magazines they subscribe to, and which television programs they watch. It doesn't hurt to expand your reach by talking to your customers or people in your field and asking them similar questions. Understanding your market is critical for any product, including information products.

Researching the information

After you know what area you want your information product to focus on, you have to research the information. In some cases, even though you may know everything you want to say, that doesn't mean you're done with this step. You should always start by making a list of everything you need in order to complete this product, even if the only thing you need is your experience.

As you prepare your list, you may want to start by creating the outline of your information product and matching up your research with sections of the product. For example, if you know that part of your product will include a contact list of professionals, one research item should be "Compile list of professionals." Every section of your product should have at least one research task, even if that task is "Think about it and write it down."

Before you finish your list, make sure that you cover the three Cs:

✦ **Current:** Make sure that your information is current. Even if you're an expert in a certain area, the rules may have changed since you last looked into it. If you're writing a guide for self-employed people doing their own taxes, for example, brush up on the new tax laws. If you're writing a guide to hot travel sites, revisit those sites and make some phone calls to make sure that everything is still open and accessible. Add a task to your research list to do follow-up, or *fact checking,* as they call it in the media.

✦ **Competition:** See what else is out there, and read up on other information products in your area. Find out what areas are being covered, how long the product is (in pages), how much it charges, and what means of distribution is being used to sell it.

Don't copy other people's paragraphs word for word. Just get an idea of the scope that they cover, and make sure that your product is competitive with (and, hopefully, better than) those other products.

✦ **Content:** What's the meat of your information product? What's the substance of the information you will charge for? Sure, you might copy some background information, some examples, and some information from a third-party source (such as the address, phone number, and mission statement of a business that someone needs to call as part of your product), but the specialized information you're adding is the reason that people are buying your product. Sometimes, the value of a product consists of the random pieces of information gathered into one document; at other times, the value lies in a streamlined set of instructions that nobody else has provided.

Organizing your thoughts

Even if you know your topic backward and forward, can you convey this information so that anyone can understand it? Some of the most brilliant people in the world may specialize in their areas, but cannot commit that information to words and pictures to explain it to others. Unless your information product is a basic directory of names and phone numbers, explain a process or product in a clear and straightforward manner.

The best way to organize all your information into a product is to imagine that you're the customer for this item. Determine which information you would need to see first. Think about what state your customers are in when they start reading your product. If you have any assumptions about what your customers have done before they start reading, make those assumptions clear from the beginning. For example, if your information product is only for people who already signed up with a company to host its Web site, make sure that you state up front: "Do not read any further until you select your Web host and sign up for an account."

Many people organize their information by using this structure:

1. **Explain the problem.**

Summarize why someone bought this product, the situation they're in, and what this product provides. "Still on the lookout for a great apartment near your work? If you're ready to find that perfect apartment, this 10-page guide walks you through all the steps and puts you on the right track."

2. **Lay out the solution.**

Start to give the "meat" of the product as you lay out the core of your information.

3. **Give examples.**

As you're explaining the situation, be sure to give lots of examples and hypothetical situations of how your information is used in practice.

4. **Summarize with a conclusion.**

Give a concise overview of what you just presented, remind readers of the most important points you brought up, and give them an action item showing what they can do after they read your product.

Use figures and illustrations to make your point. People respond to visual cues better than they do to words, so be sure to include illustrations in your information product to drive home your point. You can use computer screen shots, drawings or blueprints, or photos relating to your topic. Take a look at one artist's use of images to explain his point in Figure 3-1.

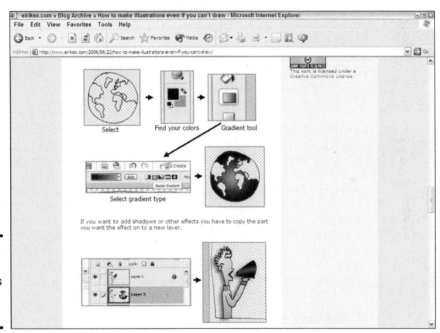

Figure 3-1:
Use figures and pictures to illustrate your point.

As you lay out your document, make sure that the sections make sense in the order you present them so that readers can logically understand the points being made. Research has shown that people respond well to a story format, with a beginning, a middle, and an end. Your information product has these three parts:

✦ **Beginning:** Explain the problem.

✦ **Middle:** Describe your solution.

✦ **End:** Give examples of using your information.

Use appendices, glossaries, and indexes to help people find specific facts quickly. This way, people can use your product as a reference guide after they initially read it.

Providing E-Books

One common way to capture and present an information product is in an electronic book, or e-book. Unlike the physical book you hold in your hands, an *e-book* is simply an electronic version of a book that you read on a computer screen or specialized reader device. Because the content of an e-book is stored in an electronic file, you have several options for storing it.

The great thing about an e-book is that you, as the creator, can choose a style for setting it up:

✦ Use chapters such as the ones you find in a physical book, with a beginning, a middle, and an end.

✦ Style your e-book as an academic term paper composed of page after page of prose, with examples, figures, and appendices.

✦ Use a long table with rows and columns of information in a directory-style format.

As you put together an e-book, its structure depends on the information you're presenting. Some e-books read like miniature books, with their own tables of contents, indexes, and chapter headings, like the management review e-book shown in Figure 3-2. If your e-book is long, consider breaking the content into clear, easy to-find headings. If your e-book is shorter than a typical chapter, an introductory paragraph is usually sufficient to explain its flow and structure.

Creating the document

Most people now use computer word processors to write their documents, which makes the creation of e-books easy. Using all the text you type, you can convert your document file into an e-book in just a few steps. If you write everything using pen and paper or your favorite Underwood typewriter, the first thing you need to do is enter all that information into a word processor, such as Microsoft Word.

The most common format for an e-book is now Portable Document Format, or PDF. This technology was developed by Adobe so that people can exchange documents without losing their style and formatting. Adobe has provided free software, the Adobe Reader, which allows anyone to read a document by using the PDF standard. Businesses around the world have adopted PDF as their standard for reading and exchanging documents. One great thing about PDF is that you can lock your PDF file and your customers can't change or edit the document. After the text is created, it's locked into place and your formatting decisions don't get lost or changed, because every customer sees exactly the same page layout.

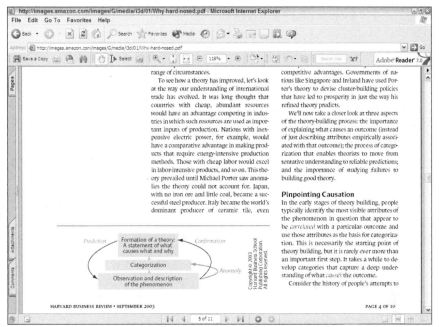

Figure 3-2:
Management review advice available in an e-book.

PDF refers to a specific kind of computer file that stores formatting information along with text and graphics. When you send the file to other people, it appears the same way to them when they view or print the file.

You have different ways to create a PDF file. Adobe sells the Adobe Acrobat software program, which allows you to create PDF files from a Microsoft Word document. You can also find software on the Internet whose only function is to convert different kinds of documents into PDF files.

To get you started in creating PDF files, Adobe offers an Internet-based utility: Create PDF. Go to `http://createpdf.adobe.com` for more information. You can get a trial subscription that allows you to create a PDF file as many as five times; then you must pay for a monthly subscription for unlimited conversions.

You can store your e-book in formats other than PDF. Microsoft created the special software Microsoft Reader, which uses a special e-book format, but that format hasn't caught on commercially. Sony and Amazon have their handheld book readers and encourage people to convert or create books for their formats. Some people use scanners to take pictures of the pages in their e-books and save each page as its own image file. The most common picture formats are JPG, GIF, and BMP. By using image files, you (the creator) can lock in the text and formatting, just like in a PDF file. You can also lay out your pages with graphics and pictures, however, even if you're not good at designing your documents with a computer.

Distributing your e-book on e-shelves

You created your e-book; now you might wonder how to hand it to your customers. In most cases, you also want to collect payment before you send the e-book to them. You can use one of these methods to distribute your e-book:

✦ Sell it directly on your Web site.

✦ Auction off physical copies saved on a CD-ROM on eBay.

✦ List it on Amazon as a product.

✦ Sell it on an information distribution Web site such as Lulu.com or ClickBank.com.

✦ Find a partner business that reaches the same customers as your target audience.

After the payment is collected, you can offer your customers several options for handing over the e-book:

✦ **Download:** Store your e-book on an Internet Web server and tie it into a Web page on that server (see Figure 3-3). When someone uses a Web browser to go to the Web page and clicks a special link, the browser asks whether she wants to open or save a file to her computer. This way, the customer can save a copy of the e-book to her computer. The main copy of the e-book always remains on the server; each time a customer clicks the link, however, a new copy is created and sent from your Web server to your customer's computer.

✦ **E-mail:** Most e-mail programs allow you to attach an e-book file to an e-mail message. After you collect payment, you create a message to send to your customer, attach a copy of your e-book, and send off the message. Just like in the download method, your original, or *master*, copy of the e-book never leaves you. Instead, a new copy is made and attached to the e-mail sent to your customer.

✦ **CD-ROM:** Even though you're dealing with an electronic product that requires no physical media, you find that certain customers still want to buy something they can hold in their hands. Many e-book creators burn their e-books to CD-ROMs and then sell those physical discs with the e-books on them. Some sites, like eBay, now require you to have a physical item to sell or auction off, so you have to create a CD-ROM if you want to sell your e-book on those sites. This method can be especially effective if the large e-book you're selling would require a long download time over the Internet. You can package your e-book CD-ROM with other documents or holders, to add some weight to your product. Or, shave the CD-ROM to the size of a business card, which makes it portable and easy to store.

Burning refers to the process your computer uses to store on disc the information that makes up a file. A special type of CD-ROM drive receives an electronic file from your computer and starts engraving, or burning, the information on the disc so that information can be read later by another computer.

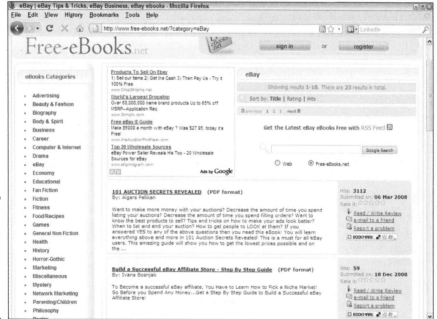

Figure 3-3:
Have people download your e-books from your Web site!

Putting Together a Webinar

Some people learn best by reading about a topic, and others learn better by having someone explain topics to them in a lecture- or seminar-style format. Although e-books can be effective in teaching people valuable information, sometimes customers require live voices or slides or drawings to complement the information. Thus, the multibillion-dollar seminar business was formed. With technology now making it easier to transmit audio, video, and text, education and technology have melded into the *Webinar,* or Web seminar.

Think of a Webinar as watching a seminar on your computer. During the seminar, you might

✦ Watch an audio feed of the instructor talking.

✦ View Microsoft PowerPoint slides on your screen.

✦ Read an outline of the presentation.

✦ Write some text notes.

✦ Use a chat window to ask the instructor some questions (or talk to your fellow seminar attendees) at the end of the presentation.

This technology is possible because of the growing number of people who have broadband connections to the Internet using cable modems from their cable TV companies or DSL connections from their phone companies. These connections allow that information — the audio, video, and text — to be carried to someone's computer as it's happening.

The easiest way to decide whether to create a Webinar, rather than an e-book, is to ask yourself whether the video and audio add value to the presentation. Does the presence of video add to the value you're giving your customer? Does your point come across better if people can see you or a live demonstration of what you're trying to do? For example, if you're selling an information product about how to assemble a motorcycle, a live video demonstration of the bike being assembled can demonstrate the process better than any book can.

In case you're not sure whether a Webinar is the right choice, take a look at your competition in that area. If everyone else is presenting Webinars, you need to create one in order to compete. Conversely, if no one is creating Webinars, you can stand out by creating one. Whoever first invests the time and resources in this newer technology will be rewarded.

Your recording session

If you ever teach a class or present a lecture or seminar, you have the ingredients for creating your own Webinar. You can simply have someone record you as you give your next seminar and then edit the video and audio to create your Webinar file. If you make your own PowerPoint slides, you can simply record yourself explaining the information and then add the PowerPoint slides to the audio file to create a basic Webinar. In this situation, you simply indicate when during the audio file to move ahead with a new slide.

One company that can help you develop your Webinar is WebEx, which handles live meetings and Webinars for a variety of people and companies. It can provide the tools and assistance to combine your video recording, audio recording, and slides to create your Webinar. WebEx employees can also help you create a Webinar to deliver information live from your laptop to an eager audience. Your customers then can connect to you by using WebEx and watch the proceedings from their computers. You can find more information by going to www.webex.com/go/demo and downloading one of its specialized demonstrations, as shown in Figure 3-4.

Figure 3-4:
Have
WebEx
show you
the power
of its
system.

This growing trend is even attracting such software giants as Microsoft, which created the Live Meeting program to help people meet virtually by connecting to a central area so that they can talk to each other, write notes back and forth, and conduct meetings without face-to-face interaction. You can go to http://office.microsoft.com/en-us/livemeeting to sign in and download a free 30-day trial version of the Live Meeting software.

Finding your audience

You have two main ways to reach your customers with a Webinar:

✦ They can watch you deliver it live.

✦ You can record it so that they can download it and view it later.

Based on how you present your information, you need a specific strategy for finding the right audience for your Webinar.

Book IV
Chapter 3

Turning Information
into Profit, from
e-Books to Webinars

If you're presenting a Webinar live, recruiting customers is similar to finding students for a live class. Pick a date and start advertising it weeks in advance. Then plan a day and time that's conducive to the audience you're reaching. If it's a business crowd, target sometime during the week and during the workday, perhaps a lunch seminar or an afternoon meeting. If you're targeting a consumer audience, a weeknight after dinner or a weekend might be more appropriate. You charge admission to your Webinar just like you do for a class, but rather than give out a conference room number, you provide an Internet link that customers can use to connect to your Webinar.

Even if you present the information live, you should always record it to sell to students down the road. Selling a recorded Webinar is like selling an e-book. The date of purchase isn't as critical, and all the necessary information is available at the time of purchase, so focus on the immediate sale. At the moment of payment, the buyer should receive access to the special Internet link to start downloading the Webinar. The recorded Webinar gives customers immediate gratification, although they don't get to ask questions while they're watching it.

Chapter 4: Paying Up with the Right Payment Options

In This Chapter

✔ **Taking credit cards**

✔ **Obtaining a merchant account**

✔ **Setting up your gateway and payment processor**

✔ **Understanding the cost of providing convenience**

✔ **Offering payment options beyond credit cards**

✔ **Avoiding fraudulent charges and other online credit risks**

*O*ne indisputable fact about running an online business is that you can't very well sell products over the Internet if you don't have a way to accept money from customers. There's really no way around it. You have a bevy of options, however.

One common solution is to accept credit cards, just as any brick-and-mortar store does. With credit and debit cards most commonly used for online shopping, customers expect to be able to pay this way. Fortunately, the acceptance and growth of e-commerce have simplified the process for online merchants. In less than a week, you can be ready to accept your first online credit card order.

Then again, not all customers have credit cards ready at their fingertips. Or, perhaps they don't want to use credit cards online for security reasons. As an e-commerce merchant, you should provide those customers with an alternative payment solution.

In this chapter, we tell you about all the payment options available to your online business, and we show you how to start setting them up on your site.

Accepting Credit Card Payments

Enabling a Web site to accept credit cards is one of the most misunderstood functions of e-commerce. A shopper understands that she has to type her credit card number into a box on her computer screen and then click the Purchase button. And, she knows that after a few seconds, she receives an approval (or not) for her purchase. Although everything that happens between these two points comes across as a mystical unknown occurrence, not a drop of magic is involved in this simple process (see Figure 4-1).

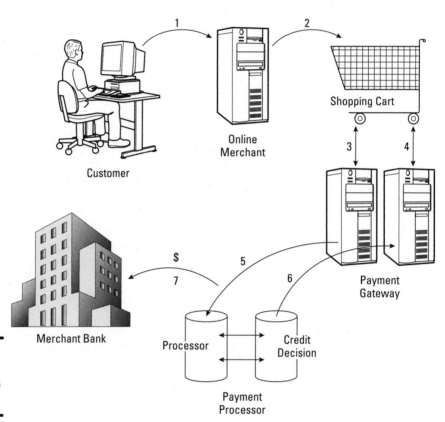

Figure 4-1:
Processing
credit cards
online.

Here's how it works:

1. A customer goes shopping on your site and puts products into a virtual cart.

Shopping cart software that you add to your site allows customers to select products for purchase. When customers are ready to check out, the shopping cart starts the process of ringing up the sale.

2. The customer pays for the product by using a credit card.

Your shopping cart program should provide an online form for the customer to complete, including personal information, shipping details, and a credit card number and expiration date (and, possibly, a verification code from the back of the card).

3. Your site sends that credit card information to a payment gateway.

   The *gateway* is a virtual gate through which information is transmitted, or passed between your site and a credit card processing site. The gateway, like the little box you use to swipe your card when you're shopping in a traditional store, is a tool for communicating information between the store and the credit card company.

4. A payment processor receives your customer's information and verifies it.

   The processor's job is to talk with the company or bank that issues the credit card. The processor ensures that the card is valid and that it has enough credit to cover the purchase.

5. The processor sends a credit decision back to the gateway.

   The processor finds out whether your customer is approved or declined for the purchase and transmits that data right back to the payment gateway.

6. Your gateway passes along the approval decision to your shopping cart and finalizes the shopping transaction.

   Your customer sees a final message saying that the purchase is approved (or not). From there, your shopping cart program can provide a receipt, shipping details, and an invitation to shop again.

   Steps 2–6 take only a few seconds, and then your customer's purchase is complete.

7. While your customer is receiving an approval message, the processor is sending the money to your bank account.

   After the credit card issuer says that credit is available, the processor makes sure that money is sent to your bank and deposited into your merchant account.

Although this process is happening within milliseconds of the approval process, you might not see the money in your account for two to three business days.

Securing a merchant account

Now that you better understand the process, you're ready to get it set up on your site. The first step is to secure a merchant account. You can choose from several resources:

+ **Bank:** You can turn to your local bank to set up a merchant account. After all, your business checking account resides there. Most banks now offer e-commerce merchant services as part of their standard small-business service packages. However, be aware of a few issues. Banks often

- Have a more rigid approval process for online businesses because they're still considered high-risk ventures

- Pass your application to a third-party company for approval (as opposed to processing and managing it internally)

- Increase your costs for a merchant account because the bank is essentially a middleman and receives a commission on the referral of your account

✦ **Direct provider:** You can access many of the same direct merchant account providers that your local bank might use. By going directly to a processor to set up a merchant account, you can cut out some of the initial costs. You can set up a merchant account with one of these processors:

- *Cardservice International:* www.cardservicesales.com

- *Merchant Warehouse:* www.merchantwarehouse.com

✦ **Third-party agent:** This type of company or independent agent offers these types of merchant account services:

- *Broker:* This person is usually an independent sales rep who makes a commission from brokering or signing up new customers. A broker who represents more than one company can help you compare and find the best rates available.

- *Online service:* Companies that once offered a primary service, such as a shopping cart program, are now including bundled access to multiple companion services. Setting up merchant accounts is among those services.

If you deal with one of the larger online services, you can take advantage of their economies of scale and find a better deal on some items. For example, sites such as Network Solutions have a merchant account program (www.merchantaccounts.networksolutions.com) and may waive set-up fees, application fees, and even deposits. They also tend to have higher approval and acceptance rates for online businesses because they target that customer base.

Choosing a payment gateway

As soon as you receive the go-ahead to accept credit cards, your next action is to choose a payment gateway.

The gateway talks to the credit card companies, your banks, and your Web site. Needless to say, the gateway plays an important role in your e-commerce equation.

If you're receiving bundled services from one source, your merchant account provider might already have a designated gateway for you to use.

That's good news because it indicates that a relationship is already established. Both ends know how to successfully come together in the middle, so to speak. Alternatively, the provider might have partnerships set up with several gateways. They simply refer you and let you select the one you want to use. Or, you might be left to search for a payment gateway on your own.

You can choose from hundreds of payment gateways, and hooking up with the wrong one can bring your sales to a halt (sometimes before they get started). Don't worry, though: You should have no trouble finding the right match. Look for a payment gateway that meets these criteria:

✦ **It's diverse.** To be effective, your gateway needs to work with all major credit cards, including MasterCard, Visa, and American Express.

✦ **It's compatible.** One of the most important requirements is that the gateway integrates with your shopping cart software. Although major gateways are already set up to talk with the majority of off-the-shelf shopping carts, it never hurts to verify that your gateway is compatible.

If your shopping cart is custom designed or is a lesser-known software, you might have to do a little programming to make your gateway communicate with your site.

✦ **It pays in a timely manner.** Each gateway has its own rules for when and how to make payment to your bank. Choose a gateway that deposits your money within a few days at most (as opposed to once a month or so).

✦ **It's supportive.** As with any service provider, make sure that your payment gateway has customer service support available at any time of the day or night.

✦ **It's accessible.** You should be able to view the status of your transactions in an online report, along with other management tools.

✦ **It's feature rich.** Payment gateways have a surprising number of features you can use (or add for a fee). Allowing for recurring billing and additional payment options on your customer accounts, and fraud-protection tools for you, are all desirable features. Even though these options might not be a big deal now, you want them available as your site grows.

When you're ready to get started, here's a list of some better-known payment gateways you can contact:

✦ **Authorize.Net:** www.authorize.net

✦ **Chase Paymentech:** www.paymentech.com

✦ **LinkPoint API and LinkPoint Connect:** www.firstdata.com/linkpoint

+ **Online DataCor Blue Pay:** www.onlinedatacorp.com/about
  onlineapp.asp

+ **Verisign Payflow Link and Payflow Pro:** www.verisign.com

When you're comparing the cost of payment gateways, be sure to look at gateway resellers, too. Some offer a limited number of transactions for free when you sign up. In some cases, you don't have to pay additional fees on your first 1,000 transactions.

Reading the fine print: Fees

When you're applying to become an authorized credit card merchant, be sure to compare service providers. Although base rates might remain similar, other unexpected fees could swing the pendulum in favor of one over another. To compare apples to apples, you need to understand the different types of fees you might encounter:

+ **Application:** Some agents charge a nominal fee for processing your application. Expect to pay at least $100.

+ **Setup:** This fee covers the cost of establishing your merchant account and can range from a couple of hundred dollars to a thousand dollars or more. A typical fee is two or three hundred dollars.

+ **Discount rate:** Each time one of your customers makes a purchase with a credit card, your merchant account provider takes a cut of the sale. The amount varies based on the type of card that's used but is usually between 2 to 4 percent.

If you're promised a much lower rate or your contract shows a very low rate, double-check the type of merchant account that's set up for you. Your account should specify Internet, mail order, or telephone sales. Because you can't swipe an actual credit card, rates for these types of transactions are consistently higher (sometimes by as much as a full point) than those for offline retailers.

+ **Terminal cost:** When you're swiping credit cards or manually punching in account numbers, you need a small electric terminal or box. You might have to lease or purchase this equipment, which can add several hundred dollars to your annual costs. For e-commerce sales, a terminal usually isn't required.

+ **Statement:** This monthly fee covers the merchant account provider's cost of compiling, printing, and mailing a monthly statement of your account. The average fee ranges from 5 to 15 dollars.

You might be able to eliminate this fee by choosing to access your reports online rather than on paper statements you receive by postal mail. When you ask your provider whether you have this option, also confirm how long online statements are available for viewing. (You print your own copies to serve as a permanent record, if needed.)

+ **Transaction:** You pay a small processing fee for each credit card transaction. This nominal amount is usually less than 25 cents per transaction. And yes, it's in addition to your discount rate!

+ **Monthly minimum:** If you expect to have a limited number of sales (maybe your business is new or you just don't expect a lot of traffic early on), your merchant account provider might establish a minimum charge level. If your sales, number of transactions, or combined discount rate and transaction fees don't exceed that minimum, the company tacks on an additional charge. In other words, the company is counting on you to process lots of orders so that it makes more money. You pay for it either way, though.

+ **Charge-back:** Whenever a customer disputes a purchase with the credit card company, the dollar amount of that purchase is taken from your bank account. Your merchant account provider might also charge you an additional fee for processing this transaction. Online orders that don't require signatures (or the physical cards to process) are especially susceptible to charge-backs.

+ **Termination:** Whether you're switching merchant providers or closing up shop, your original contract might contain a termination fee. Sometimes this fee can run close to — if not more than — a thousand dollars.

Before signing any agreement, seek out the clause that details the steps you have to take to cancel the agreement. If early termination is expensive, make sure that a companion clause specifies that you can upgrade when new features are released. Today's version of the latest and greatest feature can be quickly usurped in a few months. You don't want to get stuck paying big bucks for features that don't keep pace with your growing business.

Offering Alternative Payment Options

You might think that credit cards have a hold on the online shopping market. Indeed, the majority of customers prefer paying that way. Yet online security concerns and the demand for flexibility are driving the need for alternative options.

You receive a definite benefit when you expand your customers' payment choices. By having at least four options available at checkout, you can increase your customer conversion rates by 20 percent. Online stores that offer only credit cards as a payment source get 60 percent of their visitors to purchase something. By adding PayPal or eChecks, you can boost that conversion rate.

To put this advice in perspective, suppose that your site has 100 visitors in one day. If you offer a single type of payment source, probably 60 of those people will buy from you. Add a few other options, however, and 8 of 10 visitors will buy from you!

Gain 20 more customers by being flexible — that's a no-brainer, as they say. As luck would have it, you can offer customers more than a handful of alternative payment solutions:

✦ **PayPal:** One of the most popular alternatives is allowing customers to pay by using a PayPal account. If you already have a payment gateway, you can add PayPal Checkout Express to your Web site. As a bonus, your customers' billing and shipping information that's stored with PayPal is automatically used on your site so that they don't have to reenter information on future visits. To start using this option, go to `https://www.paypal.com`.

✦ **Electronic checks:** This service, also called *ACH processing,* allows a customer to use funds taken directly from a personal or business bank account. The funds are then deposited directly into your bank account. For you, this service represents lower processing fees per transaction than with credit cards. It can range from 29 cents per transaction to more than a dollar for each check. Increasingly, payment gateways are making electronic check processing available for your Web site. Or, you can use a third-party e-check provider, such as

  • *Electronic Payment Services' iChex:* `www.ichex.com`

  • *Pay By Check:* `www.paybycheck.com`

Before signing an agreement with a third-party electronic check provider, always compare prices. In addition to paying a per-transaction fee, you're charged a fee for returned checks. You might also be charged activation, monthly service, and integration fees for setting up the service with your existing shopping cart. These fees can run several hundred dollars. Using the service through your gateway might be cheaper.

✦ **Gift cards:** Offering gift certificates or gift cards on your site is an easy way to extend payment options while increasing your sales.

✦ **Instant credit:** If your customers could buy now and pay later, don't you think that it would help prevent shopping cart abandonment? Well, companies are now providing e-tailers a way to do just that. At the time of checkout, your customer essentially receives approval for the dollar amount of the purchase. This process usually takes no more than 15 seconds. Then the customer has a set amount of time to make the payment. Don't worry: You receive the funds immediately, as you would with any other type of payment. A third-party company handles everything for you! One such solution is offered by Bill Me Later (`www.billmelater solutions.com`).

✦ **Offline payments:** An option that's sometimes overlooked is allowing customers to send in payments by using a less technically advanced method. Although only a small percentage of shoppers are likely to use these options, it could be worthwhile. After all, it's certainly not cost prohibitive to extend these options:

- Send payment though Western Union.

- Mail checks through the U.S. Postal Service.

- Pay by phone (requires a credit card, but some customers feel safer this way).

You can use a third-party service to provide a resource for alternative payment methods for your site. iBill (www.ibill.com) offers recurring billing, pay by phone, electronic checks, and private-label credit cards. You can also charge a one-time fee to customers for using an alternative payment, which helps offset your costs.

Managing the Payment Process to Protect Your Income

Believe it or not, one day you will receive a fraudulent charge-back from a customer. You lose the money, plus handling fees charged by the credit card company.

Of course, a charge-back is only one type of online fraud you have to worry about. Dealing with stolen credit cards is another common headache.

Don't despair yet. Credit card companies, payment gateways, and processors are working diligently to help protect your online business from thieves. All you have to do is choose to implement their protective services. To help minimize your risks, search out these standard security features from your payment gateway provider:

✦ **Address verification (AVS):** Each time an order is placed, the physical street address that's on file with the credit card issuer is compared to the billing address the customer gives you with an order.

✦ **Card code verification (CCV):** Customers must enter both a credit card account number and a special three-digit code (the set of numbers that follows the card number). The code is usually on the back of the credit card.

✦ **Filtering:** You can use several security filtering tools. One type allows you to set a monetary limit for additional security checks on orders that exceed that amount. Other filters screen for suspicious orders and identify IP addresses that have excessive amounts of purchases within a short period.

✦ **Address blocking:** By using this tool, you can block IP addresses from your site. In this case, the addresses are known sources of earlier fraudulent orders.

✦ **Authorized AIM IP:** When you submit Advanced Integration Method (AIM) transactions, you can designate a server's specific IP addresses that are allowed to transmit transactions.

As a smaller online business (generating fewer than $5 million in annual sales), you typically have a lower fraud rate than large e-tailers. That's because you

✦ Process fewer transactions

✦ Validate orders manually (usually)

✦ Fight charge-backs by calling customers personally

Chapter 5: Putting the (Shopping) Cart before the Horse

Do you absolutely need a shopping cart? No. If you sell only a few items, you can easily get by with using an online order form. For example, customers making a purchase can print the form and then fax it to you. Or, after customers fill out designated boxes on the online form and click Send, the results arrive in your inbox for manual order processing.

With that in mind, here's the real question: Do you *want* a shopping cart for your Web site? Absolutely — especially if you sell more than a dozen items.

Hey, we don't have anything against Web-based forms or fax machines. Assuming that you're in the Internet game to make a little money, however, a shopping cart is an essential tool of e-commerce. This chapter helps you sort through all the latest options so that you can start selling like a real pro!

Not All Carts Are Created Equal

Today's sophisticated applications have grown into more than simple shopping baskets for online customers. And, you can incorporate quite a few tools into your shopping cart program. Your job is to figure out which features you need most, right now — and determine which features will serve you best in the long run. Before you can do either, you have to understand what's out there and what's important to use. To make this process easier for you, we divide the most sought-after features into four standard categories:

✦ Management

✦ Customer-centric

✦ Integration and maintenance

✦ Promotion and marketing

Back-end management

Each shopping cart program has a set of administration tools. Though the specifics can vary among types of software, ultimately these tools give you control of your shopping cart. Here's a list of features to look for in admin tools:

- ✦ **Administrative functions:** Passwords and options such as font size or number of items to display on a page are settings that only an administrator — namely, you — should be able to change.

- ✦ **Customization:** Choices, choices — this factor is important when you're using a shopping cart program. The more you can change colors and fonts, for example, the more likely you are to create a shopping cart that melds with the rest of your site.

- ✦ **Exporting:** Always confirm that you can export your products from the shopping cart. This feature is critical if you end up using a different shopping cart down the road and need to transfer your inventory.

- ✦ **Importing:** Having to enter your products into a shopping cart one by one is the last thing you want to do. If you have dozens of product numbers (similar to bar codes), you would be typing at your keyboard for several days! Look for programs that allow you to import your products from an Excel spreadsheet (or a similar method).

- ✦ **Inventory:** If your shopping cart feature is integrated with your own inventory system (if you already have one), you can easily manage your offline stock from your Web site.

- ✦ **Wizards:** Use these tools to customize your shopping cart and integrate it with your Web site. The wizard walks you step by step through the entire process.

Customer-centric

Which features are most important to your customers? When you're test-driving a shopping cart demo, try to view the experience from the eyes of your shoppers. Does the cart help your customers process their orders quickly? Or, does it leave them frustrated and stick you with a bad case of shopping cart abandonment? Here are some features you can include that can benefit your customers:

- ✦ **Product views:** Customers can't touch or feel your products when they're shopping online. The only qualities on which customers can base their purchasing decisions are the images and descriptions you give them. That's why you should use a shopping cart that allows you to upload multiple images for one product.

✦ **Save settings:** Can your customers save products in their shopping carts and then return later to make purchases? The ability to save these settings and others makes the shopping experience more pleasant.

✦ **Store data:** Does the cart give your customers the option to store their data? This feature prevents returning customers from having to reenter account information repeatedly. Having the option to save the data (especially credit card information) is equally important, however. Some customers would rather not sacrifice possible security risks in favor of convenience.

✦ **View order:** Your customers should be able to view complete orders as they shop or when they check out. Having to view a series of pages before they can see their total shipping costs, for example, is particularly frustrating.

Integration and maintenance

For your shopping cart to work optimally, it has to become a seamless part of your overall site. If it doesn't work, you need to be able to get help. Along these lines, you have to consider several critical integration and maintenance factors:

✦ **Access to support:** When and how is support available if you have trouble with your shopping cart? The best-case scenario is to have access to live support seven days a week. If you have to wait to get help, *your customers* also have to wait, and they aren't fond of waiting! Don't forget to ask whether you pay an extra fee for all that technical support.

✦ **Accommodation of other customer accounts:** Your shopping cart should have the flexibility to handle all types of orders — from wholesale orders to affiliates. Even if you don't need the flexibility today, you want to know that it's already built-in to your cart for use as you grow.

✦ **Communication with shipping and handling:** In addition to integrating your shopping cart with major shipping providers (such as UPS), you have to look closely at how orders are relayed for shipping and handling. Can you customize how and where the order requests are sent? For example, each time an order request is forwarded to your shipping department, can you have a duplicate copy e-mailed to another department?

✦ **Integration with your accounting software:** Perhaps one of the stickiest points of integrating accounting and shopping cart software is how well your shopping cart can relay information to your accounting program. If these two programs can't function together (or integrate with each other), your workload doubles.

Promotion and marketing

Of all the benefits a shopping cart can offer, the area of promotion and marketing probably receives the least amount of scrutiny before the purchase. Your first inclination is probably to look at how many products a shopping cart holds. Then you find out how much it will cost you. Marketing is one of the last items you consider, perhaps because it's one of those things that you just don't realize a shopping cart can do for you.

Think again! This list of marketing and promotion functions is a small sample of how your shopping cart can help you increase sales. See how many features are built into your shopping cart of choice:

✦ **Bundled products or services:** Based on buying preferences, put together groups of products. They're usually offered at a slight discount from what your customer would spend to purchase each item separately.

✦ **Coupons:** Set up coupon codes to be entered by customers at the time of purchase.

✦ **Cross selling:** Suggest similar or complementary products that customers might like when they view certain products or check out.

✦ **Data feeds:** Your shopping cart should communicate your product information with other comparison shopping sites, including Froogle, Shopping.com, Shopzilla, Shop.com, and Yahoo! Shopping.

✦ **Discounts:** Set up different types of customer groups (such as wholesale or frequent buyer) to give a discount based on buying behavior. Or, offer limited-time discounts by product.

✦ **E-mail communications:** Send newsletters or specials to your customers by e-mail.

✦ **Featured products or specials:** Highlight certain products or limited-time offers throughout your Web site.

✦ **Free-shipping option:** Offer free shipping as a marketing special. This feature can be an important competitive advantage during busy shopping seasons.

✦ **Gift certificates:** A helpful seasonal (or year-round) tool is to offer the option of purchasing and using gift certificates, or virtual gift cards.

✦ **On-site search capability:** A good search tool helps customers easily find products based on several search criteria, such as brand name, category, or generic product name.

✦ **Product reviews and ratings:** Feature additional information on product pages to increase credibility and boost the potential for purchase.

✦ **Search engine friendliness:** Use the shopping cart built-in features to better market your products in major search engines. A shopping cart might offer title and meta tags for every product page or ALT tags with keywords.

+ **Survey tools:** Find out what customers are thinking by displaying a brief survey before checkout or whenever a customer abandons a shopping cart (leaving your site without a purchase).

+ **Tell-a-friend functionality:** Customers can pass along product pages to friends and family members.

+ **Upselling:** Offer an incentive to purchase more products by upselling — for example, "Buy one, get one at half price" or "Buy two and get one free."

You don't have to use all these marketing tools. They might even be a little overwhelming for you at first. Don't worry: That's perfectly natural. We recommend using a shopping cart that has a variety of promotional features, however. As you become more comfortable, start testing the waters and increasing your sales!

Shopping Around for the Best Hosted Solution

Naturally, marketing features and administrative tools aren't the only features that can sway your decision in selecting a cart. You can make your decision based on how the cart is delivered to you (or set up for use). For instance, one easy alternative is to use a *hosted* solution. The shopping cart is then stored on someone else's server and you pay to have access to it.

Hosted shopping carts have four specific advantages:

+ **Cost:** A hosted solution is a more affordable option, especially for a first e-commerce endeavor. For a small monthly fee (sometimes for less than ten bucks), you gain access to an extensive set of shopping cart features.

+ **Simplicity:** Because most shopping carts easily integrate into existing Web sites, theoretically they should be easy to get up and running.

+ **Support:** You get access to customer and technical support. And, because it's a hosted solution, the support hours are usually around-the-clock. When your learning curve is still steep, it's nice to know that you have a place to turn for help, at any time of the night or day!

+ **Test drive:** Try it and see whether you like it. When you use a hosted solution, you don't have to make a long-term commitment. If you're on a monthly plan, you can terminate the agreement fairly easily. As long as the shopping cart has a good exporting feature, you can move your products to another solution if your current one isn't working.

Some terrific hosted shopping carts are available, so take your time in checking out each one. You're bound to find one that suits your needs. In this section, we describe three popular shopping carts to start on your search for the perfect hosted shopping-cart solution.

Of course, you might also decide to use a *storefront,* an all-in-one e-commerce solution. If you do, a hosted shopping cart is included with your storefront as part of the complete package. If this option is one you're interested in pursuing, you can discover all the details in Book VIII, Chapter 1.

1ShoppingCart

The 1ShoppingCart shopping cart has been around for a long time and has a large fan base. You can choose one of four plans ranging from $29 to $99 per month. Or, you can sign up for an annual account, from $299 to $999. Choosing the type of accounts you want is a matter of choosing which shopping cart features you want most. For example, all plans support as many as 10,000 products. And, all versions support a host of marketing features, such as ad tracking, split testing, and coupon creation.

The four plans you can choose from are

✦ **Autoresponder:** If you don't need a shopping cart — just the ability to respond to e-mail queries — this product can handle your requirements.

✦ **Basic:** A shopping cart system plus basic e-mail marketing tools differentiates this option from the Starter program.

✦ **Professional:** Shopping cart, autoresponders, e-mail marketing tools, plus affiliate tracking software make this the most powerful system you can purchase from 1ShoppingCart.

✦ **Starter:** If you don't need tools for analyzing sales, just a basic shopping cart system, the Starter product is perfect.

You can get a 30-day trial of the Professional version of the 1Shopping Cart shopping cart for $3.95. That's a small price to pay to get full access to the shopping cart before you fully invest.

Of course, you can also take a look at all features just by visiting the Web site, at `www.1shoppingcart.com/shopping-cart-features.asp`. 1ShoppingCart.com also highlights several case studies, shown in Figure 5-1, to show you how other stores have used the shopping cart software to increase sales.

GoECart

Like 1ShoppingCart, GoECart (`www.goecart.com`) provides several different plans for its hosted shopping cart. You can pay the fee monthly or yearly. A one-time payment can save you a little money, and can even reduce some of your start-up costs by waiving activation fees. Table 5-1 breaks down the costs and differences between each plan.

Figure 5-1:
See
examples of
how other
stores use
1Shopping-
Cart.

Table 5-1			GoECart Fees		
Plan	*Monthly Fee*	*Annual Cost*	*Setup Fee*	*Number of Products*	*Disk Space*
Plan II	$249.95	$2499	$299.95*	5,000	500MB
Plan III	$499.95	$4,999	$499.95*	20,000	1GB
Custom (contact for quotes)				Unlimited	1GB

*The set-up fee is based on the yearly subscription fee. A higher fee applies to the monthly subscription plan.

GoECart includes almost all its features with each plan, so you don't have to sacrifice a terrific marketing tool just because you have only 50 (rather than 1,500) products to sell. Its marketing tools are extensive, too, and GoECart doesn't charge extra for its affiliate-management feature. It's probably one of the more flexible hosted shopping-cart options.

You can try the free demo, shown in Figure 5-2.

You can see a quick comparison of GoECart and about a dozen other shopping carts by visiting the GoECart site at `www.goecart.com/shopping_cart_software_comparison.asp`.

Finding Off-the-Shelf Software

Before so many hosted shopping carts flooded the market, off-the-shelf software was your best bet for a quick, inexpensive solution. It was available from an Internet service provider (ISP), or you could license the product yourself.

An off-the-shelf shopping cart allows you to add the software to your own server. Many Web developers pursue this option and then become resellers of their particular shopping cart programs.

One big advantage for you, when you're using this type of shopping cart, is that you aren't tied to a specific Web host. In theory, that has always made managing your store easier if you switch service providers. Of course, with importing and exporting functions now a common tool in most shopping carts, it's less of a concern. Other advantages include control and price. For larger stores, the price issue is particularly important. Whereas you might pay $199 per month for a hosted shopping cart that supports 1,000 products, you might find that paying a little more for an unlimited number of products makes it easier on you as your company grows.

If you want to get your hands on an off-the-shelf cart, you can approach it in two ways:

✦ **Purchase:** You can buy software outright. Depending on the shopping cart, the price can range anywhere from $399 for a basic program to more than $5,000 for a more dynamic software product.

✦ **License:** More often than not, software vendors require that you license the use of their products. It's like leasing a car: You pay either a monthly or annual fee for the right to use the software, but you don't own it.

When you're purchasing or licensing a shopping cart, technical support may or may not be included in the price. You might have to purchase a separate technical support package, which adds to your overall cost for the product.

Numerous companies sell off-the-shelf shopping cart solutions. Here are some of the most recognized providers:

✦ **Miva Merchant (www.mivamerchant.com):** Offers all-in-one products, such as online storefronts, and individual tools, such as shopping cart systems.

✦ **ShopFactory (www.shopfactory.com):** Also provides the ability to create ready-to-go storefronts with shopping cart systems included (or sold separately).

✦ **ShopSite (www.shopsite.com):** Offers shopping cart systems at various price points for all business sizes.

✦ **PDG (www.pdgsoft.com):** Shopping cart systems with built-in search engine capabilities.

Before purchasing off the shelf, find out whether your preferred payment gateway is supported by the shopping cart. Conversely, after you buy the software, know which gateways are compatible before selecting one for your store. If you happen to choose one that's not supported, extra programming might be required!

Designing a Cart for You

Custom cart development takes place when you program (or someone you hire programs) a shopping cart that's unique to your needs.

On the bright side, you can get a program that meets your specifications in every way. And, if you know how to program or have someone willing to donate the time (or give you a steal on the price), this option can be less expensive than an off-the-shelf, or hosted, solution.

Then again, hiring someone can get expensive fast. Some programmers start at $15,000, and that amount is quickly exceeded when you add slick, gotta-have-it features. Another problem is that a customized solution can be difficult to integrate with payment gateways, or it involves at least some additional coding. Perhaps the biggest drawback is the limitation on support and ease of scalability. Every time you hit a snag, you have to go back to the developer for help. If your needs change or you discover a feature you want to incorporate, you're again dependent on your developer, which can get expensive.

**Book IV
Chapter 5**

**Putting the
(Shopping) Cart
before the Horse**

If you have a large enterprise, these issues might be small deterrents. For a small online business, your money and time might be better spent elsewhere. If you decide to delve into the custom route, look for these features:

✦ **Bid and quote.** Gather at least three bids before selecting a developer. Then ask for a final quote delivered in writing before you begin the project.

To ensure that you can compare apples to apples, provide each prospective programmer with the same list of specifications. Ask each company to develop a bid from *your* list.

✦ **Define support.** Discuss what types of setup and ongoing support are available, including when support is available and how soon a support issue will be addressed. (Support might be available only during weekdays, for example, and processing your request might take three business days!) The cost of the support should also be included in the final quote.

✦ **Determine timeline.** Be specific about the length of time involved for any type of software development project. Set a series of targets, or objectives, that should be completed by a certain date. This guidepost ensures that the project stays on track.

✦ **Get the details.** The more nitty-gritty specifics you can nail down, the better. Find out how many programmers typically work on a project. More programmers can result in faster delivery of your system, but can also add to its overall cost.

Chapter 6: Taking Inventory

In This Chapter

✔ Taking stock of the items you should make available for sale

✔ Using your research to validate your decisions

✔ Choosing price points that move merchandise

✔ Creating a winning selection with the right number of products

You probably know someone who is a fantastic salesperson. Usually, this person is described as being capable of "selling anything to anyone." Well, the Internet is similar to that top-notch salesperson. It can sell just about anything to almost anyone around the world — with your help, of course. As any good salesperson knows, however, you have to know a few tricks of the trade. The same statement holds true for selling online: To do well, you have to know a few "tricks." Or, in the case of choosing inventory, you simply need some additional information to give your business a boost.

How do you decide what to stock up on to give your business a leg up? To create the ideal inventory for your online business, always keep in mind these three points:

- ✦ **Product:** The goods or services you sell should be readily available for you to purchase and stock and reflect items of interest to your customers.

- ✦ **Pricing:** The amount you charge for your product must make it attractive to customers while also providing you with a reasonable profit.

- ✦ **Selection:** The range of products you offer your customers is more than a matter of quantity. Offer variations of the same product so that your customers can choose from alternative sizes, colors, and styles.

Fortunately, deciding which type of product to promote — and at which price — isn't complicated. In fact, several useful tools and methods can help you determine potential sales-chart-toppers. Even better, you can find most of the product information online for free.

Finding Out What's Popular By Using eBay

What does eBay have to do with the type of products you want to sell on your Web site? That might be the question you're asking, especially if you haven't planned on becoming an eBay merchant. The king of auction sites, however, has become a highly successful and proven business model that's making its way into almost every type of business, one way or the other. The bottom line is that a tremendous amount of e-commerce is being conducted by using eBay. Fortunately for you, the company wasted no time in collecting and analyzing all the valuable information about its buyers and sellers. The translation is that you now have access to a lot of useful research, and it's free!

One of the best sources of information while exploring the sellers' side (information for eBay merchants) is eBay Pulse. It tracks three major trends, which include top product searches, the largest stores, and the most watched items. The sections covering the top product searches and the most watched items list the most popular items being bought and requested by eBay visitors. You can see this information for the entire site or be more specific and view the top searches by a specific category, such as jewelry, sporting goods, or electronics. (You have lots of categories to choose from!) Similarly, you can view the biggest eBay stores, which are useful examples to study to see how they promote their products (with photos and product descriptions, for example) to find success. We suggest using this information to help keep current on which items and categories are popular and use it as a means of tracking the types of items that might be sought-after on your own Web site. To get started, visit `http://pulse.ebay.com`, shown in Figure 6-1, and dive right in!

The information is updated frequently to account for the constant number of transactions made by eBay shoppers. Each list provides an indication of which items are outpacing demand in the eBay world of online bidding. There simply aren't enough of the items on this list to satisfy all would-be buyers. Supply hasn't kept up with demand, which spells *opportunity* for you.

eBay offers another important research tool: Terapeak. This expansion of eBays's former What's Hot list has a monthly fee of $24.95, which offers basic features for free. Other features are considered add-ons, such as advanced search and research functions for a few dollars. To view and sign up for a free trial, go to `www.terapeak.com/signup`.

Figure 6-1:
Find what's
hot on the
eBay Pulse.

Hot tips for choosing the right products

When you're deciding which products to offer for sale online, ask yourself these questions to factor in the answers and reach a decision:

✔ How difficult is it to ship the product? Large, bulky products can add to your shipping woes.

✔ Will larger products, which are expensive to ship, deter customers from making a purchase online?

✔ Are you selling perishable food products?

✔ Do the food products meet all federal guidelines for food handling, storage, and shipping?

✔ Is the product fragile, and does it require special handling?

✔ How much product does a supplier require you to buy at one time to receive the best price?

✔ Where will you keep the inventory?

✔ Do you have suitable storage facilities, or do you have to pay for (rent) additional space?

✔ Is it important to you that smaller products, flat products, and information products take up less room if you have to store the inventory?

✔ If you're making custom products by hand, how long do you spend fulfilling an order? Can you keep up with demand?

✔ Are you already familiar with the product, or is it brand-new to you?

**Book IV
Chapter 6**

Taking Inventory

Putting Together All Your Research

When you're starting a new business, it's comforting to be able to validate your decisions. That's exactly what market research allows you to do. If your searches show that a potential product or service is in high demand, it's a signal that you're on the right track. Or, if you're having trouble selecting products to stock your Web inventory, the popularity listings in your research can spur your imagination.

Some established companies specialize in market research. Their background work is summarized in concise reports that forecast trends and buying behaviors. For the best results, search each company's data bank of reports for titles or topics such as e-commerce, online retailing, and e-business. Although some resources provide free information, others are pay services. Reports can range from several hundred dollars to more than a thousand dollars. For that reason, take extra care to read the descriptions and the date of the report to make sure that they have the most accurate and current information available for your purpose.

These companies specialize in market research:

+ **Ecommerce-Guide:** Provides free articles detailing online buying trends (`www.ecommerce-guide.com/news/research`). For more results, check out the Market Research section by clicking the Resources tab on the menu and then clicking the Market Research tab.

+ **eMarketer:** Specializes in providing data and analysis on trends in e-business, online marketing, and emerging technologies (`www.emarketer.com`). This site also offers free articles for limited periods, so check it frequently.

+ **Forrester:** Offers information specifically about technology and business (`www.forrester.com`). Product areas and services include data and research reports, consulting services, and community programs.

+ **Jupiter Research:** Includes an extensive collection of trend reports and advice by a team of professional analysts (`www.jupiterresearch.com`).

Pricing Your Products

After you decide which products or services you're most interested in selling, it's time to price your merchandise. Having delved into the results of your research, you probably have a good idea of which items have the best chance of selling. However, no matter how trendy or in demand your products are, setting the wrong prices might leave you with inventory that doesn't sell. In this section, we take a look at some pricing strategies and considerations to make sure that you move the merchandise directly into your buyers' hands.

When you're tagging your merchandise, the following factors are the most probable *price influencers,* or factors that affect your sticker price:

✦ **Demand:** Whether customers are seeking out your product because it either meets a need or is thought to be a desirable or trendy item.

✦ **Competition:** Not only who, but also *how many,* competitors you have, and what *prices* they have established for the same or similar products you're selling.

✦ **Market position:** How you want your business to be perceived by customers in the marketplace. For example, an upscale store with high-end products might influence pricing strategies in one direction while a larger, warehouse-type of image might warrant a more competitive pricing strategy.

✦ **Cost:** How much you pay (your expense) to create or purchase the product before reselling it to your customer.

✦ **Profitability:** How much money you want to make each time an item is sold, and after you have considered all expenses or costs associated with selling the item.

Product pricing is one of the most critical business decisions you make. Researching all the advice and pricing models offered in textbooks, or by economists, however, can leave your head spinning. Keep it simple. The basic number for you to grasp is the cost — or actual amount — of the product you're selling. This number incorporates every expense associated with your item, including the wholesale price you paid (the raw costs of materials to make the product), overhead costs ranging from utilities to Internet service fees, commissions, and packaging and shipping costs to deliver the product to your customer.

Costs or expenses that don't fluctuate are *fixed costs* and are often considered as overhead (such as rent). Expenses that might change periodically are *variable expenses.* The price of your product should cover all your variable expenses, and also help contribute toward your fixed costs.

After you understand the cost of what you're selling, you can begin making pricing decisions. Use these two common pricing strategies:

✦ **Cost-plus:** This method requires you to total the costs of your expenses associated with the product and then add an amount you want to make as profit. The resulting dollar amount represents the pricing *floor,* or the lowest price you should charge.

✦ **Value-based:** With this strategy, you're setting a price that reflects the highest amount you believe your customers are willing to pay for the product. Unlike the cost-plus method, this one considers market conditions, such as demand, competition, and the perceived benefits (or value) of your product's features.

For example, if your cost for selling a coffee mug is $4.50, should you turn around and try to sell it for that same price? No, you have to make a respectable profit. That amount depends on how much you want — within reason, of course. If you decide that you have to clear $5.50 on every mug, for example, your price is set at $10.00 per item (cost-plus pricing).

By using value-based pricing, you might be able to set a higher price based on consideration of other factors. For example, how much are customers *willing* to pay for a coffee cup? In other words, what cost does the market bear? Perhaps, in the case of an Elvis mug, its perceived value is much greater than the perceived value of other styles of cups. You might be able to sell each mug for $15.00 or more. Of course, even if your customers are willing to pay that much, they might find a better deal elsewhere. Your next consideration is to find out how much your competitors are charging for the same or similar products. If $9.99 is the top price on other sites, it might be unreasonable for you to expect to set a much higher price.

Now that you have the basic information needed to determine a baseline price for your product or service, you have to consider one more factor: your inventory.

Building Your Inventory

Choosing the best products and prices for your online business is certainly an important factor in starting your new business. You have to consider another issue too: Exactly how much inventory you should keep on hand, or how many different products you should have available for sale. The answer depends on not only the type of products you're selling but also the type of business strategy you want to execute.

Savvy online shoppers are accustomed to an endless array of choices because they can easily jump from one Web site to another. These customers are quick to make a decision about whether your site's inventory meets their expectations.

To keep the attention of most online shoppers, have a clear strategy for what type of, and how much, product you choose to offer.

We don't mean that you have to carry hundreds, or even thousands, of products to find success online. But you can follow a few distinct strategies for building an appropriate online inventory. Each one comes with its own advantages and disadvantages, as discussed in the following sections.

Stocking up as a low-price leader

Competing based on price can be a tricky situation, although it's certainly one option for an inventory strategy. If price is the primary decision-making factor in whether your customers buy, keep this advice in mind:

✦ **Provide many choices.** Offer lots of choices. Your customers are looking for good deals, and might not even have a specific item in mind when they're shopping. You have to stock up.

✦ **Change products often.** Another consideration with this type of inventory is how often you need to change out products. Even if your site doesn't see large volumes of traffic, returning customers expect a revolving inventory. If they discover that your inventory stays pretty much the same after several return visits, they stop coming back altogether.

To help avoid the *click-through* syndrome (customers quickly view all your products without stopping to make a purchase), make sure that your site offers a large variety of products that are rotated or switched out often.

Becoming all things to all people with trial-and-error inventory

This strategy is a category that swallows up many first-time online entrepreneurs. You don't truly have a strategy. Instead, you end up offering a little bit of everything, until you can form a better idea of what sells. This trial-and-error method, often referred to as offering a *chaotic* variety of products, can be cumbersome, but necessary. To reduce stress and quickly try to find the best products to keep in stock, consider these tips:

✦ **Showcase a variety of products and in limited supply.** Nothing is wrong with offering a large variety of products. To keep expenses and storage issues to a minimum, maintain a relatively low level of inventory on all products.

✦ **Rotate featured products often.** Because you're testing the waters with customer preferences, highlight different products daily or weekly. Featuring or spotlighting select items helps you quickly narrow which products your customers respond to most.

✦ **Track your results to find out inventory needs.** You want to see which types of products your customers respond to most, so maintain thorough sales records. After you have more information about your visitors' buying habits, you can begin scaling down the number of products and adjusting your inventory to provide a better selection.

Specializing with limited inventory

Specializing in a field usually leads to the best inventory strategy. And, doing so provides the most likely chance for success when you're building your online business. You might decide to deal exclusively in English teapots or carry only maintenance supply parts for the army. Artists and craftspeople are usually in this category, too. They typically work in only one medium, such as black-and-white photography or high-grade wood carvings. If specializing sounds like your cup of tea, consider the following advice when building your inventory:

✦ **Offer a select number of products.** Focus on the quality or uniqueness of the products rather than on mass quantity. You can afford to keep relatively low levels of inventory, as long as you're always searching for new items to replenish your stock.

✦ **Position yourself as an expert.** Because you deal in a narrow type of product, visitors are more likely to seek you out for your expertise. You can keep inventory levels low and charge a finder's fee or consulting fee to help customers locate similar products on request.

Keep inventories low and establish an active network with others for quickly locating similar products. Being able to direct customers to other resources, or locate special pieces in a timely manner, provides a valuable service that can also keep customers returning to your Web site.

Chapter 7: Fulfilling Expectations and Orders

In This Chapter

✔ Planning the logistics of your operation

✔ Setting up an in-house fulfillment system

✔ Outsourcing your shipping area to someone else

✔ Learning the rules of shipping and handling

✔ Maintaining your information as you pack up and ship out

Setting up your online business can be full of excitement and milestones. The true payoff, though, is best realized when that first payment rolls in for something you sold. Seeing a paper check or electronic deposit right in front of you helps cement the idea of what you're doing and provides validation of the business you created. Even though it's a satisfied feeling, you can easily see the money and think that you're done.

After the order is completed and the payment has cleared, you still need to handle one area of the sale: *Fulfillment* is simply the practice of delivering the product to the buyer after payment has been received, or *filling* the order. In a retail store, fulfillment is easy: You hand your customer a shopping bag with the purchase and the sales receipt, and he walks out the door. In an online business, you need to perform a few steps to make order fulfillment happen. Thankfully, with all the advances in Internet technology and shipping services, achieving this goal is easier than ever.

Of course, planning for order fulfillment doesn't start when the money comes through your door. In this chapter, we talk about the elements that can affect fulfillment, starting with how you set up your business. We talk about strategies you can implement to handle your product storage and organization, and how you pack and ship your items. In some cases, the best step you can take is to turn shipping over to another company and pay it to deliver your products to the right customers.

The moment you receive that payment, the clock is ticking and your customer is eagerly awaiting the item. A customer who experiences a bad fulfillment process will remember nothing else about your business, even if your Web site is well designed and the ordering process easy to complete.

Figuring Out the Logistics of Shipping

How do you set up the entire flow of your business? Start by thinking about the operations and daily tasks that make your business work. Then lay out everything and decide how the business can best operate. To help you plan all these tasks, ask yourself these questions:

+ Does my online business operate from my home or a dedicated office space?

+ Should I buy products for resale or have someone else ship the goods?

+ Does a physical store or presence have to work with my online business?

+ How many employees need access to the merchandise and system?

Track the flow of one of your items for sale from beginning to end:

+ Receive the product from your supplier.

+ Prepare the product for sale.

+ Store the product while it's up for sale.

+ Pack up the product after it's sold.

+ Ship out the product after it's packaged.

Think about when and where these events take place, to help you plan the logistics of your business. *Logistics* simply refers to how you manage the operations of your business. You might need to dedicate a room in your house, or, you might need to coordinate products and shipments through a warehouse that has different vendors and manufacturers.

The key is to set up a model that fits your business. You have no reason to buy an expensive software inventory program if you sell 10 or 20 items per month. Likewise, when your volume begins to grow, don't expect to run a multimillion-dollar venture with a pencil and pad of paper. Pick a system that lets you know at any given time where in the process your inventory is, whether it's receiving, photographing, listing, packing, or shipping.

Developing an In-House Fulfillment Model

Many small businesses take care of their own fulfillment, which means that they pack and ship their own products and send them out the door. Doing so allows these businesses to control the quality of their shipments so that they know their customers are being served. Typically, doing so makes sense: Because the inventory is on-site, orders can be packed at the source and sent out rather than relayed to some far-flung warehouse.

Setting up an in-house fulfillment model requires first having enough inventory on hand and available at your location. After you know how much inventory you need to have in stock, you can plan for the space required to hold this inventory. After you're in business a while, you know from your average order level how much inventory to have. In the beginning, you need to estimate orders and decide how many different products to carry in your store. Be sure to have enough on hand to fill initial orders.

Don't let a lack of available space be the reason that you don't carry more inventory. Different models, both in-house and outsourced, allow you to hold more products than your current available space allows.

Your relationships with your vendors help determine the amount of space that's required. If you receive shipments in batches, make sure that you have enough space available to take in a shipment and hold it until sales for that order come in. If you have a responsive vendor that can ship items in a just-in-time approach, your space requirement can be much lower.

In *just-in-time* inventory management, vendors deliver their products to you just before you need them for listing or shipping out. If you're receiving shipments just in time, you don't need to have a big warehouse to store upcoming orders. However, if your just-in-time vendor is late with a shipment, you have nothing to sell or send out to your customers.

If the space you require is more than the available space at your location, either look at temporary storage, such as a storage locker, or rent dedicated industrial or warehouse space for your inventory. If you acquire additional storage away from your location, make sure that you keep at least one sample of each product close at hand, in order to take photographs and write descriptions for your Web site.

If you rent a storage locker to hold inventory, ask the management team whether it can accept packages for you and place them in your unit. This way, you don't have to be present when your shipments come in, or worry about sending them to storage from your home.

After your space requirement is resolved, think about labor: Who will pack and ship your products? Of course, the number of orders to be packed and shipped can help determine your lucky fulfillment worker. If you're packing only a few orders a day, you or one of your employees might handle the task. As the number of orders continues to grow, consider hiring a dedicated employee to perform the fulfillment, or reassign someone to focus only on fulfillment.

Deciding to Outsource Fulfillment

Most people have a passion for the businesses they want to create. Whether someone is turning her knowledge of, and experience with, a hobby into a business or solving a need and providing a product that people want, a business owner dreams of turning a business idea into a reality. A business owner usually doesn't dream, however, of a massive shipping-and-warehouse operation (unless that person is UPS or FedEx.) Therefore, many business owners choose to outsource their fulfillment operations to someone else so that they can focus on the most important element: their businesses. After all, just because you're good at selling widgets doesn't mean that you're good at packing and shipping them.

Contrary to popular belief, you don't need to have a Fortune 500 corporation to outsource fulfillment. Small businesses around the world have outsourced this process, and many continue to do so every year. This action not only reduces the amount of space you require but also frees you and your employees to work on other aspects of your business.

Enter the *fulfillment house,* a business whose sole job is to handle the packing and shipping of other people's goods. By grouping multiple clients' shipping operations, a fulfillment house can employ fewer people to handle the volume of goods than individual companies who hire their own staffs. These fulfillment companies create state-of-the-art, computerized inventory-management systems and train their employees to be efficient in this process.

Outsourcing companies also offer specialized and enhanced service in these other areas that affect your business:

✦ **Customer service:** Every time a customer calls with a question about an order or a special request, or to have a product returned, someone has to handle the call. Fulfillment houses typically employ their own customer service teams to manage these calls. The houses worry about hiring, training, and maintaining the calls and about handling the request so that you don't have to.

✦ **Reporting:** As your business grows, you need to keep track of how many orders go out for each product line and then analyze that data. Most fulfillment houses have some sort of tracking and reporting capability built into their systems so that they can deliver reports and let you know what's going on, to help you plan for your next phase.

✦ **Scalability:** Suppose that you operate a seasonal business, such as stocking Christmas gift items, and you have to quickly grow and expand your inventory space to meet demand. Doing it yourself means worrying about reserving temporary space in September that you need to give up in early January. If you use a fulfillment service, you can draw on its resources and let it worry about finding the space. If your business grows quickly, a good fulfillment partner accommodates that growth easily.

Finding an outsourcing partner

When you're ready to outsource the fulfillment process, you're probably wondering what is the first step. After all, you probably don't just flip open the Yellow Pages and go to the *O* page, for outsourcing. Every business magazine and talk show discusses the impact of outsourcing for bigger corporations, but what about small businesses? Some outsourcing companies are specifically targeted to small-business accounts, especially online businesses.

After all, these companies know that if they can pool several inventories of small businesses, they can manage those accounts with a smaller team of trained personnel and one warehouse. In other cases, your outsourcing partner can be a similar business that has its fulfillment processes down to a science and has decided to use that expertise to make money for other companies by solving their fulfillment headaches.

As you look for a fulfillment partner, keep a few guidelines in mind:

✦ **Know your budget.** Some companies can complete a part of your fulfillment process, and others literally assume control of your entire shipping department. Know how much you can afford to spend, to guide yourself to a partner that's right for you. Understand that you're saving employee labor time and salary when you're outsourcing your fulfillment, so factor it into your budget.

✦ **Shop around.** You might find one outsourcing partner and think that you're done. Always look around and gather two or three estimates. Just like shopping around for any other type of service professional for your business, look around, get an estimate of different rates, develop a feel for the service levels they plan to offer, and see whether one company is willing to match another's price.

✦ **Factor in all the costs.** You can easily see a price quote from a company and think that it shows the total cost. Before you sign anything, make sure that you understand all your commitments and factor in all the costs. One quote might be cheaper because your company is still spending enough time and money on your end to finish the process, for example.

When you're ready to look for a partner, start by asking around: Ask your vendors, manufacturing partners, and even fellow business owners in places like Chamber of Commerce get-togethers, small-business workshops, and online forums. Internet searches on Google and Yahoo! turn up lots of leads, so do your research. See what other business owners say on message boards and in forums.

Here are some Internet companies to get you started:

✦ **Caleris:** www.caleris.com

✦ **E-Fulfillment Service:** www.efulfillmentservice.com

✦ **Fulfillment Works:** www.fulfillmentworks.com

✦ **Strategic Fulfillment Group:** www.strategicfulfillment.com

✦ **Webgistix:** www.webgistix.com

Look for a company that specializes in your area (such as Webgistix for e-commerce, as shown in Figure 7-1) or provides the reporting features you need, such as Strategic Fulfillment Group and its real-time system.

Figure 7-1:
Webgistix helps you smoothly fulfill your inventory.

You can even turn your shipping company into your outsourcing partner. UPS Logistics, for example, helps businesses around the world coordinate their supplies, orders, and product flow. The company's range of supply chain services and business technology services help take care of your fulfillment headaches. Go to http://ups-scs.com/logistics for more information.

Establishing your outsourcing relationship

After you find the outsourcing partner you want, it's time to create an agreement and determine the terms of your relationship. You have to agree on terms such as service level and the rate of customer response so that both of you agree to the level of service that your outsourcing partner provides. You need to know how quickly the company ships your products, what materials it uses in packing them, and how quickly it responds to customer requests.

Outsource some and keep the rest

Many online business owners dive into the fulfillment outsourcing question by giving up only a part of the fulfillment process and keeping the rest in-house. After all, their business reputations are on the line, so they don't want to turn over every piece and then just hope that it works. Start with a test situation (one small function), and see how your outsourcing partner handles it.

Consider hiring a college student to help you a few times a week to pack and ship orders.

It's a quick way to bring on some additional help and free up some of your time. If things work out with the student, you can bring him onboard for more hours per week, have him perform the work from his house, or even hire him full-time after graduation. Additionally, you can hire more students or part-time help and soon have your own shipping department filled with extra help.

Here are the factors in this relationship that should concern you:

+ **Reputation and service level:** Even though the outsourcing company is doing the work, *your* name and reputation are on the line with your customers. If something goes wrong, guess who gets blamed? Yep, you do! Make sure that your partner is willing to commit to a service level that doesn't embarrass you or annoy your customers.

+ **Scalability:** As you grow, your outsourcing partner must be able to grow with you. After all, you're turning to it to smoothly handle a part of your business so that you can grow the operation. If the company is struggling to keep up the pace of your business, you run the risk of your whole operation falling apart.

+ **Experience:** Your outsourcing partner's management team needs to have the right experience in the right areas to lead that company. You're paying for experience, so make sure that team members are well versed in controlling

  • Back-end computer systems

  • Customer service

  • Inventory management

  • Logistics

+ **Subject matter knowledge:** A product is a product is a product. It helps, though, to find a partner that can understand your specific product line, whether it's computer chips or dried fruit. See whether this partner has ever handled an account similar to yours, and whether it understands some of the nuances of your product line, to better anticipate any problems or questions that might arise.

Operating with an outsourced fulfillment house

When you're ready to start working with a fulfillment house, don't just sign the lowest-price contract and begin transferring inventory to it. You need to talk about how your relationship will work, what expectations you have for the company, and — believe it or not — what expectations it has of you. After all, even though you might have hired the fulfillment house to do "all the work," as the client, you still need to provide these items:

✦ **Inventory:** Most fulfillment houses take on your inventory and warehouse it at their locations. Decide how much inventory to transfer, when to do it, and when and how replacement inventory should funnel in. Make sure that you carefully assess your inventory before it leaves your business, and double-check the inventory list when it arrives. Some fulfillment companies provide the trucks and labor to move inventory; others need for you to make the arrangements.

✦ **Order information:** When orders come in, find a reliable and automated way to move that order information over to your fulfillment house. Depending on how you capture orders and which computer systems your fulfillment house uses, you can transfer orders as they occur or as a group of orders every day (in a *daily batch*). In some cases, you can have the fulfillment company operate the order-collection part of your business so that the order goes directly from customers' computer screens to the company's databases.

If the fulfillment house is taking your orders, make sure that you receive a detailed report that has all the information. After all, customer orders are the building blocks for a customer list that helps your business thrive.

✦ **Payment:** Fulfillment houses don't pack and ship your orders out of the goodness of their hearts, so they need to get paid. You have several options for handling this cost:

 • Build the extra cost into the shipping amount of your orders, and have that money transferred each time the company fills an order.

 • Have the company invoice you for a couple of months' worth of orders. You probably need to pay a reserve amount to cover initial orders.

 • If the company is taking your orders and payment, it can keep its portion of the shipping amount and pay you for the goods it ships out.

After a certain length of time, you should receive a report detailing the activity your fulfillment house has performed. Never just file the report without looking it over. This report gives you a revealing look at the flow of your business and shows you how products are moving out the door. If you're concerned about the quality of the fulfillment house's work, compare the ship dates of those orders to the times you received them, and calculate how quickly this company is processing your business orders.

As your inventory level goes down at the fulfillment house, you need to have an event that triggers the transfer of more inventory. This *inventory replenishment level* is the point at which the inventory on hand drops to zero before the next delivery from your business occurs. Many fulfillment houses can help you calculate this number because they use sophisticated computer tracking systems that monitor shipment levels and predict how long it takes to ship all inventory in their possession. They usually factor in some time to cover unexpected delays in inventory transfers or unusual bumps in your orders. When you negotiate this cushion of products with your fulfillment house, pick a level that keeps orders flowing but doesn't back up the warehouse.

If your fulfillment provider is far away from where your products are, calculate the cost of transferring inventory versus storing that inventory at the warehouse. Reducing a long, expensive inventory transfer by one per year can save you more money than the storage fees you pay at a warehouse.

Assessing the quality of the fulfillment work

When you get a sense of the quantity of work that your fulfillment partner is performing, look at the quality of its work also. Most important, determine whether your customers are happy with the packages they receive. Were the items well packed? Did packaging materials withstand the pressures of being shipped cross-country? Did your customers receive their orders in a reasonable amount of time?

The easiest way to find this information is to provide a phone number that your customers can call to report any problems. In some cases, the fulfillment house can also be your customer service partner. This way, if a problem with a customer's order occurs, a fulfillment person can go into your inventory on-site, pull a replacement set of products, ship it immediately, and let the customer know that the replacement is on its way. Make sure that you receive a monthly report of any customer service calls, and see whether that number goes up or down.

You can also go one step further: Rather than wait to hear whether a problem has occurred, reach out and ask your customers in the form of a survey. You don't want to bother them too much, but sometimes a simple survey packaged into each order can elicit some helpful feedback. Give prizes (like gift certificates) or guaranteed discounts (like free shipping on future orders) to customers who respond. You can partner with companies (like Shopzilla; see Figure 7-2) that coordinate online surveys of customers and give you the results. This way, you can uncover any problems before they get out of control.

If you notice a problem, talk to your fulfillment partner. Be direct, not confrontational. Find out the root cause of the problem, see whether it can be fixed, and inquire about how your partner will ensure that it doesn't happen again. You can never prevent all problems, but you can help make sure that they don't happen as often.

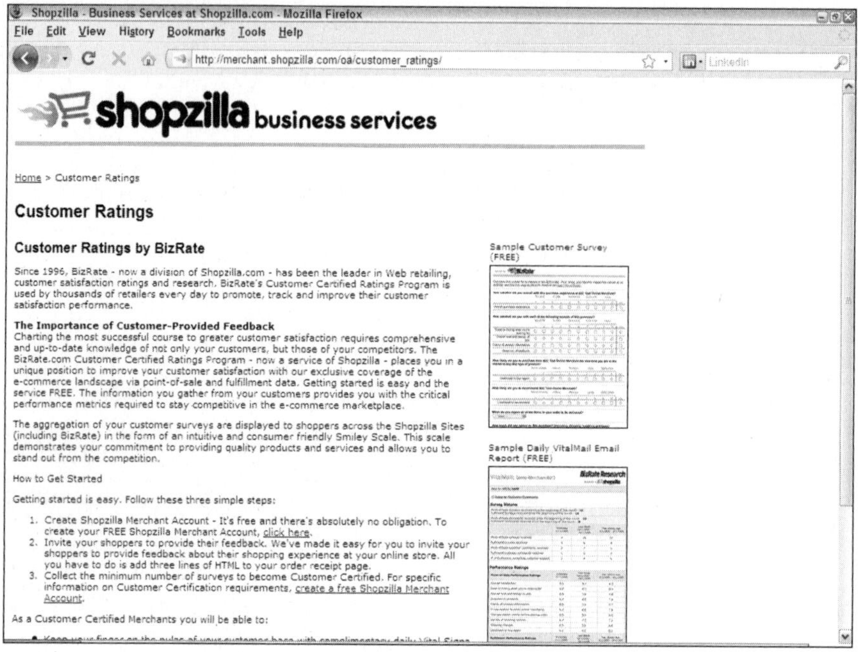

Figure 7-2:
Hire
companies
like
Shopzilla to
coordinate
surveys
of your
customers.

Shaping Up and Shipping Out

The immediate gratification that a customer feels when she orders something from your business applies also to the fulfillment of that order. Customers want to hold a product in their hands as soon as possible, and some customers are willing to pay even more to receive their order faster. Customers often have a favorite shipping carrier, or a carrier that they don't want you to use.

When those same people hear the term *shipping and handling,* they usually envision you performing these basic steps:

1. Pull an item off the shelf.

2. Put that item in a box.

3. Add packing material to fill up any empty space in the box.

4. Seal the box with tape.

5. Put the customer's name and address, and your business return address, on top of the box.

6. Ship the box.

Even though these steps demonstrate the basic flow of the shipping process, you can make it happen in many ways. If you're handling the shipment of your business orders, you can take advantage of some existing systems to make your life easier.

Giving shipping options to your customers

In the end, the best way to satisfy these different goals and ambitions is to offer multiple shipping options to your customers.

Giving customers options can mean that you offer a variety in

✦ **Shipping carriers:** You're willing to ship something by using FedEx, UPS, or the U.S. Postal Service.

✦ **Shipping methods:** If your only carrier is FedEx, for example, customers can pay for Next Day Air, 2-Day Air, or Ground (with an average delivery time of one or two weeks).

✦ **Order mixing:** A customer who orders multiple items can pick and choose which items get which type of shipping. For example, a customer who orders a heavy computer system and a light book about computers can have the book delivered to start reading the next day, and have the heavy computer system delivered by ground in two weeks.

When you offer customers these options, you (as either an in-house or outsourced business) have to be ready to use each service whenever it's needed. You have to know the common rates and link to their Web sites to find updated pricing quotes based on different weights and sizes. You also have to update your shopping cart with these different options so that customers can pick and choose.

The rewards of these efforts are best expressed in terms of customer satisfaction. Giving your customers shipping choices is like giving them product choices so that they feel more in control of the shopping experience and feel that your business is willing to cater to them. Often, an online business charges a flat fee for the lowest shipping rate and slowest delivery service. Although that strategy might work for some customers, you're missing the customers who need items immediately or by a guaranteed date.

The best example of the power of multiple shipping options is Amazon. To spur sales, it offers free shipping if you spend at least $25 on an order, and it ships items by U.S. Postal Service Ground Mail. However, customers can specify all or part of their orders to be sent a certain way, and they can pay the appropriate rate for faster shipping, such as Next Day or 2nd Day Air.

**Book IV
Chapter 7**

**Fulfilling
Expectations
and Orders**

Setting up accounts with carriers

Two truths apply to shipping companies:

✦ They always seem to break even the most carefully packed items.

✦ They're always competing for your business.

The amount of gross revenue generated by shipping online orders has become a primary means of producing revenue. Therefore, carriers are fighting to keep customers by virtue of their service — and adding new features and adjusting prices whenever necessary to succeed.

Because the shipping companies' goal is to maximize revenue, they cater to higher-volume customers. They're usually online businesses, like yours, that have a number of orders to be shipped each day, week, or month. Online businesses that are setting up accounts with one or more carriers are finding, therefore, that they have some negotiating power for better rates or more services.

To sign up for a business account, choose one of these methods:

✦ Contact the company by phone and work with a sales representative to set up your account.

✦ Go to a shipping company's Web site and look for a Business Accounts link for the appropriate forms to fill out.

✦ Go directly to a shipping company's office and ask to speak to a representative to set up an account.

When you start to talk to these companies, they ask you a number of questions to gauge your level of shipping. Determine your answers to the following questions before you start calling:

✦ How many packages do you expect to ship out in a month? How many do you send in an average week? What are your high and low numbers for a week?

✦ What size and weight are the packages you typically send?

✦ Are your customers mostly in the United States, or do you send a mix of domestic and international packages?

✦ What percentage of orders do you ship by using an Air option, like Next Day, 2nd Day, or 3 Day? What percentage do you send by Ground?

If you're setting up your shipping system from scratch, be sure to tell the company that you're providing estimates based on your initial research and by talking to fellow business owners in your field. Although you aren't bound by these numbers, the company needs an estimate to be able to set up your account.

When you start reviewing these details with the company, ask about rates and price breaks for certain shipping levels. Find out whether your current level is close to a certain price tier for shipping, and see whether you can raise your order shipments to meet that new level to save money for your business. Meeting a goal is easier if you have a measurable number to aim for.

An account with a shipping company is typically free of monthly charges, unless you add a special service. The company keeps a payment method on file so that you can accrue shipping charges and make one monthly payment. That way, you're not always paying out when you want to ship a package. Your shipping department then runs much more smoothly and you qualify for corporate rates.

After you sign up for an account with a shipping carrier, always remember to review your monthly bill. Never assume that the carrier automatically screens your bill or lets you know when you've been overcharged.

Creating online postage and labels

One of the best developments in Internet technology over the past few years (especially if you're in the fulfillment field) is being able to print postage from your computer and create your own shipping labels. Although you can still stand in line at the post office, now you can prepare packages at home or at your business and drop off addressed packages with your carrier.

If you need to buy postage for various sizes of letters or packages, you can print postage by the package or join a service such as Endicia (see Figure 7-3) and pay a monthly fee to print all the postage you need. You sign up for an account and provide a credit card number. When you print postage, these services charge your account and send to your printer a special coded label that acts as your stamp. Every month, you pay for only the stamps you print.

Here are some of these services:

+ **Endicia:** www.endicia.com
+ **Pitney Bowes:** www.pitneybowes.com
+ **Stamps.com:** www.stamps.com
+ **USPS Click-N-Ship:** www.usps.com/shipping/label.htm

For example, rather than print the stamp for a customer's order, you print a prepaid label that has all the customer's address information, your return address, and the postage paid. You stick this label to the top of the package and hand off the package to the shipping company. Every month, your account is charged for the shipping costs of all the labels you prepared.

Figure 7-3:
Endicia
helps
you print
your own
postage and
labels.

Virtually every big shipping company can now generate these shipping labels from their Web sites, including FedEx, UPS, DHL, and the U.S. Postal Service. You simply log in to a company's Web site with your account number and then start specifying customer addresses and the weights and dimensions of each order.

If you're using these online shipping tools to create labels, invest in an accurate scale that measures as close to the ounce as possible. Make sure that the scale's capacity can accommodate a large order. If you're selling only light items, like stamps and coins, a 50- or 100-pound scale is fine. If you sell electronics and computers, buy a 150- or 300-pound scale instead.

Having items picked up for delivery

After you do all the work to prepare your packages, they still have to move from you to your shipping company. In the past, you had to load your car or company van, drive down to the shipping company's office, fight for parking, honk at other cars on the road, and then stand in line to unload your vehicle.

Almost all the big shipping companies now come to you directly to get your items:

✦ **U.S. Postal Service:** If you print your shipping labels in advance and pay for your postage online, a postal employee can pick up the item on her normal route. When you sign up for the Carrier Pickup program (shown in Figure 7-4), someone picks up all your Express Mail and Priority Mail packages in a two-hour period that you specify.

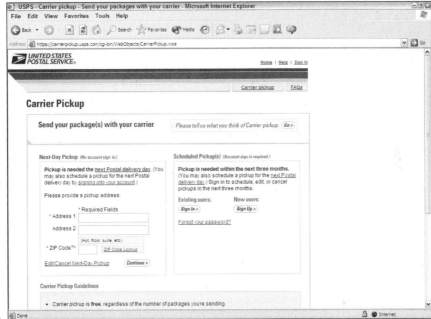

Figure 7-4: Schedule your mail carrier to pick up your packages whenever you want.

♦ **Other carriers:** Carriers such as UPS and FedEx work more on demand. If you're receiving a package from one of these carriers, you can hand off your completed packages when the driver arrives, but you have to know that the shipment is coming. For business accounts, these carriers typically offer weekly or daily pickup, based on the needs of your business. If you have a low-volume account, you're charged for this feature, and the rates vary. Depending on how many orders per month you can guarantee, however, one item you can request during your account setup is a free daily pickup. Ask your shipping company for more details.

If you're printing labels online for a given company, you can usually ask for a pickup when you create the label.

Shipping international orders

Customers around the world are communicating with each other instantaneously by using the Internet, fax and data lines, and cellphones. These methods have allowed online businesses to reach millions of new potential customers. Shipping companies have responded by beefing up their international shipping options, which gives you more options for servicing your customers.

The only shipper that reaches most countries in the world is the U.S. Postal Service. The U.S. Postal Service offers air-mail service, which can take at least a week to reach its destination country. Although the USPS offers insurance for packages to most countries, it typically doesn't provide any tracking capability. The only service it offers that guarantees a tracking number and insurance is its Global Express Mail service, which is expensive.

To see a list of countries and services that the USPS delivers to internationally, go to www.usps.com/business/international/welcome.htm.

If you want to use UPS, FedEx, or DHL to ship packages, you have to send them by some form of air mail, which can be quite expensive for heavy items. Although these services automatically issue tracking numbers, in some cases their tracking capabilities end when the packages enter their destination countries. Each country also places specific limits on package weight and dimensions. Consult each company's Web site for specific information about country-specific limits.

In all cases, you're required to fill out a customs form to document the following information about an item:

✦ The country of origin

✦ The quantity

✦ An item description

✦ The value of each product in the package

Shippers such as UPS and FedEx incorporate the customs form information into the label-creation process so that when you create your label, the appropriate shipping documents are created alongside it. The USPS uses two customs forms:

✦ **Green (Form 2976):** For packages that weigh fewer than 4 pounds (see Figure 7-5) and have no insurance.

✦ **White (Form 2976-A):** For packages that weigh more than 4 pounds or have insurance

You can now fill out USPS customs forms online by going to https://webapps.usps.com/customsforms.

In some cases, the destination country requires you to complete a certificate of origin or a signed affidavit that certifies the origin country of an exported item. Some countries also require that you

✦ Have your goods inspected by an independent, third-party organization

✦ Include a certificate of inspection with your label and customs forms

Figure 7-5:
Use this customs form to send small packages.

For more detailed information on how to send large shipments overseas, consult the International Chamber of Commerce Web site (`www.iccwbo.org`).

For smaller shipments that you send directly to customers, you typically need to classify your shipment in one of four categories:

✦ **Commercial sample:** Samples or free product trials

✦ **Documents:** Catalogs and paperwork

✦ **Gift:** Products that customers didn't pay for

✦ **Other:** Most other types of shipments

An international customer might ask you to classify a package as a gift and specify a lower amount for the value. Be aware that you can insure a package for only the value you state and that falsifying a customs document can result in fines and penalties levied against you and your customer.

Maintaining the Back End

As you grow your business, keep track of how your fulfillment operation works so that it can grow with your business. Investing in good recordkeeping enables you to not only provide customers with tracking numbers and copies of invoices but also see what's working and what's not so that you can make necessary improvements.

Deciding on a database

You have several choices for storing your business information. Many online businesses create one or more databases to store these types of data:

+ Customer information

+ Order information

+ Payment information

+ Product information

Sometimes a business owner picks a database solely because it can "talk to" the shopping cart or Web site software that the business uses. At other times, the database was installed first and the business owner wants to ensure that all other products can communicate with it. Other small-business owners organize their information by using spreadsheets in a financial program such as Microsoft Excel.

The key for you is that your database — in whatever form — needs to be accessible and searchable. You and your employees need to be able to see your data easily. You use your database to answer questions about your business (such as "How many customers do we have?" or "Which orders are ready for shipment?" or "Who still owes us money?") and to store information about how your business is doing financially.

Your order information database should list not only the products that someone ordered but also these items:

+ Carrier name

+ Internet link, if possible, to monitor the shipment

+ Invoice number

+ Order packing date

+ Shipment date

+ Tracking number

As you're setting up your business, here are some questions to help you determine which database program to use:

+ Is a database program in your budget?

+ Which programs work well with your other software systems, such as your Web server or electronic shopping cart?

+ How many people, and in how many locations, need access to the database? Are all the people in one building (or on one internal computer network), or are they spread out around the world?

+ Which software programs do you have access to?

Using handheld scanners and bar codes

Inventory tracking is a process that even a small online business can afford to implement. You don't have to be Walmart or Home Depot to use technology to help organize your inventory. You just have to spend some time setting up the equipment and codes to make it work. You can use handheld scanners that can read bar codes identified on your products to help keep track of your overall product inventory.

Here's how inventory tracking works:

1. **Make sure that each individual product for resale has some sort of bar code on its box.**

   The bar code can be either the Universal Product Code (UPC) that comes with the product or one you provide by using an inventory management program.

2. **Decide where in your warehouse or inventory area you want to store the product.**

3. **Use a handheld scanner (like the ones used in grocery stores or by delivery personnel) to scan a special bar code that represents the shelf or rack number.**

4. **Scan the bar code of the product.**

5. **Sync your scanner and inventory management software.**

Syncing occurs when two sources of information "talk" to each other electronically to ensure that both sources have the same up-to-date information.

Developing a shelving inventory system

Many online businesses buy industrial-strength racks and shelving systems for organizing their products. You can find these systems at most hardware stores, such as Home Depot and Lowes, for a couple of hundred dollars apiece (with some assembly required). After you buy and set up these racks, label each shelf properly and start storing your products on these shelves. Then, whenever you need a product, you can just walk over to your shelves and look to find the product you need. If you keep similar items together, locating and retrieving the product you need is that much easier.

Some popular ways of organizing your shelves involve grouping items by category, size, or color on one shelf or in one area. Keep different items that look similar far away from each other so that you don't mistakenly grab the wrong item for order fulfillment.

Feeding orders into the shipping department

You might think that when you receive an online order, red lights should start flashing and sirens should sound to announce the arrival of another glorious order. Although that level of drama isn't necessary, you need to make sure that your orders are being properly funneled to your shipping area so that they're packaged and sent in a reasonable length of time. You can

+ **Print orders from a printer automatically:** Then, whoever is in charge of fulfillment can grab the printout and start pulling the inventory.

+ **Print manifests or invoices (known as *pick-and-pull sheets*) from the preceding day's orders:** Items are picked off the shelves in your warehouse area and pulled into the packing area.

If you're outsourcing your fulfillment operation, you can specify that the customer receive an e-mail every time he places an order. A duplicate of that e-mail is sent to a specific e-mail account for new orders at the fulfillment house, and the employees monitor and print an order every time an e-mail is received or print a batch of e-mail at certain times during the day.

After an order is prepared and packed, the last pieces of information to capture on the back end are the package shipment date and tracking number. If you're using online postage-creation tools, that information is already captured. If you're creating your own postage and labels, be sure to keep a copy of every tracking number and shipping date and then feed that information into your order database.

Book V
Internet Security

The 5th Wave   By Rich Tennant

"Somebody got through our dead-end Web links, past the firewalls, and around the phone prompt loops. Before you know it, the kid here picks up the phone and he's talking one-on-one to a customer."

Contents at a Glance

Chapter 1: Understanding Security and Your Risks

In This Chapter

- ✔ Recognizing your liability
- ✔ Establishing written guidelines
- ✔ Setting up secure ordering
- ✔ Gaining third-party approval

Internet-related fraud accounted for more than half of all complaints reported to the Federal Trade Commission in 2007. That laundry list of complaints, combined with other losses, translated into more than $1.2 billion in losses for the year. The Internet Crime Complaint Center also had a banner year, logging in well over a million cyber-related complaints that equated to more than $650 million in losses for consumers. Who gets stuck paying these whopping bills? Well, both consumers and e-commerce merchants are vulnerable to becoming victims of cybercrime and end up eating the huge financial losses. Therefore, the burden is on you, the online business owner, to provide a safe, secure shopping environment for your customers and to protect both your customers and yourself from potential financial losses.

In this chapter, we talk about what you can do to keep your customers safe so that they continue shopping with you.

Legal Responsibility: The Merchant and the Customer

As the owner of your business, you're responsible for protecting your customers. With identity theft and fraud continuing to rise at alarming rates, credit card companies and regulatory agencies are saddling e-commerce merchants with the bill (including shipping fees and the costs of the goods). You can prevent your customers from being victims of identify theft and fraud — and thereby staying in business — by being vigilant about the credit card payments you accept and keeping your customers' information as private as possible.

Avoiding charge-backs

Most of the time, fraud comes in the form of *charge-backs*. Customers using credit cards and other online forms of payments (that access credit cards and bank accounts) can request that charges be removed. The Fair Credit Billing Act (FCBA) allows consumers to dispute purchases.

A customer can request that a charge be removed for two reasons:

✦ The card is stolen or otherwise used without the legal cardholder's permission.

✦ The customer doesn't believe that you fulfilled your obligation in delivering the product. (You either didn't deliver it or delivered a different product from what you promised.) Mistakenly delivering an incorrect product isn't a true case of fraud, but it does lead to charge-backs. It becomes fraud if you did indeed ship the correct product but the customer insists that you did not.

Unfortunately, charge-backs happen quite frequently, and proving a customer wrong is difficult for an online business. In fact, reports indicate that more than 90 million credit cards were stolen in 2007, resulting in a $3.6 billion loss to e-commerce businesses, according to Merchant 911 (described in the following section), a resource for online merchants. Because you simply don't have the same ability to authenticate or verify a cardholder's identification as you do in a brick-and-mortar environment, you get stuck with the cost of the merchandise, shipping fees (possibly), and the processing fee that your credit card vendor charges for every transaction. Those amounts add up quickly.

Fortunately, you can minimize your risk of excessive charge-backs. To avoid them, use some basic security strategies for your site:

✦ **Verify the cardholder's address.** Credit card merchants offer an address verification service (AVS) that compares the billing address a customer provides with the cardholder's name. You're notified immediately if the billing address and name don't match the information associated with the account. You can also make this comparison manually if AVS protection isn't included with your online merchant account.

✦ **Get the card verification value.** When you're completing an order from a customer, make sure to ask for the card verification value (CVV2). Because this set of numbers appears only on the customer's credit card, the customer must have physical access to the card to see the numbers. This set of numbers appears as four digits on the front of an American Express card or as three digits on the back of a Visa, MasterCard, or Discover card.

✦ **Process only approved transactions.** If a card is declined for any reason, don't process it. Although this advice seems obvious, you might be tempted to believe that the message is a mistake and try to process the order anyway.

✦ **Scrutinize e-mail addresses.** Always ask for a customer's e-mail address at the time of purchase. If the address looks suspicious, don't hesitate to call the customer and verify the order.

✦ **Be wary of excessive orders.** Buyers using stolen or compromised credit cards sometimes purchase extremely large orders or purchase several units of the same item. Call the number on the billing address to verify unusual orders.

✦ **Maintain good records.** Keep copies of an online order transaction, verification e-mails, and records of any other communication you might have with the customer.

✦ **Keep your end of the bargain.** If you experience a delay in shipping the product or the product is out of stock, notify the customer immediately and do not make any charges until the product ships. (And keep the record of the call and time, of course!)

✦ **Follow merchant-issued policies.** Whether you use PayPal or a credit card vendor to process customer transactions, be aware of its charge-back policy. Always make sure that you're following the vendor's recommendations for the prevention and dispute of charge-backs.

You can dispute any charge-back by contacting your credit card vendor directly. Before calling, be prepared to show how you complied with verifying the card's authenticity at the time of purchase. Hang in there because you might have to wait several months for a claim to be settled.

Keeping your customer information secure

Charge-backs aren't the only issue you have to worry about with online purchases. The second part of your security obligation to your customers is proving that you consistently handle their private information with the utmost care. Specifically, customers want to know how you collect and store sensitive data, including credit card numbers, Social Security numbers, birthdates, and even phone numbers.

Somewhere on your Web site (usually in a privacy or security policy), you should explain how and why you collect and save customer information. Here are the questions your customers want answered about how you hold on to their data:

✦ Do you see customers' credit card numbers before they're processed?

✦ Are credit cards processed in real time, which means that you might have access to only the last four digits of an account? Or, are they processed manually, which means that you see and have access to the full account number?

✦ How many people have access to the information?

✦ How are customer files stored? Are they recorded only as electronic files or printed for filing and storage?

✦ What precautions do you take to keep data secure? Are paper files locked away? Do you have a firewall or other security layers to protect electronic files?

✦ Are your computers password protected? Who has access to them?

✦ If you assign passwords to customer data, how are they maintained and secured?

The Federal Trade Commission and other agencies offer information to help your business comply with e-commerce policies. You can access the information from its Web site, shown in Figure 1-1, which is dedicated to e-commerce issues at www.ftc.gov.

An alliance of the leading credit card institutions created, as part of the *Payment Card Industry Data Security Standard,* a policy designed to provide some level of compliance with how your customers' personal data is processed and stored on your site. Depending on the number of online transactions you process each year, compliance can be either mandatory or self regulated (if you have fewer than 20,000 transactions per year). As with other government agency policies, failing to comply with this enforceable standard can cost you a fine of as much as half a million dollars! Book II, Chapter 1 covers this standard.

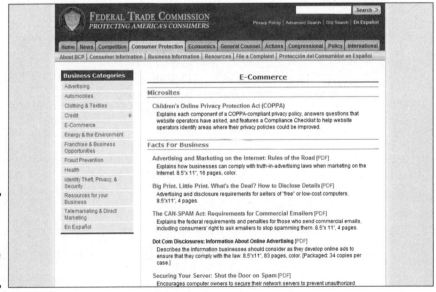

Figure 1-1:
The FTC
provides
e-commerce
guidelines.

Fortunately, certain organizations are dedicated to helping protect you and your customers from all types of online fraud. Check out these two membership-based groups:

+ **Merchant Risk Council (www.merchantriskcouncil.org):** Provides access to articles, tools, and vendors that help you secure your site. Membership fees start at $250 per year for online businesses with minimum annual revenues of $10 million.

+ **Merchant 911 (www.merchant911.org):** Educates small, online merchants about credit card fraud protection. Membership is free; the online tutorial *Preventing E-Commerce Chargebacks* costs $38. Clicking the Merchant Recourse Center tab in the menu to find it.

Defining Your Privacy Policy

When you're tackling security concerns, you have two goals as an online merchant: Do everything possible to make your site secure and safe for both you and your customers, and promote buyer confidence by letting visitors know that you take all necessary precautions to keep the online shopping experience safe.

One of the best ways to stay ahead of the security game is by being clear about your online policies. Also, regulatory agencies might want confirmation that you're looking out for your customers' best interests. Here are two types of policies you can put in place:

+ **Security:** You aren't expected to detail which type of antivirus software you're using. A security policy should explain, however, what protection is in place when you're processing customers' orders. You want to educate visitors on how information is collected, stored, and protected.

+ **Privacy:** This type of policy was once best known for letting customers know whether their e-mail addresses were shared with or sold to third parties. Privacy policies are now much more inclusive: They include details on which information is collected and why; how customers can update, change, or delete stored information; and how they can notify you if they believe that their information has been breached. When you develop your policy, consider these three categories, which can be areas of concern:

  • *Personally identifiable:* Information that connects your customer to your site

  • *Sensitive:* Information that's private to customers, such as transaction histories or e-mail addresses

  • *Legally protected:* Information, protected by law, that includes credit card numbers, financial accounts, medical records, and even education-related details

Privacy and security policies are the two types most prevalent to your site. Don't forget that online fraud and charge-backs are always at issue, too. You need to include or refer to other types of policies, especially when a customer makes a purchase. Don't hesitate to direct buyers to policies that spell out conditions relating to shipping, back orders, returns, and even customer disputes. (Book I, Chapter 5 covers these policies in depth.)

Keeping Your Web Site Secure

No matter how much online security and privacy policies are heightened, buyers are still uncertain about their online security and privacy. Research shows that people are still hesitant to give out personal information or credit card numbers to Web sites, even though e-commerce has become increasingly accepted as a viable alternative to storefront shopping. Figure 1-2 shows a snapshot of the top concerns for online shoppers in the first half of 2007, according to the Federal Trade Commission (FTC). The FTC also keeps track of which online products or industries warrant the most complaints, as shown in Figure 1-3. Although these complaints don't seem to keep everyone from buying, they provide another reason to go out of your way to make your site secure. One of the easiest and, possibly, most expected ways to do this is by using Secure Socket Layer (SSL) certificates.

SSL is a protocol, or method of communication, for scrambling information as it travels across the Internet. Any type of data, whether it's a medical record or credit card number, can be encoded so that only the authorized sender and receiver can view it. Without this protocol, the sending process would be similar to stuffing all your private information into a clear plastic bag, sealing it, and passing it around a crowded room. Even though the bag is tightly closed, anyone who has access to it can see everything inside!

Having an SSL certificate for your Web site lets customers know that their confidential information is protected when they send it over the Internet for you to process.

Using SSL is just a matter of licensing the right to use the protocol through an approved vendor and having it installed on your server. You can get a certificate directly from a private company, such as VeriSign, or (usually) from your Web hosting or domain registration company. These companies can be resellers or certified partners for organizations such as VeriSign and WebTrust. Prices range from as low as $29.95 to more than $1,000 annually. The difference in price depends on the type of certificate you choose and the level of validation attached to it. For instance, the SSL certificate on the low end of the range validates only your site's domain name. The more expensive certificates often validate these factors:

✦ Domain name registration

✦ Business owner's identity

✦ Company identity and address (possibly requiring copies of business licenses and incorporation documents)

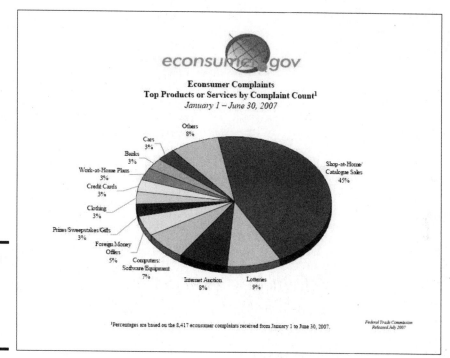

Figure 1-2:
Compare
reasons
for online
shopping
concerns.

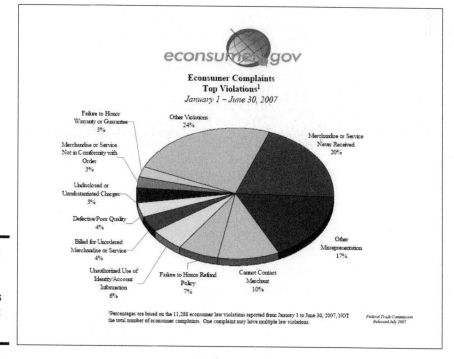

Figure 1-3:
Compare
types of
complaints
by product
or service.

The higher-priced SSL certificates also claim to provide a higher level of encryption. The industry standard is considered 128-bit encryption, and an advanced 256-bit version is available. A higher level of encryption just makes compromising (or hacking) data a little more difficult.

SSL certificates offering 256-bit encryption might still depend on the use of certain types of server and customer access to particular browsers. Check to see whether the 256-bit encryption is part of an SGC-enabled SSL certificate. *SGC (Server Gated Cryptography)* is a means of increasing the range of servers and browsers that can engage higher-level encryption capabilities.

After you purchase your SSL certificate, you're given instructions on how to activate it on your site's server. However, in many cases, your Web hosting company or a professional Web site developer can install the encryption certificate for you.

If you're not certain whether a SSL certificate is necessary for your site, or you want to find out more about it, VeriSign offers a 15-day trial SSL certificate. To obtain it, follow these steps:

1. **Go to the VeriSign site at `www.verisign.com`.**

The company's home page appears.

2. **Click the TRY button next to the Free SSL Trial link.**

A window appears that contains information about SSL certification. The window also contains several text boxes for you to complete.

3. **Enter your e-mail address, name, phone number, and the country in which you're located.**

4. **Review the enrollment and installation process for your certificate and then click the Continue button.**

5. **Complete the process by providing the following information:**

- *Technical contact:* This person is responsible for installing the certificate; you must include the person's name, title, company name, complete address, e-mail address, phone number, and fax number.

- *Server platform identification:* The type of server your site is hosted on is usually either a Linux- or Windows-based server.

- *Certificate Signing Request (CSR):* The CSR is the unique fingerprint or identification generated from your server.

Click the Help button in the upper-right corner of the page to find out more about CSR.

6. **When you're finished, click the Continue button.**

A new page appears and asks you to verify your CSR.

7. **Confirm the CSR you generated in Step 5.**

   Another page displays all the information you entered during the registration process.

8. **Review the order information and check it for accuracy.**

   If you need to correct anything, click the Edit button, which allows you to make corrections.

9. **After you review your info, click the Subscriber Agreement button and then click the Accept button at the bottom of the page.**

After you submit your completed order, VeriSign generates a trial SSL certificate and sends an e-mail to the technical contact with final installation instructions. The certificate is good for 14 days from the time of installation.

If you use an e-commerce-enabled server that's shared by others or you sign up for a storefront, you might not have to purchase an individual SSL certificate. Some companies provide encryption service to all their customers by using a single server.

Displaying Seals of Approval

When most people shop at a store online, they look for signs that the business is legitimate — particularly if it's new or located in a different city or if they're just not familiar with it. Offline, people look for a valid business license hanging behind the counter or a local Chamber of Commerce sign.

The online equivalent of the local Chamber of Commerce is a seal of approval from one or more third-party organizations. Customers feel safer shopping online with you when you post a seal of approval on your site. Table 1-1 lists organizations that provide seals.

Although these seals aren't requirements, they definitely boost buyer confidence.

You can apply for these types of seals:

✦ **Reliability:** Posting this type of seal on your site confirms that its sponsoring companies have verified information about your business. Additionally, it confirms that you agree to abide by certain online advertising and operating standards and dispute-resolution guidelines. Often, part of the qualifying process for the seal requires that you be in business for a certain length of time (usually, a minimum of a year).

✦ **Privacy:** You're eligible to display a privacy seal on your site if you meet stringent guidelines. You usually have to create and post a privacy policy and adhere to those policies, along with other industry standard recommendations. The organization issuing the seal is likely to conduct a security and privacy assessment on your site before giving you the seal.

✦ **Kids' privacy:** The Children's Online Privacy Protection Act (COPPA) hands out a seal of its own. Check out Book X, Chapter 2 for more information.

Because application and licensing fees can range from slightly less than a hundred dollars to several hundred dollars for each seal, you might not be prepared to apply for them when you're just starting your business.

Table 1-1   Organizations Providing Reliability and Privacy Seals

	Seal Type	*Reliability*	*Fees*
BBBOnline `www.bbb online.org`	Reliability or accredited	Member of Better Business Bureau; in business one year	Membership fee; licensing fee based on size of company
	Reliability or privacy	Member of Better Business Bureau; must pass privacy profile	Membership fee; licensing fee based on annual sales
Guardian eCommerce `www. guardian ecommerce. net`	Site approval or privacy	SSL certificate	Annual fee of $15.99
Privacy Secure `www. privacy secure.com`	Privacy	In business one year; must pass credit check and have privacy statement	Monthly fee, based on number of employees ($12.50 per month for one, two, or three employees)
TRUSTe `www. truste.org`	Children's privacy, Web privacy, E-mail privacy	Pass site audit	Based on annual sales

Chapter 2: Developing a Security Plan

In This Chapter

✔ **Forging a realistic plan**

✔ **Making an investment in security**

✔ **Tapping into the experts**

*Y*ou've heard the drill: Plan, plan, plan! The first step in protecting your business from an unwanted computer invasion or an IT catastrophe is developing a plan. Your plan doesn't have to be complicated or expensive. However, you do need to give your security strategy more than a passing thought. In fact, put your plan on paper so that you and your employees have a written plan of action.

The fun of thwarting a cybercrook doesn't stop here, though. After all, what good is a plan if you don't implement it? You also have to invest in a decent online security system (or two) and maybe even bring in a few professionals to ensure that you're properly prepared. If these upfront considerations are ones you've thought about — but haven't gotten around to accomplishing — this chapter has your name on it!

Making a Plan

As Paul Simon says in his classic song "50 Ways to Leave Your Lover," it's time to "Make a new plan, Stan." Only in this case, it's time to find 50 ways to leave your computer protected!

Where do you start? Whether you rework an old plan or build one from scratch, the six major components to an effective security plan are

✦ Policies and procedures

✦ Inventory and skills assessment

✦ Risk analysis

+ Existing security measures
+ Action plan
+ Resources and follow-up

In the following section, we guide you through the details to include within each of these components for your plan.

Policies and procedures

If you're part of a larger online business, you might already have a book of policies and procedures carefully spelled out, tightly bound, and neatly filed away in every employee's desk. The reality for a smaller online company, though, is that you probably haven't had time to think about formal procedures. If you're working solo, you might still be skeptical about needing to write these types of policies.

As an online business owner, the purpose of your security plan is to protect both you and your customers. By establishing and implementing written security policies, you reduce the risk of overlooking holes or flaws within the plan.

Honestly, the amount of information that has been published about how to write a security policy could fill a small room. No wonder the task of writing one has become cumbersome. However, in a smaller company, you can concentrate on the absolute basics.

Here's a baseline rule for establishing your security policies: The magnitude of how much policy you need should fit the breadth of your organization and the depth of the risk factor you want to protect.

In other words, IBM might require several hundred policies whereas you might need only five policies. At the end of the day, if either you or IBM suffers a substantial security breach because a policy wasn't effectively in place, you're both in the same boat. And we don't mean in a good way.

With that in mind, follow these steps to create your own policies (however many you might need):

1. **Write your overall goals or objectives for your security policy.**

Obviously, your ultimate goal is to protect your online business. Try breaking down that big-picture goal into a few smaller chunks of information or goals, though. Maybe you're more concerned with outside threats or establishing guidelines for employees. You might be most interested in protecting yourself legally and need written policies in place to set precedents.

2. Create a list of areas within your organization that require protection.

After each item, make a notation of which ones are better served by the implementation of a formal policy. Use the checklist in Table 2-1 as a guide to the areas that are open to possible security risks.

Table 2-1	Security Coverage Checklist	
Security Risk	*Currently Secured*	*Requires Formal Policy*
Desktop computers	❑ Yes ❑ No	❑ Yes ❑ No
Laptop computers	❑ Yes ❑ No	❑ Yes ❑ No
Employee computers (home/work)	❑ Yes ❑ No	❑ Yes ❑ No
BlackBerry, PDA, or handheld	❑ Yes ❑ No	❑ Yes ❑ No
E-mail	❑ Yes ❑ No	❑ Yes ❑ No
Bank or financial information	❑ Yes ❑ No	❑ Yes ❑ No
Server	❑ Yes ❑ No	❑ Yes ❑ No
Wireless network	❑ Yes ❑ No	❑ Yes ❑ No
Firewall	❑ Yes ❑ No	❑ Yes ❑ No
Cable modem/Internet connection	❑ Yes ❑ No	❑ Yes ❑ No
Software	❑ Yes ❑ No	❑ Yes ❑ No
Credit card numbers	❑ Yes ❑ No	❑ Yes ❑ No
Customer data	❑ Yes ❑ No	❑ Yes ❑ No
Passwords	❑ Yes ❑ No	❑ Yes ❑ No
Database	❑ Yes ❑ No	❑ Yes ❑ No
Web-based applications	❑ Yes ❑ No	❑ Yes ❑ No
Inventory	❑ Yes ❑ No	❑ Yes ❑ No
Products	❑ Yes ❑ No	❑ Yes ❑ No
Back-end system	❑ Yes ❑ No	❑ Yes ❑ No
Offices or other facilities	❑ Yes ❑ No	❑ Yes ❑ No
Other physical properties or facilities	❑ Yes ❑ No	❑ Yes ❑ No
Files or other miscellaneous	❑ Yes ❑ No	❑ Yes ❑ No
Intellectual property	❑ Yes ❑ No	❑ Yes ❑ No

3. **Determine the *scope* (number of policies) that is legitimately warranted for the size and need of your organization.**

   In reviewing your checklist from Step 1, you might find that it makes sense to combine several components into a single policy. Conversely, other areas might produce larger or more frequent risks and require a stand-alone policy.

4. **Starting with your first policy, write its purpose and provide an overview of its importance to the organization.**

   For instance, you might create a policy about who can access your primary e-mail account. Your goal might be to restrict usage to only designated personnel — and doing so is important so that confidential communications aren't compromised.

5. **Detail the scope of your policy.**

   Specify which employees or level of employees the policy applies to. Also indicate which locations, systems, and data are affected by the policy. Refer to your list in Step 2 to make sure that you include all areas that might be affected.

6. **Write the operational guidelines of the policy.**

   These are the cold, hard facts. Be specific about which actions and behaviors can and cannot happen under the policy.

7. **After the guidelines are in place, write a paragraph about how the policy should be implemented.**

   In this part of the policy, provide information such as how employees are to be notified of the policy as well as specific penalties for not enforcing the rules.

8. **Document the date when the policy was created.**

   Every time you update the policy, add the next revision date. Leave the earlier version dates so that you have a running history of the document.

9. **Repeat Steps 4 through 8 for each of your policies.**

   (Optional) You can also add details to the policy, such as a glossary of terms, or cross-reference additional procedures and policies that might also intertwine with this one.

After you finish writing all your security policies, you're ready to place them in the front section of your written security plan.

Inventory and skills assessments

One helpful component for your overall plan is to create a catalog, or *inventory*, of your equipment and the information that you're protecting. Table 2-2 serves as an inventory assessment guide, and we tell you in this section how to fill it in.

Table 2-2	Equipment Inventory Assessment Guide					
	Description or Serial Number	Registration	Username	Travels Off-Site? Y or N	Security Risk High or Low	Other Information
Hardware						
Software						
Peripheral components						
Servers						
Web applications						
Documents						

When you're filling in the guide, your final inventory list should capture the following information:

✦ **Hardware:** Record a complete list of your laptops and desktops, including supplemental information, such as their serial numbers and the names of people who use each machine. Also list any warranty information per machine. Denote which systems have DVD and CD-RW (writable CD) components. For laptops, note whether the equipment is carried off-site.

✦ **Software:** Log an inventory of your company's software. Include details such as user registration information, licensing restrictions (single or multiple user), and registration numbers. If possible, note which software is loaded on your computers.

✦ **Peripheral components:** This list might include data drives, printers, scanners, PDAs, BlackBerry and other handheld devices, portable memory storage devices, extra monitors or keyboards, networking equipment, and even cellphones.

Break out your inventory by each individual piece of equipment or software program. That way, you can compile serial numbers and registration numbers or other unique identifying factors for each piece.

✦ **Web-enabled applications:** Make an inventory of any Web-enabled programs that your business uses, whether for managing customer surveys or printing online postage. Detail which computers maintain the primary license for each application.

When creating an inventory of applications delivered over the Internet, don't overlook instant-messaging programs and music or video-related applications. You might not use them, but your employees probably have them installed. Increasingly, these programs are becoming an easy delivery method for viruses, worms, and other malicious activity. You want these programs accounted for in your inventory so that proper security measures can be applied.

✦ **Documents:** This group includes not only critical files but also your intellectual property. It might also include promotional materials stored on your computer, financial data, customer data (contracts and invoices), and current and archived e-mail messages.

After you complete this equipment assessment, turn your attention to a skills inventory. (You can add it to the bottom of your inventory assessment.) Compose a paragraph or a complete list of the security expertise that you and your employees have. You can include certifications or other applicable training, too. By conducting a skills assessment, you can see when you need to call in outside security consultants — or how much of that expertise you might need.

A skills inventory can further help you determine points of educational training needed for you and your staff so that you can develop more internal expertise.

Risk analysis

One of the most important pieces of your plan is the *risk analysis* portion, in which you identify possible security threats. This important exercise forces you to evaluate what factors hold the most potential for harming your online business. Your first action is to make a list of all potential threats that can compromise your security. Classify these security occurrences, or *events,* under the following categories:

✦ **External threats:** Include any risk that originates outside your business. You typically have no control over these events (other than being prepared to combat them if they occur):

- *Viruses and worms:* Also group Trojans horses and other harmful programs in this category.

- *Malware:* Include any type of malicious software that can be unknowingly installed on your computer from an outside source, such as spam, adware, and spyware.

- *Malicious intruders:* Consider any type of activity originating from another individual that's meant to harm you. Include hackers, former employees, competitors, and thieves. Don't forget that theft can occur on-site (at your place of business) or off-site (such as at airports and coffee houses). Comparatively, hackers steal intellectual property and data by way of an Internet connection. Hackers can also do damage by shutting down your network or your Web site.

- *Disasters:* Address floods, tornadoes, hurricanes, and fire as possible external risks.

✦ **Internal threats:** Although not always intentional, these incidents occur from within your own operations. Internal threats can do serious damage as well as expose your vulnerabilities:

- *Malicious intent:* You might have employees or other types of people with somewhat unlimited access to your assets. Unfortunately, not everyone is as nice or honest as you want to believe. Consider the possibility that a serious — and intentional — breach of security can occur right under your nose.

- *Accidents and user error:* Think of any accidents or human error that can occur. Coffee spills on laptop computers, accidentally deleted data, dropped monitors — the list is endless.

- *Failures:* Specifically, these are system failures. Whether your computer crashes, your software bombs, or your Internet connection or server goes down, these failures are all part of an unwanted security risk.

After you put on your doomsday hat and identify all possible threats that can take you down, go one step further and prioritize each one according to its level of risk. You can do this by using a hierarchical ranking system. Or, you might prefer to assign a low, medium, or high risk value for each of your items.

Ranking your risks is a subjective process that requires you to be open minded and honest in evaluating the security of your business. If you don't feel that you can be objective, consider bringing in outside help.

If you find that a risk analysis shows your business to be at a medium- to high-level risk for attacks, accidents, or failures, consider inviting a paid technology consultant to evaluate your business and offer solutions. The costs involved in improving your security pay themselves back in the long run by reducing the odds of your losing data, damaging your reputation, and putting customer information at risk.

Existing security measures

Unless you're in the planning phases for a new business, you probably already implemented some level of security. Here's the appropriate place in the plan to specify which actions to take.

Of course, you want to describe firewalls, antivirus software that's installed, and other basic security measures that provide some level of protection. However, you can add any routine security-related systems or functions you conduct. For example, you should plan to

✦ Change passwords regularly.

✦ Back up your data regularly.

+ Perform routine system maintenance and software updates.

+ Implement any physical security measures, such as alarm systems or fireproof safes.

No matter what, be honest! If the last time you backed up data was several months ago, don't include it as a security measure that you can check off your list.

Action plan

To some degree, you can consider the action plan the meat of your document. After all the assessments, inventories, and analysis, you're ready for a true plan of action!

Based on the information you collected (see the earlier sections of this chapter), you can readily spot your strengths and weaknesses in the realm of security. And now you can focus on your *points for improvement,* or *Pfls* (pronounced "PIF-fies"), which are the specific points where you find weaknesses to be corrected.

By concentrating on your Pfls, you can create a step-by-step plan of action to beef up your security. In each step, be specific. Here are examples of some of the steps that you might include in your own plan of action:

+ Purchase and install external security locks for all laptops.

+ Turn on the Automatic Update feature on all desktop computers to activate a fixed schedule for installing all new software updates.

+ Purchase a password generator and pick a date on the calendar to change passwords once per quarter.

+ Create a scheduled backup, specifically for customer data such as order histories.

Find an online service for an additional backup so that your data is stored off-site yet still readily accessible if your on-site files and backups are destroyed.

Your plan of action might include a couple of dozen steps or only a few. You have a thorough action plan when all your Pfls are accounted for and the security holes are plugged.

Compare your action steps with the security policies and procedures you already created. Your plan of action for security should take into account those policies and contribute to each one being effectively implemented.

Resources and follow up

The final component of your security plan addresses the resources (and budget) that are required to put your plan into action. Make a list that identifies all the purchases you need to make in order to fulfill your security plan. Include a price estimate for each item, even the more expensive ones. If your total is rather hefty, prioritize which ones fall under the must-have category as well as which ones can wait.

In addition to the resources that require cash, you should include all other resources used in your plan. For instance, budget the time for yourself or employees to attend an Internet security class. Even if a vendor offers this type of training session for free, attendance still requires a small investment in human resources capital.

The last piece of this section should include a timeline for change. Assign both a reasonable date for completion and a person who's responsible for each action item. Schedule a recurring date for reviewing the progress of your plan's implementation, too.

No matter how many action items you develop or how many pages your security plan turns out to be, its true worth is measured in one way: Does it work? If your plan is thorough and realistic, your answer should be a resounding "Yes!"

Creating a Budget for Your Plan

Developing a written security document is an investment in itself. If nothing else, it bears the cost of your time. But as the Resources and Follow-Up section of your security plan indicates, that's only the beginning when it comes to paying the price for security. You probably already put down a fair chunk of change but haven't tallied your investment. The typical places in which you probably already spent money include insurance for your computer equipment, antivirus software, and a good firewall for your network.

Determining how much more you need to spend depends on your circumstances. Research indicates that the average small- to medium-size business spends 5 to 10 percent of its annual IT budget on security. According to the experts, that number probably works out to a minimum of $6,000 per employee. The good news is that by 2010, 90 percent of security-related purchases are expected to go toward a single solution that addresses multiple security issues. Not only will your dollar go further, but security should also be easier to manage.

In the meantime, a truly small business (with fewer than ten employees) may find it difficult to consider spending $6,000 per employee. To come up with a reasonable budget for your business, take another look at your resources list from your security plan and determine the total value of the resources you're protecting.

Figure out how much a security breach can cost you if you *don't* make that investment. Roughly calculate the value of your equipment: all your hardware, software — everything. Then assign a value to the intellectual property you need to protect. It's probably a whopping number! For e-commerce sites, another financial factor is identity theft. You have to consider the potential dollar value of your loss if a hacker gains access to your customer information. Lawsuits and insurance aside, consider it from another perspective: If your site has a major compromise of customer data, those customers must be notified. That can be a public relations nightmare, not to mention the potential loss of future orders.

When determining your security budget, be sure to include the cost of compliance. As the owner of an online business, you may be required to implement and maintain additional security procedures to protect customer data as part of government regulations or private industry standards. Examples of these compliance issues include the Health Insurance Portability and Accountability Act (HIPAA) and the Payment Card Industry Data Security Standard (PCI DSS).

No one can tell you how much you need to spend, or should be willing to spend, on security. When deciding how much to invest for security, ask yourself these two questions:

✦ What's the value of the assets I'm protecting?

✦ Is that amount worth the cost?

Finding Security Resources

After you commit to your security budget, you can find plenty of outside resources who are happy to assist you in spending it. And you have lots of do-it-yourself opportunities, too. You have to decide when — and whether — an outside source is warranted. Then you should determine which resource is the best one for you to use.

When searching for help with security issues, you have many choices. More than likely, they fall into one of these categories:

✦ **Consultants:** Often specializing in a particular area of security, a consultant can be hired to offer an initial assessment or to assist with the complete solution. Most consultants bill in one of two ways:

- *By the hour:* Some consultants charge by the hour, which typically ranges from $80 to $300 (or more) per hour, depending on your geographic location and on the consultant's specialty.

- *Flat fee:* A consultant can also bill you a flat fee based on the scope of the project. As a general rule, the more complicated your issue — or the more specialized the expertise of the consultant — the more you can expect to pay.

✦ **Experts:** Experts can be individuals who work in a technical-support environment or who have full-time jobs in a related subject area (and advise informally or on a part-time basis). You can find experts in your vendor relationships or in community service programs for businesses (such as Service Corps of Retired Executives, or SCORE). The cost of an expert's time varies widely but usually is on the lower end of a consultant's fee. You might even find volunteers.

When paying for an expert or hiring a consultant, check out the person's certifications and ask for references. And, even if you're getting help for free, you should still ask (although it's more difficult to be selective unless you want to pay someone).

✦ **Training programs:** Call them seminars, training programs, or Webinars, these resources provide information from a classroom perspective. Rather than provide individual support, these types of programs are targeted for a large group of people. Cost for this type of instruction varies. A one-day seminar might cost $300 or $400, but a teleclass or Webcast can cost less than $30.

When attending a vendor-sponsored training program or seminar, the solutions that are offered tend to focus on that particular vendor's products. If you want unbiased guidance, make sure that someone other than a vendor or distributor teaches the session.

✦ **Self-help:** As in a training program, you can go the self-help route to seek out the knowledge base you need in order to educate yourself. The cost ultimately is a result of your time and any resources you purchase.

You have to decide which solution is right for you, and knowing when to go somewhere else is usually pretty clear. It's determined by these four key factors:

✦ **Budget:** You might have the money to spend on outside assistance, or you might be particularly budget conscious. As with the issue of time, hiring someone else and spending your labor dollars on other projects might make more sense.

✦ **Expertise:** Either you have the knowledge to resolve the issue or you don't. If you don't have the exact expertise, you must have the ability and the time to learn.

✦ **Scope:** Determine how serious the problem is and whether it's limited to your immediate network or reaches outside it.

✦ **Time:** If the issue is critical or you're reacting to a problem that already occurred, you probably want immediate action. Or, you might be taking preventive measures. If so, time is on your side. Even if you have the time, consider whether it's best spent somewhere else. You might prefer to call in the experts.

You can find a helpful chart and data sheet that explains which security tasks requires an expert and which ones are safe for you to accomplish. View it at www.microsoft.com/smallbusiness/support/articles/ what-you-can-do-to-manage-network-security.mspx.

Chapter 3: Attacked! What to Expect from the Net-Thief

*I*f you haven't been on the receiving end of an online security threat, consider yourself lucky. Even so, you probably know someone who has been affected, if not mildly inconvenienced, by a minor incident of some kind. Recent studies show that companies suffer from multiple security incidents per year from viruses, worms, spyware, and other malicious efforts. And, when companies are suffering from Internet-related attacks, they can lose an average of $2 million in revenue per attack.

That's why, as an online business owner, you need to minimize the opportunity for any type of security interference that threatens your success. Before you can defend yourself and your computer, though, you need to know what to expect. In this chapter, we review the security threats that are most likely to take a bite out of your business if you let your guard down.

Fending Off Denial-of-Service Attacks

Any time an Internet thief, or Net-thief, can prevent you or your customers from accessing Web sites and other online information or applications, it's a *denial-of-service (DoS)* attack. Okay, maybe you don't think that your Web site is large enough or popular enough to interest someone in disrupting your site. Previous DoS attacks have gone after major sites (including Yahoo!, Microsoft, and Amazon) and government Web sites, but that doesn't mean your business can't be affected by this type of malicious action.

What if the company you use for online payment transactions is attacked? Or, maybe your online banking site is hit or, worse, the company that hosts your Web site falls prey. You and hundreds of other small sites can be wiped out for several hours — or even for an entire day. Each of these is a real possibility, and each one is an example of how easily a DoS attack can prevent you from being productive or possibly even hurt your company financially.

The hard truth is that your small or midsize business is more likely to experience a DoS attack these days because it's most vulnerable. Online security is often at the bottom of a long list of concerns for smaller e-commerce sites, and you're also not investing much money in sophisticated security tools, like the big corporations are doing. That situation translates to opportunity. Intruders troll the Internet every day, looking for sites that offer security holes. Plus, DoS attack-launching tools are now fairly cheap and easy to come by, so instigating an attack has become easier. An intruder can divert legitimate traffic away from your site and drive it to other sites. The attacker may be paid every time your customers visit the rogue site, whether they intended to go there or not. With lots of dollars at stake, you can understand why the frequency of DoS attacks has spiked.

Fending off a DoS episode isn't easy. After you're under attack, your choice of responses becomes quite limited. However, you can take certain steps to reduce the chances of an attack occurring and to minimize the damage that can be done if your site suffers from a DoS attack:

✦ **Know your host.** When selecting a hosting company for your Web site, understand which security measures it has in place. Ask how your host would work with you if your site experienced a DoS attack as well as whether security experts are part of its support staff. The more prevention at the network level, the better.

✦ **Update the basics.** Individual users and their computers are also responsible for creating security holes. The best defense is to continually update antivirus and spyware programs as well as download the most recent patches (or fixes) for your computer systems. Keep your browsers updated, too — especially Internet Explorer, which has proven to be quite susceptible.

✦ **Increase capacity.** Having more server capacity to handle traffic for your site can be helpful during a DoS attack. Because a DoS attack attempts to increase the demand on your site to the level that it prevents access, the additional capacity might mitigate the damage of smaller attacks.

✦ **Report attacks.** If your site comes under a DoS attack, report it to the FBI. Attackers often use Yahoo! and other free e-mail services; the FBI might be able to trace these accounts. The FBI has created a special division, the Internet Crime Complaint Center, to address these concerns, as shown in Figure 3-1. You can access the division at www.ic3.gov.

✦ **Block traffic.** You can work with your host company to block traffic coming from suspicious or malicious IP addresses. Although you run the risk of also blocking legitimate users, this choice might be your best option.

Book V
Chapter 3

Attacked! What
to Expect from
the Net-Thief

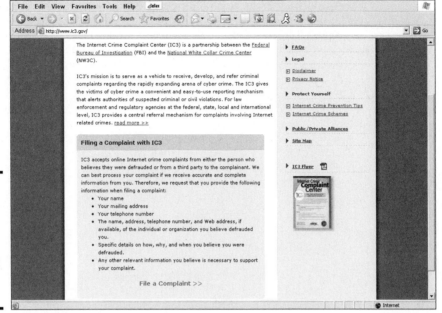

Figure 3-1:
Report
Internet
security
threats to
the Internet
Complaint
Center.

✦ **Be aware.** As DoS attacks increase in frequency and type, you must stay up-to-date on security issues. Your best defense against any attack is to be aware and knowledgeable of current threats and recommended preventive measures.

To view the latest news on cybercrime and stay ahead of potential threats, visit the Computer Crime Research Center at `www.crime-research.org`.

Deterring Hackers

Behind every DoS attack or any other harmful Internet-related threat is usually a single person or group of people responsible for starting the malicious activity. Discovering the identity of these electronic thieves isn't easy. In general, a *hacker* is anyone not authorized or given permission to intrude on or gain access to your information systems. Hackers are basically opportunists.

Some hackers are motivated by the challenge of merely trying to break through a security system and then bragging that they did it. Those hackers are typically attracted to large, high-profile, or government sites. Other hackers are excited by the possibility of making money from your site. Among the most popular methods of hacking-for-pay are stealing these elements:

- ✦ **Keystrokes:** This kind of attack might not seem like a big deal, but even inexperienced hackers can monitor and record the keystrokes on your computer. By using a keystroke logger tool, the information collected is then sent back to the hacker. Capturing this data makes it a snap to gain access to your system.

- ✦ **Sales:** Hackers divert your traffic to a rogue site (which might even look like yours) where customers spend money, in the belief that the site is legitimate.

- ✦ **Data:** By obtaining passwords to your or your customer's secure data, hackers can build a lucrative business. With passwords, hackers gain access to pertinent information, such as bank accounts, birth dates, and Social Security numbers.

- ✦ **Credit card numbers:** Hackers relish the chance to obtain your customers' stored credit card numbers. These days, those numbers can easily be resold for cash — and before anyone realizes that the accounts have been compromised.

Your data is worth a lot of money to a Net-thief! Sites that fall prey to this type of hacker are vulnerable because they're easy targets. Think of this type of breach in terms of your home's security: Although locks and alarms don't always stop thieves, they deter them. Given the choice, most bad guys break into places that are easier to get into and out of without being noticed. Your site is the same way.

If a hacker sees that you're sloppy with security, he doesn't waste any time taking advantage of you. These days, computer programs allow a hacker to scan the Internet and look for vulnerable sites.

Implementing firewalls and antivirus software certainly helps deter a hacker. You can take some additional measures to irritate a cybercrook:

- ✦ **Use uncommon passwords.** Yes, using uncommon passwords is good ol' common sense, yet most people choose passwords that are easy to remember or have special meanings, like birthdates and anniversaries. Instead, use a nonsensical or complex mixture of words and numbers. Be sure to create a different password for each application or program that you access.

For added security, use a *password generator,* which is software that creates random passwords for you. Free password-generator programs are available, or you can purchase and download these programs. This software typically ranges in price from $15 to $75, depending on whether it's for personal or business use.

- ✦ **Change passwords frequently.** Merely creating good passwords isn't enough. You have to create them repeatedly! Generate new passwords every three to six months (depending on the sensitivity of the information being accessed) for applications you use all the time. Change other passwords annually for low security-risk applications or Web sites.

Book V
Chapter 3

Attacked! What
to Expect from
the Net-Thief

+ **Keep data out of site.** Hackers can originate close to home. Whether you're working from home or an office surrounded by employees, get into the habit of protecting your information. Don't leave account numbers, passwords, and other pertinent data out in the open. Thieves lurk everywhere.

+ **Shut down your computers.** In this 24/7 world of the Internet, you're always open for business. It's tempting to leave your computers on around the clock, too. A better idea is to shut them off at the end of day to limit the possibility of unwelcome access to your system. This advice is especially good if you have a home-based business and use cable modems to access the Internet. The shared bandwidth makes you much more vulnerable.

+ **Update your computer system automatically.** Configure your computer for automatic updates to your operating system.

Avoiding Viruses and Other Malware

According to the McAfee security firm, hundreds of thousands of active virus threats are invading computers right now! Named for the germ-like nature of an illness that rapidly spreads, viruses were originally a nuisance more than anything else. Similar to thwarting hacking, programmers face the challenge of preventing the spread of irritants from one computer to another.

A *virus* is a program or piece of programming code. Viruses usually spread by way of e-mail attachments. The attachments can be Word documents, photos, games, or any other type of applications that play host to the virus. By opening the attachment, you unknowingly unleash the virus onto your computer and possibly help spread it to others. Viruses are almost impossible for you to detect without using some type of antivirus software.

The ability to hide a virus combined with its ease of distribution makes these attacks increasingly more threatening to the health of your computer and your online business. Some computer experts now refer to viruses as a part of *malware*, short for *mali*cious softw*are*. Here are some other types of malware, viruses, and annoyances to be aware of:

+ **Worms:** Unlike most viruses, worms don't need your help to spread. You don't have to open an attachment or accidentally launch a harmful program. A *worm* simply replicates itself and then spreads to other computers over a shared network. One worm that garnered quite a bit of attention a few years ago was a derivative of the Zotob worm. The worm `rbot.cbq` hit big media companies, like CNN and *The New York Times*. Taking advantage of a flaw in Windows 2000, the worm caused computers to continuously shut down and reboot. It's no fun when your business is put on a hold because of a worm — especially if you're on a deadline!

✦ **Trojans:** A computer Trojan employs the same type of subterfuge as the Greek Trojan horse. Delivered in a seemingly harmless package (usually by e-mail), it sneaks onto your computer system. Then, without your permission, it opens and performs some type of unwanted activity, such as shutting down your computer. Unlike some other threats, Trojans do not replicate themselves.

✦ **Adware:** This phenomenon started out as annoying pop-up windows that disrupted your computer surfing with unwanted ads. Now adware is big business. Someone makes money every time this advertising software displays ads for you to view.

✦ **Spyware:** Much like adware, spyware is a type of malicious software that plants itself deep into your computer system, posing as a legitimate program. It wants to stay around as long as possible so that it can collect information about you. Spyware can redirect you to certain Web sites or track and record your personal information and send it back to the spyware's originator — without your knowledge.

✦ **Hoaxes:** It isn't unusual for rumors about false virus threats to circulate around the Internet. Although these little pranks don't infect your computer, they waste your time. You can tell whether a threat is real or a hoax by noting these characteristics:

  • *Source:* If an e-mail alert came from your antivirus software provider or another trusted source, it's probably real. If it's part of a chain of e-mails being circulated by friends and family, it's more likely to be a fake.

  • *Participation:* An e-mail alerting you to this latest threat and prompting you to send it to everyone you know to spread the news is a classic sign of a hoax.

  • *Authority:* If the e-mail contains a link to a recognized antivirus software vendor or a legitimate Internet security source, it's probably real. If not, you might be participating in a virus hoax.

If you receive an e-mail virus alert and suspect that it's a hoax, check out VMyths.com at `www.vmyths.com`. This site tracks hoaxes and other overhyped computer threats.

Keeping Your Domain Name Safe

Ever since the Internet started gaining in popularity, devious minds with a creative bent have found ways to cause problems. In addition to the other methods that hijackers use to derail your sales and your business — such as virus and DoS attacks — a determined Net-thief has one more trick: stealing your domain.

Domain slamming occurs when you're tricked into moving your registered domain from one registrar to another. In this scenario, you receive an e-mail

Book V
Chapter 3

Attacked! What
to Expect from
the Net-Thief

saying that it's time to renew your domain. It even appears to be from your legitimate registrar. Unfortunately, a competing registrar has gained your information and is waiting to collect a domain renewal fee from you. Although domain slamming might be more economically detrimental to your originating domain registrar (they lose your business), it's still a hassle for you, too.

Somewhat more disturbing is the opportunity for a hacker to take over your domain by using the registration process. When a thief takes possession of your domain, you can spend years trying to get it back. And, some documented cases show that small e-commerce companies never recover ownership. Whether your domain is hijacked for a day or an eternity, here are some common problems that occur when your name is stolen out from under you:

✦ **Reselling:** Your domain name can be resold to an unsuspecting third party. Popular names can fetch millions of dollars, making domain hijacking a lucrative career for a thief.

✦ **Lost sales:** If you have an active e-commerce site that's taken over, you lose sales during the time it takes to regain ownership. Some companies have lost thousands of dollars in sales, not to mention the legal expenses involved in recovering the domain name.

✦ **Damaged reputation:** Even if you regain your site domain, you might be stuck convincing customers that it's safe to shop with you again. Or, in some cases, stolen domains are used to redirect visitors to sites that download adware or spyware onto computers. Unsuspecting customers might be hard pressed to return to your site.

Here's how domain stealing happens: If a hacker can find enough personal information about your account, he can transfer your registered domain into his name and basically take ownership of your domain in a few short hours. Most of the information needed to achieve this process can be found by simply viewing the public records of the WHOIS directory.

To prevent having personal or business information readily available for public viewing, choose to make your contact information private. The WHOIS directory then shows a third-party vendor — a *proxy* — as the point of contact and lists its information rather than yours. Your domain registrar offers the private registration service for a small annual fee, usually for as little as $10 per year.

Sadly, domain stealing is becoming more common. Domain registrars and the Internet Corporation for Assigned Names and Numbers (ICANN) continue to put policies in place that prevent or limit the damage. Still, no policy is foolproof, so here are some other tips you can follow to minimize the risk of domain hijacking:

✦ **Lock down:** Registrars offer the simple and free service of *locking down* (restricting others from making changes to your account) your URL. When registering your domain, select the check box indicating that you want to lock the domain name. If you have an active domain name, you can change its lockdown status by using account management tools or sending a lockdown request by e-mail (or phone) to customer support.

✦ **24/7 support:** Use domain registrars that offer 24-hour support or give you access to support after business hours. This strategy is important so that if you discover that your domain has been hijacked, you can start the investigative and recovery process immediately.

✦ **Standard notification:** Choose domain registration services that state standard methods of contacting you for changes or that will agree to contact you by using multiple methods (such as by both phone and e-mail).

✦ **Review status:** Frequently check the WHOIS directory to ensure that you're still listed as the owner of the domain and that your contact information is current and correct.

Staying Away from E-Mail Scams

You should be familiar with two schemes that affect the way you handle e-mail and keep your business safe: phishing ("FISH-ing") and pharming ("FARM-ing"). Both methods use unscrupulous means to find personal information or private account information about you and then use it for a hacker's personal gain.

Phishing

Phishing occurs when you receive an e-mail that seems to be from a legitimate source, such as PayPal or your credit card company. The e-mail requests that you immediately update your account information because it has been compromised or needs to be verified for other reasons. When you click the link (included in your e-mail notice), a bogus site opens that captures your personal information as you "update" the account.

Legitimate companies have done a good job of alerting users to potential phishing scams and making it easier for you to spot e-mails that don't originate with the company. Figure 3-2 shows a sample e-mail and the elements you should look for to determine whether it's real.

Book V
Chapter 3

Attacked! What
to Expect from
the Net-Thief

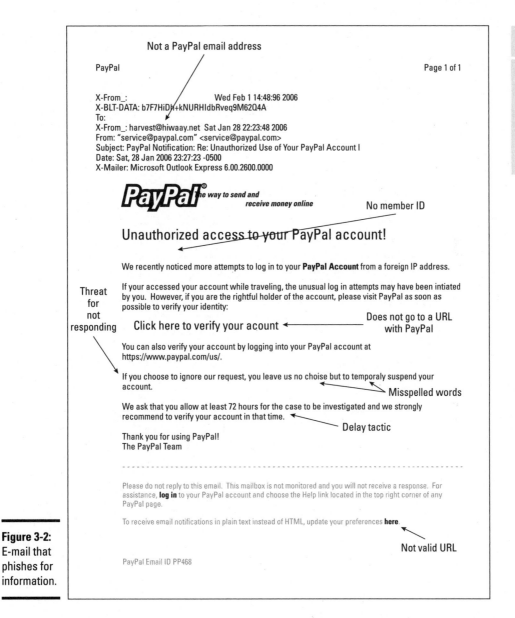

Figure 3-2:
E-mail that
phishes for
information.

Generally, though, you should be aware of these details:

✦ **Account verification:** Most legitimate e-mails from a member-based company or financial institution now include the last three or four digits of your account number. If the e-mail doesn't have any highly personalized or account-specific information, it might be a fake.

✦ **Contact information:** Check whether the contact information at the bottom of an e-mail matches the source that it's supposedly sent from. E-mail contact information should come from the company's primary URL, such as support@paypal.com — not support@paypal security.com.

✦ **Collecting data:** A legitimate request should not ask you to submit, update, or verify private and confidential information by completing an e-mail-based form or replying to that e-mail. You should be able to visit the company's Web site (without using a link in the e-mail) to update account information.

✦ **Notice of urgency:** Most phishing scams insist that you reply right away or act immediately. Bogus e-mails scare you into the thinking your information is being compromised and that you must act right now!

✦ **Contact customer support:** If an e-mail looks legitimate but you're still not certain, play it safe and call the toll-free number listed on the back of your credit card or the one listed on the company's Web site.

The Federal Trade Commission (FTC) offers more tips to keep you from becoming a victim, as shown in Figure 3-3 You can find complete information on avoiding e-mail scams from the FTC Web site at www.ftc.gov/spam. You can also find detailed tips to avoid phishing scams from the National Cyber Security Alliance at www.staysafeonline.org/content/fake-emailsphishing.

Figure 3-3:
The FTC helps you avoid e-mail scams.

Book V
Chapter 3

Attacked! What
to Expect from
the Net-Thief

Pharming

Suppose that you visit a favorite shopping site. You type the domain name, and the site pops up momentarily on your screen. You log in using your password, enter your credit card information to buy products, and perhaps fork over some personal information as part of an online giveaway — and everything seems normal. What you don't realize is that a hacker has rerouted you to a Web site that looks like the one you intended to visit, but this one is bogus. In the meantime, all the passwords and personal information you entered into the site are "pharmed" out and the data is used for malicious purposes.

You can fall victim to a pharming scam in a couple of ways. The first occurs when a virus, delivered by e-mail, compromises your computer's information. The virus can enable the computer to redirect you to a bogus site when you type a URL into your browser.

The second method is when a hacker uses *DNS poisoning,* which alters the string of numbers in your DNS (Domain Name System), causing the real URL to be redirected to a fake domain. Pharming that uses DNS poisoning is a little more destructive because it can affect a larger number of users. And, if you're an online business owner whose site has been poisoned, that destruction becomes especially costly.

Because no standard method exists for helping visitors confirm that a site is legitimate, it can be difficult to avoid becoming a victim. The best protection against pharming attacks as an individual user is to

✦ Keep your firewall updated.

✦ Keep antivirus software current.

✦ Install patches and updates to your browser.

In your Internet business, protecting your site from becoming a victim of DNS poisoning is much more difficult. In fact, there's no sure way to avoid it from happening. The best defense is to talk with the company that hosts your site, to ensure that its servers are running the latest updates of DNS software and that all patches are installed. If you have an in-house server, you or your IT manager should be responsible for the same thing.

Glossary of security threats

Do you recognize all the threats that can pose a hazard to your computer and your business? Test your security knowledge by checking out this list:

✔ **Adware:** This type of software displays ads and pop-up windows on your computer. More than just annoying, adware includes code that tracks your personal information and shares it with third parties without your knowledge.

✔ **Blended threat:** Just like it sounds, this attack incorporates several different types of threats to maximize the damage in one shot. For example, a virus might be distributed by e-mail while a Trojan horse hides in an attached file to cause further damage to your computer.

✔ **Data-driven attack:** Seemingly harmless, this threat is encoded with data that you, the user, unknowingly execute to launch an attack. This type is dangerous because it can sneak through your firewall to do damage.

✔ **DNS spoofing:** This process happens when a hacker assumes the DNS name of another system but redirects you to an unauthorized site. The domain name of the legitimate site appears just as it should, yet you're now on a different site.

✔ **Flooding:** Flooding happens when a large amount of information is directed to a particular system, contributing to a denial-of-service (DoS) attack.

✔ **Pharming:** This strategy tries to obtain personal data, such as credit card numbers, by using domain spoofing. Pharming poisons your DNS server by infusing false information that then redirects your customers elsewhere. As far as the customers know, they're still on your Web site because the domain doesn't change. Any information they provide during the visit is pharmed by the attacker.

✔ **Phishing:** In this ploy, you receive what looks like a legitimate e-mail from a large, recognizable site (such as eBay, PayPal, or Citibank). The e-mail is sent from unknown sources who hope that you respond to their request to update and verify personal and financial information from those seemingly legitimate sites.

✔ **Smurfing:** This type of software mounts a DoS attack by broadcasting large amounts of data.

✔ **Spyware:** Any software that uses your Internet connection without your knowledge or permission is spyware. It's usually distributed by using free or unknown programs that you download from the Internet. After the spyware is installed, it watches your activity on the Internet and transmits that information to other Bad Guys. Spyware can also use other information from your computer, such as e-mail addresses, secure passwords, and credit card numbers.

To discover more security-related terms and find information on protecting your computer, visit the National Cyber Security Alliance at its Web site, www.staysafeonline.org.

Chapter 4: Securing Your Site and Your Business

In This Chapter

✔ **Securing customer data**

✔ **Backing up your own data**

✔ **Adding a firewall for additional protection**

*1*f you've spent any time on a computer, you know most of the security drills about spam, viruses, and other unwanted intruders. (If not, turn to Book V, Chapter 2 to create a top-notch security plan for fending off online predators.)

However, as an online business owner, your responsibility to run a secure site is now increased in magnitude. In addition to watching out for your best interests, you must realize that your customers depend on you to take the appropriate precautions. In this chapter, we show you good security measures and provide information and tools so that you can increase protection for yourself and your customers.

Protecting against Credit Card Fraud

Operating an Internet business means that you're likely collecting, processing, and storing credit card data regularly. You therefore have to look at potential credit card fraud from two points of view: yours and the customer's.

Minimizing your own financial losses

E-commerce sites lose billions of dollars to online credit card fraud every year. VeriSign claims that online stores are 17 times more likely than offline stores to be cheated. Here are just a few of the ways that your online business can get hit with fraudulent transactions — and end up losing merchandise and money:

✦ Customers buy a product but then claim that they didn't order it (or file a similar complaint), and the credit card company deletes the charge.

✦ You unknowingly process stolen credit cards.

✦ You process invalid credit cards or cards that you should have declined.

Although you might think that the big online retailers are most at risk, smaller sites are often more likely targets because smaller sites usually have less sophisticated resources for detecting fraud. Fraudulent credit card orders increasingly account for a larger percentage of all online orders that are processed. Although it's still a relatively small percentage (less than 10 percent), that doesn't help if you're the one suffering a loss!

Protecting against online crime means that you have to stay alert, cautious, and informed. As with any security concern, seek ways to reduce your risk:

✦ **Validate credit cards.** Whether you process manually or in real-time, confirm that the credit card is approved. If a card is declined or shows up with a questionable item, resist the urge to process it anyway.

✦ **Verify suspicious orders.** Don't hesitate to contact a customer by e-mail or phone to confirm an order to validate a card number. If everything is okay, your customer will be impressed that you take this degree of precaution.

✦ **Fight excessive charge-backs.** Even if a card is valid, a customer can steal from you by refusing to pay for the product or service after receiving it. If the customer gives a valid reason (such as the product was damaged or appears to have been used or refurbished), the credit card company removes the charge. Because you have no signature on file for an online transaction, you're stuck paying the bill — plus a *charge-back* fee from your credit card company. You can challenge the claim by responding to the charge-back complaint that the credit card company sends you. You need diligence and patience to fight this type of complaint, and you won't win them all. Still, you can recover some losses, making your time invested worthwhile. (For more information on fighting charge-backs, see Book V, Chapter 3.)

If you suspect a problem or perhaps an honest mistake, call your customer directly to work it out. Keeping good records and documenting follow-up calls go a long way toward fighting chargebacks.

✦ **Add fraud protection.** VeriSign and other online payment processors now offer fraud protection programs for e-commerce sites. These services add screening features as well as links to fraud alerts to minimize the acceptance of bad orders. This service is considered an add-on, so expect to pay a monthly fee (starting around $20 or more) plus a small transaction fee on every order.

✦ **Use card codes.** As part of your ordering process, ask for the credit card verification code, which usually appears as a three-digit number on the back of a Visa or MasterCard credit card, or a four-digit number on the front of an American Express card. Asking for this information requires that the user has the physical card in hand (or at least knows the number).

✦ **Accept online checks.** You can choose to accept electronic checks or Internet checks to provide another payment alternative with fewer fraud risks. On the flip side, restricting your payment options can hurt your sales. Limiting customers to only one form of payment (such as online checks) likely can scare away many customers.

Work directly with your online payment processor to see how to further protect yourself. When selling on eBay or other third-party sites, always read the fraud policies to understand your rights as a merchant — before a sale goes wrong!

Protecting customers' privacy and financial data

Luckily, only a small percentage of customers — if any — turn out to be thieves. A bigger challenge is protecting your customers' data from the online crooks and from potential carelessness. One of these violations can land your customers' data in the wrong hands — and also land you in a lot of hot water:

✦ **Online security breach:** A lone successful hacking attempt can leave your online database of records as open game. Names, addresses, and credit card numbers — some of the most sought-after information — is easily left open at risk.

✦ **Offline theft:** Someone can break into your office and access customer files filled with personal financial data. And, don't discount *internal theft,* where the thief is someone you knowingly invite into your office space.

✦ **Sloppy disposal:** Okay, maybe you have extra copies of customer data or you decide that the statute of IRS limitations has passed and you can now get rid of old files. How you dispose of this information can leave customer records vulnerable.

✦ **Vendor carelessness:** Your security and data storage practices aren't the only factors that can lead to a mishap. Any vendor that you partner with — and who has access to your customer data — can cause a security mishap. (Think about recent scandals in which credit card companies and delivery services have mishandled or lost customer information.) How they handle data, or mishandle it, can affect your site's reputation.

The preceding list gives you some good ideas about how easily a problem can occur. Now all you have to do is make sure it doesn't. Take these precautions to minimize your risk:

✦ **Store data properly.** You probably have two basic methods of keeping data — hard copy files and online databases. Make sure that each one is tightly secured:

- *Hard copy:* Paperwork and hard copies of backup files that contain sensitive customer information must be kept in locked file cabinets, or in rooms and storage facilities with locks and limited access.

- *Online:* Online information should be password protected and have the added protection of a firewall.

✦ **Dump your data properly.** When it's time to get rid of hard copy documents, these files must be thoroughly shredded. You can even hire a professional document disposal service that will come to your location to shred documents. How convenient is that?

Before getting rid of old computers or disposing of any electronic files, erase or overwrite the machine or files (as opposed to simply deleting individual files). You can use a free, downloadable program from Active@ KillDisk at www.killdisk.com. Or, try Eraser, which you can find at www.heidi.ie/eraser, to permanently remove files from your hard drive.

✦ **Add layers of security.** Be sure to protect any type of company information, not just customer data. In addition to being preventive, showing that you have multiple layers of security processes can become a compliance issue if your data is compromised. Include these items in your layers, as shown in Figure 4-1:

- *Antivirus:* Keep antivirus software updated.

- *Backups:* Back up data regularly.

- *Checks:* Conduct regular security checks.

- *Encryption:* Use encryption tools to code information in case your data is compromised. Encryption lets you hide your data from hackers and other unwanted eyes. Only someone with the proper password can decrypt the information for proper viewing.

- *Firewalls:* Maintain active firewalls on your computers and servers.

- *Inventory:* Keep an inventory of your files.

- *Offline security:* Lock up data that's stored offline.

- *Security policy:* Write an official security policy to ensure that you cover your bases (see Book V, Chapter 2).

- *VPN:* Use a virtual private network (VPN) when sending information over a wireless connection (see Book V, Chapter 5).

✦ **Institute a notification policy.** Taking preventive measures also involves planning for the worst. Follow up your privacy policy with an internal policy describing how you will handle a security breach as well as the process for notifying authorities and customers.

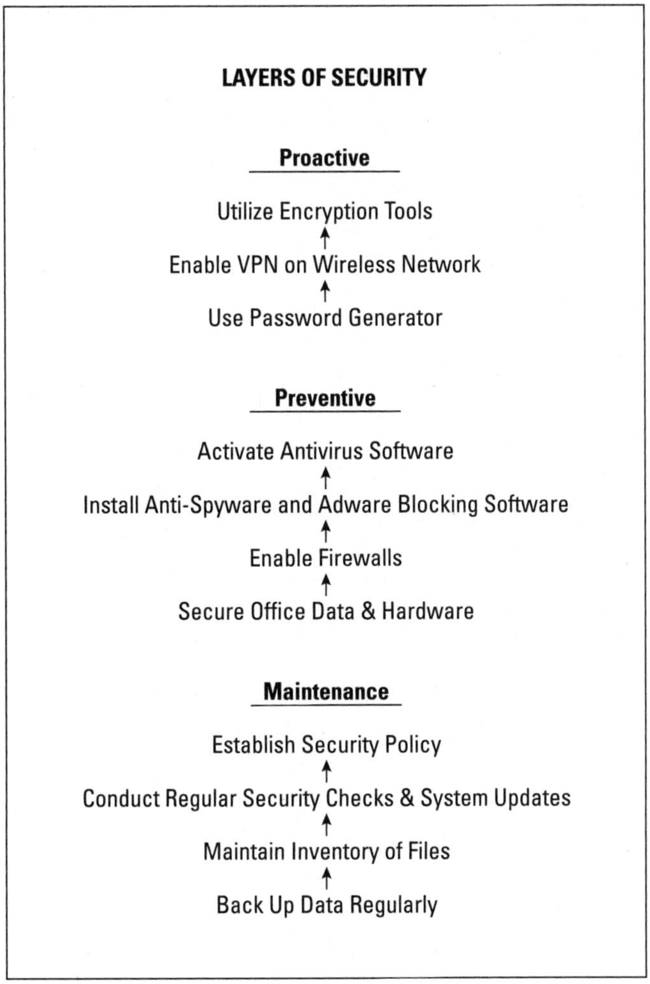

LAYERS OF SECURITY

___**Proactive**___

Utilize Encryption Tools
↑
Enable VPN on Wireless Network
↑
Use Password Generator

___**Preventive**___

Activate Antivirus Software
↑
Install Anti-Spyware and Adware Blocking Software
↑
Enable Firewalls
↑
Secure Office Data & Hardware

___**Maintenance**___

Establish Security Policy
↑
Conduct Regular Security Checks & System Updates
↑
Maintain Inventory of Files
↑
Back Up Data Regularly

Figure 4-1:
Layers of
security.

You might be a one-person show when you're starting your online business, but the stakes for messing up are the same as they are for the big guys. Mishandling, losing, or compromising customer information can cost you thousands of dollars in fines, possible jail time, and untold damage to your image as a reputable online store.

Backing Up Your Data

Stop. Take a moment and think about the information you store on your computer. Consider the amount of time you spend creating, updating, and maintaining your Web site. Now imagine that all that information disappears in a blink of the eye. Yikes!

Most of us go through our business day assuming that nothing really bad will ever happen. That's followed by the assumption that the contents of your Web site and your computer files are perfectly safe and always at your disposal. Guess again. You can lose data through human error (coffee splashed on your laptop, for example) or natural disasters, such as hurricanes.

You can prevent disasters from becoming cataclysmic by properly backing up and storing your data. Try these methods:

✦ **Store data on a removable storage device.** A common way to back up data is to save it to an external Zip disk. You can also use a Flash drive, as long as it has enough memory on it.

✦ **Partition your hard drive.** An easy way to back up files is to move them to a separate section of your hard drive. You do this by *partitioning* the hard drive, or dividing it into two or more sections. If one partition is corrupted or compromised, you can still access the second partition.

To partition your existing hard drive, use a program such as PartitionMagic software from Symantec. You can buy it for about $69 and download it directly from the Symantec Web site at `www.symantec.com/norton/partitionmagic`. Or, try the Partition Commander Professional from Avanquest Software for $49.95 at `www.avanquest.com` — type **partition commander pro** in the Search box near the top of the page.

One goal of backing up data is to have your information available in case of a disaster. If your computer is stolen or destroyed in a fire, having data backed up on a hard drive doesn't do much good. Make a duplicate copy that's not backed up as often but is saved to disk and stored in a fireproof safe or in a safe-deposit box.

✦ **Burn to a CD or DVD.** CDs and DVDs are useful options for storing data because they hold about the twice amount of an average Zip drive and take up less physical storage space.

✦ **Use a remote backup service.** One advantage of using a remote or Web-based backup service is that your data is stored off-site. If anything calamitous happens at your location, you can retrieve a copy from your backup provider and immediately restore your data. Backup services can cost as little as $10 per month and increase to several hundred dollars per month depending on the features you want and the amount of storage space required. Always shop around for the best deal.

Keep a second set of backups at your office, using a Zip disk or Flash drive. Although professional backup services have redundancy capabilities, maintaining two backup sources is just good business practice.

✦ **Back up your operating system.** If you operate Windows Vista, Microsoft includes a free backup tool to use from your desktop. It's easy to run, but you have to find a place to put the information after you create the backup. This Microsoft utility automatically looks for backup devices attached to your computer, such as an external hard drive. If it doesn't find one, it asks whether you want to save to a CD, DVD, or network drive.

If your operating system doesn't have backup capability, you can use ZipBackup software from `www.zipbackup.com`. The downloadable software costs $39.99, but you can start with a 30-day free trial version.

To back up your Windows XP or Windows Vista operating system, follow these steps:

1. **Choose Start⇨All Programs⇨Accessories⇨System Tools⇨Backup.**

The Backup and Restore Wizard starts.

Windows Vista requires you to set up Automatic File Backup before backing up data for the first time. Follow the prompts that appear onscreen to set up the auto backup function.

2. **Click Next.**

3. **Select the option for the data you want to back up:**

- *Back Up Selected Files, Drives, or Network Data:* Backs up items you specify, such as your My Documents folder, Favorites, desktop, and cookies.

- *Only Back Up the System State Data:* Backs up files that are required for your operating system to function properly.

- *Back Up Everything on This Computer:* Backs up all data on your computer and creates a system recovery disk to restore Windows in case of failure.

4. **Click Next to continue.**

5. **Name the backup file and specify the location where you want the backup file saved. Click Next.**

Click the Advanced button to configure items such as future backups, whether to verify the data was successfully copied, and more.

The backup starts.

6. **When the backup is complete, click Finish.**

The process is complete.

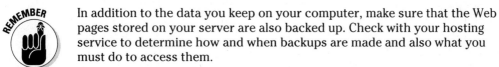

In addition to the data you keep on your computer, make sure that the Web pages stored on your server are also backed up. Check with your hosting service to determine how and when backups are made and also what you must do to access them.

Adding Firewalls

One of the best lines of defense against viruses and intruders is having a firewall installed on your computer. Think of a firewall as a security guard standing watch at all the doors and windows of your computer. The firewall monitors the traffic, decides what's safe, and then gives permission to enter. Or, if the firewall detects a threat, it shuts the door and blocks the intruder.

Firewalls are particularly important because hackers are aggressive creatures. They actively search for networks that are unprotected or have disabled firewalls. To a Net-thief, that's the equivalent of having an open invitation to browse through all the files on your computer. It also makes it easy to install harmful programs that infect or shut down your computer or that — worse — scoop up and send out pertinent information to the hacker without your knowing, such as passwords and bank account numbers.

If a pesky virus manages to break through your front lines of defense, a firewall cannot remove or quarantine infected files. You still need to run antivirus software in addition to installing a firewall.

For added security, we recommend that you

+ **Enable individual firewalls.** When your computer is part of a local-area network (LAN), most routers have a firewall installed. For the best defense, though, enable a personal firewall on each computer.

+ **Add an enhanced firewall.** Install a second dynamic firewall to gain protection from both incoming and outgoing traffic and to provide an additional layer of security. You can buy firewall software, often combined with antivirus software, starting around $40. One popular business firewall solution in particular is Zone Alarm Pro — go to www.zonealarm.com.

On a home computer, Zone Labs lets you install its free ZoneAlarm firewall. This firewall is intended for personal use only, but it's a good solution for testing. If you like it, consider investing in its ZoneAlarm Internet SecuritySuite, which is intended for businesses.

Chapter 5 : Overcoming Security Concerns in the Wireless World

*W*ithout a doubt, one of the best parts of running an online business is that you aren't permanently tethered to one location. The wireless revolution allows you to work in almost any room of your home, outdoors on your back deck, or even at the neighborhood coffee shop.

Freedom of that nature comes with a price, of course — *security risks.* Like it or not, if you're using a wireless connection, you're vulnerable. In this chapter, we show you how to keep unwanted guests off your network so that you can work in protected solitude.

Understanding How a Wireless LAN Works

Before you can protect against a security breach of any kind, consider how a wireless network operates.

In short, a *wireless local-area network* (WLAN) provides access to the Internet without the need for cables or other wires hooking directly into your computer. Instead, an access point (AP) connects other wireless devices to your local-area network (LAN). Then high-frequency radio waves transmit the signal from the LAN to your mobile computer. Figure 5-1 shows you an overview of this process.

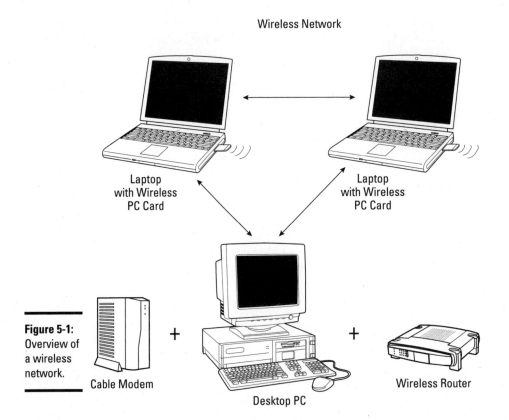

Wireless Network

Laptop
with Wireless
PC Card

Laptop
with Wireless
PC Card

Figure 5-1:
Overview of
a wireless
network.

Cable Modem   +   Desktop PC   +   Wireless Router

Wireless connections are classified by IEEE 802.11 standards, commonly known as *Wi-Fi*. The original IEEE 802.11 now has lots of other versions, all bearing the number 802.11 followed by a lowercase letter. Each letter represents different features or speeds of the wireless network. For example, 802.11b is a wireless capability that operates at 2.4 GHz. You find this capability built into most laptops, which makes it possible for you to connect with public WLANs. When buying wireless equipment, be sure to match versions. While you may still see 802.11a and 802.11b, 802.11g is now considered the most common version. In fact, most public wireless LANs (such as in coffee shops) now use 802.11g, and are continually updating the most recent versions of the standards.

Just keep in mind that whether the wireless LAN is set up in your home, in a hotel, or at a city park, the result is the same: You share a signal that's broadcast over public airwaves. Why does this matter to you? Think about your house as it sits in the middle of your neighborhood. Now imagine that your house has no walls. If you don't mind neighbors — or perfect strangers, for that matter — being able to walk through your house and root around in your drawers and file cabinets, you don't have a problem. However, if you have things you would rather not share (such as credit card numbers, passwords, and other sensitive data), being exposed to that degree can be harmful.

This might seem like a farfetched example. However, someone using a laptop or any other wireless device (portable gaming devices come to mind) can pick up and use your wireless signal from outside your home or office — without your even knowing it.

The good news is that wireless networks come with some basic protection — Wired Equivalent Privacy (WEP) — which is simply an encryption method that scrambles the information being sent out on a wireless signal. The bad news (you knew it was coming) is that WEP has some flaws. It's not as foolproof as once thought. A more secure option is Wi-Fi Protected Access (WPA). This authentication tool provides another layer of security and was designed to address the problem spots with WEP.

Any type of security measure is only a deterrent. If someone really wants access to your network, he'll find a way. In most cases, though, online thieves and hackers take a more random approach. They look for someone who is careless or naive and then take advantage of that opportunity to intrude.

IEEE 802.11 standards

When you use wireless products, these numbers describe certain attributes or features of that particular wireless network, as developed by IEEE (Institute of Electrical and Electronic Engineers):

- **802.11a:** Operates at 5 GHz with rates as high as 54 Mbps

- **802.11b:** Operates at 2.4 GHz with rates as high as 11 Mbps

- **802.11d:** Allows the wireless network to conform to networking rules in another country

- **802.11e:** Represents the addition of Quality of Service features and multimedia support to common wireless networks

- **802.11g:** Operates at 2.4 GHz Wi-Fi with rates as high as 54Mbps

- **802.11h:** Allows Wi-Fi to work with different radio frequency devices at 5 GHz

- **802.11i:** Identifies security mechanisms used with any 802.11 network

- **802.11j:** Addresses Japanese wireless regulatory requirements

- **802.11n:** Proposed standard to improve network throughput and expand rates from 54Mbps to 600Mbps

- **802.1X:** Has advanced security that addresses the flaws in WEP

Unfortunately, wireless networks can leave plenty of doors unlocked to usher in a roaming thief. Check out some of the threats that leave your wireless network exposed:

✦ **Sniffing:** Hackers use software programs called *sniffers* that scan the activity (or traffic) on a network. When a sniffer detects a vulnerability, it grabs data that's being sent across the wireless network connection.

✦ **War driving:** Using a wireless device, such as a laptop or personal digital assistant (PDA), a person literally drives around picking up unprotected wireless signals from homes and businesses. The wireless identification information (service set identifier, or SSID) is documented along with your physical address. Your information is put into an online database that lets curious thieves know that your wireless network is accessible.

✦ **Evil twin:** In this scenario, your access to a legitimate wireless access point is blocked or jammed. Then you're redirected to a second access point that's managed by a hacker. At that point, all the information you transmit is vulnerable, and thieves can even capture keystrokes to find passwords. This type of threat most often occurs in public Wi-Fi spots such as airports and coffee shops.

✦ **Wi-fishing:** Similar to the evil twin threat, thieves basically lure you to what looks like a safe access point. By using common SSIDs of public hot spots, your computer connects to a hacker's network. Again, your information becomes readily viewable; in some cases, viruses and Trojans are unknowingly sent to your system. (Read more about viruses and Trojans in Book IV, Chapter 3.)

Obviously, the real problem with these and other wireless network threats is that your bottom line is at risk. For the online thief, it's not a harmless hobby: It represents money in his pocket and out of yours! That's why investing in precautionary security measures is worthwhile.

Establishing Barriers

When protecting your wireless network, you can choose from a range of services, applications, and common procedures that can lower the risk of being compromised.

Following your common sense

Here are some basic rules you can follow to minimize your risk:

✦ **Shut down.** As silly as this method might sound, simply turning off your laptop when you're not using it reduces the chance for intrusion on your network. This technique also includes cutting the power to your cable or DSL.

✦ **Limit sharing.** Allow your networked computers to have shared access to only limited files or directories rather than to hard drives. In fact, you might want to disable file and print sharing.

✦ **Add a personal firewall.** A personal firewall installed on your laptop or on other individual computers provides another layer of protection between you and the wireless world.

✦ **Configure WPA.** Use the enhanced version of wireless encryption, Wi-Fi Protected Access (WPA). Ensure that all devices on your network are configured or set up to use WPA. If not, the less protective WEP wireless encryption becomes the default.

✦ **Disable broadcast.** You can turn off the broadcast SSID feature that automatically searches for and logs on to a wireless connection. Instead, you then have to manually enter your logon information or the name of your network.

✦ **Change SSID.** Wireless network devices that you buy are supplied with a preset SSID, which makes access quite convenient for thieves. Because this preset SSID identifies your network, you should immediately create a new SSID after installation of the wireless device. Create your SSID by following suggested guidelines for creating any password:

- *Characters:* Combine letters and numbers.

- *Length:* Use all characters allowed. (If the limit is 12, for example, use all 12 characters.)

- *Uniqueness:* Your SSID should be different from any of your other passwords.

- *Updates:* Change your SSID every three to four months.

To change your SSID, disable the broadcast feature, or configure devices for WPA, refer to the owner's manual supplied with your particular wireless router or access point.

Setting up a virtual private network

When you use a *virtual private network* (VPN), you create a protective tunnel around your wireless connection. The VPN keeps your transmission secure and also keeps out anyone not specifically granted access. To set up a VPN for your home office or small business, you can purchase a VPN server from companies such as Netgear (www.netgear.com).

Some ISPs also offer access to a virtual VPN. Take a look at Find VPN at www. findvpn.com to locate a provider of VPN services.

If you plan to work frequently at hot spots, consider signing up for a subscription-based VPN service. You can connect to a VPN for added protection in restaurants, hotels, airports, or any other Wi-Fi hot spot. Check out HotSpotVPN at www.hotspotvpn.com. A variety of pricing plans is available, ranging from $3.88 to $13.88 per month, based on your required usage.

Keeping an eye on your connection

You can also check your Wi-Fi connection to determine how safe it is. McAfee offers the free McAfee Wi-Fi Scan. To try it, follow these steps:

1. **Go to the McAfee free download site at**

   http://download.mcafee.com/us/eval/evaluate2.asp

2. **Click the McAfee Freescan link in the Free Services area on the right side of the page.**

   The next page shows a user agreement for the service.

3. **Read the agreement and click the Scan Now button at the bottom of the page.**

   Although a new page pops up that says the scan is starting, an interim page may open on some computers so that you can install the ActiveX controller that reads your computer.

   Make sure that your pop-up blocker is turned off in order for the installation to begin.

4. **Click the Install button.**

   Wait until the installation is finished. The scan automatically starts after ActiveX is installed.

5. **View the finished report that appears on your screen.**

   Pay attention to any messages in the Your Wireless Security Vulnerabilities box. You're told whether your SSID is identical to others in your area or whether your wireless router is configured with strong security. Click any links to find out how to fix problems.

No single method is best for protecting against wireless crimes. Instead, use a combination of security measures and common sense. You can never be too secure — the more the more measures you take, the better off you are.

Book VI

Boosting Sales

Tell Google about your Web site so that potential customers can find your business.

Contents at a Glance

Chapter 1: Driving Traffic, Driving Sales

In This Chapter

✔ Calculating the visitors-to-sales ratio at your site

✔ Discovering your high-volume traffic periods

✔ Marketing your site to drive traffic through the roof

You've probably heard the old saying "Build it and they will come." And, you probably know by now that this particular theory doesn't necessarily apply to your Web site. In this chapter, we show you how to calculate your site's conversion rate (how many browsers become buyers) and describe some strategies for increasing it.

Calculating Your Site's Conversion Rate

Your site's *conversion rate* is the number of visitors that come to your site and then buy from you. You *convert* a window shopper to a real buyer. That's simple enough. The concept becomes complicated, though, when you try to pin down exactly which number represents a good conversion rate.

You see a lot of conversion rate percentages thrown around — everything from .05 percent to nearly 8 percent to even 15 or 20 percent, depending on the type of site you have.

Considering that this is a numbers game, we like to take a somewhat conservative approach. We believe that 2 percent is a good conversion rate for first-time visitors to your site.

What if your site has 500 visitors per day? At a 2 percent conversion rate, that's about 10 sales ($500 \times .02$). That number seems a little depressing — unless you have some incredibly high profit margins! Based on this equation, the way to drive up sales is to drive traffic.

You can figure out how many visitors you need in order to have a healthy 2 percent conversion rate. Follow these steps:

1. **Determine the number of sales you need per day to stay in business.**

2. **Divide the number of sales by .02 (the 2 percent conversion rate).**

This number becomes your targeted goal. For example, if you want 100 sales per day, your target goal is 5,000 visitors per day.

Before you get too comfortable, keep in mind these other factors, which influence your true conversion rate:

✦ **Qualified traffic:** If you're shooting in the dark for traffic, that conversion rate becomes a sliding scale. However, by identifying visitors who are most likely to become buyers, you can put your efforts into targeting this demographic. Theoretically, you attract fewer visitors, but more of them would buy.

✦ **Site construction:** Everything from the layout and navigation of your home page to your search feature and shopping cart affect the probability that your visitors will be converted to buyers. The more intuitive, attractive, and useful your site, the better your likely conversion rates.

✦ **Quality product or service:** If you have a product or service that nobody wants, the number of visitors you can attract to your site doesn't matter. The conversion rate will lean toward zero!

✦ **Price point:** You can drive up conversion rates by using pricing strategies. Unless you can maintain price-based leverage in the marketplace, however, consider these rates falsely inflated.

Figuring Out When You Get the Most Traffic

In addition to increasing your sheer volume of traffic, to increase your sales numbers, you have to look at the whole picture. Part of navigating that landscape involves figuring out what time of day you're driving the bulk of your traffic to your site.

The average day is divided into several important time segments, called *dayparts*. This concept is important if you happen to own a business — even an online business that's open 24 hours a day.

For example, a restaurant typically receives the majority of its sales at three specific times during the day: breakfast, lunch, and dinner. It works almost the same way with the Internet, where five specific dayparts represent typical patterns of online traffic:

✦ **Early morning (6 a.m. to 8 a.m.):** Most people don't shop during these hours. Research indicates online retail buying drops by half in most cases.

✦ **Daytime (8 a.m. to 5 p.m.):** This period is one of the busiest for professionals (from 25 to 54 years old) to spend time online while working. Conversion rates for online retailers often peak between 10 a.m. and 1 p.m. That's right: Your customers typically spend their lunch hours checking out your site. Not only that — they're also willing to make a purchase.

✦ **Evening (5 p.m. to 11 p.m.):** Between the time folks arrive home from work and the time they go to bed, they apparently have enough downtime to do a little more online shopping.

✦ **Late night (11 p.m. to 6 a.m.):** This period isn't a busy one. Sure, some night owls are still looking for deals, but they're in the minority.

✦ **Weekend:** Yes, Saturday and Sunday get their own daypart! The conversion rates vary for the weekend daypart, but you can count on the peak periods being somewhat similar to weekday buying habits.

Does all this mean that you should close up shop during the wee hours of the dayparts? Of course not! After all, that's the beauty of the Internet: It's always open. Here are some strategies you can explore:

✦ **Balanced ad spending:** If you know when your customers are most receptive to your ads, that's when you want to spend the largest amount of money to get your ads shown. Similarly, you may want to decrease spending amounts during downtimes.

✦ **Increased ad revenue:** Alternatively, if you sell advertising, you may be able to make more money per impression during these busy dayparts.

✦ **Targeted specials:** Don't just run more ads during these periods. Create offers and time-sensitive pricing specials that are targeted to these frenzied shoppers. With the right offer, you may be able to bump an already strong conversion rate into an outstanding conversion rate.

You should also think about your specific site and to whom it appeals most. If most of your customers are teens, for example, the likelihood that they will buy from you during the weekday lunch hour drops. Evening and weekend dayparts may be busier for you because your customers aren't in school during these periods. However, lunchtime may present an opportunity to reach out to their parents (or to other secondary customers). Consider promoting your site's gift cards to this customer.

Balance the daypart information with what you already know about your customers. Always ask these questions:

✦ Who are my primary customers?

✦ Based on their lifestyles, when will they most likely visit my site?

✦ How can I serve them better during the specific dayparts when they're most likely to be ready to shop?

✦ What new, or secondary, customer base can I reach by taking advantage of peak dayparts?

✦ What type of offer or incentive can I create to attract that customer?

✦ How can I better serve my customers during the least-busy dayparts?

✦ What can I do to improve traffic and buying during nonpeak dayparts?

According to Jupiter Research (www.jupiterresearch.com), the two most influential factors for converting browsers to buyers are

✦ **Your site's security:** Buyers prefer to make a purchase from the site that is most secure.

✦ **Multiple options for payments:** These options include credit cards, debit cards, and PayPal.

Getting Customers to Notice Your Web Site

Getting prospective customers to stand up and take note isn't all that difficult. You have to be consistent, thorough, and unrelenting, however.

Take a multipronged approach that includes both online and offline marketing efforts. You can use these techniques to increase traffic and bump up conversion rates:

✦ **Keyword searches:** Paid keywords have proven themselves to be a cost-effective method of driving targeted traffic to your site. Check out Book VI, Chapter 6 to find out more about paid keywords.

✦ **Natural search**: Considering Web shoppers' dependency on Google and Yahoo!, getting your site to rank high remains an important way to drive traffic. We show you how to reach that all-important rank in Book VI, Chapter 6.

✦ **External links:** Increasing the number of sites that link to your site is usually a safe bet for attracting qualified visitors. Similarly, getting link referrals from online custom reviews and blogs can greatly increase traffic to your site.

✦ **Affiliate traffic:** Setting up an affiliate program can also help direct traffic your way. (Of course, you may not want to take on this task until your site is more established.) See Book IV, Chapter 2, where we discuss affiliates in more detail.

✦ **Advertising:** Paid banner advertising and direct-mail campaigns can generate just enough interest to make a visit worthwhile.

A ShopAds widget (`https://secure.adgregate.com/`) from Adgregate Markets allows prospective customers to buy a product directly from a display ad, without leaving the site where the ad appears. The ad has a secure shopping cart embedded in it, so whenever visitors see your ad on a third-party site, they can immediately click to buy the product. Talk about instant gratification!

✦ **Offline efforts:** Not everything you do has to stay online. Promoting your site offline (such as on business cards and by networking) can help drive traffic, too. See Book VII, Chapter 4 for more offline advertising ideas.

✦ **Content:** Building content on your site gives customers a reason to check out your site and then hang around long enough to buy something. We cover the different content, such as reviews, that you can provide in Book IV, Chapter 2.

✦ **E-newsletters:** Whatever the method you use to reach customers, the idea is to connect with them. After they form a relationship with you or define a need that you can answer, they will follow your lead — right back to your site. See Book IV, Chapter 3 to find out how to put together an e-newsletter.

**Book VI
Chapter 1**

Driving Traffic,
Driving Sales

Chapter 2: Special-Edition Public Relations for the Web

In This Chapter

✔ Writing product reviews

✔ Being a community leader by hosting Web seminars and sharing information

✔ Distributing free articles to build your portfolio

Although PR may stand for press release, you don't always have to draw attention to your business in the form of a press release. Publicity can come in many forms, and, by using the Internet, you can differentiate yourself and your company to attract customers in lots of ways. You probably have heard the phrase "There's no such thing as bad publicity." Well, if your customers are unhappy and they advise everyone they know to avoid your business, we're sure that it won't help your bottom line.

You must be out among the community you depend on in order to deliver customers. You not only gain a sense of what customers want and need in their lives but also connect with the community to help sell the story of you and your business. Consider the time you spend online reaching out to your community as an investment. You're building intangible relations, the goodwill that a positive company can generate, and the reason why these customers should shop with you and not someone else.

In this chapter, we focus on the publicity that revolves more around you and your product knowledge. We explore different ways in which you can indirectly promote your company while demonstrating your expertise and competence in your product's subject area. If you establish yourself as a leader or expert, customers will consider your business. One way is by using blogs, which we discuss fully in Book X, Chapter 3.

Every time you give, you receive in return. When you contribute information, opinions, reviews, or specific knowledge, people see that it's coming from the owner of Business X, not just from an individual. They believe that they can get to know both you and, through you, your business. Customers are looking for a connection, a bond, a reason to go with a particular business. Give it to them.

Writing Reviews

Most shoppers are used to seeing positive and glowing comments about a product clearly printed on the product box. They more highly value third-party independent reviews, however. After all, what company would slap the label Worst Product Ever on its product packaging? However, if thousands or millions of people are rallying because they're not happy with a product, consumers will give that action much more weight than a company's endorsements.

The independent testing organization Consumer Reports (`www.consumer reports.org`) rates everything from automobiles to computers to garden equipment. It has more than 4 million subscribers to its magazine, and an estimated 2 million people to its subscription Web site, where thousands of reviews, statistical test data, and evaluations are available for members to see. When customers are shopping online, they don't have the option to ask their local shopkeeper what she thinks about an item or to hear about how that shopkeeper helped a customer with an item that worked well (or not so well) at home. Customers turn then to reviews written online about the product, which is where you can make your entrance.

As someone with access to these products, and a history with them, you likely know more than the average person about some of the products you sell. Although you might not have used everything you sell, you have a better idea about how to evaluate a product or you gathered enough customer comments to form an opinion based on a fact.

When you write reviews, readers typically can access your profile and find out more about you. You might be surprised at the number of people who take the time to do so. Maybe they were impressed or intrigued by your comments about a product and they want to learn more. Or, maybe they're impressed by your depth of knowledge and want to know what else you approve or disapprove of. After customers identify you as knowledgeable, your opinion takes on greater weight, and so does your business.

In this section, we show you how to put those thoughts together and write some reviews of the products you sell.

Finding the best places to post reviews

The most valuable place your reviews can be posted is on your own Web site. After all, you're contributing this value to help your online business succeed and empower your customers to make better decisions. Therefore, you should incorporate any reviews you write to appear alongside the products you're selling on your own Web site.

After that, you want to spread the word about your knowledge and demonstrate to the larger community your experience with, and the professionalism of, a given product, to raise your profile as a product expert and expose new, potential customers to your company. Start by doing some investigating online, and look for Web sites that offer reviews of products you carry.

Some of these major online sites offer reviews:

✦ **About.com:** This company has been around since the early days of the Internet. Formed by a group of experts in various fields, About.com (see Figure 2-1) encompasses a network of more than 500 guides in different subjects — and 29 million visitors a month.

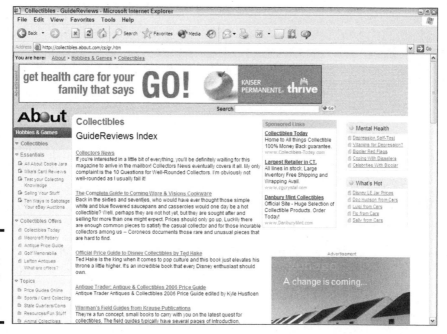

Figure 2-1:
Read about collectibles at About. com!

✦ **Amazon.com:** The world's largest e-tailer offers a wealth of reviews for its growing catalog of items. These reviews and comments are some of the drawing points for customers to this site.

✦ **eBay:** The world's largest online trading platform has been incorporating reviews and guides that its members provide. When eBay buyers are looking around for their favorite merchandise, they can read reviews, written by other eBayers, about those same products, to help make up their minds about whether they should bid on them.

✦ **News.com:** This online technology news site has amassed a growing array of product reviews for computers and consumer electronics. Underneath the editor's reviews is a section where all user reviews are grouped and averaged per product.

✦ **Yahoo! Shopping:** As one of the biggest aggregators of merchants online, Yahoo! Shopping has created product reviews to be placed alongside its wide array of merchandise, which has helped millions of consumers find the right products. The reviews are helpful, and Yahoo! lets you compare multiple items side-by-side.

Other places cater to different niches, like The Green Guide (www.the greenguide.com) for ecofriendly products and *PC* magazine (www.pc magazine.com) for computer components. If necessary, ask some of your customers where they do their research before they buy.

Every once in a while, you should check up on your product reviews to see what other readers are saying in response. Reader feedback can provide invaluable advice about whether your reviews are hitting the mark or are too confusing. Keep an open mind about their comments, and treat this strategy as another learning exercise.

In the end, you should be persistent and not overbearing. Allocate a specific amount of time per week to contribute reviews so that you don't spend all your time filling up page after page. Stay current, and approach new avenues as you have time. If you deal in brand-new products, make sure that you're one of the first people to review a product. That way, you lend greater authority to your opinion and provide your own, helpful early warning if you review an item you sell that turns out to be shoddy or unreliable.

Writing the review, section by section

After you know where to post your review, it's time to write one! You don't need an English degree to write reviews, and you don't have to carefully research, document, and stamp each one for approval. Most people are looking for honest, candid, easy-to-understand information that breaks down the essential information about a product. The best way we have heard someone describe how to write a review is this: "If a friend asked you what you thought about Product X, you could hand them your review as the answer."

Have the product in front of you when you start writing. Being able to hold up the product, scan its box, read its specifications, and experiment with the product can trigger thoughts and confirm suspicions when you're writing a review.

When you're ready to write a review, make sure that it has these basic sections:

✦ **Initial impressions:** Start by writing down your initial impressions of the product. What were the first things you thought of the first time you saw the product? What did you think about the first time you used the product? What were you hoping the product would provide, and what did you expect it to be?

Don't worry about immediately assigning a product a number between 1 and 10 or coming up with a title. These issues should be the last ones you write about, because writing the rest of the review can lead you to the ultimate ranking answer.

Your initial impressions should provide a quick summary of the product, your impressions, and a sense of whether you favor it. Someone reading only your first paragraph should see all the basic information and know whether you approve or disapprove.

✦ **Pros:** Write down the reasons you like the product, no matter how big or small the issue. Include the ways that this product is better than similar products on the market, and describe its best features.

✦ **Cons:** Write down the reasons you dislike the product. Think of the features you're not happy with or that you wish could be changed. Note whether the problem prevents you from using the product correctly or just bothers you individually. Obviously, rank the problems that affect your usage higher than your personal opinion.

✦ **Experience with the product:** Regardless of whether you love the product or hate it, does it do what it's supposed to do? If it's a digital camera, for example, does it take great-looking photos? Even if the camera is hard to use and its battery life is low, does it perform its main functions? Most products have a purpose or a use, and people want to know how this product can help them. A great-looking item might be completely useless, or an item that solves a big problem might be difficult to use.

Talk about your experience with your product in a positive way that's not confrontational. Don't say that you love it because it sells well. Say that you love it because the product is so solid that your customers love it and that's why it sells well.

✦ **Recommendations:** Would you personally buy your product? Would you recommend it to someone? Would you recommend it only for a specialized need or a certain kind of user?

After you complete all these areas, you should have a good idea of how you would rank the product on a scale from 1 to 10. You might be asked to rank certain individual characteristics on some Web sites, so consider them last too, after you think about the good, the bad, and the ugly.

The title of your review should be a one-sentence summary that captures the essence of what you're saying. The easiest titles to write are for products you absolutely love ("This product is the best thing since sliced bread!") or absolutely hate ("Don't buy this product, even if they're giving it away!"). For most reviews that lie between these two ends of the spectrum, pick a good point and a bad point, and emphasize the one you most agree with. For example, say something like "Good product for the money, but don't expect full features!" or "Product X: Adequate but in need of improvement."

TIP

Make sure that your reviews are sincere and honest. Don't rave about a product just because you sell it and you hope that a good review will boost sales. Readers will see through an insincere review, and your plan could backfire because they will go online and warn other consumers not to trust you or your reviews, opinions, or business.

Becoming a Community Leader

Building a business is not only time-consuming but also rewarding and educational. Your work, however, doesn't end with your own Web site. Interaction with the community is essential for any business, whether you hang a shingle or code a Web page. On the Internet, you have ways to participate as a business owner that lend credibility and raise the collective energy of your community, who will remember those qualities when it's time to buy.

Speaking out with Webinars

Ten or 20 years ago, you could make connections with potential customers by agreeing to speak at their Rotary Club or Chamber of Commerce meetings about your chosen subject area. The Internet and high technology have combined to create a way for you to deliver that same talk — without the rubber chicken and the echo from the borrowed sound system. A *Webinar*, (short for *Web* sem*inar*) combines video, audio, and graphics to give the audience an experience similar to sitting in a lecture hall.

When you prepare and deliver a Webinar, you can give the same set of information to an unlimited number of people in your topic area, and at any time of the day. You control the message, the delivery of that message, and all the accompanying information that goes with the message. The formatting of your presentation is always the same with a Webinar, and your presence cannot be deleted, because your image, voice, and slides drive the presentation.

One leading company that produces Web seminars is WebEx, shown in Figure 2-2. Founded in 1996 and acquired by Cisco Systems, WebEx focuses on ways to provide videoconferencing and other technologies to connect multiple people to one event. A section on its Web site is dedicated to creating these Web seminars. You can read about WebEx services and prices by going to www.webex.com/smb/webinars.html.

Figure 2-2:
Expand your
business
with WebEx
Web
seminars.

You don't necessarily have to worry about the technical aspect of producing a Webinar. See whether you can partner with a company that can handle the technical tasks so that you can focus on speaking. You're giving the company the benefit of a Webinar that it can include in its portfolio, and you can unburden yourself from the technical process of creating the event. In this case, definitely make sure that your profile is front and center on the Webinar.

Organize your thoughts for a Webinar as though you're speaking in a big lecture hall. The only difference is that people are watching on their computer screens, not from chairs physically positioned in front of you. A Webinars presenter can now host a question-and-answer session with a live audience, so it can be an interactive experience, not just another lecture.

Book IV, Chapter 3 provides more information about how you can turn a Webinar into its own profit center rather than just a mechanism for raising your profile.

Billing yourself as an expert

Given the immense amount of information and options for consumers, the easiest way for them to cut through all the noise and presentations of the high-tech world to find what they're looking for is to rely on the low-tech, time-tested tradition known as *word of mouth*. Most customers make their decisions based on recommendations from family members and friends. In the absence of a friend or family member, however, online consumers look for an expert in that area. That's where you come in.

Expertise isn't a degree that a university can confer on you; it's the real-world experience you build up in a given subject area or product category. It's up to you to share that information in a constructive way so that customers see you as the expert. After customers start asking you for advice, they find about your business. When it's time for them to buy a product, they're much more likely to choose someone they consider an expert over a nameless, faceless Web site with a slightly lower price.

To become an expert, spend some time in the places where your potential customers congregate and ask questions about your area of expertise. Two of the most popular places to frequent are discussion groups and mailing lists. Follow these general steps:

1. **Identify the discussion groups that pertain to your area.**

   Dig around, do some research, and use search engines or your favorite Web sites to see where people are gathering online to discuss topics.

2. **Join the designated groups, and find out how to participate correctly.**

   Take the time to complete the registration processes at each of these sites, and pick usernames that advertise you, not your business. If people see that a corporate name is contributing information, they might see it as an invasion for sales only.

3. **Set up your profile and signature file.**

   Make sure that your business and Web site address are clearly mentioned at the bottom of your signature file so that people can follow up if they're interested.

4. **Start looking for discussions and questions that you can contribute to easily.**

   Start by monitoring conversations and develop a sense for the tone that people use in their responses. Don't feel that you have to dive in right away. Start by providing a comment here and there, and take some time in the beginning to observe the atmosphere and get to know the major contributors.

   Don't use these places for blatant self promotion. Participate in a healthy manner, and make sure that your signature file contains a line or two about your Web business.

5. **Set up a regular schedule to contribute to one or more discussions.**

Include this process in your weekly routine so that you don't forget about it as time goes on. Maybe you spend a half-hour each Tuesday logging in to see the most active discussions. You can spend a few minutes each day and look for the most relevant discussions for your area. Find something that fits your schedule so that you have the time to participate without feeling rushed.

Make sure that each posting is free of any obvious spelling and grammatical errors. Use a word processing program, such as Microsoft Word, to write your post so that you can easily check and correct mistakes. Then copy and paste your words into the listing.

Writing Articles

When people share information, they don't limit themselves to just one or two channels. They're always on the lookout for good information. Countless sites are set up to satisfy people's need for more information, organized around every imaginable subject, discipline, passion, hobby, and criteria. Although these sites are good at organization and attracting traffic, they all usually want help with one particular area: content.

People who contribute content gain lots of exposure by sharing their information. The exposure comes from one simple requirement that you tie in to your free articles: Your name, as the author, contains a profile that links to your Web site. You allow anyone to publish, reprint, or distribute your article, as long as your profile information is attached. That way, everyone who reads these articles knows that you're the source of that information and is inclined to check out your company's Web site to see what else is out there.

Free distribution of your articles has other important benefits. As more and more Web sites pick up your article and publish it, more search engines pick up the link in your profile. Many search engines, especially Google, now rank search results based partially on how many people make references to a given Web page. Your articles create more references on the Web, and ultimately raise your ranking, so you naturally appear in a user's search results and don't have to pay as much in search engine advertising. (See Book VI, Chapter 3 for more information on search engine advertising.)

Tailoring your article topics

When you were told to write a paper in school, you probably didn't have much choice about the topic. Now you have complete control, so be sure to write articles that appeal to your customer base. You can easily fall into the trap of writing only what you know, even if that topic is nowhere near what your customers would be reading.

Writing what you know about works in the beginning, if you need some motivation to start writing articles.

As a business owner, you're already looking to stay ahead of the curve to see where your market is heading. Now you get to use that knowledge to help tell customers what to expect. You can choose from a variety of angles for your article, including these:

✦ Provide straightforward, concise explanations and examples of a new technology.

✦ List four or five non-obvious ways that a product or service can be beneficial.

✦ Create a step-by-step guide for accomplishing a specific task.

✦ Describe how to improve a (popular) way of doing something.

✦ Specify what not to do in a given area.

✦ Create a case study showing someone's right and wrong actions, and then explain why.

The best topics, sometimes, are about issues you just faced with your business or your personal online adventures. Think about how you handled a given situation. Did you learn a new trick or two along the way? Did the recommended solution pan out? Did an unorthodox method (or even the tried-and-true method) produce measurable results? If so, ask yourself this question: "Would other people benefit from what I just learned?" If so, and if you're not revealing a competitive advantage, start making notes to turn into an article.

Putting together your article

Don't be afraid to brainstorm and jot down ideas to revisit later. Your articles have to capture readers' attention, even if it's just for the first paragraph, so it has to be relevant, useful, and interesting. Most people — whether they're reading newspaper stories, magazine features, or online write-ups — see a headline, read (maybe) the first paragraph, and then move on. That's why articles have to grab you in the first paragraph.

Put together your articles in this fashion:

✦ **First paragraph:** Presents the overall picture. You need to accurately and vividly describe the situation you address in your article. If it's about a solution to a problem, first discuss the problem. Remind readers about how much of a headache this problem can cause, and detail the pain, so to speak. If you're writing a step-by-step guide, use the first paragraph to talk about the problem this guide will solve. Then make sure that you end the first paragraph by telling readers what you will say in the rest of the article.

✦ **Middle paragraphs:** Contain the "meat," or the essence, of the article — namely, the information that readers want to read. Stay away from technical jargon or low-level details or specifics, and provide an overview in plain English of what readers should do, look into, or implement themselves. Let them do the additional research of finding the specifics. Your article should identify the solution path and give readers enough information to continue investigating.

✦ **Last paragraph:** Wrap up your article with a summary of what you presented, and share either a success story or result that readers can expect afterward. If readers need to take action after reading your article, you want to leave them with an important reason to get started, even if it's an obvious reason.

The average length of an article is about 300 to 600 words, or one or two double-spaced pages in a word processor. If you're direct and to the point, don't worry about sending out a 280-word article. Conversely, if your article continues page after page, it had better be useful and not repetitive or fluffy.

Even though you're not being graded on your work, be sure to check for any spelling or grammatical errors before you send it out. Mistakes detract from the professional image you want to convey in your article, which would defeat the purpose.

If you're curious about whether your article is ready for distribution, use a small group of friends, employees, or customers as your test market, by sending them a copy and asking for honest feedback. Don't expect them to correct any mistakes; just listen to their feedback and consider their comments. A peer review usually makes a piece stronger, and a stronger article is more effective.

Handing out your articles

After you write and prepare your article with the correct profile and Web link, you need to distribute the goods. You can submit your articles to dedicated online article directories and e-zine newsletter sources, and those groups then do the work of disseminating your article to various sources. These directories stay in business by providing content to hungry Web sites and newsletters that need content to attract visitors.

Most directories have a submission process that's available on their Web sites. Submit your article to as many sites as you want. You can find a good list to get started with in Table 2-1.

Table 2-1	Online Article Directories
Name	*Submission URL*
Amazines	www.amazines.com/register.cfm
Articles Base	www.articlesbase.com/submit-articles.php
Article Marketer	www.articlemarketer.com/submit.php
Ezine @rticles	www.ezinearticles.com/submit
Goarticles	www.goarticles.com/ulogin.html
Isnare	www.isnare.com/members.php

Don't be afraid to mention the release of a new article in your blog. It adds publicity for you and reinforces the image you're presenting to your audience. It shows how you're working to keep the community informed and gives you a great reason for a new, current blog entry.

If you're already a member of niche news sites, check into submitting your article directly to them! Look for an editorial director or reporter's e-mail message in the About Us section of that Web site, and send an introductory letter along with your article. You might be offered a column or contributor status, or you can serve, at the least, as a good source to find quotes for the site's upcoming articles in your area of expertise. It all goes back to raising your exposure and achieving expert status. After all, you never know who might read your article next.

Chapter 3: Web Marketing at Work

In This Chapter

✔ Implementing a total marketing strategy

✔ Offering newsletters to lure in potential customers

✔ Advertising through a pay-per-click strategy

✔ Bringing in customers with search engine optimization

✔ Marketing your business in non-electric ways

*R*egardless of how big your online business is or will become, the power of the Web is a far-reaching and low-cost way to effectively turn people on to what you provide. One reason for Web marketing effectiveness is the power of *one-to-one marketing*. Rather than create TV ads that speak to tens of millions of people during a popular sitcom, for example, Web marketing speaks directly to your interested customers and builds a one-to-one connection between a potential customer and your business. These first-time buyers can become repeat customers who spread the word about your company to new customers, and your business continues to grow with each wave. Online sites such as craigslist grew in popularity because people came together not just to buy and sell stuff but also to find jobs, apartments, romance, and events in their geographical areas.

Many people believe that Web marketing works for only the big companies that can rent banner ads and host lavish Web sites with large e-mail distribution lists. The truth is that small businesses and entrepreneurs, just like yourself, can benefit from all the same techniques that the larger companies employ, by investing your time and effort along with your dollars. In this chapter, we show you how to use these marketing techniques to reach potential customers.

Developing a Marketing Strategy

In the early days of the Internet, you could build a Web site, get mentioned in the right places, and instantly receive a stream of customers, whether you sold sweaters or homemade apple butter. You didn't have much competition, and a hungry audience would soak up whatever they could find in the early days of the Web. Web sites and online commerce companies now sell everything that's legal (and a few things that aren't) and there's enough competition to last a long time. The days of building a Web site and receiving instant traffic are mostly over. In this section, we show you how to use branding and a targeted advertising strategy to get the word out about your business to the masses.

Hit the right concept at the right time, however, and you might find early success. When people heard of a search engine, Google, that provided relevant results, they started using it more and more. When bands could create their own Web sites and share music with their fans, who could also build their own Web pages, MySpace jumped to the top of the charts of the social networking trend.

Devising your brand

To get your business noticed, you need to come up with a basic, all-encompassing strategy. This strategy defines and drives your marketing efforts, regardless of how you do it. Always send out the right message from the start so that you don't confuse your customers and waste your money.

The first part of your strategy is to create your brand image. Your *brand image* is the message that your company portrays in everything you do, from telling people about your business to treating its customers a certain way to providing value, through your products and services. It's not one piece, but rather the overall sense that customers and your general audience get when they think of your business. Your brand is the successful combination of a memorable logo, a catchy slogan, a distinctive color scheme, and more. These elements all influence how your customers view your business, but these are not your brand. Your brand is the impression your customers have of your business.

What should your brand be? Consider these points to get you started as you devise your brand:

+ **Competitive prices:** Because you have an online business, you're not paying for expensive retail space and a carpet for customers to trip on as they walk through the front door. You can therefore offer lower prices than your offline competitors.

+ **Convenience:** Your customers can interact with the business even when they're wearing pajamas.

+ **Customize requests:** You can provide each customer's specific request or match people with similar interests.

Although we could give you more examples, the lesson here is that you have options. Pick the brand that fits with your company.

Working the brand

After you have an idea for an appropriate brand, it's time to share it with the world! Because your business operates online, you can easily promote your business online. Billions of dollars are spent each year on Web advertising (just look at Google's growing numbers), and the numbers increase each quarter.

Rather than pay for a billboard that you hope people see on their way to work, make your Web advertising stare customers right in the face — literally. You're speaking to a captive audience because the advertising is part of the screen, built into the Web page in a variety of ways. In addition, you have a better chance of having the right ad stare the right customer in the face because you can better target who receives which ad.

Because many different companies offer advertising opportunities, you want to find the right markets that best push your brand. Therefore, think about whom you want to reach with your brand. If your brand revolves around power tools and improving the home, maybe a Web site that offers cooking tips isn't the right place for you to advertise. If your company appeals to the teenage consumer, MySpace, MTV, and extreme sports Web sites are better places to start.

You can reach out through the Web and advertise your brand and company in many ways:

✦ **Paid advertising:** Many sites offer options, such as banner ads, center ads, and paid-placement spots where you can rent space based on how many people click through to your Web site. This way, you can track the *click ratio* to see how effective certain sites are to your brand, and pay only when someone who wants to find out more clicks your link.

Click ratio refers to the percentage of people who click a specific ad based on the total population who saw that ad. You calculate the click ratio by dividing the number of times someone clicked an ad by the number of times the ad was displayed. On average, click ratios can range from 0.5 or 1 percent to 5 or 10 percent on specialized sites.

✦ **Partnerships:** Rather than pay outright to be on someone's Web site, come up with a partnership deal where you and another company promote each other to your users. You can make

- *A simple deal:* You and the other company put banner ads for the other company on your own site.

- *A complex deal:* You and the other company create joint promotions and provide links back and forth.

✦ **Classified advertising:** Rather than place banner ads that advertise your company, you can take out classified ads that market a specific product or sale item. Many sites — such as Craigslist (www.craigslist.org; see Figure 3-1) or Kijiji (www.kijiji.com) and even some local newspaper online classifieds sections — allow you to post free ads.

Figure 3-1: Find what you need locally using craigslist.

✦ **Product placement:** In this newer form of advertising, you arrange to get your products mentioned and your Web site referenced by someone else. You can do it through a blog, or someone can feature a review of your product on a Web site after you send a sample.

✦ **Keyword searches:** Search engines offer advertising that can appear on the same Web page as search results. You can bid on the right to have your ad appear for a given keyword that someone types. See the section "Searching for Traffic with Search Engine Advertising," a little later in this chapter, for more information.

Big advertising campaigns don't necessarily mean big budgets. You need to think about every move that you make online, and the best campaigns start at home. Your own Web site needs to reflect the brand that you want to present to your customers. Every e-mail you send should mention your business and Web site address. When you contribute to any online discussions, chat rooms, or groups, make sure that your business and Web site are carefully displayed at the bottom of any posting you make. Small actions like these can lead to name recognition, which can lead to customer recognition and acquisition.

Reeling In Customers with Newsletters

You enticed someone to visit your site and maybe even buy something. What you really want, though, is a repeat customer. Studies have shown that getting an existing customer to return to your site is as much as six times more effective than getting a brand-new customer. You have to give people reasons to come back, and a newsletter gives them an added benefit of shopping with you and a reason for them to consider your business for their next purchase.

Newsletters are quickly becoming one of the most popular ways to promote a business. Think of a newsletter as a souped-up church bulletin or PTA announcement, made over for the Internet. Most newsletters are a combination of articles and information, with definite *plugs* for, or mentions of, specific products, sales events, or company news. Figure 3-2 shows a newsletter for Lynn Dralle, the Queen of Auctions. She gives helpful tips for selling with auctions, but also plugs her books and upcoming seminars.

Figure 3-2:
Use newsletters to provide information and increase sales.

Having a regular newsletter that people can subscribe to has many benefits. You can

✦ **Communicate with your customers.** Newsletters give you the opportunity to share why you're in business and what you can offer your customers. Although most people have trained themselves to skip over pure advertisements, reading stories or tips can break down customer defenses so that they listen and find out more.

✦ **Share information.** The products you sell have a specific use, so helping customers use the products more effectively gives your business an added value. If you sell cooking supplies, provide recipes and describe how your products help make different foods, for example. If you sell books in a specific genre, post customer reviews of the newest releases so that customers can decide whether they want to buy the latest Stephen King horror novel or John Grisham legal thriller.

Don't just fill a newsletter with product announcements, sales offers, and discounts. Then it becomes a flyer and not a newsletter. Carefully balance the content and promotion that goes into each newsletter. While some people recommend a specific balance, like 30 percent sales and 70 percent information, the key is to provide enough good information to make the newsletter worthwhile to the customer.

✦ **Build a connection.** If consumers become used to receiving from you a regular newsletter that they find helpful, they build a connection in their minds that you're now a trusted source, and they consider your business more carefully. They might think, "Oh, yeah, that's the company that sends out the Top 10 Tips that I read every week. Those people know what they're talking about, so I'll use them to order my next batch of supplies."

Creating your newsletter doesn't have to be a large and complex project full of deadlines and drama where you yell "Stop the presses!" whenever a new idea comes in. You do, however, have to do some planning, be consistent, and follow some guidelines. In the following sections, we discuss what up-front planning you need to do.

You can also check out the excellent *E-Mail Marketing For Dummies* by John Arnold (Wiley Publishing) for more information on developing and distributing your newsletter.

Decide who will write your newsletter

Many business owners think that their job is to create each newsletter and come up with all its fabulous content. If you have a staff, that shouldn't be the case. As the owner, you might want to have your own newsletter column or introduction that you sign your name to and then have different people contribute different parts of the newsletter. Decide in advance who will produce which section, because it's better to have that system in place than to scramble every time a newsletter needs to be created.

Don't forget about your customers. They can help you write your newsletter! You can include a Letters section, where customers get to share their experiences, ask questions (that you can answer in the newsletter), or be honored by you, the business owner, for reaching a certain milestone. Customers love to see themselves in print, and it shows potential customers that real people use your business.

Decide what your newsletter will cover

You need to provide different, fresh, and relevant content every time. Stay current on the issues affecting your industry by reading newspapers, magazines, and press releases in your subject area to help generate ideas.

Don't include news stories from other sources in your newsletters without their express consent. If you or someone on your staff writes the articles, you can refer to quotes or statistics from articles, as long as you cite the source in your articles.

Decide when to issue your newsletter

You need to decide at the beginning how frequently your newsletter is released: weekly, monthly, or yearly, just as long as you publish it on a consistent schedule. Readers lose interest with late or varied schedules, so pick a publishing time that you and your business can handle without much stress. You can publish on a less frequent schedule as long as you're reliable.

You also need to decide on which day of the week you will publish. Some companies target the day of new product releases to send out their newsletters. A movie and music seller might pick Tuesdays for its newsletter release because new movies and CDs hit stores that day. Another site might pick a weekend day so that its newsletter can serve as a weekly summary of events and readers can follow up when they're not at work.

Decide on a format for your newsletter

You can use a number of different computer programs to create a newsletter, although you can present it in only two main formats:

✦ **Plain-text** has words and Web links but no graphics. Although plain-text newsletters can be read by anyone and are quick to send and receive, they look, well, plain, like the newsletter shown in Figure 3-3.

✦ **HTML** has words, graphics, and design formatting to look exactly like a Web page. HTML newsletters can look cool and sophisticated but can't be interpreted by every e-mail system and can take a long time to show up onscreen.

```
USED COPIES FOR SALE AT AMAZON

Think twice before sending out f.ree review copies all over the country
-
especially New York. Here's why: They can all end up for sale on
Amazon.com by second-hand dealers--your f.ree books competing against
you.
If you are small and your pockets are not deep enough to produce enough
copies for an established distributor, be careful and selective with
review copies you send out.
--Gary N. Bourland

There is more to this phenomenon.

Many books sent to reviewers in NYC are ripped off in the mailroom and
sold to the Strand bookstore. To the basement denizens of large
buildings,
packages with books are windfall occasions.

But, the books offered at Amazon, may not be ripped off, may not be
review
copies and may not even exist.

Dan Poynter sent out just over 100 copies of The Book Publishing
Encyclopedia in PDF form via email ONLY. Within hours of the book being
posted at Amazon.com, some resellers were offering it in the paper
edition. The catch?--The paper edition did not exist.
```

Figure 3-3:
Plain-text
newsletters
display the
facts plainly.

You can create two different versions and ask your readers during the sign-up process which version they want to receive. If you want to be safe, create a clean, plain-text format, which everyone can enjoy.

Decide how to distribute your newsletter

After you create your newsletter, you have to get it to your readers. After your customer list grows beyond a few people, you can't just open an e-mail window, insert your newsletter, and send it to thousands of people at one time. You need to talk to your Internet service provider (ISP) to make sure that you can distribute the same newsletter to hundreds or thousands of people. By notifying your ISP, you ensure that it doesn't just shut down your newsletter when someone suddenly sees the increased traffic.

Send your newsletter only to people who specifically request it. Don't just spam everyone you've done business with in the past.

If you have trouble sending the newsletter through your normal ISP, you can contract a company to manage the newsletter distribution for you. This way, its computer systems handles the mailing of your newsletter and can coordinate the automatic subscriptions of new readers or the *unsubscriptions* (removals) of customers when they want to stop receiving the newsletter. Table 3-1 lists a few of these companies.

Table 3-1	E-Mail Newsletter Distribution Services
Name	*URL*
Constant Contact	www.constantcontact.com
JangoMail	www.jangomail.com
Campaigner	www.campaigner.com
Delivra	www.delivra.com
EXMG	www.exmmarketing.com

 Keep the most recent two or three issues of your newsletter available on your Web site. Not only can customers read your newsletter online, instead of relying on an e-mail program, but the search engines scan your newsletters, which can lead to more customers finding your Web site.

Automating Your Routine Tasks

How many times have you tried to reach a company through a toll-free hotline only to be put on hold or made to listen to an endless array of recorded messages? Have you pressed a number on the keypad so many times that the number has now rubbed off the button? If you're like us, you hang up and never do business with that company again.

Guard against this situation when customers interact with your online business. If they can't quickly add or delete themselves from your newsletter mailing list or respond to an e-mail or banner offer, they get frustrated and leave. They might never come back, no matter how many offers and deals you throw their way.

Enter automation. By setting up automatic processes, you can have your marketing campaign go 24/7, and with automation handling the more routine tasks, you're free to handle more business deals (such as finding the right merchandise, analyzing your sales numbers, or hiring the right staff to grow your business).

Here are some tools you can use to automate parts of the process:

✦ **Autoresponders:** This tool automatically generates an e-mail response based on an incoming request, such as when someone joins your newsletter mailing list. An autoresponder can add that person's name to the database and send him a welcome message (full of information about your company) and maybe even an introductory newsletter issue.

Don't abuse the autoresponder with every process you have in customer interaction. The last thing customers want is form letters every time they send you e-mail, especially if the form letter response has nothing to do with their original question. Reserve the autoresponder for situations that have only one expected response, like addition to or deletion from a mailing list.

✦ **Ticklers:** Send out *ticklers* (automatic reminders or updates) every few weeks with contact managers such as ACT! or Salesforce.com. Include a variety of offers in your tickler to slowly but surely encourage these contacts to try out your company and your products.

✦ **Archived information:** Sometimes, the best way you can help your customers is to enable them to help themselves. Dedicate a portion of your Web site to hold all your marketing collateral and information. Put the most frequently asked questions in this help section, and make sure that it's accessible from any page of your Web site.

Try putting your marketing material in different formats to appeal to different customers. You can turn a brochure into an audio file sales pitch, a PowerPoint presentation into a downloadable video file, or a meeting into a downloadable Webinar, for example. Each new format serves as a hook to a portion of your audience. See Book IV, Chapter 3 for more information on creating different products.

Searching for Traffic with Search Engine Advertising

If you're building a gas station, would you have it on a rural country road or a freeway off-ramp? The answer is simple: You want to position your business where your customers are located. The best businesses in the world can't succeed if their customers can't find them. That's why location and access are so important, even for an online business.

You want to position yourself where the traffic is, and nowadays most people find Web sites through search engines. Therefore, set up shop right on a search engine page with advertising, and benefit from that "drive-by" traffic.

After all, one big benefit of search engine advertising is that you know in advance what the target consumer is looking for. Search engine advertising works like this: You tie your products or Web site to specific keywords. When someone types those keywords in the search page, your ad is displayed. Figure 3-4 shows how Google displays its ads. Suppose that a potential customer is doing a search on Google for a certain brand of golf clubs. If your business sells that brand of products, your ad can appear next to the search results. Because the ad is targeted only to people who demonstrate that interest, your rate of return is higher than in a generic ad.

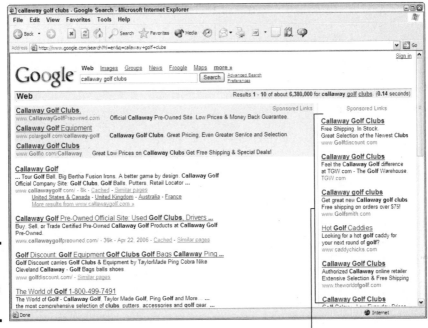

Ads

Figure 3-4:
Google
displays ads
on the right.

Although Google and Yahoo! are the two biggest companies in the area of search engine advertising, they are by no means the only game in town. Table 3-2 lists the major companies that offer search engine advertising. We show you in the following section how to sign up for Google AdWords.

Table 3-2	Search Engine Advertising Companies	
Company	*Service*	*URL*
Google	AdWords	adwords.google.com
Yahoo!	Sponsored Search	searchmarketing.yahoo.com
MSN (Microsoft)	adCentral	adcenter.microsoft.com
Miva	Pay-per-click program	www.miva.com/us
Marchex	Adhere	www.marchex.com

If your products appeal to a certain niche audience, check to see whether news or portal sites that cater to that industry also accept search advertising on their sites. Although some of these Web sites have outsourced their advertising to companies like Google or DoubleClick, the sites still control the ads that are displayed, and are usually open to some partnership or paid arrangement.

Signing up for Google AdWords

The leader in search engine ads is Google AdWords. You can use this program to create your own ads and to bid on keywords that trigger the display of those ads. When a Google user types your keywords during a search, your ad appears on the right side of the results screen in a Sponsored Ads box (refer to Figure 3-1).

Google keeps track of the number of times your ad is clicked, and you pay only for the times your ad is clicked, not the number of times your ad is displayed on the screen. Like other services, AdWords lets you set a budget, so you pay only for the ads you can afford. When your budget is used up, your ad doesn't appear any more. You even specify a daily budget so that your ad campaign can't be spent in the first day.

A Google AdWords *campaign* doesn't refer to a politician's run for office; it more commonly means running a specific ad for a given budget. Your ad campaign can consist of one ad running on Google until you spend $100, or a series of ads running for several weeks to promote a new product.

Your customization of the campaign isn't limited to just the keyword. Using Google AdWords, you can pick your target area (a city, territory, or country), and Google targets where the search user is from, whether it's from the search itself, the specific IP address of the computer, or the preferences that the user set up already. By using this targeting, you can show different ads to different territories, offer specific ads and promotions to specific areas, or even create your own test markets where only a specific group of computer users is presented with a given ad.

We discuss GoogleAds because it's popular and easy to use. All the services work similarly, so just choose the one that works best for you.

Setting up a Google campaign

If you're interested in setting up your own AdWords campaign, type your keywords and look at the ads that already appear on Google for your targeted subject area. Get an idea of the ads that you're competing against and the words they use to craft their ads. This strategy should give you some ideas for your ad.

Write out your ad copy and have two or three people proofread it before building your campaign. Also take the time to think of the right keywords to use in advance so that you're not guessing when it's time to build the campaign.

When you're ready to build an AdWords campaign, just follow these steps:

1. **Go to** `http://adwords.google.com` **and click the Start Now button.**

2. **Choose between the Starter Edition and the Standard Edition, as shown in Figure 3-5.**

    If you're planning to test the market, pick Starter Edition and select either I Have a Webpage or I Don't Have a Webpage. Help Me Create One." You can then build one text ad and become familiar with the system.

**Book VI
Chapter 3**

Web Marketing
at Work

Figure 3-5:
Choose your
level of ad
campaign
on Google.

3. **Click Continue.**

    If you picked the Starter Edition, you see a one-page form so that you can fill out all the details of your ad. If you picked the Standard Edition, you see a series of Web pages that focus on one part of the six-part setup process.

4. Pick the target area of your ad. Click Continue when you're ready.

You can pick the country where you want to run the ad and specify a local area for the ad and the language to run the ad in.

5. Specify the Web site address where you want to redirect people who click your ad.

You don't have to link your ad to your home page. You can specify a special Web page within your Web site so that you can present a special offer to only those people who click your ad. You can easily track the number of people who view that page to see how effective your ad truly is.

6. Write the ad. When you're done, click Continue.

You can use a total of 95 characters on three lines:

- *The headline:* As many as 25 characters
- *Two lines of text underneath the headline:* As many as 35 characters per line

7. Specify the keywords that will trigger your ad (see Figure 3-6).

You can specify one or more keywords that are related to the product you want to advertise. If you're looking for ideas on which keyword phrases to use, simply type your main keywords in the Want More? box and Google displays related keyword phrases that you can add to your campaign.

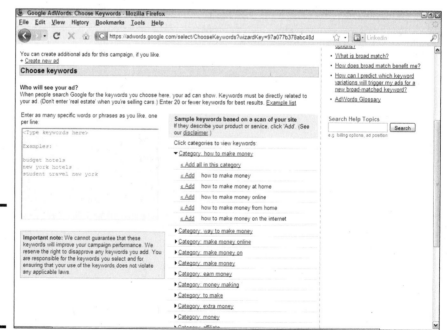

Figure 3-6:
Type the keywords to be associated with your ad.

8. **Specify the currency you're using for this ad campaign and then your budget. Click Continue.**

Pick from the options presented, or put your custom ad budget amount in the budget field provided.

Google prompts you if it thinks that your maximum per-click rate is too low and then suggests a minimum level. If you can't afford a keyword, try to come up with an alternative one.

9. **Choose to receive newsletters, surveys, and other helpful information for future campaigns. Click Continue.**

Leave the box selected if you want to receive this information. If you don't want it, be sure to deselect the box.

10. **Enter an e-mail address and a password if you need to create an account with Google.**

Google can tie your campaign to your existing Google account (if you use other Google services, such as Gmail).

11. **Answer the Google security question, and then click Create Account.**

Google sends you an e-mail containing a Web link.

12. **Click the Web link to verify your account and return to Google.**

13. **Log in to your account and provide Google with the billing information for your account.**

Just follow the prompts, or click the My Account tab and look for Billing Preferences. Google asks for your billing country and then your payment information. Read through the Google AdWords program terms and agree to them, too.

After your payment method is entered and approved, your ads begin to appear on Google almost instantly! Go to the main Google page and perform a few searches to see where your ad ends up on the results page.

Determining the right amount per click

After you set up your account, you want to know where your pricing is positioning you on the page. Follow these steps to check on your pay-per-click rate:

1. **Go to www.google.com, type your keyword phrase, and click the Google Search button.**

On the results screen, look on the right side for your ad. If it doesn't even appear, you're not paying enough to appear on the first screen; you have to click the See More Sponsored Links link to see your ad.

2. **Log in to your Google AdWords account, and click to the specific campaign.**

   Look for your campaign name among the list of campaigns (see Figure 3-7).

Figure 3-7:
Access
your Google
AdWords
campaigns.

3. **Raise the maximum amount you're paying, and click Save.**

4. **Go back to the Google results screen and refresh it.**

   You can refresh screens in most Web browsers by pressing F5. See what position your ad moves to on the page. If you see a jump in the placement of your ad, you have an idea of what your competitors have spent to get their positions, and what it will take to keep this new position. If your position hasn't jumped, your competitors are paying even more than your new amount to keep their top spots.

5. **Repeat this process to fine-tune the position where your ad appears on the page.**

   The top spot is the costliest to own, so consider whether a healthy positioning on the first results screen — albeit a few spots down — is the best economical solution for you.

Doing the math on pay-per-click

One way to determine whether a pay-per-click ad campaign will be effective is to study certain numbers related to how your online business now operates. You need to know three numbers:

- **Your average profit margin per sale:** The difference between the price the customer paid for a product and the price you paid to obtain the product.

- **Your site's *conversion ratio:*** The percentage of people who order something from you, based on your site's total number of visitors

- **Your site's *click-through ratio:*** The percentage of people who have clicked a link to get to your Web site, based on the total number of people who saw that link

Suppose that your average profit margin is $20, your conversion ratio is 5 percent, and your click-through ratio is 4 percent. If 20 people click through from an ad, one person should order and generate $20 in profit. Each click-through visitor is then worth $1 to you (or $20 × 5 percent); if you can achieve that click-through rate for $1 or less, you should have a profitable campaign.

If you're paying for the total number of ads displayed, you can calculate the value of getting 1,000 impressions (a common measurement for these types of ads) by using these numbers again:

- 1,000 impressions * 4 percent click-through ratio = 40 visitors

- 40 visitors * 5 percent conversion ratio = 2 paying customers

- 2 paying customers × $20 profit margin = $40 profit

- $40 profit / 1,000 impressions = $40 CPM (cost per thousand — M for the Roman equivalent of a thousand)

These results demonstrate why you need to know how your online business is performing before the ad campaign, and why monitoring the results after the campaign tells you whether to continue doing campaigns.

When you fine-tune your campaign, don't expect those price levels to be in effect forever. Your competitors are fine-tuning their campaigns, too, so be sure to revisit your campaign from time to time to achieve maximum effectiveness.

Deciding when to use pay-per-click

Search engine advertising is one popular way that you can drive traffic to your storefront, although it's not necessarily the right way for every business. You need to consider a few elements of your business that will affect your advertising efforts:

✦ **Your marketing budget:** If you have an unlimited marketing budget, pay-per-click is an ideal solution to generate subscribers and sales. If your budget is small, you might be better off sticking to other marketing techniques and adding pay-per-click ads to your strategy as your budget increases.

Dedicate a small portion of your budget to experiment with pay-per-click, and be ready to analyze the results after your test to see whether the results justify the cost. See the nearby sidebar, "Doing the math on pay-per-click," to figure out how to interpret the results.

✦ **Your product:** Are the products you're selling in demand and hard to find? Or, are they steady products with a limited audience? If your products sell well to anybody who can find you, pay-per-click is the way to go. On the other hand, if the awareness of your company is already high, pay-per-click might be effective only during limited promotional periods where the combination of a pay-per-click ad sending a user to your Web site and a special sale greeting can result in customers who place an order.

✦ **Your product margin:** If your product sales are slower but with a high profit margin, a pay-per-click ad can be effective as long as you get a decent conversion of browsers to buyers. Basically, if you make enough money from the sale of a product, you can afford to go find ten leads, for example, if one of those ten decides to buy. If you're operating on a razor-thin profit margin, however, you need quantity, not quality, and a targeted approach like pay-per-click might cost too much in the long run.

✦ **Your competitors:** Keep an eye on your competition, and see how they're attracting customers. If your customer base is more of a niche than a mass market, you definitely have to adopt similar marketing techniques to divert those customers to your Web site rather than to someone else's. If your competitors are using pay-per-click, you might find that outbidding them is worth the price to convert a potential customer.

Marketing Your Company Offline

Even though you're running an online business, you don't have to do all your marketing online, too. Any communication that you do on behalf of your business should feature your online store and Web address. Here are some offline media you can use to advertise and spread the word about your online business:

✦ **Business cards:** Add your Web site address, e-mail address, and Web site slogan to each of your business cards along with your name, address, and phone number. You never know who might learn about your Web site from seeing your business card.

✦ **Company letterhead or stationery:** Whenever you send a letter of some kind, whether it's a request for information, an explanation of a situation, or a thank-you note to a customer or vendor, include your Web site address at the bottom of the letterhead (see Figure 3-8).

Dear John Doe,

Thank you for your payment. It has been recorded.

Joel Elad

Owner
NewComix.Com

http://www.newcomix.com

Figure 3-8:
Work your
Web site
address
into every
document
you send.

✦ **Business flyers and brochures:** Whenever you hand out any form of paper that explains your business, you should include not only your Web site address but also a description of what the Web site adds to your business. Even if you're just reminding people that your Web site acts as a support site after a customer buys your product, the inclusion of your Web site in the brochure reinforces the Web site's importance.

✦ **Catalogs:** Something about a printed catalog encourages customers to browse and shop. Even some of the biggest e-commerce companies, from Dell to eBay, now send out printed catalogs to remind people of the goods at their online sites. Although a catalog reinforces the product line, your Web site should always be mentioned in any catalog as another easy way to order from you.

✦ **Invoices and purchase orders:** Putting your Web site address and a mention of your site features on your invoices and purchase orders can remind your suppliers and vendors to check out your Web site and maybe even recommend ways that they can assist you or transact with you online.

✦ **Voice-mail greetings:** As customers call to ask questions or place orders, part of your on-hold message or initial greeting can gently remind them that they can find more information on your Web site.

✦ **Company vehicles:** If you have company trucks or vans making deliveries for your company, why not use that big space to remind passersby that your business is now online? You might be surprised at the potential for orders to come in with the comment "I saw your Web site when your truck drove past me."

✦ **Boxes:** One way that Amazon distinguishes itself is by plastering the Amazon logo on its customized boxes and mailers. Not only do customers know instantly that their orders have arrived, but anyone around them is also gently reminded of the Amazon brand. Other retailers, like Grapevinehill (a big seller of shoes on eBay), have followed suit, and when they do so, their Web addresses are clearly marked.

If you own a retail store along with your online business, check out Book VII, Chapter 4 for more ideas on how to market the online part of your business in the brick-and-mortar counterpart.

Chapter 4: Converting Browsers to Buyers

In This Chapter

✓ Providing content to keep your customers coming back

✓ Figuring out what your customers want

✓ Creating a Web site that users enjoy

✓ Tempting your customers with good offers

*P*eople measure online businesses by using different statistics (such as total revenue, total profit, and total number of customers). Another measurement, however, exists in the online world that doesn't exist in a brick-and-mortar business: *Stickiness* indicates how many minutes a user stays at a certain Web site.

Stickiness is measured from the moment an online user first types a URL to the moment he either moves on to another Web site or closes the Web browser, including the time spent browsing around the site and deciding what to do there. The longer the average time, the stickier the Web business. The more time that people spend on your Web site, therefore, the greater the chance that they will purchase one or more of your products or interact with other customers.

Some online businesses are stickier because of their purpose. Compare businesses such as eBay or Yahoo! to a business such as MapQuest. Yahoo! and eBay offer lots of reasons for users to browse around, and MapQuest offers only a couple of reasons (maps and driving directions).

Strive to make your Web site as sticky as possible. Customers who keep coming back are more likely to buy your products — which is, of course, important to your bottom line. In this chapter, we show you how to keep your Web site fresh and buyer friendly, in addition to making your customers feel important so that you can convert browsers to buyers.

Giving Customers a Reason to Stay on Your Site

To increase your Web site's stickiness, give customers a reason to hang around, come back, or participate more in your business. Here are some ways you can make your online business stickier:

✦ **Provide original content.** This information can come in the form of articles, tips and tricks, reviews, or opinions. You can write about the hottest new product, list ten ways a customer can use a product, or share stories about how customers use your products.

One way to reuse your original content is to put that information into newsletters to keep your customers informed.

✦ **Provide discussion boards.** Allow customers to talk to each other, ask and answer questions about your product line, and get to know each other and your staff.

✦ **Provide up-to-date content.** Create a blog, maintained by either yourself or one of your employees, to provide in-depth, always changing content for your customers.

✦ **Encourage your customers to provide content.** Ask loyal customers to write reviews, guides, and anecdotes that you post on your Web site. Some businesses even have contests where the contributor of the best story every month gets a gift certificate.

✦ **Provide help and product support.** Make these items available on your Web site (see Figure 4-1):

  • A Frequently Asked Questions (FAQ) section

  • Support documents

  • Downloadable computer programs (known as *drivers*) that help certain products talk to a computer

  • Articles and schematics that describe how to install, assemble, or fix problems with your products

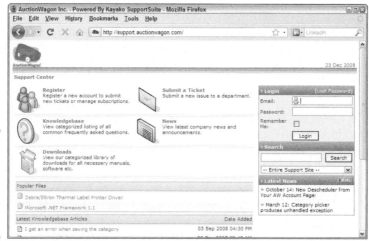

Figure 4-1:
Provide a
resource for
customers
to get online
support.

Providing your own content on your site

Regardless of what kind of business you're running, you should offer content to the buyer. Buyers want original information that they can't get anywhere else. It's like visiting a local store and persuading the owner, an expert in the field, to tell you all about products for sale and how to use them. One reason that Amazon is so successful is that it provides tons of customer and editor reviews, how-to guides, and bestseller lists.

Providing information can lead to more sales and happier customers. Start with information that matters to your customers. If you sell books, have your employees provide short reviews of their favorite new releases for the month, or write the reviews yourself. If you sell consumer electronics, perhaps you can write a guide for shopping for the best digital camera and then compare some of the top brands and discuss their features.

Book VI
Chapter 4

Converting
Browsers to
Buyers

When you provide content for your Web site, don't forget to include links and references to the products you sell. Avoid flashing banners and loud sounds; post a thumbnail picture of the product you're discussing, though, and set it up so that the customer can click the thumbnail and go straight to that product page.

You can also go "above and beyond" by providing information that anyone would want, not just your core customers. Provide links and sources to general news stories or local city guides, for example. You can specialize in an area and become the ultimate authority on it, in the hope that when people come to your site to read your content, they will stay and check out your product selection.

Getting other people to provide your content

As the person maintaining your business, you might think that you have to provide all your content, although that might not be the case. Some of the biggest online businesses rely on others to bring them the content their users depend on every day! Tap in to that global community, and encourage these people to contribute to your business:

✦ **Customers:** Besides you, who knows more about your products than your customers? Encourage them to provide stories, reviews, and opinions regarding products you sell and similar products in your area. You gain the content, the authenticity of a real customer, and the support of that customer, who feels even more invested in your business. Figure 4-2 shows a section of reviews and information provided by a customer.

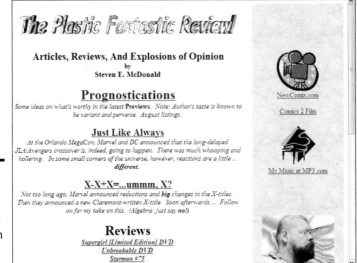

Figure 4-2:
Have your
customers
create their
own section
of reviews.

If you have a well-known or experienced customer, see whether she would be willing to write a weekly or monthly column for your Web site. Promise a featured spot on your site and maybe some credit toward her purchases, and give customers a fun reason to come back regularly to your business!

✦ **Suppliers:** The manufacturers, distributors, and suppliers you work with are usually trying to build their brands, too, so involve them in your online business. Let your customers know the newest and greatest things coming from your manufacturer, even if it's just links to its Web site and announcements about contests, promotions, or events your customers can participate in.

✦ **Media sources:** A ton of organizations can happily feed your Web site with articles and information you can post for free on your Web site. Try one of these sources:

- ArticlesBase (www.articlesbase.com)
- eZineArticles (www.ezinearticles.com)
- GoArticles (www.goarticles.com)
- iSnare (www.isnare.com)

Anticipating Customer Needs

Veteran business owners can tell you that in order to succeed, your goal should be to not just meet your customer's expectations, but to also anticipate and respond to those expectations. Online retailers are no different:

You need to read buyers' minds and figure out what they want so that you have the products to meet their demand — rather than watch your competition make off with your customers and your revenue.

You have a few ways to figure out what your customers want:

✦ **Take a look at your sales data.** Watch the purchases made through your business, to see who's buying what and how much customers are spending per order.

✦ **Monitor your customers' questions.** Whether customers communicate by e-mail, phone call, or Web form, if they're starting to ask for similar products, investigate!

✦ **Check out your competition.** See what other sites are providing, putting on sale, raising prices on, and carrying in their stores.

✦ **Look at other resources that talk about your product lines.** See what Web sites are promoting or hyping as "the next great thing" (see Figure 4-3). Read magazines, books, and newspapers, and watch TV shows about your product areas, to see what people are talking about, preparing for, and predicting for that industry.

Book VI
Chapter 4

Converting Browsers to Buyers

Figure 4-3:
Stay informed on subjects in your product area.

✦ **Go to trade groups, conventions, or organizations.** Attend trade shows for your product area, whether it's Electronic Entertainment Expo (E3) for video games, Consumer Electronics Show for general consumer electronics, or American Toy Fair for the newest action figures, to get an idea of what your buyers want next. Subscribe to these organizations' newsletters to get up-to-date information. You should always order catalogs from manufacturers that belong to these groups and ask to be on their mailing lists.

Watching customer logs

Customer orders aren't the only evidence of what customers want from your business. Because you're online, you can keep track of the different Web pages that customers view. A *customer log,* or *Web server log file,* contains information about particular pages your customers are looking at. Every time they look at another page, a new entry is created in the customer log. You can open your log and see all your customer activity.

The Web server log file is a text file that your Web site provider automatically creates and maintains for you. It keeps track of all the Web page requests your customers ask for when they browse your Web site.

When you're reading through your customer log, ask yourself these questions:

✦ What pages are looked at the most? The least?

✦ How many pages does the average customer look at?

✦ What's the last page a customer looks at before he leaves? Is it an order confirmation page, or did he give up before ordering?

✦ Are customers following the same flow through your site? That is, do they typically look at the same Web pages in the same order as everyone else?

✦ Are customers viewing the newest Web pages you provide? Are they sticking to the same core pages regardless of whether those pages get updated?

After you know this information, you can update your Web site by deleting the pages (or content) that no one is looking at. By streamlining the buying process this way, you continue to meet your customer's expectations and keep them returning.

Predicting future purchases

Mutual fund companies are notorious for this disclaimer: "Past performance is not an indicator of future returns." In the e-commerce world, however, past purchases are an excellent indicator of what customers will buy next — so much so that a company like Amazon tracks every single activity (not just purchases) performed by customers on its Web site. Your customer logs are good indicators of what your customers are looking at, and you should also look at what they're buying.

One benefit you enjoy in an online business is not being limited by physical shelf space and, in some cases, the cost of carrying the products before purchase. So, you probably offer an expansive array of products. After your orders come in, though, you want to see which products customers are ordering the most. Are these products concentrated in one or two subcategories, or are they spread out among your catalog of goods?

Obviously, if a product line is flying off the virtual shelf, you should restock it as soon as possible. If the product is a fad item, however, such as Pokémon or Beanie Babies, you don't want to get stuck with a warehouse full of that item after the fad ends.

To pick future products to stock and anticipate your customers' wants, look at what they're willing to buy from you today. As you examine past purchases, consider these dimensions:

✦ **Average price per sold item:** At what price levels are your highest-selling products? This price gives you an idea of whether limited, high-priced items or mass-quantity, low-priced items would work better for your business. After all, if your customers are used to buying the hottest computer accessories for less than $50, selling a $2,000 laptop might be out of their reach.

✦ **Average order size:** The average amount of money spent per order doesn't necessarily correspond to the average price per item. Although your customers might love your site for inexpensive items, they could be willing to purchase multiple items, resulting in a big order. They might be occasional buyers who buy expensive items. Find products that fit into your customers' average order and get them to exceed this number.

If you increase your customers' average order amount, you're increasing their value to your business. Consider new products that meet or exceed your current average order size. You want this number to go up, not down.

✦ **Luxury or necessity:** Are your customers buying entertainment products with their disposable income, or are they purchasing everyday items that they need continually? Look beyond the fad or trend, and figure out what part of their budgets you're reaching. Continue to stock products that are so cool, so cheap, or so easy to use that customers *have* to have them, or stock products that customers need or see as "automatic buys." Then they will continue to buy from you rather than look around for something better.

✦ **Technology items:** If you're selling items with lots of technology built in (even if they're kitchen appliances), always have an eye on the next model, iteration, or version. Keep enough on hand to satisfy current demand, and also acquire newer models so that customers can stay ahead of the curve or stay where they are until they're ready to buy the new model.

✦ **The 80-20 rule:** Are 80 percent of your orders coming from 20 percent of your customers? Chances are, 80 percent of the products sold come from 20 percent of the category areas. The way to make the biggest impact on your business is to increase the 80 percent of sales, so be ready to continue serving the customers of that 80 percent group.

Organizing a Buyer-Friendly Site

For a regular business, being friendly to buyers means saying "Hello" when they walk through their door, shaking their hands, and smiling at them. For an online business, friendly means creating a buyer-friendly site that makes sense to buyers and makes their lives easier. After all, they're coming to you partially because they don't want to get in their cars, fight traffic, battle for parking spots at the mall, and navigate their way through the sea of humanity just to get a new pair of jeans.

When buyers come to your Web site, provide them with a few basic pieces of information right off the bat, or else they will click their way to the next business. Go to your home page, and make sure that it answers these basic questions:

✦ What is your business?

✦ What's the primary focus of your business?

✦ What does your business offer consumers?

✦ What makes your business good enough to earn a customer's trust and, therefore, an order?

✦ How would a customer start shopping on your site?

If your opening page can't answer these questions, your Web site isn't buyer friendly. You want to be straightforward and direct with your buyers because, in essence, your business reason for existence is to help a customer with a specific need. In this section, we talk about what you can do to spiff up your Web site to offer customers a satisfying shopping experience.

Streamlining the shopping process

In department stores, the men's section is usually near the door so that guys can buy something and get out. There's a reason that all-night convenience stores can charge two to three times the grocery-store price for an item. People want convenience, especially online, so being able to grab an item and leave is crucial.

An example of an easy-in-easy-out Web site is the Amazon 1-Click system. For returning customers, Amazon already has its customers' information and can fill in all their information ahead of time so that customers can pick their items and leave. Customers return to Amazon partly because they know that they don't have to retype their credit card number, shipping address, and other information. Their accounts are already created, so they can pop in and get what they need. That's great service.

On your Web site, make sure that your shoppers can always

+ **Reach their shopping carts and accounts:** No matter where on your Web site shoppers might be, they should always be able to look in their shopping carts or check their accounts. We recommend including links to these two functions along the top of every Web page so that they're always just a click away.

+ **Access any product specials you offer from the home page:** The less hunting buyers have to do, the quicker they can add your specials to their carts and continue shopping or check out.

When you're designing the page flow of your Web site, reduce as many in-between steps as possible. If the majority of your shoppers pay by credit card, don't ask customers how they will pay. Display a page where customers can either fill in their credit card information or choose other forms of payment.

+ **Search for a specific item:** Your customers can use the search function to interact with your business by telling you exactly what they want to buy. Add to your navigation section a search box or link that appears on every page of your Web site.

Take a look at the software or Web host you're using to create your Web site, to see whether it offers a search function. Make sure that the search offers customers a focused set of results or the most relevant product.

+ **See the content on a page at a glance:** We can't stress enough the importance of clear headings and labels. Your customers are drawn to the biggest type on the page. Every page on your Web site should have a clear and relevant heading at the top, and subheadings throughout the page if you're presenting a long list of products. Look at how CNET organizes its site (see Figure 4-4) with tabs on top and a navigation bar along the left side of the page.

As simple as it sounds, make sure that headings correspond to what customers are seeing on the page. If a heading talks about clearance items and you're displaying new, full-priced goods, you will lose your customers fast as their trust in you starts to evaporate.

Figure 4-4:
Clearly marked tags and navigation buttons make CNET easy to understand.

Toning down the bells and whistles

Although you might want your Web site to look as nice as possible, cool features such as Flash movies, JavaScript programs, sound files that play automatically, or scrolling banners can slow down the buying experience and make shopping harder. Although buyers might find such effects cute the first time they visit your Web site, the effects can quickly become annoying. If a Flash movie serves as your home page, not only do you ruin your chance to be seen by the search engines, but customers who have to wait for a function to load might also feel frustrated with the slowness and try a competitor's Web site. Although some customers might enjoy it, others will drop off.

Flash movies are animated movies or introductions you sometimes see on Web sites. By using Flash technology (which was developed by Macromedia), you can create moving animations with sound in one file that an Internet browser can easily display.

A Flash movie or animation is only one kind of "bell and whistle" you can add to your Web site. Businesses use all sorts of additional features to draw attention to their online sites or spice up the user experience. Some of these include

✦ Sound files that play when a visitor arrives to the Web site

✦ JavaScript functions that load a mini-window of information on the page

✦ Java functions that load a fully functional application into the Web page

✦ Pop-out menus that cover part of the screen with a new window (also called *DHTML menus*)

✦ Animated graphics or an overuse of large, fancy graphics on the page

Some businesses, however, simply throw in these "cool factor" features without thinking about how they can affect their bottom lines; for example, a graphic designer on a project who wants to test a new feature or work on an exciting project would encourage the development of these features. Your job is to evaluate any extras by considering whether the feature is worth having in spite of these drawbacks:

✦ **It's memory-intensive.** Although more U.S. buyers are paying extra to have broadband (fast) Internet access in their homes, many people still use dialup (phone) lines. For these customers, a graphics-intensive Web site, a video or large audio file, or a large animation graphic can slow down a user's experience. Customers who get put on hold when they call a company "drop off" after they have to wait a while, and the same thing happens online. This statement is especially true for international customers because some countries don't even have broadband access.

✦ **It can display your content incorrectly.** Many of the newer features used in HTML Web pages, such as layers or JavaScript, strictly control how the content is laid out on the page. The problem with this strict control lies in older computers or different Web browser software that interprets these new commands inconsistently. Your result is that different customers may see a completely distorted and, at times, unusable Web site because the pages aren't displaying correctly; or not every element, such as an Order button, may even be displayed on the page.

Keeping Your Shopping Cart Simple

Most studies about online shopping show the percentage of online e-commerce shopping carts that are left abandoned by their users. Some statistics state that customers abandon anywhere from 45 to 90 percent of all shopping carts, for a variety of reasons:

✦ They're turned off by the high cost of either the item or the shipping and handling.

✦ They can't find all the information or functionality that they need in order to finish.

✦ They're uncomfortable registering or handing over credit card data online.

✦ They're unsure how to completely check out with their items and pay for their purchases.

✦ They're afraid to place their final orders.

For these reasons, keep in mind some helpful tips and avoid the common traps of having shopping carts on your e-commerce site:

✦ **Make it easy to find.** Sometimes, the only way for customers to even access their shopping carts is to click a link that's available on only certain Web pages. At other times, they see their shopping carts only after adding items. Put the shopping cart link at the top of every Web page (as shown in Figure 4-5). Create a second browser window that's small or always minimized, and put the shopping cart information on that screen.

Shopping cart

Figure 4-5: Put your shopping cart in a consistent location on the Web site.

✦ **Make it updatable.** Your customers should be able to add, update, and delete products in their orders at any time. When they make changes, they probably want to see their updated totals. If someone changes shipping options or picks an out-of-state address, she wants to see her final total change. Make sure that any change to an order triggers your software program to recalculate the order amount and display the revised order with a revised total.

✦ **Require no upfront information in order to use it.** If your customers can't easily add items to their shopping cart first and give personal information later, you might scare them off by forcing them to register or type lots of data first. Enable them to shop, and then require the other information before they place orders.

At some point before an order is complete, don't forget to ask "How did you hear about this site?" Provide a box for the referral name, e-mail address, or promotion code so that you can better track your marketing efforts.

✦ **Provide help from it.** Always have available on the shopping cart screen at least one Web link to a list of frequently asked questions (FAQs) about how to use the shopping cart. Nothing is worse for customers than getting stuck when they try to add something to their shopping carts and can't find any help. Don't leave customers wandering around your store aimlessly; throw them the virtual rope in advance.

You can also offer live help with chat technology. When buyers click the chat link, they can chat with your customer service representatives (or you, depending on the size of your business) and have their questions answered on the spot. Several companies offer software that augments your Web site with chat technology, such as

- RealChat (www.realchat.com)

- ProvideSupport (www.providesupport.com)

- ParaChat (www.parachat.com)

✦ **Allow customers to easily add or remove items.** A customer makes multiple decisions, usually, when he's deciding what to order. He needs the flexibility to update, add, or delete any single line item in the shopping cart without affecting the rest of the order. A customer who has to delete everything and start over is likely to just "walk out."

✦ **Protect customers' information.** When you collect sensitive information — such as credit card numbers, birthdates, or bank account information — make sure that your shopping cart is using a safe technology, like Secure Socket Layers (SSL). A customer should see a closed-lock icon in the lower-right corner of the Web browser (see Figure 4-6) to indicate that data can be safely entered on the page. If the lock is open, entering data isn't 100 percent safe on that page. Pages containing data about your products don't have to use SSL; when in doubt, though, secure the page first. (See Book V for more information about security.)

Don't just secure customers' information; tell them about it! Create a special window or Web page detailing how you're protecting their vital information. When you reassure customers that you're looking out for them in the beginning, they're more likely to buy.

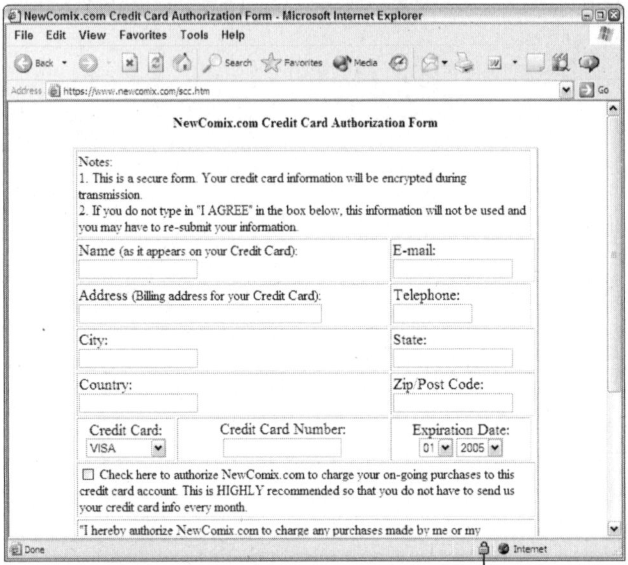

Figure 4-6:
Your
customers
want to see
the lock
for secure
transactions.

This lock indicates a secure page.

Avoiding Assumptions about Your Customers

You have to make plenty of decisions every day, and you can easily fall into the trap that you have to know everything in order to make your business work. You don't have to know everything, although you do have to know whom to ask or where to look.

When you're wondering whether the actions you're taking in your business are truly converting browsers to buyers, step back a moment to see what's going on. Pull up your Web site and click through the pages yourself. Just because the pages and offers grab *you* doesn't necessarily mean that customers will react the same way. It's a good start, though. In this section, we show you ways to see your site from the customer perspective so that you can provide them with exactly what they need.

Asking customers for feedback

Many times, your buyers know what they want — sometimes before you do. They're the ones using your products, talking to each other on your discussion board, and looking for the next great product. You should always provide a way for your customers to give you general or specific feedback using a feedback form.

Most Web sites incorporate some sort of feedback form, whether it's part of a help system or a contact system or even as part of a guest book. This simple HTML form allows customers to send comments to the Web site owners, sharing what they like and dislike about the site. You can also ask for specific feedback on your product line or ask how a customer found out about your site. Figure 4-7 shows an example of a feedback form.

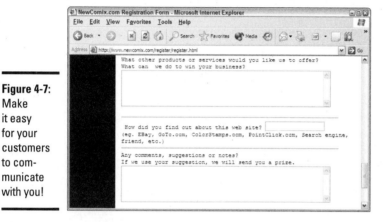

Figure 4-7: Make it easy for your customers to communicate with you!

If your most loyal customers are asking for a particular product, consider stocking it so that you don't lose them to your competition.

If shoppers want a fad item, especially one that requires a large investment, stock only what you feel that you can definitely sell. If the shelf life of a product could become very short, you don't want to blindly act on your customers' inquiries. (Just ask the businesses that are sitting on a warehouse full of pogs.)

Make sure that customer inquiries and feedback are fed into the inventory acquisition phase as quickly as possible. You have no excuse for not considering a new product line if your customers have given you advance notice about the item. Some items sell quicker than others, and you need some time to find the right distributor or manufacturer and set up an account.

Test a new product line on a subset of customers before investing too much of your inventory budget on one item. Buy enough of the product to get it in stock quickly and serve a subset of customers. Send a targeted e-mail or direct-mail piece to assess the response for the test audience. If the numbers are good, reorder more and repeat the test, or integrate the new product into your catalog.

Encourage customers to help keep you on the cutting edge by rewarding them for their feedback. Include surveys, toll-free hotline numbers, or follow-up e-mail in your communications with buyers. Make contacting you as easy as possible for them, and use giveaways, promotions, or incentives to push these customers into giving you their valuable advice.

Create a buyer council or a volunteer group of buyers that you can poll regularly to find out what customers know about a product area. Pick some steady customers that you've built relationships with, and ask whether they're interested in joining. Most will accept in order to get a feeling of ownership and to get their opinions heard.

Remembering your customers

Many online business owners get started in areas they know well and are passionate about. Then they fall into the trap of assuming that they're the perfect target audience for their own online stores, and their own preferences get in the way of doing business. If this happens to you, your bottom line — and the future flow of customers to your site — could be harmed.

When you decide which products to carry in your store, ask yourself "Am I picking these items because I like them — or because I think that my buyers will like them?" You should make decisions based on the latter part of the question because you want to put your customers' needs and desires ahead of your own. Even if you're putting yourself in the role of a potential buyer, you carry certain biases that your customers might not carry.

Stocking items that you would never buy yourself is healthy. Put your buyers' interests ahead of your own. You're not selling to yourself — you're selling to your customers! Offer products that they want to buy, at prices they're willing to pay. See the section "Anticipating Customer Needs," earlier in this chapter, to know how to find out what people are buying.

Be open to what your customers, and the orders they place, are telling you. We have met enough business owners who were too afraid or too ignorant about venturing outside their known worlds to try new product lines. Those folks usually lost great opportunities to expand their business.

If you don't have the items buyers want, they will go somewhere else to find them. And, chances are good that they won't come back to you. Buyers remember who serves them best. Respond accordingly.

Encouraging Viewers to Buy

Being available to your customers is important for people who stumble across your site while searching for something, although you usually have to ask for the sale or else it doesn't happen. You can build a clean and robust

Web site, full of exciting products, and then wonder why you aren't making sales. In the world of e-commerce, building your Web site isn't enough. You have to close the deal. Encourage buyers to place your products in their shopping carts and then commit to placing orders. You created your Web site to give them the means to do so, and now you have to give them a little nudge. In this section, we describe two techniques to convert browsers to buyers: Give them a time-limited offer, and then reinforce that offer when they're leaving your Web site.

Offering deals and promotions

Special deals and promotions are the most common way to ask for the sale because you're giving buyers a specific buying proposition. You're offering something to sweeten the deal, whether it's a discount, a free additional item, or an extra service. Usually, though, a successful deal or promotion has that all-critical time limit. You can limit these elements:

✦ **The length of time that an offer is available:** "Good for only the next 24 hours."

✦ **The number of people who can take advantage of the offer:** "Only the next 25 customers can act on this deal."

✦ **The supply of the product:** "Order now — supplies are limited."

A time limit spurs customers to act. Otherwise, if an offer is always out there, it's a regular deal, not a special offer. Figure 4-8 shows a time-sensitive, one-time only offer for a product.

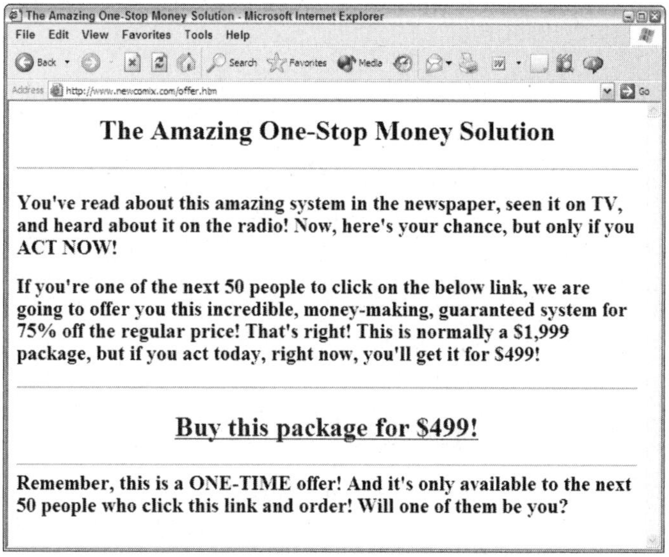

Figure 4-8: Make sure your offers include some form of time sensitivity.

The Amazing One-Stop Money Solution - Microsoft Internet Explorer

File   Edit   View   Favorites   Tools   Help

Back   Search   Favorites   Media

Address http://www.newcomix.com/offer.htm

The Amazing One-Stop Money Solution

You've read about this amazing system in the newspaper, seen it on TV, and heard about it on the radio! Now, here's your chance, but only if you ACT NOW!

If you're one of the next 50 people to click on the below link, we are going to offer you this incredible, money-making, guaranteed system for 75% off the regular price! That's right! This is normally a $1,999 package, but if you act today, right now, you'll get it for $499!

Buy this package for $499!

Remember, this is a ONE-TIME offer! And it's only available to the next 50 people who click this link and order! Will one of them be you?

You can pick from a number of events that can trigger this deal:

✦ A customer registers for the first time.

✦ A customer adds a second, fifth, or tenth item to the shopping cart.

✦ A specified length of time (15 or 30 minutes, for example) has elapsed and the customer still hasn't added anything to the shopping cart.

✦ The customer visits your Web site by using a special Web address.

Pushing to make a sale works: It forces a buyer to make a decision, and if she's getting a good deal, the impulse to buy can kick in and seal the deal. Although you don't necessarily want to be overly aggressive, you cannot just believe the line from *Field of Dreams:* "If you build it, he will come." Customers might come, but they might not shop. You have to encourage the sale.

Sending one last reminder

Many shop owners never think of the one instance in which they can ask for the sale: when a customer is leaving a Web site and moving to something else. The customer's Web browser knows when it's no longer going to your Web site, and some special commands in Web programming languages, like JavaScript, kick into gear when someone picks a different Web site or closes the Web browser window.

Some businesses owners think, "Well, if they're leaving my store, they definitely don't want anything." Your customers might just not be able to find the deal they're looking for. Or, they might want to comparison-shop before making the purchase. Maybe they just got bored because nothing unusual popped up or happened while they were shopping at your store.

The moment customers leave your site, you know a few things about him:

✦ **He just spent some time in your online business.** He browsed around, looked at some products, and read some pages. Your business is now on his mind and he has at least considered your offerings.

✦ **He had some specific interest in browsing your site.** Maybe he was looking for a product, an ad caught his eye, or he was a referral. This buyer is interested.

✦ **He's leaving your Web site, so you have little left to lose.** After all, if you present him with something more and he doesn't want it, what is he going to do? Leave? He already made the decision to leave, so what does it hurt to give him one final offer?

Your browsers are knowledgeable about, and interested in, your business and your products, and they're motivated and ready to leave. It's a perfect time to make a final offer. Call it your goodbye offer or your before-you-go offer. Display a pop-up window that encourages your viewer to consider one more rock-bottom, final price, (such as the one shown in Figure 4-9). Now is your last opportunity to make an impression (during this particular shopping session), so make it count.

Figure 4-9:
If you know
someone's
leaving, ask
him one
more time
for the sale.

Use pop-up ads sparingly on your Web site. Yes, they're annoying, and we're not saying that you should run out and flood buyers with them. You can reserve the use of the pop-up ads for goodbye offers. This way, you're not annoying customers while they shop; you're just offering one reminder as they're going out the door.

If your browsing customers are dead set against shopping, they will close this offer window just as fast as they left your site. If they were tempted to buy but remained on the fence, this goodbye offer might be enough to swing them back your way. Remember the old adage: You never know until you try. The same concept holds true when you're asking for the sale.

When you implement this offer, make sure that it appears only if the browsing customer hasn't purchased anything. You don't want a happy buyer to suddenly realize that she could have saved money if she had just tried to leave your site first. In this case, your goodbye offer should be a chance to add to an order or receive faster shipping for a lower price.

To add a goodbye offer to your Web site, add lines of code in these places:

✦ **On every Web page at your site except the order-confirmation screen, add the following lines of code to the <HEAD> section:**

```
<SCRIPT LANGUAGE="JavaScript">
function goodbye(){
        alert("Before you go, consider our final
    offer!");
        open("finaloffer.htm");
        }
</SCRIPT>
```

You should also create a special Web page to correspond to the second line in the goodbye function that contains your final offer.

✦ **On the Web pages that contain an order-confirmation screen, add the following lines of code to the <HEAD> section:**

```
<SCRIPT LANGUAGE="JavaScript">
function goodbye(){
        alert("Here's a special offer just for our
    loyal customers!");
        open("extraoffer.htm");
        }
</SCRIPT>
```

You should also create a special Web page to correspond to the second line in the goodbye function that contains your extra offer.

✦ **Add the following block of text to the <BODY> tag on all your Web pages:**

```
<BODY . . . onUnLoad="goodbye()">
```

You should add the onUnLoad section at the end of the <BODY> tag.

Chapter 5: Analyzing and Monitoring Your Customers

In This Chapter

✓ **Monitoring your Web site traffic**

✓ **Interpreting the records left on your Web server**

✓ **Using software to assemble reports on Web site usage**

✓ **Implementing techniques to gain more information from your visitors**

✓ **Asking your customers the right questions**

✓ **Updating your Web site to fix or improve performance**

*A*fter you build your Web site, your next step is to ask, "How can I make my site better?" Your initial version is rarely your current version. You create your site, watch how users interact with you, make changes, watch how users react to those changes, make more changes, watch some more, and then repeat the process. This process is ongoing as you evolve your site to meet the changing needs of your customers.

Analyzing your Web site can tell you a lot about your business that other metrics (measurements) — such as sales volume, average order amount, and repeat customers — cannot tell you. You can figure out exactly which Web pages on your site are the most and least popular. You can see how many people start with your home page, and then calculate the average number of pages a user sees before leaving. You can even find out where users come from when they arrive at your Web site and determine the last thing they see before they leave.

In this chapter, we look at the field of Web site analysis, from traffic monitoring to gathering customer feedback. We help you break down the massive amount of raw data you have on your site and turn it into useful statistics that can change your business — by using either log files or a software program. You find out which pieces of information are more important than others and how to focus your analysis to study individual user behavior. You can then use this data to make useful updates to your Web site and study the immediate and lasting effect of your changes.

The best changes that come from Web site analysis are gradual, or *evolutionary,* changes. Look at how sites like Amazon and MSN handle changes. Their interfaces don't radically change every week, although subtle and gradual changes are always being introduced, to respond to customers and enhance the shopping experience.

Tracking Trends

If you sit at an outdoor café and watch traffic drive by, you begin to get a sense of patterns. You can estimate the number of cars that drive by; determine the most popular makes, models, and colors; establish whether the cars are zooming past or crawling by; and ascertain whether they're coming in groups or as a continuous stream.

You can apply the same techniques to monitoring your Web site traffic. If you want to understand the behaviors of the traffic, you need to know the basic information and understand the trends that are occurring:

✦ The number of visitors coming to your Web site

✦ The number of *unique* visitors coming to your site

✦ Which Web sites are referring viewers to your site

✦ Which Web pages are the most frequently viewed and the least frequently viewed

✦ The number of Web pages that the average visitor sees in one visit

You can track this usage in other ways, although they mainly involve direct customer interaction. You can contact a research group to find sample visitors and perform *usability testing,* where the research group introduces a visitor to your Web site, asks her to interact with it, and then studies her activities to see whether she can intuitively find her way around your Web site, place an order, and perform basic functions. Based on these user interactions, the research group makes recommendations to you about changes you should make to your Web site to make it more user friendly or easier to use.

You can also solicit direct customer feedback through surveys, follow-up phone calls, or e-mail response forms. Many Web sites gather this feedback by contacting past customers or people who have just ordered something from the Web site, and then getting their opinions about a variety of issues. This method is useful for identifying issues that need fixing or promoting, or to add insight or qualitative information to the level of your Web site's usefulness, beyond what the quantitative information is telling you through trend analysis. Find out more about adding qualitative information in the section "Getting to Know Your Customer Really Well," later in this chapter.

Measuring Web Site Traffic

Every time your Web server receives a request from a visitor and displays a Web page for that visitor, it creates an entry for the request in a log file on the Web server. The log file records all the activity your Web site experiences. The server captures a lot of information in this file that you can then use to get a better idea of how your Web site is being used and operated by visitors and customers.

A *log file* is just a text file stored on your Web server that receives a new entry whenever your Web server has to fulfill a request from a Web browser. Sometimes, it's called the *access log file* (see Figure 5-1), and at other times the Web server breaks it into different files; for example, an error log, a request log, and a referrer log.

Figure 5-1:
Your access
log file
shows
you all the
visitors and
what they
saw.

Your log files tell you a lot about your Web site:

✦ The popularity of various pages within the site

✦ The usability of your site

✦ The types of visitors that come to your site

✦ The ability of your site to present your Web pages effectively

Defining the terms of traffic analysis

Your Web site measures a *hit* whenever a piece of your Web site, whether it's a Web page or a graphics file or another object, is sent over the Internet to someone's Web browser. You might hear this activity described as "My Web site got a million hits last month." That statement is saying that your Web site handled a million different requests for everything from text to images to audio tracks.

Although some people think of hits purely as visitors, a Web page can have, for example, nine different graphics and generate ten hits every time it's accessed. Why? When a visitor wants to view the Web page, the Web server sends out the HTML code of the page as the first request, and then the server sends nine separate graphics files, one by one, and records each of those transmissions as a separate hit.

This process is the reason that measuring hits isn't as important as other metrics. Although it gives you a good baseline to understand the level of demand, when you're talking to advertisers, finding funding, or planning a marketing campaign, a high hit count doesn't spell success on its own.

A *page view*, on the other hand, happens when a visitor views a particular page. This number, which is independent of the number of elements that might be present on a Web page, usually correlates to the number of visits to a particular page, especially on your home page.

Because most Web sites have multiple pages, you want to determine the number of visits, or *unique visitors,* that your site has. Look at the log file for some identifying information, like an IP address, and correlate that information to your page views. If you see the same IP address viewing multiple pages, you get an idea of the average number of pages viewed per user.

An *IP address,* or *Internet Protocol address,* is a series of four sets of numbers, in a range from 0 to 256, that define a computer's location on the Internet. An example of an IP address is 207.171.166.102 (which belongs to Amazon). Each IP address is unique to one computer at a time. Many users are assigned an IP address *dynamically,* which means that they're assigned a unique set of numbers the moment they sign on to the Internet, and they lose the right to those numbers when they're done. Some people, like those using cable modems or university computers, have the same IP address, or *static IP address,* all the time.

Most investors, suppliers, and employees, including you, are interested in knowing the number of unique visitors your Web site has. The easiest way to figure out that number is to implement a system where you place a text file (a cookie) on each user's computer. Turn to the later section "Storing data using cookies" to find out how to use cookies.

Public computers skew the data

Shared (or public) computers, like those you find at public libraries, Internet cafés, schools, and even some workplaces, are always on and always connected to the Internet, and they always use the same IP address to access the Internet. For this reason, your Web site log file shows every request coming from a computer as the same user. If you see 50 page views coming from the same IP address, you don't necessarily know, therefore, whether it's coming from one person or ten people.

As a result, you have to look at other elements, such as the length of time a page is served, to figure out the average number of page views per visitor. When you know an average, you can break apart a heavily used IP address to represent an average number of users. If you know that a visitor will view, on average, 5 Web pages and you get 50 page views from one IP, you can assume that the IP address represents 10 unique visitors.

Looking at your log file

Your log file resides somewhere on the hard drive of your Web site's server. Depending on the operating system that your Web server uses — whether it's Windows, Unix, Mac OS X, or a version of Linux — you can use a regular text editor to open and view the log file.

Inside your log file is a long list of entries made up of the different requests that your Web server has received and the file or information that it has sent back to the user requesting it. A typical entry looks like this:

```
208.215.179.139 - - [06/November/2008:06:01:16 -0400] "GET /
    index.html HTTP/1.1" 200 32768 "http://search.yahoo.com/
    search?p=ecommerce+products" "Mozilla/4.0 (compatible;
    MSIE 7.0; Windows NT 5.2; DigExt)"
```

`208.215.179.139`: Corresponds to the IP address of the computer from which the request was made. When you see multiple lines with the same URL, you know that either one person is requesting different files or multiple people are using the same computer.

If you want to know more information about the computer, you can do a reverse lookup of the IP address to see whether it relates to a known *URL*, or Web address. Some Web sites, like `www.dnsstuff.com`, offer reverse URL lookup services for free.

`[06/November/2008:09:01:16 -0400]`: Shows the exact date and time of the request. The `-0400` at the end refers to the offset from Greenwich Mean Time. In this case, the time is marked as the U.S. Pacific time zone.

`"GET/index.html HTTP/1.1"`: Refers to the item being requested and the method used to transfer that file from your Web server. Here, you see either Web pages (`.html` or `.htm`), graphics files (`.gif` or `.jpg`), or other content, such as JavaScript programs (`.js`), audio files (`.mp3` or `.wav`), or video files (`.mov`). Most of the time, files are transferred by HTTP (HyperText Transfer Protocol), which is the standard protocol for Web pages, although occasionally large files are sent by FTP (File Transfer Protocol).

`200`: Represents the result code for the request, or the initial response that your Web server sent back to the visitor when the request came in. The number `200` means that the request was successfully processed, or you might see `404` instead, which means that the file wasn't found.

If you're seeing numerous entries with the result code `404`, check your Web links to make sure that you're not referring people to a *dead link,* or one that no longer exists.

`32768`: Indicates the size, in bytes, of the file that was sent back. If you have lots of graphics, audio, or video files, this number is large.

`"http://search.yahoo.com/search?..."`: Shows the *referrer URL,* or the URL from which the request originated. In this example, the visitor was doing a Yahoo! search and clicked a result link to reach your Web site. You can see the search terms used. See the next section for more information on referral links.

`"Mozilla/4.0 (compatible; MSIE 7.0; Windows NT 5.2; DigExt)"`: Represents the name and operating system of the Web browser program your visitor is using to make the request. In this case, you see either a user browser, like Mozilla (which is Microsoft Internet Explorer 7.0 — or MSIE 7.0 — running on Windows XP) or a search engine robot, like Googlebot.

As you can see from these entries, you can find lots of information in your log entries. As you manually search the listings, you begin to see certain trends, like which Web pages show up most often as GET commands or which IP addresses come back week after week.

Manual scanning, however, can tell you only so much, especially if your log file measures in the thousands, or hundreds of thousands, of lines. Later in this chapter, in the section "Jam Packed: Traffic-Analysis Software," we talk about computer programs that read these log files for you and break down the information into easy-to-read statistics.

Referring to your referrer file

In some cases, a separate log file (a *referrer* file) on your computer contains the sources of all your Web page requests, as shown in Figure 5-2. The sources you see are mostly other Web sites that link to you or search engine links where a visitor has typed certain keywords and found your site as one of the results.

Figure 5-2:
See where
your Web
site visitors
are coming
from.

For example, a referrer entry like this one:

```
"http://www.somewebsite.com/links.html" - /
```

tells you that a specific Web page (`links.html`) on a certain Web site (`www.somewebsite.com`) is offering a link to your Web site, and that's where your visitor was when he clicked the link to reach your Web site.

The referrer entry

```
"http://search.yahoo.com/search?p=ecommerce+products"
```

tells you that the visitor came from the Yahoo! search engine. The beauty of this link is that you also see the keywords (`ecommerce` and `products`) that the visitor typed there to eventually end up on your site. This information alone can be invaluable when you're planning Web marketing campaigns. (See Book VI, Chapter 3 for more specific information.) If you see specific keywords or phrases in your referrer file, you know that those words are powerful terms that work on bringing people to your site.

If you're running a Web marketing campaign, you should distinguish search-result referrals from sponsored-ad referrals. If you include a keyword at the end of the link you provide for the sponsored ad, the keyword shows up correctly in the referrer file. For example, if you're linking to your home page and creating a Google AdWords campaign, you can add the link `http://www.yourwebsite.com?google` to help interpret your results.

You might also see links that come from your Web site, like this one:

```
"http://www.yourwebsite.com/page1.html"  - /page2.html
```

This line indicates that the user is on Page 1 of your Web site and is clicking to move on to Page 2.

You might also see entries like this:

```
" - "
```

Typically, this entry means that the user just typed your URL directly into her Web browser or has your Web site set up as a bookmark in her browser so that she can go directly to your site. This entry is a good thing to see because it indicates that people are being drawn naturally to your Web site without having to find it from another Web site.

Examining error logs

Error log files keep track of errors that are sometimes generated when people access your Web site. Different Web servers keep different fields of information: Some keep the date and time, the client IP, and an identifying field, like `info` or `error`. Figure 5-3 shows an error log. You're interested in the last field on each line, however, which indicates the reason for the error.

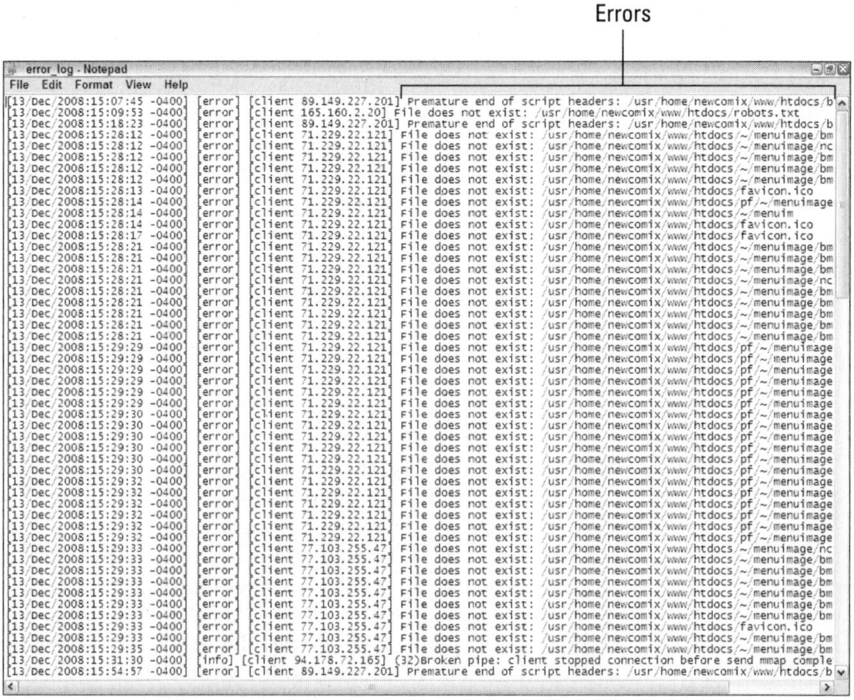

Figure 5-3: See which page requests are causing errors on your Web site.

Watch out for these messages:

✦ **Send aborted:** A visitor has stopped the transfer of the file from your Web server to her computer. This situation occurs mainly when large graphics files (or other media files) are taking too long to load on a visitor's machine, so she stops the process and moves on. If you see this message repeatedly, you need to condense the files and optimize your Web page for faster loading.

✦ **File not found:** Someone is linking to or looking for a specific file on your Web server and the Web address he's using is no longer valid. Perhaps a search engine is referencing a page that's no longer on your Web site or you advertised a specific Web link and misspelled it in the ad. When you see this message, create a Web page or file and put that file at the specified Web location or create a catchall link that points any incorrect references to the home page or a special error page.

When a search engine robot finds your Web site, it looks for a `robots.txt` file in your main Web site directory, to see whether you put any restrictions on its indexing of your site. When the robot can't find this error, you see an entry in the error log, although it doesn't mean that a problem occurred. In the absence of this file, the search engine robot program searches the entire site.

File stopped transferring: If no mention is made of the client stopping the transfer, you might have a faulty connection between your Web server and the visitor.

Although a transfer stoppage occasionally happens, if it happens repeatedly, your Web server's Internet connection isn't as reliable as it needs to be. Consider changing Internet service providers.

Checking abandoned shopping-cart logs

Typically, an e-commerce shopping cart creates a text file that contains a customer order. As the customer makes changes to that order, the shopping cart program adds or deletes from the file. When the customer checks out and pays for the order, the shopping cart converts the file into something else and deletes it from memory.

However, numerous studies indicate that Web site visitors abandon their shopping carts as much as 90 percent of the time. By looking at the shopping cart files that don't get ordered, you get an idea of how many people start the process but don't finish. You can compare this number to the number of orders you receive to calculate the percentage of potential customers that complete an order.

Suppose that you receive 50 orders for products in a month and then search for your shopping cart files and find 150 that were never processed. Your result means that 200 customers started the process, but only 50 finished, which is a 25 percent completion ratio for your visitors. When you know your ratio, you can start to take steps to improve it; we show you how in the section "Using Your Data," near the end of this chapter.

You can also find out which products are more popular by counting which ones get added to the carts. If someone took the time to physically add a product to her shopping cart, there is intent and demand for the item. You can use this information to help guide future product orders.

Scrutinizing the most common entry- or exit-page logs

Usually derivative files of the log file, the most common entry pages and exit pages focus on where people are specifically entering and exiting your Web site. In a sense, these entries tell you how your Web site functions when people use it.

Your *entry* pages detail the areas that draw people to your Web site. Maybe a product page that you thought wasn't important shows up repeatedly in this file. This information indicates that people are interested, and that you should use similar pages to bring in more people. If you're not seeing targeted landing pages that you created specifically to bring people to your site, something you did there isn't working.

Your *exit* pages show you the point in a customer's path where he gives up and goes somewhere else. Sometimes, it's the final order-confirmation screen, which is what you want to see. Most times, however, you see another page, which should encourage you to investigate why that's the case. Maybe that page gives a negative impression of your Web site. Perhaps you're encouraging your customer to check out another Web site and he's following that link rather than continuing with you. A page on your site might contain invalid, outdated, or useless information and links. This log identifies the *where;* you have to determine the *why*.

Measuring Traffic against Activity

Your Web site traffic data shows you a lot of information. To give these numbers some perspective so that you can make higher-level decisions, you have to match the traffic with other indicators of activity on your Web site:

- ✦ Number of orders
- ✦ Average order size
- ✦ Number of registered customers (if you offer registration)
- ✦ Total sales volume
- ✦ Average number of products per order
- ✦ Most common search terms (if you have your own site search engine)

The reason to compare these numbers is to give you an idea of how much your traffic is influencing your sales. Suppose that your Web site gets 1,000 unique visitors one month and you see that you're getting 250 orders from 200 unique customers that month. Theoretically, if you can double the number of visitors you receive in a month, you should see a similar increase in your orders and unique customers. Perhaps it doesn't double, but if you can estimate the benefit of bringing in more people, you can estimate the amount of money you can spend to increase traffic.

Putting together all this information gives you a complete picture of how your business is operating. Knowing these factors helps you make dozens of decisions that affect your entire business.

Jam Packed: Traffic-Analysis Software

After you get your Web site up and running, you can expect your log file to generate massive amounts of data as it records every interaction between your visitors and your Web server. As the number of visitors grows, so does the number of lines in your log file. It eventually grows to the point that you can't manually analyze the information to get your statistics. At that point, traffic analysis software enters the picture (such as Google Analytics, which you can find at `www.google.com/analytics`).

Traffic analysis software breaks apart all the log files generated by your Web server to build a summary of your Web site traffic criteria. These software programs

+ Break apart each log file entry.

+ Group together similar entries.

+ Factor out known entries, like search engine bot programs.

+ Calculate totals and averages.

You can choose from different versions and levels of traffic analysis software: basic, detailed, and enterprise or big business.

Basic analysis software

When you're using a basic analysis tool, you're looking for a program to create summaries of traffic information for a given period. Some tools, such as Urchin (`www.google.com/urchin`), provide text output. Others, for example, Webalizer (`www.webalizer.com`), WebTrends (`www.webtrends.com`), or FastStats (`www.mach5.com`), present data in both columnar and graphical format for easy viewing.

Here are some statistics that every program should produce or estimate:

✦ Total number of visitors and unique visitors

✦ Average number of daily visitors

✦ Total and average number of page views

✦ Total and average number of hits

✦ Average length of a visit (in minutes or number of page views)

Although the software you use might produce additional results, you can usually count on these categories being calculated. As an example, if you're using a free tool that creates a text summary and you requested a summary for your November 2008 traffic data, you might see results like this:

```
Period: Sat-1-Nov-2008 12:00 to Sun-30-Nov-2008 23:59 (30
    days).
Total successful requests: 2,221
Average successful requests per day: 74
Total successful requests for pages: 948
Total failed requests: 75
Total redirected requests: 349
Number of distinct files requested: 42
Number of distinct hosts served: 618
Number of new hosts served in last 7 days: 72
Total data transferred: 25,349 kbytes
Average data transferred per day: 844,967 bytes
```

This data gives you some important numbers for future demand. By looking at the total and average amount of data being transferred, you get an idea of the bandwidth you need to purchase for your Web site. You can see how many different Web pages are being looked at on your site. In this example, 42 different Web pages were requested. If your Web site has only 50 or 60 total pages, your customers are using a wide range of your site. If you have 200 or 300 pages, you need to see which pages are being loaded and figure out what to do with the rest.

You can also see more detailed information with a more powerful program, like Webalizer (see Figure 5-4). Webalizer (www.webalizer.com) provides bar graphs and summary tables to draw a detailed picture of your Web site's usage statistics, broken down by month and arranged by different criteria.

Detailed analysis software

At some point, you want to see more advanced information about how your Web site operates so that you can make targeted changes and updates to improve performance. At this stage, you should look into buying a tool like WebTrends (www.webtrends.com), Mach5 FastStats (www.mach5.com), or SmarterStats (www.smartertools.com) to analyze your log files and provide more defined criteria, such as

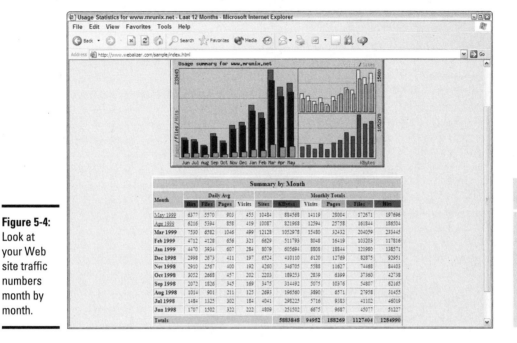

Figure 5-4:
Look at your Web site traffic numbers month by month.

✦ A detailed breakdown of page views

✦ The most common referral links used by your visitors

✦ The pages from which users are most often exiting your site

✦ The number or percentage of return visitors

✦ The most popular Web browsers used by your visitors

✦ The most popular search engines that deliver your traffic

✦ The amount of nonhuman traffic (like search engine programs)

✦ The busiest and slowest parts of the day for your Web traffic

These tools come with a number of predefined reports that help you understand your visitors' and customers' sophisticated interaction with your Web site. Figure 5-5 shows a report from WebTrends that provides a series of dashboard reports. As you change the dates of the period you want to analyze, the graphs are updated automatically. This way, you can compare traffic levels for different weeks, months, or even seasons.

Upload your log files or grant access for these analysis software programs to read your log files automatically. You might have to install these programs on your Web server to get them to work properly. Follow the setup instructions and talk to your Web hosting provider if you need specific path or filename details.

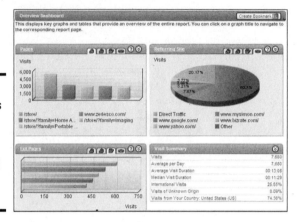

Figure 5-5:
WebTrends
provides
a series of
reports to
understand
your Web
site traffic.

Enterprise or big business

As your business grows, you might want to move up to an enterprise-level
solution, like one of these programs:

✦ **WebTrends Enterprise:** www.webtrends.com

✦ **Google Analytics (Urchin):** www.google.com/analytics

✦ **Omniture:** www.omniture.com

In this case, you want to install the service on your Web host. The key to using
these programs is being able to write your own queries to the database, which
means that you come up with your own, specific requests for summary data.

Some programs require that you know a specific computer language, like
SQL, to create your own reports. If someone in your business is focused on
information technology, have that person help you develop the language
necessary to build these reports.

Collecting the Correct Information

After people start taking advantage of Web site traffic analysis, they sometimes fall into the trap of believing that the software does all the work of
collecting the right data. You have to realize that although your Web server
collects some types of information, you can collect other types yourself. In
this section, we discuss how you can use your Web site to reach out and collect more specific information without your customers having to cough up
their Social Security numbers.

Storing data using cookies

Any Web server can create a standard file on a visitor's computer, to keep track of that visitor's activity and interaction with the Web server. That file is known as a *cookie* because it leaves "crumbs" of information that the Web server can access when the user visits that Web site. A cookie is a Web site owner's friend in many respects because it can show her what an individual user is doing on her site. You can track individual behavior and calculate unique visitors and session length much more precisely than by using log files. You can focus on one user for any length of time, from a few days to a few months, to see what he does on every visit. You can see which Web pages he looks at and the order of those pages and then correlate that information to his orders and sign-up activity.

Cookies help move your focus from a site-specific level to a customer level. When you add cookies to your server log files, you can gauge the efficiency of your marketing campaigns with precision. You can judge for yourself how effective your campaigns are so that you're not relying solely on your advertiser reports.

To turn on the use of cookies, ask your Web hosting provider to enable them for your Web server. After you do that, tell your provider which basic fields you want to use and capture in your cookies, such as

+ The visitor's IP address

+ The visitor's username or account name

+ The date and time of the visits

Your customers can refuse to have cookies stored on their computers, or they might use public computers, so their cookies won't be consistent. Even if you don't get a 100 percent view of your traffic, using cookies is much more precise than just analyzing your log files.

After you enable cookies on your Web server, your last step is to ensure that your traffic analysis software can access the cookies that your Web server leaves. That way, the software can incorporate that information into its reports and update its figures accordingly.

Adding information to your links

When you're looking at your log files, you see keywords in the string that represent a referral URL. (Refer to the section "Looking at your log file," earlier in this chapter.) Sometimes, these keywords are search terms used by visitors when they're using search engines. At other times, however, those specific terms were created for the purpose of communicating information.

You can add keywords to your URL to track the success of a marketing campaign. Add the keywords after the name of the HTML file by typing a question mark (?) and then the keywords, like this:

```
<a href="http://www.yourwebsite.com/index.html?GoogleAd1">
```

This way, when someone uses your targeted URL, the traffic analysis software can determine the number of times the keyword (`GoogleAd1`, in this example) was sent in the URL as a percentage of the total number of requests and then calculate a percentage.

If you continue to include this keyword throughout the ordering process, your analysis software can determine the conversion rate of browsers to buyers by studying how many buyers used a keyword as a percentage of the number of the browsers who came to your Web site.

Studying the path analysis

Your customers eventually follow a path of specific Web pages that take them from start to finish on your site. Although individual customers might check out different parts of your Web site along the way, they need to visit a minimum number of Web pages in order to go from a browsing customer to a paid customer. This minimum number of pages is sometimes called the *critical path* of your Web site.

Suppose that your Web site targets different levels of customers and has a special section for small-business customers. Your critical path might look like this:

> Home page→Small-business home page→Small-business catalog page→Order-review page→Order checkout page

When you identify the critical path for your customers, you can combine this knowledge with the traffic analysis you already completed to determine when and where people are dropping out of the order process. If you improve this process for your users, you should see an increased number of completed orders and a decreased number of abandoned shopping carts.

Suppose that you're studying the order checkout path. Here are some ways you can integrate all your research:

✦ If your report of the most common exit pages shows the order-review page as a common exit page, something in the order-review process might be confusing or counterintuitive to your users.

✦ If your referrer file indicates that a number of people are jumping to your Frequently Asked Questions (FAQ) page or privacy policy page from your order-review page, your customers most likely need or want more information before they check out. When they jump out of the critical path, a percentage of them never come back to the review or checkout phase. Therefore, you can integrate some of this content into your order-review page and see whether fewer people exit before completing the review page.

✦ An order-checkout page that involves multiple steps and shows people linking back and forth to the same pages could indicate that users are caught in a loop and can't break out to finish their orders. You might need to combine certain steps on one page or provide more clearly labeled links to convince customers to move forward.

Besides keeping your customers from dropping out of the order process, the other reason for studying your paths is to help you decide to redesign your Web site. Your customers eventually make their own path through your Web site, despite any warnings or guidelines you post. You can either continue to try to steer those customers or study their paths and incorporate that information into your site design so that the most common paths are recognized and supported by your Web site links and structure.

REMEMBER

Just as a river cuts its own path through the countryside, your customers will cut their own path through your Web site. You should always support that path and optimize your site around it rather than fight it and prevent customers from moving around the way they want.

Getting to Know Your Customer Really Well

If you've ever walked into a store to buy batteries, you know that the store wants to know a lot about you. The clerk asks for your zip code, and sometimes your address, even if you're paying cash. The people who run the company do this so that they can get an understanding of the customers who walk through their door and how those customers shop. Although this process can be annoying or off-putting for you, you probably accommodate the request. The store can then accurately predict, for example, which customers from which zip codes will order the most batteries.

Gathering customer information is a delicate, but ultimately profitable, venture because analyzing that information gives you razor-like focus on how your customers interact with you. Just like supermarkets that encourage their customers to use loyalty cards when they shop, Web sites are now gathering information on a customer level, independent of the traffic information that their Web browser leaves with your Web site. Because the customer is now signed in to the Web site, every activity is recorded and assigned to a customer account, which can be analyzed and aggregated without worrying about issues such as IP addresses and cookies.

As you move to understand your individual customers better, you move the focus of your data from your overall Web site statistics to your customers, where the common factor isn't your entire Web site, but rather the average customer and what she does on your Web site. Begin by having your traffic analysis program identify a unique visitor and then summarize information, such as average length of a visit or session.

Your goal is to find customer-specific patterns, not overall site trends. Collect data from your customer interactions that allow you to gain insight into customers' browsing and buying behavior. At this point, you should add tags or information on pages that matter to your customers, whether it's the order process screen or customer login screen.

Your existing customers have already told you a lot about themselves, including their

+ Names
+ Mailing addresses
+ Credit card information
+ Order lists of products

At some point, consider signing up users when they arrive at your Web site or want to learn more or do more on your Web site. Then tie that information into both the traffic and order statistics, to give yourself a true customer focus on your Web site activity.

When a customer has to log in to your Web site to use it, you can track every movement and tie those movements to a specific user ID number. Typically, users need some sort of incentive to reveal their personal information and complete a sign-up process. Some Web sites offer their members exclusive, premium content that casual browsing customers cannot access. Other sites require accounts to be created before products can be added to their shopping carts. You need to determine which special features you want to give to people who sign up with you.

When you use a sign-up process, you lose a certain percentage of browsers who could have become buyers. If you see a big drop-off in activity after instituting a sign-up process, consider assigning a guest account to your procedures. A user who wants to shop can convert a guest account to a permanent account.

Most Web sites ask for basic information whenever someone signs up for an account:

+ User's name
+ Address
+ City, state, zip code

✦ Phone number

✦ E-mail address

However, if you think beyond these basic fields, you can ask users additional questions to draw a better picture of your customers, and even to gather ideas that can influence your Web site, such as these examples:

✦ **Demographic information:** Gender, ethnicity, age, marital status, kids

✦ **Psychographic information:** Likes, brand recognition, purchase reasons

✦ **Lifestyle information:** Income, housing status, types of cars

✦ **Interests and preferences:** Favorite subjects, products, and people

Use the data to better understand what customers want and to customize content to them. On the sign-up form shown in Figure 5-6, the company asks about know the interests of its potential shoppers in order to fine-tune its catalog.

The options you present can be limited if your customers don't contribute information; if you make it required, however, you can lose a substantial number of potential and actual customers. Make this information-gathering process optional so that customers who don't want to reveal their information aren't blocked from using your Web site.

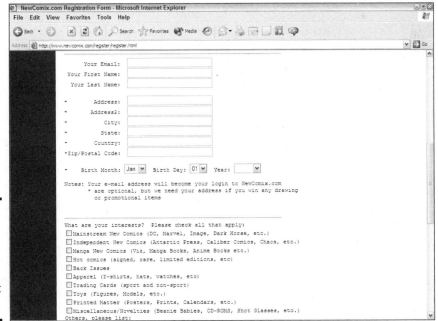

Figure 5-6:
Ask
customers
what they
like to buy
and use that
information.

Using Your Data to Understand Your Business

Collecting your Web site traffic and usage data is important for understanding your business. The true value of all this collection and analysis becomes evident when you act on the data and implement changes to your site. After all, what good is learning about a problem if you don't fix it?

Watching trends to find out average behavior

After you set up and collect your data, you have to monitor the activity levels to see trends and behavior so that you have a benchmark for comparison when you're ready to make changes. After all, if you don't know the average behavior of your Web site, you don't know where it has room for improvement.

When you study traffic and usage patterns for a longer period, look for any big changes in the data. If you see that your traffic suddenly experienced a big increase or suffered a huge drop, ask yourself what is causing big spikes or drops in your activity. Determine whether they're related to a change you made, such as an ad campaign, overall traffic, or a random event.

To fully investigate, create or access reports that give you detailed information from around the time of the change. This way, you can hunt down some big problems quickly. If the number of orders decreases and the number of error-log entries about pages not being delivered correctly increases, you know that your Web server or Internet service provider is experiencing outages. If your Web site is suddenly mentioned as part of a big news article, you probably see a spike in visitors to your site and (you hope) a spike in the number of orders placed on your site.

Other problems are less obvious to identify. Diagnosing these situations involves looking at Web page activity and seeing which statistics have been affected by the change in activity. As you look at your site, be aware of any changes you made to the Web pages, however big or small, and see whether the dates of those changes match up with the change in usage. Sometimes, a simple change disrupts an otherwise stable process and causes unexpected problems. If you watch trends, however, you can spot problems early and then fix them.

Identifying areas of improvement

You have many ways to know when something needs updating. When a road has a pothole, you know that it's time to repave the road every time your car bounces over the hole and says "ka-thunk." On your Web site, a report might indicate that traffic took a nosedive. Your e-mail account might be filled with customers screaming IN ALL CAPS that you can't keep operating a certain way.

You can also look at the data you're collecting to start making predictions before problems get out of hand. Find out which Web pages your users

✦ Gravitate to

✦ Avoid

✦ View most often and least often

Sometimes, the problem is a factor that your data can only partially identify. Suppose that your traffic report indicates that people check your Web site every morning. In addition to having traffic data, you know that your product catalog is updated only at the end of the business day, when you hear back from your suppliers. Put together those two pieces of information, and you have a timing problem because your site isn't as current as possible when visitors check out your site. They might move on if they see you as unresponsive. In this example, you have to figure out a way to update your inventory in the mornings.

Put yourself in the role of your customer. Start at your home page and try to place an order. Use your traffic and usage data to back up your assumptions about how to proceed. If you find a page frustrating to use and it shows up on your most common exit pages, you've identified an area to improve.

Don't overlook the importance of direct customer feedback for Web site improvements. Encourage regular dialogue, use follow-up surveys, and stay in contact with a portion of your customers at all times. They're usually up front about what can be improved and what has to be changed. After they identify a concern, you can research your data to choose your next step.

Deciding on a change

As you look at all your data and trends, identify an area that can be improved. Look at all factors that can influence its poor performance, and pick an element to change on your Web site that mimics a part of the site that performs well. Look at competitors' Web sites to see whether they handle the process differently. Ask customers for feedback on how you should handle the process.

When you're ready to update a part of your Web site, follow these steps:

1. **Make sure that you have a beginning set of statistics before you implement the change.**

   You need a set of data specifying how your Web site operated before the change, to use for later comparison.

2. **Make the change on your Web site.**

Many sites post notices about maintenance periods, as shown in Figure 5-7, where their sites are temporarily unavailable while new updates are posted. Typically, these updates take place during the night for U.S. customers so that the updates have the least effect on traffic. Use the maintenance period to send new versions of your Web pages to your Web server.

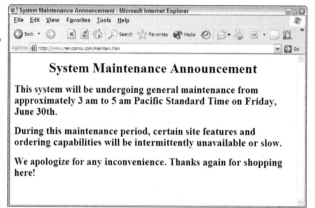

Figure 5-7:
Use a regularly scheduled maintenance period to make updates to your Web site.

3. **Gather your traffic statistics after the change is posted to your Web site.**

Watch the usage data after the new version is available, and notice whether traffic went up, as predicted, or down. Notice also whether other parts of your Web site were affected and whether orders increased.

Following up

Any change to your Web site can affect all your other processes. Therefore, you must follow up any change you make to your Web site, to make sure that you haven't disrupted anything else. You also have to study customer reaction to your changes and make sure that they benefit from them as much as possible.

Sometimes, you need to *roll back* the change (remove the update or go back to the old process). Although the techniques discussed in this chapter give you lots of insight into customer behavior, traffic analysis doesn't predict events with 100 percent accuracy. That's why you must stay flexible and judge whether any updates still provide value after they're implemented.

Chapter 6: Mastering Search Engines, Optimization, and Rankings

In This Chapter

✓ Understanding how search engines operate

✓ Convincing other businesses to link back to your Web site

✓ Telling search engines about your Web site

✓ Updating your Web pages with the right keywords

✓ Arranging your Web pages strategically

✓ Watching your search engine rankings

✓ Moving up in the search engine rankings

✓ Offering your own knowledge and experience to help your business

*I*f you earn prominent placement for your business where traffic is flowing, customers are more likely to stop by, look around, and buy something before they leave. Now, with the ever-growing and ever-changing nature of the Internet, many people are using search engines as their on-ramps, or their premier starting points for Web browsing. After all, if a potential customer thinks that she's going to end up at a search engine to find something, why wouldn't she start there? The result is that the search results are becoming the gateway to the Web, which is exactly where you want to be, offering your products to the right search results.

In Book VI, Chapter 3, we talk about marketing yourself in the sponsored ads to the right side of the standard search results page. In this chapter, we put the more valuable real estate — the search results themselves — front and center. We show you how to improve the quality of your search engine placements.

In this chapter, we discuss the inner workings of the biggest search engines and then show you how you can influence those engines in your favor. There's nothing illegal in these tricks — you're just increasing your presence in the right areas to get noticed more easily. We also show you how to stay near the top and describe more direct ways to "wave people down" in those search engine results.

Navigating the Ins and Outs of Major Search Engines

When you open a search engine Web page and type some words in the Search box, do you ever wonder how the search engine produces your search results? Do you imagine a blindfolded person tossing darts at newspapers spread over a wall? Maybe a chicken is let loose to peck its way to a few sites that are then transmitted to you. Although the true answer isn't as comical, the search engines use different procedures and methods to compare information against similar sites to come up with the all-important rankings.

Companies that figure out these procedures are the ones that continually find themselves near the top of the rankings; other businesses, which might have well-designed Web sites that are chock-full of information, get buried on Page 10 or Page 20 of the results. A few years ago, human intervention could elevate worthy sites to the top and give them featured placement. Because the placement process is almost all computerized now and computers follow rules, however, logic dictates that if you follow the rules, the computers will follow you.

The full set of rules that search engines use to order all their results are tightly guarded secrets because those rules, known as *algorithms,* set companies apart in this area. Google, in particular, uses complex rules.

The words you enter into a search engine typically aren't ordinary words. They're *keywords,* or specific words that are tied to a particular subject you're interested in. When you go to a search engine, you should give that engine the keywords, or most targeted words, that describe your search.

Search engines work like this:

1. You go to your favorite search engine, type a search term (a keyword) in the text box, and click Search to see the results.

2. Your search engine matches your search term against its database to look for relevant mentions of that keyword.

   The database is made up of countless entries of different Web pages that were gathered by either computer programs (known as *bots* or *spiders* in the technical world) or human editors.

The search engine doesn't analyze entire Web pages by scanning every word in a page against the keyword you specified. Instead, the search engine looks through *notes,* or a shorthand representation of that page. These notes (which summarize the page) are taken from such elements as

✦ The name of the Web site and particular Web page

✦ The words used in the *title* (or *head*) of the Web page

✦ The first paragraph or two of the Web page

✦ The words assigned by the Web page to represent the title and description (by using the <META> tag, which we discuss in the section "Creating <META> tags," later in this chapter)

✦ The Internet Web links that are present on the Web page

✦ The words used by other Web pages that offer a link to the Web page

In fact, the first page of the search results contains Web pages that have your search term in these places. We discuss how to insert your keywords into these various places on your Web pages later in this chapter, in the section "Placing Keywords in Key Spots on Your Web Site."

You're not limited to a single keyword. You can have multiple keywords or even phrases of keywords. However, you have a better chance of promoting a handful of keywords or phrases than trying to be the Web site that offers everything to everyone. Think about the most important or valuable phrases that your customers will use when they search for the products you sell.

**Book VI
Chapter 6**

Mastering
Search Engines,
Optimization, and
Rankings

Getting Your Web Site Noticed by Search Engines

Whether people are waving their hands in front of a crowd or smiling for TV cameras, they like to be noticed. To succeed in business, you're always told, "Stand out from the rest and be noticed." Business owners struggle with the notion of getting noticed on a finite budget. That's when creative measures come into play.

As we discuss in the preceding section, increasing your Web site's visibility on search engines involves knowing the rules they use and ensuring that your site follows those rules. Search engines don't base their rankings solely on keywords. If they did, a Web page that mentions the same word a thousand times would be at the top of their rankings. Instead, search engines also look for *references,* or how many other Web sites offer a link to a given Web page. The more links that point to a particular page, the higher that page appears on the search engine rankings, especially on Google. The reasoning is that, if other Web sites are all pointing their visitors to a particular page, that page must have more relevant content than other, nonlinked pages.

Search engines also look for content, or how much quality information you offer on your Web site. Websites that have more content — whether it's in the form of articles, calculators, reviews and guides, or just plain text — are typically given higher search result rankings than sites with little content. The reasoning here is that Web sites that offer a lot of content are more useful to someone searching out information. One big caveat here is that the higher results typically come when the content is unique to your Web site. Reprinting 1,000 articles that other people wrote can add content to your Web site, but you don't receive as much benefit as having 1,000 original articles on your Web site.

Therefore, adding original content should be one priority in order to achieve higher search engine results. Some people have a goal of writing 1 article per day for their sites. You can turn 10 or 15 minutes of writing into 365 articles after one year! Also, you can hire someone to create content for you. Just make sure that the content is readable and not stuffed with the keywords they think you need to have on your site. Search engines penalize you for having content that's overloaded with keywords, also known as *keyword stuffing*.

Having other Web sites link to your Web page is the next step. Greater weight is given to a Web page whose referring links use the main keywords for that page in the text for that link. Suppose that you're trying to promote a Web page for Arctic Technology Solutions. You have the best URL you can get for the keywords in your company name, www.arctictechnology solutions.com, and leading IT consultants link to your Web site. Now, tell these consultants to build the link this way:

```
<a href=http://www.arctictechnologysolutions.com> Talk
    to Arctic Technology Solutions! </a>
```

Notice that the clickable text that points to your Web site contains the same keywords as your URL. The search engines receive a double message that your Web site contains the text *Arctic Technology Solutions* because their computer programs read the keywords in both the HTML command and the clickable-text words.

Search engines look not just at the link itself but also at the Web site from where the incoming link is originating. Therefore, here are a couple of additional issues to keep in mind:

✦ **The more reputable the Web site, the higher value the link brings you.** Search engines typically assign a higher value to links from Web sites that are highly respected. Therefore, if you can get an incoming link from Google, Yahoo!, or one of the top ten sites on the Internet, that helps your search engine rankings much more than a link from your friend's toy review Web site. Aim for known Web sites, educational institutions, if possible, or even government agencies when applicable.

✦ **Make sure that the referring Web site is relevant to your business.** Getting reputable Web sites to link to you is important, but search engines also look for relevance. Does it make sense for them to link to you? Do your sites have something in common or something complementary? For example, having a technology review site link to your organic garden business may not be relevant, but having *Better Homes and Garden* magazine link to your garden business is relevant.

✦ **The age of the Web site name may be a factor.** Search engines check for a Web site's age by looking at the date the domain name was created in the main domain name database. The reasoning goes that, for example, if a Web site was created in the late 1990s, it has a better chance of having been around longer than a Web site created two weeks ago. Therefore, aim for incoming links from Web sites with some history. Check WHOIS (`www.whois.com`) to find the age of a Web site.

✦ **The best links are incoming only, not reciprocal.** When two Web sites link to each other in the hope of raising each other's search engine ranking, it's known as having *reciprocal* links, which carry a lower weight in their rankings. If a Web site links to you without a link back to it, that incoming link helps your ranking a lot more.

Submitting Your Site to Search Engines

Don't wait for other people to reference your Web site. The most straightforward way to make search engines notice your site is for you to tell them directly. Years ago, in the search engine submission process, Web site owners could file reports containing information about their sites and the URLs and content used on their sites. Although most of this information gathering is done now by the search engines' automatic programs, called *spiders* (because they crawl around the Internet looking for information), some search engines still allow you to submit your site.

Signing up with Google

Google sends its own programs, known as *Googlebots*, around the Web looking for new sites to add to its index. There's no reason, however, that you should wait around and hope that a Googlebot will magically land on your Web site, especially when you're just starting out. Google maintains a simple, one-page Web form that you can fill out to identify your site for its software programs to analyze.

You can identify yourself to Google by following these steps:

1. **Go to `www.google.com/addurl.html`.**

Google's Add Your URL to Google page opens, shown in Figure 6-1.

2. **In the URL text box, enter the full address of your Web site's home page.**

Don't forget to add the `http://`. You don't need to include the home page name unless it's not `index.html`, `index.htm`, or `default.html`.

3. **In the Comments box, enter a one-sentence keyword description of your Web site.**

Don't jam the box with comments. Just pick the keywords that you most want your Web site to be identified with. Don't try to shower this box with all kinds of different keywords that are on subcategory pages.

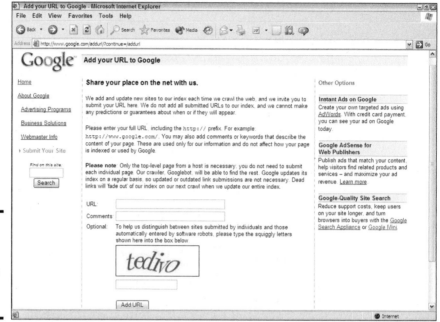

4. **Type the squiggly word shown in the big box.**

   Google adds a special "human detector" on this form to distinguish between humans filling out the form and special software programs that do it automatically. Software programs can't analyze this box because all they see is the generic name for the graphical image. Only human eyes can interpret the letters that are shown.

5. **Click the Add URL button.**

   Google gets all the information you provided and eventually sends a Googlebot to your Web site's home page. From there, it follows the links to read every page it can find and store the results.

Signing up with Yahoo!

The roots of Yahoo! are in its category search, not just a general search. Every category has an index page that contains lists of Web sites which belong to that category. Each index page also points to subcategories, each of which has its own index page. As Yahoo! has grown and bought companies, from Overture to Flickr, it has maintained the category approach to organization and also accepts submissions for its general search.

To guarantee that your submission is seen, you have to take the paid route. The Yahoo! submission process is still in human hands. The editors scan these submissions and decide what to include and where to include it. It's one aspect that sets Yahoo! apart from the other search engines.

To sign up with Yahoo!, follow these steps:

1. **Go `http://search.yahoo.com/info/submit.html`.**

You see the page shown in Figure 6-2.

Book VI
Chapter 6

Mastering
Search Engines,
Optimization, and
Rankings

Figure 6-2:
Take
advantage
of the
different
Yahoo!
submission
methods.

2. **Pick the type of content you want to submit.**

Yahoo! offers many ways for you to submit site content to its engine:

- *Submit Your Site for Free:* Your site address (although Yahoo! doesn't guarantee that it will look at it or include your site in its search engine).

- *Submit Your Mobile Site for Free:* Mobile content, if your business is geared for mobile devices.

- *Submit Your Media Content for Free:* Images and audio and video content that your business has.

- *Search Submit:* The option to put your Web site in the Yahoo! search index in about 48 hours. (You pay $49 for the first Web site.)

- *Sponsored Search:* The pay-per-click method. (Refer to Book VI, Chapter 3.)

- *Product Submit:* Specific product info to the Yahoo! Shopping directory.

- *Travel Submit:* Specific travel deals to the Yahoo! Travel Deals section.

- *Yahoo! Directory Submit:* Ensures that Yahoo! considers your site for inclusion in its category index within seven days. Although you have no guarantee that your Web site will be approved and added, it's reviewed. (Submitting for free carries no guarantees.) The cost for this program is $299; if your site is accepted, you pay an annual $299 fee to continue your inclusion.

- *Yahoo! Standard:* Your site for category inclusion in the Yahoo! main directory.

3. **Enter the URL of the Web site you're submitting.**

    Regardless of the type of content you're submitting, you enter in the appropriate box the URL of the Web site you want to submit. After you enter the URL and click Submit, the address is sent to Yahoo! for inclusion in its next robot search of the Internet.

Don't forget about Yahoo! Local, especially if your business has a retail or local outlet that sells products. Go to `http://local.yahoo.com`, and pick your area to begin. Being included in the local index ensures a higher visibility by potential customers who live in your specific area.

Submitting to other search engines

You might think that submitting your site and having it picked up by Google and Yahoo! are all you need to do. After all, who uses the other, smaller search engines? The answer is that search engines such as Google and Yahoo! do. By increasing your mention in all the smaller search engines, you get more referrals to your Web site, which leads to higher rankings on the Big Two search engines.

If you know from researching your logs that customers are using a particular search engine, you should definitely do whatever is necessary to be indexed by that search engine. See Book VI, Chapter 5 for more information on how to analyze your customer logs.

Table 6-1 lists some smaller but active search engines with free submittal pages.

Table 6-1	Free Search Engine Submittal Pages
Company	*Submission URL*
MSN Search	`http://search.msn.com/docs/submit.aspx`
Beamed	`www.beamed.com/search/AddURL.html`
WhatUSeek	`www.whatuseek.com/addurl.shtml`
ExactSeek	`www.exactseek.com/add.html`
InfoUSA	`http://dbupdate.infousa.com/dbupdate/index.html`

Many medium-size search engines — such as Ask.com and Lycos — have their own ways of accepting submissions (mainly by paid inclusion), and others have no manual submission process any more. Search engines rise and fall in popularity, just like the results they display, so do your homework and follow up with any up-and-coming search programs.

Many businesses offer, for a price, guaranteed submissions to hundreds, or even thousands, of search engines. Many links that are offered are no longer valid because companies are absorbed or go bust. Do your research before signing up with a company that makes big promises about search engine inclusion.

Book VI
Chapter 6

Mastering
Search Engines,
Optimization, and
Rankings

Placing Keywords in Key Spots on Your Web Site

You can use different methods to incorporate on your Web pages the keywords that will be viewed as the most relevant and important words that represent your page. The keywords must appear in multiple locations so that the search engine bots know that those keywords represent the content of your page.

The most important factor is, as they say in real estate, location, location, location. Sure, you can write a Web page about the hundred greatest uses for a ball-peen hammer and use the words *ball-peen hammer* repeatedly in the body of the Web page. You can find much better locations, however, than the body of the Web page, to attract the attention of search engine bots more reliably and consistently. Some locations are invisible to the Web browser, and others are hiding in plain sight.

Keywords that are invisible

Web pages are built on *HyperText Markup Language,* or *HTML.* Commands aplenty identify the information contained in a Web page. For keyword purposes, the most important tag to use in your Web page is <META>. It defines the name, purpose, author, and date of a Web page. Search engines read this tag to catalog Web pages more efficiently.

Because of this command's purpose, search engine bots are interested in knowing what information is assigned to <META> tags. They take that information with a grain of salt, however, because they know that the <META> tag info is being written by a biased source — the author of the page. Nevertheless, the <META> tag information is added into the formula for reading and interpreting Web pages.

If you're having someone design your Web pages, be sure to ask specifically whether he's defining <META> tags for every single Web page on your site. These optional tags are commonly forgotten about because they don't affect the performance of the Web page on the server.

The <META> tag is specific to only the individual Web page where the tag resides. Therefore, the information in the <META> tag for your home page is (and should be) completely or significantly different from an interior Web page that focuses on one product line.

Creating <META> tags

For each Web page, insert at least two <META> tags into the HTML for the page. More options are available, such as defining the author of the page or the last revision date of the Web page. Although you might want to define these fields for other reasons, for targeting the search engines, they're not as helpful.

Include these <META> tags as part of the head of each Web page, not the body section.

The syntax of a <META> tag works in two parts: You define which type of <META> tag you want to use by assigning a name to it, and then you assign the content for that <META> tag. For example, if you want to assign the keywords *Arctic, Technology,* and *Solutions,* your <META> tag would look like this:

```
<META name="keywords" content="Arctic, Technology,
    Solutions">
```

Unlike in other HTML commands, a closing tag isn't necessary. This line of code is sufficient. You need a separate <META> tag, however, for each type of information you want to define. Figure 6-3 shows how to separate the definition from the keywords by using two <META> tags.

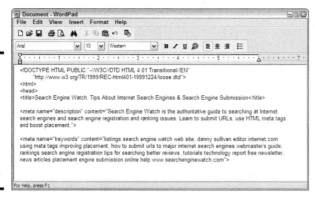

Figure 6-3:
Use separate <META> tags for different types of information.

The two <META> tags you need to include are keywords and description. For added effect, some people repeat their keywords as part of their descriptions. The search engines, though, are reading the <META> description and looking for context. A laundry list of keywords in the <META> description tag, therefore, doesn't improve your results. A creative integration can help your efforts, though.

META tags can speak foreign languages

In this global era of the Internet, your audience is no longer restricted to one region or country. Similarly, your keywords are no longer restricted to one particular language. The <META> tag has the capability to assign keywords to a particular language set, so you can have a different tag for Americans who speak English, Britons who speak English, and almost everyone in Central or South America, and in Spain, who speaks Spanish.

You can define an attribute of the <META> tag known as lang (short for *language*). The search engines implement a filter if they see the lang attribute defined and then assign the correct keywords to the specified language in the Web surfer's preferences.

If you sell soccer jerseys and sweaters, for example, your <META> tags might look like this:

```
<META name="keywords"
    lang="en-us"
    content="soccer, jersey,
    sweater">
<META name="keywords"
    lang="en"
    content="football, jersey,
    jumper">
<META name="keywords"
    lang="es" content="futbol,
    Jersey, sueter">
```

Book VI
Chapter 6

Mastering
Search Engines,
Optimization, and
Rankings

If you're selling gourmet artichoke sauces, your <META> tags might look like this:

```
<META name="keywords" content="Gourmet, Artichoke, Sauces">
<META name="description" content="Our gourmet chefs have
    picked the freshest artichokes to create gourmet artichoke
    sauces sure to liven up any artichoke recipe!">
```

Notice the repeated use of the targeted keywords as part of the context of a readable, legible sentence. Although the <META> description tag doesn't have a hard limit, using more than one or two sentences dilutes any meaning you hope to get from using the tag in the first place. Simply put, if you overload the description tag, you water down your results to the point that the search engines don't know any more what's particularly meaningful. What's dangerous is that the search engines can *lower* your search ranking result if they think that you're *keyword stuffing,* or putting too many instances of the keywords on your Web page.

Adding ALT attributes

A valuable addition to the HTML image tag is the ALT attribute. This attribute is assigned to image files that are loaded into a Web page. The ALT attribute is a description of the graphical image that's displayed on the Web page if the Web browser cannot load the image properly on the screen. Additionally, in Web browsers such as Internet Explorer and Netscape's

Mozilla, a user can hover the mouse over the image to see the information assigned to the ALT attribute.

If you're using the Firefox Web browser, don't expect to see any ALT text when you hover your mouse over the image. This program treats the ALT information as originally intended, and it's displayed only if the image doesn't load properly.

Because search engines cannot read text that's part of a graphical image, they read the ALT attribute, if it's defined, and give it some weight. Like the <META> tag, the optional ALT attribute is easily forgotten when a Web site is being designed. You should always take the opportunity to define your ALT attributes for your images because, otherwise, you're missing out on an opportunity to promote your keywords.

The ALT attribute is added to the <IMG> tag that includes an image on the Web page. If you're using a big logo image of your business that represents gourmet artichoke sauces, the command to insert the image looks like this:

```
<IMG SRC="logo.jpg" ALT="Gourmet Artichoke Sauces
    Logo">
```

Keywords that are visible

Although search engines rely on HTML commands like the <META> tag to gain an understanding of the purpose of a Web page, their computer programs are more interested in divining the "natural" meaning of a Web page, by interpreting the text visible on the page and understanding what the page itself is trying to convey to users. Therefore, make sure that the keywords that best identify your Web page are clearly used in some visible — but not obvious — locations:

+ **Page name:** Every Web page is simply a file containing HTML commands and text, and each file has to have a name. The last three or four letters of the filename after the period must be htm or html because of Web standards. Everything in front of the period in the filename is completely up to you. If you set up a page to sell tennis equipment, for example, don't use an abstract name, such as order.html. Instead, name this special page tennis.html or tennis-equipment.html.

If you're designing your Web site for optimal search engine recognition and one Web page offers two or more categories of products, divide the product line and dedicate a single page for each one. This way, you can gear everything on each page toward the specific product the page represents.

+ **Page title:** Every Web page on your Web site should have a title, regardless of the purpose of the page. This valuable space is picked up by search engines.

The worst thing you can do is leave an empty title. The second-worst thing you can do is use a vague or meaningless title, such as "Welcome to my Web site!" or "Stuff for you." Make sure that each title has the important keywords for that page.

✦ **Page headings:** Just like human eyes pick up headlines quicker than any other text on the page, computer programs read headlines and assign a greater weight to them than to the text on the page. You can be more specific in the headings than in the title — just keep the headings focused on the page content, not on your overall site.

✦ **First sentence:** The first sentence on the page is typically a summary or an overview of what the page offers. Because some search engines don't index an entire page of text, make sure that the first sentence draws a clear picture of what you intend for the page to do.

✦ **Text inside links:** Search engine bots are hungry for Web links, so make sure that any clickable text contains the right keywords for that link. The bots assign weight to those keywords because they're being referenced by the link.

In addition to adding keywords in these locations, you should still fine-tune your pages to mention your keywords throughout the text, as shown Figure 6-4. Work these keywords into the flow of the text in a way that's not jarring to readers. Don't just offer strings of keywords that don't form complete sentences. Search engine bots pick up on context, so they flag as nonessential any out-of-place lists of keywords they find.

**Book VI
Chapter 6**

**Mastering
Search Engines,
Optimization, and
Rankings**

Figure 6-4:
See how the important keywords are used throughout the page.

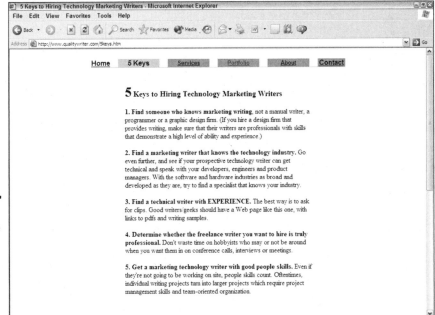

Don't display any valuable keywords as graphics files on your Web page. Search engine bots cannot scan the contents of a graphics file — only the text that's in the HTML file (or the ALT attribute for an image.) If you have to use graphics, for a navigation menu or header, for example, complement that menu with a text menu at the bottom of the page. This way, not only are you using the keywords as text, but they're also clickable text, which improves your site's ranking.

Arranging Your Pages Strategically

Your Web site is simply the collection of various Web pages that make up your overall business. Therefore, you want every Web page in your business to be well defined and serve a specific purpose. You don't want to create Web pages whose only goal is to attract search engines with keywords and defined tags. Instead, you want well-defined pages that make sense to users and search engine bots.

Keep the following rules in mind when you're constructing the Web pages in your business:

✦ **One page, one focus:** If one Web page has two or more product lines on it, consider breaking up that page so that each line has its own page. You can still have a category index page, which you can optimize with your overall business mission, and each product page can then be a launching pad for that subset of your business. The Web page shown in Figure 6-5 concentrates on one product — a garage cabinet.

✦ **Define your page**: Make sure that all your definitions, tags, and keyword mentions are at the top of your HTML source code for your Web page. Some search engines limit the number of characters per page they take, and you don't want to lose out because you added a lot of comments or JavaScript code first.

✦ **Think about keyword density**: Focus each Web page to target a select group of keywords and phrases. This technique increases the weight of each of these phrases more than when you try to use every keyword in every page (which is known as *keyword density*). When the same words are used repeatedly, search engines see this density of words and assign greater weight to the few words that are used than does an average Web site that tries to be popular for every popular keyword.

✦ **Put away the bells and whistles**: If your Web page excessively uses elements such as graphics, animation, and video or audio files on the same page as valuable product information, separate the extra features into their own section of the Web site or create two versions — one with just text and basic graphics and one with all the extras. The search engine bots give up on loading a page if it takes too long, and so will your customers.

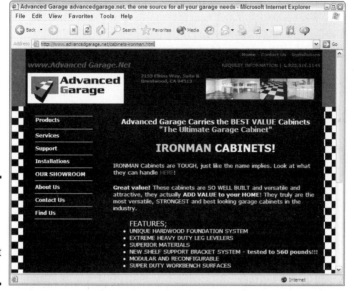

Figure 6-5:
Give every
important
product its
own product
page.

**Book VI
Chapter 6**

**Mastering
Search Engines,
Optimization, and
Rankings**

Watching Your Rankings

Although Web site pages might last forever in a search engine's database, the Web site's importance or relevancy doesn't carry over. As Web site owners try to figure out ways to improve their positions in search engine results, search engines update their systems and algorithms to reduce the effect of specific tricks that become popular.

One such practice is *keyword spamming*. Web site owners hide paragraphs of targeted keywords by matching the color of the keyword's text with the color of the Web page background. For example, the owner of a Web site using a white background puts in a block of keywords using white text. These keywords are invisible to customers browsing the Web site because the white text doesn't show up on a white background. The spiders that download the information from the Web page can see the keywords, however, and they assign weight to those keywords regardless of whether they're relevant. Search engines now compare the colors being used and eliminate those keywords, even if the colors being used are slight variations of each other.

As a business owner, you need to stay informed of the changes the search engines make to their programs, and then update your Web site accordingly to take advantage of whatever the new rules enforce. The last thing you want is to optimize your Web site based on one set of rules and then have your Web site ignored because the rules changed and you didn't update your site.

A variety of Web sites provide news, updates, columns, and information about major and secondary search engines. If you want to stay up-to-date with search engine techniques, follow some of these sites:

✦ **SearchEngineWatch.com:** This site, shown in Figure 6-6, calls itself the "Source for Search Engine Marketing," and many users agree. The company uses a variety of mechanisms — like news articles, blogs, discussion boards, and a marketplace for vendors of search engine optimization (SEO) products — to spread the word about search engine marketing. It offers a wide variety of free content and a reserved Members section (which has premium articles written by experts), an extensive archive of information, and a private newsletter. It even sponsors the Search Engine Strategies Conference and Expo, in different cities around the world, to promote the same concepts as the site.

✦ **SearchEngineForums.com:** If you're looking for a particular discussion area that covers either a general search engine (such as Google, Yahoo!, or MSN) or a discussion about a particular topic (such as link building), SearchEngineForums.com is the place for you. It has a number of discussion boards — including a section dedicated to building, hosting, and maintaining your Web site — that provide help and discussion for online-store professionals or the graphic design or database work that your Web site requires.

Figure 6-6:
This site
keeps you
up-to-date!

✦ **Yahoo Search blog:** What better way to find out what the engineers at one of the top search engines are thinking than to read their own blogs? The Yahoo! search team maintains its own blog, where they talk about everything from upcoming conferences to new functions within Yahoo! Search to cool contests and events on the Web that matter to people interested in searching. You can find the blog at `www.ysearchblog.com`.

Moving Up in the Rankings

The key isn't always to be in the top spot. Considering the enormous amount of new information that becomes indexed every day — not to mention the continual updating of search engine algorithms — you can waste a lot of time trying to stay on top by retaining the top search engine result for your important keywords.

You should have two goals for your ranking in the search engine results:

✦ A position that's high enough on the list before a potential customer sees your competitors

✦ A position among the first page or two

Most people who are presented with multiple pages of search engine results typically skim the first page and try a few links. A few of them then go to the second page and try more links. After the second or even third page of results, however, if the destination sites aren't close to what the user is looking for, that person typically enters a new string of keywords, sees a different set of results, and tries again.

You can earn a prominent spot by using keywords in the right spots or partnering with a business to link to your Web site. If you're interested in staying ahead of your competition, though, read these next few sections. We show you how to find your rankings and then how to keep an eye on your competition.

Knowing where you stand

You can't know where you're going unless you know where you are. Your first job is to understand what the search engines know about your Web site. Search engines provide a growing number of tools that that can open a window into their databases and show you what they now know about you.

Exploring the Yahoo! Site Explorer

As one of the oldest search engines on the Internet, Yahoo! has built an extensive database of the structure of the Web. Web pages are classified by category and subject as well as by the links that point to the page themselves. Yahoo! uses all that information and its own algorithms to construct search results.

**Book VI
Chapter 6**

Mastering
Search Engines,
Optimization, and
Rankings

Yahoo! offers the Site Explorer tool, which shows you all the information it has about a specific Web site. If you don't have a Yahoo! account, you need to create one. Follow these steps to use Site Explorer:

1. **Go to `http://siteexplorer.search.yahoo.com`.**

   The opening page for Site Explorer appears.

2. **Enter the URL of the Web site you want to analyze in the text box, and click the Explore URL button.**

   The `http://` is already filled in, so you don't need to enter it.

   You have several options for URLs to enter:

   - *awebsitename.com:* Analyze all subdomains as well as the main www server.

   - *www.awebsitename.com:* Analyze only the main www server of the Web site.

   - *www.awebsitename.com/dir/:* Analyze a subsection of the main Web server.

   - *www.awebsitename.com/dir/page1.html:* Analyze a specific page on the site.

   After you enter the domain and click the button, the results screen is displayed.

3. **View all the pages in that Web site, displayed in their natural search order.**

   The default view for the Site Explorer results lists all Web pages found in the domain you specified. After we entered `http://www.dummies.com` in Step 2, we saw a page similar to the one shown in Figure 6-7. The results include the 33,910 pages within all subdomains of Dummies.com. You can click the `Dummies::Home` Web page title to see the page or click Cached to see the stored Yahoo! version of that Web page.

4. **Click the Inlinks link to see how many Web sites offer links to your specified domain.**

   Inlinks view shows you the Web pages that offer a link back to the domain specified in your search. When you're analyzing your own Web site, this resource is invaluable for seeing who's offering links back to you. Don't be surprised to see pages within your Web site showing up on this list. This feature shows you all the inlinks, not just the ones that reside outside your Web site.

Finding your Google PageRank

One way that Google decides how to order its search engine is by assigning every Web page a specific PageRank. The term *PageRank* was invented by the Google founders to represent the popularity of a Web site, from 0 to 10, based on the number and quality of other Web sites that offer links back to the Web site in question.

Figure 6-7:
Explore
Dummies
pages on
the Web.

**Book VI
Chapter 6**

Mastering
Search Engines,
Optimization, and
Rankings

The PageRank algorithm and concept, which have been patented by the founders of Google, rank Web pages by using a vast link structure to indicate the value of a page. Google PageRank interprets a link from Web Site A to Web Site B as a vote for Site B (from Site A). PageRank then looks at the quality of Site A, the voter, and other factors of both pages to determine an ultimate rank.

Google offers a way for Web site programmers to search its database with an automatic query and return the PageRank value for any submitted URL. For a quick way to find out the Google PageRank for your Web site, go to one of these sites:

✦ `www.urltrends.com`

✦ `http://google-pagerank.net`

✦ `http://whatisyourpagerank.com`

You can always see the Google PageRank of a Web site by installing the Google Toolbar on your own computer. To add the toolbar, follow these steps:

1. Go to `http://toolbar.google.com` to install the toolbar.

 2. **Click the Options button.**

 3. **Click the Browsing tab, and select the PageRank option.**

 4. **Check out your PageRank and compare it your competitors.**

Seeing what your competition is doing

No analysis of your Web site is complete without looking at your competition. If your Web site is the only one in your given area, this step is unnecessary. Chances are, however, that you have more than one competitor and you're trying to figure out how to steer customers to your site and away from the others. You have to recognize the difference between these two types of competitors:

✦ **Direct:** These businesses are the same size as yours and offer a similar (or almost identical) product mix to your target set of customers.

✦ **Indirect:** This type of competitor happens to sell some of the same products you sell (divisions of a big retailer, for example).

You can learn about your competitors by going online. Visit your competition's Web sites to see their Web page design and find out what they offer to customers. Also ask yourself these questions about your competition:

✦ Which keywords are they using in their Web site names?

✦ Which keywords are showing up in their Web page titles and headings?

✦ Which <META> keywords and descriptions are they using? (In your Web browser, choose View⇨Source to see the HTML source code.)

✦ How many other links point back to their Web sites?

✦ What are their Google PageRanks?

Don't cut and paste any info from a competitor's Web site. That site has an automatic implied copyright the minute it's created and posted on the Internet. Although you can observe and apply techniques or concepts, you cannot plagiarize the text or reuse a site's graphics or photos without permission.

As you're reviewing your competitors' Web sites, note the techniques they use that you don't now implement. Then compare their search engine results to your results on multiple search engines. Concepts that work well on one engine might not be picked up on another site. Find out what works, and avoid what doesn't.

Creating your own referrals

Some Web site owners have decided that if they can't get other Web sites to offer a link to them, why not build their own links? The sole purpose of some

Web sites is to serve as part of a newly built network to promote a central site. When you go to these referral sites, it's quite obvious in some cases that they're built for only one reason. As search engines have adapted their rules, they ignore sites whose only purpose is to link to someone else.

The right way to achieve your own network is to build a series of targeted, focused content sites, each of which feeds into your main e-commerce business. Suppose that you sell pet supplies. Rather than add original content solely to your e-commerce site, you can set up targeted Web sites about dogs, cats, birds, fish, gerbils, and hamsters. You can then focus on building up these Web sites by becoming an authority or expert in these areas. After you have fellow enthusiasts hooked on your information, you can then refer those people to your e-commerce site when they're ready to buy something.

Getting another Web site to cross-promote with you is easier when it's exchanging links with a content site, not with an obvious potential competitor. You can always offer excerpts of your content on the e-commerce site, in case your repeat customers come straight back and want to read something first.

You can even promote your products on sale at places like Facebook, LinkedIn and other social networking, blog, or profile Web pages. Each third-party Web site has its own restrictions, so follow up to be sure before you launch something with a questionable link.

Discovering Editorial Opportunities with Engines

The Open Directory Project (www.dmoz.org) is a free directory of the entire Web that's organized by human editors. According to its description, the Open Directory Project is "the largest, most comprehensive human-edited directory of the Web." This directory is built and maintained by an enormous worldwide community of volunteer editors who have to adhere to certain standards and practices. One fundamental aspect of this directory is that the information is completely free and will remain free as long as people contribute to it.

As the Web continuously grows, the Open Directory Project approaches the massive amount of information one section at a time. These volunteers, or *netizens* (Inter*net* cit*izens*), organize a list of Web sites related to a small piece or subject. They promote the good sites and omit the bad ones. The netizens then present their findings to the greater community, where other netizens also can review and update their work.

This process creates an ever-changing, ever-evolving site that's constantly being looked at with human eyes as the collective "brain" of this community comes up with the most valuable and useful links and sources.

Book VI
Chapter 6

Mastering
Search Engines,
Optimization, and
Rankings

Where do you come in? Well, chances are good that you have gained some specific knowledge about the product areas in which your business operates. If you share that knowledge with the Project, you identify your business as one place people can go.

You cannot make an empty gesture to the Project, where you reference your Web site just for the sake of being referenced. Being included in the Open Directory Project creates a high Google PageRank incoming link for your Web site, which means that the Project gets bombarded with requests all the time. Make your contribution count and it will be worthwhile!

Signing up with the Open Directory Project is simple. Follow these steps:

1. **Go to www.dmoz.org.**

2. **Find the category you want to contribute to.**

3. **Click the green Become an Editor link, shown in Figure 6-8.**

   If no link is available, pick a more focused subtopic that offers this link.

Your work is reviewed by other people after you resubmit it to the project. Therefore, if you don't contribute a valuable and concise guide, your work is deleted or rewritten and your business doesn't see any benefit.

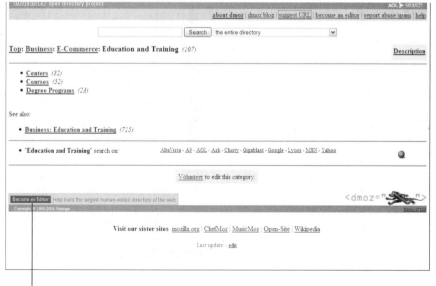

Figure 6-8: Become an editor on the Open Directory Project.

Click to volunteer with the Open Directory Project.

Book VII

Retail to E-Tail

Deliver coupons by cellphone.

Contents at a Glance

Chapter 1: Knowing When to Put Your Store Online

In This Chapter

✔ **Deciding whether a Web site can help your business**

✔ **Perfecting your timing when you're launching a site**

✔ **Building on your store's existing identity**

✔ **Mapping out the details for your online move**

✔ **Putting your inventory on the Web**

*O*nline retailing has celebrated more than ten years of selling on the Net! Having weathered the demise of innumerable dotcoms in 2002, and even surpassed offline sales in the past few buying seasons, online retailing has proven to be a successful business model. You might have put off launching a Web site because of costs or other reasons, but there has never been a better time to join the online revolution. In this chapter, we explain what you need to do to make the transition from your brick-and-mortar store to an online store.

Making the Decision to Move Your Store Online

While you're thinking of taking your business online, ask yourself this basic question: Why do I want to move my business online? If you're making the move online only because everyone else is doing it, you might want to think about it a little more. Of course, you should make the move — but for the right reasons.

You're ready to get serious about building an online site when that site can help you reach a specific goal that makes your business stronger. Typically, these reasons include

✦ **To expand:** Going online opens another channel for selling your products. If your site is executed properly, it helps increase your revenue and profit potentials — a standard goal for any business.

✦ **To control the cost of growth:** Comparatively speaking, expanding onto the Internet can be much less expensive than opening another physical location. Additionally, an online store potentially reaches a national or an international customer base rather than confines you to a limited geographic area. You reach more customers for less money! That's smart business.

✦ **To create awareness:** Your site is an extension of your marketing efforts. It becomes a permanent, online advertisement for your brick-and-mortar store. Sometimes, you might have a site solely to support your other marketing or PR activities. If you're already getting a lot of exposure through your current marketing methods, you need a place to direct prospective customers for more information. Either way, customers won't easily forget about your store when you're continually communicating with them, both online and offline.

✦ **To drive traffic:** No matter how much, or how little, inventory you offer for sale online, you're ultimately building foot traffic to your store, too. Your site is an interactive marketing tool. For example, to attract new customers, you can use paid and *localized* (targeted to your local market) keyword searches and search engine optimization (refer to Book VI, Chapter 6). And online coupons, e-mails, and e-newsletters become incentives to purchase (online and off). You decide where you want to direct the traffic!

Ultimately, your reason for starting an online store must make sense as part of your business strategy. As with any other decision, this choice deserves your deliberate and considerable attention.

Unfortunately, some offline entrepreneurs haven't thought through their online strategies. In fact, they don't have strategies. This type of storeowner is chastised by customers for not having a Web site. Eventually, the store-owner gives in and decides to buy a domain name and throws something up there just so that he can say "I have a site!"

Here are the four worst reasons to move your company online at any time:

✦ **Your customers are demanding it:** If you're not prepared to do it the right way, having a hastily developed Web site won't appease your customers.

✦ **Your competitors are all online:** If you're not ready to invest in the components that you need in order to create a quality site, your customers will find your competitors more enticing, anyway.

✦ **You finally have the money:** Saving up for the amount that you budget for a site is one thing. Haphazardly deciding to spend some of your profit just because it's available is another thing entirely. In reality, if e-commerce is an important part of your strategy, you can find the necessary money to fund it at the right time, according to your plan.

✦ **You need business:** If your retail sales are way down, you might think that moving your store online is the only answer. Having a Web site isn't a cure-all for what ails your business. Instead, e-commerce is only an element within your business. Therefore, if your offline store is already flailing, your online version is likely to face equal — if not greater — struggles.

For the most part, the reasons in the preceding list represent pressure points. And, when you can't take the pain any longer, you finally respond.

Someone (or something) else is then calling the shots and deciding what's best for your business. Don't give in to this kind of pressure. Instead, think about the timing of your decision and take control!

Finding the Right Time

To find the right time to make the move online, you have to step back and analyze the situation as objectively as possible. Does creating an online store truly fit into your business plan right now? In what ways would an online store contribute to your short-term and long-term goals? Is there a better time to move your business online?

In addition to your internal store goals, you have to consider external factors. What are the current market conditions for your industry? In what general direction is the national economy heading? If your customers aren't spending right now, you might want to conserve the money that you originally budgeted for your site development. On the flip side, if market factors are pushing the demand for your type of products, you might want to bump up the development of your site by a few months.

Make time to track industry trends, both online and off. Regularly check out the issues by reading trade magazines and following industry-related research. Start with the Gartner group at www.gartner.com.

Taking into account seasonal latitude

As a retailer, you probably have a particularly busy season, when you earn the majority of your revenues. Your busy season might be the end of the year when most holiday shopping drives sales. Or, if you sell recreational items, such as bikes or swimming pool accessories, the summer is probably when you gear up for brisk business.

Your products are most in demand during this period, which can affect your plans for starting a site in two ways:

✦ **Development time:** Building a site takes time. Even if you're outsourcing the work, you're intricately involved in the process. And, creating your first online endeavor during your store's most hectic time of year is a bad idea. If you're already loaded with work, you're likely to make hasty site-related decisions or drop the project altogether out of sheer frustration. You can offset this potential for disaster by planning around your store's busy time.

Start working on your site right after your busy season ends. Although you might anticipate a development timeline of only a few months, many events and circumstances can delay or extend that deadline. Beginning site construction at the close of your business's high point gives you plenty of cushion before that busy time rolls around again.

✦ **Launch time:** Planning to launch a site during your seasonal high point isn't a grand idea. You need time to test the site to see how it works and to find and correct errors. Sure, you and your developer test most of these items before you take the site *live* (the point at which you put it on the Internet). But, plenty of minor glitches go unnoticed by everyone but your customers. If you launch the site before your busy season begins, you have more time to respond to these customer issues and resolve them. And, because fewer customers are likely to be affected by the problems, you can keep the issues contained.

Don't be shy about letting your customers know that your site is new. Make a point to ask for feedback and suggestions for improvement, or to be notified of trouble spots. Reward customers who send you information. You can give them coupons or other small gifts to thank them for their time.

Timing your launch around an event

Similar to seasonal timing, other events can influence when you decide to launch your site, such as an annual event that your store participates in. You might think that an event where all your potential customers are gathered is the perfect time to unveil your site. Keep in mind, though, that perfect timing isn't always as perfect as it seems.

Of course, you might insist on coordinating your site's debut with an event-driven date. If so, here are some points to keep in mind:

✦ Double the amount of time that you think you need for your site's development.

✦ Add another six to eight weeks to that date to allow for testing and customer feedback.

✦ Don't commit to using your site for event-related promotions (just in case).

✦ Avoid using event-specific merchandise in the launch of your site.

If your store's online premiere is tied to an immovable date, hope for the best — and always plan for the worst!

Dedicating manpower

You need to find the time for a project the size of a Web site launch. Regardless of what else you have going on in your business (and your life), at the end of the day you have to dedicate your time to the cause.

Although you can hire out the bulk of the development work for your site, you need to be involved in a long string of commitments during the process, including these tasks:

✦ Find and hire a Web site designer (two to three weeks).

✦ Define the scope of the project (eight to ten hours).

✦ Decide on the site design (one to two weeks).

✦ Choose a shopping cart solution (one week).

✦ Coordinate payment-processing options (one to two days).

✦ Select inventory to stock your online store (ongoing).

✦ Create a site launch campaign (one week).

You get the idea — you're going to be busy!

Take a look at your average day and then tack on another two to three hours to it, to allow for managing site-related tasks. The time that you devote to your site includes meetings with your design team and your staff, and the time you need for decision-making. Block off at least half a day on the weekends for site work, too. You probably need to use this schedule for about three to six months.

Bridging Your Offline Store with Your Online Store

All too often, a retailer is eager to have an e-commerce alternative and then takes a somewhat haphazard approach. Most traditional entrepreneurs who are unfamiliar with the Internet tend to view the physical store and the online store as two separate and very different entities. When you treat your brick-and-mortar store and your online store differently, customers have two different experiences with your company. And, those customers become confused about which experience truly represents your brand.

Seamlessly bridge your brick-and-mortar store (your company's history) with your online store (your brand's future). With this approach, you can provide a single, cohesive user experience. Focus on these three critical areas: identity, image, and, integration.

We also show you how one company — Williams–Sonoma — does an outstanding job of meeting these three objectives.

Finding your identity

Identity incorporates all the physical characteristics that your customers associate with your store. It's your logo, your color palettes, your store layout, and any other details that contribute to your store's distinctiveness.

When you visit Williams–Sonoma, you see a lot of soft, muted, neutral colors as a backdrop on the walls. The color scheme is simple and understated. The occasional pop of color springs from the products themselves, neatly arranged as part of the in-store displays. The online version of the store has the same feel to it: A crisp white background lets featured products grab the spotlight.

Creating an image

Image incorporates not only the physical appearance of your store but also how customers perceive it. Is it considered a high-end retail store with select, but pricey, items? Or, is your store an eclectic mix of trendy yet unique gifts? Are you known for exceptional customer service? Or, do customers enjoy browsing in a low-key environment? All these details contribute to your store's image, and you want that image to carry over to your online store.

One thing that sets apart Williams–Sonoma is that it provides helpful information, often in the form of in-store demonstrations and cooking classes. The store has created an image of being a solution provider for upscale kitchen products. It has carried that image online by including recipes that incorporate cooking ingredients or products for sale on the site. The site also uses quality graphics to show you its finished product.

Integrating your shopping cart

Perhaps less visible to the customer is (ideally) the functionality of your site on the back end. In particular, you need to consider how your online inventory is managed. Your goal is to integrate the back end to work alongside your offline inventory system. For example, if a customer orders a product from your site, that product should be in stock. If it's not, you want that information to be available to the customer at the time of the order.

The technology choices you make (such as which inventory-management solutions and shopping carts you use) ultimately determine the types of buying experiences your customers have on your site. (For more information about and shopping carts and inventory management, refer to Book IV, Chapters 5 and 6, respectively.)

We really can't tell you how or whether the Williams–Sonoma online shopping cart is tied into a particular store's inventory or whether it's integrated with a shipping warehouse. Frankly, as a customer, you don't need those details. The William–Sonoma Web site gives you a good example of shopping-cart functionality, though. If the site has additional information about a particular product, a message appears at the top of your shopping cart before you check out. You can find out whether you need to expedite shipping for a holiday-themed item to arrive by a particular date or how long a product on back order might take to arrive.

Making a Flawless Transition

Granted, a national retail chain probably has a much larger budget for a Web site than you do. Even so, your smaller store can embrace the same concepts that the big boys use for a smooth, effective online transition. The best way to make this transition is to plan.

Adding an e-commerce component to your store is similar to planning a big party or a major event. Part of your plan is already in place. You already have an approximate timeframe for making your project a reality. To make it more manageable, break that timetable into three smaller chunks, or *stages:* orientation, implementation, and evaluation. For each stage, create a checklist of activities that should occur during that stage.

Stage 1: Orientation

When you're talking about moving your store online, the Orientation stage includes everything from conducting initial research to evaluating and choosing the best vendors and software applications.

Some of the tasks that you should accomplish in this stage include the ones in this list:

+ **Identify and research your competitors.** Check out the competition's sites, and even purchase items to get a feel for how their shopping carts work. Put together a list of products and price points (refer to Book IV, Chapter 6). See the section "Building an Inventory," later in this chapter, for more information about this step.

+ **Set up your Web site.** Research a hosting solution, pick a domain, and set up your server. (To find out about these tasks, refer to Book III.) Then figure out how to integrate your existing back-end solution with your online processes.

+ **Decide on payment options.** Determine which forms of payment (credit cards, PayPal, or gift certificates, for example) that you want to accept on your Web site. Contact your bank provider and ask about its options for online transactions.

+ **Evaluate shopping vendors and other customer service.** Decide whether you're going to provide live or e-mail-based support.

Take a look at Figure 1-1 to get an idea of how to start a checklist of the tasks you need to accomplish during this stage.

Stage 2: Implementation

In the Implementation stage, you move from just thinking about your Web site to making it happen. You're building the site, integrating your back-end systems, and creating offline and online marketing tools to use.

Take a look at all the research you compiled in the Orientation stage, and start making some decisions:

+ **Set a budget and a schedule.** Create these items to keep track of your money and your time.

E-tail Pre-Launch Checklist

Action Item	Result/Resources	Decision	Notes
Identify all competitors			
Research competitors			
Extensively view their sites			
Purchase products online			
Test customer service functions			
Return a product to determine how it's handled			
Maintain list of similar products/price points offered			
by competitors			
Review industry trends			
Check for domain availability			
Determine options for hosting solutions			
Compare pros/cons of third party hosting verses			
internal servers			
Locate top three shopping cart products			
Compare prices			
List capabilities			
Note limitations			

✦ **Approve the site design.** Create the *copy* (text) for the site and gather any content from other people, such as reviews and testimonials.

✦ **Go live with the site and register with search engines.** Start making your URL visible to the public.

Figure 1-2 shows how to set up a checklist to keep you on track while implementing your site.

Stage 3: Evaluation

Technically, after your site is up, the Evaluation stage never ends! You need to continuously test, review, and revise your site to maintain its functionality and appeal.

Here are some elements that you want to keep your eye on after your site goes live:

✦ **Site performance:** Check how long individual pages take to load, how many page views you're getting (refer to Book VI, Chapter 5), and whether all your links are working.

✦ **Shopping cart:** See whether the cart is working as it should.

✦ **Shipping and handling:** Make sure that orders are being fulfilled in a timely manner and that customers are happy with your service.

Figure 1-3 gives you an idea of how to start a checklist for this stage.

Implementation Checklist

Action Item	Person Responsible	Current Status	Implementation Date	Completed? __ Yes __ No
Set budget				
Create development schedule				
Develop marketing plan				
Register domain				
Hire Web developer (if applicable)				
Contract wtih Search Engine Optimization specialist (if applicable)				
Approve site design				
Approve site map				
Obtain Web hosting service				
Purchase additional hardware (if applicable)				
Initiate vendor agreements (payment processors, fulfillment, and so on)				
Select shopping cart software				
Create product list for initial launch				
Set prices				
Choose product images				
Add image tags				
Write product descriptions				
Upload products to shopping cart				
Create all Web copy				
Develop FAQ				

Figure 1-2: Keep your online store on track during development.

Post-Evaluation Checklist

Function/Area	Last Update	Current Status	Describe Known Problems/Concerns	Corrective Action	Complete By
Site Performance					
Load times					
Page views					
24/7 Access (no down times)					
All applications working properly					
Working links					
Landing Pages					
Home page					
Information current					
Graphics loading properly					
Internal/external links working					
Policies current					
Individual product pages					
Product Images					
Product Descriptions					
Customer Reviews					
Supporting Content					
External Links (to other sites/reviews)					

Figure 1-3: Conduct regular evaluations on your site.

**Book VII
Chapter 1**

Knowing When to Put Your Store Online

Building an Inventory

A big part of planning for a successful transition online involves selecting the right inventory from the start.

The pressure of choosing the best products to sell on the Internet might seem like a daunting task. Unlike other e-commerce sites that are starting from scratch, however, you have a distinct advantage: product mastery. You not only have an existing inventory, but you also know it intimately. You understand exactly what sells and what doesn't.

Consider the number of conversations you have had with customers over the years. Because of that feedback, you have a firm grasp on why your customers like a product and what they might need to know about it before making their final purchasing decisions.

That's exactly the information you need in order to move those same products online without missing a beat!

Follow these steps to begin building your online inventory:

1. **Pull together a list of your current inventory.**

    We hope that you have this list already. If not, you need to create an up-to-date and complete inventory list.

2. **Separate your current inventory into categories.**

    For example, you can group products according to which areas will help or hinder how well they sell online. These categories include

    - *Top sellers:* Items that are at the top of your moneymaking list

    - *Exclusive items:* Items that are truly unique, hard to find, or handcrafted

        If you're an approved reseller or licensed dealer for a particular product or brand, check your agreement for any conditions or terms on how or where you can sell.

    - *Shipping weight:* Heavier or bulkier items that are more expensive to ship

        You don't have to eliminate items that might be too bulky, and thus too expensive, to ship. Instead, make those items special orders and have customers e-mail or call for quotes that include shipping. Or, make the products available only for in-store pickup.

    - *Availability:* Items that are in stock or readily accessible from the manufacturer or supplier

    - *Drop-ship capability:* Items that can be shipped directly from the manufacturer or supplier, which saves your inventory space

3. **Rank your inventory.**

   List items in order from those most suitable for selling online to those least suitable. Suitable items are easy to ship, not unusual in size or shape, and are generally items that are nonperishable. Food items and products such as flowers that are perishable can sometimes be unsuitable for online sales unless you have the fastest delivery methods possible.

4. **Go online and find as many Web sites as you can that sell items similar to those in your inventory (starting with the products at the top of your list).**

   Make a record of these sites so that you can watch them as you prepare to build your store. Study the sites and determine how they compare to your store and future site. How are the competing sites branded? Are they easy to find in the search engines? Do they ship globally? What advantages and disadvantages does your store have in comparison to these stores? What do you like or dislike about how they promote the products?

5. **Compare the sticker prices of the actual products. Mark on your inventory list the products that are price competitive.**

   When you're comparing prices, factor in all the pricing considerations, including sales tax and shipping-and-handling fees.

6. **Review your inventory list and reprioritize, if you need to.**

   Move or drop those items for which you don't have a strong competitive advantage. Bump to the top of your list the products that make you shine.

   Keep this data. It not only helps you decide which items are ideal for your online inventory, but can also help guide you in promoting your products later.

7. **Determine the number of products you want to sell online.**

   Revisit your strategy. If the purpose of your site is to sell merchandise, then the more products, the better. If you're just promoting your brand, starting with a smaller amount of products might work fine. Or, you might be limited in the number of products that your shopping-cart program allows (without investing more money in a shopping cart).

   Rather than delete items, consider adding ones that aren't part of your current store inventory. Especially if vendors can drop-ship, there's nothing wrong with adding to the list, if it makes sense.

8. **Apply the *customer factor* (any customer-related information that can influence an online purchase).**

   Here's where your years of customer interaction come in handy. Evaluate the products through the eyes of your customers. Which items are difficult to sell because customers need additional information?

Can you present that information in an online product description? (Or, maybe the product sells even better online because you can give the customer additional product detail.) If the customer might see some aspect of your product in a negative way, now is the time to delete an item from your online inventory.

9. **Delete any products based on their image — or, rather, a lack of one.**

Sort through your inventory and figure out which products have photos available from a vendor or manufacturer. The quality of the product images on your Web site directly reflects the image of your store. If a high-resolution, quality photo doesn't exist, you have two choices:

- Drop the product from your online inventory.

- Spend the money to hire a professional photographer.

Although amateur pictures taken with a digital camera might work on eBay, it's probably not the quality customers expect from a retail store. Hiring a professional photographer is worth the investment.

Ask your vendor whether any marketing program incentives are available that could help offset the cost of a photo shoot. For example, you might agree to feature certain products on the home page of your site or use them in your store's offline marketing materials. In return, you might be eligible to participate in a vendor's marketing reimbursement program (which can equal several hundred dollars for a small retailer).

You need to take pictures that feature several different angles of the product. Most products sell better if a customer can see multiple views of the item; if the site offers the option to show a product being used or positioned in a setting; and if a customer can zoom in on the picture for a more detailed view.

Chapter 2: Understanding the Differences between Real and Virtual Customers

*I*f you expect your in-store customers to be identical to your online customers, you may be setting yourself up for a nasty fall. Sure, the two types of customers have some similar characteristics. But the reasons that someone buys from your retail location can be quite different from how, why, and when that person chooses to shop with you online.

Perhaps you're wondering whether these differences really matter. The short answer is yes! Your job is to entice customers to buy. To do that, you have to get to know your customers — both online and offline. In this chapter, we cover the differences between offline and online customers and how you can accommodate both of them.

Comparing Online and Offline Customers

When you launch an online store, your ultimate goal is to change the way your customers shop. Whether that means getting them to buy more or buy more often, you're hoping that your online store provides the incentive to make that change. But before you can change your customers' behaviors, you have to understand them, especially in the area of e-commerce.

Once accidental or happenstance, most online shopping is now quite purposeful. Your customers are making a conscientious decision each time they make a purchase online. To better understand their decisions, compare some of the reasons that your customers might shop in your store (real customers) as opposed to shopping online (virtual customers).

Customers showing up in your brick-and-mortar store expect these features:

✦ **Security:** Your customers may think that shopping in your store is more secure than giving out credit card information on your Web site.

✦ **Guaranteed delivery:** Sometimes, purchasing a product is a time-sensitive issue. If customers need an item in their hands by a certain time or date, shopping online may become an afterthought. This need-it-now mentality is especially true during a holiday rush.

✦ **Instant gratification:** Waiting for a product to ship isn't everyone's idea of shopping. Sometimes, customers need or want an item immediately, and shopping in a store gives that instantaneous gratification.

✦ **Loyalty:** The customers are familiar with your store and feel a connection. They often translate that into a perceived relationship with you and your employees, and these customers are quite loyal to your store. It makes them feel good to shop with you.

✦ **Service:** Having access to personalized service is a big plus for many traditional shoppers. These customers typically believe that shopping in a store is the only way to find that level of assistance, and they don't realize (or believe) that they can find quality sales support online.

✦ **Only option:** Some customers simply don't consider other buying alternatives. They may think that in-store shopping is the only option because they aren't comfortable or familiar with the Internet or don't have online access or just aren't aware that the option to shop online exists (with your particular store).

✦ **Try it before you buy it:** Some customers need to see, touch, or try on products before making a buying decision. In this case, shopping over the Internet doesn't do the trick.

✦ **Avoid extra charges:** Shipping cost is the main factor working against online shopping. Many customers decide to shop offline simply to avoid having additional shipping and handling fees tacked on to their purchases.

Virtual customers have the following expectations from your online store:

✦ **Research first:** Shopping online provides the opportunity for detailed research before making a final purchasing decision. Shoppers can find product reviews, read customer feedback, compare brands, and then make a purchase — all in a matter of minutes. Research shows that male customers are especially prone to do a little digging before they start buying online.

✦ **Hard to find items:** An item may be out of stock in a store, or it may not even be available locally. Shopping online provides access to products that aren't otherwise readily available.

✦ **Niche/specialty items:** Customers are frequently drawn to online stores because those stores provide access to specialty items, including vintage goods, collector's items, or any other type of exclusive or niche product.

✦ **Convenience:** Round-the-clock shopping is tough to beat. These customers enjoy the flexibility that comes with virtual shopping — and knowing that the store is never closed.

✦ **Value:** Although shipping costs may be of concern to an in-store shopper, an online buyer may factor in such issues as the cost of gas and time.

✦ **Price:** Comparing prices and finding the best deal online is a snap these days. That ability to get the lowdown on a price point for any given product is the reason that many buyers head straight to the Internet to shop.

✦ **Extended inventory:** Frankly, retail stores traditionally have limited shelf space. On the other hand, a Web site can house a virtually unlimited number of products — okay, maybe not unlimited, but your choice selection is typically a lot more than in traditional brick-and-mortar locations. (And products can often be *drop shipped* — ordered and shipped directly from a manufacturer or supplier.) Because many Web shoppers believe that they have access to a wider product selection online, e-commerce stores are often their first stop for shopping.

What Your Online Customers Expect from You

Customers shop online for many reasons (see the previous section to read about some of those reasons). But you need to recognize another underlying difference between real and virtual shoppers: Online customers have great expectations for your e-tail location. Sure, all customers are particular and — dare we say — demanding, but the Internet has raised the bar. It's up to you to make sure that your online store performs. In the following sections, we talk about what online customers expect of you.

**Book VII
Chapter 2**

Understanding
the Differences
between Real and
Virtual Customers

Round-the-clock hours

Most customers expect your store to be open 24 hours a day, seven days a week. Granted, meeting this need seems like a cinch. After all, after you put your site out on the Web, it's . . . there. Right? Unfortunately, running a store 24/7 involves a little bit more work. Your customers are used to having 100 percent access to online stores, whether it's midnight or midmorning. Here are a couple of site-related tasks that you may want to consider:

✦ **Customer support:** Can your customers contact you in the middle of the night and expect to receive an answer? Or, will prospective buyers receive help only during normal business hours? Ultimately, that's your call. But you have to decide the rules up front and then let your customers know.

✦ **Routine maintenance:** Maintenance includes any factor from your server going down (and your store being temporarily offline) to a glitch in your payment gateway provider that may prevent credit cards from being processed. When you're open for business around the clock, it helps to have a backup plan for all the things that could go wrong when you're not at the helm. Customers aren't much concerned with those problems — it's just as easy for them to sail over to a competitor's site to find what they want when they need it.

To ensure that your online store is always running and fully functioning, try a 24/7 site-monitoring service. Server Check Pro from Keynote NetMechanic monitors your server every 15 minutes and immediately reports problems. You can try the service for free for eight hours. Register at www.net mechanic.com/products/SCP_FreeSample.shtml.

A variety of payment methods

Accepting multiple forms of payment is an absolute necessity online. Customers may be more forgiving when they shop in your retail location, because they can whip out a checkbook or cash. In the world of Web retail, customers simply leave your store and surf over to a competitor. Of course, online payment options extend beyond traditional bank cards. See Book IV, Chapter 4 about the wealth of payment options you can make available to your customers.

Everything a customer could want, plus the kitchen sink

Virtual inventory is a big component in e-commerce. It doesn't matter whether you store all your products in a warehouse behind your retail location or have orders drop-shipped from a supplier. Customers want you to provide a large selection of choices, including everything you have available in your retail location. In addition, customers expect you to be well stocked — at all times.

If a product is on back order or temporarily out of stock, your customers expect to be notified before they start the checkout process.

Some shopping cart programs have a feature that displays a message when a product is running low, such as "Only 2 Left." If your software can't display such a message, manually add the disclaimer "Almost Out" to your product description when inventory of your best sellers gets low.

Details, details, details

Savvy Web shoppers are spoiled by the amount of information they can find at the stroke of a key. But too much information can overwhelm customers and distract them from purchasing. Thus, your challenge is to anticipate which information a shopper really needs (and wants) to know about a product and then provide that info (and only that info) in a succinct and accessible manner. The following list gives you some of the most sought-after product information:

✦ **Product descriptions:** Listing the color and style of a coffee table is helpful, but if you leave out its dimensions, customers will hesitate to make a purchase. You need to make all the details of a product available to your customer. The trick is to offer the information in layers. In other words, give a brief description of the product, along with a photo, but then give customers the option to click a link for more details or additional photos.

✦ **Reviews:** Customer reviews came into vogue after Amazon.com made them popular on its own site. Providing easy access to reviews by experts or other credible sources (such as magazines) is also a hot demand from online customers.

✦ **Delivery options:** Customers want to understand, at the absolute least, the different methods of delivery your site offers. This information includes the provider of the service (the U.S. Postal Service, UPS, Federal Express, or some other shipping company), the delivery options (for example, Express or Ground), and the cost. In addition, if you're using a private shipping company, customers want to have access to a shipping number and a direct link to track the delivery status of their packages.

✦ **Contact information:** Make sure that customers can always easily find your phone number and e-mail address. (And then make sure that you respond when a customer contacts you!)

✦ **Return policies:** People seldom ask about return and exchange policies before making a purchase at a brick-and-mortar store. The customer doesn't think about these policies until he's back at the store, standing in line to return the item. But online shoppers usually figure that they should get the scoop long before they make that final purchase. Especially when buying clothing or perishable items, your customers want to be reassured that they can get a fair deal if something goes wrong when they receive the products.

Methods for coping with the holiday rush

Having your return policy clearly accessible is certainly a plus during a busy holiday season. But that's just the bare minimum. Keep in mind that customer expectations really peak at holiday time. And not just at Christmas — your business probably has a seasonal period when demand peaks. Whenever your holiday rush occurs, you can prepare for it in the following ways:

✦ **Offer rush deliveries:** Your delivery company may not have a problem with rush delivery, but you need to make sure that you can get the items packed and out the door to meet the hectic pace.

✦ **Extend delivery times:** Again, you just need to handle those last-minute orders that arrive the day before (or the day of) the major holiday. Whether or not you can extend your delivery times often

**Book VII
Chapter 2**

Understanding
the Differences
between Real and
Virtual Customers

depends on whether you have enough help behind the scenes to keep filling those orders.

✦ **Stock up on inventory**: There's nothing worse than running out of a hot item and finding out that you can't get more in until after the holiday. You may want to go a little heavy on your inventory or alert your suppliers to the potential of increased demand.

✦ **Bulk up on service representatives:** Customers don't hesitate to ask for help when it comes to holiday shopping.

Although the busiest retail season is typically November and December, other holiday periods also drive sales. According to recent research, online sales heat up during Valentine's Day, Easter, and Mother's Day (for example).

Flexibility

When you have both an online and offline location, you're in a unique predicament. The good news is that you have the opportunity to substantially boost your sales because you can address customers from both ends of the spectrum, so to speak. The flip side is that customers expect you to be more accommodating.

Returns are an example. If a customer buys from your Web site, she may want to be able to return the item to your store. If this return method doesn't work for you, think about how you can go out of your way to make your policy clear at the time of purchase. Similarly, if you have a special promotion in your store, customers expect to get the same deal online. (The opposite applies, too.)

As long as you give your customers plenty of options for shopping in all your locations, you may have a distinct advantage in the marketplace. Lamps Plus.com has a Store Locator feature (see Figure 2-1), which helps customers find information about any of its many brick-and-mortar locations across the west coast. Each location page includes a detailed map and store phone number, along with a photo of the actual store.

Superior customer service

At the heart of the difference in shopping online, as opposed to in a store, is the customer service. The level of support that you provide your online customers is one of the single most influential factors in whether those customers return to your site to buy again. You probably don't doubt that superior service is important in your store. But a high level of service is even more important online because customers are limited in their ability to interact with your products. Customers depend on you to provide as much information about a product as you can so that they can make an immediate buying decision. They can't pick up a product and examine it up close. If you don't have enough detail on your Web site or a customer has an unusual question, you want that customer to be able to reach you.

Figure 2-1:
Allow online customers to find your offline store.

Fortunately, offering exceptional customer service from your site has gotten pretty darn easy. The technology is readily available, and implementing it doesn't cost you an arm and a leg. Here are a few of the ways you can reach out to your customers:

✦ **E-mail:** One of the easiest ways to provide customers with information about your products is by letting them contact you by e-mail. You can make shopping easy by posting a customer service e-mail address throughout your site. And remember to respond in a timely manner — within a 24-hour period.

Use an automated responder to automatically generate a return e-mail which notifies your customer that you received the e-mail she sent. In the confirmation e-mail, include the typical waiting period for a response and give a phone number as a quicker alternative for contacting you.

✦ **Phone:** Clearly posting a direct phone number so that shoppers can access customer support is an absolute must. If you can swing it, get yourself a toll-free number! If you don't have a 24-hour support line, be sure to post the normal operating hours of customer service.

✦ **Live chat:** Although some online shoppers like the anonymity that the Internet provides, many more demand instantaneous support, such as they might find in your brick-and-mortar store. To answer that need, consider offering "standby" customer support representatives through live chat technology. This tool helps customers immediately connect to a person who can answer their questions (either through an instant-messenger-style format or audio over the computer).

**Book VII
Chapter 2**

Understanding
the Differences
between Real and
Virtual Customers

Most live-chat software providers offer a free trial if you purchase the software directly from their Web sites. You can find one of the least expensive products by using Livehelper (`www.livehelper.com`).

Figure 2-2 shows the customer service options that Lampsplus.com offers, which include e-mail, live chat, personal callback, and a toll-free number.

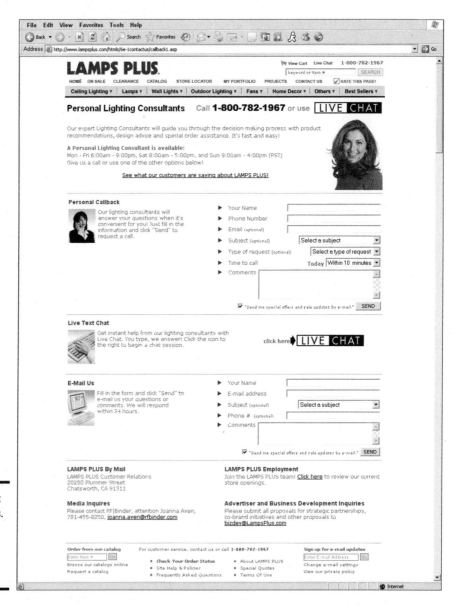

Figure 2-2: Lampsplus.com gives customer service options.

Establishing Patterns

Getting customers to buy from you (at any location) comes down to establishing buying patterns. You help form your customers' buying patterns by helping them develop the habit of coming to *you* as opposed to a competitor. After you understand your customers and what they want, you're in a position to start creating that pattern. To establish a buying pattern with your customers, you need to achieve three things as an e-tailer:

+ **Information source:** Your site is a place to shop, but it's also a resource for product information. After you establish yourself as an authority on your product lines, customers begin making a conscious decision to go to you first.

+ **Buying opportunities:** Experienced Web shoppers aren't looking strictly for information. They want a reason to buy, too. You can give them access to regular specials or limited-time-only offers, exclusive sales, and select or new merchandise to convince them to buy.

+ **Reliability:** In addition to providing a good inventory and terrific customer service, the entire buying process at your site has to pass muster — from the time your customer pulls up your home page to the point that the purchased product is delivered to her doorstep. When you have the opportunity to prove yourself as a reliable retailer (and use that opportunity), customers get used to coming to you to shop.

**Book VII
Chapter 2**

Understanding
the Differences
between Real and
Virtual Customers

Chapter 3: Window Dressing for the Online Display

In This Chapter

✓ Revealing your store's unique identity

✓ Organizing your store so that customers can find anything

✓ Designing a site that convinces your visitors to become customers

As a brick-and-mortar retailer, you probably gave a great deal of attention and thought to your store's appearance — the selection of paint colors, the placement of shelving, and even the way each product is positioned for display. You probably agonized for days, if not weeks, over each decision — and for good reason, too.

Major retailers spend a substantial amount of time and money sorting through the same details. And, when they find that perfect look, it becomes a blueprint for every store that follows.

Why go to all this trouble? Your goal in creating a positive shopping environment is to increase your sales. That process begins with the look of your store. And, the way products are arranged contributes to that overall feeling or mood. Customers will buy more if they're comfortable shopping in your store, can find what they need, and are treated well. The same statement holds true for your online store. So, in this chapter, we show you how to map out your very own online-store blueprint!

Creating the Right Look for Your Online Store

Imagine for a moment that one of your customers is blindfolded and brought into your store (without knowing where she is being taken). After the blindfold is removed, the customer should be able to tell that she's in your store. For example, do you carry specialty products or a line of signature items? Do you use bright, unconventional colors on the walls?

Transferring your physical image, or *identity,* to your online store is a major part of creating the right look for your site. As with anything else, you can go overboard. That's why we recommend starting the process by picking out a single element that you believe customers most readily identify with your store. The main factor that makes your store special may be one of these features:

✦ **Architectural element:** Maybe the shape of your store's building makes it stand out. Or, perhaps you designed the interior with special features, such as high vaulted ceilings, curved walls, or dramatic windows. Sometimes, the physical appearance of your location leaves a lasting impression.

✦ **Color scheme:** The interior and exterior of your store may be filled with soft, muted tones or wild and bright, eye-popping colors. Either way, these telling color combinations may provide your customers with a strong association with your store.

✦ **Location:** Some stores take their images directly from their surroundings. For example, you may be located in a trendy, upscale part of your city. Or, maybe you're part of an eclectic revitalization of a downtown area. Then again, your customers may know you best as "that shop by the beach!" Your store may be associated with a vacation hot spot or well-known tourist destination.

✦ **Theme:** Your store may be created around a particular theme, such as birthday parties or business travel.

✦ **Event or activity:** Perhaps you hold an annual event that's closely tied to the image of your store. Or, maybe you have certain ongoing activities that draw attention.

✦ **People:** Every once in a while, a store is less about the products it sells and more identifiable with the person who owns it. So maybe you're a pseudocelebrity — or an outright famous person! Either way, if that's the case, your personal image may be most closely tied to the image of your store.

✦ **Selection:** Superstore retailers are known for offering a wide variety of products. Although you may not compete at that level, you may be best known for your extensive selection of a particular brand or type of product.

✦ **Price:** Ah, price. You may be on the superexclusive high end or the rock-bottom low end.

✦ **Customer service:** During a time when many stores compete on price alone, retailers (particularly smaller ones) that focus on customer service receive lots of attention. If customer service is your forte, that may be what customers remember most about you.

✦ **Niche:** Maybe you specialize in Mexican pottery, collectible Disney products, or nostalgic items from the 1950s. If you have a streamlined product base that appeals to a highly targeted customer base, you can bet that this specialization makes up your total image.

Your offline store identity gives you a starting point for your Web site design. As you build your site, if you get off-track from the image you want to project, this element gives you a clear place to return. It's a guideline.

Similarly, after you begin promoting your online store, having a single element related to your image gives you a useful tie-in for advertisements, promotions, and marketing materials. And, even though this identifier is what you're best known for in your local (offline) market, it can become a unique selling point in a crowded online marketplace.

Creating the Perfect Shopping Experience

The right image is just the beginning. The look of an online store can be nearly flawless, but after you open that door (or enter the Web site), you may find a different story. Regardless of your store's image on the outside, if customers have difficulties with the actual shopping experience inside, you can quickly lose those customers.

As a shopkeeper, you have to make great strides to carry your complete image from the outside in. For an online store, that inside image is all about organization.

For example, any large bookseller probably has thousands and thousands of books packing the shelves and tables of its store. Yet every book has its place. Each one is neatly categorized according to subject matter, release dates, clearance items, sales, or even product type (books, magazines, greeting cards, and gifts, for example). With all this managed chaos, the store still has room for wide aisles, chairs and sofas, and an entire coffee shop!

When you visit the online version of the bookstore, you should find the same strategy at play. The navigation provides clear choices that mimic the categories you find in the store.

To achieve this level of detail online, start by taking a tour of your brick-and-mortar location. Think about all the ways that you categorize products to make shopping (and inventory management) easy. These categories often include

+ **Brand name:** People shop by designer labels and other recognized brands.

+ **Product type or style:** These distinctions can even be product categories within categories. For example, a drugstore might carry makeup, books, and school supplies. You can divide the categories further by lipsticks and eye shadows, bestsellers and bargain books, and pens and notebooks.

+ **Price:** Though it may be more difficult to do in your offline store, you can allow online customers to sort products based on price (from high to low or from low to high).

✦ **Sale or clearance items:** Everybody likes a bargain. Your customers are no different, and they appreciate when a bargain is easy to spot.

✦ **Discontinued items:** These products won't be produced any more, and especially with collectibles, customers want to know that they won't be able to find these items on the shelves (real or virtual) any more.

✦ **New releases (or just in):** Books and DVDs aren't the only items that are classified this way. Products are continually being updated, or new items are introduced within a product line. Even if an item isn't hot off the press for the manufacturer, it may be the first time you have it in your store.

✦ **Solution:** Increasingly, products are categorized by the problem they help customers solve. In books, you can find an entire section of self-help categories, for example. You can probably categorize your products in a similar fashion (for example, kitchen tools and bathroom cleaners).

Organizing your products in categories

However you categorize products, carrying your retail store's organization through to your online store isn't difficult. It just takes some, well . . . organization.

You may not realize (or may have forgotten) how and why you placed your products the way you have in your brick-and-mortar store. Follow these steps to refresh your memory and come up with a plan to organize your online store:

1. **Draw a diagram of the inside of your retail store.**

Your diagram doesn't have to be drawn to scale. But the drawing should clearly show the layout of your store, including shelving units, display cases, and doorways.

2. **On a separate piece of paper, make a corresponding list of all the items you have displayed.**

This step helps you make an inventory of everything that's placed out on the floor (where customers shop) and detail where it's displayed. Label shelves and tables in your store diagram with numbers or letters. The corresponding list should indicate which products are stored where, and you should include why you organize them that way.

3. **Create a list of your top-selling items.**

Pull this list from your store's inventory and sales reports. When you have your list, look to see where those top-selling items are located in your store. Do you see any noticeable patterns?

4. **Identify your merchandising hot spots.**

Your *merchandising hot spots* are the places that receive the most attention because of their physical location within the store. Items next to your cash register, in your front window (if you have one), and near the front door where customers can see them when they walk into the store are all examples of merchandising hot spots.

5. **Group your products into categories that you want to use online.**

Take your preferred product groupings and incorporate them into your Web site's site map. Basically, you're merchandising your online store by using the identifiable trends from your offline location.

One product can appear in several different categories. Your shopping cart software should allow you to easily cross reference items in multiple categories.

Offering a search function

In addition to creating a plan for the layout of your online store, you can offer customers another critical organizational function: a Web-based search tool.

You're probably familiar with using Google or Yahoo! to search the Internet for keywords. Well, online stores have found that the same kind of tool is a true boon to business. Again, think about it in comparison to your store: A customer can come in and ask a sales associate where something is located in your store. Online shoppers, however, have to depend on using the clues on your site's menu bar. Including a search function on your home page eliminates customers having to guess in which category they can find a certain product.

Not all search functions are created equal, especially when your online store deals with thousands of products. Make sure that customers can search by using the smallest detail (such as a brief product description, a brand name, or even color) and still find what they want.

Look for a search tool that

+ **Searches by a specific keyword term:** If you type a specific keyword, such as `cereal dispenser`, the search returns all similar items. Figure 3-1 shows the search results on Organize.com.

+ **Sorts the results:** Customers should be able to sort their search terms. Organize.com allows them to search by price, category, and relevance (see Figure 3-2). The additional sorting function prevents a large number of results from overwhelming customers.

Figure 3-1:
A search
should
return all
products
similar to
the search
term.

Figure 3-2:
Customers
can sort
the results
further.

✦ **Displays similar or complementary items:** When customers click a
product, they should see a list of items that they might be interested in
buying, based on the original search term.

✦ **Show customers specific banner ads or promotions:** Customers should
see ads targeted specifically to them, based on the results of their keyword searches. Targeted ads can convert more buyers to your site.

Beyond Window Shopping: Designs that Lure Traffic

A good site design makes attracting buyers to your site much easier. Not only do the aesthetics of your site matter, but you also need functionality. These elements can keep your site's traffic flowing (and, you hope, converting to sales!):

✦ **General appearance:** Research indicates that shoppers are more likely to purchase from a site that has a professional and trustworthy appearance. Although nothing's wrong with fun and wacky (if it fits your product), just make sure that you also show that you're responsible. For example, clearly display your terms of agreement, return policies, and contact information, and make sure that you have a reliable shopping cart program.

✦ **Remove clutter:** Resist the urge to pack your site's pages full of information, promotions, and product choices. When a site has too much going on, a customer becomes overwhelmed. Rather than buy, the customer flees.

✦ **Simplicity:** Keep both the graphical design of your site and the information you provide simple. The phrase "less is more" is one to take to heart when selling online.

✦ **Good navigation:** A sure way to convert visitors to buyers is with your site's ease of navigation. Shoppers should be able to move from one place to another on your site relatively easily. And, your navigation system should be fairly intuitive so that a customer clearly understands how your site is structured.

✦ **Links:** Set up your site so that customers don't have to click many links to reach their destination.

✦ **Layered information:** You may want to give customers the option to go deeper into the site in order to find more detailed information. You simply have to provide the details in layers. Usually, you see layering when a product is displayed with a photo and general description. If a customer wants to know the item's exact dimensions or see alternative views of the product, he can do so by clicking the next link (or layer) of product detail.

✦ **Cash register:** From an easy checkout process to the opportunity to *suggestive sell* (offer up similar products or useful items, such as batteries), the function of the cash register — or shopping cart — program is one of the most important elements of good design.

✦ **Product display:** Provide customers with clear headlines, good images, and detailed information. The basic information, such as an item's price and how to purchase it, should be clearly displayed.

✦ **Special promotions:** Offering discounts or limited-time offers is a good way to convert buyers. But these specials don't do you any good if a person can't find those offers or the offers aren't in line with what a person is buying (or shopping for). Carefully place targeted promotions within your site to make them effective.

Having good design and the right image for your Web site isn't that different from what you already do in your brick-and-mortar store.

Chapter 4: Making In-Store Customers Loyal Online Shoppers

In This Chapter

✔ Pairing your storefront and your Web site in your customers' minds

✔ Making in-store customers an online offer (they can't refuse)

✔ Supporting and informing your customers

✔ Giving customers a starring role

Some people who operate traditional brick-and-mortar storefronts don't consider what others may see as obvious: the connection between their storefront customers and their online business. These store owners may be concerned that if the brick-and-mortar customers start using the Web sites, customers may stop visiting the store, buy less often, or even forget about the store altogether.

A customer is a customer is a customer, whether she walks through the front door or pulls up the home page of the Web site.

In reality, the more options you give your customers, the better chance you have of keeping them. Having your in-store customers take advantage of your online business can increase revenues — both in-store and online — and create a longer-lasting, more valuable customer overall. Although some businesses have shut their doors permanently and moved online, most store owners find a healthy mix of the two venues. And, the increased range of options that this dual presence offers customers makes ringing up purchases at both sites more appealing to those customers.

In this chapter, we describe how you can go about grooming your customers to embrace both in-store and online buying. Specifically, we tell you how to introduce your offline (in-store) customers to the power and potential of also shopping with you online. We detail some strategies and techniques you can use to take advantage of the dual mediums and how they can feed off each other.

Benefiting Customers (And Your Business) with In-Store and Online Synergy

Customers look at an online store much differently if they know that a physical storefront goes along with it. Sometimes, a customer just likes knowing that he can drive down to a real building and talk to a real person if something goes wrong with his online order. At other times, the cleanliness, professionalism, or range of options that your physical store shows off tells the customer, "Hey, Joel's Electronics knows its stuff. Buying online from the Web site is just like walking through the store." The goodwill that you generate in-store acts in your favor online, and these venues come together in your customers' minds in the following ways:

✦ **A physical presence builds customer confidence:** Your in-store customers form an impression about your business before they even walk through the door. The mere fact that you have a physical presence gives many customers the confidence that you're a reputable business, and that feeling can encourage them to trust your online business as well. Many stores, sometimes called *pure plays,* operate only online and don't have the chance to build up confidence until a customer completes a successful transaction with them.

One of the best examples of a successful pure play e-tailer is Amazon. com. Amazon built its business from scratch and never allowed customers to interact with it physically. Because of this lack of physical presence, Amazon cannot expand its market share beyond Internet users.

✦ **Selling your goods online makes your store always open:** This is the always-on effect of the Internet. Customers can shop in your online store 24 hours a day and 7 days a week, from the comfort of their homes and their favorite pajamas, without the hassle of getting ready, driving down to your store, fighting traffic, finding a parking spot, and dealing with other customers walking in front of them as they wait in line to pay and leave (in order to get back in the car, fight traffic again, drive home, unload — you get the idea).

Your online store has to be always on and available to take orders. Unlike your physical store, which has specific opening and closing hours, your online store must stay open to serve customers at their convenience. You can't close it for other than brief periods (which you may need to do in order to perform maintenance on your Web site software). Because your online customers may shop at nonstandard hours, you need to have your store hosted on an Internet server that's supported around the clock, in case a problem crops up at 2 a.m. And, if you run your online store from home over a high-speed connection, make sure to always leave that computer on and connected.

✦ **An online store gives your customers access to unlimited shelf space:** Anyone who has had to rearrange an in-store aisle display knows how valuable that retail floor space can be, and most stores have to carefully plan how to use every last square foot without overwhelming the customer. Online stores suffer from no such physical restrictions. You can offer one or one million items on the same site with the same amount of screen space, and you can store the actual inventory in less expensive warehouse or industrial space rather than in the costly retail space.

Enticing Customers to Your Online Offering

Of course, for your in-store customers to become online shoppers as well, they have to know about your new store location (online, that is!). So use the advantage of having that customer in your brick-and-mortar store to advertise and promote your e-store. Whenever you make an in-store sale, you have the perfect opportunity to inform and entice that customer with the lure of the Web.

Publicizing your Web presence

Make a big deal about your move to the Web by showing off the name of your online business — and the *URL* (Web address) of your online store — in your physical store and in all the transactions that take place there. We're not saying that you have to draw 6-foot letters on every wall or plaster every window with gigantic URL addresses, but you definitely have to incorporate your online store name and URL into all your store literature and promotional space. This opportunity to promote your e-store includes items such as

✦ **Business cards:** Leave your business cards (with your e-store name and address highlighted) next to the cash register and throw one into the package with every customer's purchase.

✦ **Sales flyers:** Integrate your Web site address into every flyer, most likely along the bottom. Add a blurb on the flyer that says "Check us out online at. . . ." Even include online discount codes on the flyer that allow the customer to shop online during the sale at the same discount.

✦ **Cash registers and counter displays:** In addition to keeping your business cards prominently displayed next to the register, add a small sign to your cash register, and perhaps add a small counter display with a brochure or one-page flyer that someone can pick up and read while waiting to check out.

✦ **Outside windows:** These panes of glass are always visible and can include a sticker or display mentioning that you're online. This technique is especially valuable if you get a lot of foot traffic, such as at a shopping mall or strip center.

✦ **Receipts:** Customers may throw away your shopping bags, your business cards, and your sales flyers, but they're likely to look at their purchase receipts again — at least once. Include your Web address on the receipt, and check out the section "Showing shoppers the money," later in this chapter, for more ideas about using receipts.

✦ **Shopping bags:** When it's time to reorder those shopping bags with your name and logo, insert an extra line that mentions your URL address.

✦ **Company delivery trucks:** Add an extra decal or section that features your URL address and your online store.

Mentioning your online store's name isn't limited to including it on literature and promotional materials. Train your sales associates to casually mention your online store when talking with customers. This reference can be a simple statement made to customers during checkout — for example, "Hey, you can also check out our Internet store at Myonlinestore.com." Or, when a customer asks about an item, have your employees say, "You know, we're out of that item here, but you can order it from us on the Web at Myonlinestore.com."

Some stores have added computer kiosks that allow people to shop the online store while at the physical store. What a perfect way to connect these two shopping opportunities in your customers' minds! Besides access to online items, an in-store kiosk has another advantage for shoppers: ready-made customer support. If customers have questions about online shopping while at the kiosk, they can receive immediate and personal help from an in-store sales associate.

Displaying your online goods in-store

Although promoting your online store presence is the first step, it surely isn't the last. Some store owners have an interesting tendency to hide their online-only merchandise at the back of the store because customers can't buy it immediately and take it home. We think that store owners are missing a valuable opportunity: Take advantage of your customers' immediate presence by showing off the items you have for sale online, whether these items are part of your online inventory or are unique items that you're selling on an online auction, such as eBay.

Make sure that any online-only items that you display in-store are clearly marked with a note along the lines of "Hey, find me online at Myonlinestore. com" or "This product is up for sale under my eBay ID myonlinestoreid." Some people even print little cards or slips of paper with the information on how to find that item online so that customers can take the slip with them for reference when shopping at home. The physical presence of merchandise with the sign not only reminds in-store customers that you're online as well; it also allows customers to see, hold, feel, move around, and inspect the item before they buy it.

When creating these helpful shopping slips for your customers, don't forget to include directions to find items through the special links of your affiliate programs, as we talk about in Book IV, Chapter 2. You can earn more money when your customers follow these links.

Definitely pay attention to the reactions of customers who look at your online-only items. Here are some ideas for handling questions and gleaning information from these reactions:

✦ **If customers ask whether they can buy an item right away (in-store!):** Tell them why it's only available online. Online auction items are the easiest to explain because you can say something like this: "Well, this item is so unique that I want all my customers to have an equal chance to purchase it. The fairest way to give everyone an opportunity is to list it in an online auction on eBay."

✦ **If you're selling something online that you pay for only after the customer has ordered it:** Tell your customer, "I'm testing this new product by ordering it from someone on consignment. That's why I need for you to order it online." If enough customers insist on being able to buy this item at your store, their input becomes valuable sales data about which products to carry in-store!

The feedback and opinion sharing related to your online offerings can help both your real and virtual stores improve. And, making improvements based on the feedback shows your customers that you're listening to what they say and using their input, which can lead to greater loyalty and enthusiasm.

Showing shoppers the money

Every store owner has an opinion about the value of coupons or special discounts. But most owners agree that offering special values definitely helps generate additional sales — otherwise, you would never see all those half-off sales or the gobs of weekly coupons that arrive in your mail. Generating sales for online stores is no different, and one of the best ways for you to introduce your in-store customers to your online store is to offer a coupon or special discount that they can use only online.

The following list describes a couple of ways you can offer specials that may entice customers to your online store:

✦ **Print a special card that you slip into every customer's bag:** Use this card to invite shoppers to check out your online store and save 10 percent on their first order. You can have your sales associates hand out to your best customers a special coupon offering free shipping if they buy from you online. Or, you can have a display next to the cash register telling people that your online store is offering a new product this month at a special price.

✦ **Print special discount or coupon information directly on your sales receipt:** We tell you to print your online store's name and Web address right on your sales receipts (see the section "Publicizing your Web presence," earlier in this chapter), and we think that you should do the same with online discounts or coupons. Check with your cash register's maker and find out which capabilities your register has to generate special codes or discount offers that print with a customer's normal receipt.

If you decide to print special discount codes on your in-store customers' receipts, don't forget to update your online store with the new discount code before you start handing out those receipts. Don't risk the wrath — or, worse, the lost confidence — of the online shopper whose discount code doesn't work!

Your discount or coupon doesn't have to be a complete giveaway. Many companies tie the discount to a form or survey that the customer fills out online. This way, you entice in-store customers to answer a few questions about your online store, and when those customers finish the survey, they receive a special code that they can use for their discount. A helpful example of this survey incentive comes from the fast food industry: Restaurants print a special receipt with a survey URL and code, and everyone who fills out the survey also enters a drawing for money or earns free food on a future visit.

Providing a Positive Shopping Experience

The best way to encourage your in-store customers to also shop online is to make sure that all your sales processes work together. How customers buy goods from you — at the cash register or by way of an Internet Web browser — shouldn't affect how they can interact with you. When you combine the capabilities of your in-store and online processes, you can offer some interesting advantages to your customers that an online-only store never can.

Keeping friendly, flexible policies

Making the sales process smooth for your customers and giving them options for how the process works are effective ways to cultivate customer loyalty. Make sure that your online shoppers can pick up at your physical store any (or most) items that they buy online. Although many people thoroughly enjoy the convenience of shopping online, a lot of them are unwilling to pay the shipping charges to have items delivered to their house.

For other shoppers, the emphasis is on immediate gratification. That is, they see items online, click the Buy button, pay for the items with their credit cards, and want to receive the items right away. In-store pickup allows these impatient shoppers to do just that — and it gives you a chance to sell them more items when they arrive to pick up their online purchases. Even big businesses are encouraging in-store pickup. For example, Wal-Mart provides free shipping when customers order products at Walmart.com and use the SiteToStore option to pick up their items from their local stores.

Offering impeccable customer support

You can never go wrong by keeping customer support and convenience in mind. Offer a return policy stating that customers can bring items they purchased online back into your physical store for a refund or credit. This way, you not only save the postage cost of having items mailed back to you, but you also gain the face-to-face opportunity to help customers and smooth over any perceived problems from the purchases they initially made. If you already have your physical store open for business, why not take advantage of it to offer superb customer support?

Some customers who shopped online for convenience don't want to get in the car and drive over to return the item. But at least you offer the option, and letting customers know that they have the opportunity for in-store returns is comfort enough. Who knows? They may walk in to return an item and walk out with a shopping bag of new items.

Enlightening your shoppers

For many customers, in-store interaction is the best part of their shopping experience. They take the time to come into the store so that they can ask questions, gain knowledge and expertise, or hear the opinion of the "expert" in that field — namely, you as the store owner or manager. Online stores build that type of interaction through the use of newsletters, which you may already produce for your brick-and-mortar store. These newsletters can be a mixture of articles, tips and tricks, featured items, and anything else related to your store — whether it's an in-store promotional event or a feature on your employee of the month. Here are some ideas for promoting online activities with your newsletter:

✦ **Feature your online store and any special online promotions.** You may only need to display the store's URL where customers can see it, and maybe print a discount code or highlight a special Web page. If you want to expand your coverage to either increase sales for your online store or encourage a shift in offline shopping behavior, you can include profiles of online store items, online auctions for the store, or testimonials about an online sale. Doing so provides an important and powerful reminder to your customers about your online store, such as the familiarity they now have when walking into your store.

✦ **Have printed copies of the newsletter available at the store.** You may want to include a newsletter with any in-store purchase. You're not forcing the interaction — you're simply making in-store customers aware of the different options they have when shopping with you.

✦ **Offer customers the opportunity to sign up in the store for a free monthly newsletter that's delivered to their e-mail addresses.** You can simply place next to the cash register or information desk a clipboard with a sign-up sheet for the customer's name and e-mail address. Or, you can have the sales clerk ask for an e-mail address during checkout and receive permission from the customer to send out the newsletter. The best way to entice people to agree to receive your newsletter is by offering a discount or promotion or special advice that they can find only in the newsletter.

Making Your Customer the Star

We encourage you to make your customers the stars of your show. One way you can encourage in-store customers to check out your online store (and, you hope, check out with some purchases in their online shopping carts) is to involve them in the online presence. Take pictures of your retail store and your in-store customers, and feature these pictures in your online storefront. Do surveys of customers who shop both in-store and online, and feature those testimonials on the Web site.

Most people love to see their name in lights — whether it's a neon sign or a backlit computer screen — and if your customers know that they might (or will be) featured, they will not only log in to see it but (chances are) also tell their friends, neighbors, co-workers, and even their daughter's soccer team about it.

Making your customers the "stars of the show" builds excellent word-of-mouth advertising, and the feedback that you receive from surveys and testimonials gives you valuable data about how to improve or update your online store. Putting your in-store customers in the spotlight also shows your online customers how fun, personal, and interactive your physical store can be, which may create the bonus effect of turning loyal online shoppers into loyal in-store customers.

Chapter 5: Staying Local, Getting Mobile with M-Commerce

In This Chapter

✔ Understanding different types of mobile commerce for retailers and e-tailers

✔ Sending text alerts

✔ Building business with mobile coupons

✔ Targeting local customers online

*I*n an increasingly competitive environment, you have to make every possible effort to reach customers and convince them to buy from you. For storefront locations, you need to not only reach out from your Web site but also draw local online shoppers to your location. This is where mobile commerce — *m-commerce* — offers unique advantages to both e-tailers and traditional retailers looking to extend their brands online.

For the most part, m-commerce refers to the way companies use cellphones or other mobile devices, such as PDAs, to market and sell to customers. If you own a cellphone, chances are good that you have already experienced mobile commerce. Here are some examples:

✦ Pay a bill by entering a specific code into your cellphone.

✦ Vote for a contestant on a reality show by texting a short numerical message.

✦ Receive a text message from a favorite store, alerting you to an exclusive bargain.

All these examples demonstrate m-commerce, and more applications are on the way. In fact, the value of mobile transactions is expected to exceed $300 billion by the year 2013, according to Jupiter Research (www.jupiter research.com). That's not all: IMS Research indicates that the number of active mobile banking and payment-service users is also set to increase by more than 662 percent, by 2012!

One reason for these staggering predictions is technology. Many mobile phones can access the Internet and make transactions with speeds and functionality similar to those of a desktop computer.

You can find more about mobile commerce from the Mobile Marketing Association at `www.mmaglobal.com`.

In this chapter, we offer you a glimpse of how m-commerce is poised to change the way customers buy in the future and how you can capitalize on existing mobile applications to increase sales now.

Distinguishing Between Different Types of Mobile Commerce

Here are some ways you can now use mobile commerce, all of which we discuss in greater detail in the following sections:

✦ **SMS alerts:** Short Message Service, or SMS alerts, is one of the most popular methods of mobile commerce. Companies use SMS to send short text messages to their customers' cellphones. As an example, *Allure* magazine sends subscribers who have chosen to receive text alerts daily or weekly messages about contests and bargains. The goal is to drive subscribers to the magazine's Web site, to keep them actively engaged with the magazine and potentially drive subscriber rates for their magazine.

✦ **Text to buy:** Some savvy marketing companies have begun testing an instant gratification type of application for mobile commerce. With text-to-buy, companies place traditional advertisements for a specific product on billboards, in television or radio commercials, and in print ads. Included in the ad is a special numerical code (usually a short string of numbers or letters). The consumer enters the code into a cellphone and buys the product.

Text-to-buy ads are an effective way to strike while the iron is hot, or to get a customer to buy while he's thinking about the product he just saw in an ad.

✦ **Mobile coupons:** Some people may still be reluctant to make a purchase by using a cellphone, but you can still reach out to them. By using mobile coupons (m-coupons), you can send coupons to customers by cellphone. Customers can then go online or to your physical location, provide the coupon code, and make a purchase. Just like that, the customer gets a good deal and you get a bump in sales.

Although not all these examples may be readily available for your online store, you can expect the trend to grow.

Twitter

Another unique way of using the cellphone to communicate with customers is Twitter (www.twitter.com). This young technology company has rocketed into the spotlight as a way for individuals and companies to hold and follow short conversations with each other. Unlike having a conversation with just a single person, Twitter allows an unlimited number of people to follow your conversation and lets you follow or track dozens or hundreds (or more) of conversations by others. It was created based on asking the question "What are you doing?" Entries at Twitter (which is set up similar to a blog in appearance) are short text messages — no more than 140 characters — which makes them easy to use with mobile devices. Users must register with Twitter and then identify conversations they want to follow or start their own conversations.

As an e-tailer, your customers can follow weekly, daily, or even hourly updates on the status of a release of a hot new product, such as a video game. Or, a traditional retailer might be opening a new store or hosting a special event, and customers can follow updates about it by using Twitter. As this free service continues to develop, look for innovative new ways to turn occasional customers into a community of loyal followers for your brand!

To find out who might be looking for information about your store or site, use the Twitter search function to track conversations by inserting keywords. For example, if your online store is MyPlace.com, just enter that name into the search box and Twitter pulls all current and archived conversations in which your site's name is mentioned. It's a helpful way to find out what customers are (or aren't) saying about you and your products.

Sending SMS alerts

Sending short text messages over a cellphone is an easy and affordable way to communicate with customers. It works especially well for these tasks:

✦ Send reminders about an event, a product, or a service.

✦ Create immediate awareness.

✦ Send special offers.

There is a growing number of companies that offer SMS marketing services. Try one of the following:

✦ **WebText** (www.webtext.com): Offers pay-as-you-go pricing. Typically, per-message prices start at 11 cents for U.S. customers.

✦ **Red Fish Media** (www.redfishmedia.com): This company has a range of mobile marketing and SMS services as part of its Blue Water message delivery program. Prices vary depending on the program and number of emails.

✦ **Cardboard Fish** (`www.cardboardfish.com`): Offers a number of marketing options for SMS services. Pricing starts at 20 cents per message for U.S. customers.

Advertising with text-to-buy

Text-to-buy ads give customers an easy and immediate way to purchase your products by using their cellphones. Here are some companies that offer this service to e-tailers:

✦ **4Info (`www.advertising.4info.net`):** Works with many large businesses and e-tailers. Using this ad service, you can send customers text messages with links back to a mobile Web site to

- Make purchases.
- Link back to a live support person in a call center.
- Click to view a product video.

✦ **Cross Link Media (`www.crosslinkmedia.com`):** Offers several different solutions as an advertiser and claims that mobile advertising has return rates 15 times higher than other online advertising.

Distributing mobile coupons

According to a report from Jupiter Research, 30 percent of people surveyed showed interest in receiving coupons on their cellphones. Half of those interested in coupons also showed interest in receiving offers from local retail stores. Whereas other research shows that a majority of consumers are still unaware that this type of capability exists, most, after they learn about it, want to know which online businesses use m-coupons. That's an indicator that the demand for mobile coupons is likely to continue growing as they become more mainstream.

Some of the companies that provide m-coupon distribution services are described in this list:

✦ **Cellfire** (`www.cellfire.com`): Customers access your coupons by downloading the Cellfire application to their phones. The advantage that this company offers is that it provides nationwide coverage but can deliver your mobile coupons to specific zip codes.

✦ **Plum Reward** (`www.plumreward.com`): Unlike some of its competitors, Plum Reward specializes in working with brick-and-mortar locations. In fact, the company sells a small piece of hardware, similar to a debit or credit card scanner placed in stores. Customers then enter their cellphone numbers into the device to begin receiving offers specific to that particular store. Although the service is free for customers, you pay an ongoing monthly fee in addition to the initial equipment cost.

✦ **Proximity Media** (www.proximitymedia.com): This mobile coupon solution uses Bluetooth technology to deliver coupons to customers. It's a little more complicated than other solutions but is a viable option.

✦ **Sacaya** (www.sacaya.com/m_coupons.html): Taking m-commerce one step further, this site truly provides mobile coupons on demand. A customer using this service sends a text message to any of the registered advertisers and requests a coupon. Advertisers send targeted offerings back to the customer in a text message.

✦ **XtraCoupons** (www.xtracoupons.com): Using this mobile coupon application, users scroll through a list of available stores and choose the coupons they want. After a user is in a store, he can access the coupon code by using his phone and let the store clerk enter the code. Figure 5-1 shows you how this application looks on a cellphone. The service is free for customers, and you, as an advertiser, pay a small monthly fee.

Book VII
Chapter 5

Staying Local,
Getting Mobile
with M-Commerce

Figure 5-1:
Deliver coupons via cell phone.

Localizing with Ads

One advantage that mobile commerce offers is the ability to reach customers in a specific geographic region. The concept of *localization,* or local advertising, isn't restricted to mobile applications. If you're an e-tailer with brick-and-mortar locations, local search can mean big business for you. As competition and market conditions tighten, local paid search is expected to grow as an important advertising strategy for retailers. Local ad revenues for 2009 should reach $13.6 million with annual increases of 22 percent or more.

In this process, also referred to as *geotargeting,* your business ads appear as part of search results that are based on a specific geographic location. Plenty of sites use the concept of local marketing, such as craigslist and Angie's List, and even the online yellow pages. However, in the area of paid local search, the two most well-known outlets are Google and Yahoo! These search engine competitors have taken online advertising to a new level. Both have geotargeting programs that provide paid search results based on a user's computer IP address, which can be associated with a specific physical location. Google can provide local search results down to a city level. However, Yahoo! is in beta testing for a service that can target consumers by zip code.

Google AdWords

Using Google AdWords is comparable to placing an ad in your local newspaper. You purchase a specific amount of space (or ad size) for a set dollar amount in order to entice customers to come into your store. You can even specify a section of the paper in which your ad should appear. For example, if you have a sporting goods store, your ad might appear in the sports section of the newspaper. Google works almost the same way.

In this case, your ad is displayed in the search engine based on a prospective customer's search results. Suppose that someone uses Google to search for soccer balls. Your text ad, typically a few sentences long, shows up on the right side of the screen with other sponsored ads, as shown in Figure 5-2.

Unlike with traditional newspaper ads, with Google AdWords you choose the keywords that trigger your ad to appear and you decide how much you want to pay for the "ad space." When you use AdWords, you aren't paying for a certain ad size but, rather, for a certain number of hits on your ad. In this process, known as *cost per click,* or *CPC,* you pay only when prospective customers click your text link.

Geotargeting takes CPC one step further. You also might decide that you want your ad to appear *only* when the prospective customer is searching from a specific location, or city. For example, if your sports store is based in Raleigh, North Carolina, and someone in that area searches for soccer balls, your ad appears. If the person clicks your ad, you're charged the amount that you agreed to pay. You can pay as little as a few pennies for each click, or it can cost several dollars or more.

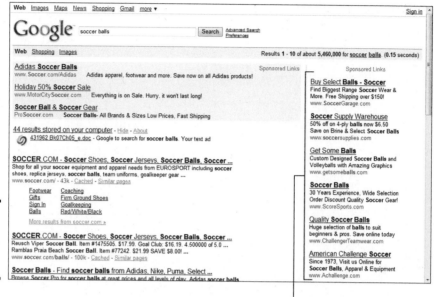

Google ads

Figure 5-2:
Drive traffic
with Google
AdWords.

If you set the price, or CPC, that you're willing to pay (as we just mentioned), you may be wondering why you would ever agree to pay a high dollar amount. It's simple: Because you're basically bidding on the price of the ad, or in this case, the CPC, your price correlates with the popularity of the key-word on which you're bidding. The more popular your keyword is or your keywords are, the more people are willing to pay for them, which drives up the price. You might still choose to bid a smaller amount for your CPC, but that means your ad will appear a fewer number of times. To be competitive, you may have to pay a higher CPC.

You can limit the cost of your keywords by bidding on specific words or phrases, as opposed to choosing more general terms. Rather than bid on soccer balls, for example, bid on a specific type or name-brand soccer ball. Or, use a phrase such as `soccer balls for kids` or `youth soccer balls`. You see fewer results, but they should also lead to a more qualified buyer for a smaller ad price.

Google AdWords is almost entirely free to use, and it requires no contracts or minimum spending requirements. You pay a nominal activation fee (approximately $5), but that's it. Otherwise, you're charged only when someone clicks your text ad. Google offers a Starter version and a Standard version of AdWords. Although the two versions are similar, the Standard version allows you to

+ Create campaigns for multiple products or Web sites, using multiple sets of keywords

+ Target multiple locations at once (instead of only one zip code, or city, for example)

+ Use images, video, and audio with the ad, as opposed to only text

+ Gain access to various advanced planning and budgeting tools

+ Set daily budget limits (for greater control) versus monthly budget limits

Both versions cost the same. We recommend that you begin with the Starter version because it's simpler to use (it has fewer features and options). You can decide to upgrade at any time, for no additional charge. And, you get to keep the same account so that you don't lose any historical data when you upgrade.

You can extend the value of organic localized search results by taking advantage of Google's free mapping feature. When someone searches for a keyword that brings up your Web site in the *organic,* or regular, search results, you can choose to add a map, an image, or even a video to the link for extra impact. Sign up for Google Maps at `http://maps.google.com/maps`.

We show you how to sign up for Google AdWords in Book VI, Chapter 3.

Yahoo! Search Marketing

Much like other search engines, Yahoo! offers the chance to bid on keywords and attract prospective customers by using paid, localized search results in the form of text ads, like the one shown in Figure 5-3. You should understand a few key differences between Yahoo! and Google, as described in this section.

Perhaps most significant is that Google captures approximately 63 percent of the U.S. search market share, according to ComScore (`www.comscore.com`). Yahoo! usually pulls in just over 20 percent of the search market. (The remaining percentage is divided among sites such as Microsoft, Ask, and AOL.) These numbers certainly don't mean that your paid search is less effective with Yahoo!, but it does mean that you're reaching a smaller portion of the overall market. Even so, more than 47 million people still use Yahoo! daily and approximately 42 billion searches are conducted monthly. For that reason, among others, we think it worthwhile to participate in Yahoo! paid searches.

The other differences aren't as dramatic. Yahoo! charges a larger registration fee — approximately $30 for a one-time, nonrefundable initial deposit. However, Yahoo! recently introduced a localized paid search option that lets you geotarget prospective customers by zip code (compared to the city level, as with Google). This feature of Yahoo! Search Marketing is in the beta stage, so it's being tested and its results aren't guaranteed. What a big step for localized search, however! Additionally, Yahoo! lets you set daily budgets for your ads, based on the CPC you want to pay, with no long-term obligation. You can calculate an estimated CPC or bid by using this Yahoo! tool (see Figure 5-4).

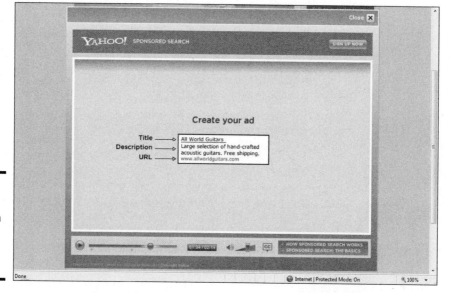

Figure 5-3:
Place a
text ad with
Yahoo!
Search
Marketing.

Figure 5-4:
Calculate a
maximum
CPC for your
text ad.

Try out the tool at `http://sem.smallbusiness.yahoo.com/search` `enginemarketing/marketingcost.php`.

Follow these steps to start advertising with Yahoo! Search Marketing:

1. **Go to the Small Business home page on Yahoo! (`http://small` `business.yahoo.com`) and click the Learn More link on the Market Online tab in the center of the page.**

   A new page opens that provides information about search marketing and advertising online.

2. **Click the Sign Up button in the upper-right corner of the page.**

   Another page opens that outlines the steps to bid on keywords.

3. **Click the Target Customers by Geographic Location tab, and choose a target area from the drop-down menu.**

   After you choose an area to target, such as by city or zip code, the next page that opens lets you fill in details.

4. **Decide whether to target by zip code or by city. Then click the Submit button. Confirm your choices and then click the Next Keywords button.**

   If you're targeting by zip code, you can include as many as 250 zip codes.

5. **Enter the keywords you want to target in your advertising. Then click the Next Related Keywords button.**

   You can enter as many as 50 keywords or keyword phrases. A page opens listing similar or related keywords that you can choose to add to your previous list. The related keywords list also shows the estimated number of monthly searches for each keyword, to help you determine their popularity.

6. **Click the Next Pricing button at the bottom of the page.**

   You see a page labeled Tell Us How Much You'd Like to Spend.

7. **Enter a daily spending limit for your account and a maximum CPC price that you're willing to pay for each keyword.**

8. **Click the Next Create Ad button and write your ad.**

   This step lets you develop your text ad, preview it, and even see tips for writing better ads. To create your ad, enter the ad title, a brief description (no more than 70 characters), and a url that links the ad to your Web site.

9. **After you finish writing your ad, click the Next Review button.**

This step provides one last look at your text ad and lets you edit it or change the CPC rate or daily budget. You're also asked to log in to or create a Yahoo! account with a username and password.

10. **Click the Activate button to start displaying your ad.**

Before your ad goes live on the search engine, you're asked to provide a credit card to be billed for the total amount that's accrued on your account.

That's it! You're ready to sell online with Yahoo! Search Marketing.

When you spend a monthly minimum of $1,000, you can request a Yahoo ad specialist. That person helps you build a campaign, including selecting competitive keywords, writing ads, and determining the ideal maximum CPC. Ask for a specialist if you plan to spend at least this amount on your campaign.

**Book VII
Chapter 5**

Staying Local,
Getting Mobile
with M-Commerce

Chapter 6: Troubleshooting the Transition to E-Tail

In This Chapter

✔ Developing a return policy and sticking to it

✔ Figuring out how to make your back end work online

✔ Bringing together your brick-and-mortar and online stores

✔ Increasing service and sales with alternative payment options

As you move your retail store online, you can always hope that things will go perfectly. In reality, you can expect a few minor bumps along the way. This chapter talks about navigating over the bumps and avoiding the big potholes after your site goes live.

The good news is that your customers probably won't even notice most of the known bumps. The rest of the bumps, you can overcome. The secret to surviving is planning now for those situations most likely to cause you stress.

Handling Returns in the Store from Online Sales

Suppose that you have store policies already in place, but it's now time to update your return or exchange policy. Given today's high rate of fraudulent activity, you're probably already wary (if not suspicious) of customers who hightail it back to your store with merchandise in hand.

Now you have to add the return of online orders to the mix. After your online store is up and running, someone will certainly make a purchase on your Web site, and the purchase might be the wrong size or be damaged or be in a style that the customer doesn't like.

Before you can decide how to handle the return, you have to ask yourself how you want to respond to it. If your goal is to work with your customers and make them happy, you want to develop a customer-friendly policy.

On the other hand, you may be most interested in protecting your bottom line. In that case, you can approach the online return policy in a way that's most convenient for you.

Here are some decisions that you need to make about return policies:

✦ **Customer-friendly policy:** If you're taking this route, your policy might stipulate that you

- Pay for return shipping (or reimburse the customer for it) if a purchase is sent back by mail
- Accept the return with no questions asked
- Give a complete refund or exchange the item
- Request (but not demand) a copy of the original receipt

✦ **Bottom-line policy:** When cutting corners is your biggest concern, protect yourself with these rules of return:

- No returns are made without an original receipt.
- Issue only store credit or an exchange of equal value.
- Limit the time for which returns are accepted (within 30 days from date of purchase, for example).
- Do not accept returns on sale, clearance, or discontinued items.
- Returns should be made from the location where they were purchased (no in-store returns for online purchases).

When sending items to your customers, pack a Return/Item Exchange Request form inside the box. Make sure that the form provides complete instructions for returning an item and states your return policy. Customers wanting to return an item can use this form to provide basic information (such as name and address) and a reason why they're returning the product.

Merging Existing Back-End Systems with Online Requirements

By the time you launch your Web site, you typically already have a lengthy history. You have established customers, extensive sales data, an inventory management system, in-store policies, point-of-sale systems, ordering guidelines, and a host of vendors and suppliers at your beck and call.

Having that much structure and information definitely plays in your favor because you're not starting from scratch when you move into e-commerce. But integrating all these systems and procedures to an online business can present a few challenges to your back end.

A successful brick-and-mortar store, Garrison Confections, launched its e-commerce site with a nice look and a fairly standard back-end shopping cart solution. The online store worked fine initially, but as the site became more popular, it couldn't handle the increased traffic. The owners had to come up with a new back-end solution.

The company made two critical decisions about how to handle this transition period. First, it outsourced the project to a local Web development firm. The second part of the equation involved making the decision to invest the necessary money to make the upgrade happen. A small business can't easily spend thousands of dollars, but as a part of the overall business, paying for a new back-end solution made sense.

This time around, the site is better integrated with the company's back-end process, making the money that the business paid to rework its site a worthwhile expenditure. Figure 6-1 shows a glimpse of the updated Garrison Confections site and ordering system. You can also check it out in full at www.garrisonconfections.com.

Figure 6-1: The Garrison Confections online store.

Managing inventory

One of the biggest headaches for an e-tailer is handling inventory levels in a way that's least disruptive to both you and your online customer. At the heart of the matter, you need to make sure that your online store can communicate with your existing inventory system.

Here's an example of what typically happens when you have a kink in your inventory management. A customer goes to your site, places an order, pays for the order, and then expects it to be delivered according to your shipping policy. You receive the order and start filling it, only to find that the item is out of stock. Now you have to communicate with your customer and let him know that the product is on back order. As you know, this situation isn't ideal. For a better alternative, implement a system that communicates inventory levels with all your primary points of operations, including

✦ Point-of-sale system (your retail location)

✦ Online shopping cart

✦ Call center

✦ Warehouse

When investigating these different operations, make sure to determine whether each one can work with your inventory management system. The best solution allows any (and possibly all) of these operations to communicate directly with your software inventory management system to allow for a real-time updated tracking system of what you have in stock and what you need to reorder.

Fulfilling and shipping your orders

Chances are good that your store has already encountered the need to package an order and ship it somewhere. Depending on what type of store you have, you may do it regularly (with catalog or telephone orders, for example) or only occasionally. But imagine that you suddenly have to ship out anywhere from 10 to 100 different packages every day. How does that affect your already hectic schedule? Do you have employees that can be dedicated to handling the process? Or, does the idea of shipping orders evoke the image of you having to stay up late at night, digging for boxes, printing labels from your computer, and trying to meet last-minute pickup schedules?

Another concern with an increased number of shipments is space. Think about your existing location. Do you have dedicated space for packaging? Is it a space that in-store customers can see? Or, is it a separate offsite warehouse space? Regardless of where you ship the product from, how do you confirm that an order has gone out? Do you have computer software set up to show that information, or are you keeping a manual checklist?

As you can see, you have a lot of questions to consider for what seems to be quite a simple process. Placing one of your products into a box and shipping it out to a customer isn't difficult. But it's more time consuming than you probably think.

One solution is to outsource the shipping-and-handling portion of the operation. Another option is to have many of your items drop-shipped to customers from your suppliers. However, you can also keep this function in-house, if you want. Check out Book IV, Chapter 7 to find out more about your shipping options.

Tracking your orders

You may already have internal systems for tracking customer orders. But now that you're selling online, you need to provide your customers with direct access to the status of their orders, particularly after those orders ship. You can minimize the number of calls and e-mails that you receive from customers by allowing them to directly check on a delivery. Anything that helps reduce your workload is a good thing! The truly good news is that the major shipping companies provide free online order-tracking tools for you to incorporate into your site. Try these shipping companies:

✦ **DHL** (www.dhl.com): As a registered customer, you can use the DHL tracking tools and send automated e-mail messages to customers. The messages include information so that customers can track the status of their orders.

✦ **FedEx** (www.fedex.com): Use the FedEx InSight tool to track shipments. You can see all your inbound and outbound shipments, and the tool gives real-time updates of any potential delays. To let your customers track their orders, use the Invite feature.

✦ **UPS** (www.ups.com): By far, UPS offers the best online-tracking tools for your customers. The delivery company has developed a set of applications that you can integrate directly into your Web site. By using UPS, you don't need to send customers e-mail messages with directions on order tracking or direct them to another site for tracking. Customers can check the status right on your site. Before starting the process of connecting your site to UPS, use the UPS Online Tools Integration Checklist to make sure that you're prepared to implement the applications on your site.

UPS offers tracking tools that use both HTML and XML programming. To implement XML-based applications on your site, you may need to hire a programmer who's familiar with Java (a programming language).

Maintaining site performance

Before you decide to sell your inventory online, you may already have some type of Web site. Sure, it's probably more of a brochure site that shows your logo and maybe a photo of your retail location and offers prospective customers a map to help them find your store. If that's the case, your site probably doesn't see a whole lot of traffic. And even you probably don't look at it that often. Well, after you enter the world of e-commerce, that situation is likely to change.

Now that you're an official e-tailer, you need to understand your site's performance capabilities. For example, how much traffic can the site handle? If you exceed a particular limit of bandwidth usage, does your monthly hosting fee increase? What about the site design? Is it optimized for the best viewing in varying screen resolutions? Can a customer using a slower Internet connection shop your site as easily as a customer with a broadband connection? How well do product images load? These questions are just a sampling of the site performance issues that can surface as you begin selling online.

Deciding How to Handle Integration

Even if you're a smaller store, site performance, inventory management, and order-tracking solutions suddenly becomes major elements within your new business model. Even so, you probably start off needing to make only minor changes to your current way of doing business. That way, you have a chance to see what works and what doesn't, and you can then figure out what you need to change. This trial-by-error process is common.

However, if you already have sophisticated back-end processes or you're more of a mid-size retailer, you may want to plan ahead. In fact, you may find it worthwhile to hire a consultant to help you survey your systems and find the best hardware and software match to smoothly integrate your online operations.

No matter the size of your site, you can get a jump-start on the installation and integration of your hardware and software by using these four checkpoints:

✦ **Review:** Make a list of all areas of your store operations, from your cash register (or point of sale) to your inventory system. Take a close look at how you currently handle each of these operations.

✦ **Analyze:** You can begin deciding how, if at all, your current systems will translate to an online process. Can you use the software programs that you already have with your e-commerce site? Or, is your software designed only for a traditional retail store? If you use manual programs, those programs can quickly get bogged down after your site experiences its first phase of growth.

✦ **Decide:** After you have an idea of how well your existing procedures may or may not hold up, you have decisions to make. For example, are you ready to invest in new systems? Where will you get the money for upgrades? Are you comfortable managing your e-tail operations in-house, or do you need to bring in the professionals?

✦ **Investigate:** If you decide that you need a new software program or want to outsource some of your operations, start looking at your options. Begin familiarizing yourself with current terminology, leading technology vendors, and the typical price ranges for various back-end solutions.

One thing is certain: You won't find a shortage of experienced vendors ready to help you transition into the world of multichannel retailing. The systems in the following list are worth looking into to help integrate your offline location with your online store:

✦ **CORESense** (www.coresense.com): CORESense offers multiple products that range from real-time inventory management to fulfillment and marketing.

✦ **Epicor** (www.epicor.com): Epicore retail solutions include a cross-channel order management system, which helps you provide real-time inventory management between your store's inventory, Web site, catalog, and even kiosk. It can link your site and in-store point-of-sale (POS) system to a call center.

✦ **VCommerce** (www.vcommerce.com): A provider of back-end solutions to some of e-tail's biggest players, VCommerce offers a complete package for retail integration. Included among its features is drop-ship management for multiple suppliers, inventory management, and order and transaction management. Though it caters to larger companies, it offers competitive pricing, including the ability to bundle services at a fixed-rate fee.

✦ **NetSuite** (www.netsuite.com): Using the Real-Time Dashboard software, you get an instant and detailed look at all areas of your business, online and off. You see such indicators as sales orders, pending shipments, and inventory levels. It's one of several products designed to help you manage the back end of your small, multichannel business. NetSuite offers a free trial, too.

Extending Payment Options to Virtual Customers

The goal of providing a variety of payments is to take away an obstacle that may prevent customers from buying from you. However, the increasing competition for online sales is forcing e-tailers such as yourself to always be on the lookout for new payment options.

For a list of vendors for your online business needs, check out the Internet Retailer vendor list, which includes many payment processing vendors, along with other valuable resource categories. You can check it out at www.internetretailer.com/eRetailing/vendor_list.html.

Whether customers purchase from your store or Web site or by e-mail or phone, the future of e-tailing comes down to two principles:

✦ Continually connect with your customers.

✦ Always give your customers options.

Buy now, pay later

Extended payment terms, deferred terms, or instant credit — call it what you like, this payment option is gaining popularity as an alternative online payment solution. This type of credit basically allows a customer to delay paying cash out of her pocket at the time of purchase.

Deferred billing is the same as the offline promotion of "90 days same as cash." Allowing customers to take advantage of this type of payment can truly help your business if you sell higher-end items or want to increase your per-customer average sale. Customers often seek out this option during the holiday season, when they're already in a cash crunch. To set up a deferred billing arrangement, start by talking with your bank or merchant provider.

Another option that's exceeding expectations for e-tailers is the Bill Me Later program offered by I4 Commerce. This program is basically instant credit. Your customer gets approved for a certain credit limit and then receives a billing statement through the mail or by e-mail to pay the balance. Your customers like it for the following reasons:

✦ **Speed:** At the time of purchase, Bill Me Later asks your customer only for his date of birth and the last four digits of his Social Security number. (I4 Commerce uses this information to make a quick credit check.) Approval is returned in a matter of seconds, in most cases.

✦ **Security:** Because Bill Me Later doesn't require giving out extensive information or using credit cards, some customers view it as a safer way to make a purchase.

✦ **Fraud protection:** I4 Commerce offers "zero fraud liability" to consumers who use Bill Me Later. Customers don't have to pay for purchases they didn't make.

As an e-tailer, you're bound to like Bill Me Later for these reasons:

✦ **No risk:** I4 Commerce accepts all the risk when extending credit to your customers, so you don't have to worry about losing anything if a customer doesn't pay.

✦ **Affordable:** When we last checked, the processing fee for a Bill Me Later transaction was still slightly less than for most credit cards.

✦ **Sales boost:** Based on what I4 Commerce says is the norm, online merchants are experiencing both higher ticket averages (customers spending more per visit) and increased repeat purchases from existing customers using Bill Me Later.

Customers can simply look for the Bill Me Later logo on your Web site (see Figure 6-2). By clicking the link, the user opens a new page to start the application process. To explore this credit option for your customers, you can visit I4 Commerce at www.i4commerce.com.

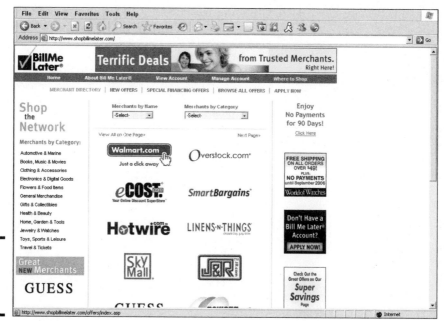

Figure 6-2:
Look for
the Bill Me
Later logo.

Check alternatives

A more common payment method involves your site accepting various forms of checks, or even money orders. With Internet checks, you work through an independent processor that accepts money from a customer's bank account and then deposits it into your merchant account, usually in fewer than 15 days. You can check with your payment processor to find out whether it offers this type of service. Another solution is offering Automated Clearing House (ACH) processing that transfers money directly from a customer's checking account to your merchant account, usually within 48 hours. Again, if you want to use this method for your online store, start by checking with your payment processor or bank.

Book VIII
Storefront Selling

The 5th Wave   By Rich Tennant

"How many times have I told you that you can't sell your brother on eBay?"

Contents at a Glance

Chapter 1: Instant E-Commerce with Storefronts

In This Chapter

✔ Exploring standard storefront features

✔ Determining the price for storefront convenience

✔ Analyzing your storefront options

*O*ne of the easiest ways to get started selling online is by using a store-front solution, or e-commerce-in-a-box, in which all components necessary to build and manage your store are conveniently gathered in one place.

Because storefronts have become increasingly popular, the solutions they provide have become more diverse and less expensive. The result is that you have a bunch of viable, and reliable, options. The most difficult part of choosing one is sorting through them all to find the best one for you. This chapter explains the most popular features of storefronts and helps you make a decision about which storefront would work best for your business.

Some storefront solutions have recognizable names. We cover Amazon.com in Book VIII, Chapter 2; Yahoo! in Book VIII, Chapter 3; and eBay in Book VIII, Chapter 4.

Knowing What You Want: Features

When choosing your online store, make sure that the following three essential elements are included. Together, these functions help qualify the store-front as a true all-in-one solution:

✦ **Shopping cart:** This back-end feature allows customers to browse for, select, and purchase products. (If you want to know more, Book IV, Chapter 5 compares specific shopping-cart features.)

✦ **Payment processor:** The virtual cash register. Of course, customers need a way to pay you during checkout for the products they want. A storefront solution should give customers multiple options. You need to consider whether the storefront's payment processor can integrate with your existing payment processor. (Book IV, Chapter 4 gives you some useful tips for selecting a payment gateway for your site.)

✦ **Hosting solution:** You need a place to host your actual store. Your hosted shopping cart, however, doesn't have to share the service you use for your primary Web site. But one of the benefits of a storefront is that hosting is included in the deal, eliminating additional Web site hosting fees.

These bare necessities are just the tip of the iceberg when you're selecting features for your storefront. You may already have an extensive shopping list of your own, special preferences. If not, start by separating the features that you want into groups based on what you truly need from a complete storefront solution. Classify those features by these three areas of need: performance, product merchandizing, and administration features. All three are described in the following sections.

Performance

Unfortunately, performance is the area of a storefront that you don't always think about until something goes wrong or isn't what you expected. Yet it's truly the backbone of your operations. Paying special attention to these performance-related issues when selecting your storefront is ultimately worth your time:

✦ **Speed:** A lot of factors contribute to the speed of a storefront, and it isn't always easy for you to determine how it will fare. The best way to find out is to visit some of your storefront's featured sites and see for yourself whether a lag in processing time occurs.

You can also sort through a storefront's community forum section to see whether other storeowners have complained about the storefront's *processing speed,* or the load time for pages.

✦ **Storage:** You want adequate disk space and bandwidth transfer available for your site. Even if your storefront starts small, you need room to grow without being immediately penalized with a higher rate. As a point of reference, mid-level priced storefronts provide about 10GB of disk storage.

✦ **Security:** Proper security is an essential part of e-commerce. Before purchasing your storefront, understand what type of services or protections are offered to guard your store.

✦ **Product quantity:** Many storefronts place limits on the number of products you can sell. Which storefront you choose often turns into a price-based issue. The good news is that even with limitations on quantity, your monthly fee typically supports a fairly substantial number of product listings (sometimes as many as 60,000). But don't assume that you automatically get that support. Be aware of SKU code (the inventory product number) limitations and whether you face additional charges for exceeding a certain number of products.

✦ **E-product delivery:** If your storefront supports electronic products (e-books and CDs, for example) they can be delivered by way of customer-initiated downloads. You can also sell memberships electronically. The ability to download some products in digital format (such as PDF files or music files) is growing, and you should definitely consider offering these kinds of products because they require no warehouse space and can offer substantial profit margins. See Book IV, Chapter 3 for more about selling e-products.

✦ **Import and export tools:** This feature lets you transfer large numbers of products into or out of the storefront. Storefronts with this feature commonly let you dump products into the storefront from an Excel spreadsheet, for example. This feature can be a timesaver if you have a lot of inventory.

✦ **Support:** Having access to the storefront's technical support team can be your only lifeline at times. In the best possible situation, full tech support is available 24 hours a day, seven days a week.

✦ **Templates:** One benefit of turning to a storefront is that you have access to templates. If you aren't a savvy Web developer, predesigned Web page templates are supposed to make it easy to open your store. But for templates to truly be of value, the storefront needs an extensive array of template styles available and should also allow for minor customization (of font style and colors, for example). This ability to customize lets you take advantage of the template but still provide a storefront look that's all your own.

Try to use a storefront that offers at least a hundred (and preferably more) template designs. Before making your final purchase, check to see that it offers a wide variety of styles and themes.

✦ **Wizards:** The storefront solution should offer a setup wizard to guide you through the process of building and customizing your storefront. Ideally, the wizard takes your store setup from start to finish without any major headaches. If you don't think that the wizard is intuitive to use or you have difficulties working with it, it negates one of the biggest advantages of using a storefront — simplicity!

Spend time on the storefront's demo section, and tinker with the wizard before making your final decision. If the demo isn't fully functioning, contact a sales representative. Ask the person to give you live access to the store-building tools for a week or so. This access gives you a chance to test-drive the real wizard.

Product merchandizing and marketing

A stellar storefront solution should provide a host of tools that assist you in promoting products (offering ideas based on past purchase histories, for example), and marketing them (by e-mailing brochures, for example) to your customer base. After all, these features ultimately help you move more products and bump up your sales revenue:

Book VIII Chapter 1

Instant E-Commerce with Storefronts

✦ **Product images:** Ideally, customers should be able to view multiple images of a product before making a purchase. To make several images of a product available on your site, the store's product gallery has to allow for more than one image to be uploaded and viewed per product.

✦ **Customization component:** One recent major online trend is letting customers customize products. You can customize a product by adding a monogram, engraving messages into the product, and modifying a color or style, for example. Because customizing is potentially a persuasive purchasing feature, your storefront should allow customers to add customizing instructions in its shopping cart program. Offering the ability to customize products during the shopping cart phase of a purchase can provide additional profits in the form of impulse purchases.

✦ **Cross-selling (or upselling):** This feature allows you to promote similar products on a single page. In other words, when customers add one product to the cart, you can then recommend or suggest that they may also like another product. Also referred to as *suggestive selling,* cross-selling occurs during the checkout process, where you recommend additional products or services to the customer, based on the existing purchase. Cross-selling is a standard technique to raise the amount a customer spends in one visit to your store.

✦ **Discount pricing:** You may want to be able to set up special groups that can be assigned different prices. For example, you may want to offer a 10 percent discount in February to active military members and their families. Or, you may want to allow certain resellers to receive a different price than your public customers. This feature lets you distinguish among types of customers and charge them different prices.

✦ **Promotions:** Coupon codes, gift certificates, and any other special offerings can be set up as incentives to buy for your customers. The complexities of this feature vary, so take a close look at what each storefront solution can and can't do. As an example, some storefronts allow you to deduct only a certain percentage rate or a flat dollar amount. Other programs allow promotions such as buy-one-get-one-free (or half price).

✦ **E-mail marketing:** Staying in touch with your customer base is a surefire way to drive up sales. And, storefronts seem to offer a wide variation on this feature. For example, one storefront solution limits the number of e-mails that can go out within a certain timeframe.

✦ **Search-engine-friendly:** Search engine optimization (SEO) is being continuously integrated into storefront features. Having your individual product pages (or the images) tagged is an increasingly important element to helping your pages show up in the results at the search engines. See Book VI, Chapter 6 to find out more about search engine optimization.

✦ **Shopping feeds:** Similar to search engine marketing, your e-commerce store needs a way to hook into Froogle (Google's shopping comparison site) and other popular shopping sites. Called an *XML-data feed*, it allows you to pull results from these types of sites into your own in the blink of an eye.

✦ **Widgets:** You can easily use these add-on features or applications in your storefront to help market, promote, or sell. Widgets are pieces of code that you drop into your storefront and that don't require additional programming to implement.

✦ **Affiliate sales:** An affiliate program may have various levels or attributes assigned to it. So you often need something different from the coupon feature that accounts for this need. Book IV, Chapter 2 covers affiliates in depth.

Be prepared to pay extra for an affiliate sales monitoring feature. Several major storefronts offer this feature as an added module or plug-in for your store.

Administration features

To do your job properly, you have to manage some behind-the-curtain activity. Access to administrative tools lets you oversee these processes. The following list shows the most common features that you'll be grateful to have included with (or added to) your storefront:

✦ **Inventory management:** You need, at the very least, to keep track of your inventory levels and ensure that your existing inventory systems work cohesively with your storefront. Ideally, you should use real-time inventory tracking.

✦ **Accounting system integration:** Look for storefronts that can sufficiently communicate data between your storefront and your accounting package. If this option is available, it's typically set up to integrate specifically with QuickBooks (a financial software package).

✦ **Reporting functions:** Ah, the sales reports — and more. Your storefront solution should be able to track sales, returns, and invoices, among other things.

✦ **Payment system:** Yes, a storefront needs a payment gateway. But perhaps equally important, your storefront needs to include a range of payment gateways for your customers to use. PayPal, Visa, MasterCard, American Express, Discover Card — these options are the basic ones. Make sure that your storefront's gateway accepts multiple forms of payment because payment options can combat *shopping cart abandonment,* the phenomenon that occurs when visitors leave your site without purchasing the items they placed in their carts (virtually abandoning their shopping carts).

**Book VIII
Chapter 1**

Instant E-Commerce
with Storefronts

✦ **Tax calculation and reporting:** Like it or not, you probably have to deal with taxes online. Taxes can be a complicated issue because amounts vary by county and state. By identifying storefronts that are already set up to add taxes when required, you can save yourself much trouble.

✦ **Multiple currencies:** You can use a feature that allows customers to make purchases with any type of currency. If this option comes as an add-on storefront product for an additional charge, you can probably wait before investing in it — the cost may not be an absolute necessity at this point.

✦ **Integrated shipping tools:** UPS, FedEx, and DHL are among the most popular U.S. delivery systems for packages. And, to get your customer's product delivered, you need to ensure that your storefront can talk to one or more of these organizations. Your storefront doesn't have to integrate with all the shipping options, but it should at least work with the one your site uses most.

✦ **Analytics software:** Along with other tracking and reporting functions, your storefront should help identify your traffic patterns, along with your customers' data on how they use the pages of your site. A good analytics program built into the storefront can give you many of those answers.

Realizing What You Can Have: Cost

Most storefront solutions claim that the sky is the limit on functionality and scalability. They're not far off. But, as you probably realize, your budget ultimately becomes either the enabler or the deterrent.

Figure out what you can afford. After you do that, you have to decide which elements you can't live without. As you consider what's most important, keep in mind the way that storefront solutions are typically priced:

✦ **Monthly fee:** Most often, you're provided a monthly price for using the service, which should include your monthly hosting cost, too. You can cancel most monthly agreements at any time, as long as you follow the store's termination procedures.

✦ **Annual fee:** You have the option of prepaying for a year's worth of service. You usually receive a slight discount, as compared to paying the monthly fee. The service may also waive any setup fees, and you might receive other perks (such as a certain number of Google AdWords for free).

When you sign up for a storefront annual account, you're prepaying for a year of service in advance. You can always cancel your agreement before the 12 months end. But, in most cases, none of your money is refunded, so you lose the money that you prepaid for any remaining months.

✦ **Tiered pricing:** Storefronts typically use a tiered pricing structure to suit all levels of need. They group benefits and features into different types of pricing plans. For example, if you need less disk space or fewer features, choose a basic plan for a lower monthly fee. But if you want the whole shebang, choose the more expensive plan (often called a gold or premium plan).

✦ **Product capacity pricing:** Similar to tiered pricing, some storefronts may divide plans by the number of products you want to support. So you may be able to get the benefit of all features in every plan and pay only according to the number of product listings.

✦ **Module fees:** You may find that you can receive additional services as part of an add-on module. These modules cost extra and may be priced as a monthly service or a flat annual fee.

✦ **Activation fee:** You probably have to pay for some sort of setup or activation fee at the time that you sign up for the service.

Activation fees are often waived when you sign up for an annual account or premium account. But you can sometimes convince someone to waive these fees by signing up over the phone rather than online. Let the customer service rep know that you're willing to sign today if he can drop some of the upfront fees. It never hurts to ask!

Deciding how much you can afford to pay (and the way you want to pay for it) comes down to determining what you need. When figuring out what you can afford, start by considering how many products you want to sell and the amount of disk space you may need. After that, it's a matter of which features are most important to you.

But you can also break down the numbers another way. Look at how many products you have to sell on a monthly basis to cover the cost of the storefront. For example, you might choose a mid-level plan that costs $149 per month. It includes an extensive list of features and supports as many as 10,000 products. You have only 75 products, and your average amount of profit for each one is around $9. That means you have to sell at least 17 products per month just to cover the cost of your storefront.

On the flip side, you might choose a lower-level plan. It may support only 100 products and have fewer features. But it costs only $25 per month. Using the same profit margins, you now have to sell only three products each month to cover your storefront costs.

So, if you're just starting out in e-commerce and don't have any built-in traffic, the lower fee means fewer monetary risks. It's all a matter of figuring out what's most important to you!

**Book VIII
Chapter 1**

Instant E-Commerce with Storefronts

Shopping for Storefronts

After you know which features you want and figure out what you want to pay, you're ready to find a storefront solution. You don't have a shortage of options, but here are some possibilities to look into:

✦ **Quick Shopping Cart:** You might not know it from its name, but Quick Shopping Cart is a complete storefront solution from GoDaddy.com. What makes this choice popular is its price. The economy plan is only $9.99 per month, and that price includes hosting. The downside is that it supports only 20 products. But you can choose the next level, which supports 100 products and costs only $29.99. For $49.99, you receive unlimited product support and 2GB of disk space. For the price, it has (by far) the most extensive list of features — too many to begin to name. Get the full scoop by visiting `www.godaddy.com/gdshop/ecommerce/cart.asp`.

✦ **MonsterCommerce Merchant:** Using this storefront from Network Solutions, you can create a standard monthly account for as low as $49.95 or upgrade to a professional version for $99.95 per month. The plans support as many as 300 and 100,000 products, respectively, and include plenty of payment processing options and standard features. Not bad! Plus, the professional version has lots of extra features at no additional costs, including custom feedback forms, customized product searches, mailing lists, customer reviews, and a feature for selling electronic products, such as e-books. The site also makes nightly backups of your store, which is quite a helpful security feature. MonsterCommerce has created a very easy-to-use storefront but still provides a significant amount of customization. Go to `http://ecommerce.networksolutions.com/shopping_cart_features_menu.asp` for a complete description.

✦ **Volusion:** This storefront offers five different pricing plans, ranging from $19.95 per month for as many as 20 products to $99.95 per month to support an unlimited amount of products. All prices include hosting on RackSpace servers, and the same impressive list of features is included with each plan, although bandwidth allotments vary according to price. You can check out this solution at `www.volusion.com/ecommerce-web-hosting.asp`.

✦ **Hostway:** Formerly known as ValueWeb, Hostway now offers a bundled all-in-one storefront solution featuring MerchantManager as its shopping cart. The solution includes all the standard features needed for an e-commerce site, plus it offers extras (at no additional cost) such as podcasting tools, streaming media capability, and daily backups. This all-in-one solution is available for 99.95 a month. To find out more, take a look at its site at `www.hostway.com/web-hosting/ecommerce/index.html`.

Chapter 2: Mastering the Amazon

In This Chapter

✔ **Listing items for sale in the Amazon.com Marketplace**

✔ **Going pro with a Pro Merchant seller's account**

✔ **Getting on board other Amazon.com opportunities**

*I*t may be a jungle out there, but Amazon.com has strategically cleared a path for the willing netrepreneur. That wasn't always the case. You might recall the days when Amazon.com was launched and the idea of putting an entire bookstore online to make a (substantial) profit garnered its fair share of skepticism. The only thing about the site that got any attention back then was the big, wooden door that the company's founder, Jeff Bezos, used as a desk! Well, a few things have changed.

Consider that Amazon now expects to earn around $19.52 billion in sales in 2008. That's not too shabby for a guy who didn't have a "real" desk. What's more exciting is that the site has continued to create business opportunities for people like you by selling products on Amazon.com. Having a slice of that billion-dollar pie probably sounds good!

Amazon has established multiple selling strategies for you to use: Marketplace, Pro Merchant, WebStore, and aStore, to name a few. In this chapter, we show you how to pick a sales model and follow the instructions that Amazon.com has carefully laid out for you.

Joining the Marketplace

Selling in the Amazon.com Marketplace is by far the quickest way to make some cash on Amazon. Considering its fee structure and setup, the Marketplace is a basic selling opportunity that will suit you if you want to sell only a few items. This clear-cut process has no start-up costs, which is an ideal way to get your feet wet if you haven't sold on Amazon previously.

After you register in the Marketplace, you can post a new or used item for sale. Your item is then listed alongside the same brand-new product sold on Amazon. Figure 2-1 shows an example of how a used item appears on the same page as the new version of that item.

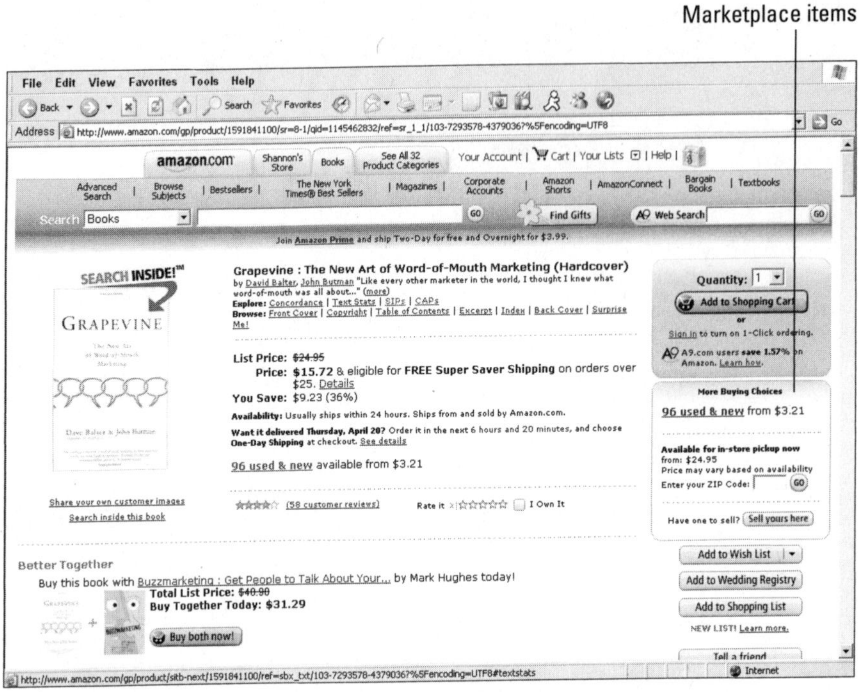

Marketplace items

Figure 2-1:
Marketplace
items show
up on the
Amazon
product
pages.

Customers can choose to buy the new item from Amazon or buy it instead from you. When a customer decides to purchase from you, he adds the product to his shopping cart and pays for it on Amazon.com (like a normal purchase). Amazon then sends you (the seller) the customer's order information and you're responsible for shipping the product. Your Amazon seller's account is credited for the purchase amount, and then you receive a check from Amazon for the items that sold. (Although total amounts show up in your account immediately, checks are distributed every 14 days.) That's it!

Amazon doesn't charge you any money to list an item. But you pay a fee when the item sells. Here's a list of the fees that Amazon deducts from your sales price:

✦ **Commission:** Amazon bases commission costs on the category in which your item is listed. The commission percentages break down like this:

- *Automotive parts and accessories*: 12 percent

- *Cameras and photos:* 8 percent

- *Cellphones and accessories:* 15 percent

- *Computers:* 6 percent
- *Electronics* (including items such as printers, scanners, and the like)*:* 8 percent
- *Everything Else store:* 15 percent
- *Musical instruments:* 12 percent
- *Watches*: 13 percent
- *All other product lines:* 15 percent

✦ **Transaction fee:** Amazon charges a flat fee of 99 cents for each item sold (which is waived for Pro Merchants).

✦ **Variable closing fee:** This fee is the Amazon equivalent of a handling charge. The amount varies based on the shipping method and product category. Table 2-1 lists the Amazon closing fees.

Table 2-1	Amazon Marketplace Variable Closing Fees	
Category	*Domestic Standard Shipping Cost*	*Domestic Expedited Shipping Cost*
Books	$1.35	$1.35
Music	$0.80	$0.80
Videos (VHS)	$0.80	$0.80
DVDs	$0.80	$0.80
Video and computer games and software	$1.35	$1.35
Electronics	$0.45 + $0.05/lb.	$0.65 + $0.10/lb.
Cameras and photos	$0.45 + $0.05/lb.	$0.65 + $0.10/lb.
Tools and hardware	$0.45 + $0.05/lb.	$0.65 + $0.10/lb.
Kitchen and housewares	$0.45 + $0.05/lb.	$0.65 + $0.10/lb.
outdoor living	$0.45 + $0.05/lb.	$0.65 + $0.10/lb.
Computer	$0.45 + $0.05/lb.	$0.65 + $0.10/lb.
Sports and outdoors	$0.45 + $0.05/lb.	$0.65 + $0.10/lb.
Cellphones and accessories	$0.45 + $0.05/lb.	$0.65 + $0.10/lb.
Musical instruments	$0.45 + $0.05/lb.	$0.65 + $0.10/lb.
Office products	$0.45 + $0.05/lb.	$0.65 + $0.10/lb.
Toy and baby	$0.45 + $0.05/lb.	$0.65 + $0.10/lb.
Everything Else	$0.45 + $0.05/lb.	$0.65 + $0.10/lb.

Book VIII Chapter 2

Mastering the Amazon

The advantage of shopping in the Marketplace is obvious for your customers: They receive the same product (used or new) at a discounted price. For you, the benefit is the ease of the selling process.

If you're already an Amazon customer, the site automatically displays how much you can potentially earn by selling in the Marketplace. It calculates the resale value of your most recent Amazon.com purchases (though, of course, you can sell more than just your Amazon purchases). Click the Sell My Stuff link on the site's home page to find out how much you could potentially make from your past Amazon.com purchases (see Figure 2-2).

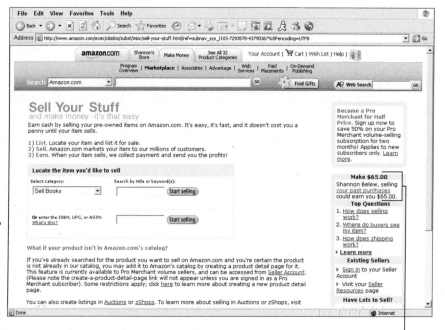

Figure 2-2:
Past
purchases
add up to
easy money.

The total

To get started with the Marketplace, follow these steps:

1. **Go to Amazon.com at www.amazon.com.**

2. **Scroll down and click the Sell Your Stuff link on the Features and Services menu tab on the left side of the home page.**

   A new page appears that briefly describes the selling process. It also contains a search tool you can use to look up the product you want to sell. You can sell only products that Amazon sells.

3. **From the Select Product Category drop-down menu, choose a category that fits your item.**

For example, if you're selling a book, choose Books.

4. **Search for the product you want to sell by using one of these methods:**

   - *Search by Title or Keyword text box:* Enter the title of your product or a keyword describing it.

   - *Enter a code in the Search By ISBN, UPC, or ASIN text box:* Enter an identifying code. You can find the International Standard Book Number (ISBN) or Universal Product Code (UPC) on the back of your product, or look for the Amazon Standard Identification Number (ASIN) on the item's product information page (see Figure 2-3).

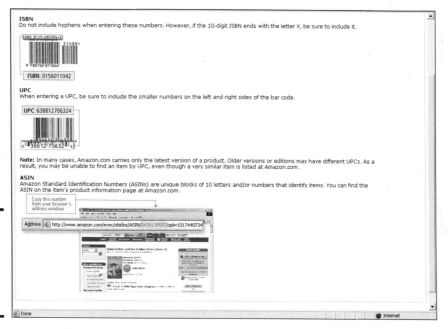

Figure 2-3:
Find the ISBN, UPC, or ASIN for your product.

**Book VIII
Chapter 2**

**Mastering
the Amazon**

5. **Click the Start Selling button.**

   A new page appears that lists Amazon.com products that contain the title or search term you used.

6. **Identify the correct product from the returned list and then click the Sell Yours Here button, which appears to the right of the product.**

7. **Double-check to ensure that you have the right product.**

   The item must be an exact match. Amazon.com requires that you sell the exact match to the product being sold on its Web site. For example, you should make sure to match items by the correct edition (if it's a book) or color (if it's a product).

REMEMBER

TIP

8. **From the Condition drop-down box, select your item's condition.**

Your choices include terms such as New; Used — Like New; Used — Very Good.

Click the Condition Guidelines link to find out how to select and describe the proper condition of your item.

9. **Enter a few comments about the specific condition of your product in the Add Your Comments about the Condition text box.**

You can enter as many as 1,000 characters. Use this opportunity to further describe your product, as shown in Figure 2-4. The additional information can increase sales.

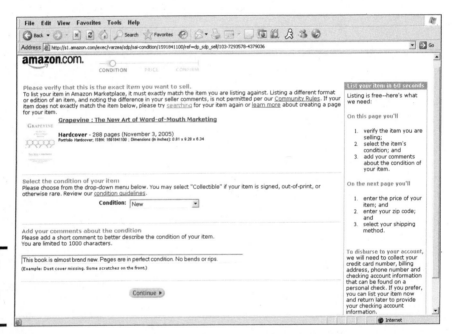

Figure 2-4:
Describe
your item's
condition.

10. **Click the Continue button at the bottom of the product condition page.**

The next page walks you through the final details of readying your product for sale.

11. **Enter the price for your item in the Enter Your Price box.**

For comparison, Amazon shows you its current price and other Marketplace prices for this item in the Pricing Details for Your Item box, which is on the right side of the page.

12. **Enter in the Quantity On-Hand box the quantity of the item you're selling.**

13. **Enter your zip code in the Enter Your Location box.**

You're shipping your item from this location.

You don't have to enter this information each time if you include it in your Seller's Account. Amazon automatically pulls your zip code from your account information. To add or change this preference, click the Editing Your Seller Preferences link.

14. **Choose the ways in which you're willing to ship the product.**

You're automatically required to provide standard shipping methods. But you can offer expedited and international shipping options, too. The correct amount is credited to your account to cover the shipping method that your customer chooses.

15. **Click the Continue button when you finish.**

16. **Enter your e-mail address and password into the appropriate boxes to register to accept payments from Amazon.**

You have to provide this information only once. If you already registered with Amazon to accept payments, skip to Step 18.

If you don't already have an account, click the I Do Not Have an Amazon. com Password button and follow the instructions for creating one.

17. **Follow the prompts for registration.**

You have to supply a valid credit card number, a U.S. bank account number, a U.S. phone number where Amazon.com can reach you directly, and your billing address.

If you're already an Amazon customer, your customer account information is automatically used for the registration process, speeding up the process significantly. But you always have the option to change or update your information.

To complete the registration process, you must be available to receive a verification phone call from Amazon.com. You enter the phone number where you can be reached, and then you respond to the automated prompts when called. Completing the verification process takes about 30 seconds.

When the registration process is complete, you return to the final page to finish posting your listing in the Marketplace.

18. **Review your complete listing as it appears on this final page. Click the Submit Your Listing button.**

You can make changes to your listing by clicking the Edit button in the upper-right corner of the page before clicking the Submit Your Listing button.

Book VIII
Chapter 2

Mastering
the Amazon

Amazon sends you a confirmation of your listing to your designated e-mail address. Then you simply wait for the item to be sold. After 60 days, if the item doesn't sell, Amazon removes it from your listings. You don't pay any fees if your item doesn't sell.

If you have a Pro Merchant account (see the next section), you can leave the listing on Amazon.com until you choose to remove it.

Achieving Pro Merchant Status

Realizing that you might want to increase your sales potential by using Amazon.com, the site established the Pro Merchant account. You're a primary candidate for this type of account if you sell more than 40 orders per month. And, it has grown into a competitive alternative to the eBay Power Seller program. As a Pro Merchant, you're still selling in the Marketplace: The way your listings look, the options for where the listings appear, and the way you post your items for sale are the same (see the section "Joining the Marketplace," earlier in this chapter, for details about selling in the Marketplace).

However, when you become a Pro Merchant seller, you gain a few definite advantages:

+ **Reduced fees:** The 99-cent transaction fee is automatically waived for all Pro Merchant accounts. All other commissions and fees remain, however.

+ **Bulk listing capabilities:** Designed for sellers of large inventory, the Pro Merchant account provides tools that make it easier to load and manage multiple listings. Included among the tools are

  • *Inventory Loader:* Modify, delete, and upload thousands of products at one time.

  • *Book Loader:* Match and upload books considered to have pre-ISBNs. Rare, collectible, or out-of-print books are in this category.

+ **Continuous listings:** Your listings never expire. You keep them posted until an item sells or you decide to remove them.

+ **Management functions:** You gain access to various reports that show the status of your account at any given time. These reports allow you to view all account activity (including items that shipped) for periods of the past 15, 30, or 60 days.

+ **Fraud protection:** Amazon offers a payment fraud protection program to help eliminate fraudulent products. It also offers an A-to-Z Guarantee program that protects both the customers and you, in case something goes wrong with an order.

Of course, unlike your basic Marketplace listing, opening a full account comes at a price. Amazon.com charges $39.99 per month for a Pro Merchant account (although it sometimes offers limited-time-only discounts for the first couple of months of service). Additionally, several categories require special approval from Amazon before you can begin selling. These categories include apparel, automotive parts, beauty products, cellphones and accessories, gourmet food, jewelry, personal computer, shoes and accessories, and watches. If you're selling in the toys-and-games category, you must also plan ahead. Amazon doesn't accept new sellers in that category during the holiday season, which usually starts in late October and runs through early January.

Needless to say, opening a Pro Merchant account can truly pay off. You have access to several different types of inventory reports, including

✦ **Open Listings:** In this report, you view all items that are available for purchase, including the items you marked as Coming Soon. You can also make changes to this report, using an Excel file, and then reload your updated listings.

✦ **Open Listings Lite:** Sometimes, you don't need to see all the information — only a few key points. This report allows you to make updates to your listings quickly and then reload the changes. The Lite report shows you this information: *seller-SKU number* (a unique number you use to identify a product you sell), quantity, price, and product ID.

✦ **Open Listings Liter:** The Open Listing Liter is scaled down even further than the Open Listing Lite report. One quick glance at this report provides you with access to only these two items: seller-SKU number and quantity.

✦ **Order Fulfillment:** Create a quick report of all products that have been purchased. You also see the buyer information (such as shipping address) so that you can send out the orders in a timely fashion.

✦ **Sold Listings:** You see an extensive report of all your product listings that have sold, even if payment may be still outstanding.

✦ **Cancelled Listings:** Just as it sounds, this report shows which items are no longer "in the hopper" because Amazon has cancelled them. Not included are any items that may be sold out, that the Inventory Loader purged, or that you may have nixed.

To sign up for a Pro Merchant account, look for the Start Now link, in the Have Lots to Sell section on the Sell Your Stuff page.

REMEMBER

Although Amazon handles the payment process between you and your customer, you're responsible for any returns or refunds. If a seller requests a refund, he has to ship the item back to you. And, you have to absorb the cost of the shipping. All refunds can be handled directly from your Amazon.com merchant seller account.

Book VIII Chapter 2

Mastering the Amazon

Taking Advantage of Other Selling Opportunities with Amazon Web Stores

Amazon has cleverly created several opportunities to make money using its site, products, and technologies. Truly, there's an opportunity for just about everyone. In addition to those we discuss earlier in this chapter, Amazon has two other programs, or Web stores.

The first, an aStore, is the simplest to get started. In fact, you don't even need your own inventory to sell using this method. Instead, Amazon allows you to examine its entire inventory of products and select which ones you want to sell. You sell them from a storefront that Amazon provides to you, at no charge. You can add the storefront to an existing Web site you already own or create a unique domain name (an *URL*) especially for your new Web store. Did we mention that it's entirely free?

What's the catch? Each time a product is sold, you earn only a small commission. In other words, you probably won't get rich serving as the Amazon. com middleman, but you can earn a few extra bucks.

Because the site has such an extensive selection of products, you can also use this option as a no-cost method of testing different types of products and how they might sell on your Web site, before investing in similar types of inventory. It's also a useful quick-start way to start selling products on a new site or on a blog for an extra revenue source.

Figure 2-5 shows an example of an aStore that 365Beach.com added to help sell beach-related products from the extensive Amazon inventory of products. To start creating this basic Web store and selecting products, go to `https://affiliate-program.amazon.com/gp/associates/astore/main.html`.

Another selling opportunity comes in the form of the Amazon.com WebStore. This branded e-commerce store is complete with everything you need to sell online. It uses the same back-end platforms that power the Amazon.com site. In addition to selling your own products, you can also extend your offerings and place Amazon merchandise for sale in your WebStore. Pricing starts at $59.99 per month, and Amazon charges a 7 percent commission on every item that's sold. However, unlike selling in the MarketPlace, you face no set-up or listing fees. Basically, WebStore is an alternative to other storefront selling solutions, but it comes with the name recognition of Amazon and allows you to piggyback, not only on its technologies but also on its promotional and marketing strength. Figure 2-6 shows how Home and Living (`www.homeandliving.com`) uses a WebStore for its e-commerce site. You can sign up by going to `http://webstore.amazon.com`.

Figure 2-5:
Add an
Amazon
aStore to a
site.

Figure 2-6:
Use a
WebStore to
sell online.

Chapter 3: Let's Hear It for Yahoo!

In This Chapter

- ✔ Setting up a Yahoo! e-commerce store
- ✔ Adding products to your store catalog
- ✔ Designing your store Web pages
- ✔ Comparing package solutions
- ✔ Calculating the fees for using Yahoo! Merchant Solutions
- ✔ Using marketing systems to bring in more customers
- ✔ Evaluating the success of your Yahoo! store

*O*ne big advantage of using Yahoo! Small Business is how easy the site makes it for you to create your own store. At all stages of the process, Yahoo! walks you through all the steps necessary to create, design, fill, and maintain your own store. Because it's one of the biggest and oldest Internet companies, Yahoo! can provide peace of mind by offering reliable solutions. Over the years, smaller companies have folded or changed or were acquired by other companies, so customers of these companies aren't sure what to expect. With Yahoo!, though, you know that your Web site will be fully functional and available, and live to see the next day, because Yahoo! professionals provide the technical expertise to keep all their Web sites running smoothly.

In this chapter, we talk about the many features that Yahoo! stores offer you, the basic platform of the small business solution, and how you perform basic navigation and item creation processes. We cover the different packages offered and describe how Yahoo! makes its money with this service. Finally, we talk about how you can make more money with your Yahoo! store, whether it's from marketing, customer relationships, or data analysis.

We can't cover all you need to know about starting a Yahoo! business. To delve into Yahoo! even more, check out *Starting a Yahoo! Business For Dummies*, by Rob Snell (Wiley Publishing).

Why Open a Yahoo! Store?

Although you can order different levels of solutions with Yahoo! (as you can read elsewhere in this chapter), a powerful base platform comes with every solution. Here are ten functions that every business can enjoy with Yahoo! Merchant Solutions:

✦ **Built-in shopping cart:** You can put an unlimited amount of products into your Yahoo! store, and its shopping cart software presents those items to your customers and lets them add them to, or delete them from, their own shopping baskets. Then the software interfaces with shipping companies and tax tables to show customers all their costs when they check out.

✦ **Customizable sales reports:** In case you want to see how your business is doing, Yahoo! gives you a whole set of customizable reports so that you can see what's selling, what's clicking, and what's being searched. You even see which Web sites send you the most traffic and which Web pages on your site are the most viewed.

✦ **Inventory tracking and alerts:** If you don't want to sell out of your hottest product or you need an e-mail alert when your available inventory gets too low, Yahoo! has you covered. It manages your inventory and automatically e-mails you if your inventory falls below a predetermined quantity.

✦ **Unlimited space and bandwidth:** If you have large image files or audio or video, you can relax. You get an unlimited amount of storage with each account and an unlimited amount of bandwidth available to send those massive files each time a customer comes a-knockin'.

✦ **Your own subdomains:** Maybe you want to create distinctive names for parts of your Web site or add subdomains so that you can have `shop. yourwebsite.com`, `ebay.yourwebsite.com`, or even `customer. yourwebsite.com`. You get as many as 500 subdomains per account, so choose wisely.

✦ **As many as 1,000 business e-mail accounts:** Yahoo! gives you the power to create as many as 1,000 unique business e-mail accounts. Each of these accounts comes with an unlimited amount of storage. Now your employees, temporary employees, family members, vendors, suppliers, or whoever needs a business e-mail from you can get it.

✦ **Secure (SSL) technology:** With Yahoo!, your customers can enter information safely because you can create secure Web pages by way of Secure Socket Layer (SSL) technology that encrypts sensitive data (such as credit card numbers) when customers transmit that info to you.

✦ **Credit card verification tools:** If you're worried about credit card fraud, use the Yahoo! free Risk Tools to help verify whether the card is real or stolen — before you send your customer's credit card number to be processed.

✦ **Norton AntiVirus and SpamGuard screening:** To keep your files and e-mail as clean as possible, Yahoo! uses Norton AntiVirus and SpamGuard software to scan and destroy viruses, spam, pop-up ads, and other nasty annoyances of doing business on the Internet.

✦ **Automatic backups of your Web site:** Yahoo! takes a snapshot of your Web site at regular intervals and lets you go back and forth between those versions. If you accidentally lose data, you can restore the last version quickly. Yahoo! making the backups without even asking or reminding you.

Setting Up Shop

When you ready to set up a Yahoo! store, follow these steps:

1. **Go to the Yahoo! home page (www.yahoo.com), and click Sell Online from the Yahoo! Small Business area, as shown in Figure 3-1.**

You can also go to http://smallbusiness.yahoo.com/merchant.

Figure 3-1: Yahoo! guides you to its online sales solutions.

The Yahoo Merchant Solutions page displays the most popular package that Yahoo offers: the Merchant Starter plan. (Two additional packages — Standard and Professional — are recommended for established e-commerce or offline businesses.) We discuss the prices and benefits of these packages later in this chapter, in the section "Selecting a Yahoo! Plan."

Yahoo Small Business offers more packages than just its Merchant Solutions. If you want to build a regular Web site, buy a domain name, or sign up for online marketing services, you can do so at Yahoo! Small Business. Find out more at `http://smallbusiness.yahoo.com`.

2. **Click the Sign Up button.**

3. **Enter a domain name for your Yahoo! store (see Figure 3-2).**

You should have a Web address in mind, but don't worry. If your first choice is taken, Yahoo! offers you several suggestions of available domain names similar to your request. If you already bought a domain name, simply click the link labeled Already Have a Domain Name? Use It with Your Order.

Figure 3-2:
Enter the domain name for your Yahoo! store here.

4. **Log in to Yahoo!**

If you have a Yahoo! ID, simply log in to Yahoo! for this step, and Yahoo! uses that information.

If you're new to Yahoo!, create a Yahoo! ID by clicking the Create One Now link. You see the Yahoo! one-page sign-up form. Enter your personal identification, such as name, birthday, e-mail address, credit card information, and billing address. Pick a user ID and password.

5. Enter your billing information.

You have to enter a credit card number to leave on file for Yahoo! to bill you monthly for your Merchant Solutions package. If you're new to Yahoo!, you need to verify your billing address for the card.

6. Review your options (see Figure 3-3) and then click the Continue button to finalize your order.

Make sure to choose wisely because it costs more money to go out and buy another domain name, for example.

Figure 3-3: Specify your options correctly.

Managing Your Yahoo! Services

After you sign up with Yahoo! Merchant Solutions, you can control all aspects of your account. Go to http://smallbusiness.yahoo.com and sign in with your Yahoo! ID to open your account home page (see Figure 3-4).

Figure 3-4:
Access
all your
account
controls
from one
screen.

From there, you have access to the four main parts of your account:

✦ **Store Manager:** Use this main screen to build, maintain, and update your store.

✦ **Web Hosting Control Panel:** Find out about your Web hosting space and how much room you still have in your account. You can download the SiteBuilder tool from this link (see the later section "Opening Your Store for Business" for more information) or create your own blog to appear on your Web site.

✦ **Domain Control Panel:** You can handle all aspects of owning a custom domain name for your online business. Here, you can update your domain registration, add more unique URLs to your overall business, and organize the sections of your Web site to appear as subdomains on your site.

✦ **Email Control Panel**: You can manage all your business e-mail accounts in this area. Create a new e-mail account, see how much space all your e-mail accounts are occupying, and set up a special e-mail account (a *catchall*) to receive mail that has been improperly addressed to someone at your business.

As your e-mail addresses are increasingly circulated, you run the risk that those accounts are being added to spam lists. The catchall can result in an overflowing account of spam; if that occurs, don't assign the catchall to any account.

Opening Your Yahoo! Store for Business

You're on the road to setting up your Yahoo! store, and no plan is complete without your home base of operations. For your customers, your home page is their central hub. For Yahoo! Merchant Solutions, that launching pad is the Store Manager page. When you log in to your account and click the Store Manager link, your main Store Manager page opens (see Figure 3-5), from which you can control almost every facet of building your store.

Figure 3-5:
Control your store from one page.

Constructing your catalog

What's a store without products? Yahoo! has the central program *Catalog Manager,* which lets you enter your products for sale and also tracks the inventory level as people place their orders. You can update your inventory at any time, organize your inventory by different product tables, and even upload your entire product catalog all at one time.

When you want to add a product to your database, follow these steps:

1. **From the Store Manager page, click the Catalog Manager link.**

   The main Catalog Manager page is displayed.

2. **Click the Manage Your Items link to add a new product.**

   If you already have a file (such as an Excel spreadsheet) that has your catalog inventory ready to go, you can upload the entire file and create your catalog in one step. Click the Upload Items link and then click the Upload button to send the file directly to your catalog database. Make sure that the file matches the Default table in your Store definition. See the tutorial at `http://lib.store.yahoo.net/lib/vw/catalog tutorial.html` for more information.

   The Default table of items that you defined in your store appears.

3. **Click the Add Item button.**

   This step opens the one-page Add Item form that Yahoo! provides.

4. **Complete these fields:**

   - *ID:* This is a unique ID identifier, in letters or numbers or both.

   - *Name:* Enter the name that you want your customers to see as the name of your product.

   - *Code:* This visible code identifies your product, like a UPC code.

   - *Price:* Every item must have a numeric price.

   - *Sale-price:* When you use this field, the sale price overrides the regular price, and your customers sees both prices, with a line through the regular price and the sales price highlighted.

   - *Orderable:* Set this option to Yes if you want customers to be able to order the product.

   - *Ship-weight:* Put the numeric weight of your item in this field. You can define the unit of measurement in your store settings.

   - Taxable: Set this option to Yes if you collect sales tax on this product.

5. **Enter the details of your product:**

   - *Image:* Specify the path where the digital image of your product is stored on your computer and upload it to your store.

   - *Options:* If you offer the same product in different sizes or colors or other options, don't create individual entries for each option. You simply enter your options, one line at a time, as a string of words with the option name and then the different options, like this:

     Size Small Medium Large

     Color Red Blue White Black

Do not use any internal punctuation, such as a comma, between the options. Yahoo! is looking for a space between each option.

- *Headline:* If you don't want customers to see the name of your product, you can add a headline here that replaces the name.

- *Caption:* Enter all details in this field (similar to an item description).

- *Abstract:* Think of the *abstract* as your summary, or a shorter version of the caption that your customers see when browsing your store.

- *Icon:* Specify and upload a thumbnail (picture file) to use when linking from category pages to your product page. This icon should be in GIF or JPG format only.

- *Inset:* (Optional) Specify a second thumbnail if you want.

- *Label:* Highlight a special feature of this item, such as new arrivals or sale items.

- *Download:* If you're selling a downloadable product, like an e-book or a music file, upload the file to your store so that Yahoo! can send it to your customers when they order it from your store.

6. **Click Save to store the item.**

    If you enter multiple items one at a time, you can click the Save and Add Another button instead to repeat the process.

7. **Repeat Steps 3 through 6 for any additional products.**

Opening the doors

When you want to open your store for business, Yahoo! walks you through its four-point checklist:

1. Research and plan your site: See what you like and dislike from other Web sites and come up with a plan for your Web site. See Book III, Chapter 2 for more info on developing a Web site design.

2. Build your store. You need to construct the Web pages that display your products. Building the actual store requires some design work, and Yahoo! provides you with three ways of building the actual pages you need:

    - *Store Editor:* Yahoo! has hundreds of special templates you can use to build all the necessary pages of your Web site. From the Store Manager page, click the Store Editor link; then choose from the pre-designed templates and assign the locations and attributes of your products to the page.

    - *SiteBuilder:* You can download SiteBuilder software from Yahoo! to your computer and then use drag-and-drop technology to build your Web sites. The SiteBuilder Store Products Wizard walks you step by step through the process of creating individual product pages, multiproduct pages, and the overall category pages to hold your products. Use this software to create your thumbnail images and navigation bars, and then publish your work to your Web site with a few clicks.

- *Dreamweaver Extension:* If you or your professional Web designer wants to use advanced Web design software such as Adobe Dreamweaver, Yahoo! has a special Dreamweaver extension that you can download and use with the program. This special plug-in allows you to create store tags that you insert into your pages, using Dreamweaver, and those tags then reference your catalog so that the page is automatically filled in with matching products whenever a customer views your Dreamweaver-built Web pages.

3. Set up payment processing. You need to decide how you want to handle payment processing for your store. You can use an online payment processing service (such as PayPal) or consult your bank to open a traditional merchant account to accept credit cards. You can find more about payment processing in Book IV, Chapter 4.

4. Set up and publish order settings. Click the Publish Your Order Settings link to set up your checkout form. Define your shipping and tax rates when applicable. The reason you have to publish your changes in Yahoo! is simple: When you're working on your store, your customers don't see the changes until you're ready to publish your changes, whether updating your catalog, store design, or order settings.

Selecting a Yahoo! Plan

As we mention throughout this book, rarely does a one-size-fits-all solution exist for building your online business. Yahoo! offers different levels of its Merchant Solutions service to coincide with the size and scope of your business. The beauty is that as your company grows, your Yahoo! plan can grow with it while you can move up the scale to a more robust set of services.

With other services, you have to pick your features *à la carte* by cobbling together a plan. Yahoo! gives all its merchants quite a strong foundation, offering enhancements for its larger clients to fulfill the needs of a growing customer base. Yahoo! has years of experience in offering different tools — such as e-mail, Web hosting, and marketing support — and those refined tools help make these packages that much more accessible.

Starter package: Starting out

Don't let the name fool you — the Yahoo! Starter package isn't a stripped-down, bargain basement tool that holds only five or ten products. This package provides quite a rich set of features and is an excellent jumping-on point for new e-commerce retailers.

With the Starter package, you get the ability to build your own store, host any number of products, and design your site by using Yahoo! tools. Some of the more advanced marketing and reporting techniques are reserved for the more expensive packages, but most small businesses wouldn't even need them.

Standard package: Moving up

The medium Yahoo! solution is its Standard package, which contains all the basic features of the Starter package but offers more advanced features that bigger e-commerce stores need to run their enterprises.

Some of the benefits you receive in the Standard package mean that you can

+ Receive orders by fax or e-mail (rather than just e-mail)

+ Send your order data in real-time to your own databases or applications

+ Export orders to UPS WorldShip shipping software

+ View the most popular search topics and paths taken by your customers on your Web site

+ Offer trackable Web links to affiliate or advertising programs

+ Offer gift certificates and coupons for your Web site

+ Feature special software to cross-sell your goods within your Web site

Professional package: Building on solid ground

As e-commerce Web sites grew, Yahoo! needed a solution for its biggest customers, especially for store owners whose stores grew past the magic million-dollar number in sales per year. Although rich functions are important to bigger Web sites, you should care mostly about *scalability* — the ability to grow your Web site's capability to match an increased amount of customers or demand. Therefore, Yahoo! created the Professional package for its Merchant Solutions.

The Professional package focuses on providing the right amount of capabilities to make sure that the customer's Web site brings in millions in sales just as smoothly as they were bringing in their first few orders.

Breaking Down the Fees

With Yahoo! Small Business, you incur fees the moment you sign up and decide to use the system. Whereas some companies charge a one-time fee for creating an e-commerce site or provide free tools in exchange for ad placements or ownership, Yahoo! Small Business works on a subscription model. You pay every month that you use its solution. Your payment to Yahoo! consists of a few types of fees:

✦ **Setup:** At the time of this writing, Yahoo! charges a $50 setup fee regardless of the plan you select. Look for promotions when this fee is waived; check partner sites, such as PayPal.com or JoelElad.com, for special deals to have the setup fee waived and 25 percent deducted from the regular price of your first three months of service.

✦ **Monthly:** Yahoo! Small Business charges a fixed monthly subscription fee for using its solution. The price varies by plans:

  • *Starter:* $25.97 for the first three months and $39.95 per month after that (with a partner promotion as just described)

  • *Standard:* $129.95 per month

  • *Professional:* $299.95 per month

✦ **Transaction:** In exchange for using its rich features (like the shopping cart and order checkout system), Yahoo! also takes a transaction fee for every sale you make in your store. Yahoo! takes a percentage of your sales, depending on the package that you select. As your sales go up, the percentage goes down:

  • *Starter:* 1.5%

  • *Standard:* 1.0%

  • *Professional:* 0.75%

This fee alone can determine your package level. For example, if you're getting at least $80,000 in sales per month, you should upgrade to the Professional package. The cost savings of the lower transaction fee easily pays for the extra monthly cost of the package.

Yahoo! provides a number of functions with its Merchant Solution packages, but the company charges extra for some added services. Table 3-1 outlines some of these extras, which are mainly useful for larger or rapidly expanding businesses.

Table 3-1	Additional Fees
Service	*Fee*
Private domain registration (hide Web site ownership)	$0.75 per month
Extra e-mail accounts for your business	$10 for 20 accounts
Search engine advertising programs	Varies by program

Growing with Your New Business Partner

After you use Yahoo! tools to build and run your Web site, you're probably ready to expand and grow your business further. That's why Yahoo! partnered with a number of companies that can help any online business grow, and those companies provide special discounts for Yahoo! Merchant Solutions members.

Marketing programs

There are so many ways to reach out, through the Internet and in the physical world, to spread the message of your business. Most people find that their biggest limitation is time because there are many more programs than there are hours in the day. That's where automation comes in. When you grow your plan, Yahoo! provides you with some ways to automate important merchandising features.

Shopping directory listings

If you're already using one of biggest search companies to manage your Web site, why not tap into its networks? Yahoo! has its huge Yahoo! Shopping, and you can pay to have your items listed as a part of this directory. An estimated 50 to 60 million shoppers use Yahoo! Shopping every month to find all sorts of products.

As a Yahoo! merchant, you qualify for a 20 percent discount when you submit your products to the Yahoo! Shopping directory. You then pay only when a potential customer clicks a product link of yours, whether that link showed up in its search results or after the customer read one of the Yahoo! Buyer Guides. Because Yahoo! can verify your status, it acknowledges your listings with a special Certified Merchant status and includes your items under the Buyer Protection Program for its customers. This way, the customers whom you reach are protected when they shop with you, which should encourage more spending. Yahoo! even bumps your text listings within its Buyer Guides to the top portion as a bonus, and lets you offer an Express Checkout so these potential customers can shop quickly with you.

To sign up with Yahoo! Shopping, open your Store Manager page (refer to Figure 3-5) and click the Yahoo! Shopping link in the Promote section.

You don't have to stop with the Yahoo! Shopping directory. Your Merchant Solutions package works with tools that Yahoo! provides to interface with Shopping.com and Shopzilla (two large shopping-comparison Web sites on the Internet), where you can pay per click to be mentioned in their product directories.

Search engines

As we discuss in Book VI, Chapter 6, search engine advertising is important. You can position yourself at the right moment when a potential customer is looking for your products. Yahoo! offers you the chance to take out ads in its Sponsored Search program so that you can present targeted ads that link back to your Yahoo!-powered store.

On your Store Manager pages (refer to Figure 3-5), simply click the Yahoo! Search Marketing link in the Promote section. You have to sign up for Yahoo! service, Search Marketing, and pick a starting budget for your campaign. You then specify which keywords you want to bid on and how much money you're willing to spend per click. Yahoo! does the rest.

Why stop with paid search engine ads? Yahoo! automatically submits your Web site to its search engine, but at what speed? Yahoo! offers a Search Submit Express package that allows you to send multiple URL addresses into its search engine for review, starting at $49 per year for the first URL. You can also pay $299 to have your entire site submitted to the Yahoo! Directory Search for inclusion so that people searching the extensive Yahoo! directory can see your directly on the right category pages. Although Yahoo! doesn't guarantee absolute inclusion, it does guarantee speed: Yahoo! promises to review Directory submissions within seven days.

Customer relationship management

You can build connections with your customers in lots of ways. The power of an online business is that you can reach your customers directly, one by one, rather than rely on a network of distributors, middlemen, and retailers to connect products with customers.

Yahoo!'s Standard and Professional packages allow you to offer features on your store like gift certificates and coupons. You can also provide automatic discounts to your customers, whether it's a one-time promotion, a reward for their first purchase, or an incentive to come back for a new order. Yahoo! keeps track of all the logistics so that you can provide a simple code to your customers that acts as a gift certificate or discount coupon and also update your customer's orders when needed.

After you get to know your customers, you begin to see what else you can sell them. *Cross-selling* offers a complementary product that fits well with the original purchase. For example, when you see a customer buying a CD recorder drive, you can reasonably assume that he needs blank CDs to record on. Yahoo! has a special cross-selling engine that lets you decide which products are offered to your customers when they pick any product in your store.

This feature is available only with the Standard and Professional Merchant Solutions packages.

You simply click the Cross-Sell feature from your Store Manager page (refer to Figure 3-5). You then specify rules that display products that complement what a shopper is buying. For example, you can set a rule that your batteries should be displayed every time someone orders a portable CD player.

Report results

You must think that we love reports, the way we talk about them repeatedly in this book. We are fans of reports for one basic reason: You don't know where you can go if you don't understand where you've been. Yahoo! offers a number of sales reports to help you track what's succeeding and what isn't, so pay attention to these reports and make smart decisions about how to grow your business.

Sales reports

The lifeblood of any online company is its orders. Your Store Manager provides easy-to-find statistics in the middle of its offerings. You can click the Sales link to display a chart of the orders you've received and the items that have sold. You can click the Reports link to see preformatted summaries of customers, orders, page views, and income from your store, by the month, week, or day. You can even export that data to Excel if you want to do further number crunching.

If you're interested in doing your own data analysis with Excel, check out *Excel Data Analysis For Dummies*, 2nd Edition, by Steve Nelson (Wiley Publishing).

After you see your customers' orders, you can then see how they found you in the first place. Click the References link to see a report of all visits your Web site has received. For each visit, you see the *referring URL*, which is the Web address your customer was viewing before coming to your Web site. Yahoo! even ties together the orders that came from these links so that you can see the revenue per visit. This information gives you an idea of how valuable a new customer can be — so that you know how much to spend to get that new customer to return.

If the referral URL is from a search engine, pay attention to the URL closely. You see the exact search terms that the visitor typed in the search engine to find you. Knowing these words should definitely influence your search engine marketing campaigns.

One report that you don't see often on e-commerce platforms is the Yahoo! Repeat report. Yahoo! tracks repeat customers, showing you how often those repeat customers come back to you and the items they ordered. After you know your core set of repeating customers, you can cater to them more effectively and grow sales through them. When you watch your repeat customers' orders, calculate their value to your business by watching the trends of which items move the best, what your active customers are buying daily, and the key ingredients of how recently they spent, how frequently they spend, and how much they spend.

Path reports

Your sales reports give you a useful picture of how your Web site is doing overall. Your next level of reports should tell you about the individual customer so that you can see what to update to appeal more to that specific sale. Therefore, Yahoo! gives its bigger merchants (Standard and Professional packages) the ability to watch customers and see how those customers use your site.

Imagine if you could follow a grocery store customer around the store. You could see which aisles she walks down, where she stops to examine a product, which items she scoops off the shelf and decides whether to put in her shopping cart, and whether she leaves the store after making a purchase or just walks out, leaving with a half-empty cart in Aisle 7.

Yahoo! has a special Click Trails report that gives you the same ability to follow your Web site customers, if you have a Standard or Professional merchant account. This report shows you the exact path a customer takes in your store, showing you each page he sees as well as the link he clicked to open the next page. You can follow that path to understand which parts of your store enjoy the most traffic as well as which parts aren't seen. With this knowledge, you can put your valuable merchandise where your customers virtually walk.

Of course, some customers don't wander and browse. They type search words and try to go directly to the product page they need. To track this type of customer, Yahoo! also shows the most frequent words in your own Web site's search engine (not the main Yahoo! site). You see a ranked list of the top search terms that your customers use every day to find your specific products. You can then take this list and ensure that your inventory matches accordingly. It all comes back to matching the right product with the right customer.

Chapter 4: Making eBay THE Way

In This Chapter

✔ Figuring out the basics of eBay

✔ Getting your eBay experience going

✔ Starting an eBay auction

✔ Opening an eBay store

*I*n the past decade, eBay has grown from a quiet, small online bazaar into the most powerful consumer trading platform on Earth. Although other Internet companies grew overnight into sensations and burned out of existence just as quickly, eBay has remained profitable from the first month it started charging users.

eBay is an effective way to gain customers, establish cash flow, and turn over some inventory. The beautiful part of eBay is that it handles many routine tasks that you need to handle by using e-commerce: the trading platform, Web site, and software needed to transact the sale. The one thing that eBay can't provide, however, is a guaranteed stream of customers or income just on its own. Building an eBay business requires some work and effort, however, combined with a number of strategies and tactics.

In this chapter, we show you how to get up and running on eBay with auctions. Then, when you have your feet wet, we detail how to advance to the big leagues with a dedicated eBay store.

Running an eBay business doesn't require that you focus all your efforts on eBay. eBay can simply be one channel for selling goods and making money, or you can use eBay to start your business before you launch your own Web site. In this chapter, we present a plan for building steady, constant sales through this channel, and you decide how you want to use eBay, based on your total online business strategy.

Understanding How eBay Works

Online sales usually involve four key elements: product, price, seller, and buyer. On eBay, rather than pay a fixed price, buyers compete with one another to win the item in a bidding system. If you've ever been to a live auction, you know that buyers raise their bid price until one bidder remains, and then that highest bidder pays the top price and receives the item. On eBay, members place a bid electronically rather than raise a paddle.

Here's the basic flow of how an eBay auction transaction works:

1. List an item for sale on eBay. See the "Setting Up an Auction" section, later in this chapter.

2. A buyer places a bid on eBay for your item, indicating the highest price he's willing to pay.

3. The buyer with the highest bid at the end of the auction's time period wins the item, and eBay sends an e-mail to you and the highest bidder.

4. You send the highest bidder an invoice, indicating the total for the item sold, including shipping, handling, and sales tax (when applicable) and how you accept payment.

   If you need to set up your accepted forms of payment, see Book IV, Chapter 4.

5. The buyer sends you payment.

6. You mail the item to the buyer. See Book IV, Chapter 7 for more info on shipping products to your buyers.

7. You and your bidder can leave comments about your transaction, known as *feedback,* on eBay. See the "Leaving feedback for your buyer" section, later in this chapter.

Getting Started on eBay

Signing up for eBay is easy, and it's free. Your account can be used to browse, bid, and sell on eBay. The main requirement is that you have to be 18 years or older. Just fire up your Internet browser and go to www.ebay. com and follow these steps:

1. **Click the Register button.**

   The Enter Information page appears.

2. **Enter your personal information and click Continue.**

   You're required to give your full name, address, phone number, and e-mail address, which eBay keeps on file if it needs to communicate with you.

   The Your User ID and Password page appears, as shown in Figure 4-1.

3. **Enter your User ID and password.**

   Every eBay user has to have a unique ID. Think of the ID as your "name to the world" for doing business on eBay. It can be a variation of your own name (like johndoe1), the name of your business (mybusiness.com), or the name of a category where you plan to sell (buddyselectronics).

Figure 4-1:
Create your
user ID and
password
to use on
eBay.

[Screenshot of eBay.com - Registration: Enter Information - Microsoft Internet Explorer]

Your User ID and Password - All fields are required

Create an eBay User ID

[ ] [Check Availability of User ID]

Your User ID identifies you to other eBay users. Learn more about eBay User IDs

Create password

[ ]

6 character minimum See tips

Re-enter password

[ ]

Secret question   Secret answer
[Pick a suggested question... ∨]   [ ]

You will be asked for the answer to your secret question if you forget your password.

Date of birth
[--Month-- ∨] [--Day-- ∨] Year [ ]
You must be at least 18 years old to use eBay.

Terms of use and your privacy - All fields are required

[ ] I agree to the following:
• I accept the User Agreement and Privacy Policy.
• I may receive communications from eBay and I understand that I can change my notification preferences at any time in My eBay.
• I am at least 18 years old.

[Continue >]

Click the Check Availability button to see whether the name you want has been taken. If it's taken, eBay prompts you for information and suggests some ID names that are available.

You aren't permanently stuck with your first choice. eBay allows you to change your user ID once every 30 days.

Your password should be something that no one can randomly guess. eBay requires that your password be at least six characters long, but you need to pick a combination of letters and numbers that isn't your user ID, family member's name, or a common word that someone can guess.

4. Pick a secret question and supply your answer.

To help prove your identity in case you forget your password, eBay asks you the secret question you selected and looks for the answer you supplied.

Your mother's maiden name is a valuable piece of information that banks and credit cards use for verification, so you may not want to select that question here.

5. Enter your date of birth.

Using the drop-down boxes, select the month and day of your birth date. Then type the four-digit year of your birthday. No bouncer will check your ID, but you have to be at least 18 to legally do business here.

6. Agree to the Terms and Conditions and then click Continue.

Book VIII
Chapter 4

Making eBay
THE Way

If there's a problem with your address, phone number, or user ID selection, eBay prompts you with an error and returns you to the previous step.

Otherwise, you see the Check Your Email page, which indicates that an e-mail has been sent to the e-mail address you provided.

7. **Open your e-mail and click the activation link.**

If, for some reason, your e-mail system doesn't support clicking links from the e-mail message, you can confirm your registration by going to the registration screen at `http//:pages.ebay.com/register`.

Your confirmation page is displayed, and your eBay account becomes active!

After you register on eBay, you have to perform some additional details before starting your first auction or opening a storefront:

✦ **Sign up for PayPal:** PayPal, the eBay version of online payment processing, lets you send or receive money based on your online sales, on or off eBay. You can maintain an account on PayPal for free — you pay only a transaction fee (typically 2.5 to 2.9 percent) when you receive a payment. Go to `www.paypal.com` to sign up.

You can also sign up for a merchant account from your bank, where you can process credit cards directly. You must have either a PayPal or merchant account if you want to sell on eBay, and PayPal is the most recommended payment method. According to research from eBay, 90 percent of all eBay auctions offer PayPal as a payment method, and 80 percent of all transactions are paid for through PayPal.

✦ **Set up a dedicated bank account:** Both eBay and PayPal require you to provide a credit card number and your bank account information in order to create an account. We recommend setting up a second bank account at a smaller bank and getting a Visa or MasterCard debit card through this account so that you can keep track of your eBay activity separately from your main banking transactions.

✦ **Set up an About Me page:** Use this page to advertise your own online store, talk about your online sales activities, and detail your reputation for doing business on the Internet. You can include a picture on this page, whether it's an image of your retail storefront, your company logo, or one of your products.

To create your About Me page, click the Community button at the top of any eBay page. At the bottom of the page, click the Create an About Me Page link (see Figure 4-2). You can either insert your own Web page HTML code or answer some questions and post your description, photo, and information about yourself.

✦ **Research your competition:** You can find out how to price your items, see which items are selling well, and determine which ones to stay away from. In the Search box, which is in the upper-right corner of every eBay page, type the words that describe the item you want to sell and click Search. To see past sales, select the Completed Items Only check box after you perform your first search. You can then sort these past sales by price, from highest to lowest, and see a snapshot of how your item has sold on eBay in the past couple of weeks, by seeing the most successful sales first. You can also sort by distance to see how nearby competitors are doing, or sort by oldest or newest listings to get a sense of price levels over time.

Research not only helps show you what to expect as a price for your item; it can also give you the following useful information:

- Which keywords to use in describing your item
- Which category on eBay to place your item in
- Which features you should mention about your item
- The current level of supply and demand for this item on eBay

Here are the main questions you should answer while doing research:

- Are the items I want to sell doing well on eBay?
- Are the prices the items are selling for enough for me to make a profit?

If the answer to either of these questions is No, you may want to find other items to sell instead, before you invest time and money on a product line that's wrong for eBay.

Figure 4-2:
Create your own profile page or About Me page.

Create an About Me page.

You can take advantage of lots of other eBay features and options that we don't cover here. Check out *eBay Business All-In-One Desk Reference For Dummies,* by Marsha Collier (Wiley Publishing), for your authoritative and complete reference to using eBay.

Setting Up an Auction

A sale on eBay is, basically, an auction. You know the kind: *1, 2, 3, Sold to the highest bidder!* But rather than wave their hands enthusiastically, bidders place a bid on your auction by using their computers.

You set up an auction by getting an item or a product you want to sell, writing a description of the product and taking photos of it, and creating a Web page with all the basic information about that product.

The reasons you want to set up an auction are many, but here are some of the top ones:

+ **Auctions attract people's interest.** Shopping on eBay has become more than a matter of buying items. It's now a form of entertainment, with bidding, competing, and winning. After people bid on an item, they're more likely to follow the auction to its completion and stay emotionally invested in acquiring the item.

+ **Auctions get more attention.** Although eBay is selling a lot of items at fixed prices, the primary avenue of sales is still the auction format. When people search on eBay, the first thing they see is a list of auctions that match the search. When you use an eBay store, the buyer has to go directly to you before seeing your items. When you use an auction, the entire community can see your items for auction by making a simple search.

+ **Auctions move merchandise faster.** When you sell items on your own store or by using an eBay store, it can take days, weeks, or even months to find the right buyer. With an eBay auction, you can sell an item in one to ten days and find your high bidder, and some interested underbidders, much quicker. Think of the auction as a call to action, and the buyers decide to respond.

+ **Auctions cost the seller only money per item, not per month.** When you operate an eBay store, you're paying a monthly fee regardless of how many items you sell. In an eBay auction, you're paying only a small fee to list the auction, and another fee if the item sells.

+ **Auctions let you test the water.** Rather than launch a full-blown store for your items, you can run a few eBay auctions and gauge the interest of the buying community. You can get an idea of success before investing in Web site design and programming.

Of course, auctions have some drawbacks. The fees involved in running auctions can add up if you're continually trying to sell something that receives no bids. Although a short timeframe of the auction helps move inventory, it's also quickly forgotten in the minds of the buyer. You have to run a lot of auctions to build the constant presence needed in order to remind buyers of who you are. Without repeat buyers and the constant flow of goods, it's hard to build a sustainable flow of revenue by putting up random auctions every week. Auctions provide an excellent piece of the overall e-commerce business plan, however.

The easiest way to get started on eBay is to plunge ahead and set up an auction. Look around your business inventory for something that you want to sell and follow these steps:

1. **Click the Sign In link at www.ebay.com.**

2. **Enter your user ID and password in the appropriate boxes and click the Sign In Securely button.**

3. **Click the Sell button at the top of any eBay page.**

   The Choose a Selling Format page appears.

4. **Type a few words that describe your item and click Search.**

   The first step in selling your item is figuring out which category should be assigned to your auction item. eBay has more than 50,000 unique categories, organized in more than 30 categories, such as Antiques, Art, and Books. After you click Search, eBay prompts you with a list of the most likely categories where your item belongs.

   If the list of suggested categories isn't accurate, click the Browse Categories tab and search eBay's category structure yourself to find the most appropriate subcategory for your item.

5. **Pick your category and the appropriate subcategories, and then click Continue.**

   The main auction page opens, where you describe everything about your item for sale.

6. **Enter these elements:**

   - *Title:* Incorporate the most frequently used keywords about your item so that buyers who search eBay's database for items like yours can find it.

   - *Item Specifics:* Enter specific details depending on what you're selling. (For example, every shoe has a size, width, and color.) The more details you enter in the boxes provided, the more easily buyers can find your item.

7. **Scroll down the page to the Bring Your Item to Life with Pictures section.**

8. **Click the Add Pictures button to attach any digital photos to your auction. Scroll down to the next section when you're done.**

Book VIII
Chapter 4

Making eBay
THE Way

When you click the Add Pictures button, a second window opens, asking you to identify where on your computer the pictures for the auction are located. After you pick those pictures, click the Upload button to close that window and send the pictures from your computer to eBay.

9. **Enter a description in the Describe the Item You're Selling section. When you're done with the description, scroll down to the next section.**

   Remember to add not only a description of the item but also all your policies about payment and shipping methods, as well as a return policy. Use the buttons that eBay provides above the Description window to add bold, italic, or underlined text as well as bulleted or numbered lists.

10. **Enter your starting bid (or a fixed Buy It Now price), and set the duration and items in your lot. When you finish with this part, scroll down to the next section.**

   You can either enter the starting price of your auction (and assign either a Reserve or Buy It Now price, or both) or click the Fixed Price tab and sell your items for a fixed Buy It Now price. eBay now allows you to sell items at a fixed price for up to 30 days at a time.

11. **Choose which payment methods you're willing to accept for your item and which shipping options you're willing to provide (see Figure 4-3). Scroll down to the next section when you're done.**

Figure 4-3: You decide where in the world you're willing to ship your item.

For payments, you can accept PayPal, a credit card (using your merchant account) or ProPay. For shipping, some options you can choose from include whether you're willing to sell your item only to customers in the U.S. or around the world. If you don't want to ship something (such as a heavy piano), pick the Will Not Ship — Local Pickup Only option.

You must enter a flat price for shipping or click the Calculated tab and let eBay calculate your postage costs based on the weight and the buyer's zip code. Your only other options are Freight Shipping or Local Pickup Only.

12. **In the last section, define your sales tax rate and return policy and provide any additional checkout instructions to your customers. Click Continue when you're done.**

13. **Review the possible listing upgrades that eBay offers you for your auction. Make sure that your title and Gallery thumbnail photo appear correctly in the sample. Look over the information you entered and the choices you made.**

14. **If everything looks good to you, click Submit.**

    Your listing goes live on the eBay site. If you want to fix something, click the Edit Listing link to return to the previous page and make corrections before clicking Submit.

If you're selling a similar item, you can click the Sell a Similar Item link to create a brand-new auction, with all the information fields already filled in. You simply make the changes necessary for your second item and submit the new auction in a fraction of the time it took you to complete your first listing!

Maintaining your auctions

You receive a free tool to help manage all your eBay activities, both buying and selling. The My eBay tool is accessible from the top of any eBay page: Simply click the My eBay button. Think of My eBay as your personal dashboard for monitoring your eBay buying and selling activity.

If you click the All Selling link, you see the Selling home page and its distinct sections:

- ✦ **Selling Reminders:** Your to-do list showing what to complete
- ✦ **Scheduled Items:** The items you're going to sell later
- ✦ **Selling Totals:** Your summary of sales
- ✦ **Items I'm Selling:** Your items still up for bid on eBay
- ✦ **Items I've Sold:** Items that received at least one valid bid and are completed
- ✦ **Unsold Items:** Completed items that didn't receive any bids

When you click the Items I'm Selling link, you see a live snapshot of all items you have for sale on eBay: auctions, fixed price, and store inventory items. This page shows you a lot of information about each item you're selling:

✦ The current high bid

✦ The number of bids that have been placed

✦ The amount of time remaining in the auction

✦ The number of people watching your item

✦ The number of questions people have

When your item has completed the bidding stage, it appears on another page within My eBay: Items I've Sold. This page provides you with a visual checklist of tasks you need to complete after the winning bidder has been determined. For every item, there are five icons along the right side of the screen. When you complete one of these steps, the icon is colored purple. This way, you know what needs to be done on each item you sold.

Leaving feedback for your buyer

Because eBay buyers typically don't meet sellers, they require a level of trust to buy something sight unseen. eBay builds this trust by maintaining a feedback score, allowing the buyer to see the trading reputation of any other eBay member instantly. Buying on eBay gives you a way to build a trading history and a positive reputation, which can help you as you start to sell on eBay.

For every transaction you participate in on eBay, whether you buy or sell, you're allowed to give feedback to the other party when the sale is over. This feedback is aggregated into a numerical score for every eBay user, along with a feedback record made up of comments from other users, as shown in Figure 4-4.

As a buyer, you can now leave three kinds of feedback for a seller:

✦ **Positive:** Increases the feedback score by one

✦ **Neutral:** Doesn't affect the feedback score up or down

✦ **Negative:** Reduces the feedback score by one

The seller is allowed only to leave positive feedback for the buyer or to report the buyer for not paying for the auction. The feedback system is a way to report whether people complete transactions reasonably and fairly. It isn't supposed to be a complaint or vendetta forum, although some users see it that way. Positive feedback is left when the transaction was handled satisfactorily or if both parties worked out an agreement to resolve the transaction. Neutral or negative feedback should be reserved for only those transactions where sellers grossly misrepresent themselves and do absolutely nothing to correct the situation.

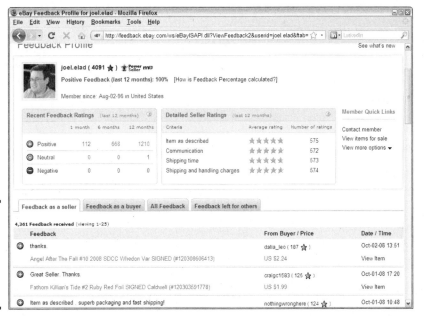

Figure 4-4:
Feedback
becomes
your instant
reputation
on eBay.

In addition, buyers can rate their sellers on four different dimensions of the transaction, using a scale from 1 to 5. These Detailed Seller Ratings, or DSRs, are designed to weed out the bad sellers and reward the good sellers. The buyer can rate the seller based on these criteria:

✦ **Item as described:** How closely does the item resemble its description in the auction? (A score of 5 means the same item, and 1 means grossly different.)

✦ **Communication:** Did the seller communicate with you, as the buyer, sufficiently during the process? (A score of 5 means yes, and 1 means silence.)

✦ **Shipping time:** How quickly from your payment (as the buyer) does the item arrive to you? (A score of 5 means a quick turnaround time, and 1 means that you're still waiting six weeks later.)

✦ **Shipping-and-handling charges:** Did the seller charge you a fair price to package and ship the item to you, based on the category average? (A score of 5 means that it was reasonable, and 1 means that it was outrageous.)

Every buyer's feedback is then aggregated and shown on the seller's feedback page as a set of stars, from 1 to 5, as long as ten buyers have responded in the past 30 days. Sellers are given a Final Value Fee discount for DSRs higher than 4.6 on all four dimensions, but their accounts are suspended if any DSR falls below 4.3. A PowerSeller loses PowerSeller status if any DSR falls below 4.5.

Staying successful on eBay

Follow these guidelines to become successful on eBay:

✔ **Set up a template with your policies:** Use the description section of an auction listing to detail your policies for doing business. Mention the condition of the item, the payment methods you accept, how you plan to ship the item, any return policies you offer, and any other legal policies.

✔ **Write clear, organized descriptions:** Provide all the information your buyers want to know when they're making a decision about whether to buy your item. Make sure that your description makes sense and guides the buyer toward decision. And, make sure that any description of an item you're selling contains the condition of the item (its functionality, make, manufacturer, brand name, and model number) and its physical characteristics (color, size, and weight).

✔ **Define your shipping and return policies clearly:** eBay now requires all sellers to specify defined shipping costs for all auctions, a defined handling time to process the auction, and a defined return policy for each auction. Therefore, think about your policies in advance, research the items your competitors are offering, and ensure that every auction you create has all its policies defined.

✔ **Add photos to your listings:** If a picture is worth a thousand words, it's worth even more on eBay because the buyer doesn't get to see the item until the bidding is over. Therefore, you want the best pictures you can produce: Blurry or dark photos just scare buyers away, and pictures that are too large take too long to appear on the screen, which can also turn buyers away.

Feedback cannot be altered after it's given, so think carefully before giving feedback. If you're having a dispute with the other party, try to work out the situation before leaving feedback.

Every member's feedback score is represented next to her user ID, along with color-coded stars after the score reaches 10. Multiple feedback from the same person within the same week increases the score by only 1, so if Aunt Sally buys ten items from you at one time, it raises your score by only one point. If she buys one item per week, you receive multiple feedback credit for multiple sales, even if it's to the same person.

Opening an eBay Store

An eBay store is an interesting combination of eBay sales and your own e-commerce store. Think of owning an eBay store as owning a small shingle underneath eBay's massive marketplace.

With an eBay store, you benefit from these features:

✦ **A dedicated e-commerce storefront:** You can direct your customers to one place, which you can advertise on anything printed material you send out to any customers worldwide. Then you can see exactly which pages, which items, and which deals your customers looked at the most, so that you can see what's working and what's boring.

An eBay store can significantly increase your sales because it gives you another mechanism for reaching customers. Every time you sell an item on eBay through an auction, you can point the winner (and all your other bidders) to your eBay store to buy additional merchandise. You can list thousands of items in your eBay store that would cost too much to auction individually.

✦ **The chance to sell items on eBay at a fixed price:** You don't have to take a lower bid as you may with an auction that lasts only as long as 10 days. Post your item for the price you want and wait for someone willing to pay that price. Your store inventory can last for months, so there's not as much pressure to offer low prices to attract bidders.

✦ **List items in your store for months at a time:** If something doesn't sell right away, you don't have to list it again in an auction. You can keep it in your store until it sells.

eBay Stores give you a place to sell your products online under a fixed address, but they also come with many other features to make your business more successful. Here's a look at five features that can assist you with running your eBay store:

✦ **Accounting Assistant:** This new Web site function can export all your eBay and PayPal information directly into QuickBooks (accounting software).

✦ **Store referral credit:** Promote your items outside eBay. When a customer comes directly into your eBay store by using a targeted ad link that you create and promote, you can have credited to your account as much as 75 percent of the eBay final commission assessed on that item!

✦ **Advertising templates:** You can download these templates to create everything from business cards to stationery and envelopes to flyers that advertise your store in magazines, newspapers, and other print media.

✦ **Coordinating active customer lists:** The e-mail newsletter function also helps you handle the mass e-mail of marketing items, such as your monthly newsletter or sales announcements.

✦ **eBay's traffic reports:** Find out exactly which pages within your store receive the most traffic, which search words are used most often inside store searches, and which inventory items are selling most quickly.

Have we sold you on running an eBay store? Well, before you do so, you need to know that you have to pay eBay some additional fees for the glory. Your very own eBay store costs some money, from $15.95 to $299.95 per month, depending on the functionality and placement you want for your store. If you're running a small business, you can do quite well with the Basic package or the slightly more expensive Featured package, which includes bonus features for marketing and tracking your store. If you want your store to become an anchor in a certain category, with quality placement and features (think of an anchor department store in a mall), you may want to consider the (pricey) Anchor store plan. After you pay for any store subscription, adding items to your store costs about 3 to 10 cents per listing per month that it's listed. When the item sells, you pay a sliding scale commission to eBay.

Setting up shop

You retain a lot of control with your eBay store and get to study your customer's shopping habits. If you're ready to have your own eBay storefront, here's what you need to know.

You have to have a feedback score of 20 or a PayPal account in good standing to open an eBay store. Try to build up your score and gain some experience before opening an eBay store.

Before you open your store, make sure that you have these items lined up:

+ A good name picked out for your store because it can be (and usually should be) different from your eBay user ID

+ A store inventory sufficient to make having a store worthwhile

+ The knowledge that you can handle the extra work of selling merchandise at any given time, not just when a batch of auctions is over

When you're ready, go to `stores.ebay.com`, and follow these steps to open your store:

1. **Click the orange Open My Store button.**

   Log in with your user ID and password if you need to.

   A Subscription Level page opens (as shown in Figure 4-5).

2. **Pick your subscription level.**

   Your buyers won't know your store subscription level because all the core functionality comes with the basic platform. Most PowerSellers who are starting out pick the Basic option ($15.95 per month) and move up to the Featured level when they want to do more online marketing with their stores.

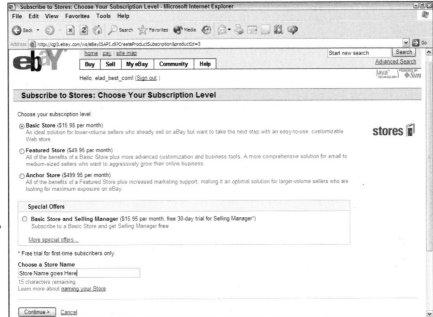

Figure 4-5:
Choose
your store
subscription
level.

3. **Enter your store name and click Continue.**

You can use as many as 35 characters for your store name, so choose
wisely. Don't infringe on any copyrighted name, especially the word
eBay, with your store name, but make it memorable.

The Provide Basic Information page opens.

4. **Enter a store description.**

Provide a short, 300-character description of your store. Only text
is allowed, so write one to two sentences and use the appropriate
keywords to describe what your store will sell. eBay sends this store
description to the search engines, so pick your words carefully.

5. **Pick a graphical image for your store and click Continue.**

eBay offers a multitude of free banners and artwork that you can use to
add a picture to your store home page. If you have a custom-designed
logo, you can upload it, or maybe you can use a picture of a retail storefront you maintain.

6. **Agree to the terms and click Subscribe.**

Your store is live!

**Book VIII
Chapter 4**

**Making eBay
THE Way**

Managing your store

After you sign up for an eBay store, it's time to get in there, spruce it up with some colors, logos, and products, and open it for business! At any time, you can manage your eBay store by clicking one of two links:

✦ From your store's home page, scroll to the bottom of the page and click the Seller, Manage Store link.

✦ From the eBay Stores home page, click the orange Manage My Store button.

The Manage My Store page opens, as shown in Figure 4-6. From there, you have access to the main features of your store, including but not limited to the ones in the following list:

✦ **Store design:** Use the Display Settings option to pick from many preformatted templates that you can use for your eBay store design. You can define as many as 300 custom store categories, such as Top Picks of the Month or Gifts Under $10. If you want to add several pages to your Store, such as a policies or shipping page, you can do so by using the Custom Pages link.

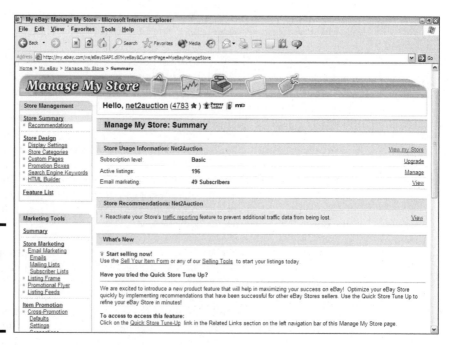

Figure 4-6:
The central hub for updating your eBay store.

✦ **Store marketing:** You can control any e-mail marketing campaigns you want to run regarding your eBay store. eBay helps coordinate any lists of customers you build. eBay also coordinates the mass e-mailings of newsletters and special promotions for you, and helps design flyers and distribute product information for you. See Book VI, Chapter 3 for more general information about running an e-mail marketing campaign.

✦ **Item promotion:** When you link your items and set cross-promotion rules, this function controls it all. You can specify rules and preferences for how your items should be cross-promoted throughout your store, and set up favorites to appear as featured items on your store's home page.

✦ **Logos and branding:** When you have a custom logo, use this function header to upload the logo to customized e-mail messages that you use to communicate with your customers.

For a full, in-depth explanation of maximizing your eBay store experience, you can't go wrong with *Starting an eBay Business For Dummies*, 2nd Edition, by Marsha Collier (Wiley Publishing). It's full of tips, tricks, and techniques that you can use to make your eBay store shine.

Becoming a PowerSeller

eBay has a special term for people who sell a steady amount of merchandise every month, earn a high amount of positive feedback, and comply with all eBay listing policies: *PowerSellers*. eBay has different levels of PowerSellers, starting with Bronze ($1,000 per month) and going all the way up to Titanium ($150,000 per month). Every PowerSeller has to maintain at least a 98 percent positive feedback rating with a minimum of 100 feedback comments earned on their account, and create at least four listings per month. When you qualify, eBay sends you an invitation to accept your PowerSeller status. After you become a PowerSeller, you qualify for special benefits, such as Extended Seller Protection, where eBay and PayPal protect you as a seller if a buyer pays with PayPal and you can provide proof that you shipped out the item.

eBay calculates your sales level using a three month average. If your average sales level drops below the PowerSeller minimum, eBay gives you one month to increase your sales; after that, you lose your PowerSeller status. However, after you increase your average sales, you can be reinstated.

Although not all PowerSellers focus on the same categories or use the same means to rack up impressive and steady sales, they typically share one bond (the reason that their sales jumped to the next level): "the sale."

Most PowerSellers can tell you about the single item they sold early on in their eBay trading experience — usually an item that they had little faith in or little money invested in. Someone might have put the item up for sale under an eBay ID and waited. Maybe the person watched the bidding every day or every hour or forgot about it completely. But the seller never forgot the thrill of seeing the high bid when the auction was over, and that's how that person became hooked, by investing the time and figuring out the different techniques to work their way up to PowerSeller status.

After you achieve PowerSeller status, your focus is on every sale, not just a single memorable sale, and on keeping track of a growing number of sales and customers. Many PowerSellers look into using a third-party tool to help manage their sales. You might try a program, such as Auctiva (`www.auctiva.com`), that can help you manage listings and sales activities. If you carry a large volume, try an Enterprise solution from ChannelAdvisor (`www.channeladvisor.com`) or MarketWorks (`www.marketworks.com`) that manages your sales across eBay and any other channels where you sell online and combines every sale into easy-to-read reports.

For the ultimate source in third-party tools, check out eBay's Solutions Directory at `http://solutions.ebay.com`.

Joining the Reseller Marketplace

After you become a PowerSeller, eBay gives you access to a special Reseller's Marketplace, where you can buy wholesale lots of goods from reputable sellers. eBay allows only PowerSellers to buy and sell in this marketplace, so you don't have as much competition from other eBay sellers.

You can find preapproved large sellers, such as Belkin, who sell everything from laptops to clothing in large quantities. It works just like eBay's main marketplace, where you place bids for the lots you want to buy. Unlike when you search for a reputable wholesaler, eBay screens the sellers that want to participate in this marketplace before they can put something up for sale. Thanks to eBay, you have a secure marketplace to buy large quantities of salable merchandise to ramp up your sales.

You can find more information about this marketplace by going to `http://reseller.ebay.com/ns/home.html`.

Chapter 5: New Storefronts, New Opportunities

In This Chapter

✔ Discovering auction sites beyond eBay

✔ Using storefronts to sell to your town

✔ Selling on demand with CafePress

✔ Spotting other storefronts that are worth your attention

The big-name storefronts, such as Yahoo! and eBay, remain forerunners as online wealth makers. They have the clout to help you pull in numbers and make the sale, but both are struggling to hold their leading positions as the business models evolve. That leaves the door open for new competitors. Sometimes, being successful comes down to your ability to spot the next big thing. In this chapter, we give you an overview of some lesser-known auctions and storefront sites. It's worth your while to investigate each of these rising stars within the growing storefront community.

Highest Bidder Takes All with Auction Sites

Online auction houses have certainly proven themselves to have a viable revenue model. Admittedly, eBay has garnered the lion's share of the attention (which Book VIII, Chapter 4 covers). But several other auction sites can produce strong results for you. Some of the eBay competitors on that growing list include

✦ **Bonanzle** (www.bonanzle.com): This eBay alternative, shown in Figure 5-1, offers not only a marketplace for a wide variety of products and categories but also a host of advanced features. Some of its more popular features are a price estimator, live chat, and image cropping for posting photos of your items — and you can easily import items you may have listed on eBay or craigslist. Listing items for sale on Bonanzle, along with as many as four photos, is free. A modest final offer value fee includes the final selling price of the accepted offer plus any shipping fee that exceeds $10. However, for products valued at less than $1,000, the fee doesn't exceed $5, and the maximum final value fee is $10. The low fees and extensive features are helping Bonanzle earn a reputation for providing true competition to once-loyal eBay sellers.

✦ **Etsy** (www.etsy.com): Although this auction site is limited to selling handmade products, it's still a viable place to sell your wares. Allowable products include any handcrafted items, hobby or craft supplies, and vintage items. Fees are reasonable. You're charged 20 cents for each listed item, and a final sales price, or final value fee, of 3.5 percent is also added to your fees.

✦ **PlunderHere** (www.plunderhere.com): With its free basic membership, this auction site keeps growing its number of listings (see Figure 5-2). Selling options include both traditional auction bidding and fixed pricing, in buy-it-now fashion. As a seller, you can also create your own store and pay no listing fee for as many as 2,000 items. Upgraded stores range from $5 to $40 per month. As on other auction sites, enhanced listings are also available for various charges, such as a video upload feature that costs one dollar per listing. A flat 2.5 percent final value fee is added to your costs.

✦ **WeBidz** (www.webidz.com): This auction site also has a substantial variety of product offerings, although its look is probably more dated than some of the other auction sites. Given the inexpensive pricing, that's okay. Basic listings are free, but you can upgrade to fee-based enhanced listings, most for less than a nickel apiece. You pay no final value fees or any other charge for creating your own basic store with as many as 250 items.

Figure 5-2:
This auction site is increasing its listings.

✦ **Wensy** (www.wensy.com): One of the biggest benefits of this small but growing site is that neither buyers nor sellers pay any fees. As stated on the seller's registration page, it's 100 percent free!

Saying no to listing fees

One hot topic that comes up when you discuss auction sites is fees. Listing fees, along with other pre- and post-sale charges, suddenly became much more important when eBay aggressively began raising its own fees. Even sellers once loyal to eBay began looking for other online auction sites. If you're just getting into the online auction business, you now have a host of choices for sites with zero listing fees. If having to pay listing fees may stop you from auctioning, visit one of these online auction sites, none of which has a listing fee:

✔ At WeBidz (www.webidz.com), enhanced paid listings are optional.

✔ eBid.net (www.ebid.net) charges a 2 percent fee whenever an item sells.

✔ MyAuctionPlanet (www.myauction planet.com) has free stores and no final value fee when an item sells.

You can find a lot of great scoop on all the online auction happenings from AuctionBytes at www.auctionbytes.com. This online resource covers news about auction sites ranging from eBay to OnlineAuctions.

Localizing Storefronts with LiveDeal

Through auctions or otherwise, the Internet gives you the potential to reach out to customers all across the world. Yet many online storefront owners are beginning to focus on targeting a more local customer — one who's right in their own backyards. One way to go local online is by selling in the equivalent of a newspaper's classified section. Sites such as LiveDeal (at www. livedeal.com) have already begun to fill this niche (see Figure 5-3). The site already boasts more than 13 million business listings with more than 1 million products and services listed. Not bad for a site that hooks up local buyers and sellers!

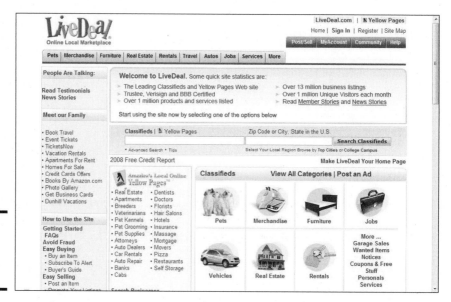

Figure 5-3:
Selling locally on LiveDeal.

Of course, you can't get rich selling stuff in online classifieds listings, but making big money isn't the real purpose of online classified sites. They're designed to facilitate connecting individual buyers and sellers. So why bother, you ask? Diversification.

To grow your storefront's sales, you have to take advantage of several different selling formats. eBay's top PowerSellers use this strategy. Their products don't show up in a single place; they diversify by promoting and selling in multiple locations. You want to sell to multiple targeted communities. Online classifieds sites let you do just that, through both listings and targeted advertising.

When you're focused on e-commerce sales (as opposed to single listings), LiveDeal offers a Super Seller program. The site recommends registering for a Super Seller store account if you have more than 10 items to sell. With this type of account, you also gain access to special support features. For example, service reps can guide you through the bulk-listing process when you want to load more than 100 items as a Super Seller.

Incorporating LiveDeal into your online strategy allows you to reach out to potential customers by region, city, zip code, and even IP address. Both you and your customers receive several benefits:

✦ **Eliminate shipping costs:** Your prices become more competitive when customers have the choice of local pickup because shipping fees are no longer a factor.

✦ **Sell large items:** Furniture, cars, and even real estate become easier to sell when you can target customers locally. These bulky or cumbersome items are no longer a shipping nightmare. Plus, local customers can check out the merchandise personally, which increases the chance of a quicker purchase on big-ticket items.

✦ **Gain more immediate sales:** Some estimates show that online retailers lose sales because products aren't immediately available to the buyer. Localized selling gives customers quick access to products, which means more sales for you.

Unlike auction sites, classified listings typically charge a one-time fee. In the case of LiveDeal, you pay no setup or listing fees. But you can expect a small charge for a category listing. A service category listing costs $9.95 for 30 days. In the Auto category, you have to open an account that holds a $250 deposit. And, every time you receive what the site classifies as a valid and unique lead, you're charged a flat rate of $20. You can receive a valid lead by either e-mail or phone.

LiveDeal offers a variety of paid marketing features to help market your listing. One of the best deals is paying to have your item promoted on the site's home page for 30 days for only $19.95.

Creating Instant Products with CafePress

If you don't happen to have any existing merchandise to sell at auction, you can create products by e-merchandising. The site that does e-merchandising well is CafePress (www.cafepress.com).

**Book VIII
Chapter 5**

**New Storefronts,
New Opportunities**

E-merchandising is similar to having a blank slate to create your own, customized products — and you don't have to buy and stock truckloads of inventory. You can make multiple products and then sell them one at time — or, rather, on demand. (Naturally, customers can buy more than one item if they want!)

Discovering the benefits

CafePress provides you with a long list of products, such as T-shirts, coffee mugs, messenger bags, and other apparel. Stores also provide the ability to sell books (printed on demand) and CDs. You use your own graphical design, text, or audio to create a one-of-a-kind product. CafePress even hosts a complete store for you on its servers. The best part about this whole deal is that the site takes care of everything for you. Your job becomes marketing your products (and CafePress even provides support to help with your marketing efforts). Here's what CafePress does for you:

+ **Inventory:** Because the base products are bought and warehoused through CafePress, they're ready and waiting as soon as an order, however big or small, comes in.

+ **Storefront:** You're given the tools to create a complete online store. You can even use a URL with its server or get one of your own.

+ **Order processing:** When setting up a store, you use the CafePress built-in shopping cart and payment processors. You don't need to have a merchant's account to sell!

+ **Printing:** CafePress prints your designated design on each item.

+ **Packing and shipping:** The site also handles all back-end functions for you, including shipping and handling.

+ **Customer service:** From fielding general questions to handling product returns, CafePress manages it all for you, even providing a toll-free number to customers. For example, if a customer wants to place an order by phone or isn't satisfied with a product and needs to return it, CafePress handles it all for you, in full.

+ **Reporting functions:** To keep up with sales, returns, commissions, and other functions, the site has an extensive online reporting function. You can access it at any time to see a snapshot of how your store is performing.

+ **Payments:** Similar to an affiliate program, CafePress tracks your sales and earnings (the difference between the cost of the product and the price you set). After you accumulate at least $25 in your account, the company sends you a commission check.

✦ **Marketing support:** Through your CafePress store, you have access to several marketing tools, including creating a newsletter and e-mail marketing campaigns.

✦ **Traffic:** Because CafePress is also set up as a community of shopkeepers, your store is always listed on the site's marketplace. So customers can find you (by accident or on purpose) by visiting the main CafePress shopping pages. (Of course, your sales are always stronger when you market your site directly.)

At CafePress, each product has a base price associated with it. That price covers the cost of the product itself, the printing, and all other related services and overhead. From that base price, you then set the price with which you sell that product to your customers.

Suppose that you decide to sell a large coffee mug with your logo and another clever saying on it. CafePress sells the finished product to you for $12.99. If you want to make $3 on each sale, you price the mug at $15.99. Each time it sells, you earn a $3 profit.

Another advantage of using CafePress is that you don't have to pay for the product until someone actually purchases it from you. Even then, CafePress simply deducts the base cost from the total sale price and then passes the difference along to you.

CafePress gives you a couple of options when setting up your store:

✦ **Basic:** A free site gives you access to many CafePress features. You don't have a limit on the number of products you can sell. And, you don't have a limit on the number of basic shops you can open. However, each shop comes with only one page.

✦ **Custom:** This next step up from the Basic level costs $4.99 per month. For that fee, you can create a highly customizable store with an unlimited number of pages or product variations (see Figure 5-4). You also gain access to some exclusive products and customization tools that aren't available in a Basic shop.

You can see a complete comparison between the two store types at `www.cafepress.com/cp/info/sell/shops/premium4`.

As with most e-merchandising sites, CafePress also offers an affiliate program. You can earn a 15 percent commission on all products sold by linking to the marketplace or by referring others to set up a store.

Figure 5-4:
A CafePress
custom
store.

Registering with CafePress

You can set up a store on CafePress in a flash. When you're ready to start, follow these steps to open your first CafePress store:

1. **Go to CafePress at `www.cafepress.com`.**

2. **Select Start Selling Now from the menu bar at the top of the home page.**

3. **Click the orange Open a Shop button.**

   The Join CafePress.com! page appears. You have to become a member of CafePress before opening a store. (Don't worry: Membership is free!)

4. **Complete the form.**

   You need to fill out basic information, including creating a password for your account.

5. **Read the Terms of Service agreement and then click the Join Now button to continue.**

   Another form page appears on your screen.

6. **Answer the questions about the type of site you want to open and click the Open Your Shop button.**

7. **Choose whether you want a basic or custom shop.**

   Scroll down to read the differences between the two shop types. We recommend starting out with a basic shop @md you can figure out the nuances of selling on CafePress without having to pay a monthly fee. When you're ready to increase your options, you can upgrade to a custom shop at any time (with no additional charges other than the cost of the upgrade).

8. **Create a shop ID.**

    This part of your shop's name is used in your URL. If you go with a basic shop, your URL is tagged onto the end of the CafePress address, like this: `www.CafePress.com/`*`YourShopID`*.

9. **Create a name for your shop and enter a URL that you want customers redirected to after they finish shopping.**

    Your shop name appears at the top of your store, such as Kathy's Kollectibles. Customers identify you by this name.

    The redirect URL can be your shop's home page or a different Web site you own. You want this page to reopen after a customer's order is processed.

10. **Answer a few more questions about your new shop.**

    Let CafePress know whether your site's content is suitable for kids. You can also choose to have your site listed by search engines and made available to the public in the CafePress marketplace.

11. **Read and agree to the shopkeeper's agreement and then click Submit.**

    A welcome page for your new store opens. Your URL is confirmed on this page, too.

12. **Click the Build Your Shop button when you're ready to add products to your store.**

Fantastic! With the registration process complete, you can view the shell for your store and upload products to your shop!

Setting up your store

After you register for your site, a Product landing page opens. This page shows you two choices: Set store settings or add products.

Select the Set Store Settings option to define your settings. Selecting this option walks you through a series of pages that ask you to choose a template, describe your site (using descriptive keywords), and upload your logo. You can square away your site settings in about 10 to 15 minutes.

 Save time and set a default pricing option as part of your store settings. You choose how you want all your products priced. For example, you can choose to apply a 50-percent markup on everything or use a tiered markup (low, medium, high), based on pricing models for each product. (CafePress has suggested pricing for its items and recommends that you don't vary much from these prices.) You can also set an exact dollar value for the markup. By choosing one of these defaults, you don't have to individually price each of your products when you add them to your shop.

Adding images and products

After you set up your store, you can start adding products. We suggest browsing through your choices to familiarize yourself with all the products. And, if you're new, start by uploading only one or two products until you're comfortable using the features. You may want to start with a T-shirt and coffee mug because uploading images for each of those items is easy. Uploading these images gives you a good feel for what to expect when you start working with other products (that often require more image resizing to fit an unusual product surface or shape).

CafePress provides an extensive image-creation and -sizing guide for each product. To help you out even more, the site features an online tutorial — the Image Workshop. It ensures that you use the properly formatted image for the best visual quality on your product. You can access the guide at `www.cafepress.com/cp/info/help/images.aspx`.

To start populating your store with products, you first have to upload your images. To upload them, follow these steps:

1. **Go to the CafePress.com home page (`www.cafepress.com`) and click the Your Account link in the upper right corner of the page.**

   If you're already logged in, go to your account page.

   A new page opens, where you can log in to your CafePress shop.

2. **Enter your e-mail address and CafePress password, and click the Sign In button.**

   The home page for your shop appears, as shown in Figure 5-5. It's divided into several categories.

3. **To add an image, click the Images link in the Media Basket section.**

   The page on which you can see your stored images appears. If you don't have any images saved, this page is blank. You can also add and store audio files and other documents on this page.

4. **Click the Upload New Image button on the far right side of the gray menu bar.**

   Your screen now shows several menu boxes that allow you to browse and search for images you stored (see Figure 5-6).

   Carefully ready the important image guidelines and the copyright and use information on the right side of the page. You don't want to be in violation of any of these rules.

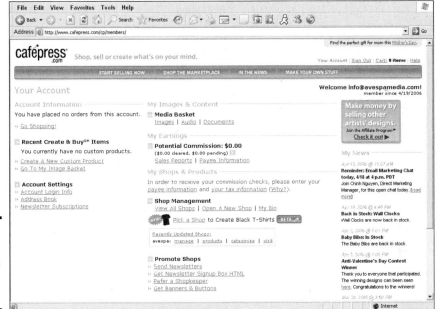

Figure 5-5:
Your
account lets
you create
a shop.

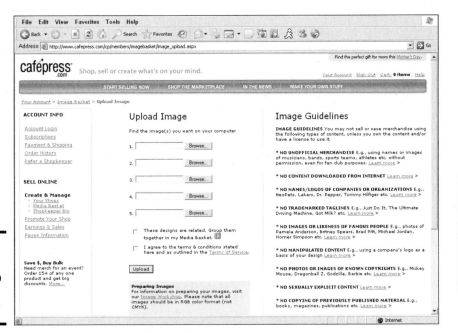

Figure 5-6:
Browse
your files to
upload an
image.

5. **Click the Browse button to find the image you want to use. (The image should be one that you've stored as a file on your computer.)**

   Your image is placed in your media basket, where you can view it. You can add as many as five images at one time.

6. **Check the check box labeled I Agree to the Terms and Conditions Stated Here and Outlined in the Terms of Service. Then click the Upload button.**

   If you want to group your images, select the check box labeled These Designs Are Related. Group Them Together in My Media Basket.

You can improve the searchability of your products by adding tags to your product images. By attaching descriptive keywords to the image, you improve the likelihood of your product being found during a search for similar keywords or topics. You can add tags by clicking the Tag Them Now link at the top of your media basket.

CafePress occasionally empties the media baskets, which gets rid of unused images in its basic shops. Always — always! — save copies of your image files somewhere other than in your shop's media basket, or else you risk losing those files!

After you upload images, the next step is to add products. Follow these steps:

1. **Click the Your Account link in the upper left menu to return to your administrative home page.**

2. **Click the Product link in the Shop Management area.**

   This link is one of three that appears next to your shop's name.

   The page that asked you to set up your shop opens.

3. **Click the Add 1 or More Products link, which appears under the shop settings.**

   You see images and descriptions for all product categories that CafePress offers.

4. **Click the Make Selections link for one of the product categories.**

   We suggest choosing a mug to start your store.

   A window opens and shows you images of all relevant products in stock, along with their listed base prices.

5. **Choose a product and click the Add Selections button.**

   The Products to Be Added box on your products page shows the product you choose.

6. **Repeat Steps 4 and 5 to add more products.**

7. **Select the image you want to use on your product by clicking the Select Image button.**

   A new page appears that displays all the images you previously uploaded into your media basket.

   You have to save as part of the image file any text that you want added to your product. If you want a graphical image and text to appear as a single image, you have to save the image file the same way. The image appears on your product just as it does in the file.

8. **Choose the image you want to use by clicking the Select Image link under image on the right.**

   The product page reopens, and your selected image appears above the product box.

9. **Highlight the products you want to add to your shop. Then click the Add These Products button.**

   The next page shows a picture of your products. All active products appear on this page at the same time.

   If you don't see any product names after adding the image, return to the Shop Management section and click the Manage Products link. This link opens the product page that displays all the products you're customizing.

10. **Click the Edit button on the product you want to sell.**

    This step opens a new page, again displaying the product with the selected image. On this page, you can change the image size and rotate the image to the location where you want it placed on the product.

11. **Click the Next button and begin entering a product description.**

    This page allows you to edit product information. Follow the prompts to write a caption and a detailed description of the product. Then set the price.

12. **When you finish writing your product description, click the Save and Finish button.**

The product page reopens. From there, you can choose to continue adding products or close the product page. You're finished!

To view your shop, return to the Shop Management area and click your store's URL at the top of the page.

For more features, and to customize and add pages, upgrade to a custom shop. In the meantime, use the rest of the marketing and promotional features to help market your site. You can access all tools from your site's home page.

Book VIII Chapter 5

New Storefronts, New Opportunities

To ensure that in your store is listed in the most appropriate part of the marketplace, don't forget to categorize it. You can let CafePress know which type of store (Merchandise, Books, Software, or Music) you have and who your customers may be.

Comparing Features to Find the Best Deal in Storefronts

More e-merchandising storefronts, such as CafePress, are popping up every day. For the most part, the features and benefits offered by all the sites are fairly similar. One site hasn't truly pulled enough ahead of the others to say that it's the one that will become the eBay of e-merchandising. Admittedly, many sellers prefer CafePress. But you can find other sites worth delving into. In the following sections, we describe two that offer a few interesting alternatives.

Spreadshirt

Spreadshirt launched in Germany in 2002, but it has opened United States and other European locations for its base of operations. Spreadshirt has established several avenues for you to make money:

+ **Design Shop:** You can create a fully functioning store of your own for free. This opportunity gives you access to all the Spreadshirt products and apparel, and you upload your own images to create truly customized products. You set the commissions you want to earn for each product, up to $20, which is added to the cost of the item (Spreadshirt sets the base cost).

+ **Design Premium**: Upgrade your design shop for $10 per month. This option allows you to run a store without any Spreadshirt-hosted ads running on the store pages. You also gain access to a few additional features.

+ **Marketplace:** You can offer your designs and products for sale in the Spreadshirt Marketplace and earn a 20 percent commission on every product or design that's sold, by either you or another shop.

Along with offering multiple revenue earnings models, the site has other advantages, too:

+ **Brand-name products:** Your customers may be pleased to discover that your custom products are printed on established name-brand wares. Included among the names are Hanes, Fruit of the Loom, and American Apparel.

+ **Extensive apparel options:** The Spreadshirt collection of T-shirt styles and other types of clothing is the mainstay of its product inventory.

✦ **Print on dark color:** You can choose from a variety of dark-colored T-shirts to print on. This site has the much-sought-after black, red, gray, and other shirt colors.

✦ **Sell globally:** Because Spreadshirt has its roots in Germany, it's only natural that it provides a global sales strategy. You can choose to sell through a U.S. or European store. To sell in both places, you have to open two separate stores.

To start selling at Spreadshirt, go to www.spreadshirt.com. You can open a shop in only a few minutes, and then you just upload your own, custom products to sell!

Zazzle

Rather than help you sell your wares in stores, Zazzle.com (www.zazzle.com) offers galleries to display customized products that are for sale. You can choose to design products and keep them in a private gallery, accessible only to you. Or, you can contribute to the public gallery and allow your work to be sold. You can also take part in a new feature and choose to sell others' designs and receive commissions for those items.

When your products are placed in the public gallery, two things happen: Zazzle sets the price of all products and you receive a straight 15 percent royalty on anything that sells. (Your limited control on pricing is probably why Zazzle isn't considered an actual store.) However, the incentive package it added lets you to earn as much as 34 percent commission, based on the volume (in dollars) of products you sell.

The other interesting twist is that you can let other people use and tweak your creative works (text or art) and make it their own. You retain the copyright to all your work, no matter what. But this option lets others put their stamp on it. Theoretically, this opportunity is supposed to increase the probability of your work being sold because the extra personalization has wider appeal.

As for product selection, Zazzle now offers a variety of merchandise you can customize. Choose from apparel, cards, posters, coffee mugs, and even skateboards. You can also choose from a wide variety of colors and styles for the apparel products.

Among the other beneficial features is an intuitive wizard for creating products that walks you through the process step by step. So, the overall design and image-upload process is fairly simple. The shopping cart is also a useful feature for customers (see Figure 5-7). A customer can click the product she wants to buy, and an image of that product immediately appears. Then the customer can select the size and quantity she wants. You can also choose for the cart to display the customer's total cost as she select products.

Book VIII
Chapter 5

New Storefronts, New Opportunities

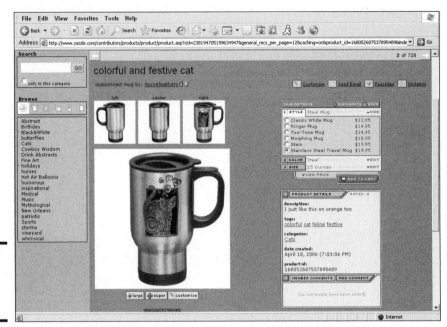

Figure 5-7:
Shopping
is easy at
Zazzle.

Another feature that sets Zazzle apart is that it gives you access to a wide selection of licensed (and public) images that you can use on your products. These images include Disney characters, superheroes, and more artistic images pulled from state libraries.

You can increase potential earnings by joining the site's affiliate program. By placing a link to Zazzle on your primary Web site, you earn 15 percent commission from any purchase made from a referral (which can come from a Web site, your e-mail, or a blog, to name a few possibilities). If customers happen to buy your customized products, you receive both the 15 percent affiliate commission for the referral and the 15 percent (or more, depending on your sales volume) royalty from your products (for a total of a minimum of 30 percent).

Book IX
Fundraising Sites

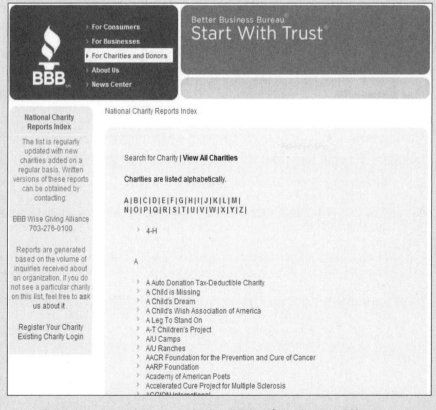

National Charity Reports Index

The list is regularly updated with new charities added on a regular basis. Written versions of these reports can be obtained by contacting:

BBB Wise Giving Alliance 703-276-0100

Reports are generated based on the volume of inquiries received about an organization. If you do not see a particular charity on this list, feel free to ask us about it.

Register Your Charity
Existing Charity Login

National Charity Reports Index

Search for Charity | **View All Charities**

Charities are listed alphabetically.

A|B|C|D|E|F|G|H|I|J|K|L|M|
N|O|P|Q|R|S|T|U|V|W|X|Y|Z|

> 4-H

A

> A Auto Donation Tax-Deductible Charity
> A Child is Missing
> A Child's Dream
> A Child's Wish Association of America
> A Leg To Stand On
> A-T Children's Project
> A/U Camps
> A/U Ranches
> AACR Foundation for the Prevention and Cure of Cancer
> AARP Foundation
> Academy of American Poets
> Accelerated Cure Project for Multiple Sclerosis
> ACCION International

Register your charity with the BBB Wise Giving Alliance.

Contents at a Glance

Chapter 1: Raining Donations: Why Not-for-Profit Is Big Business Online

In This Chapter

↳ Increasing value with e-philanthropy

↳ Spreading the message and convincing decision-makers

Did you know that four of ten donors *always* go online for information before making a donation? According to the ePhilanthropy Foundation at www.ephilanthropy.org, online giving for nonprofit organizations grew from $250 million in 2000 to more than $6 billion in 2006. And, estimates show that the amount raised online continued to increase by nearly 20 percent in 2007! With e-giving exceeding expectations, one question remains: What are you waiting for?

Now is the time to bring your organization online and expand its Web presence. If you're unsure about how to accomplish these goals, don't worry. In this chapter, we explain why online giving is appropriate for your cause and how to get everyone else in your organization on board.

Determining How Your Organization Can Benefit

E-giving, or e-philanthropy, refers to the concept of charitable organizations raising money from online donations. An evolving concept since it first came in vogue in 2000, it's no longer simply a means of asking for money over the Internet.

E-philanthropy is now a recognized strategic tool that you can use for your nonprofit. This method of marketing touches all outreach initiatives and specifically encompasses these six areas within an organization:

✦ **Awareness building:** An effective online presence targets your internal (or existing) membership base *and* your external (or potential) audience. You can increase awareness for a specific campaign or for your overall mission.

✦ **Donor development:** You're using the Internet to not only target one-time contributors but also build long-term donor relationships.

✦ **Membership retention:** The combination of targeted e-mail communications and a useful Web site is a proven means of generating membership renewals for your nonprofit.

✦ **Volunteer and client recruitment:** Your organization thrives on financial contributions and the support of volunteers. Fortunately, your site can serve as a recruitment tool for both entities. Additionally, if your nonprofit is service based (such as debt management or tax preparation assistance for senior citizens), an online strategy can help you reach the audience most in need of your services.

✦ **Board outreach:** Although your board members are technically part of your volunteer base, you should consider board outreach and development to be a distinctive area within your organization. A fully integrated and well-maintained Internet initiative is an increasingly important method for keeping your board committed to your cause.

✦ **Grassroots activism:** The Internet is increasingly used as a way to elicit action at the basic level. From online petitions to e-mail campaigns, response rates are rising among the masses, and the effort is paying off!

These are the key areas in which online initiatives should be regularly infiltrating your organization. Consider how each segment provides additional benefits to your cause, and then take a closer look at what your organization gains when it actively solicits online donors.

Savvy e-philanthropists have three characteristics in common:

✦ **Generosity:** Current research indicates that online donors are twice as likely to give to your cause, and they typically give twice as often as offline contributors.

✦ **Curiosity:** Online donors seek out information; they're eager to learn about your organization and its activities. Most important, these Net donors turn to the Internet for facts, figures, and general information before making their final giving decisions. In return, a donor who makes an informed decision takes the first step in forming a lasting bond with your organization versus a one-time random act of giving.

✦ **Loyalty:** The members of your nonprofit with whom you stay in touch over the Internet are highly likely to stick around. Therefore, if you're fostering the relationship, chances are good that your multiyear renewal rates will increase.

Convincing Your Board of Directors

After you're committed to using an online strategy to grow your donor base, the next step is convincing the rest of your organization that it's the right thing to do.

Persuading your board that e-philanthropy is a timely solution is easier than you think. You might just have to spend a little more time moving progressive ideas through the approval process. Consider the usual reasons that board members tend to reject or stall a new idea:

**Book IX
Chapter 1**

**Raining Donations:
Why Not-for-Profit
Is Big Business
Online**

+ They're fearful of the unknown — especially where technology is concerned.

+ They're convinced that the costs outweigh the benefits.

+ They have decided that someone else has a more compelling argument against it.

If you understand these three points, you can arm yourself with the power of persuasion. People engage in many spirited debates over the proposal of innovative concepts, yet plenty of fantastic ideas are eventually rolled into action because someone embraced a plan of persuasion and stuck with it.

Not every board fights the incorporation of an extensive Internet strategy. Heck, people might even line up to take turns making this idea a reality. However, if your board tends to closely scrutinize a plan before rubber-stamping it, you might find the information in this section especially helpful.

Tying the Internet strategy into your mission

One characteristic that all directors of nonprofits share is their belief in an organization's mission. Because the mission is usually the catalyst that prompts a member to get involved, use that synergy in your favor. With every point you make in support of e-philanthropy, tie that initiative directly into your mission statement.

Developing an online strategy

In a 2004 survey of nonprofit organizations, 92 percent of respondents said that they have a Web site. Only 24 percent, however, have a written online strategy. Many organizations still view the Internet as a one-time fundraising shot and continue to treat their sites as separate entities. That's not exactly a good argument to convince a board to invest its organization's precious dollars.

Instead, if you're ready to get your board of directors on board, make sure that you have a plan with a detailed and all-inclusive strategy.

Use the six points we outline earlier in this chapter, in the section "Determining How Your Organization Can Benefit," and feel free to add any others that might pertain specifically to you. Create an Internet marketing plan that incorporates each one. From donor development to member retention, don't hesitate to use them all. Your proposal is illustrating that the Internet is more than a single action item and proving it to be a component of the bigger picture. With this strategy in hand, you're ahead of the game when the board gives your plan the green light!

Providing a budget-friendly proposal

When you present your proposal to your board members, expect them to search for the price tag for implementing your project. That final number is often a deal breaker for an organization with a limited budget. (What non-profit does that statement *not* apply to?)

Be sure to take advantage of your organization's 501(c)3 status. (Not doing so is the single biggest mistake that many organizations make when pricing technology.)

Whether you're building or updating a Web site or purchasing back-end components to add to an existing site, follow these three simple rules:

+ **Ask vendors for a discount or special pricing for not-for-profit organizations.** Companies are usually willing to work with nonprofits, although it's not a price point that's typically advertised.

  Always get multiple bids (from separate companies) for each service or technology, and use the same *specs*, or list of requirements. Then compare the prices, apples to apples, before making a final decision.

  Never go with the first or only quote you receive. This may seem like common sense advice, but we can't stress enough that shopping around can inevitably save you money.

+ **Use your board of directors as a resource.** Board members might have access to the services or technologies you need through a company they own or work for, or because of their own, special skills. Services and equipment are often donated or sold at rock-bottom prices.

  When a board member performs a service, such as updating your Web site, ask for a written contract. The contract should specify, as with any other vendor, start and finish dates, the scope of work and project details, and a review-and-approval process for signing off on the finished project. In case something goes wrong, the contract protects both sides. Even better, it can help avoid an uncomfortable situation with a board member.

+ **Check the Internet for organizations (both for-profit and not-for-profit) that have technology programs specifically for nonprofits.** An untold number of resources offer free or discounted technology, and related services, to the nonprofit sector. In Book IX, Chapter 2, we provide detailed information about several of these programs and the companies that sponsor them.

  If you qualify for one of the technology programs, be sure to list your actual cost in the budget proposal. (Even if equipment is free, you might have to pay shipping or installation.) Then show a comparison of the bids you received from other commercial vendors. Board members appreciate seeing this type of cost savings. Just knowing that you found a good deal can sometimes sway the vote in your favor.

Book IX
Chapter 1

Raining Donations:
Why Not-for-Profit
Is Big Business
Online

Offering case studies

Not everyone is a risk taker. In fact, most people tend to be conservative when they do new things. That's why boards especially love to hear other success stories before jumping into the unknown world of technology, and that's why we encourage you to find *case studies*, or examples of organizations, that benefit from using a real Internet strategy.

To increase the chances of your examples being well received, choose these types of case studies:

✦ **Mirror images:** Feature organizations that are as similar as possible to yours in size, budget, mission, or donor profile.

✦ **Matching projects:** Pick examples that use technology, or overall strategies, similar to what you're proposing.

✦ **Multipurpose:** Case studies should demonstrate more than a single point of success. Ideally, the strategy should result in multiple benefits. Even better, the study should also tout recurring, or lasting, benefits for the organization.

You can find technology case studies in several ways. Talk with other organizations in your community, read a few national newsletters or magazines targeted to philanthropic organizations, or check out the Web sites of nonprofit consultants who frequently list detailed case studies for prospective clients to view. Network for Good provides access to case studies and white papers for online fundraising: `http://www.fundraising123.org /nonprofit-marketing`.

Recruiting an expert

Plenty of experts specialize in both nonprofits and the design and implementation of Internet strategies. If you're uncertain about your own power of persuasion, consider inviting an expert to discuss the issue with your board. Even if you give an overview of the proposal, try to have a consultant on hand to answer likely questions.

A consultant who offers to speak to your board for free usually hopes to eventually be hired. If you have no intention of engaging the consultant's services (even if the technology proposal is approved), be honest about it. Instead, negotiate a reasonable hourly fee to cover the consultant's time.

Garnering positive peer pressure

Hiring a professional isn't the only way to find support for your proposal. Other board members or staff members might be willing to jump on your bandwagon. Identify possible candidates, and find at least one other person to help champion your cause. Finding someone whose opinion is respected, or who has a knack for generating positive peer pressure, obviously helps.

Getting specific

You know that more than one board meeting might be necessary to make a decision about something that encompasses a large strategy. To help your cause, offer to assign ownership to another individual or to a committee that can gather additional information between meetings. This strategy also helps spread the burden of conducting the final research. Additionally, suggest that the plan be implemented over a specific period. If you split the project into specific stages, the overall goal appears more attainable. Figure 1-1 shows a sample timeline you can use for implementing the project.

Figure 1-1:
Employ a
timeline to
show that
your goals
are realistic.

Internet Implementation Strategy Timeline (approx. 34 weeks)

Start date: February 1
Decision date 1 (board approval of budget): March 1
Decision date 2 (accept technology vendor proposals): May 1
Decision date 3 (board approval of revised site/online giving campaign): September 5
Implementation date (site goes live/kick off first e-philanthropy campaign): October 1

Action items targeted for completion by designated week:
Week 1: assign ad hoc committee
Week 4: verify/define goals for Internet strategy; identify needs for updated or new Web site; finalize budget
Week 12: research desired technology solutions; identify possible technology vendors; request and review proposals from Web developers; select of Web developer and/or technology vendors
Week 16: select first e-philanthropy giving campaign using updated site and technology solutions
Week 18: review first draft of proposed site revision (aesthetic design with site map)
Week 24: give all approved content, photos, and graphics provided to Web designer
Week 26: finalize marketing plan for online campaign
Week 30: present new/revised site for board approval, along with initial online giving campaign
Week 31: develop all elements of campaign (including offline support materials)
Week 32: implement final changes/corrections to site
Week 33: pre-launch site internally (not for public access); test all features and make necessary changes; publicly announce upcoming public launch of site and kickoff of fundraising campaign
Week 34: public launch of new site and first online giving campaign

Chapter 2: Adding Online Moneymakers to an Existing Site

In This Chapter

✔ Evaluating your site structure to decide which elements are plausible

✔ Researching technology resources

✔ Selling to the highest bidder as the ultimate e-fundraising tool

✔ Adding easy fixes to increase online donations

*B*y now, you might have noticed two separate movements from the early days of the Internet (its first ten years, or the period from which it's just now emerging). The first movement was filled with *innovators*, or sites considered to be Net pioneers, such as eBay and Amazon and even smaller companies that happened to develop exciting and useful applications delivered online. The second movement, occurring simultaneously, was filled with folks who thought that brochureware constituted a good Web site.

Unfortunately, most people are in the latter group, where someone turns the equivalent of a marketing pamphlet into a 3- or 4-page Web site, checks off that action item on a to-do list, and then never again (or rarely) touches the site. Does this situation sound familiar yet?

If so, you're not alone. This description fits the position that many of your nonprofit peers are in right now. The good news is that you're committed to change. You're ready to bring your site into the next decade and fully embrace the opportunity of online fundraising. In this chapter, we arm you with information about your options, and the costs involved, so that you can make an informed decision and start raising funds.

Determining Which Features Your Site Can Support

You probably have a basic Web site now. Its pages might explain your organization's mission, highlight a few of your annual fundraising events (along with a few fuzzy photos), and list the names of your board of directors and officers. Then again, you might have developed a more detailed site structure and haven't yet implemented any type of online fundraising tools to go along with it.

Regardless, the first step in this process of adding money generators is to conduct a detailed analysis of all aspects of your technology, support resources, and site framework. Your primary objective is to realize current capabilities and address possible limitations.

If you have already implemented or designed a general technology plan, you can pull from it much of the information you need in this analysis. On the other hand, if you don't have this type of plan, the information you collect in this analysis can be transitioned into that document.

For this purpose, we recommend taking an inventory, of sorts. Break down your situational analysis into eight function areas. The chart shown in Figure 2-1 is an overview of these areas of interest.

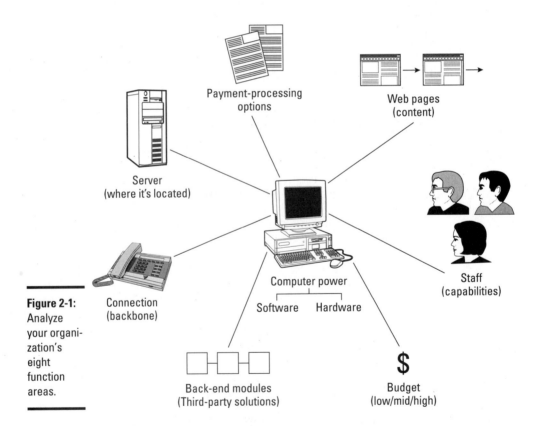

Figure 2-1: Analyze your organization's eight function areas.

Payment-processing options

Web pages (content)

Server (where it's located)

Staff (capabilities)

Connection (backbone)

Computer power

Software   Hardware

Back-end modules (Third-party solutions)

Budget (low/mid/high)

Testing your backbone (connections)

Begin your technology analysis by taking a closer look at the power of your in-house computer connection. Are you still using dialup to log on to the Internet? Or, are you using a faster connection from a broadband-enabled service (typically, either DSL or cable)? Jot down the status of your current connection speed. If you're on a slower connection, note whether you can upgrade your connection.

You might believe that your connections speed doesn't matter and that only your potential donors' connections matter. Well, designing a site that's accessible to as much of your target audience as possible is always a concern that deserves your attention. Internally, however, connection speed matters, too. For instance, your connection can influence the type of third-party services you can add to your Web site. If you want to use *Web-enabled* technologies (services delivered over the Internet), for example, accessing your provider for online reports and other features can be difficult if you're not using a fast broadband connection. And, the inability to increase your connection speed can cause you to look to a different type of fundraising solution for your site.

Deciding on your computer needs

When it comes to hardware and software, a couple of different main theories exist:

✦ **Buy only what you need and nothing else:** The idea is to buy items later when they become a necessity. You don't spend money on a larger display screen or a wireless mouse and keyboard, and you don't splurge for extra memory.

✦ **Buy as much as you can now rather than later:** In this theory, you get a better price by bundling all the components you need rather than buying them individually.

Both concepts are valid, and the one that you need to take into consideration depends on where you buy your hardware and software. Some vendors give discounts when you bundle printers, LCD screens, and other items with your basic purchase. Other vendors sell only bare-bones systems (just the basics) for extremely low prices, but these systems typically cannot be customized and are sold "as is". Shop around with your list of requirements (divided into items you must have and the ones you can do without) and then do business with the vendor who can give you the best deal.

Locating your server

You need to identify the physical location of your site's server for your technology analysis. If your server is in-house, it's located on the physical premises you maintain. Otherwise, it must be hosted off-site, through a vendor, which is typically the case.

Now comes the tricky part. How much do you know about that server? For example, can you identify its operating system and whether it's Windows or Linux based? What you do or don't know about the server can hinder, or slow, the addition of fundraising elements to your site. Several small-business owners sign hosting contracts only to learn later that their company servers didn't support the specific language used to develop their Web sites.

Your answers to the following basic questions about your server can affect whether you can add future fundraising solutions to your site:

+ **Is your server a database?** What type is it? For example, MySQL, Microsoft Access, and SQL 2000 are the more popular choices. Does the database have size limitations?

+ **Which development languages are supported?** Does your server include ColdFusion MX7, .NET, Perl, PHP, or Java? Are you charged extra for supporting some of the languages, or are they all included in your regular fee?

+ **What are the limitations on your server's disk space?** What's the cost to add space, if needed?

+ **Do you have *root* (admin) access to the server, which allows you or your technical staff to make changes?** What are your host company's policies regarding technical support for changes that relate to the server? What are the tech-support fees for that type of assistance?

+ **Is the host company partnered with other application vendors, such as shopping cart providers?** On the upside, your server might already be set up to handle some of these applications, and perhaps even at a slightly discounted fee. On the downside, if the partnerships are exclusive, your host company might prohibit you from adding other (competitor) applications to the server.

Although you aren't expected to be the technical expert in this area, having this basic information written down and accessible is valuable as you begin evaluating applications from other vendors. You should have a good idea about whether the features are likely to be readily (and inexpensively) compatible with your site's server.

Processing payments

If you represent a nonprofit organization, you probably already accept donations. The issue for your technology analysis is *how* you accept them. If you accept only checks and cash, you should also have a merchant account with your bank or some other means of accepting credit card transactions. You might already accept debit and charge cards too, even if it's only offline. Well, your analysis is the place to spell it all out and put your cards (so to speak) on the table. Include a thorough description of the types of payments you accept, how they're collected and processed, and which company or bank processes them.

Use this part of your analysis to start conducting some research. For instance, maybe you have a merchant account but don't process payments online. Check with your merchant provider and your bank to explore what you have to do to collect payments through your Web site. If you're uncertain about which questions to ask or what your options are, we explain the ins and outs of payment processing in Book IV, Chapter 4.

Tracking back-end modules

The module-tracking portion of your technology analysis is, more than any other part, a straightforward inventory. You need to know what types of applications and capabilities your site already has and whether to use these features.

In addition to considering the use of shopping carts, databases, and online form pages, think in broader terms to answer these types of questions:

✦ Do you use a contact management system to keep track of donors and volunteers?

✦ Is a system in place for collecting and storing e-mail addresses?

✦ Is e-mail now gathered from visitors to your Web site, or do you only collect addresses offline?

Try to compile a thorough list of all back-end applications. Note whether you use each particular feature, detail how you use it, and identify the name of the vendor you obtained it from (if applicable).

One important reason for this part of your analysis is compatibility. As you add features, be sure not to replicate one that you already have.

Although we're specifically discussing the addition of online fundraising applications, a company might want to sell you, or encourage you to use, other services or features that are compatible with (or accessories to) the fundraising feature. Knowing what you already have helps prevent duplication and added costs. In addition, a vendor for one of your current applications might also offer fundraising applications. By checking with those providers first, you might be able to use those tools and receive a guarantee that they're compatible with some of your existing applications.

Mapping your site structure

Mapping your site structure is extremely easy. In fact, if you have a current site map of your Web site, this section of your technology analysis is partially complete.

Review your existing Web site page by page and create a site map of your pages, as shown in Figure 2-2. The map, similar in structure to an outline, uses hierarchical ranking to show how the site flows, or how subpages are linked to primary pages. Unless your site has hundreds of pages, this task isn't difficult.

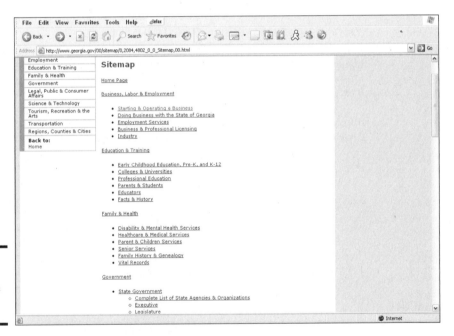

Figure 2-2:
Create a
site map of
your site.

Print a copy of each page of your site. The hard copy of your site is useful for reference and planning purposes.

As you begin selecting online fundraising tools, use these pages to begin reconstructing your site to accommodate and promote the placement of those tools. Rather than have to completely rework your site structure, you only have to identify the places where a visitor to your site is most likely to see and participate in the fundraising effort.

Determining staffing capabilities

Your staff members and volunteers comprise an important resource for your analysis. Not all organizations have a technical-support person on staff, so here's your chance to thoroughly analyze the strengths and weaknesses of your support base. Start this section of your analysis by making a list of your staff members and regular office volunteers. List each person's skills and educational background as they apply to technology.

Even if you have a full-time technical-support position in-house, you should still take an inventory of everyone's skill sets. It's a terrific opportunity to tap in to hidden talent or uncover the need for a future training session.

Paying the piper: Your budget

The final piece of your analysis is probably the easiest to create. Identify your current budget for technology and Web site development. If you already have a line item in your annual report for this element, make a note of the number. Don't stop there, though: Detail whether this money is truly available for use. Is it already spent or earmarked for another project? Are there any restrictions on how the money can be spent? Be realistic about how much money is available or when it might be available.

If you don't have money already designated for technology upgrades in your budget, try to calculate a workable amount. Rather than use an actual dollar amount, assign a range. If you're broke, call it like you see it: Give it a low-end designation and assign it a range from zero to a few hundred dollars. A good midrange amount is usually from $1,500 to $5,000. Consider the high end to be anything over $5,000 and realistically capping out around $10,000. Depending on the size of your organization, your numbers might be bumped up by several thousand dollars. You get the idea, though.

One reason that we prefer to assign a range for a budget analysis is that it makes a discussion with other people more palatable. If board members and other decision-makers know that you're looking within the "low-end range" of the scale, you're not immediately pinned down to a specific dollar amount. Likewise, when you're requesting price quotes from vendors, you feel less pressure to have to name the exact high-end dollar amount you can spend. Identifying a range that's budgeted for the project usually feels more comfortable.

Adding an Auction to Your Site

It's no secret that the world has fallen head over heels in love with online auctions. (eBay has almost single-handedly proven it!) As an active part of the nonprofit sector, you probably know that auctions have long been a staple of charity fundraising. Silent auctions are especially popular as stand-alone affairs or as add-ons to dinner galas and other live events. Thanks to the power of the Internet, the buck (literally) no longer stops there.

Your organization now can increase the reach and earnings potential of your typical event-specific auction by putting it online. As with other fundraising tools, online auctions come in all shapes and sizes, so you can find the perfect fit for your organization.

Third-party auctions

From one point of view, this type of auction — the "effortless" auction — is by far the easiest type for your organization to participate in. All you have to do is have your organization selected as a recipient charity. The auction itself is promoted and managed entirely from another company's Web site. These companies continually auction off items and then ration the proceeds to their approved nonprofits. Two examples are BiddingForGood.com and eBay.

The philanthropic auction service BiddingForGood.com, run by cMarket Online Auctions (www.cmarket.com), is essentially an online community working for nonprofits. It promotes an ongoing auction of items that include furniture, clothing, collectibles, event tickets, and even celebrity items, which are sold from its Web site at www.biddingforgood.com. After the auction for each item ends, the proceeds go to the charity that provided the item or that was selected to receive the proceeds from the item. The site can host an entire auction for one charity or raise money from single auction items and donations. So far, the site has helped raise more than $48 million for schools, communities, and national charitable organizations.

The eBay Giving Works program is open to any approved charitable organization. To date, the program has raised more than $150 million from eBay auction items. It teamed up with MissionFish (www.missionfish.org), a nonprofit auction-management solution that works exclusively with other nonprofits.

When you apply for and receive certification from MissionFish.org that recognizes you as a legitimate charity, you're in the system. eBay sellers can choose to donate anywhere from 10 to 100 percent of an item's winning bid to the charity of their choice. When a seller agrees to donate even a portion of the auction item's proceeds to your organization, a special ribbon icon is placed next to the item so that bidders know that the auction is part of a fundraiser or charitable donation. The ribbon icon is easy for bidders to spot, as shown in Figure 2-3.

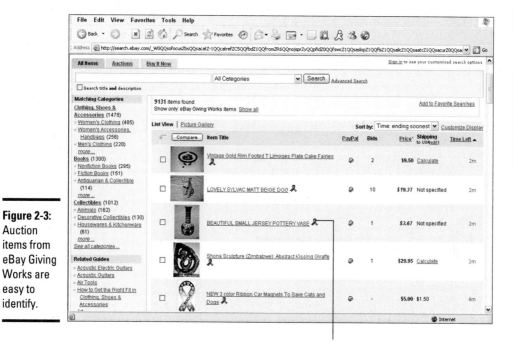

Figure 2-3:
Auction
items from
eBay Giving
Works are
easy to
identify.

eBay charity ribbon

As a bonus, any seller can choose to donate to your cause by selecting it from a list of certified charitable organizations and then designating it as a donation item after listing it on eBay.

You can decline proceeds from any auction item listed in your name. Watch for notifications each time a new listing appears. All you have to do is respond through your MissionFish account and request that the item be cancelled. It's removed from the listing within 24 hours.

You don't have to depend on the generosity of strangers. You can encourage your own members and longtime supporters to auction items on eBay and then donate the proceeds to your organization.

Normal eBay listing fees apply to a seller's auction item when the total donation is less than 100 percent of the winning bid. If your seller chooses to donate the entire profit, the only fees are a nominal $3 administration charge that goes to MissionFish and a credit card processing fee that's now listed at 2.9 percent of the value of the item.

Although this simple process is a favorable alternative to managing your own online auction, you have to consider a few other pros and cons:

✦ **Donation tracking:** eBay offers a password-protected Web page that reports all fundraising activity for both the seller and your organization. Because not all auction Web sites offer a donation-reporting feature, though, decide whether it's a necessity for you.

✦ **Delivering donations:** Every auction site has its own policy about when and how to deliver funds to your organization. For example, eBay transfers funds to your bank account. You usually don't see the donation for at least a month after the auction ends, though. Other auction Web sites send checks with final donation amounts, which are mailed either monthly or quarterly. Don't count online auction proceeds from third parties as immediate revenue.

✦ **Confirm receipt:** In most cases, the Web site (or a partner organization) that's managing the auction takes responsibility for issuing tax receipts. However, always confirm that this is the case, and keep the site's contact information nearby. If a benefactor has trouble getting a receipt, you then know where to direct her for help.

✦ **Promoting the auction:** As with any fundraiser, find out how auction items are promoted, and then ask whether the site offers other tools or resources to let your organization help promote the auction. Sometimes, you can do something as simple as add a logo to your Web site. Or, perhaps e-mail-based tools can be used to prompt bidding.

eBay Giving Works offers your organization the chance to promote an auction event by placing your logo on both the eBay site and the MissionFish site. You're chosen on a first-come, first-serve basis, and information must be submitted at least two weeks before your event. For complete information on how to participate, check the eBay Promote Your Listings page for nonprofits: `http://ebaygivingworks.com/ns/sell-resources-promote.html`.

Direct auctions without the middleman — almost

In the *direct-selling* form of the online auction process, *you* are the seller *and* the recipient. (One example is offered through the eBay Giving Works program.) You auction off your own items, such as excess inventory or old office equipment. On eBay Giving Works, eBay provides the auction structure and reporting features, and you handle the rest.

Of course, you can take the direct path and fully manage your own online auction. You still need the support of a vendor, though, at least for the back-end technology. In exchange for your use of the technology and other accompanying services, you can expect to pay a setup fee, a one-time usage fee, and a percentage of sales from each auction item.

cMarket Online Auctions, an online auction software-and-services provider have run more than 5,000 auctions and helped raise more than $50 million for nonprofit organizations. The company's Auction Manager service allows organizations to set up and manage their own online auctions. In exchange for a one-time fee, you can run unlimited numbers of auctions for 12 months, including a template for setting up the auction catalog and access to tools to manage and promote the auction. The company estimates that nonprofits earn as much as $5 for every $1 invested. cMarket services have been used by organizations such as the national Parent Teacher Association (PTA), the Leukemia and Lymphoma Society, and the Glaucoma Research Foundation. You see an auction for Glaucoma Research in Figure 2-4.

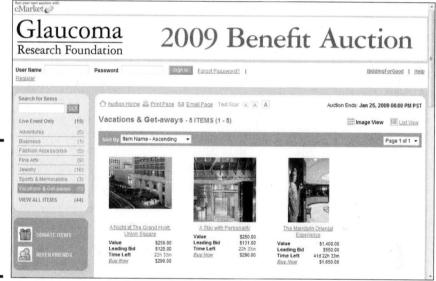

Figure 2-4:
Check out the auction Web site for the Glaucoma Research Foundation.

cMarket and other online-auction software providers usually offer supplemental services and features that you can add for an additional charge, such as enhanced tracking and reporting features or additional technical support. It all depends on your needs and on your budget.

Lots of other companies offer online auctionware and compatible services. These three companies can get you started:

✦ **BenefitEvents:** www.benefitevents.com

✦ **GoBid Auctions:** www.gobid.ca

✦ **AuctionAnything.com:** www.auctionanything.com

Online fundraising doesn't have to have the same grand *scope,* or large scale, as an auction has. As anyone who has pulled off this type of event can tell you, it still requires lots of work.

Soliciting Donations on Your Site

Just as some sites manage auctions on behalf of different charities, some organizations solicit online donations for charities. Adding your nonprofit's name to the list takes only a few minutes.

Connecting with online giving sites

Online giving sites, or *charity portals,* typically work with thousands of different types of charities. The portal actively solicits online donors, and then individuals choose which charities receive the donations. In some case, these sites also distribute their databases of nonprofits to larger entities, in an effort to increase giving potential.

A few of the largest, and most widely recognized, charity portals are

✦ **JustGive.org:** www.justgive.org

✦ **Network for Good:** www.networkforgood.org

✦ **CanadaHelps.org:** www.canadahelps.org

You pay no registration fee when you sign up with any of these three sites. However, they all deduct a small percentage of each donation (usually 3 percent) to cover their credit card processing fees. As for online reporting features and the transfer of donated funds to your organization, these items vary with each organization. You can check the FAQ section of each site to find more information on each organization's specific policies.

Adding your nonprofit's name to each site's list of charities takes only a few minutes. When you're confirmed as a recognized charitable organization (typically within 48 hours), you're automatically listed on the site. You can also place on your Web site a link that directs your members to the charity portal. Then, when visitors to your site want to make a donation, they just click the appropriate link.

To be able to participate in any of these three charity portals, you first must register with GuideStar, which is part of Philanthropic Research, Inc., a widely recognized nonprofit. Charity portals use GuideStar to certify nonprofits in good standing.

You gain other advantages by registering with GuideStar. Because sites such as JustGive, Network for Good, Schwab Find for Charitable Giving, and American Express also use the GuideStar database of charitable organizations to supplement their online databases for giving, you can be automatically listed within several charity portals. The GuideStar site alone now attracts more than 5 million visitors each year. That's a lot of potential donors for your cause!

Registering with GuideStar is a two-part process: You set up an account and list your organization within the GuideStar system. When you're ready to get started, follow these steps to set up your account:

1. **Go to the GuideStar Web site at `www.guidestar.org`.**

2. **Click the Register button on the site's home page.**

You see an online form on a new page that requests basic information in order to set up an account.

3. **Set up your GuideStar account by filling in these fields:**

- *E-mail:* Enter your e-mail address, which also serves as your username.

- *Password:* Enter a password with at least seven characters, and then confirm your password in the Re-Enter Password field.

- *Are You a Nonprofit Manager?* Select Yes if you're responsible for the account.

- *Organization:* Specify which kind of nonprofit organization you are.

- *Zip Code:* Provide your zip code.

- *Select User Type:* Select Grantmaker, Personal, or Professional. Click the What Type of User Am I? link to find out more.

- *Your Industry:* Select the industry that best describes your organization.

- *How Did You Hear About Us:* Select how you heard about GuideStar.

4. **Click the Submit button at the bottom of the page.**

After your registration is verified, you can list your organization with GuideStar:

1. **Click the Nonprofit Resources tab at the top of the page.**

2. **Click the Update Your GIF link on the right side of the page.**

3. **Enter your e-mail address and password.**

A new page appears that shows the employer identification number (EIN) for your organization.

4. **Click your EIN.**

If your number isn't displayed on the page, enter it in the EIN box on the same page.

A new page for your specific organization appears.

5. **Click the Update GIF link.**

6. **Fill in the GuideStar information form.**

This form asks for detailed information about your organization, including fiscal information, funding goals, mission statement, and other critical information. You can update the GuideStar form at any time.

7. **Click the Submit button at the bottom of the page.**

   You're listed in GuideStar within 48 hours!

If your organization is an exempt nonprofit recognized by the Internal Revenue Service (IRS), you might already be listed on the GuideStar site. Although the basic listing is pulled from your IRS Form 990, it doesn't include full details about your organization. Complete the GIF (GuideStar Information Form) to ensure that as much information as possible is available about your organization.

After registering with GuideStar, you can visit the online charity portals to complete the personalized registration process for each site.

Adding Donate Now buttons

More than a dozen reputable sites provide you with the ability to accept online donations on your Web site, without having to open a merchant account for credit and debit cards. These sites work by providing you with a Donate Now button to place on your Web site. Visitors to your site click the button to contribute to your cause. The processing sites take care of the rest of the process on your behalf, by transferring donations into your account (in some cases, by mailing monthly or quarterly checks).

All three of the charity portals we describe in the preceding section offer this option. Their only fee for this service is the 3 percent deduction from the donation total, to cover the processing fees charged by the credit card companies.

The types of additional fees charged by some Donate Now button services can include

✦ **A one-time setup charge:** Can be as much as $1,500

✦ **A monthly service fee:** Normally ranges from $15 to $25

✦ **A transaction fee to cover individual charges:** Might be a percentage of the donation or a flat fee

You have to shop and compare services. Some fees might include services that you don't need, so you're better off selecting another, lower-cost provider. Here's a sampling of the Donate Now button service providers you can explore:

✦ **BlackBaud:** Designs software for nonprofit organizations (www. blackbaud.com)

✦ **CharityWeb:** Provides e-commerce solutions for nonprofits (www. charityweb.com)

✦ **LocalVoice:** Develops software for nonprofits and other organization types (www.localvoice.com)

Many of these sites can provide a range of services, products, and consulting help tailored to the needs of your nonprofit. Check out some of their other products while you're on their sites.

Shopping for a good cause

Another growing phenomenon in the world of e-philanthropy is the development of *charity malls*. After visitors shop for products and services in these Web site communities, a portion of the proceeds is donated to the shoppers' charities of choice.

The reason that these malls are becoming an increasingly effective way to raise donations — especially for schools and other small nonprofits — is that many of them are partnering with widely recognized retail brands, such as Lands End and Barnes & Noble. You can easily encourage your membership base to shop online (at the stores they would normally frequent anyway) and then donate to your organization.

One advantage of these sites is that registration is quick and easy. You don't have to provide much detailed information, as you do when you sign up for GuideStar, for instance. These sites have a couple of downsides, too. Marketing this type of fundraising option falls completely on your shoulders. Unlike in the charity portals, individuals are less likely to randomly donate to your organization just because it's listed at these malls.

The other possible disadvantage is that many charity malls don't require organizations to be registered as nonprofits. For larger, recognized nonprofits, this detracts from the overall idea of shopping for a cause. However, they're still worth checking out. If you're interested, you can visit these charity malls:

✦ **iGive** (www.igive.com): Allows you to register your nonprofit to receive donations from purchases on iGive-sponsored e-commerce sites.

✦ **YourCause.com** (www.yourcause.com): List your nonprofit so that it can receive donations from e-commerce sites.

✦ **We-Care.com** (www.we-care.com): E-commerce sites that are partners with CharityMalls.com provide a list of nonprofits for consumers to select and make a donation.

Chapter 3: Getting the Donor Base to Come to You

In This Chapter

✔ Attracting visitors to start building a donor base

✔ Preparing your online strategy for attracting donors

✔ Moving your current supporters online and boosting activity

✔ Networking online for a good cause

*W*ouldn't it be wonderful if you could put up your site, post your mission statement, and then watch as the generosity of strangers poured in for your cause? Well, it can happen — but not quite as easily as that! Getting people to donate to your cause takes effort on your part, mixed with a little bit of time and skill.

Creating a healthy online donor base is similar to organizing any other major fundraising campaign or event: It requires event planning, the ongoing help of volunteers and staff, a good marketing campaign, and (almost) flawless execution. In this chapter, we show you how to transfer those offline fundraising skills to your online efforts.

Building an Online Donor Base from Scratch

As with any commercial Web site, your online success depends on attracting customers. In this case, those customers are your donors, supporters, or constituents. At the end of the day, your goal is to bring these qualified visitors to your site.

These people are actively interested in your mission and are prepared to invest money, time, and good will in your cause. To find and keep this online donor base, try these three actions, which we call the *G.E.E Whiz factor:*

1. Get your site noticed.

2. Engage passersby.

3. Establish a relationship.

It sounds simple. In truth, it *is* simple. The only difficult part is that many fantastic causes reach donors by way of the Internet, and, ultimately, your organization is competing with each one of them. That's why the ones that are the most successful in e-philanthropy are the ones that best communicate the G.E.E. Whiz factor.

Get your site noticed

Develop a strategy to put your Web site on the radar map. This step requires actively promoting your site to existing members of your organization and introducing it to prospective donors from around the globe. The Humane Society gets noticed, for example, by giving prospective donors helpful information and links to more articles.

The Humane Society also gets noticed by providing articles to other sites, such as the Pets911 site (www.pets911.com). This site has a prominent link to the Humane Society logo, where a prospective donor can find more information on how to get involved (see Figure 3-1).

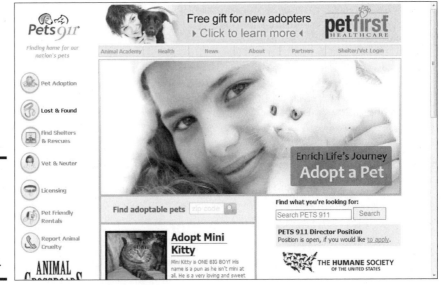

Figure 3-1: Putting your logo on partner sites helps increase your traffic.

Engage passersby

Give visitors to your site a reason to be involved in your organization *right now*. Rather than simply post your mission statement, use the site's home page to highlight one of your success stories. Show how other donors have made a difference, and then list specific actions that visitors can take to help create another success story.

Take a look at the Humane Society home page, shown in Figure 3-2.

Figure 3-2:
Engage donors with multiple ways to get involved in your cause.

The page lists many ways for potential donors to become engaged with the site:

✦ Click a link to simply make donations.

✦ Find out how to write to their congressional representatives to help pass animal-protection bills.

✦ Find information on hosting parties to raise money for animals.

✦ Help provide relief for animals affected by the hurricanes.

Establish a relationship

Getting people to take action once is a worthy goal; convincing them to become long-term donors is your real goal. To do that, use your Web site to keep people informed, to give them updates about how donations are being spent, and to expand their involvement into other areas of the organization.

The Humane Society brings home the G.E.E. Whiz factor by establishing a relationship with its donors. The site invites donors to join its online community, as shown in Figure 3-3. Donors can sign up to receive regular information from the organization and also to customize their preferences. They can receive information that interests them, and the organization can keep donors informed about issues that they're likely to continue supporting and funding.

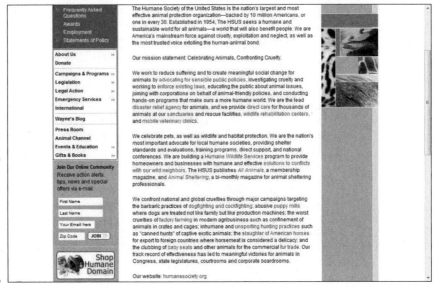

Figure 3-3:
Keep donors coming back by keeping them informed.

Putting Together a Plan to Reach Donors

After you have a good idea of what it takes to get your site noticed and to keep visitors coming back for more (see the preceding section), you can put together a plan for your own online efforts. Your plan should include these action items:

✦ **Identify your prospective donors.** Whom do you want to target? Be specific — an "Everyone" response doesn't count. What does your typical contributor look like? Include descriptors such as age, gender, marital status, personal interests, or any other factors that typically reflect your most faithful donors.

✦ **Determine the desired donor actions.** What do you want people to do after they find your Web site? Are you interested solely in cash donations? Or, are you soliciting in-kind donations and supplies? Perhaps you want to recruit volunteers, too.

When you determine all the possible actions, rank them in order of importance. Then you can decide how to place, or showcase, the opportunities within your site.

✦ **Describe the rules of engagement.** How can you capture (and keep) the attention of your visitors? For example, consider the content you use on the site. Have people shared testimonials or success stories of how your organization has helped others? Use these stories to pique visitors' interest, and follow them with instructions on how to get involved.

Visitor awareness building and education are probably expected at this point. In fact, now you want to use those objectives to help elicit a specific online action — whether that's making a contribution or having someone send your link to a friend.

✦ **Define your donor pool.** Geographically, where are your prospective donors located? Does it matter to you? Your organization might have a national or an international appeal, or your mission might benefit a regionalized population. Even if your scope is limited, other people might be interested in your cause. What about people who move away from your city and still have ties to the area? What about others who are simply affected by your cause? Deciding where your donors are likely to come from, or how far out you want to go to reach them, is an important element of your online marketing efforts.

The Internet readily allows you to localize your marketing efforts, if you choose. Or, you can decide to cast your net far and wide. If this issue is important to you, use geographic descriptions in your <META> tags and page titles. That way, your organization is more likely to turn up in location-based results in search engines.

✦ **Establish donor hangouts.** You want to create online marketing opportunities for your cause. To do that effectively, you need to know where your prospective donors are likely to hang out online. You can use these sites (blogs, for example) to place banner ads, buy keyword advertising (paid searches), and post press releases.

✦ **List giving partners.** Exchanging links with sites that complement yours is an effective way to expand your reach. You can also partner with other sites by offering to provide content, place informational links to research, or simply promote a fundraising event.

✦ **Provide action opportunities.** Keep your donors involved by giving them lots of options to participate. Your plan should detail the ways in which someone can not only donate money but also take action that makes them feel connected to your cause for the long haul.

✦ **Specify follow-up.** Plan to stay in touch with your online donors. E-mail messages, electronic newsletters, podcasts, blogs — the list is almost endless. You can use some or all forms of communication (online and offline) to stay in touch with donors and build lasting relationships.

Converting the Faithful

Although most online plans attack the issue of recruiting new donors, don't forget the ones who are already most familiar with you.

Unless you have a recently launched nonprofit organization, you should have a fairly long list of existing supporters, which typically include

- ✦ Previous donors

- ✦ Full-fledged members or active donors

- ✦ Participants in, or attendees of, earlier fundraiser events

- ✦ Board members and volunteers (past and present)

- ✦ Community supporters and sponsors

If you played your cards right, you collected the e-mail addresses of these folks over the years. Even if you never had reason to use those addresses, you should still have them on file.

You should have your list of supporters in a database with at least their names and current mailing addresses. Regardless of whether you ever fully took advantage of this resource, you're now in a great position. Obviously, these people represent a built-in group of followers. If nothing else, they're already aware of your organization and its mission. All you have to do is use your online initiative as a tool to step up their level of giving and involvement.

A great deal of recent e-philanthropy research indicates that people who give to charities over the Internet are likely to donate more — and do it more often. If you can convert a percentage of your offline contacts to online contributors, donations to your site might increase.

To see that happen, you have to reach out to everyone on your current list of names. Your objective is to get them active online.

Despite the fact that online giving continues to prosper, not everyone on your list is up to speed in Internet giving. Some donors are always more comfortable sending donations by snail mail (sent by way of the U.S. Postal Service) or being involved face to face, so continue to provide those options.

How do you decide whether someone is willing to receive your message online? You have to ask, of course! To start converting your faithful followers, do the following:

- ✦ **Send an electronic invite.** Use your data bank of existing e-mail addresses and send a request for donors to visit your Web site. Making them aware of the site — and the ways they can stay involved online — is the first step in conversion.

- ✦ **Reach out the old-fashioned way.** Send a postcard, make an announcement in your print newsletter, or write a letter. If all you have is a street address, reach out with traditional mailers and invite donors to check out your organization online.

✦ **Register constituents online.** For your next fundraising event, let folks register online. You then have the opportunity to collect updated e-mail addresses and get them accustomed to communicating with you over the Internet.

A few issues are still at play here. What happens if that piece of snail mail sits in a pile unnoticed? Too bad you didn't have the recipient's e-mail address! Then again, maybe your list of contacts contains old, outdated, or incorrect e-mail addresses, which are useless anyway.

One solution for these types of obstacles is to pay to obtain valid e-mail addresses from your list of constituents. Several companies now offer services in which they match information about your existing list of donors with their current e-mail addresses. You don't have to have existing e-mail addresses in order to use the service — this type of company can cross-reference information from other e-mail databases in order to find valid e-mail addresses.

You're likely to find one of these three types of services helpful in your online business:

✦ **E-mail appending:** You can cross-reference online databases to find someone's e-mail address when all you have is a name, phone number, or street address.

When you're choosing a company for e-mail-appending services, make sure that its process complies with guidelines issued by the Direct Marketing Association (DMA) and the Association of Interactive Marketing (AIM).

✦ **E-mail validating:** Your list of existing e-mail addresses might be outdated or contain errors (such as typos) that make them invalid. Companies can now verify e-mail addresses for you.

✦ **Reverse appending:** If you're collecting e-mail addresses online, the addresses might be all the information you have on prospective donors. A reverse appending service matches e-mail addresses with valid street addresses.

Dozens of legitimate companies offer e-mail appending and related services. Prices for these services vary; many of them charge based on the number of valid e-mail addresses they find. One company that specializes in assisting nonprofits, Blackbaud, estimates that organizations usually convert 20 to 30 percent of their total donor lists to valid e-mail addresses. DonorPerfect (at www.donorperfect.com) and DonorWorks (at www.donorworks.com) are also viable programs.

After you get someone's valid e-mail address, you still must obtain permission to send the recipient information about your organization (even if you already had the name in your records). The company performing the appending services should work with you to provide a final *opt-in,* or permission-based, list of valid e-mail addresses.

Reaching Out to People Surfing for Charities

Obtaining working e-mail addresses is only one component of building an active base of online donors. Regardless of how many names you already have, you want to reach out to as many potential donors as possible.

Fortunately, a growing online trend is opening the door to millions of socially conscious Internet users. *Social networking* is a form of socializing through virtual communities. Although some of the most recognizable social networking sites are geared toward entertainment, dating, and fostering friendships, a derivative group of the social networking sites is specifically focused on charitable giving and on philanthropy in general. These sites connect individuals, or large groups, who share an interest in various causes. In addition to highlighting current nonprofit news and topics of interest, members can share their experiences in community message boards. Social networking sites also allow members to create their own personal pages (for free) to discuss the causes in which they're active, to create and circulate online petitions, to donate to featured organizations, and to learn about different types of nonprofits.

Check out the sites in this list:

✦ **Care2:** Care2 (`www.Care2.com`), which has approximately 5.7 million members, is one of the growing number of sites that are proliferating social awareness online.

✦ **Charity Guide:** The editorial content on this site (at `www.charity guide.org`) highlights how members can make a difference in 15 minutes, a few hours, or over several days.

✦ **Charity Navigator:** A special feature of this site at `www.charity navigator.org` is that it rates charitable organizations from its database of more than 5,000 organizations. Members can even track and compare charities on their own, personalized Web pages.

You must understand what makes outreach through social networking different from other types of outreach. At these sites, you don't plaster Donate Now buttons across personal pages or aggressively solicit for paid memberships to your organization. Instead, these sites provide a forum to educate the public about your cause. Think of that forum as a low-key, grassroots type of marketing tool, and get creative!

For example, at Charity Guide, the Canadian organization Teddies for Tragedies is featured in the section about how to make a difference in a few hours. An article briefly explains the organization's mission and then explains how someone can knit or crochet a teddy bear and donate it to the group. The article, shown in Figure 3-4, grabs attention by using a photo of a finished teddy and then provides links to sewing patterns and to the organization's Web site.

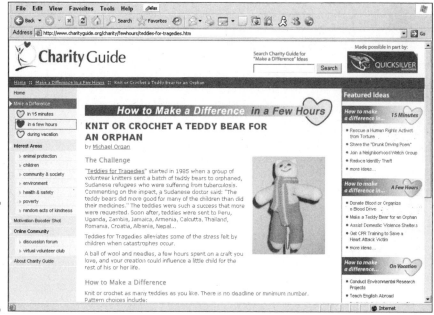

Figure 3-4:
This site
shows
people how
to make a
difference.

You can get involved with these types of sites and spread your organization's mission in several ways:

✦ **Sign up.** Become a member of the site. (Signing up is usually free.) Create your own, personal page to discuss your cause, connect to similar groups, and send messages to friends in your online network.

✦ **Actively contribute.** Join the discussions on the message boards. Find out what people are talking about, and when it's appropriate, let them know what your organization does and how they can get involved.

✦ **Provide content.** Submit articles for the site's content, send press releases, and forward news briefs with information pertaining to your cause (such as the status of current legislation).

✦ **Become a sponsor.** With millions of active and vocal members, your site's marketing dollars are likely to go far when you become a sponsor or paid advertiser on these types of sites.

✦ **Submit your charity.** For sites that keep logs or reviews of nonprofit organizations, always send in the necessary information to keep your cause on the list.

With the exception of paid advertising, nonprofit organizations can face limitations on how, when, or whether they can actively or directly solicit for membership or donations. Always read the FAQ (Frequently Asked Questions) section of the sites, and review their terms and agreements to ensure that you follow the rules for promoting a specific cause.

Chapter 4: More Online Marketing Strategies for Nonprofits

In This Chapter

✔ Enlisting the help of others to ask for donations

✔ Simple solutions for collecting the dough (again and again)

✔ Strategies to pique curiosity, provide purpose, and elicit action

*I*n discussions of marketing strategies for nonprofit organizations, the term *marketing* can encompass many different activities: donor development, fundraising, education, awareness building, and public relations, for example.

For marketing purists, not all these items belong in a marketing discussion. Right or wrong, they all become part of a nonprofit's marketing mix. In this chapter, we clarify what marketing means for nonprofit organizations, including taking advantage of opportunities that lead to growing your organization, through online monetary donations and other contributions.

Asking for Donations

Online marketing provides more than one chance to ask directly for money (or whatever else your organization needs). You can even ask for donations repeatedly. The person on the other end won't even bat an eyelash. If you don't like asking people for money, the Internet allows you to easily fundraise.

People checking out your Web site expect to be asked for donations. Often, they're the ones who have sought you out. Become comfortable with the idea of using the Internet to ask people to give — over and over again. E-philanthropy provides a host of methods for doing so.

Multiplying donation buttons on your site

One of the most overlooked online marketing opportunities is the Donate Now button, which is typically a single button (or link) on the home page of a site. Clicking the button displays an online form page where a visitor can choose to contribute. Nowhere else on the site is a prominent request for help, however.

You can increase the potential for a donor response by increasing the number of places on your site that you ask for support. Note that we don't endorse randomly scattering Donate Now buttons throughout your site. Instead, take an integrated, thoughtful approach, and follow these pointers:

✦ **Be position-savvy.** Visitors to your site view numerous pages. Make sure that donation buttons or links appear in as many spots as possible. Visible areas of your site include

- The navigation bar

- The upper-right corner of each page

- The lower center of the page

- Banner ads along the top or sides of the site's pages

Ask in different ways. Rather than repeat the phrase Donate Now on every page, use different terms that draw attention, such as these examples:

- Make a Difference

- Help Change a Life

- How to Contribute

- Ways You Can Help

- Get Involved Today

- Click to Contribute

✦ **Latch on to content.** When you share a success story on your site or spotlight someone in need, ask for support. In addition to placing a button following the content, include links to donate within the article.

✦ **Associate with a specific giving opportunity.** Consider the types of visitors your site attracts and why they're interested in learning about your cause. Someone might be more likely to give if your request is tied to a specific area of help. For example, you can link a request for a donation directly to research funding or to provide meals for a family in need. Be specific.

✦ **Highlight alternatives.** Not everyone wants to, or can, charge a $50 donation to a credit card. Instead, offer information about how to participate in a fundraising event or write a member of Congress to speak out on an issue. The Save the Children site (shown in Figure 4-1) provides a variety of opportunities to help: For example, philanthropic children can request a money box to raise money in their classrooms or homes.

✦ **Make a final plea.** Before a visitor leaves your site, display a final request for help in a pop-up window. Rather than ask for a cash donation at this point, ask the person to register to receive additional information on how they can support your organization. Collect only a name and an e-mail address, to keep the process quick and unobtrusive. You can then automatically send e-mail with specific requests for donations.

Figure 4-1:
Ask often,
and provide
giving
choices.

This type of follow-up e-mail is the perfect time to spotlight a story about your cause and then ask prospective donors to sign up for your newsletter. Even if they don't donate directly from your e-mail request, you can keep them informed and grow their activity level.

Passing the hat (pass-alongs)

As you might know from working with volunteers, sometimes these people are most passionate about your cause. Because their enthusiasm and dedication are infectious, not long after they start working for your cause, they recruit plenty of their friends and family members. In the corporate world, this concept is referred to as creating *buzz*, or word-of-mouth marketing; people in the nonprofit world call it *pass-along* marketing.

Suppose that 5 people who are drawn to your site discover something useful or important about your organization. They not only want to help but also share the site with others. If each of those individuals tells 10 more people they know and perhaps at least half of those people then choose to educate 10 of their friends, your cause has been shared with at least 105 people in that short cycle!

If your cause can motivate just one person to act, your site can also provide the tools to help that person spread the word to others. Here are two simple techniques:

✦ **Add a link or button on your site that asks visitors to send information to a friend.** A visitor who clicks the button can forward a message from you to a friend.

✦ **Allow site visitors to send free e-greeting cards to their friends.**
Include in every card a link that the recipient can click to donate. You
can also build your network by requiring the sender to sign up for your
network. The Make-A-Wish Foundation takes this approach, as shown in
Figure 4-2.

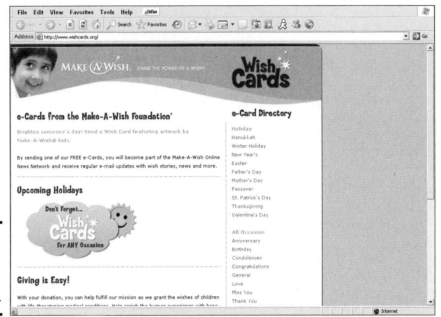

Figure 4-2:
Send a
greeting
card to
invite giving.

You can purchase software to implement your own program for sending
e-greeting cards. eCardMAX at www.ecardmax.com offers ready-to-
install software starting at $150. Or, you can work with a technology
company that offers a suite of services especially for nonprofits. Convio
(www.convio.com) offers an e-card program as part of its suite of
services.

Building personalized pages

Expanding fundraising tools for volunteers and event participants is another
growing online trend. The easiest way to do it is to offer personalized Web
pages to promote specific fundraising events (such as walk-a-thons).

Personalized pages are typically "miniature" Web sites that constituents can
build themselves by using templates (or a selection of preformatted Web
pages). A page usually includes an organization's logo, information about
its cause, event details, and the personal story of the fundraiser. Pictures
and the real-time tracking of donation goals can also be added to the site, as
shown in Figure 4-3.

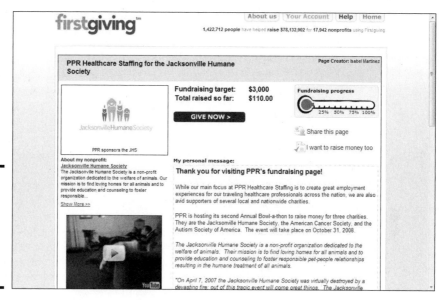

Figure 4-3:
Add your
own
fundraising
pages to
increase
donations.

Firstgiving.com (www.firstgiving.com) offers this type of service. In this case, your nonprofit may qualify for a free basic account that includes most features. Your organization can also register for a branded premium account for an annual $300 subscription fee, which gives you an unlimited number of pages for your supporters, access to event registration tools, and other advanced features. In addition to charging the base fee, the company charges a credit card processing fee (2.5 percent) and a small percentage (5 percent) of donation totals. However, Firstgiving provides these services in exchange:

✦ Creates on-demand reports showing the funds that are raised

✦ Collects donations and handles on-payment processing

✦ Provides unlimited support

✦ Manages online event registration

This unique solution helps supporters who are hesitant to fundraise in person or contributors around the globe.

Highlight your fundraisers' pages on your organization's main Web site, and provide prominent links directly to their personal sites. This way, you can easily offer prospective donors (visitors to your site) a specific, personalized way to give.

Because these sites often contain personal information (including e-mail addresses), always get your volunteers' permission to post links from your site.

Circulating donation links offline

One way to increase the value of any type of volunteer effort (personalized fundraising pages or any other method) is to distribute your information by way of other established networks that your volunteers belong to, such as these examples:

+ Churches

+ Credit unions or banks

+ Employers

+ Member-based organizations or clubs

+ Professional associations

Although most organizations and almost all companies maintain no-solicitation policies these days, you can occasionally find loopholes. For example, employers tend to make exceptions if their employees are contributing to good causes. Similarly, if an employee or a spouse suffers from a health issue (such as diabetes or cancer), a company is often willing to promote the nonprofit organization associated with that person's problem. Co-workers and peers are also more likely to donate to your cause when they know that they're supporting someone they know.

Here are a few ways to circulate news about your cause and increase visits (and donations) to your Web site:

+ **Create a newsletter.** Write a brief article about your volunteer and how that person is helping your organization. Your article can describe anything from raising money for a bike-a-thon to heading up a clothing drive. Include a Web address where people can learn more and donate. If you create an electronic newsletter, provide an active link to your site.

+ **Use the company's intranet.** An *intranet* is a private Internet site for an employer or organization that's unavailable to the general public. Employees or registered members access the intranet for news, general information, and critical updates. Provide a brief description (similar to a newsletter article) along with a button or link to your organization (see Figure 4-4). You can then place the link in a prominent place within the intranet site so that other employees or members can reach you and make donations.

+ **Produce a member bulletin.** This regular e-mail notification goes out to employees or members of an organization. Or, you might produce a non-electronic (printed) notice that's circulated in pay stubs or at meetings. Again, spread your message along with your Web site address to encourage others to get involved or make donations.

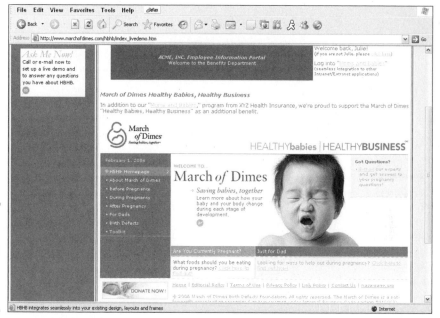

Figure 4-4:
Intranets
are effective
online
marketing
tools.

Cross-promoting

Not all donation requests have to originate from your site. You can take
advantage of *cross-promotional marketing* strategies, too. In these programs,
you work with another organization in a way that benefits both of you.

One type of charitable giving program, administered by major credit card
companies, plays off the popular reward programs offered as incentives to
cardholders. If you have a credit card, you know that many companies allow
you to accumulate reward points. You earn points based on a percentage
of the dollar amount you charge to your card. For example, every $100 you
spend earns 10 reward points. You can then redeem your points for a gift;
for example, 800 points might qualify for a $100 gift certificate to your
favorite spa. Several companies now allow you to trade points for a charitable
contribution of a specific dollar amount. What an idea!

Unlike in formal partnerships with card companies, some programs simply
require you to enroll. The American Express donation site (shown in
Figure 4-5) is an example. When you're ready to enroll, visit www.american
express.com/give. After you're approved, you can add a Donate Now
button with the American Express logo to your Web site. Visitors who click
the button go directly to the card company's donation site to redeem reward
points for your organization or to make donations by using the American
Express card.

Figure 4-5:
Reward
points can
be donated
to your
nonprofit.

Before enrolling with the American Express donation site, you must be listed
with GuideStar.org (see Book IX, Chapter 2). You also need to have your
employer identification number (EIN) handy to start the registration process.

Making Donating Easy

With a little help from your friends (and their friends), your online fundraising
efforts are bound to be a success. However, it's ultimately your job to make
it easy for anyone to get involved. The key is to not only get the attention
of would-be donors but also eliminate any barriers that might prevent them
from contributing. Your Web site provides a backdrop for combining simplicity
with donor-building strategies. Look into these features:

✦ **Automated membership renewals:** When you're using your site to
  market for membership fees, do yourself and your new member a favor.
  Rather than ask for a one-time membership fee, give your donor other
  options, such as these:

  • *A multiyear membership with an incentive:* Ask your potential donor
    to pay now to sign up for a three-year membership, and you'll give a
    bonus gift or discount.

  • *Automatically membership renewal:* Gain permission for your
    organization to automatically renew the membership each year by
    charging the fee to a designated credit card.

✦ **Recurring donations:** Donations made by credit cards is one of the simplest solutions you can ask for in online fundraising. Another option for incorporating this service is to set up the processing of recurring donations. This set dollar amount is then regularly (weekly, monthly, or even semiannually) charged to a credit card. Credit card companies sometimes offer this service directly from their Web sites, or you can manage the process internally.

✦ **Simplified employee matching programs:** When someone makes a contribution to your organization, doubling the donation can be a no-brainer. All you have to do is

- Verify that the donor's employer has a matching program.

- Get the right form into the donor's hands.

- Make sure that the form is submitted.

- Ensure that the employer cuts a check to you.

Even if this process sounds simple, it can represent a lot of work that your supporters might not be willing to do. Or, you might even overlook or forget the follow-up process. By implementing an automated donor matching program on your Web site, you can immediately see your intake increase, in one of two ways:

- *Donor verification:* Provide a link from your site to an employee matching database. The donor can verify that his employer participates, review the procedures for getting it approved, and review any conditions to the matching program.

- *Nonprofit verification:* Your organization verifies the participation of the donor's employer, *and* you use the information in the database to submit forms on behalf of the donor.

The DonorPerfect.com site offers online applications for each of these services. The Gifts Plus Online module gives your nonprofit access to more than 8,000 matching programs so that you can complete the process for your donors. Or, you can include the E-Match Donor link on your site so that donors can access the information on their own. Both programs are priced as annual subscription fees based on the number of users. A low monthly subscription fee is also available for smaller nonprofits. Find more information at `www.donorperfect.com/fundraising-software/donation-processing.asp`.

✦ **An easing of the burden of making nonmonetary donations:** Does your organization accept clothing, food, toys, or even cars? These items aren't easily collected from a Web site! You can simplify the donation process, however: Try partnering with a third-party collection center to pick up donated items. Allow your site's visitors to schedule a pickup online, or at least fill out an online form to start the process. You can also list drop-off spots that accept these donations for you. Better yet, consider allowing visitors to make online monetary donations that are then used to purchase items you need.

It might seem like you're doubling your own efforts to simplify the process of making online donations. Before you think that it's not worth your effort, take a look at how one nonprofit turns nonmonetary items into a big treat — literally — for everyone! The Treats for Troops online gift shop, shown in Figure 4-6, is stocked with premade gift baskets, individual sweets, and nonperishable items that you can donate. Supporters visit the site at www. treatsfortroops.com to go shopping and then click their mouse buttons to pick the perfect treats to send. Since the site began operating in 2003, it has sent more than two tons of goodies around the world, which shows the potential success you can have when you make online giving a breeze.

Figure 4-6:
Go shopping for a donation at this site to send treats to troops.

Chapter 5: Legal Considerations for Nonprofit Organizations

In This Chapter

✔ Selecting a gatekeeper for online compliance

✔ Writing and posting important policies

✔ Handling must-do registrations and guidelines

✔ Signing up with a governing organization

As the owner of a registered nonprofit organization, you're accustomed to the issue of compliance. Filling out annual reports for the IRS, issuing tax-deductible receipts to donors, and distributing legal waivers to volunteers are all a small part of your legal duties.

Fundraising over the Internet is no different. When you go online to seek donations, certain responsibilities come along with it. Some of the issues we discuss in this chapter are internal compliance activities. Even if an action item isn't mandated by a government entity, it's still something you should do. Other issues mentioned in this chapter are legal requirements. If you're venturing into e-philanthropy for the first time, this chapter is required reading. Even if you know that you're up to speed with the latest online regulations, consider this chapter to be a review.

Designating Responsibility

You know who takes the legal heat when something goes wrong: Your board of directors is ultimately in charge of the well-being of your organization. Even so, responsibility follows an internal chain of command. Depending on the size of your nonprofit, that chain of command might include an executive director, an entire paid staff, or a group of directors and volunteers structured by committees.

Now that you're entering the realm of online donations, similar legal responsibilities and consequences apply. Although your board accepts these legal responsibilities, you should assign responsibility for your Internet initiative to a designated individual or committee within your organization. By incorporating this position, you're developing both internal expertise and an internal watchdog for your online operations.

We recommend having an internal watchdog, for two reasons:

✦ **Branching out on the Internet is most likely new territory for you and your cause.** Initially, you have to turn to outsiders for consultation and guidance. If you find good start-up assistance and develop a holistic Internet strategy, however, you find that online fundraising increasingly becomes a larger part of your overall revenues, resources, and image. Internet fundraising might grow from occupying 1 percent of your organization's pie chart to eventually meeting or exceeding the 50 percent mark. That amount is an extremely big piece of your pie to not have internal expertise assigned to it! Likewise, growing its contribution to that level takes a long time unless an insider is championing the initiative.

✦ **Industry watchdogs, individuals, the media, and the federal government are increasingly scrutinizing online fundraising.** That's a good thing — you want the playing field to be as fair and ethical as possible. Otherwise, as donors see more scams and corruption from supposedly legitimate charities, they subsequently decrease their online generosity. Scams will happen to some degree, no matter what. That's why you have to go out of your way to promote your organization's high standards and continue building long-term, trusting relationships with online givers. Keeping pace with external watchdogs is generally helpful so that you're not surprised by changing policies and procedures.

You can choose an individual staff member or director or assign responsibility to an ad hoc committee (that you hope will become a permanent committee after your by-laws are adjusted). Although a larger, national organization might have the funds to hire staff members for this position, a smaller organization can still build this internal expertise by giving an employee the added responsibility.

When you're selecting the appropriate person, you don't have to look for someone with existing or extensive knowledge of the Internet. She should be comfortable with the Internet and technology in general, though. The biggest factor, by far, is that the person you choose should be willing, able, and enthusiastic to learn.

Try to recruit a person who can — and will — assist your organization for a lengthy period, to cut down the amount of time you spend having to continually reeducate and retrain. Some organizations are successful in recruiting permanent volunteers when hiring extra staff members is out of the question. Usually, these retirees, home-based parents, and professionals don't have full-time paid positions.

The designated individual should focus on keeping policies and procedures in compliance with any local, state, or national guidelines. An Internet strategy liaison can further benefit your organization by serving in these added capacities:

♦ **Point of contact (POC):** As the "go-to" person for questions regarding your online fundraisers, your designated POC should be responsible for overseeing or understanding all parts of your Internet strategy. The POC fills out the forms and updates any registrations on third-party sites, and assists your members, donors, and staff members with online fundraising issues.

♦ **Trainer:** As your organization adds online fundraising tools and features or participates in online events, your Internet strategy liaison should be available to train other staff members, directors, and volunteers.

♦ **Researcher and trend watcher:** In a quickly changing environment, having someone responsible for keeping up with the industry makes sense. Researching proposed policy changes or spotting innovative online tools for fundraising is incredibly important assistance to have.

♦ **Advocate:** Just as you or others in your organization are championing the cause of bringing your nonprofit into the area of online fundraising, the need for that advocacy will always remain. Having someone who's knowledgeable and excited about the role of e-philanthropy helps further your cause in the long run.

Creating Online Policies

When you shop online, you probably notice links to the legal section on many sites. You often see online privacy policies, user agreements, return or exchange policies, and other protective verbiage. After you begin your online fundraising endeavors, you too need to create certain policies to display on your site and to provide some basic information to visitors.

Include these items:

♦ **A privacy policy:** A privacy policy is a requirement. It's a statement that tells your visitors whether and how you collect information about them, such as e-mail addresses or name and physical addresses. It's also the place to let people know whether you're tracking their visits to your site through the use of cookies or other tools. If you're collecting information, tell them how you use it, and state whether you share that information with others. A link to your privacy policy should be clearly displayed on the home page of your Web site. For help with your online privacy policy, the Better Business Bureau offers a sample policy that your organization can use as a guide. You can find it at `www.bbb online.org/privacy/sample_privacy.asp`.

♦ **A security policy:** Similar to a privacy statement, your security policy lets visitors know how you store and protect their personal data. Although this policy is optional, you should use one if you collect donations online. In it, you explain how credit card data and other personal information are stored and protected. If you use a Donate Now button or another outside source to process online payments, let patrons know and then provide a link to those sites' privacy and security policies.

- ✦ **A COPPA statement:** If your nonprofit appeals to children or if you suspect that children might visit your site, you need to comply with the Children's Online Privacy Protection Act (COPPA). Regulated by the Federal Trade Commission (FTC), it helps protect children and dictates how or whether a Web site can collect information about children, particularly those under the age of 13. The FTC provides guidelines for compliance and a children's online-privacy statement to post on your Web site. You can find details at the FTC Web site at www.ftc.gov/privacy/privacyinitiatives/childrens.html.

- ✦ **An explanation of funds:** Describe how donations are used within your organization and specify exactly where all the money goes. Online donors appreciate knowing that their charitable contributions are put to good use. If money can go toward separate endowments, lifetime-giving opportunities, or other distinctive areas within your nonprofit, now is a good time to explain to donors. If donors can contribute in other ways (such as giving supplies, clothing, or food), break down those items into categories and display them so that donors readily understand their giving choices.

- ✦ **Form 990:** You might want to create a policy allowing visitors to view your IRS Form 990 online. Although you're not required by law to provide this information, it assures prospective donors of the legitimacy of your site. If you don't want to post this information on your Web site, provide a link to GuideStar at www.guidestar.org, where visitors can view your form by searching the site's database. To find out more about GuideStar, turn to Book IX, Chapter 2.

- ✦ **Contact information:** As the owner of a nonprofit, you must clearly provide contact information to your site's visitors. Providing an e-mail address is helpful; offer a phone number and mailing address, too. Then prospective donors can reach you if they have more questions. Seeing your full contact information prominently displayed on your Web site is also reassuring.

IdeaList.org is a terrific resource for information on all types of questions about nonprofits. Check out the IdeaList FAQ (Frequently Asked Questions), particularly the section on regulation — you might find other policies or statements that you want to add to your site. You can view the site at www.idealist.org.

Registering Your Charity

The most critical registration task you can do is to complete the individual state registration process. If you collect donations from people outside your organization's home state, you must register with the other states. This procedure is part of the individual states' solicitation laws, and compliance isn't optional. A few exceptions exist because only 40 states now require charities to register individually. See www.irs.gov/charities to view the list of states. Each state differs in how it requires registration, so we can't give you details on how to do so. Try an online search using your state name and the search terms **register**, **donations**, and **charity**.

Fortunately, a collaborative effort was created to make filing a little less burdensome on nonprofits. The National Association of State Charities Officials, in cooperation with the National Association of Attorneys General, created a unified registration statement (URS) to make multistate registration simple. The organization provides a registration kit in PDF format, which you can download from its site at www.multistatefiling.org. After you complete the information, you can submit the form to multiple states to register your organization.

The unified registration statement kit isn't accepted by Alaska, Colorado, Florida, Oklahoma, or the District of Columbia. If you use the URS kit, you aren't in compliance with these states and must register directly with each one.

If you use a Donate Now button service or participate in an online charity portal, you need to register with *all 50* states. These organizations solicit donors all over the United States, in addition to Canada and other international locations. If you don't register with all states that require it, you can face serious penalties and stiff fines.

If you need more information about what you have to do to collect donations, the IRS Web site for charitable organizations (shown in Figure 5-1) has information on various tax and compliance matters at www.irs.gov/charities.

Figure 5-1:
The IRS
provides
compliance
information
for your
charity.

Gaining Seals of Approval

Another step you can take to maintain compliance is to sign up with entities that govern charities. We discuss two in this section: the Better Business Bureau and Charity Navigator.

Although these programs might cost you additional time and money, they're well worth the investment. As a respectable charity, you want prospective and existing donors to know that you have high standards and are in compliance with mandated regulations. Providing this level of assurance only helps to expand the success of your online fundraising initiatives.

In addition to national ranking and approval systems, some regional and statewide organizations keep up with the progress of your charity. For instance, Maryland Nonprofits offers a certification program for participating organizations. It awards a Standards for Excellence seal to area nonprofits that qualify under its peer approval process.

To find out whether your state has a similar program through a recognized nonprofit association, check with the National Council of Nonprofit Associations. Its Web site, at www.ncna.org, has a membership list of all state associations that you can view for free.

Better Business Bureau

The Better Business Bureau (BBB) is a nonprofit organization that works to monitor and improve the solicitation of funds. A few years ago, it developed the BBB Wise Giving Alliance (www.give.org). This online charity-evaluation and -report system gives donors another reliable source for information about causes. The BBB specifically offers the program to national organizations or to organizations that solicit contributions in multiple states. If you're a smaller charity, you can still participate by way of your local BBB office. Register with Wise Giving Alliance by clicking the Charity Reports and Standards link on the left side of the page. Click the How Charities Can Enroll link at the bottom of that page, and then provide the requested information for your local BBB.

The organization's Web site maintains an up-to-date database of reports and financial information on select national organizations. You or your donors can scroll through the list of archived charities on the Wise Giving Alliance Web site (shown in Figure 5-2).

An optional program you can participate in is the BBB Wise Giving Alliance Charity Seal Program. If you meet the approved accounting standards adopted by the program, you can post the Alliance's seal of approval on your Web site. The seal lets prospective donors know that you're in compliance with national giving standards. If you decide to apply for the seal, you must also sign a licensing agreement and pay a sliding-scale fee based on the size of your organization (which is based on the amount in donations you took in during your last fiscal year).

Figure 5-2:
Find out whether you're listed in the Wise Giving Alliance charity report.

Even if you don't participate in the seal program, your organization might still show up in the BBB online database of charity reports.

Charity Navigator

Although Charity Navigator (www.charitynavigator.org) doesn't hand out a seal for Web sites, it doles out stars in its rating system of U.S. charities. It helps people and businesses evaluate the more than 5,000 charities (their reputations and financial well-being) and is itself a nonprofit and doesn't accept donations from any of the charities it monitors.

The information is pulled from an organization's IRS Form 990. The nonprofit organization uses an established set of criteria to weigh first the financial side of your organization and then the administrative side. In other words, it assigns values to your financial statements, fundraising efficiency, administration overhead, and ratio of working capital, to name a few. Your scores are then combined into a ranking system based on stars. As with hotel rating systems, the more stars you receive, the better. Whether you want to be ranked or not, your organization is likely to be ranked by Charity Navigator. If you aren't already listed, you can become a registered member of the site and request that your charity be reviewed. To become a member, click the My Tools link to join as either a member (you can use Charity Navigator's services) or as a charity (you can request your charity to be considered for review).

If your site receives a 4-star rating, you appear on the Charity Navigator list of 4-Star Charities. Because the group doesn't have a logo to add to your site, contact Charity Navigator to get permission to link to its site from yours.

Book X
Niche E-Commerce

Earn a living in Second Life!

Contents at a Glance

Chapter 1: Discovering Niche Markets

In This Chapter

✔ Narrowing your product focus

✔ Figuring out which niche market has your name on it

When you start an online business, the Internet offers plenty of untapped markets for you to explore. These markets are segments within existing industries that have a lot of potential because they haven't yet become saturated by sellers. You can certainly find this potential in *niche markets,* which are smaller, more defined segments of an existing market. You can tap into one of these healthy, vibrant market subsections after you glean a few basic guidelines for working with a niche product. In this chapter, we show you how you can access these niche markets and sell to their loyal customers.

Deciding to Sell a Niche Product

When thinking about a niche market, imagine the market in terms of a pie. The whole pie represents an entire market — one that's usually well established. But cut out one piece of that pie, and that piece becomes a smaller market all on its own. You no longer concentrate on selling the entire pie. You now narrow your focus to that single slice.

The pet industry serves as a real-world example. As a whole, pets represent a multibillion-dollar industry, with more than $10.5 billion that was expected to be spent in 2008 on pet supplies and medicine alone, according to the American Pet Products Manufacturing Association. Within that total market is pet insurance, which is a much smaller, but growing, niche.

Research shows that pet owners spend close to $1,000 per year on veterinarian bills. But surgeries or the need to treat serious illnesses can cost more than $5,000 per procedure. Despite these high costs, fewer than 5 percent of pets in the Unites States are insured.

If you're keeping up with the math, therefore, 95 percent of that market is up for grabs. And, pet owners are obviously willing to spend on this niche service offering: In 2007, owners spent $195 million on pet insurance premiums (a 21 percent increase in the prior year's spending) — with only nine pet insurers in the marketplace. That number shows a true demand in this niche. To answer the demands of this customer base, Web sites such as QuickCarePetInsurance.com and GoPetPlan.com now offer online quotes and enrollment to pet owners. Even if pet insurance now makes up only 2 percent of the total pet market, that's still a lucrative piece of pie that these companies can enjoy.

Pet insurance may be a relatively small piece of the industry, but it also represents a significant amount of untapped potential. That's a niche market.

As you see, a niche market can be financially substantial, especially for a small online business. Naturally, you get to enjoy these advantages in a highly targeted market:

✦ **Defined customer base:** If you do your homework, you usually have no trouble identifying your customers. And, because you're dealing with a narrow focus, you can get to know your customers extremely well. You can respond to their needs and wants much more easily, thereby creating loyal customers.

✦ **Bigger bang for your buck:** Because you're selling to a target group of people, you can stretch your marketing dollars further. Rather than invest in mass advertising, you can place less expensive banner ads on smaller Web sites that attract your exact audience. Targeted e-mails and podcasts are definitely budget-friendly for sites of all sizes.

✦ **Pursued specialty:** When you provide products that are hard to come by, your customers often seek you out. Your job is to make the best of your search engine optimization (see Book VI, Chapter 6). Then prospective customers can actively search for and find your site when they use the finely honed keywords related to your niche.

✦ **Positive word of mouth:** Word-of-mouth marketing (WOMM) is powerful, especially within a tight-knit community of customers. When these niche buyers find a quality provider of products or services, you can bet that they talk to everyone else within their circle of like-minded friends.

Not to burst your bubble, but you should consider these few disadvantages, too:

✦ **Limited customer base:** You're marketing to a much smaller group of potential customers. If the number of prospective buyers is too small, you can quickly reach market *saturation,* in which the pool of sellers is enough to satisfy the pool of buyers.

✦ **Restricted product expansion:** Finding new products to sell that complement your niche can be challenging. In a specialty market, you may find yourself stuck with the same product, even as sales begin to taper off.

✦ **Dreadful word of mouth:** Suppose that you make a few mistakes as you start growing your niche business. The same word-of-mouth marketing that could have been quite advantageous now becomes a killer. Because your customer base is small, negative comments can do a lot of damage to your site's sales. And, the widespread use of blogs and community boards makes it especially easy to spread the negative online word to a connected community of buyers.

To offset bad word-of-mouth marketing, be even more aggressive in quickly resolving customer complaints. Follow up every order with a personalized e-mail. Invite customers to share the results of their online shopping experience with you. If a customer has a problem, your attention to him (even after the fact) mitigates the damage, and this attention often redeems you in the eyes of your customers.

The disadvantages shouldn't deter your plans for a niche business. The benefits far outweigh any of the minor risks involved. But those risks give you all the more reason to be thorough in selecting the right niche to pursue. After all, if the interest hadn't been there, pet insurance could have bombed. Instead, the timing was right, and this niche has left animal lovers begging for more.

Finding Your Niche

Almost every established industry has a single piece of pie waiting to be divvied up. When searching out your online niche, here are some general guidelines to follow (to help you remember them, notice that the first letter in each term spells out the word *niche*):

✦ **Notice:** All too often, niche markets are in plain sight — ripe for the picking. Some people see them, and others walk right by. So, stop. Pay attention to your personal interests and those of your friends and family. After all, you're consumers. Take a look at which services or products you want or need that larger companies aren't providing. Watch for new trends, too. Find out what people are talking about, and determine what's hot and different right now. Trends are often predecessors to an emerging niche.

✦ **Investigate:** If you think you've hit on a great idea, it deserves an adequate level of attention. Research the larger market from which your niche originates, and determine whether it's a growing market. Check annual sales and identify top performers (the large companies) in that market. Find out what analysts and researchers are saying about possible spinoff segments of the market, and determine whether these industry experts have spotted the same niche that you noticed.

✦ **Competition and customers:** As with any other market, you have competitors in a niche. Do a little digging to uncover how many others are already servicing the market. If you have zero competition, you may want to reevaluate the demand.

Put your prospective customers under the microscope, too, and find out who they are. Be specific. Note whether they're single men with dogs, for example, or working mothers with young children. Figure out their preferences, current buying habits, and available income. The more you know about the people you're serving in this niche, the better chance you have of successfully marketing to them down the road.

Find out whether your competitors are catering to only that particular niche or whether it's just one more piece of their overall businesses. If your niche is only a piece of the competitors' pie, you have a possible advantage. You can specialize in the niche and become the expert.

✦ **Hypothesize:** Before you launch your niche-focused site, you need to test your theory. Maybe you developed the perfect product. It answers a definite need, and research shows that there's money to be made. To be sure, you have to test, test, test. Conduct small samples to find out whether people are truly interested. You have to know whether they're willing to pay for it, whether it answers their needs, and whether they're ready to buy from a new online resource.

✦ **Execute:** Create a solid plan for selling to your niche market. Sometimes, reaching this type of customer proves to be more difficult than marketing to a broader customer base. After all, you're talking about highly targeted and specific customers. Not only do you have to work harder to locate them, but one misstep in your marketing efforts can also destroy your credibility. An effective selling strategy clearly communicates how your product answers a specific or unique need for that niche customer.

Niche customers are often quite knowledgeable and passionate about the niche that your product or service addresses. Can you speak their language? Talking the talk means being up to speed on current terminology, hot topics, and issues of importance.

Draw in your customers by providing timely, informative content on your Web site that supports the products and services you offer for that particular niche.

The Internet definitely provides an exciting opportunity to sell to a niche market, and often the opportunity is right under your nose. Many online entrepreneurs stumbled onto a niche market out of sheer necessity. In some cases, the market lacked a product that provided a much-needed solution. In other instances, a niche market started up because an existing industry or market changed as the Internet matured. To stay ahead of the game, entrepreneurs identified smaller segments within their markets that weren't being served.

The Knitting Zone (`http://knittingzone.com`) is a shining example of how a need for a product can carve a healthy niche from a larger, existing market. The craft-and-hobby industry is a market of more than $31 billion, but knitting is experiencing a resurgence in popularity with hobbyists and represents a healthy portion of the overall hobby market. The Knitting Zone is taking advantage of that niche demand and meeting a specific want within that industry as a wholesaler of knitting yarn, supplies, and software. The Knitting Zone, shown in Figure 1-1, sells its products all over the Unites States and has a close-knit fan base.

Figure 1-1:
The Knitting
Zone targets
a unique
niche.

Look through these e-newsletters and online resources that track trends and future niches to help get you started carving a nook for yourself:

✦ **Ecommerce-Guide Daily:** www.ecommerce-guide.com/news

✦ **IconoWatch:** www.iconoculture.com

✦ **Stylephile from Variety:** www.thestylephile.com/blog/330000033.html

✦ **TrendHunter:** www.trendhunter.com

✦ **TrendTracker:** www.smallbiztrends.com

✦ **TrendWatching:** www.trendwatching.com

Chapter 2: Discovering Niche Trends That Pay: Children and Boomers

In This Chapter

✔ Unlocking the minority report of the under-18 crowd

✔ Getting to know the over-50 market

I n this chapter, we take a look at two niche markets: Children and baby boomers.

Children make up a fairly large market of potential online customers, and there's no reason why you can't take a piece of that market — as long as you can keep them interested in what you have to offer. We show you how to tackle the marketing strategies to reel in children — and most importantly, their parents.

Another growing segment of the market is baby boomers. A record number of people were born between 1946 and 1964, and they eventually received the baby boomer label. Today, these baby boomers represent one of the fastest-growing markets.

Marketing to Children

Children are typically divided into these three distinct groups, based on age:

✦ **Kids:** Although children who are 7 or younger don't always have enough independence to shop by themselves, they're influential in their parents' final purchasing decisions. Parents want to please their offspring and usually give 'em what they want.

✦ **Tweens:** Children between the ages of 8 and 12 are now considered a target market unto themselves. These kids have outgrown "baby" items and are starting to emulate the trends made popular by their older counterparts (teens).

+ **Teens:** Ranging in age from 13 to 17 (and some marketers go all the way to 18), this group is typically more mature. Savvy-shopping teens usually have greater decision-making abilities with less adult input. And, many teens have hefty amounts of money to throw around, from working part-time jobs or from receiving an allowance from their parents (or both!).

All three groups share at least one characteristic: Many kids are adept at using computers. Tweens and teens are particularly comfortable surfing the Internet and embracing technology for multiple purposes — including shopping online. To give you an idea of how teens embrace the Internet, check out some facts from a recent Pew Internet and American Life Project study:

+ Approximately 21 million teens (ages 13 to 17) are online.

+ More than half of teens using the Internet do so every day.

+ Close to half (about 9 million) of online teens buy online.

Pew Internet has a lot of good research to help you better understand the market of kids and teens online. You can even read the entire report, "Technology and Teens," for free on its Web site: www.pewinternet.org/pdfs/PIP_Teens_Tech_July2005web.pdf.

Attracting a fickle customer

Perhaps one of the toughest challenges in selling to kids is simply keeping them interested. Kids are often among the first consumers to get excited about a new product and help it skyrocket to success. Unfortunately, their enthusiasm can pass quickly, and they're equally willing to shun an item after they tire of it.

To decide which products your online business should promote to children, given this level of market uncertainty, you can search for items in one of the following broad categories. At least for the next few years, these product areas are expected to remain hot, hot, hot for kids of all ages:

+ **Technology:** Kids love technology. Think about where the iPod would be today without its young audience of fans. The fantastic factor about kids and technology is that this relationship usually helps create other industries and products, too. You may not have created the iPod, but you can easily sell accessories to go along with one. Technology and anything related to it equals opportunity in the kid market.

+ **Interactive services:** Kids use the Net in a big way. And, their expertise and the amount of time that they spend online will only increase over the next decade. That's why any service (for fun or otherwise) delivered by way of the Internet has a shot at success with kids. Online gaming has rocketed into a full-blown industry of its own, thanks in large part to the kid market.

✦ **Sports:** Kids and sports are almost inseparable. A record number of kids now play on local sports teams, and sports span the gamut of this market, appealing to young kids, tweens, and teens. Whether you sell sports gear online or promote e-books targeted to improving your game, even your most fickle kid customer can't resist this category.

✦ **Customization:** Kids like having the option to customize a popular product to their specifications. From shoes to jewelry, tweens and teens seem particularly fond of slightly tweaking a mass-produced item and calling it their own. This area has potential to grow, especially as more brand-name retailers offer online customization of products.

✦ **Decor:** This product category is definitely hot right now, including stylish home products to decorate kids' bedrooms or teens' dorm rooms, and fun accessories that dress up school lockers and a teen's first car. Decorating personal space feeds into the desire of children to make things their own.

Keeping 'em coming back for more

No matter what you choose to market to kids, you have to deal with the issue of how to keep those little shoppers coming back to your site. Follow these guidelines to help turn your young customers into repeat buyers:

✦ **Add products:** It almost goes without saying — introduce new products, and do it often. Period.

✦ **Offer a twist:** You can update older products by offering them in new colors or styles. Or, after you identify a particular product that sells well, offer companion products.

✦ **Change your site:** In addition to the products you sell, the site itself needs a frequent facelift. You don't have to redesign your site. Instead, try adding fresh images, updating content, and switching colors occasionally.

✦ **Create a community:** As the popularity of social networking sites demonstrates, kids thrive on interacting with other kids. Sites that (safely) offer the opportunity for kids to communicate online or that can build a sense of identity for a particular group keep kids coming back.

✦ **Grab opinions, give rewards:** You can include quick polls, top ten lists, and other surveys that solicit the opinions of your customers on your site. (These features also help create a sense of community.) Kids also like to be rewarded for patronizing your site. Free downloadable games, coupons, loyalty shopping rewards, freebies, and giveaways are sure to please.

If kids like your site and your products, they tell their friends. Why not make it easy for them? Let your loyal customers pass along some of your site's freebies to their friends by way of e-mail. If you make sharing easy, you attract more attention — and future customers.

Reeling in the parents

Like it or not, moms and dads continue to play a role in their children's purchasing habits, even as the kids approach early adulthood. How, or how much, you involve parents in the online selling process typically depends on two things: age and product.

Age

Exactly how old is your target customer? Generally, the younger the child, the more information you want to provide for parents:

✦ **Kids:** Parents usually have the final authority on all purchases when young children are involved. But don't forget that these kids (especially as they reach school age) are fairly avid computer users. Have sections on your site that meet the wants of the children, as well as a section that addresses the needs of the parents. Barbie.com, for example, gives young girls a place to play online games related to its core product: the Barbie doll. The site also has a separate section that targets parents, as shown in Figure 2-1.

Figure 2-1:
The Barbie site appeals to both kids and parents.

✦ **Tweens:** After a child enters the tween stage, the parent/child relationship begins to change and your site has to respond appropriately. Parents still have a great deal of control, but their input becomes more of a filter. At this age, kids and parents are truly making decisions together. If you're marketing to tweens, you don't have to devote an entire section aimed at parents, but you may want to reassure adults that you're safely marketing to kids.

✦ **Teens:** If teens are your market, you probably don't need any messages targeted to parents. After all, these kids want the site to be all about them. And, they certainly don't think that they need Mom or Dad hovering in the background. WakeUpFrankie.com (`www.wakeupfrankie.com`) specializes in linens and room decor for teen girls, and every part of the site's design is made to appeal to the 13-to-18-year-old market. The site uses bright colors and lots of images, and it incorporates content that speaks to its teen customers (see Figure 2-2). *Note:* The site doesn't even mention parents!

**Book X
Chapter 2**

**Discovering Niche
Trends That Pay**

TIP

If you have a product that appeals to more than one targeted age range, divide your site by age. Create sections for each age group so that kids and parents can quickly find the appropriate spot and start buying!

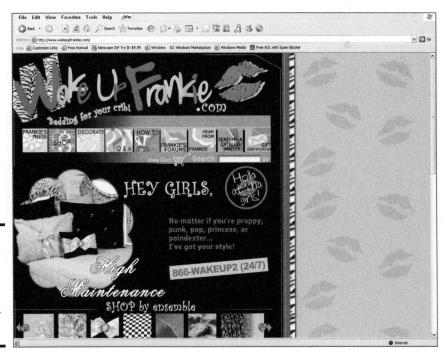

Figure 2-2:
When targeting teens, your site should reflect their style.

Product

The type of product you sell can determine how you involve, or market to, parents. One of the best examples of a product deciding the parents' role is clothing. Rarely do young children visit online clothing sites. In most cases, parents do all the shopping. Therefore, you might have a site designed in fun, age-appropriate colors because it matches the tone of the product line, but you're ultimately selling to parents.

Reading the small print: Important policies to consider

We can't cover the basics of selling to kids without sharing one of the biggest rules of running an online business: Always clearly post privacy policies and terms of agreement for your users. (You can find more details on these policies in Book II.)

Posting and following a privacy policy is the number-one rule when you're running a site targeted to kids. The Children's Online Privacy Protection Act (COPPA), passed by Congress in 1998, oversees children's privacy on the Net.

The primary goal of COPPA is to ensure that you're acting responsibly when you collect information online from children under the age of 13. In a nutshell, you can't request even a hint of personal information from a child without first notifying his parents and getting their permission. If you have one of the following two types of Web sites, the COPPA Rule applies to you:

✦ **Children's site:** You have content, products, or services specifically designed for children. Your site also

  • Is a *for-profit,* or commercial, Web site

  • Collects personal information from children under the age of 13

✦ **General site:** Your online business can offer any type of product or service, but COPPA applies if you

  • Have a section on your main site targeted to kids or specifically designed to appeal to kids

  • Knowingly collect personal information from a visitor under age 13

Generally, you have to follow seven basic requirements for communicating with preteens, using the COPPA Rule:

✦ **Post your privacy policy.** Make your site's policy on protecting a child's personal information easy to spot on your home page. Don't be afraid to use a little extra real estate to make this policy stand out.

No matter which type of site you run, always clearly post a privacy policy on your site for customers to read.

✦ **Notify parents.** When children want to receive fun stuff from your site (or you want information about them), obtain parental permission first.

You're allowed to collect a child's name and her parent's e-mail address in order to request parental consent. Check the Q&A portion of the Federal Trade Commission's COPPA site (www.ftc.gov/privacy/coppafaqs.htm) for the lowdown on getting parental consent.

✦ **Protect data.** Any information you collect must remain private, secure, and protected. It's your obligation!

✦ **Offer a choice.** After you notify parents that you want to collect information about their children, make sure they know they can say No.

✦ **Provide access.** At any time, a parent can request to take a look at the information you have on file for their children. Be sure to open those files if a parent asks!

✦ **Keep in touch.** Stay in contact with parents. Give them the opportunity to *opt out,* or discontinue receiving information.

✦ **Allow participation.** No matter what, you can't restrict a child's access to your site if a parent doesn't want to give up personal information.

You can avoid tempting the Federal Trade Commission (FTC) to slap fines on you by deciding not to collect personal information. Instead, get parents involved. Communicate directly with moms and dads if you have messages for their children.

If you fail to comply with COPPA, you and your site can be penalized by the FTC. If you make the necessary changes, you still have to pay a fine. Previous cases have involved fines as high as $30,000 or more.

To ensure your compliance, the FTC has created an informational site filled with details about COPPA. You can check it out at www.ftc.gov/kidzprivacy. Because the site is targeted to both kids and adults, it also gives you a good example of how you can design a fun yet functional site (see Figure 2-3).

With everything that you have to worry about, selling to kids can seem a little overwhelming. If you take the time to plan your strategy, however, and make sure that your legal *i*'s are dotted and *t*'s are crossed, it's truly a fun market!

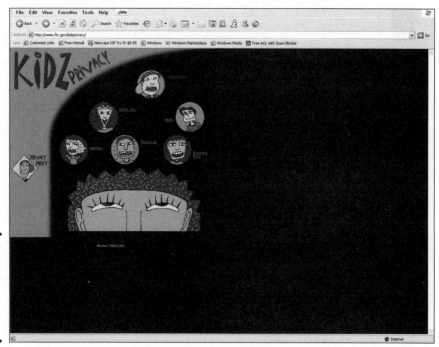

Figure 2-3:
Sites can be designed to attract both kids and adults.

Understanding the Baby Boomer Market

After baby boomers hit the big Five-Oh, they become part of another interesting demographic — the over-50 market. The U.S. Census Bureau projects that this special population will grow to 97 million strong by 2010!

This group is also notorious for spending billions of dollars — online and off. With approximately 36 million of the over-50 market having computer access, that shopping bent bodes well for online businesses that court the boomer generation!

Before targeting your business to the over-50 customer base, you need to know some things about this group. Boomers are lucrative customers, if you understand these traits. They are

+ **Open minded:** Research indicates that boomers are willing to try new products, regardless of who makes them. Sure, like everyone else, they have their favorites, but these consumers aren't bound by brand alone. That's important. This flexibility means that you have room to introduce alternative products or services to boomers, and they're likely to receive the message.

✦ **Value conscious:** Everyone likes getting a good deal, especially consumers over the age of 50. We're not talking about bargain basement shopping, though. Research shows that although this group is willing to spend money, they want to know that they're receiving a value in return. That value can range from a quality product for the price to a fantastic experience that makes the money worth spending.

✦ **Influenced by peers:** Friends tend to have lots of opinions about their buying experiences, and boomers seem particularly interested in hearing from their comrades. In fact, the over-50 market is quite receptive to opinions from their peers. And, those opinions frequently influence the boomers' final buying decisions.

✦ **Self confident:** Friends and family aren't the only ones with valuable opinions. People over 50 trust themselves, too. A person's experience with a product or service greatly affects future purchasing decisions. That's not to say that you can't make an honest mistake and be forgiven. But this group thinks carefully before spending more money at your site if you've already let them down.

✦ **Research advocates:** Before buying, this market wants the scoop on products. And boomers are willing to invest whatever time necessary for a little pre-purchase investigation.

Make consumer research available on your site when targeting over-50 consumers. Add sections for product reviews and customer feedback. Then provide a Buy It Now button at the end of the review to make purchasing easier.

✦ **Willing to spend:** The over-50 market has plenty of disposable income. Even better, people in this group have a propensity to spend it — if they're moved to do so!

Designing your site to attract aging customers

As much as we want to give you a one-size-fits-all rule book for targeting the 50+ market, we simply can't, because this group of consumers is so diverse.

But you can rely on one undisputable fact about selling to the over-50 market: It's as much about having an appropriately designed Web site as it is the type of products you sell. By making a few conscientious decisions, you can improve your site's appeal to over-50 customers.

Background and colors

Research shows that your site for the over-50 crowd is better served by sticking to some standard color rules:

✦ **A white background color works best.** White is simple and crisp, and it makes text easy to read.

✦ **Certain elements need color.** Captions, headlines, and ads can use color — use brighter, bolder selections.

✦ **Black text reads well.** Stick with black text for articles and product descriptions.

✦ **Minimize your use of blue and green.** Avoid using too many blue and green tones, especially from the lighter color palettes.

✦ **Use only a few colors.** Keep the number of color selections to a minimum.

✦ **Maximize your use of contrasting colors.** They're more pleasing to the eye, and they make information on your site "pop."

Text and fonts

The prevailing mindset says that if you target older consumers, you have to use huge text on your site. This idea isn't exactly true. The overall goal is to increase the readability of your site. Follow these tips for better readability:

✦ **Avoid placing text on top of blocks of color.** Use black text on a neutral (preferably white) background.

✦ **For primary text, such as main content, use a larger font.** Try 12 or 14 points.

✦ **To grab attention in headlines and captions, use a large font.** Try 14 or 16 points.

✦ **Use case wisely.** Place captions in ALL CAPS for emphasis, but use lower-case letters for other text.

✦ **Use leading appropriately.** Add extra spacing between lines of text so that your content isn't cramped.

✦ **Choose a sans serif font for your text.** Arial and Helvetica are good choices.

You can find plenty of nouveau twists on the classic sans serif fonts, some of which you can see in Figure 2-4. Explore these new alternatives on sites such as Linotype (www.linotype.com).

Links and buttons

Every spot on your Web site serves a purpose, especially links and buttons. URLs placed within the site serve as links to help visitors move within your Web site. Buttons also guide people through your site's structure. You can enhance the functionality of these features, making it easier for boomers to get around, by using these tips:

✦ Visually differentiate between links that the user has or hasn't visited.

Having a link change color after a user clicks it is a common method to indicate a link that has been clicked.

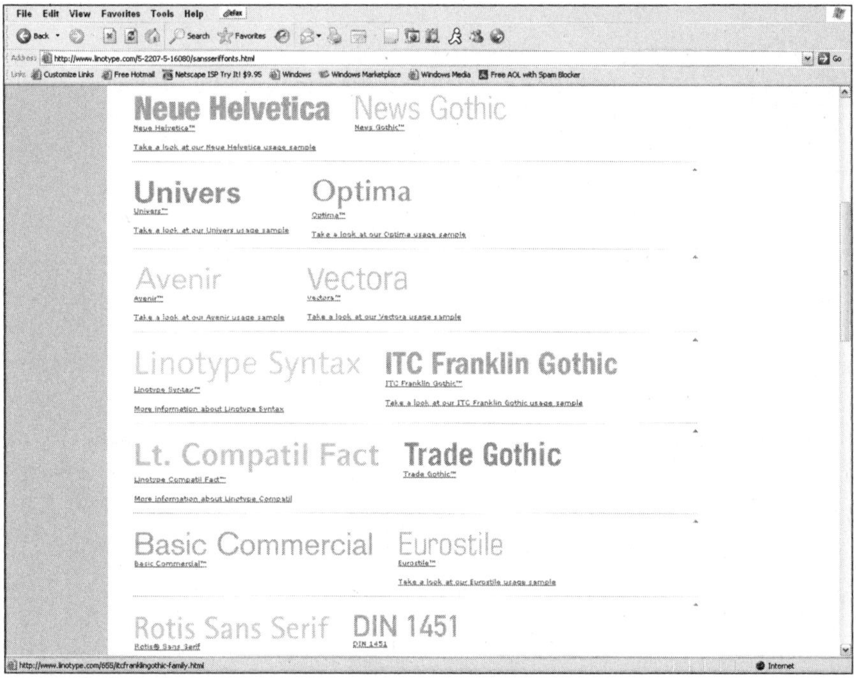

Figure 2-4:
Use updated versions of the classic sans serif fonts.

✦ Place a series of links in a bulleted list.

✦ Be descriptive when labeling links. Use keywords and specific phrases to describe the link, as opposed to using the phrase *Click here.*

✦ Make the clickable areas of buttons and graphics larger than the button or graphic itself. A consumer should be able to click the mouse on a target area that surrounds the image (as opposed to clicking exactly on the image itself).

Site structure

The key word for organizing your site is *intuitive.* You want boomers to be able to easily (and instinctively) locate information and products throughout your site. To make your site structure boomer friendly, follow these guidelines:

✦ **Location, location, location.** Keep your most important information or content in the upper-middle areas of each page of your site, especially the home page.

✦ **Limit scrolling.** Not all online shoppers appreciate excessively long Web pages.

✦ **Avoid excessive clicking.** Don't make shoppers click or double-click excessively to navigate through your site.

Try incorporating expandable menus in your site to show page options. Usually, these submenus appear whenever your mouse cursor moves over a specific button or link. Unlike with drop-down menus, you don't have to double-click to open expandable menus.

✦ Display a directory of topics (shown as a group of links) at the top of your pages. When you group link choices and make them all visible at one time, your visitors can easily move throughout your site.

In reality, many of these design rules for the over-50 market translate to good design for everyone. For the most part, these guidelines come from a lot of research done on boomers. Organizations such as AARP now promote these design tools as recommended standards for this market.

Keeping baby boomers buying from you

Boomers aren't as decrepit as you may think. As their active lifestyles demonstrate, they're far from it! And although they may qualify for the classic senior discount at many businesses, you can use a number of better ways to reward those customers who fall in the 50-to-64 age range:

✦ **Provide enhanced service.** Excellent customer service is a plus for any age group. This market is no exception. Dazzling your customers with extreme care and attention is better than any $5-off coupon.

✦ **Offer targeted promotions.** Rather than give a general discount, you can create a personalized promotion that zeroes in on the interests and needs of each special consumer.

✦ **Give out loyalty rewards.** Boomers may be open to trying new brands, but don't hesitate to reward them when they decide to stick to yours. Frequent-buyer discounts, special giveaways, and other product-based rewards help convince customers to come back to your site.

Finding a niche within the baby boomer market

Accepting a gold watch upon retirement and settling into a comfortable recliner is no longer the status quo. This generation is bursting at the seams to stay active, fit, and involved. If your version of an online store for boomers is centered on denture creams and motorized wheel chairs, you had better think again. Customized accessories for Harley-Davidson motorcycles and NASCAR paraphernalia are more likely the speed for this group. Here are a few other areas with great appeal to the over-50 market:

✦ **Business:** Boomers are working longer than their predecessors. They're also controlling their professional destinies by starting businesses of their own. Online sites that help boomers further their careers and businesses are finding a healthy niche.

✦ **Convenience:** The do-it-yourself (DIY) trend is passé for boomers. Many of them think that the convenience of having someone else do tasks is worth the price. Any type of product or service that saves time is a winner in this market.

✦ **Cosmetics:** On average, boomers consider themselves 12 years younger than their actual birth date indicates. Both men and women are willing to invest in helping their outsides appear as healthy as their inner selves feel.

✦ **Customization:** Boomers are a diverse bunch who often reject any type of labels. You can't pigeonhole this group into any single category. One 55-year-old may be retiring while another is launching a new business. Those two people may be the same age, but that doesn't mean that they're experiencing the same things. The good news is that this individuality opens up another lucrative online market opportunity for you. Customization, specialization, a niche within a niche — call it what you like. Focusing your product base to a boomer's current lifestyle circumstances, rather than to an age-based generalization, often equals profit.

✦ **Home decor:** Thanks to the interest in second homes and vacation properties, boomers have many houses to furnish. This demand creates a lucrative market for stylish household appliances, upscale linens, and many other decorative household items.

✦ **Recreation:** Boomers can always find time for play. Recreational items, ranging from RVs to Vespa scooters (and everything in between), fit nicely with the active, adventurous lifestyle of most Boomers.

You don't have to sell a 16-foot RV to find success in the recreation category. Instead, focus on a smaller niche, such as specialized accessories for the large vehicles.

✦ **Romance:** Unfortunately, divorce for couples over 50 is on the rise. The number of newly single 50-somethings has led to an influx of increased dating among this age group. Online dating services are booming, along with other sites that help boomers explore a second (or third) chance for love.

✦ **Technology:** Many people believe that the over-50 market has a technology phobia. That may be true for seniors who are at least age 65. But boomers have been working with computers for a while now, and in the area of the latest high-tech gadgets, they have money to burn.

✦ **Travel:** Helping boomers explore exotic locations has proven to be a good strategy for several online travel sites. Any product or service that makes traveling more comfortable and enjoyable can result in a winning e-business for you.

The moral of this story is simple: You have an unlimited number of market opportunities when you're wooing the over-50 niche, so use your imagination and have fun with this exciting group of online consumers.

Chapter 3: Blogging for Profit

In This Chapter

✔ Developing value for your blogging persona

✔ Identifying revenue opportunities

✔ Choosing the perfect blog platform

*B*logs are online diaries or journals of thoughts, observations, and comments about people's lives and the world around them. Not only did individuals jump on the blog bandwagon, but the business world also quickly saw the value of having this type of forum, too. Companies have adopted blogs as a way of promoting products and services.

Perhaps most important is that many companies that create and maintain blogs enjoy a healthy financial return on their efforts. That's right: Bloggers are making a lot of money for simply sharing their thoughts and opinions.

In this chapter, we show you how to turn a blog into a viable business. And, with thousands of blogs and hundreds of tools now available to help any aspiring *blogger* (the person who writes a blog), you can easily get started.

Creating Value

The first rule of finding success as a business blogger is to provide value for readers. To better understand this concept, consider the top benefits that blogs offer to you and your business:

✦ **Current information:** Although Web sites are an effective way to disseminate information, their content doesn't change as often as people want. Magazines are published monthly, and most newspapers are published daily. The Internet allows instant communication, and people want to hear the newest information immediately. Although many online news sites are now updated throughout the day, blogs enjoy the reputation of being the most actively updated news sources. A good blog posts multiple entries per day or even an entry per hour. (This frequency of updating information can also help your blog rank higher in online search results.)

✦ **The ability to connect:** The power of many blogs lies in the power of communication. On one level, bloggers are able to provide Web links to articles, reviews, or even other blogs. The bloggers become an army of reviewers, by recommending to others which articles to read and providing summaries. On a more personal level, bloggers and readers often communicate with each other by *commenting,* or leaving messages, following a particular blog post. This almost-instant two-way communication technique keeps readers engaged in a blog.

 Readers who use the RSS (Rich Site Summary) feed on your blog can choose to receive updates from it as new posts are added. Promoting a RSS feed on your blog is another way to keep visitors engaged and coming back to your site. To get started for free, try using FeedBurner (www.feedburner.com), owned by Google.

✦ **Less filtering:** Blogs have sprung up to cover almost every topic imaginable. Traditionally, nonblog media organizations have to decide which stories to mention in a limited amount of space or time and don't always provide detailed information. On blogs, readers have a broader array of information to choose from, and it's often more in depth. Additionally, blogs provide links to other resources and background information.

 One requirement of maintaining a blog is having extra time. Your blog readers expect that you will continually update your blog. If you create a blog with great fanfare and then wait months to post new entries, you quickly lose favor and even irritate your potential audience for wasting their time.

Finding your voice

When you create a blog, it needs two components:

✦ **Topic:** When you're selecting a topic, decide whether you want to share news and information about a specific industry, type of product, or notable trend. Or, you might decide to make your blog more personal by selecting a topic such as the journey you're taking to run your business, by discussing health concerns, or by sharing ideas about raising kids. No single correct topic exists, so pick something you're passionate about. Of course, because you're planning to earn money from your blog, you should also choose a topic that has wide appeal to a large number of people. Along those lines, if you're adding a blog to an existing business site, blog about topics that relate specifically to that business or its products and services.

✦ **Tone of voice:** Establish a tone of voice that's also unique to your blog. Keep in mind that blogs are conversations between you and your visitors. The information you post, or your blog entries, should reflect your own voice. In most cases, blogs don't abide by the typical rules of formal business writing. Instead, a blog's tone should be

- Casual

- Friendly

- Informal

- Inviting

- Informative

That's not to say that you shouldn't use good grammar or check for correct spelling. It just means that you should write your blog as though you're having a one-to-one conversation with a friend. Your particular blog voice is then further defined by your personality. It may be a little more humorous, satirical, or to the point. Just make the voice yours.

Although one person should coordinate all blogging efforts, a good blog can and should have multiple contributors. This includes feedback, or comments, from your readers. To encourage feedback, be sure to allow public comments on your blog.

Check out *Buzz Marketing with Blogs For Dummies,* by Susannah Gardner (Wiley Publishing), to find out how to generate more buzz and encourage your audience members to contribute their voices to your blog.

Content, content, content

The best way to create and maintain value for your blog is by adding content. According to a 2008 report from Pew Internet and American Life Project (www.pewinternet.org), 73 percent of American adults use the Internet, and 42 percent of those users read blogs. That's a lot of people looking for a lot of information. If they find your blog, how do you keep them interested — and keep them coming back? Content.

Two types of content are used in blogs:

✦ **Blog posts:** It's extremely important that you frequently add new posts. Although some people may encourage posting an entry at least once a week, we recommend a more frequent schedule. Blogs with heavy traffic, for example, may post a new blog entry three to five times in a single day. This number of entries may seem like a lot, but don't worry: Most blog entries may consist of only a few sentences, with a larger post, the equivalent of an article (around 500 to 1,000 words), posted at least once or twice per week. Because blog posts are typically stamped with the date and time they go live, visitors can easily tell whether you're adding fresh content to your blog site. Therefore, in addition to the quantity of blog posts, it's important to have current, frequently updated entries.

Make sure that the content you post is relevant to your readers. If readers aren't interested in your content, they don't come back, no matter how many times you post.

✦ **Links to more detailed information or articles:** These links can be to content on someone else's Web site, but, ideally, the links point to articles on your own site. Not only does this strategy keep visitors on your site, but the additional pages of content also provide more opportunities for search engines to find your site and to earn ad revenue. To find out more about search engines and how they help attract visitors to your Web site, read Book VI, Chapter 6.

Earning Money with Google AdSense

One of the most popular ad-based revenue streams for blogs comes from Google. Its AdSense program makes it relatively simple to display advertising links that complement your blog's topic. In other words, Google's AdSense crawls the content on your site and then matches it with ads that target related products or services. Not only is it easy to use (and requires no selling on your part), but the ads are also more effective and more likely to generate revenue because they're selling products that relate to your blog.

To sign up for AdSense, follow these steps:

1. **Go to www.google.com and click the Advertising Programs link.**

2. **Click the Sign Up button to start the registration process.**

You need to provide details, such as your name and mailing information and the name of your Web site, and accept Google's policies.

3. **When you finish the form, click the Submit Information button.**

A page appears that shows all the information you completed on the form. You're asked to verify that the information is correct.

After you confirm that the information is correct, you cannot go back and change the Payee name (the person to whom future checks are paid).

4. **If you don't already have a Google e-mail address or AdSense account, enter a valid e-mail address and choose a password for your account.**

Google sends you a confirmation message. It includes final instructions to submit your application, or your Web site, for review and approval by Google.

5. **Access your account and set up payment information.**

6. **Select the types of ads you want to run on your site, identify specific keywords for targeting ads, and choose where on your site you want the ads to appear.**

Figure 3-1 shows an example of how Google ads may look on your blog.

Google AdSense

Figure 3-1:
Google
AdSense
adds
revenue to
a blog.

Freelance blogging

One way to earn money as a blogger is to blog for someone else. This concept is the equivalent of being a freelance writer who is paid to post regular blog entries. In some cases, you may be responsible for a specific blog topic. It's similar to having your own blog, but someone is paying you to maintain it. Similarly, a larger corporation can hire you to post to one or more of the company's blogs. In this example, an investment firm may hire you to blog regularly about money-related topics; or a technology company may pay you to talk about a specific product. In either case, you might use your own name, or you might ghost-write the blog as an employee of the company. How much can you expect to earn? We have seen companies pay as little as a few dollars per post, pay by the word or the length of post, or pay a flat monthly fee of several thousand dollars. In some cases, blogging communities may also allow you to host a blog topic and pay you by sharing ad revenues. In other words, you earn a percentage of the company's ad revenue, which is influenced by how popular your topic is and how well you drive traffic to the blog.

If you prefer to work for yourself, you can earn money by generating ad revenue for your own blog. Basically, you sell ad space on your blog. This strategy is similar to the way you might use display ads as a moneymaker for any type of Web site. You can find out more about how to do it in Book IV.

Choosing a Blog Platform

As with other online business opportunities, one of the biggest advantages of starting a blog is its extremely low overhead. In fact, many of the available blogging software and tools are completely free.

If you already have a Web site, talk to your hosting company to see whether you can integrate a blog into your Web site. This way, the blogging audience that comes to your blog can easily cross over to other portions of your Web site, which just might lead to a sale.

If you're starting a blog from scratch and don't already have a Web site, a variety of free and modestly priced blogging tools are available.

Although plenty of free tools are available to start a blog, you might have to pay a modest monthly or annual fee if you plan to use your blog to make money. You might want to start with a free version while you set up your blog and become comfortable using it, and then upgrade to a paid account when you're ready to build revenue for the blog.

Check out these free sites to start a blog:

✦ **Blogger** (www.blogger.com): A free blogging site, Blogger provides templates and has no restrictions on the number of blogs you can maintain. See the next section to sign up for Blogger.

✦ **WordPress** (www.wordpress.com): One of our favorite blogging tools, WordPress has become one of the most widely used blog software programs. WordPress is free, but offers access to upgraded features for as little as $10 per year, in some cases. Although it occasionally runs ads on your blog, you can opt out of ads for a small annual fee. One WordPress feature lets you access your blog from your mobile phone or PDA.

You can start with the hosted version (wordpress.com) and then upgrade to the self-hosted version (wordpress.org). You can then grow into your blog and business and you don't have to switch your blog to a different host.

✦ **LiveJournal** (www.livejournal.com): This site is free to use also, but you have to display ads from Live Journal on your blog. You can also sign up for a paid account, which offers access to more features.

✦ **TypePad** (www.typepad.com): As the owner of a commercial service, you pay a monthly or annual fee to have your blog reside on the TypePad server. Rate plans start at $4.95 per month, which includes access to most of the service's advanced features and widgets. One particularly nice thing about TypePad is that it allows easy integration with third-party e-commerce tools or vendors, including eBay, Amazon, and PayPal. TypePad also has a tool that lets you easily add display advertising. With a seemingly endless supply of template designs, this tool is ideal for starting a revenue-generating blog.

✦ **Movable Type** (www.movabletype.com): One of the most powerful blogging options is Movable Type software, which you have to install on your computer. An open source version of the software is available for free, for complete flexibility. You can also find free and paid versions for individuals and companies. If you want complete control of your blog or want a blog that's part of your Web site, check out Movable Type.

When selecting a blogging platform, check to see whether the tool lets you export content if you decide to move to another blogging tool. You don't want to build months, or even years, of posts, only to lose them if you find a better platform for your blog.

If you have an existing Web site, you may want to integrate a blog into that site rather than maintain a separate URL for a blog. When deciding on a blogging platform, see whether it can be easily integrated into your site. Most blogs can be added by using various levels of programming to make it happen, but if you don't have that skill set and don't want to hire a programmer, make sure that the instructions for adding a blog to your existing Web site are clear.

Signing up with Blogger.com

One easy-to-use tool is at Blogger (www.blogger.com), shown in Figure 3-2. It provides a simple signup process for creating your blog, and even has a detailed tour of how the system works.

Figure 3-2:
Get your free blog at Blogger.

Follow these steps to create a blog:

1. **Click the Create Your Blog Now button on the Blogger home page (www.blogger.com).**

2. **Enter the following information:**
   - *Username and password:* Use this information to log in to your Blogger account.
   - *Display name:* Type the name you want to appear on your blog.
   - *E-mail address:* Enter the address that you want Blogger to use to communicate with you; the address doesn't have to appear on your blog.

3. **Select the Terms of Service acceptance box and then click Continue.**

4. **Enter the name and address of your blog.**

   Don't worry about making any permanent decisions about your blog name; you can always change it later. All Blogger addresses start with blogger.com, so your address *yourblogname*.blogger.com.

5. **Enter the verification word and then click the Continue button.**

   This step ensures that you're a real person and not a software robot. You see a graphical image of a distorted word that you have to type in the box provided.

6. **Select a template.**

   Choose a template based on a color scheme and layout. Click the Preview Template link to see a sample design.

7. **Click Continue.**

   Blogger creates your blog and displays the message Your blog has been created!.

That's it. Now just enter your content and you can have your own blog.

Getting started with WordPress

Another easy blog platform is WordPress, as shown in Figure 3-3. It provides access to many templates and features, all of which are easy to use. One of the many advantages of WordPress is the ability to integrate the free version of the blogging platform into an existing Web site. Of course, the blog can also be your entire Web site, if you prefer. To get started with WordPress, follow these steps to sign up for your own blog.

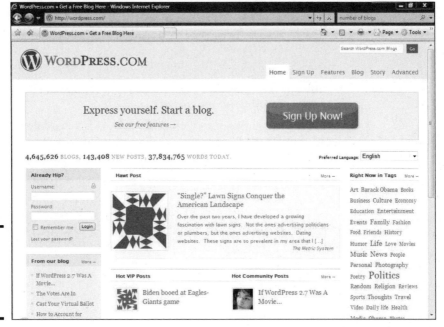

Figure 3-3:
WordPress
is an easy-
to-use blog
tool.

1. **Click the Sign Up Now button on the WordPress home page at www.wordpress.com.**

2. **Enter the following information:**

- *Username and password:* The username, or the identity you create to access your blog in the future, is also used as the name of your blog and in the URL. For example, if you choose DormDecorating101, your URL becomes www.dormdecorating101.wordpress.com.

  If you don't want to use WordPress to host your blog, during the registration process, choose to create only a username (to start) rather than specify that you want a blog identity. After your username is established, you can then go on to access the WordPress software and develop your blog using its tool.

- *E-mail address:* Use an e-mail address that you check often, because it's where WordPress sends you updates and other important information.

- *Legal agreement:* After reading the terms of agreement, you must acknowledge that you have done so and agree to the terms, in order to continue the registration process.

3. **Confirm the name of your blog and accept the WordPress privacy terms.**

4. **Click the Sign Up button.**

    An e-mail is sent to your account.

5. **While you wait for your e-mail to arrive, update your profile by providing a short bio about yourself.**

6. **When your e-mail arrives, click the URL that's provided to activate your WordPress blog.**

7. **Choose to sign in to your blog, and enter your username and password to access the blog dashboard (as shown in Figure 3-4).**

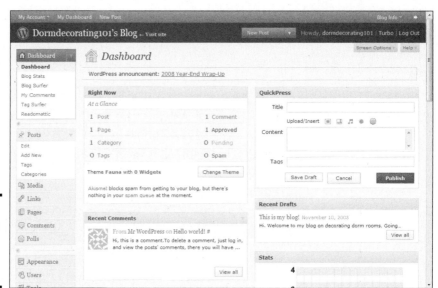

Figure 3-4:
Dashboards
let you
manage a
blog.

8. **Click the Design tab on the menu at the top of the page and select your *theme*, or look and style, for your blog.**

    You can preview as many styles as you like. When you find your favorite, click the Apply Style button. Your blog is automatically updated with that design, as shown in Figure 3-5.

    When selecting a theme, look for design options that are widget-ready so that you can add widgets or extra features to your blog. You also want to choose a theme that has two or three columns, to allow room for display advertising and other features. When previewing available themes, a description indicates these types of details for each theme or style.

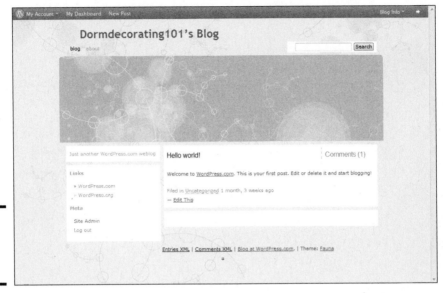

Figure 3-5:
Select a
look for
your blog.

9. **Click the Write tab at the top of the page, and write your first post.**

Figure 3-6 shows you what it looks like when you write a post.

10. **When your post is finished, click the Publish button to send it live for the world to see.**

Figure 3-6:
Write a
post in your
WordPress
blog.

That's it. You're on your way to having your very own WordPress blog.

To help search engines and other bloggers more easily find your blog post, add tags to it. *Tags* are keywords found within your post that someone may also search for when looking for information about a particular topic. For example, if you write a blog post about refrigerators you can keep in your dorm room, you may want to include tags for `refrigerators, mini-refrigerators`, and `dorm rooms`.

Chapter 4: Socializing (And Profiting) in Second Life

In This Chapter

✔ Understanding the difference: Worlds, communities, and games

✔ Getting a (Second) Life

✔ Deciding how to earn a living in 3D

Social networking and online communities are among the fastest-growing trends among online niche markets. You may have heard of MySpace or Facebook. If you aren't familiar with the concept of online socializing, think of it in terms of attending a big networking event where hundreds or thousands of professionals might go to meet, mingle, build relationships, and drum up business. Of course, lots of different types of online social networks exist, and they aren't always focused on business activities. Some communities are created solely for socializing, others are created for a specific group (such as business executives), and others are developed as a support network for a particular group (such as moms).

Because these types of online networks attract so many eyeballs (or visitors), you can potentially make money, directly or indirectly. In this chapter, we discuss the different types of online communities, along with some of the ways in which you can profit from them. In particular, we introduce you to Second Life, which has already proven itself to offer legitimate moneymaking opportunities to its members.

Introducing Other Worlds

Different types of online communities exist. Although they're often lumped into the social networking category, that grouping isn't entirely accurate. In the following sections, we introduce you to three types of online communities you should explore:

As in real life, each of these online communities offers very real threats and hazards. Because you're interacting with people from around the world, you expose yourself to virtual strangers. As a result, all these communities, games, and social networking sites have had their share of problems. To reduce your risks, always read a site's policies, privacy statements, terms-and-conditions documents, and general member guidelines. Stay safe!

Social networks

In its truest form, a social networking site provides a central hub where individuals or groups can exchange ideas, share information, and build relationships. Among the best known social networks are

✦ **Facebook:** www.facebook.com

✦ **LinkedIn:** www.linkedin.com

✦ **MySpace:** www.myspace.com

Typically, these sites host mini-pages, or subpages, within the overall community for individuals. For example, your personal page can be filled with information about yourself, along with photos and videos. You can add links to friends' or associates' pages, leave messages for one another, blog, and much more.

To give you an idea of how popular these communities are, consider that research shows that the most popular social networking sites have experienced year-over-year growth of 75 percent or more. In fact, in the first half of 2008, both MySpace and Facebook attracted more than 115 million visitors worldwide per month (per site). That's a lot of social interaction!

Massively Multiplayer Online Role-Playing Games (MMORPG)

Massively Multiplayer Online Role-Playing Games (MMORPG) or Massively Multiplayer Online (MMO) are based on online communities. Often, the games are created around a fictional place, or world, and individual members, or players, control fictional characters within the game. Because the games are played online, you interact (in real time) with other players from around the world. The objective of the game is typically to collect tools and booty (treasures) that aid your advancement in the game, until you finally reach the highest "level" or accomplish a specific goal.

Two of the best-known MMO games are *Azeroth* and *World of Warcraft,* and dozens of other games boast hundreds of thousands of members.

Although we're talking about games, you can profit from them. For example, when advanced players sell a game's virtual tools or treasure on eBay for real money, lower-level players can purchase those tools, which help them advance quickly in the game. Right or wrong, many gamers have wracked up some significant (and real) coin in exchange for some virtual ones.

Virtual communities

Some virtual communities have been hugely successful in blurring the lines of reality. These sites, unlike MMOGs, usually don't have an element of game playing. But, unlike social networks, they offer a higher level of interaction because the socializing occurs in a 3D environment.

One of the most advanced of these virtual communities is Second Life. This 3D world was started by a small company, but the community has been developed (literally) by its members. Rather than have a single Web page, as you would on MySpace, in Second Life you can create a virtual character that moves through its communities as you build houses, start businesses, make friends, and sell products. The rest of this chapter discusses in detail how you can earn a real living in this virtual community.

Navigating the Basics of Second Life

Second Life is an online world created in 3D. As a member, or resident, of Second Life (shown in the following section, in Figure 4-1), you're represented by a 3D character known as an *avatar*. Using this character, you can buy, sell, or rent land, build houses, open businesses, shop, and attend events and concerts. It's similar to real life, but it takes place in another world. This online world is also filled with smaller communities, cities, and neighborhoods. It has islands (public and private) and other real-world landscapes. Your avatar not only interacts with other avatars (by way of text-based conversations) but also has a voice, which adds another level of reality.

At the time this book was written, Second Life consisted of nearly 16 million residents who collectively own approximately 2 billion square meters of (virtual) land!

We understand that participating in Second Life requires that you absorb a lot of information, and the information presented here is just for starters. Fortunately, within Second Life, you can visit many places to find detailed and helpful information. We recommend that you check out the following spots:

✦ **Showcase:** Find an overview of exciting and popular places to visit in Second Life at `http://secondlife.com/showcase`.

✦ **Support:** Find answers to typical support issues, obtain detailed information about common functions and features within Second Life, or access support for tougher problems and concerns. Visit `http://secondlife.com/support`.

✦ **Policies:** Second Life offers detailed policies, terms of service, and safety guidelines at `http://secondlife.com/policy`.

Whether you're interested in socializing or earning some extra cash, there's a lot to learn about Second Life — certainly more than we can fit in this single chapter. Before jumping in with both feet, take some time to explore the various online help centers within Second Life and become accustomed to this massive 3D world.

Check out *Second Life For Dummies,* by Sarah Robbins and Mark Bell (Wiley Publishing) to find detailed instructions on becoming an active resident of this virtual community.

Signing up with Second Life

Of course, before you can start making money in Second Life, you need to sign up for an account. Second Life offers a free membership, or you can upgrade your account status to gain special benefits, such as being able to purchase certain types of land.

Second Life has two types of accounts:

+ **Basic:** This free account gives you access to all areas, stores, and events in Second Life. You can also develop or create items. However, if you open two or more basic accounts, you're charged a monthly fee (approximately $9.95) for every account you open after the first one.

+ **Premium:** This membership level, at $9.95 per month, lets you buy land and build on it. If you're interested in earning money as a developer, or in any other area that requires the purchase of land, you need a premium account.

Save money on your membership fee by paying in advance. For example, paying quarterly for your membership translates to a $7.95 monthly fee. Annual memberships are $6 per month, but you must pay for the full 12 months when you join.

When you're a premium account member, Second Life gives you a small stipend (or income) for maintaining a character. Even with this type of premium benefit, we encourage you to register first for a basic account and use its free access to explore Second Life and become comfortable it. Then you can make the monthly investment in a premium account.

To get started, follow these steps:

1. **Go to `www.secondlife.com` and download the Second Life file.**

   You see the download link on the home page. You also can download this file, also named Second Life Viewer, at the end of the registration process.

2. **Go back to the start page featured on the file you just downloaded, and click the Sign Up for Account button in the lower-right corner of the page.**

   See Figure 4-1. Or, simply click the Get Started button on the Second Life home page.

   You can also go to `https://join.secondlife.com`.

Figure 4-1:
Get started
with Second
Life for free!

3. **Provide the following information:**

   - A starting look for your avatar.

   - A first name.

   - A last name from a list of available names. (You must select a last name from a predetermined list of family names in Second Life.)

   You don't need to spend a lot of time choosing a body and style for your character. You can change the look of your avatar at any time.

4. **Provide your e-mail address and contact information, agree to the terms of service, and click the Create Account button.**

   Second Life sends you an e-mail message.

5. **Click the URL in the e-mail to confirm your new account and launch the Second Life viewer.**

   If you didn't already download the Second Life viewer, continue to Step 6. If the Second Life viewer is successfully launched, you know that the file was loaded and you can skip to Step 7.

6. **Download the Second Life viewer, if you haven't already.**

   You see the option to download the viewer after you finish setting up your account. If you have problems loading the software, check the system requirements for Second Life. Help is always available in Second Life. You can go to the demo area to learn more, as shown in Figure 4-2.

Figure 4-2: Visit the demo area in Second Life to find out more information.

7. **Log in using your avatar name and your password.**

8. **Read, review, and sign another terms-of-service agreement. Click the I Agree button to start Second Life.**

9. **Start exploring Second Life.**

   Congratulations! You're officially a member of Second Life.

TIP

You can receive additional help in moving your avatar and other basic functions by using the pop-up menu that appears on the login page, as shown in Figure 4-3.

Figure 4-3:
Let the
pop-up
menu guide
you.

Modifying your avatar

During your time in Second Life, you're represented by a personalized avatar — your 3D character. During the registration process, you pick a basic avatar character from the available selection of available avatars. By the time you take your first steps in Second Life, you have a basic avatar. It doesn't have to end there, though: You can completely change your avatar.

To modify the look of your avatar at any time, choose Edit⇨Appearance or right-click your avatar and choose Appearance.

Here are the avatar characteristics you can change:

✦ **Shape:** Select the gender of your avatar and choose a physical body size and appearance.

✦ **Skin:** Select the color of your avatar's skin, and even wrinkles or tattoos.

✦ **Eyes:** Select every aspect of your avatar's eyes, from the color of the iris to the shape and angle of slant.

✦ **Clothing:** You can select your clothes and accessories, from shirts and pants to shoes and scarves. You can also create a file, or closet (so to speak), of clothing items so that you can select and change outfits. Of course, this area grows as you buy — or make — more clothing within Second Life.

✦ **Attachments:** To change your avatar's appearance, you can also attach other items to it that you find or buy in Second Life by using the inventory feature.

In addition to looking good, your avatar provides your transportation in the game. Avatars can walk, fly, and even transport between destinations (which are assigned by specific URLs). The menu within Second Life provides you with all these options, so moving in-world (within the program) is just a matter of using the arrow keys on your keyboard or selecting specific function tabs on the menu. It's easy! If you have trouble, your avatar can visit Help Island (the in-world support center) as shown in Figure 4-4. Use the navigation tool that's available to your avatar to go to Help Island at any time.

Figure 4-4:
Your avatar can visit Help Island.

To visit Help Island, follow these steps:

1. **Click the Inventory button at the bottom of the screen.**

   The button appears while you're logged in to Second Life.

2. **Type** Help Island **in the search box.**

   It appears at the top of the inventory window.

3. **Double-click the box labeled landmark.**

   It appears as a result of your search.

4. **Click the Teleport button.**

   It appears in the new box that opens, and your avatar is automatically transported to Help Island.

Table 4-1 lists the most common tasks your avatar performs.

Table 4-1	Common Control Functions for Your Avatar	
Task	*Control Key or Combination*	*Menu Command or Function*
Walk	Left- or right-arrow key	N/A
Run	Ctrl-R	Main menu⇨World⇨Always Run
Fly	Page Up (PgUp) key	View⇨movement controls
Chat	Enter *<type message>* Enter	Chat *<type message>* Say
Teleport	N/A	Map⇨Select Location⇨Teleport

Getting your hands on Linden Dollars

To participate in the booming virtual economy, you need a little spending money. The Second Life economy uses Linden Dollars, or Linden$, as its source of exchange. Don't be fooled: This fake dollar has real value! In fact, you need to use real U.S. dollars (or another legitimate foreign currency, such as euros) to purchase Linden$. Fortunately, the program has a healthy exchange rate. For example, recently you could purchase more than 2,600 Linden$ for ten U.S. dollars.

You can buy and sell Linden$ to other residents on the Linden Exchange (LindeX). The rate of exchange, or value of Linden$, varies based on market value. For that reason, when purchasing Linden$, you should shop around to find the best exchange rate.

Economies of scale

As in any community open to commerce, Second Life has its own inworld economy. To give you an idea of how lucrative this virtual economy is, take a look at some recent data released about Second Life.

Residents spend a lot of money in this virtual world. In fact, the value of resident-to-resident transactions (or spending) is expected to top $408 million (in real U.S. dollars) for 2008.

Thousands of its residents maintain positive incomes, and many earn six-figure incomes. Second Life already boasts a real-world millionaire, who made her fortune in Linden Dollars by buying and selling property in Second Life.

Enterprising online entrepreneurs can expect to make anywhere from a few dollars per month to more than US$5,000 per month. (More than 200 people did so in October 2008.)

Obtaining Linden$ is simple. You can use one of three primary methods:

- **Market buy:** Specify the amount of U.S. dollars you want to spend to purchase Linden$. You can either enter the amount in U.S. dollars or enter the number of Linden$ you want to purchase. When you click the Buy Now button, Second Life searches for the best exchange rate and automatically calculates how much you need to spend (in U.S. dollars) or how much you can purchase in Linden$. You can obtain Linden$ by using a market buy at `https://secondlife.com/currency/buy.php`.

- **Limit buy:** You can limit the number of Linden$ you want to buy or set a minimum on the exchange rate you want to accept. The LindeX matches selling rates with your specifications to make the buy. To make a limit buy, visit `https://secondlife.com/currency/buy.php` on the Second Life Web site.

- **Inworld buy:** While you're within Second Life, you can access your Linden Dollar balance and choose to purchase more. Just look at the bottom of the screen for the account-balance symbol that's visible while your avatar is logged in to Second Life. When you find the symbol, click the L$ button next to your current LindeX account balance. A Buy Currency menu opens and you can enter the number of Linden$ you want to purchase. The value of the Linden$ purchased in Second Life is the same as if you conduct a market buy on the Linden Exchange.

To purchase Linden$, you have to add credits to your member account. You need U.S. dollars in your account to pay for any Linden$ you agree to purchase. Second Life uses PayPal (verified accounts only) and accepts other major credit cards. Paying the US$25 minimum amount is necessary for adding credits to your account so that you can purchase Linden$. To add money to your account, or buy account credit, select the Increase Credit link under the Linden Dollar section of the account menu. You must be logged in to access this section, and your billing information for your account must be updated (which means there is a valid credit card number of PayPal account that is on record and can be billed).

Earning a Living in Second Life

After you become comfortable keeping your avatar on the move, it's time to earn a living. (We think that this is the fun part!) As in real life, you have lots of ways to make money (or, in this case, Linden Dollars). You can use real money to purchase as many Linden$ as you will ever need and never have to work for a living! But where is the fun in that? Second Life gives you a chance to earn a modest living by doing basic jobs or to find real wealth (online and off) by building your own business.

You can often find job opportunities in the Classifieds section of Second Life, or sometimes you can find out about jobs from other residents by participating in Second Life forums. If you choose to open a business or have a particular skill set you're offering (such as being an event planner), you must market your abilities within the game in order to sell your wares or services, just like in real life.

A couple of restrictions apply to businesses in Second Life. Its gambling establishments are no longer legal, and individuals cannot open or manage banks. Other than that, Second Life career and business opportunities are almost endless.

Unskilled labor

The category of unskilled labor is self explanatory: These jobs require no true skill or talent. Your avatar might do something as mundane as sit in a "chair" at a location (to make it seem busy). As you might expect, unskilled labor positions typically don't pay well, and may even be hard to come by. Here's a look at some jobs considered to be unskilled:

+ Dancer at a club or party

+ Shop clerk

+ Ad model (a rare position that requires a large investment of time and money to make your avatar look good)

+ Security (including bouncers at clubs or general security guards)

Skilled labor

Whenever you're looking for an opportunity to earn a better living, explore jobs that require skilled labor. The pay is typically much better, and there's often a larger demand for avatars to fill these types of positions. The job guidelines in Second Life specify two types of skilled labor:

✦ **Classical:** Requires a specific skill that you have in real life that might directly relate to this 3D world (such as computer programming)

✦ **Business owner or freelancer:** Uses real-life skills that may not apply directly to Second Life but can be used to make money

Here are some examples of skilled-labor jobs within Second Life.

✦ **Builder:** Includes architects for 3D homes, furniture designers, and vehicle designers

✦ **Animator:** Requires a high level of real-world skill to animate objects for use within Second Life

✦ **DJ:** Spins tunes at parties and events that are hosted in Second Life

✦ **Event host:** Takes care of hosting duties at events that happen in Second Life

✦ **Fashion designer:** Creates clothing and accessories for avatars in Second Life

✦ **Scriptor:** Uses a programming language to script movements and interactions for avatars

✦ **Texture artist:** Graphical designers (often in real life also) who work with inworld builders to add designs and textures to houses, furniture, cars, and other items

Within these categories are lots of smaller skilled-labor positions. If you happen to possess some of these real-world skills, you can put them to good use to earn a real income in a 3D world.

Entrepreneurs

Starting a business within Second Life produces perhaps the greatest level of opportunity — and the highest level of fun. This category, considered by Second Life to be classified as part of the skilled-labor area, includes business owners, freelancers, and land barons (the equivalent of real-world real estate brokers).

As an entrepreneur, you can use skills such as designing avatar clothing or furniture and open a 3D business. As you might expect, you can buy or rent property, as shown in Figure 4-5, to use as a storefront.

Figure 4-5:
Buy or rent
storefronts.

Among the many opportunities as a business owner, Second Life entrepreneurs can take on these jobs:

✦ Architects

✦ Avatar stylists

✦ Builders

✦ Clothing boutique owners

✦ Dance club or night club owners

✦ Freelancers

✦ Furniture store owners

✦ Landscapers

There's really no limit to what you can do, if you tap into your own areas of expertise and match them with market opportunities.

 Second Life is divided into different geographic locations, such as cities and neighborhoods. Each one has its own, distinct personality and characteristics, and also different levels of traffic and popularity. Before buying, renting, or building, do your market research to determine whether your proposed location is an ideal fit for your intended business.

As a land baron or real estate agent, you can make a good deal of money in Second Life. The 3D world's first real-world millionaire was a successful land baron. Excelling in this role requires that you be

✦ Knowledgeable about the various areas of Second Life

✦ Aware of the qualities that make an area special or popular

✦ Skilled at negotiating

Most land barons make their money by purchasing land areas wholesale, at auction, and then reselling to residents. You may also want to buy land and develop it with landscapes, buildings, and other features to make it more marketable.

Selling your wares in the Marketplace

Second Life offers a range of tools to help you design and create objects within this 3D world. To discover more about the tools and how to use them, we suggest that you visit the Second Life Knowledge Base, by visiting `http://secondlife.com/support` and then clicking the Knowledge Base link, under the Support menu on the left side of the screen.

When you're ready to sell your objects, you have a couple of options:

✦ Open a store and place items in it for sale, as we mention when we discuss opportunities for entrepreneurs. However, you don't have to own a store in order to sell your stuff.

✦ Find buyers for your virtual wares and services in the Xstreet SL Marketplace, which is similar to a Classifieds section, as shown in Figure 4-6. To access the online Marketplace in Second Life, go to `http://xstreetsl.com` and click the Marketplace tab on the menu at the top of the page.

Before buying or selling virtual wares in the Marketplace, you must register as a new user for the Xstreet SL Marketplace. Simply click the Login to Purchase or List Items link at the top of the Marketplace page to open a login and registration page. Then click the new registration link and complete the form by using your avatar name and your real e-mail address.

Figure 4-6:
Sell virtual
goods in
the Market-
place.

Approximately 20 different categories in the Marketplace include everything from gadgets and home-and-garden utensils to animations and services. When selling your wares, simply select the category that's the closest match to your product or service.

There's no fee for placing a basic listing in the Marketplace, but Second Life charges a commission, ranging from 3 to 5 percent, after a transaction is completed. You can also enhance a basic listing by paying a nominal fee for bolding captions, adding a border, or featuring your listing on the Marketplace home page.

Are you ready to sell at the Marketplace? To do so, you must first become an official merchant by setting up a magic box, which provides a place to store your virtual wares and a means to transfer items to other avatars, after you purchase them. Getting a magic box is easy! After you register as a new user in the Marketplace, you can obtain a box (for free) or download one (again, for free) at

```
https://xstreetsl.com/modules.php?name=Marketplace&file=item&
    itemID=14129
```

You also need a secure place within Second Life to permanently keep your magic box. If you don't already own land, or have a safe space to keep your magic box, Second Life can provide a place for you. Referred to as magic box hosting, it's free for 60 days. You pay a nominal monthly fee (50 Linden$) after the first two months of service. To get started, you must contact Support at the Second Life Marketplace and request magic box hosting. Someone from Support contacts you, usually within 72 hours, and provides additional instructions to set up your magic box and begin selling.

When you're ready to start selling, Xstreet SL offers merchant tips to help you sell in the Marketplace. You can find these tips at

```
https://xstreetsl.com/modules.php?name=Conent&pa=showpage&pid24
```

Other income opportunities

Building a business takes time. It's rewarding, though! While you're building, you can supplement your income with the following elements:

+ **Stipend:** When you join Second Life as a premium account member, you're paid a weekly stipend. This small "salary" is automatically deposited into your account. (When we last checked, it was about 300 Linden$ for premium accounts.)

+ **E-commerce:** If you have either inworld products you're selling or real-life products, you can offer them for sale outside Second Life. To find out more information, check out Book VIII on storefronts.

+ **Linden Exchange:** Similar to the stock market in the real world, Second Life offers the opportunity to become a broker for the Linden Exchange by buying and selling Linden$ transactions. You must invest a large amount of money because, in order to be profitable, you must buy large sums of Linden dollars (to receive a better exchange rate) and then resell them in smaller amounts to individuals.

Book XI
E-Commerce Advanced

The 5th Wave   By Rich Tennant

Contents at a Glance

Chapter 1: Overhauling the Business

In This Chapter

✓ Identifying when your business needs a change

✓ Inspecting falling numbers

✓ Taking your first steps toward renewed success

*H*ow do you measure the success of your Web site? As with any business, you should identify key performance indicators (KPIs) that closely match your primary objectives. These indicators may be based on profitability, sales revenue, or even customer service goals. According to a poll of small-business owners, two of the biggest indicators of e-commerce success are positive feedback from customers and the amount of *traffic,* or visitors, the site receives. The survey also revealed that the number of sales leads and the amount of total online sales are also considered important KPIs. However you choose to define success — it is indeed important.

Equally important is understanding that success has eluded you and deciding that your online business needs an overhaul. In this chapter, we show you the signs indicating that it's time for change, and we explain how to start putting your business back on the right e-commerce track.

Paying Attention to the Signs

Wouldn't it be nice if you could start your business, launch your Web site, attract lots of customers, make plenty of money — and never have to change a thing? If you have owned an online business for a while, you know that that's not the way it works. The Internet industry is constantly morphing, and so are the rules for growing a thriving online business. That's why the secret of long-term online success is recognizing the signs of change — both good and bad — and being able to adapt.

If your Web site has any of the following characteristics, you might need to reevaluate your business:

✦ **A drop in search engine rankings:** A good, high-ranking position at Google or Yahoo! is often the lifeblood of an online business. If your site begins to slip or inconsistently maintains its position after several years on top, something is wrong. Although the problem might be an optimization issue, don't discount the possibility that your site is losing relevancy.

✦ **An outdated look:** You notice that the visual look of your site is now considered a design relic from the dot-com era. Your competitors have stripped away the black backgrounds from their sites and adopted clean, crisp images. It's time for you to do the same.

✦ **A lack of ongoing maintenance:** You can work in your business every day and still overlook the simplicity of good site-keeping. Broken links, expired coupon offers, and irrelevant or dated content are all indicators that you haven't been paying much attention to detail.

✦ **Fluctuating market conditions:** All types of issues in the world influence your business, either positively or negatively. The fluctuations that most closely relate to your industry or customer base obviously affect it the most. These factors include, but are not limited to, increased competition, changing product trends, regional or national economic indicators, supplier costs, customer demand, and pricing issues. A significant change in your market space can dictate a change in your online business operations.

✦ **Overlooked technology upgrades:** Overlooking technology upgrades (whether you're updating antivirus software or installing a new version of a content management system) is detrimental in the world of e-commerce. Allowing technology innovations to bypass you is a definite signal for change.

✦ **Nose-diving profitability:** This factor isn't one of the more subtle signs that it's time for Plan B. When revenue falls, overhead increases, and your bottom line pays the price for it all, you know that regrouping is a necessity.

✦ **A variation in visitors:** Is your site losing customers? Are your traffic counts falling or becoming less consistent? Or, are you noticing an influx of visitors from a different source or customer base? Fluctuations in site traffic and activity warrant a reaction.

This list of signs pointing to change isn't exhaustive. It's a starting point, though, for conditions to search for within your own business.

To make sure that you don't overlook anything, conduct a thorough *business change evaluation*. This system first establishes a baseline for your business, based on your KPIs (such as sales, visitors, and available products). Using the baseline, you then can evaluate other possible influences on your business.

Your goal is to take a "snapshot" of all your business indicators and determine which ones are driving change. Create a checklist by following these steps:

1. **Write a detailed description of your e-commerce business.**

   Include as part of your description the specific products or services you sell both online and offline. This description should provide a complete picture of your business.

2. **Describe your existing customers.**

   Be sure to include as much classifying information as possible about your customers. Details such as age and household income are bonuses. If you don't know those types of details, classify customers according to their product interests or purchases, or even by how they find your site. For instance, determine where customers come from: ads, other site referrals, or offline.

3. **Break out your revenue structure.**

   In this step, list the ways or places in which you earn money. Break down the list by month for the past 12 months. Then complete a year-over-year comparison for the past three years (if the data is available). Show the numbers in percentages of total sales. If you have a brick-and-mortar store, include revenue from your offline sales too.

   If you're keeping up with your monthly profit-and-loss statements as part of your accounting procedures, you can pull these numbers directly from those statement histories.

   For a more immediate snapshot of what the numbers mean, show the results in the form of bar graphs or pie charts. This type of visual aid is often helpful for comparison purposes.

4. **Generate a traffic analysis of your site.**

   Break out the numbers in the form of a monthly comparison for the past 12 months, and then by year for the past three years. Include the total number of *unique* (different) visitors and *page views* (the number of pages requested within a particular period).

5. **Make a list of all areas that affect your business or influence change, either positively or negatively.**

   You can group the items by category as they apply to your site, such as marketing, sales, product development, or content.

6. **Categorize each item as positive or negative based on how it influences your site. Then explain why you chose that indicator. Beside the explanation, note whether you responded or reacted to the change.**

As you finish this section, you can identify areas where change is occurring and determine whether you have adequately adjusted to them.

You might be tempted to believe that you already know this information or that this process is oversimplified. We can't emphasize enough the power of writing down this information in one place, for your review.

The purpose of making a meaningful evaluation is to help you identify holes in your current online business strategy. Then you use the information to target a market weakness or opportunity that you might have overlooked.

Keep this completed chart on hand as you continue through the overhaul process. Figure 1-1 shows an example of a checklist.

Business Change Checklist

Indicator	Type of Change: (Positive/Negative)	Why?	Responded? (Y/N)	If yes, how?
SITE				
Site design is outdated	_____	_____	_____	_____
Dated/old graphics	_____	_____	_____	_____
Broken links	_____	_____	_____	_____
Content not fresh	_____	_____	_____	_____
Expired coupons/offers	_____	_____	_____	_____
Defunct affiliate programs	_____	_____	_____	_____
New technologies released	_____	_____	_____	_____
INDUSTRY/MARKET CONDITIONS				
Increase in competition	_____	_____	_____	_____
Decrease in competition	_____	_____	_____	_____
Fluctuation in economy	_____	_____	_____	_____
Change in product/service	_____	_____	_____	_____
Change in consumer demand	_____	_____	_____	_____
Supply costs update	_____	_____	_____	_____
Pricing update	_____	_____	_____	_____
New vendors/partners	_____	_____	_____	_____
Customer (profiles) different	_____	_____	_____	_____
SEARCH ENGINE RANKINGS				
Dropped rank (out of Top 10)	_____	_____	_____	_____
Removed from rankings	_____	_____	_____	_____
Consistently moving down	_____	_____	_____	_____
Inconsistent rankings	_____	_____	_____	_____
Inconsistent rankings across various search engines	_____	_____	_____	_____
Keywords outdated	_____	_____	_____	_____
No active optimization activity	_____	_____	_____	_____
Variation in site visitors	_____	_____	_____	_____
Traffic/page views changing	_____	_____	_____	_____
MARKETING				
Offline advertising reduced	_____	_____	_____	_____
Less/more online advertising	_____	_____	_____	_____
Changed # of referring links	_____	_____	_____	_____
Updated promotions/offers	_____	_____	_____	_____
OPERATIONS				
Major fluctuation in profits	_____	_____	_____	_____
Outdated business plan	_____	_____	_____	_____
Revenue resources altered	_____	_____	_____	_____

Figure 1-1:
Your checklist for evaluating change.

Qualifying for a Makeover from Lagging Sales

One no-fail indicator that your online strategy needs help is steadily falling sales. The issue always boils down to numbers — the number of products sold, the number of site visitors, and the last number on your bottom line. They're all connected, and that connection has everything to do with sales.

The wonderful thing about the Internet is that you have immediate, and often real-time, access to online sales transactions. At any hour of the day, you can determine exactly how many dollars your Web site is generating. You then know whether your business is having a good day. What happens, though, when it's not a good day, or a good month?

If sales are down, start by asking yourself two basic questions:

✦ Do I need to pull in more visitors?

✦ Do I need to convert more visitors to buyers?

Sure, sometimes you answer Yes to both questions. Typically, though, your problem stems more from one reason than the other. Either the number of people coming to your site has decreased and your sales are affected, or the proportion of sales to the number of visitors is off because people are leaving your site before making purchases. After you decide which issue is most responsible for weighing down sales, you can begin addressing the problem.

Book XI
Chapter 1

Increasing the number of visitors to your site

If you need to increase the number of visitors to your Web site, concentrate on these areas to give sales a lift:

✦ **Search engine optimization (SEO):** Reexamine the search engine optimization techniques used for your site (see Book VI, Chapter 6). It's a necessary part of ongoing site maintenance. If your site isn't optimized correctly, however, its chance for a solid ranking in the search engines goes out the window. And, it's not only a matter of rankings. Customers searching for your specific site can be disappointed when your site doesn't pop up in their search results. Perhaps you haven't provided the best possible information to make a match during a typical search request.

✦ **Marketing strategies:** Letting routine marketing activities slip in priority in the daily chaos of managing an online business is easy. Diminishing numbers of visitors are a wake-up call to get back to basic marketing concepts. Create an online newsletter, or send out a fresh round of promotional e-mail to your existing customer database. You don't always have to dangle deep discounts in front of them. Sometimes they simply need a reminder that you're still out there!

Overhauling the Business

✦ **Paid advertising:** Spend a little dough and pump up the number of site visits. Google AdWords, pay-per-click advertising, and paid listings or banner ads on other Web sites are quick fixes to help generate traffic. If you're already spending money in these areas, look for new sites to place advertisements, or experiment with buying some different Google AdWords.

✦ **Linking opportunities:** When was the last time you asked someone to exchange links with your site? Spend an hour or two searching for sites that are compatible with or complementary to yours, and ask to swap links.

Link swapping isn't just an effective way to increase traffic to your site — a quality link exchange helps increase your site's value with search engines. That's a bonus!

✦ **Public relations:** Are you creating awareness of your site by engaging in effective public relations strategies? What was the date on the last press release you distributed? Phone a few reporters and suggest a story relating to your business. When your site's traffic flow is slowing, now is not the time to be shy.

Not all news has to be based on good news. Think creatively and turn your *problem* into a relevant story idea that's timely and grabs attention. For example, a national report on decreased consumer confidence and spending could tie in nicely to a recent dip in sales for your site. Be sure to put a positive twist on how you're combating the issue. For instance, send the message that your site's competitive pricing is sure to win over customers now that they're more careful in their spending.

✦ **Offline promotions:** Whether or not you have a retail location, use traditional offline marketing to create an immediate boost in your online traffic.

Go to a networking event and hand out your business cards. Arrange for a speaking engagement at a meeting of a community organization or at a regional trade show. Create flyers or professional brochures and distribute them in stores that are complementary to (and not a competitor of) your site.

Converting more visitors to buyers

Maybe the number of visitors to your site is on target. Instead, you need a boost in converting window shoppers into full-fledged buyers. In that case, focus on offering these features to start sales flowing in a positive direction again:

✦ **Functionality and usability:** You might be surprised to discover how cumbersome shopping on your Web site can be. Viewers leave sites if they tire of trying to figure out how to check out. At other times, the problem is all about site design. In Book XI, Chapter 2, we explain how to update your site design and functionality to make it friendlier to customers.

✦ **Graphics and copy:** One issue that derails a sale quickly is a lack of information about your products. Ensure that your Web copy provides customers with enough detail and that your pictures are of good quality, and not grainy. Thumbnail photos provide clear, crisp images.

✦ **Credibility:** Skepticism and uncertainty plague online shoppers, especially when buying from unfamiliar sites. Create trust and credibility by making customers aware of who you are and why your site is a safe place to shop.

Boost consumer confidence by displaying your contact information prominently throughout your site. Providing your phone number and physical address in addition to your e-mail address shows customers that you can be reached for questions. For an added vote of confidence, clearly post privacy policies, FAQs, and return and exchange policies. Be upfront with customers about what they can expect when they do business with you!

✦ **Customer reviews:** In addition to your own credibility, that same level of trust can be extended through the words of other customers. Recent data shows that the buying decisions of online customers are heavily influenced by the opinions of other buyers. When you allow buyers to rank the quality or value of a product (even if they didn't purchase it from you), write a review of the product on your site, or even link to a review offsite, other prospective customers will take notice.

✦ **Product selection:** Sometimes, declining sales are a result of an outdated or limited choice of products. In Book XI, Chapter 3, we discuss in greater detail the idea of expanding your product lines.

✦ **Payment options:** Customers want not only a wider product selection but also payment options. Maybe your site is set up to accept payments only by PayPal. After being in business for a while, you have to accept other methods of payment, such as credit cards, debit cards, and online check processing. See Book IV, Chapter 4 to find out the payment options you can offer.

In addition to accepting payments for orders online, allow customers to pay offline. Hesitant customers might prefer placing orders by phone or by printing order forms and mailing checks.

✦ **Affiliate programs:** You might be used to signing up for other sites' affiliate programs to add a little revenue. Why not create an affiliate program of your own? Products and services with more forgiving profit margins are ideal ways to boost revenue for both you and your online allies. Or, if you don't want to worry about tracking specific products, offer a flat percentage (or referral fee) on *any* sales that come through one of your affiliates.

✦ **Pricing:** Drop by competitors' sites to find out what they're charging. A drop in sales can indicate that you're not keeping up with current pricing strategies.

To check out the competition, use online price-comparison guides. Try PriceGrabber at `www.pricegrabber.com`, Froogle at `www.froogle.google.com`, and CNET Shopper at `http://shopper.cnet.com`.

✦ **Buying incentives:** Whatever you call them — coupons, discounts, free shipping, limited-time offers, or special sales — these kinds of incentives to purchase often nudge browsers to act.

✦ **Upselling:** People in the restaurant business use this strategy to extract another dollar or two from customers at the time of purchase (for example, asking about dessert after a meal). You can do the same for online sales. Before a customer completes the checkout procedure, offer to add another item. Display it and offer it at a one-time discounted price. Impulse buys based on the power of suggestion are powerful. And they don't hurt sales!

Knowing Where to Start

When you're deciding which changes to implement, you can base part of your decision on an outstanding resource: your customers! Implementing a customer survey is a quick way to get the facts about your site. Keep these suggestions in mind when you're conducting this type of online research:

✦ **Identify the basics.** Pick only the most critical information that you want to discover about your site. An all-inclusive survey becomes long and complicated, so choose only three to five areas. Including more areas in your survey warrants bringing in a professional to administer it.

✦ **Keep it simple.** Web surfers have limited time and limited attention spans. Your best results come from keeping a survey simple and short.

✦ **Offer an incentive.** Always thank customers for taking the time to share their opinions. Better yet, offer a small incentive (a discount on their next purchase, for example) in exchange for feedback.

✦ **Select your customers.** Determine who will take your survey: potential customers or loyal customers who know your business.

SurveyMonkey (`www.surveymonkey.com`) offers a full range of survey products and template options that start at just under $20 per month. It also offers a free basic survey option that's ideal for quick surveys or for small sites.

Chapter 2: Redesigning to Win New Customers

In This Chapter

✓ Evaluating your Web site design for improvements

✓ Creating a plan to update your site

✓ Informing customers of proposed changes to gain feedback

✓ Making your site more accessible and user friendly

✓ Adding ways for customers to interact and learn

*I*f you have ever seen a pair of bell-bottom jeans or another article of vintage clothing, you probably understand the old adage "What looks good today may not look good tomorrow." Styles and trends change with the times as different generations adapt to different looks, fashions, and designs. When people are living in the moment, they think that the current style will become a classic and always be accessible. Then they look back in a few years and wonder what they were thinking.

The same principle applies to Web sites and Internet businesses. Although nothing lasts forever, the changes happen more quickly than ever because the Internet is always evolving, so you have to be responsive. Before the Internet became popular, companies redesigned their marketing efforts only every year or two. With the fast pace of the Internet, companies have been reinventing themselves every three to six months, or, occasionally, even more often.

Web design is a continually changing and evolving concept. No guru sits on a mountaintop and decrees, "This year, all Web sites will use blue Courier Type 12 font with a polka dot background!" Instead, the collective nature of the Internet means that people look at each other's designs, and as time progresses and new styles are introduced, some are favored and mimicked by other sites while others stay on the fringe and refuse to adapt. Some higher-level trends seem to ripple through the Web community every year or so, and the bigger or commercial sites usually adapt to these trends after they become more mainstream.

In this chapter, we talk about those trends and how they should affect your own Web site. We show you how to examine your current design, compare it with the design of your competitors' sites and sites in the community at large, and then adapt your site. We also describe the benefits of that adoption. You discover how to interpret new capabilities and decide what to include in your own site to stay current with the times.

Updating an Outdated Look

Some Web designers can look at any Web site and accurately predict when that site was originally designed. Just as a beehive hairdo represents the 1950s, certain Web designs evoke a particular year or era in the life of the Internet. Certain Web site themes over the years have become the telltale signs of a site's age. These Web page elements still exist but have mostly disappeared from the Web:

✦ Pages with a black background and white text

✦ Frames that section off the information into distinct areas on the screen

✦ The Under Construction graphic, with a stick figure digging a ditch

✦ Graphical buttons that don't have any text labels associated with them

✦ Animated GIFs (pictures) and scrolling text along the bottom of the screen

✦ Splash screens (animated pictures) or Flash graphics that you have to watch before the home page is displayed

You have no way to accurately predict the next big trend in Web design. Therefore, after you launch your Web site, keep an eye out for newer design trends and decide on a regular time interval to update any outdated design issues for your site. Consider it spring cleaning for your site: Throw out the old designs and hang up some new ones.

 If you're ever wondering where certain design techniques are becoming outdated, check out five or ten of your favorite Web sites. The design technique disappearing from those sites is an early indication that your site is in need of a change.

Giving your designs a purpose

The overall question you should keep in mind when you evaluate your Web site is

> Does my Web site effectively communicate my business message?

Every design decision you make should revolve around this question. After all, unless you're building a hobby site or an artistic site, your site needs to serve your business needs. If your site isn't communicating clearly to your customers and window shoppers, you're unnecessarily limiting your potential and harming the bottom line.

You might find that Web designers and programmers are eager to implant the hottest new technology in your Web site, on the assumption that customers will want the technology because it's new. As time passes, these designers figure out that e-commerce design involves finding out what visitors want *and then* fulfilling those customer needs.

A perfect example is the Flash introduction, where a company's home page displayed an animated clip that resembles a movie trailer. Even if this introductory clip was slick and impressive, the Flash intro created a barrier between visitors to the Web site and the information they were seeking. After numerous visitors and customers told site owners that they didn't want to see this feature, it started to disappear.

Communicating your business message quickly, concisely, and cleanly on your company's home page is more important than ever. Web surfers spend only a few seconds evaluating a new site before they make up their minds and decide to stay or leave. Your home page has to catch a potential buyer's attention and give that person a reason to stay.

Changing for the sake of change

Suppose that you evaluate your Web site and that its design is still relevant and appealing to your customers. Because the Web is changing fast, however, you might want to redefine your site design simply to seem current in the eyes of your customers. After a while, even the cleanest site interfaces can look old and tired because customers repeatedly see the same screens, buttons, and graphics. Sometimes, a company updates its site just to look up-to-date because doing so gives the impression that the company is reinvesting in its site and trying to keep its customer base interested.

These updates don't have to be radical redesigns of your current site. You can simply pick one facet of your site design to alter across the board, such as these examples:

✦ **Font type:** Change an existing font type throughout the site.

✦ **Color scheme:** Alter the color scheme enough to show a difference without making the site unreadable.

✦ **Navigation bar:** Update the navigation bar with a different visual template. Use tabs across the top of the screen rather than buttons along the left side, for example.

✦ **Company logo:** Unveil a new company logo that gives your Web site a fresh new look.

✦ **Shortcuts:** Add shortcuts from your home page to popular sections of your site.

Telling customers about the change

As you're redesigning elements on your Web site, remember that your customers will be on the receiving end of these changes. Keep customers involved when you're changing your design so that they know what to expect and when to expect it.

Changing the floor plans

Have you ever noticed that your local grocery store likes to move everything around from time to time, with no apparent rhyme or reason? You enter the store, ready to go to Aisle 9 to pick up some rye bread and sourdough rolls, only to find salad dressing and olives. The store does have a rhyme and a reason for the move, and it has to do with learned patterns. Studies have shown that shoppers develop, over time, a specific path through a grocery store to pick up only the items they need and then head to the checkout stand.

When a store changes its entire layout, shoppers are forced to break their standard paths and evaluate every aisle again. In doing so, shoppers are exposed to new items that they previously might have walked past and might now consider adding to their carts.

The same concept applies to Web site shopping: Your customers might learn a specific path to the products they always order from you and then head to the checkout line. By changing the navigation of your site, you force customers to browse a little while longer while they learn their way again. Then you introduce them (you hope) to products they didn't know about but simply must try.

Beware: If you change your flow too drastically or too often, resulting in customers not finding anything or adjusting too often to a new process, you may notice a lot of abandoned virtual shopping carts and declining orders. Practice change in moderation.

When a change is being made in road construction, road signs are clearly marked. Sometimes, signs are put up in advance to warn motorists of upcoming road or lane closures, and cones or guidance markers move vehicles away from and around areas of construction until they're ready for use.

We're not saying that you have to display bright orange signs on your Web pages. You can put small messages or links on the home page, to let customers preview new designs. Add an announcement to your site to let people know when to expect a new design. Take a look at the LinkedIn home page shown in Figure 2-1. At the top of the page is a message for users to check out the improved People Search function, which allows LinkedIn users to find other professionals easier.

Figure 2-1:
LinkedIn announces a new, improved search function.

The more notice you give, the less shock your customers experience when the change occurs. Customers have certain expectations about doing business with you, even if they don't say it. The more feedback you solicit from them as you redesign, the less chance that you need to abort those changes if your customers disagree with your decisions.

Involve your customers in your redesign decisions because your Web site (and the action you take to maintain it) is, in the end, a reflection of your business. Provide a responsive, friendly, and professional site, and your customers will infer that your company is the same. Conversely, if you abruptly make changes that make the customer experience more difficult, you and your business will earn the image of being unresponsive, undependable, and uncaring.

Customers like doing business with people and companies that they like personally and can relate to on some level. On the Web, customers can move around quickly from business to business because of the level of choice that's available. They stay, however, with companies they identify with and with companies that exhibit qualities (such as style, professionalism, quality, or friendliness) that customers aspire to maintain in their own lives.

Deciding what to update

When you're ready to update the design of your Web site, here are some general guidelines you should follow:

✦ **Watch the competition.** Spend some time examining sites that handle graphical design well, to see how the sites are built. If the sites are using new techniques, take notes and find out whether the new design is showing up in more than one place. Check out your competitors' sites to see which designs they're using. Compare those designs to your site design, to see whether other designs look more appealing.

Your competitors can evaluate your site just as easily as you can evaluate theirs. Spend some time evaluating them routinely, to see how quickly they respond to a new situation. Your goal is to have other sites respond to your changes rather than you play catch-up with their redesigns.

✦ **Check for consistency.** Go to your business home page and make sure that all your category and subcategory pages have the same design and graphics. As Web sites change, not every page is updated. You might have added to your Web site some new sections that don't incorporate the newest site design. If you don't check for consistency, you might have four or five different versions of your design coexisting on your site and confusing your customers, which reflects poorly on your company image.

✦ **Test for compatibility.** If possible, test your current site on different computers with different Internet browsers. Although Microsoft Internet Explorer is still the dominant Web browser, a growing number of people use the Mozilla Firefox Web browser (www.firefox.com),

Google's Chrome browser (`www.google.com/chrome`) or the Apple Safari browser (`www.apple.com`). If you see errors while using an alternative browser, find out what's causing the error and update your site accordingly.

✦ **Familiarize yourself with new technologies.** Many times, the limitations your site faces are due to the technology available to you. As the Web becomes more sophisticated and Internet browsers can handle new tools, your options for implementing advanced design techniques on your site begin to expand. Talk to your Web site designer or do some research on the Internet to see which new technologies are reaching the mainstream. (The sites `webdesign.about.com` and `www.webstyle guide.com` have some helpful articles.)

✦ **Talk to your customers.** If you truly want to know the current state of your Web site, talk to the people who use it all the time: your customers. Pick a subset of recent customers and send them a survey asking what they like and dislike about your site. Alternatively, you can also include a comment area in the checkout process so that customers can write their comments as they're buying products.

Rolling back changes

Web site customers overwhelmingly reject design changes. NewComix (`http://newcomix.com`) specializes in selling comic books, action figures, DVDs, and other entertainment merchandise to customers who order these products long before they're released. These *presales* (advance orders) allow the company to offer deep discounts because everything that's ordered is sold. The site started in 1998, launched a redesign in 1999, and by 2002 figured that it was time for a change.

Because the NewComix product line is visually oriented, the new design incorporated lots of graphics and images to show off all the newest character designs for popular characters such as Spider-Man, Superman, Batman, and the X-Men. These graphics were incorporated on top of an extensive catalog list of approximately 4,000 items per month and some brand-new content sections, such as user reviews.

When the new site design was introduced, NewComix customers were outraged. Many of them, especially overseas customers, were still using dialup connections to the Internet. Although the new graphics looked impressive, they caused the site to load at unbearably slow speeds. The Web site was practically unusable, which threatened sales because it was the only way to place orders.

After the NewComix owners heard from their customers about these problems, they quickly reverted to the old style and limited their image selection to only a few essentials. Even as broadband penetration improves, NewComix now keeps a simple interface to allow its customers to shop quickly and easily.

The point is to identify what's working, what isn't working, and what's possible to implement in your site design. After you have an idea of what you want to do, you have to create some different scenarios for your redesign. They can range from simple page updates to a slightly redefined user interface to a complete tear-it-all-down-and-start-over total site makeover. Weigh these scenarios against your current available budget and your overall plans for the site. After all, if you're going to completely change your business model, for example, you might want to delay any site design changes until then.

If your resources are limited, focus immediately on any errors that are occurring and all wildly inconsistent Web pages. When you have more time and resources, you can worry then about updating your Web page styles.

Increasing Appeal

Have you ever walked past a storefront and wondered what was sold inside the building? A dimly lit store with an abstract name, a window covered in a painted design or series of posters, and a confusing display can be quite misleading. Imagine the difference you experience if you have a clear view inside the business and you see an inviting entrance that encourages you to walk in and informative signs that clearly display pricing, selection, and store hours. A powerful redesign doesn't just look new — it's also appealing to your customers.

Although some Web sites are chock-full of information and deals, if users can't easily find what they're looking for — or understand what they're seeing — they move on to one of your competitors. Web sites that appeal to customers make their information clear, concise, and easy to find.

Giving your customers search capability

The Internet is all about searching. Look at some major companies on the Web:

✦ **Google and Yahoo!:** Are primarily search engine companies

✦ **eBay:** Lets you search through millions of items

✦ **Amazon:** Has a highly searchable catalog of media

People don't just browse around any more; they actively search for what they want. The question you have to ask yourself is "Can my users search through my business?"

The search box is quickly becoming the item that retailers must display first and foremost. This way, regardless of how you organize your Web site, customers who know what they're looking for can come to your home page, enter a search term, and go directly to what they want.

In the past, Web sites put the search box in its own section of the site and customers had to click to it from the home page. Many designers have since moved the search box to the home page and eliminated a painful step to encourage people to try out the site.

If you don't have a tool in your toolkit (or your site designer doesn't have one) to make a search box for your site, don't worry: Google makes a free tool that allows you to offer search capabilities.

To add a Google search box to your site, just follow these steps:

1. **Go to Google Custom Search Engine at `www.google.com/coop/cse/`.**

2. **Click the Create a Custom Search Engine button.**

   The page shown in Figure 2-2 appears.

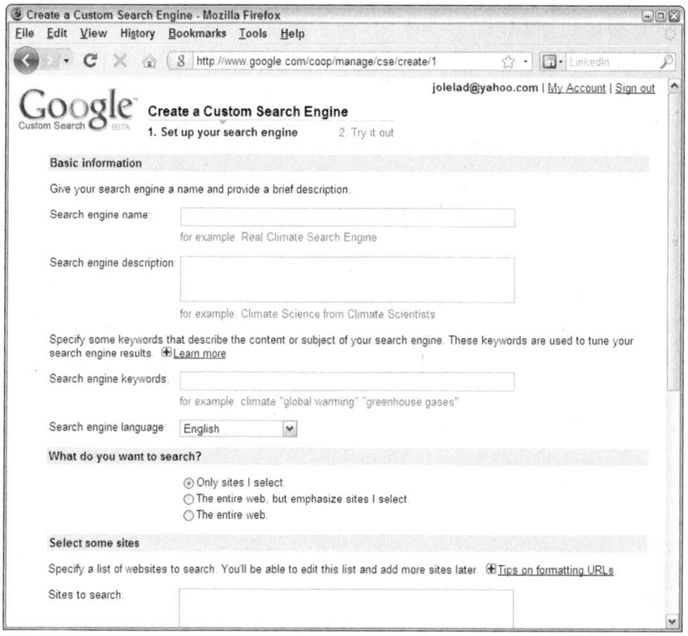

Figure 2-2: At Google, you can name and describe your custom search engine.

3. **Give your search engine a name.**

4. **(Optional) Enter a description for your search box in the Search Engine Description text box.**

5. **Scroll down and make sure that the Only Sites I Select option is selected under the What Do You Want to Search heading.**

6. **In the big Sites to Search box, enter the URL of your Web site. Scroll down to the Select an Edition section and click the Standard Edition radio button.**

7. **Click the Terms of Service link to read the terms of service for offering this function on your Web site. Click the Back button in your Web browser and select the I Have Read and Agree to the Terms of Service option.**

8. **Click the Next button.**

9. **Test your new search engine on the next page that appears, by typing sample queries and seeing the results.**

10. **Click the Finish button.**

    A page listing your search engines appears (see Figure 2-3).

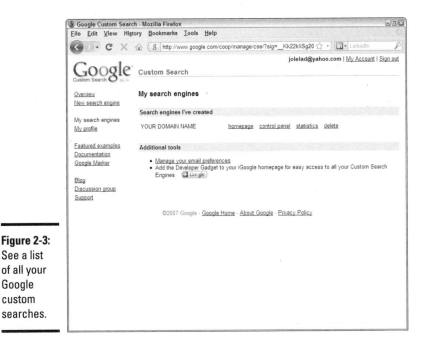

Book XI
Chapter 2

Redesigning to Win New Customers

Figure 2-3:
See a list
of all your
Google
custom
searches.

11. **Click the Control Panel link on the line for your domain search engine.**

    The search engine detail page appears.

12. **Click the Code link.**

13. **Copy the HTML code from the box that's provided.**

    In each case, Google displays the HTML code necessary to display the box as part of your Web page (see Figure 2-4). Simply highlight the code with your mouse and copy it to your computer.

Figure 2-4:
Google
offers free
HTML code
to put a
search box
on your site.

14. **Open the HTML file for your home page and insert this code.**

If your Web designer maintains a site for you, send her the code you just copied. Decide where you want to put the search box (the top or left side of the page works best), move the cursor to that point, and paste the text you copied in Step 13.

15. **Save the HTML file and upload the changes to your Web server.**

Talk to the Internet service provider (ISP) that hosts your Web site about how to change your Web pages. You can edit a page while it's sitting on either your server or your home computer. Then send the changes to your ISP by using an FTP (File Transfer Protocol) program.

Adding content

People nowadays want to read good content wherever they go on the Internet. E-commerce businesses that focus solely on selling products are finding that they have to add more information to entice people to check them out. The key is to provide clear, well-written, up-to-date, and accurate information that offers some value to the reader.

Look at the content on your site. Does it need to be updated? Could it be better written? Look at the information that people are reading on your site, and look at the questions you receive from your browsers and customers. If you're not particularly skilled in editing, have some friends, employees, or colleagues look it over and make suggestions.

You should also look at potential ways you can add to your content, such as these examples:

✦ **Add a section featuring reviews and recommendations for products you're selling.** When customers have to decide what they want to buy, they like reading about other people's impressions, experiences, and opinions. When you provide reviews, you give customers a reason to come to your Web site, and one less reason for them to look elsewhere when it's time to buy.

✦ **Relate customer success stories and experiences.** When you highlight actual customers that have used your business, you provide a sense of validation to new customers by showing them that other customers are happy with you. Your current customers will want to come back to see whether you featured them. Customers can also learn from each other through the common bond of your products, which gives your business more value and helps you build repeat business.

✦ **Provide articles you wrote for other sites.** One way you can market your business online is to write articles that have the effect of referring people to your business. Why shouldn't those articles appear on your own site first? See Book VI, Chapter 3 to find out how to write well-written articles.

If you don't have time to write articles, tap into free article databases, such as ArticlesBase.com or EzineArticles.com, to run other people's articles on your site.

✦ **Tell the personal story of your business.** Customers are always interested in knowing more about the people who work behind the scenes in a business. You create a sense of trust and purpose when you add some personal information, because then you're putting a "face" to your clean, well-laid-out online business. If people get involved after hearing your story and the reason your business was created, their purchase becomes a form of support because they're buying from a real person who has goals, desires, friends, and a family.

✦ **Write short biographies of you and your employees.** You can add a personal touch without revealing sensitive information. Take a funny or humorous approach to make it stand out. Have your employees contribute their own bios and interests so that they feel some ownership in the project. Share stories that can be used for a company newsletter, especially motivational and success stories. You want to maintain a professional business, but you can add the human element and inject some fun and personality, too.

Creating a user community

You might have had the experience of turning to someone at a big department store and asking a question, only to find out that you're talking with a fellow shopper. Or, maybe you overheard a conversation and you pointed another shopper to the correct aisle to find the item they were looking for that day. User interaction is a common aspect in the retail industry. Customers have a similar interest, which is why they're in the same store together. They can talk about their interests and how the products affect them, and even share advice about good and bad purchases.

In the online world, more and more businesses are adding their own virtual community meeting places to their Web sites. Mostly, these places are in the form of discussion boards and chat rooms, where people can gather and discuss issues that are relevant to the business or that just interest them.

You, as a business owner, can enjoy several benefits by connecting your customers:

✦ They might be quicker to respond to a new customer's question or concern and can give detailed answers.

✦ They have one more reason to spend time — and their hard-earned dollars — at your site rather than at someone else's.

✦ As browsers and customers hear about potential uses of your products from other customers, they might be more inclined to purchase those products themselves. Because they're already on your site reading about it, your site is their first choice for buying it.

✦ By keeping an archive of customer communications, you're building a knowledge database of questions, answers, and experiences that can help solve future customers' problems.

You can find several free discussion board software tools. Look on the major search engines for a tool (search for **discussion boards**) that works on the operating system for your Web server. Talk to your Web designers or IT staff members to see whether they have access to any ready-made discussion board or chat room software.

One way to encourage people to use a chat event right away is to create certain events that revolve around a specific day or time. You can unveil your new chat room software by hosting a "town hall" or open meeting with your business's CEO or visible board member, where customers and general browsers can ask questions and receive immediate responses. You or an employee can host a workshop where you explain a new feature or business that's being rolled out on your Web site.

Running a poll

You can also offer polls or surveys so that customers can vote on questions of the week (or month) that you devise. You can make polls fun by asking about customers' favorite stories in the news or have the polls tie in slightly to your business by asking people about their favorite products.

Use your polls and surveys as valuable customer research. Present a few new product lines and ask customers to vote on their favorites, where the winner of the poll results in your new product line. You add excitement and involvement for your users, and they feel like they have some ownership in your business.

If you don't have a software tool available for offering polls, try `www.free polls.com`. Although it hosts your survey, it lets you display the poll and collect votes on your Web site.

Update your poll regularly, to avoid making your site look stale and outdated. Nothing turns off customers like seeing a 4-month old poll on the home page. It makes the whole site look old and unprofessional.

Making Your Web Site Functional

Web sites used to be limited in the functions they could offer to customers. You could display *static* (fixed) Web pages, have forms e-mailed to you with text fields of information, and have customers sign a guest book. Now your site can be fully interactive, where each Web page is built on the spot based on a customer's specific needs. Your site can talk to other computer systems automatically, link back to your own database to read or write information, and process everything from data to audio and video.

Just because Web sites now can do lots of complex functions doesn't mean that you should put all these functions on your site. Pick a series of functions that serve your business needs and your customer wants. The point of Web site functionality is to support the user experience.

Updating your Web site in a timely manner

Many businesses find that, as their Web sites become more and more complex, they rely on a single person or company to make all their site updates. This situation not only is a bad strategic decision (because it locks you into this entity if you want to keep using your own site) but can also seriously jeopardize your chances of keeping your customers.

Customers are looking for sites that are continually updated with fresh, important, up-to-date content. Businesses that want to succeed have to be able to respond to changes in the market quickly, go after new business opportunities and satisfy a curious, fickle audience with varying demands. All these tasks require the ability to quickly update your site and its content, and relying on one person or business slows down the process. What if your Web designer gets sick or is away on vacation? What if you have to post a critical announcement over the weekend and your Web design company is closed? What if your designer is so busy changing someone else's site that your site isn't updated for weeks?

Your company should always be able to make some changes, especially content changes, to your own site. Why pay a Web programmer lots of money to change some text? Instead, pay that person to develop a function where you and your employees can send changes to the site that are updated automatically.

If you allow your employees to update your company site, be sure to install some sort of screening process, where a serious change has to be approved by either yourself or a manager. You don't want an angry employee's changes to be plastered all over your site.

Building smart navigation tools

We talk repeatedly in this book about the importance of a good navigation system on your Web site. Maybe you have a vertical row of links or buttons along the left side of your page or a series of tabs along the top. Take it one step further: Determine how sophisticated your navigation bar is and whether it helps customers move around the site.

When a customer uses the navigation bar to go to a particular section, can the customer see, from the navigation bar, where he is on your site? When you first arrive at JCPenny.com (see Figure 2-5), the tabs are the same color. When you click the Shoes tab, however, it's displayed in a different color from the rest, to make it stand out (see Figure 2-6). Your navigation system should be responsive to the choices a customer makes and should allow a customer to move anywhere on your site from any page on your site.

Figure 2-5:
The tabs on the navigation bar are the same color.

Figure 2-6:
The Shoes tab is a different color, which indicates where you are on the site.

One way that Web sites show a shopper's progression is to display information showing the context of a current Web page within the entire site structure. This process is known as following a *bread-crumb trail,* which is a string of different page labels within a site. A user can return to the page by clicking the specific "crumb." A trail might look something like this:

Home→Catalog→Men's Clothing→Jeans

Displaying a trail of crumbs shows customers how you group information on your site and how you establish a *hierarchy,* or order, of Web pages. In addition, your customers can move up and down the hierarchy much more easily.

Your site navigation system should remain intuitive while being able to directly open the pages that customers need. They shouldn't need lots of explanation or training in order to navigate around your site. A customer should be able to open your home page and instinctively know what to click or how to proceed.

Your site is reaching a global audience, not just your neighborhood or city. Therefore, you can't be overly dependent on the language you use, because foreign visitors won't know all the words. If you see that you're getting a lot of international traffic, consider adding symbols or pictures alongside your words so that people can navigate without a language barrier.

As the owner or operator of your Web business, you probably know your site by heart and can easily move around in it. What about new visitors, though? Gain a fresh perspective sometimes by having a stranger (or a friend who has never used your site) test your site. You can hire some companies that can handle this *usability study* for you. The key is to gather a new visitor's impressions about what makes sense and what doesn't so that you can update your site and navigation system accordingly.

Usability, in the area of computer applications, refers to the effectiveness and ease of use that people find when they interact with the computer. If an element has high usability, people can easily learn about it and remember how it works, and they find it visually satisfying, efficient to operate, and helpful to use when things go wrong.

Building your customer history

One reason that people still go to local shops and pay higher prices for products is the familiarity they feel when they're shopping in a store. The owners or employees know their shoppers' faces and call them by their names, so they can recommend new products because they know the shoppers' purchase histories and likes and dislikes, and can recommend products accordingly.

This high-service model works for many small businesses, and you can convert this familiarity to your site with some added functionality. Basically, you want to make a customer's previous purchases (perhaps within a time limit, such as one or two years) available to the customer after she logs in to your site. If the purchases are available to shoppers, they're available to you, the store owner, and you can provide analysis. From analysis come recommendations and suggestions, perhaps tied into an automatic marketing offer based on the customer's purchase pattern.

For example, if you know what your customer's previous orders are and you see that he's ordering something you predicted, you can offer similar goods at a package discount to encourage sales. When your customers can go back to your site and view their past purchases, they can answer questions on their own without involving you as much. They can also look up their order histories, and your shipping department can record the tracking numbers in your software or Web site tools. If your customers can answer their own questions or find answers without hearing back from you, you can focus on other customer service issues more quickly and efficiently.

Implementing this function means that your Web site software has to have a way for customers to create their own accounts, and a database to store customer information and order information so that it's ready to be displayed on your own Web site. The customer account should have some form of password protection, and should potentially store customer address and payment information.

You can integrate this software by looking for customer relationship management (CRM) software that works with your e-commerce software. Check out either the latest edition of *Microsoft CRM For Dummies,* by Joel Scott, or *Database Development For Dummies,* by Allen Taylor (both from Wiley Publishing) for ways to implement this integrated technology.

Chapter 3: Expanding Products to Increase Stagnant Sales

In This Chapter

✔ Determining when to modify your line of products

✔ Restructuring your inventory

✔ Testing the waters for the best replacement inventory

*I*f you own a mature online business, you must master two tasks to maintain success. First, you have to nourish (or *feed*) your site in a way that keeps it healthy, productive, and growing. Second, you have to perfect your timing, by creating a feeding schedule for your site and recognizing when it needs nourishment and care in order to expand.

The sale of products (or the lack thereof) is a good indicator of how well you're doing on both counts. If your site has been around for a while, you know that stagnant sales say a lot about your online business. And, what they say usually isn't good.

If that's your situation now, this chapter is for you! We explain how to fine-tune the feeding schedule, adjust your inventory, and change your product mix to rev up your sales — at the right time.

Figuring Out When to Expand Your Product Line

With inventory, you're never deciding *whether* to drop a product; rather, you're deciding *when* to do so. Think about the last time you went grocery shopping. Did you notice that most food items had Sell By (expiration) dates stamped on their packaging? If a product's Sell By date has passed, the product shouldn't be purchased. Instead, it's eventually replaced on the store's shelves by a fresher product.

Most products (food or otherwise) have expiration dates, or at least life spans, because at some point, for whatever the reason, products are no longer valid. In marketing terms, a product's life span is referred to as its *life cycle* (see Figure 3-1).

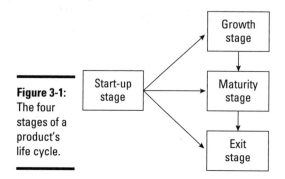

Figure 3-1:
The four stages of a product's life cycle.

Typically, a product's life cycle is defined in four stages:

✦ **Start-up:** As you introduce a product to the market, you're defining the product's place among your customers and building awareness for it.

✦ **Growth:** In a product's expansion phase, you're increasing sales, developing the customer base, and exploring alternative markets for growth.

✦ **Maturity:** When a product hits its prime, you have to protect its market share. You might notice more competitors at this stage. After a product hits its peak, try to eke out profitability for as long as possible.

✦ **Exit:** In a product's stage of decline, its sales are steadily decreasing and interest in it has waned. You have to decide what to do with the product — eliminate it, repackage it, or update it.

Not every product experiences all four stages of development during its life cycle. A product can move directly from the start-up phase to the exit phase, for example.

You can follow the upcoming steps to plot revenue and help determine when to phase out one product and introduce another. You have to decide when to drop a product, however. Unlike food items, not all products have Sell By dates stamped on them. *Your* job is to determine when a product is past its prime.

A logical starting point for determining when a product has outlived its shelf life is to conduct an inventory analysis. When you're ready to start this process, follow these four steps:

1. **Make an exhaustive list of all your current product offerings.**

If you stock products, you can use a recent inventory list for this step. The most important task is to make sure that your list notes every product you offer on your site.

Make a few notes about each product. You can include details such as

- Product locations on your Web site
- Product-specific promotional offers or coupons
- Other sites that link to specific products
- Ads or reviews that mention specific products
- Other details that you believe are pertinent to each product

2. **Plot the sales history for each product.**

   You should chart sales weekly, monthly, or annually. We suggest reviewing monthly sales over the past year. For older products, you can then chart annual sales for the preceding two or three years. (Likewise, for newer products, you might want to break the total monthly sales into weekly figures.)

   When you're tracking a product's sales history, show the data in the form of bar graphs, line graphs, or other types of charts so that you can more easily visualize the product's progression within your overall inventory.

3. **Determine the percentage of sales for your inventory, by following this method:**

   a. Divide the annual sale (in dollars) of the product by the total annual sales for all products.

   b. Multiply that number by 100.

   Your equation should look similar to this one:

   $7525.00 (product X) ÷ $72,346.00 (total sales) = .10401 × 100 = 10.41%

4. **List the products in descending order.**

   The list is then organized from highest to lowest percentage of sales.

5. **Match one of the four stages of the life cycle to each product.**

   For example, products with sales that have steadily declined and account for a lesser percentage of your sales are probably in the Exit stage.

By the time you complete your list, you should see a clear picture of your inventory that shows how much, or little, each product has aged.

Limited-appeal products

Just as some consumable products have a limited use, other products have limited appeal. Usually, you know that these products are temporary fads and that demand for them will wane after their novelty wears off.

Unless you're at least a certain age, you might not realize that someone once made millions of dollars by stuffing a rock into a box and selling it as a Pet Rock. Other examples of trendy products are T-shirts, bumper stickers, and coffee mugs printed with catchy phrases that reflect a current event. If you were selling a shirt with a witty slogan about the 2008 presidential campaign, for example, it naturally had a limited life cycle and should be replaced.

Limited-use products

Before you axe all the products classified in the Exit stage, as we describe in the preceding section, you have to consider a few other factors. As you might expect, sales history isn't the only indication of how well an item is selling or why its popularity is declining.

Some items — such as food, diapers, razors, or pet care products — have limited uses. After a product is consumed or applied, for example, it's all used up. Theoretically, this type of item should maintain a steady stream of sales because customers must replenish it.

If sales drop steadily, you have to consider the possibility that other factors are in play — for example, product quality, customer service, branding, or awareness (such as whether customers remember that they ordered a product from you).

Technology-based products

As technology advances, products become dated or defunct or their appeal lessens. If a new version of a technology-based product is released, the earlier edition can automatically be doomed for the clearance bin. Do your customers really want to purchase the Xmark1000 from you when they can have the advanced Xmark2000 for just a few dollars more?

Auxiliary products can force this change, too, as in the case of video games and game systems. The release of new games often coincides with the release of an updated game system. The catch is that the new games are compatible with only the new system. If the video games are popular enough, they drive sales of the updated game systems. In turn, the popularity of the earlier game system declines. Although the original system can take a while to become truly extinct, its value and marketability decrease.

You might decide that this type of product is in its final stage and should be replaced. Or, you might view it as a product entering its mature stage and decide to market the older system to a customer base that's more concerned with price and function than with the latest, greatest technologies.

Product marketing

Your marketing or promotional efforts can expand or shorten a product's life cycle. In fact, the theory of product life cycle is a marketing concept that's typically used in developing marketing campaigns for new products. By using the product life cycle concept, marketers can better respond to each stage of a product and increase (they hope) the overall product life cycle and its revenue.

Find out what you can do to prevent a decline in your product sales. Think about whether you actively promote products, and how often and in what ways you promote them. Before scratching a product from your inventory list, you might need to reevaluate your promotional strategy for that product.

Product positioning

Product positioning influences a product's sales and life cycle. Think about the physical location of an item (or, rather, its image) within your Web site. Do you rotate multiple products into premium spots on your site? Is a product positioned with similar items so that shoppers can easily find it? Or, is the product buried deep within your online store, waiting for someone to stumble over the right link? Even if a product is popular, if customers have trouble getting to it, your sales will suffer.

Price points

Setting the correct price for your product is essential. You can bet that a product that's priced incorrectly from the start will go straight to its exit stage in no time flat. As a product matures, though, its pricing also must be reevaluated.

Conversion rates

By using e-commerce (and effective analytic software), you're in the unique position of being able to track almost all your customers' movements, not just those initiating from ads. It's the equivalent of following someone around your store and watching as she picks up an item to look at it and then puts it down and moves on. You don't know exactly why she didn't buy it; you just know that she didn't. Online, when you direct a customer to a particular product page, you count it as a visit. If the visitor purchases the product, you count it toward a positive conversion rate.

You contribute to a higher or lower conversion rate for a particular product. Your site-design decisions, linking choices, and marketing efforts all factor into a conversion rate.

Suppose that your product has a history of low sales. You do a little research and find that even though the number of visitors to the product page is decent, the conversion rate is quite low. Do you cross the product off your list? Not yet.

Before you write off a product as a nonproducer, double-check all factors that affect the conversion rate. Here are two suggestions:

+ **Take a closer look at the product page.** Determine whether the page has enough information to allow a customer to make the decision to purchase — whether size and color options and the price can be quickly obtained, for example. Some critical details might be omitted from the description, or the product photo might be small or fuzzy or cannot be enhanced. These factors can cause a potential buyer to remain a window shopper.

+ **Track all pages that link to the product page.** Find out, for example, whether customers expecting to find one type of product are finding a much different product when they click through to checkout. You don't want them to believe that that they were misled or oversold.

Take a look at Book VI, Chapter 1 to find out how to calculate the conversion rate.

Replacement or Expansion: The Art of Culling Your Inventory

When you decide to drop products that aren't selling well, you can take two approaches to adjust or refresh your inventory, as described in the following two sections.

Replacing one product with another

One strategy for refreshing your inventory is to replace nonperforming products: Get rid of one product and immediately substitute it with a new one. Your replacement products should meet these criteria:

+ **They're complementary.** Look for items that are a good fit with the theme or focus of your site. You want products that continue to be relevant to your target customer.

Resist the temptation to add products that require marketing to an entirely different customer base. That's almost the same as starting a brand-new business, and it can permanently derail you!

+ **They're price competitive.** The price points of replacement products should be within the range of your current pricing structure. You don't want to introduce a high-end luxury item if your site is more of a midrange store. Similarly, you want to search for products that can be competitively priced on the general market. If you can find the product from other online sources for significantly less cost, you will have difficulty competing.

Always compare prices before adding products. PriceGrabber.com at www.pricegrabber.com lets you view current rates online for a particular item. Or, download a price-comparison toolbar, such as Dealio (www.dealio.com), which you add to your browser. It automatically displays comparison pricing when you search for products online, including eBay items.

✦ **They're appropriate for markup.** Choose products that are priced right for you, too. An item can be costly to you if the wholesale price is too high, or if you have to buy a superlarge quantity to make the price feasible. These items throw off your normal markup strategy and leave you paying for it — literally!

✦ **They're deliverable.** When you search for products now, the world is truly at your feet. You can send anything from almost anywhere and then resell it. If delivering a product to your customer becomes difficult or takes too long, however, it costs you business. Your site should feature products that can be quickly shipped to customers without hassles or delays.

Expanding your product line

You can refresh your inventory by simply expanding it. Here are a few expansion tactics:

✦ **Concentrate on expanding a particular product line.** Perhaps your inventory analysis reinforces what you already suspected: One particular brand of products sells particularly well. Suppose that you're a reseller of spa products (hair and skin care) and you realize that the three Bumble and Bumble brand products on your site consistently sell well. After dropping your five worst-selling products, you decide to expand the Bumble and Bumble line. You have no reason to search for other brand-name products; just build on the one you already have.

Expanding on a popular line of products is also a useful marketing opportunity. Make the most of it. Promote not only the new products but also the fact that you're expanding the entire brand.

✦ **Accessorize your bestselling products by adding items that complement one of your top products.** Perhaps you sell electronics and games and find out that the PS3 game system by PlayStation is one of your three best-selling products. When you beef up your inventory, concentrate on PS3 companion products. You can expand your line of PS3 video games, memory cards, controllers, and any other items that work with it.

Accessorizing is similar to the promotional strategy of upselling. When you see a product that your customers want, add supplemental products that might also interest them.

✦ **Scale back the number of your products.** This strategy narrows your focus so that you can concentrate on a select group of your top sellers, no matter which brand or category they're in. In other words, eliminate the dead weight. Then start promoting the heck out of your best-performing products to increase sales.

For example, you might have 75 items for sale, and your inventory analysis shows that only a dozen of those products make up a clear majority of your sales. Combined, the other 63 items account for fewer than 15 percent of your total annual sales. If you get rid of the majority of your products and stick to the 12 bestsellers — along with marketing — you should see sales increase without the hassle of working with a large number of products.

Finding New Products

No matter what strategy you use to replace products, you first have to find new ones that shine. Fortunately, you can look in certain places to narrow your choices:

✦ **Vendors:** If you already work with regular suppliers, ask them what's selling. Your vendors know which items they can't keep in stock because of demand and which ones are lagging. Suppliers usually have a good idea of which type of new products are coming in, and can suggest ones that fit well with your site.

✦ **Customers:** Your customers know best. Or, at least they know what they're willing to spend money on. Do a little online polling or send a short e-mail survey to find out which products your customers want to see on your site. They're usually quite willing to share an opinion or two.

✦ **Competitors:** Check the clearance section of a competitor's site to see which items didn't sell, and take a look at deeply discounted items to see which items might be on their way out. Don't forget to see which items are being heavily promoted.

✦ **Trade shows:** These events are filled with product distributors showcasing their latest product offerings. Often, you can even detect a theme for upcoming releases. For example, you can see which colors are hot or which product categories distributors are pushing. Not surprisingly, manufacturers are all usually pushing the same items, so you can easily spot the next trend.

✦ Trade shows and markets are also an opportunity to chat with suppliers and gather detailed information. The atmosphere is much more casual, and distributors and members of their sales force are eager to talk.

Of course, after you make your decision about which products to add, the real proof is in the pudding (as they say). With that proverb in mind, it certainly doesn't hurt to literally put your judgment to the test. You can run online tests for a product by using one of these methods:

✦ **Forced placement:** Try featuring only a single product on your home page. This strategy forces visitors to view the new product so that you can more easily monitor click rates and conversions when you're introducing a product. If you're uncomfortable promoting one item, you can also place the promotion in a premium spot on your home page.

✦ **Rotate promotions:** Alternatively, you can run internal promotions on your site and rotate new products with your popular staple items. Use banner ads, pop-up ads, product reviews, or testimonials, and then rotate the promotions throughout your site (not just on the home page).

✦ **E-mail customers:** Introduce new products in an e-mail campaign to your targeted customers. That way, you can quickly gauge customer reaction to your latest product selection.

✦ **Keywords:** You can also place external advertisements to drive visitors for product testing. The most effective method is paid keyword searches. Because these target visitors are already searching for your particular type of product, or something similar, this method is an effective way to test the waters for purchasing behaviors.

✦ **Sample offline:** Give a few samples to friends or family members, and ask whether they would buy the product or have bought one similar to it already. If so, find out where and for how much. You can even have an informal focus group check out your product online. You can watch as its members visit your site and search for the new product. Find out from them what they think of your product, whether the promotion you used was effective, and whether the product image on your site accurately portrays the product. Honest feedback offline can help put you on the right track online.

Even a well-researched and thoroughly tested product isn't a sure bet. However, implementing these strategies as part of your product expansion truly helps you beat the odds.

Chapter 4: Bringing Former Customers (Back) Home

In This Chapter

✓ Understanding why loyal customers don't return to your site

✓ Creating offers that elicit a renewed response to buy

✓ Pampering customers with top-notch service

✓ Thanking customers for their loyalty

"**I**f you love someone, set them free. If they come back, they're yours." Hah! That quote might have worked for novelist Richard Bach in the 1970s, but it won't work for your site. When you're fighting for customer loyalty (and retention), nothing could be further from the truth.

In fact, lost customers rarely magically reappear without any effort on your part. Although you might be tempted to ignore an occasional customer departure, it can be an expensive mistake for your online business.

Consider that gaining a new customer costs approximately five to six times as much as keeping an existing one. Even if you allot the majority of your marketing dollars and attention to trolling for new customers, you should also spend some of your marketing budget on keeping existing customers happy.

What happens when existing customers get fed up and decide to leave? Is it too late to show them that you care? Not at all! This chapter shows you how to woo back lost loves ('er, customers) and ensure that they remain yours for keeps.

Figuring Out Why a Customer Left

Before you can hope to win back former customers, you need to understand what hastened their departure in the first place. Although you might think that every situation is unique, customers leave for a variety of reasons:

✦ **Product dissatisfaction:** Among the top customer frustrations is the poor quality of a product (or service). Maybe it didn't perform as expected, didn't fit properly, or was poorly made — the reasons are endless.

✦ **Poor service:** Customer service is one of the most influential factors in maintaining customer loyalty. Allowing one bad service experience, or a string of experiences involving consistently mediocre service, is a sure way to drive away paying customers.

✦ **High prices:** Technology increasingly allows online customers to compare price points with little effort. Customers who install price-comparison toolbars or check out online shopping sites that root out the biggest bargains can easily be lured by good deals — especially if no other compelling issue, such as brand loyalty or customer reward programs, makes them stay. Another price issue driving customer decisions is that if they can no longer afford your product, they search for affordable alternatives.

✦ **Difficulty in buying:** One of the biggest customer-loyalty roadblocks you can create is making it difficult to do business with you. Making changes that help you manage your online business can also inadvertently make buying more difficult for customers. An update can leave your site navigation cumbersome or make your checkout procedure more time-consuming.

✦ **Apathy:** You lose customers because you fail to be memorable, or to make them care. On the surface, you fail to create a sense of identity or loyalty to your site. Dig deeper and you find a lack of offers or promotions that prompt customers to buy. Apathy can further evolve because you don't add new and exciting products or because your site and its content are stale and outdated. Customers are left with a feeling that you don't care about your business.

✦ **Site awareness:** Your site isn't demanding the attention of your customers. In most instances, this problem is tied directly to a lack of marketing, advertising, or direct communication with customers. In turn, they have forgotten that you're out there.

✦ **The lure of competitors:** Deep discounts, blowout advertising campaigns, and promises of extra perks and rewards make competitors look good. Often, those techniques are just good enough to steal away even the most loyal customers.

✦ **Evolving needs:** Sometimes, customers simply outgrow the need for your product or service. Or, they no longer have a compelling reason to use it. If you specialize in maternity wear, for example, you will lose that customer eventually (specifically, in three or four months).

✦ **Lost contact information:** Often, you can't reach online customers because their contact information has changed, especially e-mail addresses, which change frequently. Or, maybe your site's search engine rankings drop and customers can't find *you* any more. For one reason or another, your relationship with an online customer can quickly become an elusive one.

✦ **A rebel attitude:** Some customers strongly believe that variety is the spice of life. They're loyal to no one, and their buying behaviors are erratic at best.

Instituting countermeasures

The reasons that some customers leave are often beyond your control. However, you can counter those situations.

If your site is small, you probably have a tough time competing purely on price with larger sites. Your best strategy is to ensure that you offer some other equally powerful value point, such as one of these examples:

✦ **Exceptional customer service:** Finding online stores that exceed expectations remains a rarity. Filling that gap within your product space can offset even a price differential that you face with competitors.

✦ **Specialized expertise:** If you address a niche, you can easily retain customers because of your narrowly focused expertise. See Book X to find out how to become a niche business.

✦ **Payment plan alternative:** A customer who can buy a digital camera for $50 less on another site will be tempted to go for it. If you offer a creative payment plan, however, such as spreading out payments or allowing full payment later, you can compete.

Service providers, such as BillMeLater (`www.billmelater.com`) and eLayaway (`www.elayaway.com`), make it easy and affordable to add payment plan alternatives to your site.

Customers whose need for your product has changed will stop buying. That can't be helped. You can turn around even this situation, however.

One strategy is to expand your product line to address your customers' *next* set of needs. If you sell clothes to expectant mothers, for example, you can add items especially for children. You can also become a "go-to" source on a broader topic, by introducing content on your site or distributing an online newsletter that offers tips and advice on motherhood — not just maternity. Your goal is to stay connected to your customers. That way, if their needs change again, you want to be the one they go back to. They're also more likely to refer you to other people who also need your service.

To entice fickle customers, you can set up an aggressive marketing campaign and stellar (deep discount) incentives.

Asking for reasons that customers leave

You might be wondering how you can *know* the reason that a customer left. You simply have to ask. Whether you hire a professional or take on the task yourself, you can get the scoop from a former customer in several ways:

Signs that a customer might jump ship

Don't wait until a customer leaves to finally take notice. By paying attention earlier, you can anticipate trouble brewing in the distance. Here are some warning signs that a customer is getting ready to defect:

- ✔ **A drop in orders:** A sure sign of customer dissatisfaction is a sudden or steady decline in orders.

- ✔ **An increase in returns:** Cross-reference customer order histories with return rates. A high number of returns or exchanges can shed light on unhappy customers.

- ✔ **A spike in complaints:** An increase in your service calls or e-mails, or in the use of your online real-time support, can indicate a growing problem.

- ✔ **Unresolved complaints:** Similarly, customers who have outstanding or unresolved concerns are likely to start shopping with competitors soon.

- ✔ **An increase in online chatter:** Monitor blogs, community forums, and social networking sites to find discussions about your online business. If a customer has a valid complaint, others usually spread quickly alongside it.

- ✔ **A drop in response rates:** If your purchasing incentives sent by e-mail or direct mail have gone unnoticed, you have a problem. A steady decline in the response rate to these types of offers usually means that customers are shopping elsewhere or are frustrated because the offers don't address their needs.

- ✔ **Bounced e-mail:** This situation is a sure sign that you're losing a customer. Even if it's just a mistake (a customer changes an e-mail address or forgets to update an account), it means that you're losing touch with her and she doesn't even have the opportunity to respond to you.

- ✔ **Opting out of e-mails:** Customers who take their names off your mailing list are sending you a clear message. Respect their wishes, but use the opportunity to ask why they're no longer interested in receiving offers from you.

✦ **E-mail:** An e-mail message targeting former customers can be a quick way to deliver a brief survey. Keep your survey limited to three to five questions. Start by asking for the last time the customer remembers purchasing from you (because he might not realize that he's considered a lost customer). Then start determining the possible reasons for the absence.

Always include a toll-free phone number and a link to your online customer-service page. Encourage customers to call and share with you the details of their shopping experiences. An open invitation to complain can garner much more information than a brief survey.

✦ **Direct mail:** Mailing former customers a more extensive survey is a legitimate way to uncover the details of why they left. You can also use direct mail to invite customers to call and talk to a customer service manager about their experiences with you. In both cases, getting a response requires offering some type of incentive (such as a gift card) in exchange for their time.

+ **Call:** In Internet-based companies, picking up the phone to contact customers is often a forgotten option. Although some former customers might not appreciate the intrusion, you might find that feeling to be the exception and not the rule.

+ **Focus groups:** Gathering a small group of former customers and questioning them in depth can be revealing. Knowing how to extract the answers you're looking for takes experience, so we advise hiring a professional marketing firm for this endeavor.

Offering Customers Incentives to Return

Whatever the reason for your customer's departure, your objective is to win them back. Enticing a customer to return means showing them that you've changed. You listened to their critiques and paid attention to what went wrong, and, most importantly, you're ready to make amends.

Many marketing experts use the *lifetime value (LTV)* concept to quantify what a customer represents to your company. Basically, you determine how much money your customer spends with you over a certain period, and then, when you factor in expenses and other considerations, you know that customer's relative value.

Unfortunately, we could fill an entire book explaining lifetime value. Instead, you need to understand why it's worthwhile to invest in winning back your customers, regardless of the dollar value of that effort. Winning back customers is worthwhile for these reasons:

+ **Cost:** If it costs you $100 to get back a former customer, it would cost at least $500 to win a brand-new customer.

+ **Profit:** Existing customers often account for more than three-fourths of a site's revenues.

+ **Familiarity:** Educating former customers on the benefits of your site takes less time. They're already familiar with your business, your products, and your service.

+ **Upselling:** After you win back a customer, you're more likely to increase the average value of her purchase or to upsell to another level of product or service. On the other hand, it takes more time to achieve the same result with a new customer.

+ **Referrals:** You're not only gaining back the value of a customer but also "netting" the value of all other customers that this one refers to you.

+ **Brand strength:** Loyal customers increase the strength and value of your overall brand.

To find out how to calculate a customer's LTV, check out How to Compute Your Customer Lifetime Value from Database Marketing Institute at www. dbmarketing.com/articles/Art251a.htm.

A tailor-made offer

Inviting a lost customer to do business with you again involves far more than simply offering an apology for messing up the first time. More often than not, you just have to connect with your customer's needs again. What better way to do that than to present a personalized offer?

Being able to make this type of offer assumes that you have built, in a database, good historical data that details the customer's preferences. (If you do that, this task isn't difficult.)

Most e-commerce shopping cart software now includes database functions for storing and acting on customer data. Or, you can extend that capability by importing the data into a more powerful database (or customize your own). An online database service provider from Caspio (www.caspio.com) is a flexible solution that doesn't require programming.

To customize an offer, start by looking at your customer's buying history. Review the products or services she bought most recently and frequently. If the data is available, you also want to find out which offers she responded to most often. Some examples are a percentage-off coupon code, an offer to buy one and get one free, a limited-time offer, and the option to purchase on a deferred-payment plan. When you have this information, you're ready to create an offer tailored to the consumer's preferences!

For the best results, create the offer *after* you survey to determine the customer's reason for leaving. This way, the enticing offer you construct appeals to the person's present interests or needs and isn't based solely on old (or changed or outdated) buying habits.

A targeted offer

Customizing an offer for every departed customer might appear excessive. However, you can create ready-made targeted offers, such as these examples:

✦ **Deep discounts:** An offer of a deep discount on the next purchase gives your customer a chance to experience it again. You can include a coupon code to buy one item and get one for free or half the price.

✦ **A reasonable discount on the next purchase:** Consider a 10 to 15 percent discount on the next purchase, depending on the price point of the product or service you sell.

✦ **A gift card or free gift:** Offer cash up front with no strings attached — a gift card for ten dollars' worth of product, for example. Or, send a small product as a gift to show a customer that you're serious about winning him back.

✦ **Invitation to participate in an event:** For example, if you offer customers a special podcast or an informational Webinar related to your site or product, they might just buy something from you.

Enticing Customers to Stay

Figuring out why customers no longer purchase from your site is only half the battle of winning them back. To win the war, you have to take care of returning customers and ensure that they don't leave again. That's harder than it sounds because, after you have customers back "in your pocket," you can easily take them for granted.

If you offer a sensational deal to only *new* customers, your loyal customers may feel left out and underappreciated.

Well, your customers are spending money with you. They're faithful to (or have a renewed faith in) your brand. This section helps you figure what you can do for them.

Giving them blow-your-socks-off service!

You can bet that if you finally win back a customer, you had better not disappoint her. The first area you're graded in is customer service. No longer can you squeak by and maintain the status quo. After wooing a lost customer, you have to step up your game.

Status quo service involves doing what is already *expected* of you, such as in these examples:

✦ Provide a quality product (or service).

✦ Give the basic information that's necessary to make a purchasing decision.

✦ Be available for questions or support.

✦ Make the ordering process simple and efficient.

✦ Deliver the product as promised.

✦ Make post-purchase support readily available.

✦ Clearly post customer policies on your site.

✦ Honor your policies and terms of agreements.

That's the *minimum* service commitment required from you. It keeps your customers satisfied but doesn't make them feel special. Fantastic, *blow-your-socks-off service* keeps your customers loyal. This type of service might include these activities:

+ Anticipate customer needs by using shopping cart and database functionality.

+ Communicate regularly with customers to keep them informed about related topics and up-to-date on the latest trends.

+ Ask for customer feedback, and then respond to it.

+ Provide easy-to-find links on every page to access online customer service.

+ Offer real-time support (live customer service over the Internet) and other, traditional options (such as toll-free numbers and e-mail).

+ Allow customers to choose the type of information or promotions they want to receive based on their interests or needs.

+ Follow up purchases with personalized thank-you notes.

+ Offer worthwhile incentives to buy more.

+ Make it easy to change orders or agreements.

+ Be flexible, to address the changing needs of your customers.

For more helpful tips on how to excel in offering outstanding customer service, check out *Customer Service For Dummies,* by Karen Leland and Keith Bailey (Wiley Publishing). It contains lots of tips to help you exceed customer expectations.

Rewarding loyalty

Customers appreciate being rewarded for their loyalty. You can reward customers with these special benefits:

+ **Personalized coupons:** Offer discounts on products targeted to customers' specific interests (based on past buying habits).

Send personalized e-greeting cards to your customers on their birthdays, for example. Including a coupon code for a special offer targeted to your customer is an effective way to reward loyalty.

+ **Freebies:** Occasionally give a free upselling product or other perk to reward loyal buying behavior.

+ **Inside information:** Give special access to sales or new products *before* a new customer receives it.

+ **Buyer's club:** Customers get a special offer, a gift, or money back every time they reach a certain purchasing level at your site.

✦ **Frequent shopper:** No matter how much or how little the amount you choose, customers appreciate some type of monetary reward for buying regularly from you.

✦ **Special events:** Invite loyal customers to special online or offline marketing events (for example, cooking classes, forums with experts or celebrity guests, and training Webinars).

Don't let a lack of funds stop you from rewarding customers. Get creative. For example, if you can't afford to give a free gift to 100 customers, 2 customers might be a manageable number of recipients. When customers spend a certain amount of money each month, enter their names in a drawing and select 2 customers to receive gifts. Make a big deal out of the drawing by sending an e-mail to everyone on your customer list and posting the winners' names on your Web site.

You really have no limit on the type of reward program you can offer customers. The only downside is that the program can become difficult to manage, especially as your business grows. That's the time to enlist the help of a professional.

Luckily for you, many skilled and reputable companies specialize in the development and management of customer loyalty programs. Look into these companies:

✦ **Corporate Rewards:** www.corporaterewards.com

✦ **Elliance:** www.elliance.com/Services/loyalty-programs.asp

✦ **Online-Rewards:** www.online-rewards.com

✦ **Profit Point:** rewardforloyalty.com

WebLoyalty.com at www.webloyalty.com offers a free customer-loyalty incentive program that's perfect if you're a small or start-up e-tailer with fewer than 50,000 customer transactions per year. When you use this affiliate rewards program, your customers receive coupons for $10 off their next purchases on your site. They also receive a free 30-day trial to a WebLoyalty. com program that offers discounts to other companies. Customers can later join the discount program for a small fee, which is how WebLoyalty.com makes its money. Customers who join continue to receive a monthly coupon to your site, and you earn money from the affiliate referral fee. Everybody wins!

Saying "Thank You"

One of the most overlooked customer rewards is the simple expression of thanks. As the owner of an online business, you can show appreciation to your customers in many ways:

✦ **Post order landing pages.** After your customer completes an order, send an entirely new page (or *landing* page) created specifically to say "thank you" for the order. Surprisingly, many sites still overlook this opportunity.

✦ **Send automated thank-you notes.** Use an autoresponder program to automatically send a thank-you e-mail to your customer immediately following each purchase.

The option to send automated e-mail messages (and order confirmations) is already built into many shopping cart and e-commerce software programs.

✦ **Send thank-you notes in shipments.** Customers appreciate opening their shipments and finding thank-you notes right on top.

✦ **Post delivery e-mail.** After an order is scheduled to be delivered or a ship date is confirmed, send an e-mail expressing thanks. Sending the thank-you note after the order has arrived is also a good time to ask for feedback on your customer's shopping experience.

✦ **Send personalized cards.** Just because you run a Web site doesn't mean that you can't communicate the old-fashioned way. Send loyal customers a thank-you card by way of the U.S. Postal Service to seal your relationship.

✦ **Make phone calls.** Let your customer service department (even if it's just you!) make a few calls rather than just receive them. Phoning customers to say thanks provides the opportunity to make a direct connection with your customer.

Any time a thank-you is issued, offer an incentive. You make the customer feel special while inviting the person to do business with you again.

Chapter 5: Revisiting Marketing Strategies

In This Chapter

✔ Reviewing your company's past year and campaigns

✔ Involving everyone in your marketing strategy

✔ Analyzing your mistakes openly

✔ Learning from past failures and successes

✔ Growing your marketing efforts in the right areas

✔ Tailoring your efforts to fit your company

✔ Working with partners on new campaigns

*W*hoever said that nothing lasts forever was definitely thinking of the Internet. Strategies, trends, and perspectives changed at lightning speed over the years, as more and more people began to use the Web in different ways and companies responded to meet those ever-changing needs. In the beginning, the strategy was all about grabbing attention for a site. Then the strategy moved from attention to conversion, as the all-important order volume dictated the online focus of a business. Now, your strategy to get customers should contain a mixture of providing quality content, ample variety, and competitive prices.

As these strategies shift, you must update your marketing strategy. What worked well a few years ago might not work now, or maybe it does. Examine your successes and failures and compare them with your overall industry, and then with all Web businesses, to form an idea of what to do next. If you stay ahead of the curve, you stand a much better chance of adapting to changes in the Internet business and surviving while others march on, unchanged, and watch their businesses fade or close.

In this chapter, you find out how to make a tough assessment of your business by looking at past advertising efforts, gathering their strategic points and lessons, and matching your future plans with the marketing strategies you need in order to get there by creating new plans (or *campaigns*). We show you how to look at both successes and failures — because both elements contribute to a healthy future. Finally, we focus on the issues that will affect you the most and suggest ways you can tailor a custom solution.

Reviewing the Progress Report: An Annual Tradition

What is it about a year that makes us want to look back? Every December and January, we find ourselves watching Year in Review specials (which recap the past year in news, entertainment, and sports), reading movie critics' Top Ten lists for the year, and listening to the State of the Union address. Something about these summaries, or examinations of what has happened in the past, helps all of us understand what's coming next. Companies do it throughout the year by issuing their annual reports, as they prepare their financial statements and make comments about "looking forward" to the opportunities and challenges ahead. The Small Business Administration (SBA) even prepares reports and analyses on different industries that you can read, as shown in Figure 5-1.

Figure 5-1: The SBA does the homework for you in various industries.

No matter what size company you're running, seeing a report of the past year always helps you judge how you're doing. You can easily become so caught up in the day-to-day operations of your company — adding to your catalog, fulfilling orders, and answering questions — that you might not want to stop. We recommend looking at this type of assessment, though, so that you can see where you've been and ensure that you're headed in the right direction.

Don't feel that you have to wait for January 1 to assess your company. Pick a date that's close to the 12-month mark that doesn't interfere with any heavy workload for your company. For example, if you're an online retailer of gifts, don't do this examination in October or November while you're trying to capture your holiday market; try January or February instead, when you're recovering from the holiday rush.

Getting the right reports

As an online business owner, you probably generate mounds and mounds of paper. Over the course of 12 months, you probably generate enough invoices, plans, receipts, marketing materials, and other paper products to wipe out a tree or two. When you do your yearly review, you might not know where to start. Here are some common report types you should take a look at:

✦ **Financial:** Any business generates some form of cash flow and has a balance sheet. You definitely want to construct some form of profit-and-loss (P&L) statement to see whether you're making money, breaking even, or losing money slowly — or quickly. (Figure 5-2 shows as example of a P&L statement.) You want to see how much of your revenue is eaten up by costs and whether certain costs are growing faster than others.

Figure 5-2: Add up your revenue and expenses to figure out your profit or loss.

```
Creating a Profit and Loss Statement - Microsoft Internet Explorer
File   Edit   View   Favorites   Tools   Help
Back                        Search   Favorites   Media
Address  http://www.va-interactive.com/inbusiness/editorial/finance/intemp/income.html          Go

                          XYZ COMPANY
                       STATEMENT OF INCOME
                FOR THE YEAR ENDED DECEMBER 31, 2002

               SINGLE - STEP INCOME STATEMENT
            Revenue:
               Net sales..                              0
               Interest income.                         0
               Gain on sale of equipment.               0
               Total Revenue.
            Costs and expenses:
               Cost of goods sold.                      0
               Selling expenses.                        0
               General and administrative expenses.     0
               Interest expense.                        0
               Income taxes.                            0
               Total cost and expenses.
            Net income..
               Reset Values              Calculate Totals

Sample Multiple-Step Income Statement
```

✦ **Customer:** If you're not keeping track of your customers, in some form or another, you really need to start. You have to see whether your customer database is growing, and in what demographics. Maybe you're noticing numerous repeat buyers or one-time-only buyers, or maybe certain product categories are picking up, in terms of quantity, compared to others. You're looking for a healthy increase in the quantity and quality of customers.

✦ **Inventory:** Determine how quickly you're sending merchandise out the door. We don't just mean packing and shipping. If you weren't buying new inventory, how long would it take to sell out? Are you holding on to products forever, or turning over inventory often? You want to ensure that you have enough inventory to last until the next order comes in but not so much that you can't get rid of it without selling at a huge discount or making a generous donation to charity.

✦ **Marketing:** Take a look at the marketing campaigns you launched in the past year. What avenues did you use? Whom did you reach? How many people visited your site? Even more importantly, how many customers ordered something, and how many of them returned? In the end, how much did you spend? Although you can compute all sorts of ratios, in the end your report has to be able to answer this question: "Did I make more in profit or awareness than I spent on marketing?" That's the bottom line: If you're spending $50,000 to make $10,000 extra in profit, that's not the way to survive. Although you can spend some money to build brand awareness, most of the time you need to spend that money to generate orders and profit.

Sharing your progress report with your team

When you review all the numbers and campaigns for your business, you must make sure that your whole team understands the situation. If you're running a business by yourself, this issue isn't critical. If you have employees, independent contractors, family members, or friends helping out, spend a little time going over the basics with them.

We're not saying that you should rent a private bungalow for a three-day retreat to assess your business. (There's nothing wrong with that strategy, though. We hear that Maui is nice.) Allocate some time during the workday for a meeting. You can take everyone out for dinner or have a weekend barbecue at your house.

If you want your event to remain social, don't bring any PowerPoint slides with you.

The point is to cover your company's highlights, its highs and lows of the past year, the successes it has achieved, its challenges ahead, and the direction it's heading. Ask for feedback or for employees to share their success stories and memories of the past year.

Getting your team involved ensures that

✦ Everyone has a clear understanding of your company's progress.

✦ Employees feel some company ownership because you share the situation and ask for their help and opinions.

✦ You gain a sense of whether your employees agree with your assessment and rally behind the cause or just nod and stay silent.

✦ You gain a new perspective on the health of your company, from the stories and experiences of your employees.

You should never allow one of these gatherings to turn into a cold, finger-pointing assessment of where the company went wrong. It's not about blame — you're assessing the situation and agreeing on a plan to move forward. If the situation starts turning negative, move the conversation to another topic and focus on the company's successes and future plans.

Figuring Out What Worked and What Didn't

You can plan and research and make a great effort to present your company and your products to your customer base, and sometimes it just doesn't work. (Few people get everything right on their first try.) You can invest in a product line that turns cold the moment you try to sell it, and your marketing message can miss your audience completely or even attract the wrong crowd.

Mistakes happen — it's what you do about them that makes the difference. You can easily hide from missteps, blame them on something or someone else, and ignore their results. That strategy, however, is probably the worst thing you can do. You should instead look closely at every mistake and treat it as a learning exercise. Although the exercise might be expensive, if you analyze it correctly, it can make money for you down the road because you won't make that mistake again. Some people call this process "the most valuable education you can give yourself."

Analyzing a failure

Admitting that you made a mistake is difficult. Spending time and effort picking apart your campaign and determining the root cause of the failure might be even more difficult. Some business owners respond to mistakes by simply avoiding those areas altogether and shifting their focus elsewhere. They often believe that if they try to enter a new market and the campaign fails, it must not be right for them after all, so they should shift gears and try something else.

When you make a mistake in a campaign — and spend no time trying to learn why — the mistake contains no value and no lesson learned. It can even be detrimental to the future of your business. After all, you spent some time planning this effort, so the key is to find out the difference between your planned expectations and the reality of the situation.

When you discover this "disconnect" in your analysis, you can update your plans and benefit from the mistake. Here are some issues that might come up:

✦ **Bad implementation:** Your marketing message wasn't formatted correctly or contained the wrong price, link, or information. You can learn from this type of mistake immediately and then implement careful screening to avoid it the next time you put together marketing materials.

Always include yourself in any marketing lists that are sent out, whether it's a direct-mail, telemarketing, or e-mail effort. Simply insert your address, phone number, or e-mail address so that you can judge any messages resulting from your marketing campaign. If you're relying on outside parties to handle your marketing, make sure that they're doing their jobs.

✦ **Wrong price:** Your initial research into price points neglected to include a competitor who was underpricing you. Your special price wasn't competitive for your customers when they added such extra costs as shipping and handling.

✦ **Wrong audience:** You thought that certain customers would love a new product but it didn't appeal to them. You got your customers interested, but the "call to action" to purchase something wasn't compelling enough or easy to find.

When you evaluate a campaign, look for issues that would turn you off if you were a customer. Start at the beginning and pretend that you know nothing about your business, to see whether the campaign makes sense to you. Determine whether you're expecting customers to make the mental leap to a certain page when you're not drawing a clear connection.

Bring in other employees, or even friends and family members, to walk through the same campaign and express their opinions. Sometimes, a fresh perspective is all you need to determine a potential weakness.

The key is to find the weakness or drawback in your plan without placing blame. Treat this process as a learning exercise for you and your employees so that your next effort is that much stronger. Don't dwell on a mistake, except to make sure that you don't make exactly the same mistake again.

Examining a success

Although the reason that a marketing campaign was successful might seem obvious to you, it's worth exploring which elements brought you that success. That way, you can apply those valuable lessons to the other parts of your business and future campaigns. As the saying goes, "Learn from the best!" Why shouldn't you learn from yourself when you do something right?

Some people are afraid of overanalyzing something that made money, because they fear that they will disrupt some magical chain of events that made it possible. The reason that you look a little harder is so that you can make it happen again. Although every success is important to building your company, long-term success comes when you can repeat a valuable campaign and make it successful again.

Sometimes, the answer to the success of a campaign becomes apparent afterward, such as in these examples:

✦ You picked a new product line to promote, and the products became red-hot right around the time of your campaign. Your success came not necessarily from the technique, but, rather, from having the right product.

✦ Your promotion found the right price point to induce lots of purchases. You tested a lower price point and saw a wide adoption rate. Your success came from picking a level that guaranteed you some profit while increasing the volume of products sold.

**Book XI
Chapter 5**

At other times, determining the success of a promotion requires additional investigation. Businesses commonly send out follow-up surveys to select groups of customers who took advantage of particular marketing campaigns. This type of survey should contain questions that pinpoint the buyer's motivation, such as

**Revisiting
Marketing
Strategies**

✦ "What encouraged you to make this purchase today?"

✦ "What were the top two or three reasons for you to buy something?"

✦ "How important were price, selection, presentation, and message to your decision to buy?"

✦ "What aspects of the offer being made were the most appealing?"

You should also leave at least one or two non-purchase questions, where you're looking more for customers' general comments rather than offer-related answers. Your goal is to find out which parts of your marketing message worked and which parts can be improved. Sometimes, the answer lies in a combination of the right product, price, message, and audience.

Be sure to keep track of the positive feedback you receive after a marketing effort. Whenever you find a message or an offer that encourages people to leave positive comments after the fact, you discover something that connects directly with your customers, to the point that they spend extra time telling you how good it is.

Customer success stories and positive feedback also makes excellent content for future promotions. Whenever customers give you rave reviews, thank them for their comments and ask permission to reprint their quotes on your Web site. Most people love receiving the extra attention and seeing their names in print. If some of your customers ask that you use only their initials or first names, you should accede to their wishes.

Changing Plans for a Growing Company

Former IBM chairperson Louis V. Gerstner, Jr., had a favorite small-business comment: "I've never met a small company that didn't want to become a big company one of these days." Most business owners nod and smile when they hear this bit of wisdom. The goal of starting your own business is usually to have the business grow to the point that you can quit your other job, hire people to maintain the day-to-day aspects of your business, and have the time and resources available to pursue your own dreams, whether that's traveling, resting, or starting more businesses.

As your company grows, you realize that the same processes you used when your company was small don't truly apply to a bigger business. You can't run your expenses by using pen and paper any more, and you need to consult or hire a CPA or an accountant — or maybe even a chief financial officer (CFO) — to coordinate your finances and file all the appropriate paperwork. Your inventory systems have to become more formal because pen and paper and "mentally keeping track" of your products don't apply to a 20,000-square-foot warehouse full of products that are selling at hundreds of orders per day.

The same concept applies to your marketing strategies. At first, your goal is probably to raise brand awareness of your company, find some initial cash flow to sustain your business, and gain more customers and market share. After you start seeing sustained results — after you're achieving a certain level of sales and revenue without massive or unprofitable sales — you have to start shifting your marketing strategy to that of a mature company.

Focusing on specific elements of your strategy

One of the first shifts in marketing strategy should occur when you start concentrating on part of your business rather than on the entire company. An individual product line might be worthy of having its own marketing efforts, or each product line might bring in a piece of your overall sales.

Shift your marketing focus to center on a particular unit of your company. This way, your message can be concentrated on a single product line rather than on the expectation that customers will check out all the products your company offers. Pick a target sales level based on past sales of that one unit, and don't assume that you will attract any extra traffic to the rest of your site.

Even though you're more focused in your campaign, bringing in customers eventually lifts the other areas of your business, as some of these people become repeat customers in multiple areas. Don't rely on getting this business to make the campaign successful. Consider it the icing on the cake.

When you send out your marketing message, present your brand name and make the theme of your message related to one unit, not to the company in general (as shown in Figure 5-3). At this point, you're no longer selling your company, necessarily. You're selling the product and providing a reason to buy it immediately. For example, if your initial campaigns focused on this message:

> Hey, check out HotNewSpicySauce.com for all your spicy needs!

a newer campaign might be

> Get the best-tasting chipotle salsas around at HotNewSpicySauce.com!

Figure 5-3:
Go for the specific product sale rather than the Web site.

Testing your ideas

Opportunity comes when you least expect it, and that statement definitely rings true when you operate your online business. You never know when you're going to get the opportunity to load up on a new product line, to offer a deep discount on some reliable bestsellers, or even to branch out into something only partially related to your current business. After all, as you gain a loyal set of customers, you have the chance to capture more of their dollars by providing similar goods that appeal to them.

When you see the opportunity to either bolster your current product areas or branch out into new, uncharted waters, you should consider doing some test marketing campaigns to see how your customers will respond. In some cases, if the new product area is wildly different from your current brand, create a new subsidiary or partner company and build up that new brand name.

Pick a subset of your customer base, or partner with another company to market to its users. Then create a campaign that focuses on this new product line and reinforce the connection between the new product area and your existing brand. If you're creating a new brand, make some sort of connection that lets people know that your business is recommending, but not necessarily carrying, this brand.

For example, if your business is a leading supplier of video games for the Xbox 360 system, you might have the opportunity to carry a variety of toys related to both video games and superheroes. You could create a new company named The Master Toy Supplier and create a specialized campaign that says, "Hey, gamers! We've created a special deal just for you at Master Toy Supplier."

Test marketing has several benefits, beyond the obvious one of determining whether anyone wants to pay money for your product. You can form an idea of people's interest and response rates, and find out whether your product brings any good or bad reactions from your customer set. This new product area might be well served by specialized competitors, and the best price in the world won't diminish your customers' loyalty to their suppliers. You benefit much more by finding out this information from a test-marketing campaign than by investing heavily and hoping that the product will sell down the road.

Automating your campaign

Business owners measure the success or failure of their first marketing campaigns by keeping track of orders using pen and paper, or maybe a Microsoft Excel spreadsheet. As the size of your business and marketing campaigns grows, you have to make sure that everything is recorded properly so that you can go back and analyze the data in whatever way you need.

This process becomes especially important when you start having multiple campaigns running at one time. Suppose that you're using e-mail marketing to promote a few product lines that you're carrying and you're using direct mail or telemarketing to continue to build brand awareness and add to your customer database. With both these campaigns running, you want to know exactly which source is delivering that new customer to your Web site so that you can determine separately the profitability and success of each campaign.

Here's how it works:

1. You assign each campaign a specific code or keyword.

2. When you build your e-mails, you assign a link that includes the code or keyword to the product you're selling.

3. When a potential customer clicks the link, it goes directly to the product page on your Web site.

4. Your e-mail marketing program then counts how many times the keyword shows up in the links that people use to access your Web site and matches that number against the orders placed on your Web site. That way, the program can determine important measurements, such as the *click-through ratio*, or the percentage of people who saw the ad and clicked it to go to your Web site.

After you start automating your campaigns and relying on individual, targeted codes for each campaign, you can follow your prospects throughout your site to see how your campaigns are working together. You can follow, for example, how a customer who clicked in response to Campaign A might have checked out three or four more Web pages on your site and responded to Campaign B for something completely different. This data becomes quite useful as you plan future campaigns and figure out which campaigns you can combine.

When you rely on these automated tools, you gain other benefits, too:

✦ Your employees can spend more time on other parts of the business rather than generate e-mails and count results.

✦ The automated tools handle the mundane tasks of resending e-mails when an error occurs and collecting e-mail verification receipts from customers who open your e-mail.

✦ These tools usually provide built-in reporting capabilities so that you can view results without you or an employee having to summarize the data and calculate results.

You're in the business of selling something, not generating marketing campaigns. Although these issues are important to your business, your time is better spent building your business rather than on handling the details of a marketing campaign. Outsource any tasks you can in order to allow you to focus.

Finding Your Place in the Market

You can quite easily sit in a room with fellow business colleagues and say, "Hey, let's do what Google does!" or "Let's take the same approach to this problem as Microsoft does" or "What would Yahoo! do in a situation like this?" Some of the business concepts now practiced by the largest companies are sound, and others simply do not apply to the area you occupy. Although you can easily latch on to a good idea or latest trend, it's more important to understand why that trend is useful, to see whether you can apply it to your company.

Your business has to offer something unique to distinguish it from your competition. If you practice the same techniques, marketing messages, and focus as everybody else, your message begins to blend with everyone else's. After you become part of the crowd, determine what motivates your potential customers to shop with you rather than with someone else.

Focusing on your strengths

In the area of competition, you shouldn't follow other companies' techniques that highlight your weaknesses. If you provide a high level of service and charge a premium price for your products, following the techniques of Walmart is counterproductive to your business. Its effort to provide the masses with merchandise that matches its slogan, "Always Low Prices — Always," doesn't help you if you lower prices only occasionally to compete with Walmart during a sale.

Therefore, focus on competitors that share a common strength, in order to adapt your campaigns. If you're a "high-service" company, perhaps you should study a company such as Nordstrom or Coldwater Creek to see how their marketing messages are reinforcing the service levels they provide.

When you look at competitors, keep the size of your campaign in perspective. Because Nordstrom can appeal to millions of customers in its database, certain campaigns might be profitable because they need only a small percentage of customers to respond. In your case, however, you might need campaigns that appeal to a larger set in order to break even.

Emphasizing quality, not quantity

As you're planning new marketing campaigns and your budget becomes a real issue, you have to start asking yourself about the best way to move your message through all the "noise." You might tend toward trying to reach the largest audience possible and to hammering out the message, in the hope that enough people respond to each effort to be profitable.

As your business and customer set grow, your goal should be to achieve quality, not merely quantity. Suppose that you're paying for a banner ad that receives 50,000 impressions from 50,000 distinct users. If the ad contains an offer so focused that it creates an impulse for a response right away, it's the right technique.

If your ad requires multiple impressions to "wear away" at your potential customers' screening process and convince them gradually to try you out, you should invest in multiple impressions among a smaller, focused group of participants. Rather than pay for 50,000 random banner-ad impressions, you might pay for 5 targeted placements inside a newsletter that goes to 10,000 enthusiastic group members in your product area.

Some research shows that customers need to hear something a minimum of five times before they remember it. That's why radio and TV ads continually repeat phone numbers, for example, so that you call in and order.

Increasing your profit, not buzz

In their quest to gain attention, companies routinely shift their marketing strategies to stand out by creating advertising campaigns designed to be slick, funny, or appealing. Some large companies can afford this approach to preserve their brand awareness or announce new initiatives. Most companies, however, need a measurable result from their marketing — typically, an increase in orders, customers, or profit.

When you plan a new marketing campaign, always try to include something to differentiate yourself. Make sure that you're also persuading customers to take some sort of action. Ad campaigns to generate buzz, or a coolness factor, tend to cool off over time and provide no lasting benefit — or increased revenue, which is necessary for the next effort.

Not every campaign you create has to be solely about orders. Maybe you're launching a new weekly newsletter for your business, and the purpose of your marketing campaign is to increase the number of subscribers. Although you don't enjoy an immediate bump in orders, a newsletter can bring loyalty and repeat customers and pay off over time.

Borrowing Strategies from Others

Your company is typically not the only player in your market that's having an effect. Therefore, to see where you're going in your industry, you must learn from the fellow companies in your industry. After all, you can't compete if you don't know what the other players are doing. Your customers will compare you to the competition, so know where you stand and update your plans accordingly.

Stealing a page from your competitor's playbook

Evaluate your competitors and understand how their marketing strategies are reaching consumers and affecting their buying decisions. Start by identifying the largest companies in your area that directly compete with you for customers, and then move on to companies that indirectly compete with you.

Always be informed of your competitors' new promotions by signing up for their newsletters and promotions. Use a free e-mail account from Yahoo! or Hotmail so that your competitor doesn't see your company's Web site on its e-mail list.

As you scope out your market, start developing a sense of the overall feel that your competitors present as their marketing message, and look at the ways they use to communicate that message. Then ask yourself these questions to compare their strategies with yours in these areas:

+ **Appeal of the campaign:** What's eye-catching, unique, or appealing about their messages? Are they more current or relevant than you?

+ **Product selection:** Do your competitors carry a bigger or wider selection than you, or do they focus on one niche?

+ **Price and promotion:** Where do your competitors' prices fall in comparison with yours? Do they rely on pricing promotions to lure the initial sale?

+ **Customer policies:** What kind of return, payment, and shipping policies do they have? Are they more flexible or generous than yours?

+ **Additional services:** What bonuses do other companies offer their customers? Do they provide free delivery, gift wrapping, bonus items, or customization, for example? Do they offer something that you don't, or can't, provide?

+ **Tactics:** Are other companies sticking to the same marketing mediums as you are, whether it's print (direct mail or coupons), TV or radio, outdoor billboards, or Internet marketing? Have they found some new, clever way to distribute their marketing?

When you evaluate your competitors, you begin to learn more about your own company and where you can play up your strengths and take advantage of any perceived weaknesses you find in your competitors. Making this type of evaluation regularly is a healthy strategy because your competitors are also evaluating you and changing their strategies. Make an honest evaluation so that you know where you stand — and not where you *think* you stand.

Updating your strategy for survival

There's a difference between adding a marketing message to stay competitive and updating your campaign to compete more effectively. If your customers see a new technology or offering as essential to doing business, you need to add the same element in order to effectively compete, not just stand out.

When real-time credit card processing on Web sites was unveiled, it was a cool bonus for customers who could pay instantly after ordering a product rather than fill out a form online and wait for the e-commerce owner to process the credit card at a later date. Now, if an online retailer doesn't process the customer's credit card instantly, its customers see the business as "behind the times" and inefficient and leave for another online retailer that has the real-time processing. Therefore, borrowing this technique becomes essential for survival.

This concept also applies to marketing strategies. If your customer base is mostly concerned with features, hammering a message about price makes you seem out of touch. Conversely, if you're selling a product that people view as a commodity, you have to either make some alteration and focus on the difference or focus on the lower price you can provide.

Here are some ways you can differentiate yourself through marketing:

✦ **Combine products and services.** Maybe you can extend a product you're offering by adding a service that no one else does. Perhaps you can customize a clothing item you're selling to match each customer's wishes. This way, you make the product and your business more valuable to the customer.

✦ **Package different items.** Rather than be a retailer of goods, be a solution provider. Combine different products that fill a similar need into an "all-in-one" solution for your customers. They will pay for the convenience of putting everything in one basket and reward your business for supplying their needs.

✦ **Extend an offer.** If you can extend a promise to your customers, use it as your message when you market yourself. Blockbuster converted its strategy of renting movies into a guarantee that the newest releases are always available. Domino's became known as the pizza place where your order is delivered in 30 minutes or less or your pizza is free.

✦ **Conquer a niche.** Maybe an area of the market isn't being properly served. Even if your business goal is to serve more than one niche, conquering an area gives you a hook for doing business. A customer might say, "Oh, yeah, that's the place that handles the small-business market well. Hmm, maybe I should think of it for my business." (We discuss niche markets in more depth in Book X, Chapter 1.)

Book XI
Chapter 5

Revisiting Marketing Strategies

✦ **Provide a personal touch.** Sometimes, the little things make a big difference. If you do something unique that benefits your customers, they remember you for it. For example, an antiques seller includes a little homemade gift with every order she sells online. Some of her customers become more excited now when they order because they can't wait to see their cool gift.

Partnering with other companies

As your business grows, you should always consider an opportunity to partner with other companies in your industry. We're not saying, however, to go out and ask your direct competitor to engage in a joint advertising campaign. Consider creating partnerships with companies that reach the same audience as you, to leverage each other's positions and gain (you hope) more customers and orders in the process.

Here's how this strategy works. The target audience of Mountain Dew is quite similar to the video game crowd. Therefore, Mountain Dew partnered with the Microsoft Xbox 360 gaming system to put on contests and promotions on both their Web sites, as well as exclusive content that both sites get to promote to their users. Both companies share the customer information, and use their products to promote the other company.

Start by evaluating your own network. Perhaps you work frequently with a certain vendor and see that you're both reaching the same market, but in different ways. Be sure to do your research before proposing any deals: You don't want to do business with any company that might negatively affect your image or pick a partner that your employees or customers don't support.

Be sure to consult your customers, business colleagues, or employees. If there's a natural fit, where you both bring something valuable to the other party, you can create quite a successful partnership.

Just make sure that both companies benefit and share the costs. The last thing you want is to do all the work and have your partner walk away with all the new business.

When you network with other companies, pick up whatever strengths or innovations they come up with, to see how you can adapt your own organization. Sometimes, the result of making an effective alliance is gaining a valuable education for yourself.

Chapter 6: Hiring Experts to Get Business Rolling Again

In This Chapter

✔ Knowing when to seek a consultant to guide you

✔ Finding an advisor who knows your business

✔ Choosing the right professional to work with you

✔ Creating binding contracts to define the rules of engagement

✔ Approaching change with realistic requests and firm goals

*B*elieve it or not, many of the Internet's most successful Web sites have already celebrated ten years of being in business. That milestone is significant for any company, and especially for those early e-commerce pioneers. You might recognize a small handful of them, such as Amazon and eBay.

Obviously, though, not everyone on the Net found that same success. Your site might be one of the smaller ones that have been around just as long as Amazon but are still struggling to keep their heads above water. If that's the case, you might need a new strategy and a little kick in the pants! Or, perhaps your site is among the well-established and formerly lucrative sites whose sales have recently stalled. You're a good candidate for bringing in expert advice and revamping your game plan. In this chapter, we explain how and when to bring in professional advisors, set realistic goals, and make a new plan.

Bringing In the Pros

Most online business owners are used to taking risks and calling the shots — alone. That's why the hardest part of being a netrepreneur is realizing that you don't have all the answers. The second most difficult part is to understand when to turn for help, when you finally admit that you need it!

If you're unsure whether your site warrants outside help, trust us: Ailing businesses leave plenty of clues to that answer. If any of the following problems sounds familiar to you, you might need some outside help:

✦ **Declining sales:** A steady drop in online orders is a sure sign that something is wrong. It doesn't matter how many products or services you offer — if overall sales decrease month after month, you're losing precious dollars.

A sharp and immediate decline in online orders is treated differently from sales that drop steadily over a long period. If you suddenly lose a disproportionate number of sales, first check out these issues before you start panicking:

- Your site lost its search engine rankings.

- Your site or server is temporarily down.

- You had a security breach.

✦ **Stagnant sales:** If your online orders aren't growing as your business matures, you have a problem. You might see an occasional spike in sales on a new product or from new customers. Stagnant sales mean that you're losing loyal customers, however, which means that you're either not attracting new visitors to the site or not adding enough products to account for attrition. No matter the reason, it's money out of your pocket!

✦ **Recent management or partnership changes:** Dissolving a relationship with a business partner or experiencing a high level of management or employee turnover is often a sign of more serious issues lurking in the background. Making bad decisions, experiencing limited or no growth, and tolerating a hostile work environment are issues that can scare away business partners and employees. Your business is in need of a fresh perspective.

✦ **Difficulty in attracting new visitors:** Don't blame the search engines! Web sites with strong search engine rankings can have trouble increasing their numbers of visitors. The same percentage of visitors consistently hovers over your site. Why? Lots of possible reasons can explain why your site isn't attracting more eyeballs. The bottom line is that if your site isn't gaining exposure, it's time for you to find out why.

✦ **Fewer visitors to your site:** Even worse than being unable to attract new visitors is watching your numbers decline — steeply or not. If the drop is consistent and it isn't occurring over a holiday weekend or as part of a seasonal slump, it's time to stop the bleeding.

✦ **Increased customer complaints:** If your customers take the time to complain, consider yourself lucky. An increasing number of complaints is one of the best indicators that something is wrong with your site, your product or service, or your customer service. And, not all customers are kind enough to tell you about it — they simply go somewhere else to shop!

✦ **Added competition:** A decade ago, most sites didn't have much competition. Now, thousands on thousands of sites are targeting your customer base. Even if you don't think that you're taking a direct hit from competitors, they're eating into your site one way or another.

 ✦ **Profit void:** Depending on how well you maintain your accounting procedures, you might not immediately realize that profitability is an issue. As
you watch sales come in and you pay your expenses, everything seems
okay. Of course, as a more established online business, you analyze the
numbers closely (we hope!) to allow the real story to surface. When the
amount of money you clear begins to decrease (or isn't increasing), you
have to find out why and correct it.

These red flags are the most common sign that your business is in need of a
tune-up. Of course, sometimes a flag is just the tip of the iceberg. You might
be experiencing several problems simultaneously, and some are naturally
more critical than others.

Looking at the age of your business

Whether you enlist professional help depends on how long your business
has been around and what's appropriate for that stage in its life span. A
start-up company (in its first year or two) naturally experiences problems.
It's in the early phase of establishing *baselines*, or the indicators that show
what's normal for your site. In other words, you begin to see patterns
emerge in sales trends and traffic patterns during this stage of your business. You also experience the ups and downs that come along with a brand-
new endeavor. Minor problems are to be expected.

If your online business has been around for five years or longer, you
should have a definite feel for what's considered a minor bump in the road
and what will stop you in your tracks. Figure 6-1 shows how the Fairfax
County (Virginia) Office of Business defines the business life cycle and
what challenges you might face during each stage of the cycle. You can
check them out at

www.fairfaxcounty.gov/dpsm/osb/four_phases.htm

By the time you have been in business online for five years, your baseline
numbers are established because you have a consistent track record in
maintaining profitability, making sales, keeping visitor logs, and tracking
other customer- or product-related trends and data. For example, if you sell
trampolines over the Internet, you know to expect a dip in orders during the
winter months. If you see significant dips in the warmer months across consecutive summers, though, that's not a good situation — and you need help.

If you have a mature site that has been doing business online for nearly ten
years, you're probably even more tuned in to subtle indicators. Slight variations in profitability, a loss of visitors to specific pages on your site, or an
inability to increase sales during a typically good time of year for your product line immediately cause concern. Your instinct tells you that these problems aren't going away.

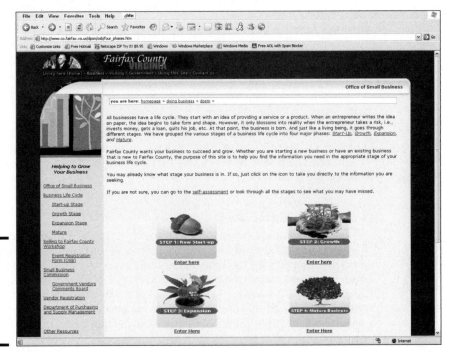

Looking at the severity of the problem and attempts to solve it

The truth is that you're not going to call for help at the first sign that your site is starting to tumble. And, you don't have to. You have to consider how bad the problem is before you panic. One summer of decreasing trampoline sales might be a fluke. A consecutive or long-term drop in orders during the peak selling season, however, can cause outright worry.

Consider which actions you have taken to correct the problem. What have you done differently to correct a negative trend? Have you consulted peers, customers, or trusted personal advisors about the problem?

Only when you have exhausted all potential solutions — and free resources — is it time to pay for an outside advisor.

Looking at your skill level

Sometimes, regardless of what the problem is, finding an answer is simply outside your skill level or experience level. The Internet evolves rapidly, as do the rules of the game for e-commerce. And, as an online business owner, you're already wearing many hats. Because you can't be expected to keep up with every area of e-commerce (or every general small-business issue), your site can benefit from bringing in a security expert, a search engine optimization specialist, a tax advisor, or any other professional who specializes in a particular field and knows it inside out.

Looking at the timing

A critical part of determining the severity of a problem on your site is deciding to what degree time factors into resolving the issue. If you have a bit of a cash flow cushion, you might be able to work only on the problem for a few months. Then again, you might have a rapidly depleting bank account or seasonal deadlines; a competitor might be launching a site soon; or other time-sensitive factors might demand that you find help immediately. Timing is everything, as they say!

If you aren't sure whether a steady decline in sales is affecting your competitors or is specific to your site, check with a reputable member-based association, trade journal, or research firm that tracks the sales cycles and trends affecting your industry. You might discover that the problem is industry-wide. Start by visiting *E-Commerce Times* (www.ecommercetimes.com) for a snapshot of factors influencing online businesses everywhere.

Book XI
Chapter 6

Hiring Experts
to Get Business
Rolling Again

Matching the Right Advisors to Your Business Needs

Half the battle of fixing a problem with your site is realizing that it has a serious problem and needs help. Before you can tackle the other half of the problem, though (solving it), you have to find the right person to assist you.

First, take a look at the different types of help available to you. Here are your options, depending on the severity of your problem, the amount of resources you have to spend, and your personal comfort level in seeking outside consultation:

✦ **Trusted advisors:** You can usually find two types of trusted advisors:

- *The people closest to you whom you already turn to regularly for help:* They might be family members, college roommates, or former co-workers.

- *A structured set of advisors:* If you've been in business for a while, you probably have in place a board of directors or an informal panel of business professionals who offer you advice occasionally. Or, perhaps you belong to, and network with, a group of professionals within your industry and you serve as resources for one another.

✦ **Free resources:** These nonprofit organizations, government-sponsored entities, and membership-based associations typically offer counseling and business advice at no charge (or for a nominal fee or donation). These groups often consist of retired executives or employed professionals who enjoy mentoring and advising others.

The Service Corps of Retired Executives (SCORE), which bills itself as Counselors to America's Small Business, is one of many organizations that offer free resources. (See Figure 6-2.) It offers online training and guidance from its membership of retired professionals. Be sure to check out its Business Tools section, which is designed to give you immediate support. You can visit SCORE at www.score.org.

✦ **Professional consultants:** The defining characteristic in this category of resources is that you pay money for the services you receive. Additionally, these people have specific expertise in the area in which you need assistance. You also have a formal relationship with a paid consultant because you sign a contract for services. Professionals can be independent consultants, or you can hire a larger consulting firm or associate firm.

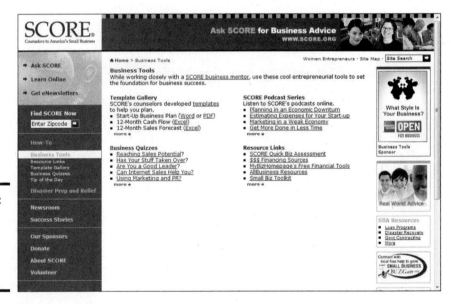

Figure 6-2:
Get help from the SCORE business toolbox.

Use the stable of resources you probably already cultivated in the course of running your business. If a trusted advisor has expertise in your area of need, go to that person for help. If your problem is more complicated or you don't know anyone in that field, tap in to other free resources. Exhaust your free resources before shelling out money for professionals.

Choosing the Right Consultant

After you decide that you need help, you have to choose a specific consultant who best suits you and the needs of your site. Finding the right consultant is tricky because in most cases, you're forming a long-term, intimate relationship with the person.

You're putting your trust in this person to help guide the future of your business, and that process gets personal. At times, you might feel uncomfortable because the consultant questions your management style, the direction of your online business, and even your routine daily tasks. The person's honesty and your willingness to listen are critical, however, to turning your site around. Trust and experience are not only important but also crucial to finding a good match between your consultant's style and personality and your style and personality.

To ultimately achieve a good relationship, carefully consider these issues when you're hiring an outside consultant:

+ **Expertise:** Knowing that you have to match a consultant's area of expertise to your problem is a no-brainer. Regardless of whether you need someone who specializes in search engine optimization, Internet security, or long-range business planning, however, verify that the person has the educational and professional credentials to back it up. That evidence can include formal education, on-the-job training, professional certifications from accredited affiliations, and any other applicable and verifiable background information.

+ **Experience:** The consultant should share with you any accomplishments and successes with other projects or clients. Request detailed specifics on the consultant's experience with other clients and the results he achieved.

  Don't ask for only finished results. Discuss the processes and methods used to reach those goals. By listening carefully, you discover a great deal about the consultant's approach to solving problems, in addition to confirming whether he met the intended goals.

+ **References:** Never accept a consultant's word and stop there. Do a little digging. Ask for references, and call them. Talk about what that client liked and disliked about the relationship with the consultant. If you can, contact one of the consultant's previous clients whose name wasn't offered as a reference.

  Be fair to the consultant, too. Ask which projects didn't go well and why. Find out which client relationships didn't last. Trust us: Disastrous projects aren't always the consultant's fault. Sometimes, a client isn't willing to listen or to make recommended changes. In that case, success is hard to come by with any consultant!

Book XI
Chapter 6

Hiring Experts to Get Business Rolling Again

+ **Philosophy:** Discuss the consultant's belief about what makes a project work and what doesn't. Find out exactly what she deems a successful client relationship and what she needs from you in order to accomplish that goal. Then decide whether you can agree to those terms.

+ **Working style:** Uncovering a consultant's working style involves understanding his approach to problem solving. Does he require full 24/7 access to you, your employees, and the online business? Or, does he use more of a hands-off style and want to deal directly with you? Will he take a while to analyze your situation from a distance? Or, does he prefer to jump right in and get his hands dirty from the start? You need to decide whether you can live with, and agree, to the consultant's approach in helping resolve your problem.

Check out these resources to find the right match for you:

+ **Institute of Management Consultants USA at `www.imcusa.org`:** Search the member directory for a consultant in one of its 24 chapters nationwide. Consultants specialize in a variety of fields, including finance, technology, marketing, logistics, manufacturing, and human resources.

Before making your final hiring decision, verify whether your consultant is a member of a professional association for consultants, or if he has any applicable certifications.

+ **Independent Computer Consultants Association:** Find consulting and associate firms across the United States at `www.icca.org/finda consultant.asp`. You can search according to area of specialty, firm or independent professional, or state.

+ **Guru.com:** Hire an independent consultant on a project-by-project basis using this global Internet site for freelancers (`www.guru.com`). Check the Business Consultants category for a complete list of available professionals and specialty areas.

+ **Organization of Search Engine Optimization Professionals:** Locate a search engine optimization consultant or an Internet marketing consultant from this organization's consultant directory at `www.seopros.org`. It has a list of consultants from 11 countries, including the United States.

Defining the Relationship

When you settle on a professional consultant, you can establish the rules of the game. Remember to fine-tune the working relationship in the form of a contractual agreement. Make sure that your contract covers these items:

✦ **The scope of the project:** Agree on clear goals and the expected outcome. Determine whether the consultant will identify the specific problem, solve the problem, or both. Then decide on a start and finish date for the project (within reason, of course).

✦ **The price:** When you hire outside help, expect the person to be upfront and clear about fees. Understanding the cost of the project is a big part of making your final decision to hire. If the fee is based on an hourly rate, don't be afraid to ask for the estimated number of hours to complete the job. Or, you might prefer to negotiate a flat rate that covers everything, regardless of the number of hours it takes to complete.

Keep on your toes to avoid being surprised by a huge bill. Check to see whether travel expenses or other incidentals are covered in the hourly rate or the flat-fee amount. You also need to find out how and when the consultant bills you. Do you pay half up front, or is the total amount spread out over several months? When does the consultant invoice you, and when does he expect payment?

✦ **The process:** Understand what the consultant expects from you, and which information he needs for you to provide to get the job done. Find out whether he expects to have access to your financial information, your Internet passwords, and your customers. You also need to know his specific methodologies for meeting the goals you have set. Now is the time to find out.

✦ **Working parameters:** You need to understand the consultant's time availability and how much is allotted to your project. Find out how often he provides a status report, whether you need to set up space for him inside your office for a long-term project (or whether he works only off-site), and how you can reach him after hours in case of an emergency. Be specific so that both you and the consultant understand the expectations.

Ensure that your consultant operates as a true independent contractor (under the terms established by the IRS) and not as an employee. Otherwise, you can be fined and have to pay back employment taxes.

✦ **A confidentiality and nondisclosure agreement:** Nondisclosure agreements are a standard but necessary practice. In the simplest of terms, a nondisclosure agreement tells the consultant what topics about your company he can and cannot discuss outside the organization. The goal of these documents is simple: Prevent the consultant from sharing your private matters with customers, competitors, or any other source that might benefit from the information — or cause you to adversely suffer because it was made public.

✦ **A written contract:** Spell out the agreed-on terms in a written contract signed by both you and the consultant. Then put the contract in a safe place!

**Book XI
Chapter 6**

Hiring Experts
to Get Business
Rolling Again

✦ **An escape clause:** An escape clause is a common practice these days. It provides an option for getting out of an agreement if the relationship doesn't work. Find out the penalty for using the escape clause. Terminating a contract early usually involves a monetary charge. Alternatively, check out the conditions that allow the consultant to bail on you. He might leave you high and dry with no recourse for recouping your money!

Always take out your magnifying glass and read the fine print.

Overcoming Great Expectations and Still Getting Results

If you poll small-business owners, most would probably say that the majority of their experiences with consultants were positive, but that more than a few didn't work out well. The relationship might have been frustrating for both the company's owner and the consultant because of a simple misunderstanding — or great expectations. *Great expectations* happen when either the owner or the consultant is unrealistic (or both are unrealistic) about the results that can be achieved.

You can avoid unrealistic ideals about the consulting process and still achieve tangible results with these techniques:

✦ **Set specific, achievable goals.** Identify the most critical problem and agree on which goals must be met to correct it. Avoid taking on more than three or four major goals during a given period.

✦ **Break each goal into action items.** By dividing each goal into a list of action items or a to-do list, you understand better what you need to do to meet the goal. These items should be specific actions that can be completed by a specific time.

✦ **Assign responsibility.** Designating who is responsible for each action within a goal prevents confusion and frustration. If you don't assign responsibility, you can easily assume that someone else will take care of the item, although it never gets completed.

✦ **Determine a timeline.** After digesting what's needed in order to turn the site around, you and your consultant must agree on a reasonable time frame for accomplishing each goal.

✦ **Know the cost.** The best-laid plans quickly go astray if you don't know and agree to the costs of implementing them!

You hired a consultant because you have a problem. Maybe you messed up along the way and a problem needs to be corrected. Or, perhaps you didn't fully understand how to grow your online business to the next level. Either way, the issue has taken quite a while to develop. It takes more than a day or two, therefore, to undo the damage or to correct your path toward success.

When you bring in a consultant or advisor to help your business, make a commitment to the following ten phrases. They can help you avoid being disappointed by great expectations:

+ Agree on the problem.

+ Set reasonable goals of what it will take to correct the problem.

+ Be realistic about the amount of time, effort, and money required to fix the problem.

+ Remain honest and open, and respectful of the process.

+ Accept responsibility for the past.

+ Commit to doing what it takes to change your future.

+ Remember that it's not personal — it's business.

+ Know that the result is for your benefit.

+ Be patient, but be determined and unrelenting.

+ If you don't like it or it gets too difficult, you can decide to stay where you are and keep spinning your wheels.

**Book XI
Chapter 6**

**Hiring Experts
to Get Business
Rolling Again**

Chapter 7: Transitioning a Small Site into Big Business

In This Chapter

✓ Mapping out your growth options

✓ Investing in the next level of technology

✓ Figuring out what to do after you hit the big time

✓ Creating your final strategy

Truthfully, plenty of entrepreneurs are satisfied with their online businesses staying small. For the rest of us, growth is the carrot that's continually being dangled in front of us. In this chapter, we share the strategies and resources that allow you (and your site) to finally take a bite out of that carrot.

Seeking Out the Next Level of Your Business

Entrepreneurs can tell you that the process of growing your business almost always starts out the same way — by planning for it.

Before transitioning your online business to the next level, you have to identify exactly *what* that next level is. You have to put all your options under a microscope and decide which one makes the most sense to pursue. What are your choices? Well, each of the most common paths to growth has its advantages and disadvantages.

Expanding the business

An obvious choice is to add products or services to your existing site. The purpose is to use variety to attract a wider customer base while bringing in larger revenues. This strategy is certainly the one that many entrepreneurs implement regularly, whether they realize it or not. But, after you consciously identify it as your preferred growth strategy, you can become more aggressive and targeted with your actions.

Here are the pros of expanding your business:

✦ You retain full control of the business, just like always.

✦ You can explore different areas, which can be fun for an entrepreneur.

The cons of expanding your business are that they

✦ Can take more time to show results

✦ Might require a large investment in back-end systems to support added inventory or a product base

We discuss ways to expand your product base in Book XI, Chapter 3.

Acquiring other sites

Buying existing sites is another fairly typical development strategy. You can easily start by making a list of competitors' sites that might be worth purchasing. Also, look at sites that complement your current business. These noncompeting sites offer products or services that are different yet still a good fit.

Of course, the larger or more established a site, the higher its asking price. Sometimes, a better strategy is to identify up-and-coming sites or sites that (like yours) have also remained small.

The pros of acquiring other sites are that they

✦ Provide a quick way to expand or diversify

✦ Introduce your current site to a wider customer base

The cons of acquiring other sites are that they

✦ Usually require substantial out-of-pocket cash

✦ Sometimes aren't for sale, so it takes time to convince their owners to negotiate a price

Becoming an affiliate or a partner

Maybe you're not ready to purchase another company outright. A better solution might be to expand through partnering opportunities or affiliate programs. For example, you might partner with a national membership-based organization as the sole provider of a particular service or product.

Expanding your business through partnership agreements is a good idea. You're typically unrestricted in the number of partners you have, and you retain control — and can cancel an agreement if the partnership doesn't work.

In a similar arrangement, starting your own affiliate program becomes a viable option. Unlike in a partnership, you're developing a specific program that another site can replicate in exchange for a commission.

Although an affiliate program is often associated with e-books and other content products, it's a viable delivery method for almost any product or service. You even see traditional e-commerce stores offering a flat percentage of revenues to affiliate sites that sell their products by using links. Or, you might see payroll services companies that create affiliate opportunities. In that case, the affiliate earns a flat dollar amount for every customer referral that comes through the site.

To make affiliate programs attractive (and worthwhile) for others to participate in, you should have a viable product to promote and pay out a decent commission.

The pros of going the affiliate or partner route are that they

+ Are relatively easy to set up

+ Are inexpensive to develop

+ Are compatible with almost any type of business (whether it's product-, content-, or service-oriented)

+ Can produce a quick return on sales

Here are the cons of going the affiliate or partner route:

+ Brand control becomes an issue (primarily with affiliates), as you lend your name for others to use.

+ Administrative duties increase (monitoring affiliate sales, cutting checks, and distributing 1099 forms, for example).

+ You're essentially marketing two companies now (your original concept and your affiliate or partner program).

In Book IV, Chapter 2, we discuss signing up for affiliate programs.

Going international

Expanding your operations outside your home country is a proposition that's both exciting and scary. This strategy becomes easier when you have, or a partner has, experience in working outside the United States. However, the return on the investment can be lucrative. Products can become oversaturated in the ever-competitive American market. Yet, overseas, the product might be a relatively new and sought-after item with few — if any — distributors.

The pros of taking your business internationally are that they can

+ Have more opportunity for growth and increased sales in foreign countries

+ Achieve global name recognition

Here are the cons of taking your business internationally:

+ Language barriers can complicate the process.

+ Selling the product might require setting up foreign distributors and manufacturing plants.

+ Laws and regulations vary by country, which adds another layer of compliance.

Bringing in financial partners

Recruiting a financial partner might be a desirable option for your site. If you do it correctly, you end up with needed money for growth and a business partner who has expertise that you might not possess. Finding a financial partner is a little different from simply going out and finding money to support your expansion because you're taking on an actual partner in this scenario.

Unlike a bank or another lender, a *financial partner* is a person who has a say-so in your business. She participates in both operational and financial decisions. You can consider angel investors, depending on the arrangement, and venture capitalists as examples of investment partners (see Book I, Chapter 4). More than likely, your financial partner will end up being a former co-worker, a business associate, or a friend or family member.

The pros of finding a financial partner is that the person

+ Provides needed capital to upgrade and expand your site

+ Introduces fresh, alternative ideas from an experienced financial partner

Here are the cons of including a financial partner:

+ You sacrifice some control (and ownership) of your business.

+ The situation can become ugly if you find out that you don't share a united vision for growth.

+ Your partner might bail out at an inopportune time.

Going public

The good old days have a bit of nostalgia connected to them. You might remember the heyday of the dot-com era, when companies went public with shares breaking Wall Street records. Well, even if it takes more work (and a good battle against skepticism), going public remains a viable option for your Internet business. Google certainly has proven that the dot-com magic is still viable.

Here's the catch: You have to follow the same game plan as any other company that wants to go public, which includes these tasks:

✦ Create a sustainable business concept that's capable of keeping shareholders happy over the long haul. Your financial statements must be in tip-top shape, and you must have a critical strategy in place to support sustained growth.

✦ Take a closer look at your employees, vendor partnerships, and customers, and then begin investing in some heavy hitters (if you haven't already).

✦ Attract executives who are knowledgeable about the process of going public, and who have substantial experience with recognizable companies. You also need to partner with, or sell to, big-name vendors and customers. The more attention your company gets, the higher your public stock will be.

The pros of going public with your company are that you

✦ Increase its net worth (you hope)

✦ Jump into the "big leagues"

The cons of going public with your company are that

✦ The process is complicated, time consuming, and expensive.

✦ You get no guarantees.

✦ A *venture capitalist* (a firm or person that prepares your company to go public) might ask you step down as CEO or president if your skills aren't a match for taking your company public.

You usually don't decide to go public overnight. If you're on this path, you will experience some lower-level rounds of fundraising first. During that time, you typically work with angel investors and work your way up to venture capitalists.

Passing on your company and retiring

For some owners, passing the company on to a family member might qualify as following an exit strategy rather than making plans for growth. We disagree. In this particular strategy, you're in essence growing your heir, who in turn grows the business. The first step is to decide whether you have a next-generation family member interested in taking over your business. Then you have to take an honest and objective approach to deciding whether that person has the necessary skills or talents. At this point, it's like hiring an employee whom you plan to groom for a management position. Obviously, it's not always easy to be objective.

The upside is that you might find an untapped resource who has a terrific energy level and pushes you!

The pros of handing off your business to someone else are that

+ You continue to have a lifeline to the business, even after you step away from it.
+ The person brings a fresh perspective that can accelerate your site's growth.
+ Your business stays within your family.

The cons of handing off your business to someone else are that it

+ Can take several years to "groom" an heir
+ Might hurt your relationship or cause increased tension in the family
+ Stays within the family. (Yes, this one is also a pro — family has a tendency to have both positive and negative aspects in running a business.)

Selling your site

Selling your site is considered an exit strategy. Yet, selling your site is sometimes the only way to grow it.

You might be tired, tapped out of money, and looking for a way out. Maybe you recognize that your site has fantastic potential and you lack the experience and knowledge to make it happen. You might also have a limited window of opportunity, or you simply might not have the resources to expand your site within that optimal time frame.

Listing your site for sale online

You can advertise that your business is for sale or search for a prospective buyer on these Web sites:

✔ **BizBuySell.com:** `www.bizbuysell.com/sell`

✔ **BizByOwner.com:** `www.bizbyowner.com/Public/SellABusiness.aspx`

✔ **BizQuest.com:** `www.bizquest.com`

✔ **BusinessBroker.net:** `www.businessbroker.net/services/listings.ihtml`

✔ **BusinessMart:** `www.businessmart.com/1`

✔ **Entrepreneur.com:** `www.entrepreneur.com/tools/detail/157050.html`

✔ **MergerPlace.com:** `www.mergerplace.com/mp/visitor/sellers/listing/create`

Keep in mind that developing a plan to identify a buyer is quite different from someone unexpectedly calling you with an offer. If selling is your strategy, preparing your business can take as long as six months to a year. If you have a smaller site, or have been lax in sticking to a management regimen, you need a few months just to clean up your organizational act!

Depending on your asking price and the current market, finding the right buyer can take another year (or longer). This time frame is where you see the difference between selling as an exit plan and selling as a growth strategy. When expansion by selling is your goal, finding the right buyer match is critical. A professional broker can help you identify key characteristics.

Generally speaking, you want to look for someone who has these characteristics:

✦ A shared vision for your site

✦ Experience in taking a business beyond the start-up phase or past the early-growth years

✦ Peers in the industry who can substantiate her reputation and skills

✦ Verifiable liquid assets and net worth to invest in the business beyond the purchase price

You can locate a reputable business broker through BizBuySell (`www.biz buysell.com`). The site has a free, searchable database that's broken out by state, as shown in Figure 7-1.

Book XI
Chapter 7

Transitioning a Small Site into Big Business

Figure 7-1:
Find a business broker.

What to do before your site goes on the market

Although the decision to sell might come easily to you, preparing your site for that transaction doesn't happen overnight. Check out this to-do list before you hang a For Sale sign on your business:

- Put your financial house in order with a set of audited financial statements.

- Meet with your accountant to discuss tax strategies for a sale.

- Have a professional valuation conducted to determine a feasible asking price.

- Contract with a business broker who has experience in selling Internet companies.

- Review all vendor agreements, equipment leases, and miscellaneous contracts, and then take a thorough inventory.

- Make sure that written policies and procedures are in place and are being strictly followed.

- Update all back-end functions (as long as doing so doesn't require a significant cash investment).

- Work on increasing the number of visitors to your site and the average length of time they spend there.

- Hire an expert in search engine optimization to improve your position at search engine sites.

- Step up your PR activities to get attention. (Unlike in the area of marketing, PR gives you more exposure for the money.)

You don't have to work with a professional to sell your site. However, a broker often has extensive contacts of potential buyers and can speed up the selling process. Regardless, selling your site might be the ideal opportunity for you.

The pros of selling your company outright are that you

+ Receive a potentially large chunk of change for all your hard work

+ Remove the burden of growth from your shoulders

+ Open doors to try something else

Here are the cons of selling your company outright:

+ If you stay with the company, you lose control.

+ If you leave outright, you have to start a new business from scratch, find a job, or retire.

+ You have no guarantee that the buyer will succeed in growing the site.

+ Because payment terms might be spread out, realizing the full sale price can take a while.

✦ The buyer may require you to sign a non-compete clause, which means you cannot compete with the buyer by starting another business in the same industry for many years. Given that your experience is heavily tied to the company you just sold, this could limit your opportunities in the future.

✦ The business could go under before you collect all your money, leaving the site wiped out and you fighting in court for restitution.

Selling your domain

An alternative to selling your entire business is to sell only its URL. A popular domain name can fetch a pretty penny, which can help you expand your site.

Suppose that you have a limited amount of money to invest in any type of tools for growth. However, a key asset is your domain name. You can, in theory, sell the domain — to provide a needed influx of capital — and retain, as a condition of the sale, the rights to all content and services. That way, you move the content to another domain and use the money from the sale to build up the new site.

This strategy is particularly feasible if you already own a domain for a smaller site that has a similar theme or customer demographic. Of course, unless you have another domain name in your back pocket, starting over might be difficult.

The pros of putting your domain name up for sale are that you

✦ Engage in a quick process that can have a high monetary return

✦ Retain ownership of your content, products, or services

✦ Gain capital to reinvest in a new site

Here are the cons of putting your domain name up for sale:

✦ The purchaser of your domain can develop a competing site that uses your old URL.

✦ The purchaser can use your domain name for a less-reputable type of site or as a gateway to a scam site.

✦ You lose traffic, search engine rankings, and ratings for your previous site.

Dealing with Accidental Success

Ahh, sweet success. Admittedly, the term *accidental success* is a bit humorous. Ask any rock star or well-known actor about an overnight boost of fame. The honest ones don't hesitate to explain that *years* of hard work preceded their "accidental" good fortune.

The same concept holds true for any online business owner. Imagine finding yourself in the throes of a major public relations blitz, with skyrocketing sales following close behind. The reality is that you might be unprepared to handle the level of business that this scenario brings. But we guarantee you that your success is no accident!

How do you prepare for an onslaught of hard-won business? After all, if your site is merely mentioned by Oprah or featured in a short segment on CNN, your URL can be rocketed into the glare of the spotlight (in an extremely good way). Before you know it, you would have back orders and your site would be bogged down from the jump in visitors. You wouldn't be able to get UPS to pull into your driveway fast enough. Lest this blitz of good fortune turn into your sudden demise, you had better be ready.

The following list describes both immediate and short-term actions you should take when opportunity comes knocking at your domain:

+ **Identify your pressure points.** Determine where the biggest demand for your time or resources is coming from. You might be beseeched by the media for interview requests and can't make it to the phone. More than likely, your production and distribution cycles have kinks, and you have to get (or keep) products stocked at the higher demand levels. Also, your customer service functions must handle the incoming request load. Maybe your biggest problem is figuring out how to pack and ship this steep increase in orders. After you identify your most immediate (and demanding) source of frustration, you can begin developing a solution.

+ **Hire temporary help.** When your manpower runs out of "man," you have to call in the cavalry. Going from a solo operation to one with a dozen employees is daunting, however. It takes time to screen and hire people and put benefits in place. The solution is to hire temporary workers to provide an immediate boost to your productivity levels, without the hassle. Use a professional staffing agency to quickly add qualified and prescreened workers. An added benefit is that you can pull back on staffing levels if demand slows down.

+ **Outsource certain tasks.** After a sudden influx of orders, the most economical solution (for both the short and long terms) is to outsource some of your functions. As the owner of a small site, you're probably used to processing each order and then packaging and shipping the product yourself. Factor in a 50 percent to 75 percent increase in orders, and you can no longer physically keep up the pace. Combat the problem by finding a local call center that can take over functions related to customer service. Or, try contracting with a distribution center to warehouse your products and handle order-packing and -shipping functions. See Book IV, Chapter 7 to find an in-house or a third-party solution to your packaging and shipping dilemmas.

✦ **Adjust the back end.** Another victim of your site's growing pains is the back-end function. From your shopping cart program to inventory control, the programs that were once suited for a start-up site can quickly become antiquated. To survive an unexpected sales rush, work with your vendors to make minimal improvements to your existing support systems. Then schedule time to research advanced products and features that can be better scaled to your new sales levels. We discuss all your back-end solutions in Book IV, Chapter 7.

✦ **Seek funding.** The changes you have to make to your business require money. Even if you decide not to invest in new equipment or tools, you need money to handle inventory spikes and hire staff. One of the best things you can do is take a trip to your bank — or other lender. As long as your credit score is reasonable and your relationship with the bank is good, establishing a line of credit is an easy way to gain access to cash. A *line of credit* is basically a loan with a preestablished limit. Rather than take out the full amount at one time, you can withdraw money in smaller amounts only when you need it.

✦ **Talk, talk, talk.** Now, more than ever, you need to communicate with vendors, distributors, employees, and customers. Take time out for daily or weekly 10-minute staff meetings. Take the opportunity to share operational changes and find out about problems that might otherwise fly "under the radar" in your stepped-up pace of activities. Let customers know about back orders, shipping delays, and any other minor problems that are surfacing. The worst thing about overnight success is that if you don't address concerns effectively, you lose the customers who came to you during this crunch time of good fortune.

 Take notes when you're talking to customers, especially when they have a positive comment or a success story concerning your product. Turn these stories into case studies or testimonials that you post on your Web site, and use them as offline marketing materials, too.

✦ **Spend wisely.** We hope that your burst of success is proportionate to the rising number in your bank account. With years of hard work behind you, you might be tempted to splurge. Instead, think of this influx of funds as investment capital and put it back into your company as much as possible.

 Meet with your accountant to review or update your financial strategy. A substantial increase in revenues, and subsequent expenditures, brings along plenty of tax implications. Ask your accountant to discuss your options to maximize the use of your money.

✦ **Take it to the next level.** With momentum on your side, consider leveraging it a little further. With increased recognition and revenues, you have a good shot at negotiating partnering opportunities, developing another line of products or services, and riding out a wave of expanded publicity. Use your moment in the spotlight to further establish your site's brand and position it for the future.

Purposefully Making the Next Move

Whether your site is growing because of fate or strategy, your next move should be well thought out. Follow these strategies:

✦ **Assemble an advisory board.** You might already have a formal board of directors that you assembled immediately after you incorporated. In that case, consider the value of expanding your board and adding individuals with specific expertise. If you're not comfortable bringing on directors, assemble a somewhat less formal *advisory board*. This group of professionals from your network meets regularly to review your business goals and provide guidance. Similar to when you have a board of directors, look for people with experience who complement your strengths and weaknesses.

✦ **Update planning tools.** Oh, you know that we're going to say it: Growth means digging into that old business plan and marketing plan. You know which ones we mean — the ones you threw together half a decade ago because everyone said that you had to have them. Those people were right: You need both documents, even though they're long overdue for an update. Use the old plans as a foundation to reassess your current goals and strategies.

✦ **Focus on long-term financial planning.** In addition to working more closely with your accountant, seek input from a financial planner or a CPA who specializes in your industry. You're no longer simply moving from one tax year to the next. As both your company revenue and personal income increase, you want to make calculated decisions about your money.

✦ **Stay current.** It's all about the research. Growing companies tend to put up walls around themselves. By not paying attention to what's happening in the world around them, they are quickly outpaced by more innovative businesses. The best way to ward off this curse is to become a vigilant researcher:

   • Watch for developing trends.

   • Read business and trade publications.

   • Talk with peers in your industry.

   • Attend trade shows.

   • Skim the Internet for information that might affect your site.

   • Keep an eye on your competitors.

✦ **Find a mentor.** You might not want to invite your closest competitor to have coffee with you, and getting the CEO of Google on board might be a little farfetched. You can, however, look for sites that embody your philosophies and implement similar growth strategies. Approach the founder or president by e-mail, and see whether she's open to answering some questions. (Be honest about why you're contacting her!) Striking up an online mentorship is easier than you might think.

✦ **Participate in industry activism.** As a small-business owner, you have to focus primarily on your site. Your number-one priority is figuring out how to make your site work, which can be isolating at times. As you expand, you're in the position to broaden your horizon. Make a point of joining national industry associations or professional organizations within your local community. Get involved with issues that affect your business and your peers' businesses. Table 7-1 highlights a few of the national member-based organizations that cater to Internet professionals and small-business owners.

Becoming active in your professional community and your industry associations is also a proven and powerful networking tool.

Table 7-1	Associations for Online Business Professionals	
Organization	*URL*	*Annual Membership Fee*
Direct Marketing Association	`www.the-dma.org`	$1,500
eMarketing Association	`www.emarketing association.com`	$175
Internet Council	`http://internet council.nacha.org/`	$2,500
National Federation of Independent Businesses	`www.NFIB.com`	$300
Shop.org	`www.shop.org`	$2,750
Search Engine Marketing Professional Organization	`www.SEMPO.org`	$299

Index

X

Y